MW00784303

The Hereditary Sheriffs of Galloway; Their "forebears" and Friends, Their Courts and Customs of Their Times, With Notes of the Early History, Ecclesiastical Legends, the Baronage and Placenames of the Province
Volume 1

HEREDITARY SHERIFFS OF GALLOWAY

Printed by R. & R Clark

FOR

DAVID DOUGLAS, EDINBURGH

LONDON   . SIMPKIN, MARSHALL, HAMILTON, KENT, AND CO , LIM
CAMBRIDGE . MACMILLAN AND BOWES
GLASGOW   JAMES MACLEHOSE AND SONS

THE HEREDITARY

SHERIFFS OF GALLOWAY

THEIR "FOREBEARS" AND FRIENDS
THEIR COURTS AND CUSTOMS OF THEIR TIMES

WITH NOTES OF THE EARLY HISTORY, ECCLESIASTICAL
LEGENDS, THE BARONAGE AND PLACE-
NAMES OF THE PROVINCE

BY THE LATE

Sir ANDREW AGNEW, Bart.

OF LOCHNAW

VOL. I.

EDINBURGH
DAVID DOUGLAS, 10 CASTLE STREET
1893

EDITOR'S NOTE

WHEN my Father died a few months ago, this second and enlarged edition of the *Sheriffs of Galloway* was practically finished. The whole of the MS. was in the hands of the printer, and some of the early proofs had already been returned for correction. Under the circumstances, his family were anxious that a work in which he had taken such a deep interest, and to which he had devoted so much labour, should, if possible, be brought to completion. The warm encouragement and advice of Mr. David Douglas has made this an easy task.

As it was mainly a question of revising the proof-sheets, and as I had written out the whole of the MS at my Father's dictation, it was thought that the work had better be done by me. I have done my best to keep the book free from slips, whether in the printing or in the sense; and with the valuable help of Mr. George Stronach, one of the assistant librarians in the Advocates' Library, who kindly undertook to verify the quotations from old records, whether French or Latin, I trust all preventable mistakes have been avoided.

It can scarcely be hoped that in a work of this kind, especially in one which deals so largely with the etymology of local names, some errors should not have crept in, which only the special knowledge of the Author could have detected. Had he lived to see the proofs, these errors would no doubt have been observed and rectified. If any such, therefore, are discovered, I trust they will be attributed, not to the Author, but to the fact that the book has had to be published without his personal supervision, which alone could have ensured its absolute accuracy.

CONSTANCE AGNEW.

LOCHNAW, *November* 1892.

PREFACE

HAVING rushed prematurely into print many years ago, as a natural result the volume abounded with errors of omission and commission

Happily the very extravagance of some of the mistakes induced gratuitous assistance for their correction. As, for example, a statement hazarded that "the Agneaux, once numerous, were now entirely extinct in the country which was the cradle of their race," led to a mild remonstrance from the Bocages of Normandy, to which the volume had found its way, that their Scottish representative had not only ignored but annihilated them.

Correspondence led to explanations and an exchange of visits, as agreeable as they proved fertile in results. The charter-chest of the Château Isle Marie and the departmental archives of St. Lo yielded documents innumerable, from which not only details were to be gathered as to the family in France, but particulars as to their settlements in England.

The clue thus found, the identification of the Norman branches in their English domiciles was an easy matter. In the English State Paper Office, exchequer rolls from Parliamentary writs, commissions, summonses, etc., afforded abundantly the information we required; and now knowing in what direction to look, many further particulars were to be gathered from the exhaustive works of our English county historians, and of these more especially Bloomfield and Chauncey.

In our former publication many family papers and official notices were overlooked, and many sources of information which were really open to us were either unknown or unthought of. Prominent among these were :—

1. *Notes Historiques sur la Seigneurie, le Château et la Paroisse d'Agneau*, François Nicolas de Bosque, St. Lo, 1857.

2 *Nobiliere de Normandie*, 2 vols., royal quarto, E. de Magny, 1862.

3. The Pipe Rolls, Parliamentary writs, etc, all accessible in the State Paper Office, though few then had been published.

Whilst since that date official publication has been made of the Lord Chamberlain's and Lord High Treasurer's accounts in Scotland, as well as of the Great Seal Register

And the *Chronicles of the Picts and Scots*, ably edited by Mr. W. F. Skene, have been officially issued from the Register House.

Previous also to our publication, Chauncey's *History and Antiquities of Hertfordshire*, folio ; and Bloomfield's *History of Norfolk*, five vols., folio, had been published in last century, and these have been largely quoted

Since our publication there have appeared M'Dowall's *History of Dumfries*, 1867 ; Fordun's *History*, Notes by Skene, 1871-72; Wyntoun's *Chronicles*, Notes by Laing, three vols., 1872-79; *Lives of St. Ninian and St. Kentigern*, Bishop Forbes, 1874; *Annals of Viscount and 1st and 2nd Earls of Stair*, Murray Graham, 1875; Skene's *Celtic Scotland*, three vols., published between 1876-80. *Correspondence of Sir Patrick Waus* (a model of good editing), Mr. Vans Agnew, 1882 ; *Chronicles of Lincluden*, M'Dowall, 1886.

Of older works, I have found extremely useful the *Annals*

of Scotland, by Sir David Dalrymple, Lord Hailes, as much
for its intrinsic merit as the accuracy of its reference to the
older chroniclers facilitating closer examination.   The edition
quoted was in three vols. octavo, 1797.

The early history of Galloway being inseparable from that
of Ayrshire, not only in family notices but as respects the
names of places, we have treated of Galloway in its largest
extent, and have looked for examples as far north as the Water
of Irvine.

As for place-names, this subject alone is approached with
diffidence, well knowing how tentative many attempted explanations necessarily must be; protesting, however, against the application of the sneer laid against oracles of old to those interested
in this branch of philology—Μάντις ἄριστος ὅστις εἰκάζει
καλῶς (the best guesser is the best prophet).   Any one attempting to explain the names of a district of which he knows
nothing, by mere guessing from the sound, will soon find himself
in a mess.   Personal inspection, if possible, with local and
historical knowledge, are indispensable to anything like an
approach to correctness.

My thanks are due for the many useful suggestions made
from time to time by the Bishop of Down and Connor; as well
as to Dr. Joyce for his extreme courtesy, although we are
personally strangers, in so fully and kindly answering the
many troublesome queries in the long correspondence I inflicted
upon him.

For the actual force of many of the roots I am much
indebted to the late Dr. Thomas M'Lauchlan, who over and
over again revised my notebook.

As also to my much lamented friend John Campbell of
Islay, who was much interested in Celtic research; Rev. George
Wilson, Glenluce, Rev. Andrew Urquhart, B.D.

Besides which an historical account of the Kennedies from charters at Culzean, privately printed, was kindly given to the author by Lord David Kennedy, and a MS. collection of notices of the Agnews in Ireland was sent for perusal by the Rev. Classen Porter.

Adamnan's *Columba* being considered especially valuable, as well as those given by Mr. Skene in his *Celtic Scotland,* Dr. Joyce's *Names of Places in Ireland,* Sir Herbert Maxwell's *Studies in the Topography of Galloway*, and certain suggestions have been obtained from Bannister's *Names of Places in Cornwall,* Ferguson's *Northmen in Cumberland,* and Miss Yonge's *Christian Names* The dictionaries principally relied upon are O'Reilly's, with Supplement by Dr. O'Donovan, 1864 (Irish); Armstrong's Gaelic Dictionary, 1825, M'Leod and Dewar's, 1831. for pronunciation, Neil M'Alpine's, sixth edition, 1872; Owen's Welsh Dictionary, 1826; and William Spurrell's, third edition, 1872.

The name of Galloway, although so constantly in the mouths of its inhabitants, is so entirely ignored by map-makers that we may state that, although in early times its bounds extended to the river Irvine northward, as well as eastward of the Nith, for many centuries its limits have been confined to the counties of Wigtown and Kirkcudbright. From before the wars of succession Wigtown has been a sheriffdom; while Kirkcudbright, from the days of the Douglasses to very recent times, was under the jurisdiction of a steward (whose duties were identical with those of a sheriff). Hence the true Gallovidian rarely names "Wigtown" or "Kirkcudbright," but calls the whole district "Galloway," distinguishing the former as "the Shire," and the latter as "the Stewartry."

We are well aware that the circle is a most limited one to which a History of the Sheriffs of Galloway can be of any interest whatever ; but, in accordance with the homely proverb that " what it is worth doing at all, it is worth doing well," I have spared no pains to make the record of Galloway events, as well as the doings of the family of its Sheriffs, during the period they presided in its Courts, as complete and as accurate as possible, and as such to offer it as a legacy to my descendants, who, a century or two hence, may give a kindly thought to the compiler.

LOCHNAW, *November* 1891.

CONTENTS

CHAPTER I

A.D. 79 to 794

CHAPTER II

A.D. 794 to 1124

CHAPTER III

A.D. 1124 to 1161

CHAPTER IV

A.D. 1161 to 1234

CHAPTER V

A.D. 1234 to 1360

CHAPTER VI

CHAPTER VII

CHAPTER VIII

A.D. 1000 to 1460

CHAPTER IX

A.D. 1084 to 1360

CHAPTER X

A.D 1365

CHAPTER XI

A D. 1365 to 1366

CHAPTER XII

A.D. 1366 to 1424

CHAPTER XIII

A.D. 1424 to 1440

CHAPTER XIV

A.D. 1440 to 1455

CHAPTER XV

A.D. 1455 to 1484

CHAPTER XVI

A.D. 1484 to 1498

CHAPTER XVII

A.D. 1498 to 1506

CHAPTER XVIII

A D. 1506 to 1510

CHAPTER XXV

A.D. 1584 to 1598

CHAPTER XXVI

A.D. 1598 to 1616

CHAPTER XXVII

A.D. 1616 to 1630

LIST OF ILLUSTRATIONS

VOL. I.

Chateau D'Agneaux
Normandie

CHAPTER I

FROM THE ADVANCE OF AGRICOLA TO THE RETREAT OF THE NORTHUMBRIAN SAXONS

A.D. 79 to 794

> Three forward bands of Novant
> Three kings wearing golden torques —TALIESSIN.

> Ad terram Pictorum qui Niduari vocantur.
> BEDE, *Vit. Sanc. Cuth.* c. 11.

> Picti qui vulgo Galweienses dicuntur.
> RICHARD OF HEXHAM

THE word Galloway is derived from "Gallgaidheal" (*d* mute), the Celtic name for its people.[1] The Cymric equivalent of this was Galwyddel (the *dd* pronounced *th*), whence the Latin Gallwethia applied to the province, softened to Gallovidia, and anglicised Galloway. But though the term Galwyddel is that usually applied to Galwegians by the British bards of the sixth century, the name by which they are best known in current history is "Novantæ" (Greek Νοváνται), meaning the Nith men,—the Celtic "Nydd" on Roman lips changing to "Novius,"—whilst in low Latin the Cymric equivalent for the Pictish "Nyddwyr" was represented by "Niduari."[2]

---

[1] Dr. Reeves, Bishop of Down and Connor, once wrote to the author: "Your Galloway is a compound word which is found in the Irish annals and implies something like 'stranger Gael' 'stranger' not implying the Gael in a strange land, but a hybrid race"

[2] "Ptolemy terms the Nith, Novius: as the name Nith is the equivalent

The so - called Welsh bards (who were mostly Strath-clyde Britons), the nearest neighbours of the Galloway Picts, call them synonymously "Peithwyr," "Galwyddel," and "Novant."

Mr. Skene, with a stroke of his pen, scatters to the winds the cobwebs which had long darkened the threshold of Galloway history, and exposes the mistakes which, made when philology was young, have been reproduced and even aggravated by later authors Of these, the most opposed to fact are :

1st, That the Novantæ were Britons (Cymri), not Picts.

2d, That the Galloway Picts, known to medieval history, were not descendants of the Novantæ found there by the Romans, but Irish Dalaradians or Cruithne, who swarmed across the Channel in the eighth and ninth centuries, dispossessed, exterminated, or absorbed the Novantæ, and changed their place-names. Whereas, on the contrary, the race encountered by the Romans were undoubtedly Picts, written of as such ("Peithwyr" and "Novant") by Cymric bards, within a century of the Roman occupation ; and there is no authority whatever for saying that they were ever subdued, or even invaded in force, by any Irish tribe , still less that they disappeared.[1] In short, our paradox is this, that the Galloway Picts generated the wild Scots of Galloway !

Chalmers gives two reasons for believing in this early annihilation of the Novantæ · the one inconclusive, even were

of Ptolemy's Novius, so Bede's Niduari is the exact equivalent of Ptolemy's Novantæ, both meaning the 'gens' of the Nith "—*Celtic Scotland*, i 132

Nydd is a common river name, meaning spinning or whirling in eddies

[1] " Chalmers states dogmatically that Galloway was colonised in the eighth century by Cruithnigh from Ireland, followed by fresh swarms from the Irish hive during the ninth and tenth , and this statement has been accepted by all subsequent writers as if there were no doubt about it *There is not a vestige of authority for it.* The only authorities referred to by Chalmers consist of an entire misrepresentation of passages from the Ulster Annals '682, Bellum Rathamoire Muigeline contra Britones ,' '702, Bellum campi Cuilinn in Airdo ' Now both these battles were fought in Ulster. Rathmore or great fort of Muigeline, which Chalmers supposes to be Mauchline, was the chief seat of the Cruithnigh in Dalaradia, and is now Moylinny , and these events were attacks by the Britons upon the Cruithnigh of Ulster, not attacks by the latter on the British inhabitants of Ayrshire."—*Celtic Scotland*, i. 132

there no evidence to the contrary, the other depending on an entire misconception The first being, That the Irish topography corresponds more directly with that of Galloway than that of Scotland proper. The second, That Irish annals represent the Irish Picts obtaining a great victory over the Britons at Maigiline, which he renders Mauchline. Now the correspondence of names on the two sides of the Channel is simply accounted for by the circumstance that the Dalaradians who inhabited the land opposite Galloway were Picts as well. Again, while a victory of Irish Picts over the Damnii at Mauchline would have little concerned the Novantæ in any case, the argument derived from it is at once disposed of by the discovery that the scene of the battle was Moylinny in Antrim, not Mauchline in Ayrshire. Britons were invading Ireland, not the Irish Scotland,[1] the Galloway men having no part in the fray.

Accepting the dates which Mr. Skene assigns to the movements of Agricola, as related by Tacitus, it was in the year of our Lord 79 that his legions "surrounded the estuaries, and explored the lands and forests north of the Solway." When crossing the Nith they encountered a new race, differing from those (the Selgovae and Brigantes) they had left behind, whom they wrote down Novantæ.[2]

From the valley of the Nith the Romans marched westward through the territory of this same people, which they found extended continuously to the Irish Sea. Meeting with little opposition, and masking the native strongholds by fortified camps, they pushed forward to the "Doon of Kildonan," whence the legionaries gazed with wonder at the serrated outline of the Mourne Mountains, which, like giant's fingers, seemed to beckon them onwards to new worlds across the stormy waters.

---

[1] Scotland is here used in its modern sense · the Scots of that day were Irishmen, a colony of whom, known as the Dalriad Scots, colonised Argyle

[2] No doubt adapted from a native word The "Nydd" becoming Novius. So the Selgovæ were the hunters, from Celtic "Seilg," the Brigantæ (Cumberland and Lake district), hillmen, from Celtic "Bre," whence the vernacular "biae " The Selgovæ and Brigantes were British, the Novantæ Picts

Fragments of rectangular parapets, as well as place-names, point unmistakably to Roman stations established in this advance:[1] such as the Moat of Urr,[2] Castlecreavie, Bomby, Sypland, Dunrod, Dromore Castle on the Dee, Castramont, Longcaster,[3] Rispain, and Kildonan just mentioned.

This Doon and its surroundings deserve a moment's notice. The discovery of the rectangular outline (one-half of which has been levelled by the plough), which proves its Roman origin, is due to the intelligent research of the Rev. Andrew Urquhart. This ascertained, it is curious to note how the surrounding place-names, the meaning of which had been long as much unsuspected as the existence of the fort, seem to fill in the story of its construction. Above it, we find mapped Kirklauchlane, and short scrutiny is required to convince us that " Kirk " is here the not unusual corruption of *Caer*, and that this was a stronghold commanding a harbour and a town ; the name of the former being " Portespittal " (Spideal, suggesting here rather a place of entertainment for travellers than a refuge for the sick),— and the latter represented by " Nashantee " (na sean teach), the old houses—*old* perhaps a thousand years ago ! whilst the Roman fort or " Doon" has for centuries been known as Kildonan," that is, a dedication to St. Donan, whose date is 17th April 616 in the kalendars, suggesting that this was once a centre of population—although port, tower, camp, church, and hospice have long alike lain silent.

Ptolemy's British place-names are doubtless those supplied by Agricola's officers, and their Celtic roots are easily recognis-

---

[1] " He surrounded the subjugated tribes with forts and garrisons , and the remains of numerous Roman camps still to be seen in Dumfries, Kirkcudbright, and Wigtown, attest the extent to which he had penetrated the country The position of these illustrates in a remarkable manner the expression of Tacitus : " Praesidiis castellisque circumdatæ "—*Celtic Scotland*, i. 48

[2] Thirty years ago outworks, seemingly erected by the Romans, remained near the Moat of Urr. Three silver coins were found there—one of Hadrian, one of Commodus, and several legionary spears.—*Old Stat. Acc.* xi 69.

[3] " Castra and Chester always indicate Roman occupation On a Monreith estate map of 1777, a rectangular outline on the hill of Drumtrodden is marked ' Roman camp,' all traces of which have disappeared under the plough."—Maxwell's *Topo. of Galloway* (Camford)

able through their Greek or Latin dress.   The Rhynns and Mull
of Galloway being mapped by them Novantum Chersonesus and
Novantum Promontorium, proves beyond doubt that these men
of the Nith occupied the whole of modern Galloway.[1]

Other names are Rerigonium, evidently the same as the Caer
Rheon (Cathair Riaghan) of the bards, and Rerigonium Sinus is
their Llwch Rheon.   In the suffix of Vanduara we have Ayr,
Clota is the Clyde, Abravannus, the confluence (Aber or
Inbher) of the rivers, seems to be that of the Luce and Piltanton in
the Bay of Luce;   Lucopibia is the Isle of Whithorn (though it
is an extraordinary confusion of ideas to suppose that Ptolemy
was thinking of Ninian's white house);[2] Fines Æstus is the
estuary of the Cree;[3] Deva, the Dee, the black stream, Carbantorigum or Carbantium, possibly Kirkbean; Novius, the Nith;
Corda, Caer, the fort, with Sean prefixed, now Sanquhar (sean
caer), the old fort; Ituna, the Solway, from "Tonn," a tidal
wave.

The neighbours of the Novantæ are respectively mapped as
the Selgovæ, or hunters (Seilg), the Brigantes, or hill-men (Bre),
and the Damnii or Damnonii (damh, an ox), the cattle-breeders

Whilst mapping the province, the Romans seem to have
brought civilising influences to bear.[4]   This is proved by well

---

[1] One of the most perverse of the popular errors current in Galloway history
is that the Novantæ were bounded eastward by the Dee ; thus, as well as that
as to their nationality, arising from a neglect of finding the true root of the words
Thus Camden, suggesting that Novantæ was abridged from the Welsh "nant,"
low in a vale (*Brit* i 363), those who followed him assumed they were Welsh,
that is British, and entirely overlooking the Novius or Nydd, they failed to per-
ceive that Novantæ and "Niduari" *must* alike hail from the Nith.

[2] And was not able to spell it properly if he did ! if so, it should be Luco
kidia

[3] In the so-called Ptolemy's Atlas, reproduced "Ienæ Æstuarium" (Wigtown
Bay) ; but Mr Skene asserts that earlier editions have "Fines Æstus" (*Celtic
Scotland*, 1. 66).   If so, the Fines is a translation of Cree (crioch, a boundary) ;
a similar translation is "Longus" in Argyle for the "Add" (Abhuinn fhada), the
broad stream.

[4] "The following winter (*i.e.* 79-80) was devoted to reducing the turbulent
character of the natives to quiet submission "—*Celtic Scotland*, i. 44

Mr Skene connects with this date the description of Tacitus. "Having spread a
general terror through the country, he suspended his operations that the barbarians
might taste the sweets of peace a fierce people running wild in the woods would
be ever addicted to warfare. Agricola encouraged the natives to build temples,

authenticated facts of doings of St. Ninian, at a date prior
to their final departure   Their appreciation of the Christian
religion, their reception of strangers, their desire for instruction,
and the security to person and property evidenced by the completion and endurance of Ninian's works, prove the Novantæ of
the fourth century to have been under the reign of law.   The
greatest of St. Ninian's works not being the little church built of
stone ("more insolito Britonibus "), but the conventual establishment, humbler in material (a closely packed cluster of wattled
huts)—the mother, nevertheless, and model of the sixth century
monasteries of the Scoto-Irish Church.   Here a seminary,
known variously as Candida Casa, Magnum Monasterium,
Futerna, the House of Martin, Alba, and Rosnat, attracted
youths of high birth from far beyond the bounds of the province ; and during the following two centuries it was the
resort of those leaders of thought—of almost European reputation — known as "Secondary Saints."   Among these were
Tighernach, Eugenius, Malidh, and almost certainly his uncle
Patrick, Mancennus, Medana, Ciaran, Nennius, and Finian
of Moville   There cannot be a doubt that of the original
Candida Casa, the Isle of Whithorn was the site ; its penin-
sular position, as described by Ailred,[1] as well as the very name,
Ros-nat (nocht), "the bare point," being wholly inapplicable to
the inland priory and cathedral church ;—built by Fergus, and
not before the twelfth century.

Another work proving the existence of a central authority,
and requiring organisation and skill for its execution, was the vast
rampart, the ruins of which bear variously at different points,
the names of the "Deil's Dyke"[2] and "Picts' Dyke" or "Picts'

courts of justice, and commodious dwelling-houses, to establish a plan of
education, and give the sons of chiefs a tincture of letters "—Tac *Vit. Agri* 20

[1] Ailred, who frequently visited the place between the year 1140 and 1165,
writes of Ninian as "selecting for himself a site in the place now called Witerna,
which, situated on the shore of the ocean, and extending far into the sea on the
east, west, and south sides, is closed in by the *sea itself*, while only on the north
is a way open to those who would enter."— *Vit. Nin.* c 3

[2] This ancient fence is invariably eight feet broad at the base, with a foss on
the north side. The Deil's Dyke commences at Loch Ryan, on the farm of Beoch,

Wall." Carried in a right line, over marsh and moor, forest, mountain, and flood for full fifty miles between Leffnoll, an outwork of the citadel on Loch Ryan, and Sanquhar, the old strength upon the Nith—it extended, as Taliessin puts it,

" Between Caer Ryan and Caer Rywg "[1]

The erection of this dyke was, as Mr. Skene suggests, probably accomplished before the final departure of the Romans in 407   It was obviously reared as a barrier between the Novantæ and their neighbours the Damnii—their southern and western frontiers being defended by the sea, and their eastern by the Nith   We thus find their original territory included the modern shires of Wigtown and Kirkcudbright; with the parishes of Holywood, Dunscore, Keir, Glencairn, Tynron, Penpont, and a part of Durisdeer, in that of Dumfries.

As the Romans seem to have overrun Galloway with little bloodshed, so they seem to have maintained amicable relations with the Novantæ.   For two hundred years after they retired we glean notices of the province from church calendars and Irish chronicles, giving us continuous lists of kinglets, whose existence, though open individually to doubt, yet in the aggregate may be held to be founded upon fact.   And it is remarkable—if not absolutely conclusive as to their accuracy—that most of the so-called kings have impressed their names upon the soil.[2]

First we have Sarran, who, according to the *Book of Bally-mote*, established his power over Saxons and Picts, married

---

thence by Braid Fell, Cairnzerran, Kylfeddei, by the north end of Loch Maberry, Kirkcalla, Ochiltree, Glenvernoch, (a hill fort of large dimensions here,) Knock-ville,—crosses the Cree,—Terregan, Dranandow, between "the Thieves" and the Nappers, Auchinlech, Talnotrie, Craignelder, Craigencally, Garrary, Knockreoch, Auchenshinnoch, and passing Glencairn, Tynron, and Penpont, is nearly entire on the farm of South Mains, opposite Sanquhar —Train, *App. to Mackenzie*

[1] *Book of Taliessin*, 10.   Caer Ryan is Rerigonium, the modern Innermessan , Caer Rywg, Sanquhar, the fort on the Crawick.—*Four Ancient Books of Wales*, i 270

Leffnoll, "halfpenny land of the wool" (Leithpheigan).

[2] Riaghan or Rheon, Lachlane, Torquil, Donachie, Trost, Dermot, are to be classed with those mighty men anterior to Agamemnon, over whose memory has closed an endless night—"carent quia vate sacro."   They made their mark in

Babona, daughter of Loarn, son of Erc, and by her had, with three other sons, Leurig and Cairnech, and, after victory and triumph, "died in the House of Martin." [1] Leurig succeeded him, Cairnech being abbot of this House of Martin or Monastery of Rosnat. The date approximately 440

Leurig after this extended his power and forcibly built a fort within the precincts of the monastery of Cairnech his brother, that is, the Isle of Whithorn. Cairnech remonstrated, Leurig scoffed, whereupon the Abbot incited his cousin, Murcertach, son of Erc (afterwards King of Ireland), to dethrone his brother, which he did, and also killed him.[2] Cairnech then went to Ireland, and introduced monachism there, on the model of Rosnat, which had now attained to great note   This must have occurred before 478.[3]

Murcertach, or Murdoch, whose name, "sea-warrior," is an appropriate one to the invader of Galloway, afterwards ruled there.[4] The age of Leurig and Murdoch coincides with that of the somewhat mythic Medana, of St. Patrick, and of his popular nephew Mahdh (from whom the stream

their day, and their names are indelibly attached to places of strong defence, as Caer Ryan, Kinklochlane, Kilquhockadale, Murdonachie, Ardtrostan, Craig-dermot.

[1] *Book of Ballymote, Chron of Picts and Scots*, 52   Mr Skene there identifies the House of Martin with Candida Casa in the Isle of Whithorn

[2] In the Irish Nennius this relation follows that of the departure of the Romans, and immediately precedes the mention of Vortigern's invitation to Hengist and Horsa, A.D. 449.

[3] To Cairnech is attributed the introduction of monachism into Ireland , he is mentioned as Bishop of the House of Martin, in other words, of Candida Casa. From this date we frequently find saints (of the second order) resorting thither for the purpose of being trained in the monastic life.   Among others, Tighernach of Clones and Eugenius of Ardstraw, natives of Leinster, who had been carried off by pirates and brought to Britain, were sent by the king, at the queen's intercession, to a holy man, Monennus, and trained by him at the monastery of Rosnat, which is also called Alba, or white.—*Celtic Scotland*, ii 46 , quoting Colgan, *Vit. Tighernach*, etc.

[4] "Then he thrust his battle staff into the king's side, and returned to the cleric with his head, and said, 'Here is thy brother's head for thee, O Cairnech'; and Cairnech said, 'Leave me the bone, and eat thou the marrow.' Then he took hostages and power in the land for seven years, as also the sovereignty of Britain and Cat and Orc and Saxony."—*Book of Ballymote*
Murcertach, "the sea-warrior," is Murdoch in Scotland

which supplied his baptistery is named "the Water of Malzie"); of Bridget, and St Lassair (mother of Finnian of Moville), whence our numerous Kilbrides, and Killeser   In 525 A D. we find a King Drust, the loose doings of whose "one perfect daughter, Dustric,"[1] as a pupil of the great monastery, is the subject of a penitential hymn by St. Mugint, which, as Bishop Forbes well remarks, sheds a *remarkable* light on the life—half monastic, half social—at Whithorn.[2]   Dr Stuart connects this King Drust with a vitrified fort in Anwoth, called "Trusty Knowe"   This would give additional point to the quatrain in O'Clery's Calendar commencing—

"Trust, king of the eastern confluence on the strand"[3]

Contemporary with Drust was Arthur of the Round Table, his name is supposed to be reflected in Loch Arthur, whence, after fighting his twelve battles, he turned northward   Taliessin's line—

"Beyond Caer Wydyr they saw not the prowess of Arthur,"[4]

seems confirmatory of this, and "Caer Wydyr" to point to the vitrified fort of Castle Gower ("Gwydyr," glass, a term applicable to vitrification, being easily convertible to Gower).

We find no notice of a direct successor to Drust, but the death of a king Cendaeladh is recorded, A.D. 580, whose name was preserved till comparatively recent times in that of the parish and lake of Loch Kendellach.   The parish is now called New Abbey, and his name is almost unrecognisable in that of the lake itself, now corrupted to Loch Kinder

The years of Cendaeladh's reign, and twenty following, are those of the "Welsh Bards," whose heroes are contempo-

---

[1] O'Clery's *Calendar*, 1 November   [2] Introduction to *Life of Ninian*, xli.
[3] "Ant-'saoir" is translated "free bay" by Mr. Skene, "the noble confluence" by Dr. Todd   But "t'soir" means also "of the east", and "Trusty Knowe" overlooks the confluence of the Cree eastward of Whithorn
[4] Arthuret on the Carwhinelow has nothing to do with Arthur, the roots apparently being "ard" and "rod."   Carwhinelow is a corruption of Caergwenddoleu, named from a Cymric prince, whose hill-fort overlooked it.

rary princes, scions of two royal lines: namely, that of Coyl Hen (the old King Cole), whence the place-name Kyle,— and that of Ceredig (the Coroticus of the Epistle of St Patrick). The line of Coyl are termed in church history the Pagan faction, though, more correctly, they were simply unorthodox Of these were Gwenddoleu, Cymbelyn, Morcant, Urien, and Gwallawc, nephew of Caradawg (from whom we have Carrick)

Of the line of Ceredig those contemporary, were Rydderch Hael, Elydyr, and Aeddan Vradog

The two opposing factions, with such forces as each could muster, met in deadly combat at Ardderyd (Arthuret), A D 573, the respective commanders being Gwenddoleu and Rydderch Hael, Cendaeladh probably assisting the former.

The Christians were entirely victorious. St Kentigern, Rydderch's bishop, who had fled from persecution, was now recalled to his diocese Glasgow (the Penryn-Wleth of the bards), called Gulath by Jocelyn; whence soon after, "going forth, he cleansed from the foulness of idolatry and the contagion of heresy the land of the Picts, now called Galwethia." [1]

We need not follow the complications of the period,—a score of kinglets perpetually at war, constantly changing sides, some- times allied with the Novantæ, sometimes against them,[2]—but we may mention one who, whether as enemy or ally, equally won and retained the admiration of the Galwegians—Gwallawc, the hawk of battle,[3] latinised Galgacus   There was of course more than one Galgacus, as there was certainly more than one

[1] Jocelyn's *Life of St Kentigern*, ch xxxiv (a hill called Gulath by the water-side near his home, ch. xiv.)

[2] A few years before, according to Nennius, there were Urien, Rydderch, Gwallawg, and Morcant fighting against the Northumbrian Saxons

[3] *Black Book of Carmarthen*, 32

"Gwallawg, the horseman of tumult, would drive onward."—*Red Book of Hengist.*

   " The rich plains from Caer-Clud to Caer,
      The support of Penprys and Gwallawg."—*Book of Taliessin,* xi

The bards of the Four Ancient Books of Wales are Myrddin or Merlin, Aneurin, Llywarch (whose son is believed to have built Caerlaverock, Llywarch's fort), and Taliessin, ("the bright browed bard of Urien and Owen")

Caractacus; and Boece, mixing truth with fiction, and with a
total disregard for dates, adopting the local tradition that
Gwallawc reposes beneath the standing stones of Torhouse,
represents him to have been the King Galdus, who, expelling
the Romans from Galloway, reigned over a united Scotland, and
dying at Wigtown, was interred with great pomp in the neighbourhood, many huge pillars being raised above his sepulchre,
and by a decree of Parliament in the year 103, the province was
named Galdia,—whence Galloway,—in his honour.[1] It is unnecessary to refute the absurdities of this relation. It was a
thousand years later before there was a united Scotland, or the
pretence of a National Parliament. As real incidents in his life
we may give a list of battles fought by Gwallawc, of which
Galloway was certainly the scene, the date being the latter half
of the sixth century.

"A battle in Agathes.
A battle of trembling in Aeron.
A battle in the wood of Beit.
A darting of spears—a battle in the Marsh of Terra [2] with the
    dawn."

In "Agathes" we recognise Cairn Agathe in New Luce,
"Gath," "a dart or javelin," suggestive of the "darting of
spears", "Aeron" is Glen-iron; the "Marsh of Terra" is that
crossed by "the Stepping Stones of Glenterra;" and "Beit" is
Beoch, overlooking Loch Ryan—the four battlefields all lying
to the south of the Deil's Dyke.

Following Cendaeladh was Eochaidh Aingces (the cursing or

---

[1] "Galdus deceissit fra the incarnation of God cin yeres. Many huge pillars
was raisit about his sepulture . . and that his memory never sall peris, *be decreit of
Parliament,* wes commanded that the lands named afore Brigance (!) sall be in
time coming Galdia—in our days Galvidia—be corruption Galloway."—Boece,
bk iv ch 2

[2] *Book of Taliessin,* xi. Almost by intuition Mr Skene recognises in the
"stepping-stones" of Glen-terra "the marsh of Terra" The stepping-stones led
across a marsh ; there are also "standing stones," no doubt, marking the field of
battle (*New Stat. Wigtownshire,* article 'Inch'). Terra is "Teamhair," meaning a fortified enclosure commanding an extensive view

fretful), whose daughter married Eochaidh Buidhe (the yellow-haired), son and heir of Aidan Vradog, king of the Dalriad Scots. This second Eochaidh being expelled from his own kingdom of Argyle, the Gallovidians accepted him as their sovereign, apparently in right of his wife. His greatest recorded feat was leading the Gallovidians across the Channel to assist the Dalaradians, or Irish Picts, against the Dalriads, or Irish Scots, in which he was entirely successful, though his sons had come from Argyle to help the Dalriads, and two were left among the slain.[1] The former Eochaidh's name appears in Kilauchy, and the latter's in Cragauch, usually called "the Tawer" (Teamhair)—an intrenched hill-fort, a perfect example of the meaning implied by this Celtic word, "an intrenched position commanding a distant prospect."[2] It seems possible that Lochnaw may rather mean Eochaidh's Lake than the Lake of the Ford; the name differs little phonetically from Lough Neagh, notoriously named from another Eochaidh, and the site was exactly such as chieftains of his day affected for their strongholds.

Eochaidh Buidhe's death is chronicled, 629.[3] A son of his, Donald Breac (the swarthy) had succeeded to the throne of Argyle on his brother Conadh Cerr's death in battle. He had another son, Donald Donn (the brown haired), who may possibly have been a king of Galloway, but whoever Eochy's successor was, he seems to have courted and accepted the suzerainty of the Northumbrian Saxons.[4]

[1] "Cath Fedhaeoin, A D 629," Tighernach "The battle of Fedhaeoin was fought between the Cruithnigh and the Dalriads. Eochadh Buidhe was here on the side of the Cruithnigh, and opposed to two of his own sons, one Conad Cerr being king of the Dalriads, and two grandsons of Aidan were slain."—*Celtic Scotland*, i 241

[2] O'Donovan Cormack's *Glossary*

[3] *Annals of Ulster*.

[4] The following names of places retain those of kings of Galloway, and although any individual instance may be fairly open to dispute, their being all recoverable can hardly be fortuitous .

c. 440 Harran, Sarran, Ciaran	Chipper Harran, corruptly Chapelheron
440 Bobona, his Queen .	Cairn Baber
440 Luirich . .	Castle Larrick.
476 Murcertach, or Murdoch	Murdonachie, Dunmurchie, Murchies Wa's
525 Trust, or Drust	Trusty Knowe (a vitrified fort), Ardtrostan.

It was during this reign that, A D. 639, Sabina, an outraged maid of royal blood, crossed the channel from Ireland, as it is said, upon a boulder, landed in the Rhynns of Galloway, probably at Port Nessoch, and leaving her stone currach on the shore, crossed the Isthmus, and encamped in a wood near Loch Ryan.   Here, on lighting a fire, the glitter of her bracelets attracted the cupidity of robbers lurking near, who, rushing upon the party, were miraculously paralysed by a gesture of her "holy boy," Cuthbert, whose saintship was here first asserted. Next day mother and son embarked in a neighbouring creek, on a ship of ordinary build, and sailed for the north [1]   Place-names wonderfully corroborate the details of the legend,[2]—the site of the first encampment being "Killiemacuddican," its northern corner "Culchintie," and their port of embarkation "Portencailzie," their first stopping place Kirkcudbright-Innertig, now Ballantrae, their next Kirkcudbright-Innergarvan, now Girvan [3]

c. 580 (died) Cendaeladh	. Loch Kendelach
580 Eochaidh Aingces	Kilauchy, Craigauch Castle
610 Eochaidh Buidhe	Auchlannochy,[1] Tower of Ciaigauch.
629 Donald Donn	Castle Donnell

[1] "Miro modo in lapidea devectus navicula apud Galweiam in regione illa, quae Rennii vocatur in Portu qui Rintsnoc dicitui, applicuit —Post haec curroc lapidea in Galweia derelicta, navim aliam subit "—*Libellus de Nativitate Sancti Cuthberti*

[2] Given in full, *Celtic Scotland*, ii. 203.

"Killiemacuddican" (Coile-mo Cuideach-an) means the ' wood of the saintly little Cuthbert."

"Culchintie" (cul teinte), "the angle of the fires," where, according to tradition, any faggots of wood being thrown ignited spontaneously.

"Portencailzie" (Port-na-cailleach), the "nun's port."

Besides Kirkcudbright-Innertig, which is now Ballantrae, there was Kirkcudbright-Innergarvane, now Girvan, probably marking their camping-places on the shore

The incident of the fire is placed in the legend farther northward, but the name "Culchintie" seems decisive

[3] The first stood at the influx of the Tig into the Stincher ; in a charter of Robert III, 1404, it is called "Sancti Cuthberti de Invertig " At the same date Girvan was granted to the monks of Crossraguel as " Ec[a]. de Sancti Cuthberti de Invergarvane "

---

[1] Each-lann Eochy—Minigaff   Eochy's stable.   So Stable-alane seems to be anglicised Gaelic, Alan's-stable   Stabul is a living word in Gaelic and Irish

Meanwhile the Northumbrian Saxons were extending their power northward, Edwin, their king, having permanently imprinted his name on the Castle Rock of the future capital of Scotland—"Edwinesburch," as it is written in the foundation charter of Holyrood. Under Edwin, the Saxons had driven the Strathclyde Britons out of all the country between the Cheshire Dee and the Derwent, and, seizing the Isles of Anglesea and Man, opened up alliance with the Galloway Picts, thus taking them in flank. Without entering into the complications of Saxon History, we need only say, that though Edwin was killed, and his throne seized by Eanfrit in 633, the alliance between the Northumbrians and Gallwegians was continued by the new king; and we have evidence of its being in full operation under Oswald (the saint who received a Scottish education at Iona), who succeeded him the following year. It was with the assistance of the Gallwegians that Oswald gained his crowning victory near the Bay of Ayr, the site of which is supposed to be marked by the church of St. Oswald of Turnberry,[1] which gives name to the parish of Kirk Oswald.[2]

The fraternisation of the Galloway Picts with the Saxons is the subject of frequent allusion by the Welsh bards.

Taliessin scornfully exclaims:

> " Angles and Galwyddel,
> Let them make war."

And ventures a prophecy, sadly belied by events:

> " I will predict, before the end,
> The Brytton uppermost of the Saxon "[3]

From 634, for one hundred and seventy years, the Gallwegians remained true to the Northumbrian Saxons, their admitted overlords. The tie being the stronger that it was self-imposed. The

---

[1] *Caledonia,* iii 532.   [2] *Old Stat Account,* x. 474.
[3] *Book of Taliessin,* 1. The Brytton—the Strathclyde Britons. Mr Skene remarks that "there was here a combination of the Britons of Alclyde and the Scots of Dalriada against the Angles and the Pictish population (of the west) subject to them "—*Four Ancient Books of Wales,* i. 284.

Galloway Picts could not hold their ground against their more powerful Cymric neighbours without such an alliance, offensive and defensive.   Oswald, who by this arrangement was practically King of Galloway, was killed in 642 at Oswestry, and succeeded by his brother Oswy, and he in 670 by his son Egfrid.   In both these reigns the Saxons extended their conquest greatly over the Picts of Lothian and Fife; and it was these, and not the Galloway Picts, who made a determined attempt, in the commencement of Egfrid's reign, to throw off the Saxon yoke. Galloway, on the contrary, was over-run by the combined forces of these northern Picts and Britons, and Dalriad Scots from across the Channel, against whom the Gallwegians made common cause with the Saxons.   The trustworthy Bede[1] tells us that, to keep the Irish employed at home, Egfrid sent an army into Ireland (of course through Galloway), who ravaged its eastern shores; and that, coming himself in person, driving, as we otherwise learn, the British and Pictish kings Oan and Bridei out of the south, he followed them too far, and, becoming entangled in mountain passes, was defeated at Dunnichen, near Perth, in the following year.[2]

The untrustworthy Boece gives as an episode a minute account of a battle on the sandhills beyond the confluence of the Luce and Piltanton, which, from its anachronisms, has been generally discarded as fabulous. But place-names so entirely agree with his relation, that we are disposed to think that one of the battles hinted at by Bede was really fought here, though many of the incidents, markedly that of King Egfrid's death, were fictitious, and the facts inverted.   It was the aptitude of Boece for furbishing his story with actual local traditions, but which he used as he chose, — utterly regardless of accuracy, —that gave his history such a hold over all Scotland in an uncritical period, ingleside oracles accepting his spurious version as undoubted.

The scene opens on Dunskey Castle, occupied by the Scots

---

[1] Bede, *Eccles. Hist.* iv 26   [2] *Celtic Scotland*, i. 264

and Northern Picts under Bridei, besieged by Egfrid and the Galloway Picts.   Oan, king of the Strathclyde Britons, advanced on Egfrid's rear, obliging him to raise the siege.   In the words of Boece, as rendered by Bellenden :

"Edfred send ane buschement of Saxonis in the Scottis landes. . . . Sone eafter, ambassatouris wer send be Eugenius to Edfred desiring redres, be quhom was answerit 'That he wald invade the Scottis with mair trubil than afore, but ony redres' . . . Eugenius . . . heirand that his ennimes wer to cum in Galloway, he gaderit ane gret power, to prevent thair cuming. Yit, afore his cuming the Saxonis and Pichtis wer lyand at the seige of Donskene, the strangest castel of Galloway in thay dayis Edfrid be haisty cuming of Scottis, wes constranit to leif the seige, and met thame at the river of Lewis in Galloway quhilk was that time, be inundation of snawis, boldin above the brayis. The battalis junit haistely with equale hatrent.   Edfred exhortit his men to remembir thair anciant virtew, and to vincus thair ennimes only be violent force.   Siclik, Eugenius ceissit not to pas about his folkis, exhorting thame to schaw thair invincibill curage, that they micht rejose the palme of victory.   Quhile the Saxonis and Scottis war fechtand thus in maist fury, the Pichtis fled to the nixt mote.   The fleing of Pichtis dejeckit gretumly the curage of Saxonis, for thay dred that thir Pichtis suld cum on thair backis   Nochtheless, King Edfred exhortit his folkis to perseveir in ithand battal   And quhen he was spekand maist specialy, he rasit up his visour, to be the mair fervent in speche, and incontinent he was doung throw the heid be ane ganye (arrow or dart), quhair his face was bair, and fel to the ground.   The Saxonis, seand thair king slane, gaif backis; on quhom followit the Scottis with lang chace, and drave tham to the river of Lewis, quhare mony of thame perist, and few of thame tane." [1]

Among the sandhills where the battle was fought, there is a "mote" mapped Knochencrunze (cnocan-Cruithne) "the

---

[1] Boece, bk. ix ch xxiii

Picts' Knoll." Their line of retreat lay across the dangerous
ford still called " Droch Dhuil," the devil's bridge ; from there
up Ballochjargon, the red or bloody pass, and the point where
fugitives thence would reach the Luce is Craigfolly (creag-
na-fola), the rock of the blood, a name which seems translated in " Bloody Wheel," a little farther up the river. The
scene of action among the sandhills forms a part of the farm
of Torrs, and here arrow - heads and spear - points are being
constantly discovered.[1] The difference between the true and
spurious versions being that Boëce reverses the issue of the
fight; it was Oan and Bridei who fled, Egbert and his
Galwegians who wielded the " red pursuing spear."

Egfrid was succeeded in 685 by an elder natural brother,
Aldfred, who had been educated in Ireland by Adamnan, the
biographer of St. Columba. And on Aldfred's succession he,
being then Abbot of Iona, sailed round the Galloway coast on
his way to Bamborough, to plead with his former pupil for the
release of Irish captives brought there by Egfrid's General
Berct. His biographer thus relates a miracle worked by this
saint on the shores of the Solway,—which he terms " Tracht
Romra "[2] (the exact equivalent of the Bardic " Tawne " and the
Roman " Ituna "), The Frith of the Sea Swell.

" At Tracht-Romra the strand is long, the flood rapid,—so
rapid that if the best steed in Saxon-land were to start from the
edge of the tide when the tide begins to flow, he could only
bring his rider in by swimming. The Saxons in authority were
unwilling to permit Adamnan to land. ' Push your currach on
shore,' said the saint, ' for both land and sea are obedient to
God.' The clerics did so. Adamnan drew a circle with his
crozier round the currachs. God rendered the strand firm under

---

[1] The arrow-heads, knives, spear-points, and other lethal weapons described
as found on the Farm of Torrs, in the *Archæological Collections of Galloway*,
vol. 1 p 3, in an article contributed by the Rev. J. Wilson (of Glenluce), may
all be spoils from the battlefield of Knockencrunze

[2] "Tracht" is glossed "the sea" as well as the shore (O'Reilly), "Romra,"
"springtide," "swell of the ocean" (*Ibid*); "Tonn," Gaelic and Irish, "a
tidal wave."

them, and forming a high wall of sea around them, the place became an island. The tide roared past them to its limits, and did them no harm." [1]

This description points to a dangerous sandbank opposite Colvend, known as "Barnhourie," [2] which is completely covered only at spring tides, and this not being so on this occasion may be held by the sceptical to explain the miracle.

Aldfred is reputed to have been the first literary prince of his race, to have ruled Galloway with justice, and preserved peace till 705, when he was succeeded by his son Osred.

In 716 the crown was wrested from Osred by a cousin of the blood-royal, Conred, who held it for two years, when in turn he was deposed by Osric, a brother of Osred.

Osric dying in 729, Ceolwulf, brother to Conred, seated himself upon his throne. Ceolwulf has left his mark in Galloway history as the founder of the bishopric of "Hwitern"

Individuals of the Scoto-Irish Church had often been styled Bishops of Candida Casa, which is the equivalent for Whithorn, but the title referred rather to the church and monastery than to the see, which was now for the first time constituted territorially. Its bishop was a suffragan of York, an arrangement which held good till the middle of the fourteenth century. [3]

As to the present bishop, Bede writes: " In the province of Northumbria, where King Ceolwulf reigns, four bishops preside · Wilfred, in the church of York; Ethelwald, in Lindisfarne, Acca, in Hagulstad (Hexham), and Pecthelm, in that of Candida Casa, which, from the increased number of believers, has lately become a see, and has him for its first

---

[1] *Irish Life of Adamnan.* Also Introduction to Adamnan's *Columba* (Reeves).

[2] "Odhar," genitive "huidrie," brown or dun, is often applied to legendary cows The famous *Leabhor-na-h'uidre*, the "Book of the Brown Cow," was so called because written on the skin of the pet cow of St Ciaran. Many places derive their names from such legendary cows, and so possibly may Barnhourie —See Joyce, ii 280

[3] "Michael, who died in 1359, is the last Bishop of Whithorn whose submission to the Church of York is on record."—Bishop Forbes, Preface to *Life of Ninian*, p. lv.

Prelate."[1]   The "increased number of believers" suggests increased activity in Saxon colonisation.   The Galloway Picts had been Christians centuries before their overlords, but the newer converts pretended now to greater orthodoxy, that is to say, they looked to Rome rather than Iona.   The main points of contention between the two churches being as to the form of the tonsure and the calculation of Easter; the Galwegians, as members of the Scoto-Irish Church, adopted the tonsure and accepted the Easter of the Eastern Church, and the victory of the Romish over the Scottish Church in Galloway, as dependent upon Northumbria, is solely to be ascribed to St. Cuthbert, its active advocate, who had died in the reign of Aldfred, A.D. 687, as Bishop of Lindisfarne.   We need hardly say that the dedication to himself of "Cuthbrectes Cyrc" gives its name to Kirkcudbright, the occasion probably being his visit to the Niduari Picts,[2] as recorded by Bede.

With the consecration of Pecthelm, Bede brings his valuable history to a close · "The Picts,"[3] he tells us, "are at peace with the English nation, and rejoice at being united in peace and truth with the whole Catholic Church. The Scots,[4] satisfied with their own territory, meditate no hostilities against the English.   The Britons, though they from innate hatred are adverse to the English, and from wicked custom oppose the appointed Easter of the Catholic Church, though in part their own masters, and elsewhere brought under subjection to the English, can in no way prevail as they desire   Such being the peaceable disposition of the times, many of the nobility, as well as private persons, rather incline to dedicate both themselves and their children to the monastic vows than to study martial arts.

[1] Bede, *Eccles. Hist.* bk. v. ch. xxiii.
[2] Bede, *Vit Cudb* ch ix   It was at this time, when Prior of Melrose (*circum* 661), "that he went to the land of the Niduari Picts, or Picts of Galloway, then under the dominion of the Angles. .   The traces of this visit have been left in the name of Kirkcudbright."—*Celtic Scotland*, ii 208.
[3] Bede, *Eccles. Hist.* bk v. ch. xxiii. It is to be remarked that there were Eastern, i e Lothian Picts as well as the great northern nation. Bede uses the word Niduari to distinguish those of Galloway.
[4] That is, the Dalriad Scots of Argyle.

This is the present state of Britain, in the 731st year of the
incarnation of our Lord, in whose reign may the earth ever
rejoice and the islands be glad."

In proof that Bede had read aright the signs of the times, it
is on record that only six years later (737) King Ceolwulf
resigned his crown to his cousin Eadbert, to end his days as
a monk of Lindisfarne.   During Eadbert's reign, Galloway was
invaded by a Celtic pretender, Alpyn, son of Echach.[1]   The
Galwegians rose against him *en masse*   He conquered the
greater part of the country, till he was confronted by Innrechtach, a native chief, near Kelton on the Dee.[2]   Here he was
completely routed and forced to fly.   His retreat was, however,
carried out in an orderly manner, till, as he was in the act of
leaving the province, fording a stream at the entrance of Glen-
App, in the midst of his bodyguard, a single man sprang upon
him and struck him lifeless from his charger[3]   The stone which
marks his sepulture still preserves his name.   From time
immemorial it has been named in charters as a landmark—
Laight-Alpyn.   The pillar-stone itself is the "Laight," whilst
Alpyn is still recognisable in the name of the beautiful glen, near
which he fell.   Saxon troops now came, though rather late in
the day, to the assistance of Innrechtach and his Galwegians,
who, following on Alpyn's retreating force, drove them entirely

---

[1] This Alpyn is not to be confounded with Alpyn, father of Kenneth, who
flourished exactly a century later   Alpyn, son of the Scottish Dalriad king
Echach by a Pictish princess, became king of the Northern Picts in 726
Expelled from this throne in 728, he took refuge in Argyle, and there obtained
the throne.   Again expelled from Dalriada, he seized upon the Pictish territory
of Galloway, where he was slain after having subdued it.—Skene, Preface to
Chron. of Picts and Scots, p. clxxxvi.

[2] Mr. Skene suggests Kirkcormac as the scene of this battle, which is called
in the *Annals of Ulster*, Drum Cathmail —*Celtic Scotland*, i 29

[3] Cesty fust tue en Goloway, com il le auoit destruyt, de vn soul hom qi ly
gayta en vn espesse boys en pendaunt al entree dun ge de vn ryuere, com
cheuaucheoit entre sez gentz —*Chron. of Picts and Scots*, 198.

"The name of Laicht Alpyn really belongs to the farms of Meikle and Little
Laicht, on the eastern shore of Loch Ryan . . On the very line of separation
between the two counties is a large upright pillar-stone to which the name of
Laicht-Alpin, the monument or grave of Alpin, is actually appropriated "—*Ibid.*
clxxxv

out of Carrick,[1] with which as a base, Eadbert so well improved his advantage, that by 754 he had annexed "all Carrick,
with the plain of Kyle[2] and other regions," to his kingdom of
Galloway.   Eadbert was succeeded by his son Osulf in 757,
but already the power of the Northumbrians had culminated.
Osulf was murdered by Ethelwold, who grasped Osulf's crown,
only to have it snatched from himself in 765 by Alchred.   He
was dethroned by Ethelred, a son of Ethelwold, and Ethelred
again by Elfwold, the brother of Alchred, in 778.

In Elfwold's reign the monks of Candida Casa entertained
a distinguished visitor, in the person of Alcuin,[3] tutor of
Charlemagne, a scholar of European celebrity.   Elfwold
was murdered by his troops in 789, and was succeeded, but
for a year only, by Osred, his nephew ; when Ethelred, who
had been dethroned ten years before, reappeared, killed the
two sons of Elfwold, to secure himself against a second expulsion,
but was himself murdered in 794.   Meantime, whilst the royal
house of Northumbria was crumbling to its fall, aspirants to
dominions wider than theirs were taking their departure from
the Sound.   The horizons of the British Isles, east and west, were
darkened by the sails of the dragon-prowed war-galleys of the
"Gentiles," as the Church chronicles styled the Norsemen.   A
cry went up from the cloisters of Lindisfarne in 793, to be
re-echoed a few years later from Iona, and the Saxons withdrew
from Galloway at their approach.[4]

The Saxon colonists during these long years have left few
traces of their occupation in place-names.   It is difficult, no
doubt, to distinguish Northumbrian Saxon from the kindred

[1] "744   Factum est prælium inter Pictos et Britones."—Simeon of Durham
[2] "750   Eadbertus campum Cuil, cum aliis regionibus, suo regno addidit."—
Continuation of Bede
[3] 782   Alcuin presents a holosericum for St. Ninian's body.   Ethelbert was
then Bishop of Whithorn, consecrated at York 777 —Forbes, Preface to *Life of
Ninian,* p 44.   Keith's *Scotch Bishops*
[4] We have thus followed fourteen sovereigns of the days of the heptarchy :
Oswald, Oswi, Egfred, Aldfred, Osred, Cenred, Osric, Ceolwulf, Eadbert, Osulf,
Ethelwolf, Alchred, Elfwold, Osred, and Ethelred, all acknowledged as head
kings (Ardrigh) of Galloway.

Norse. But leaving to the Vikings such distinctive roots as by, garth, gil, nes, oe, tun, wark, seat, we may assume ton, ham, mearc, cyrc, float, beorg when in the form "berry," and "wic" when an inland station, to be Saxon test words.

The Rosnatense Monasterium, or Candida Casa of earlier chronicles of the Irish Church, had its name permanently Saxonised by its Northumberland overlords to Hwitern (one of the surest proofs of undisputed possession), which to this day it practically retains.

Cuthbrectes Cyrc was the oldest form of Kirkcudbright, founded in Saxon times — Kilcudbricht being its contemporaneous Celtic form.[1] So, Kirkdale is from Anglo-Saxon "Cyric-doel" (not "dale" or Celtic "dol"), the church portion— the glebe. "Fleet',"[2] or "float," indicates a naval station, and we may presume that the Northumbrians had an arsenal in the estuary of the Cree, ever since called the "Fleet,"[3] and another on the Irish Channel, at Float[4] The Saxon form of "wic" we find in Stennoch (stein-wic), and in Wig (now Castlewigg), behind it—Wigtown being Norse (the tun or station in the bay of the Vikings or Creekers; as is the Wigg, their naval station in Lochryan). "Ton" tells its own tale in Aggiston, Engleston, Ingleston (Angles'), Preston (the Priests'), Carlton (Ceorl, the churls or husbandmen), Gelston (Gyles), Levingston (Leofwine's), Myreton (by the mere), Broughton ("broch," the fortified ton, —a form peculiarly Northumbrian), Orchardtons (villa residences of officials, with garden attached).[5]

[1] Simeon of Durham writes it Cuthbrectis Church . . . in an old Manx poem it is Keelchoobragh

[2] "Fleot," a place where vessels "float." In Norse also "fleet" , in French the suffix takes the form of "fleur," as Harfleur

[3] It is to be remembered that the Strathclyde Britons had successfully disputed the occupation of the Borders and Cumberland with the Saxons, whose communications with the Galwegians were therefore only by sea—from Lancashire, Anglesea, and the Isle of Man, to their ports on the Irish Channel or the Solway

[4] Float is preposterously said to be so called from wreckage of the Armada, and of a piece is the tradition that the little horses called Galloways were the produce of a stallion which escaped from the said vessels "Flote" is to be found in charters a century before the Armada was built. Galloways were a native breed, famous a thousand years before.

[5] "Ortgeard" in Northumbrian Saxon meant a yard for orts, or wyrts, i.e.

"Ham" appears in Edingham (Edwine's home), Cunning-hame (Coning's—a proper name; or possibly the king's). In Penninghame the "ing" might represent the family of Penn,[1] though it was probably a "penny land." Botel, now Buittle (a mansion), marked the seat of a man of importance.

"Mark" in later times indicates rates of taxation, as Three Mark, Half Mark; but the Saxon "merk" meant a boundary, as Mark on the Marches of Carrick, Mark Bredden, the Britons' March, Mark Broom (a broom bush doing duty for the "mearc treow," the march tree, so frequently named in Saxon charters).

"Inks" is certainly taken from the Anglo-Saxon "inge," glossed "pratum" and "pascuum,"—a common meadow,—but in Galloway is always applied to low lying land on estuaries, within high-water mark.

"Holt," another test word, appears in Chapelshot, Buittle, the chapel wood.

vegetables, herbs, or roots: an enclosure for apples, cherries, or other fruits is a comparatively modern meaning of the word.

[1] As Pennington, in Hants and Lancashire.

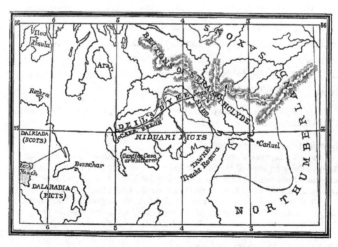

RELATIVE POSITION OF RACES AT THE PERIOD.

CHAPTER II

A D. 794 to 1124

"And they burned the churches, the heathen Dane,
To light their bands to their boats again."
Harold the Dauntless.

THE fleets of the Galls bore onwards, tales of their violence preceding their arrival. They rounded the Mull, and had soon enveloped the peninsula of the Novantæ in its full extent, from the entrance of Lochyran to the estuary of the Nith.

The Saxons had disappeared. The Galwegians were utterly unable to cope single-handed with the amphibious warriors. The fanes of their saints, especially their Candida Casa, the centre of the religious life of the province, lay absolutely at their mercy, and, to human ken, seemed absolutely doomed. But whether or no St. Ninian's spirit, hovering above his ancient shrine, miraculously interposed, certain it is, that the brand which in Norse hands elsewhere symbolised sacrilege and slaughter, in Galloway became emblematical of the torch of Hymen. No bard has sung, no chronicler told the story of this fraternisation; but whilst the Galls, black and white, overran other districts "as fierce wolves, killing not only sheep and oxen, but choirs of monks and nuns," in Galloway, and there alone, they entered into the closest fellowship with its people, sought their daughters in marriage, and enrolled their sons in their martial ranks.

The Galwegians, on their part, proved apt pupils in pillage and piracy. Irish annalists term them "the foster children of the Norseman," and within a generation of the unholy alliance, Macferbis the Sennachy describes the Galloway Picts as "a people who had renounced their baptism, and had the customs of the Norsemen"; and bad as those Norsemen had been, the "Gallgaidhel" were worse.[1]

But although, both before and after their coming to Galloway, the Norsemen were notoriously burners and robbers of churches, it is an undoubted fact that they spared Whithorn. It seems generally to have been taken for granted that the great monastery then disappeared, to be revived in the priory built by Fergus farther inland. But there is proof positive that eighty years after the arrival of the Norsemen the identical Monastery of Rosnat existed as a religious house.

The Bishop of Lindisfarne, in carrying the relics of St. Cuthbert, to save them from desecration by Norsemen on the east coast, embarked in 870 at the Derwent to sail to Ireland; but driven back by a storm, he perforce took refuge at Whithorn, and was lodged along with his precious burden by the brethren there — a statement strengthened rather than invalidated by the legendary addition, that during his stay a copy of the Gospels which he had lost in the storm was washed up uninjured on the beach.

The belief in such a miracle was strictly conventional, and the legend dovetailed in good faith into the story, substantiates

---

[1] Fragments of Irish Annals, an. 852   *Chron. of Picts and Scots*, 403.

"During the latter years of Kenneth's reign, a people appear in close association with the Norwegian pirates, who are termed 'Gallgaidhel'   The name was certainly first applied to the people of Galloway   It seems to have been applied to them as a Gaelic race, under the rule of 'Gall,'[1] or foreigners."— *Celtic Scotland*, i. 311

But although the word Gallgaidhel is first used in chronicles at this period, the bards applied it to the Niduari Picts as early as the sixth century. The Norse sagas change the word to Gadgeddli.

---

[1] "Gall" simply means "stranger," "foreigner"   The Norsemen are "the Galls" of the chronicles of the period , later, the Anglo Normans   There were Fingalls and Dugalls: the "fionn" (white, fair-haired), Norwegians , the "dubh" (black, dark-haired), the Danes

the geographical fact that the monastic house was *on the shore*, and also the historical one, that the fraternity were still resident there, enjoying under Norse rule an immunity denied to monks by Norsemen elsewhere [1]

Their rule, indeed, seems to have been with the hearty acquiescence of the Galwegians, the overlords bearing themselves rather as protectors than conquerors, and interfering little with the internal government and customs of the Picts.   But if they colonised little inland, they established themselves strongly on the seaboard, the Galloway cliffs bristling with forts, its bays guarded by carefully constructed camps, which became the basis of operations against English and Irish, and often against their own fellow-countrymen.

A thousand years have not obliterated the marks of their busy spades, and the names of many of their haunts still remain unchanged, such as " Wigg" in the sense of a naval station in Lochryan, formed by a curious bank of gravel, running like a natural breakwater for half a mile into the sea, bearing the old Norse name of Scar,[2] in its primary meaning of " cutting," " dividing," not the secondary one of a sea cliff.

The well-known Sea-King's Camp at Larbrax is locally called Kemp's Walks (" wark," old Norse " verke," a fortress).   They had a large station in Monreith Bay, a fortress on Castle-Feather of great extent, and a look - out post at Burrow Head.

Burrow Head commands the approach to the Isle of Whithorn, as Borgue to the entrance of the Dee; both forts being at the extremity of the capes forming Wigtown Bay.   Their very names have a Saxon ring, Buruh being suggestive of

---

[1] " In 875-883, Eadwulf, Bishop of Lindisfarne, and Eadred, Abbot of Carlisle, wandering with St. Cuthbert's relics, resolved to embark at the mouth of the Derwent and go to Ireland   They were driven back by a storm to Whithorn, where his book of the Gospels, lost in the tempest, is found in safety "—Bishop Forbes's *Life of St. Ninian*, p. xlv.

[2] The primary meaning of " vic " in both Anglo-Saxon and Norse is a station the Anglo-Saxon a station or land, hence a village ; the Norse a station for ships, hence a bay.—Taylor, *Words and Places*

" Skera," old Norse, " to cut " or " divide "

entrenchments, and the Norsemen seem to have extended the name of Beruvik, to the Bay in which the Isle (really the *presqu'ile*) of Whithorn[1] is situated.

At the confluence of the Bladenoch the Norsemen had a strongly-fortified station. The old form of its name seems to have been · Wigginton, or Wyggeton, and its prefix seems rather to be Viking than "vic;" that is, the "bay-men," or Creekers, not the "bay" itself, a name which would be somewhat colourless.[2]

Cruggleton Castle, one of their most pretentious works, was probably of a later date. They impressed their own tongue on the island of Hestan, equivalent to the Celtic Auchness (each inis), and "the Horse Isles," translating both, is mapped on the opposite shore—Southerness also, Southwick (the southern point of the province), and Gill-foot on the strand of Troqueer, where their galleys rode on the smooth water of the Nith, bear traces of their occupation.

The Norsemen having fraternised with, rather than conquered, the Galwegians, we find the latter boldly intervening in the quarrels of their more peaceful neighbours,—British, Scottish, and Northern Pictish,—and this with effect, the Norsemen supporting their foster-children both by land and sea. Indeed they appear to have turned the scale in favour of Kenneth when he founded the kingdom which developed into Scotland, although for the present Galloway formed no part of it.[3]

This Kenneth MacAlpine, who seems to have had hereditary claims on both the Scottish Dalriad and Northern Pictish, had undoubtedly also Galloway blood in his veins, and, according

---

[1] Kari Solmundson, when abreast of Dublin, puts about, "sails north to Beruwick, and fared up into Whitherne."—*Nials Saga.*

[2] Worsaae considers Wicklow to be Viking-low.

A John of Wigginton (as also a laird of Broughton) was a commissioner for Edward Baliol's private estates, and for long after this the word was written with three syllables, Wyggeton

[3] Up to the end of the tenth century Scotia meant Ireland. Kenneth's kingdom was, correctly speaking, Alban, not Scotland, and when Scotland superseded Alban, the Scottish kingdom was limited to the district north of the Firth of Forth, excluding Caithness and Sutherland.

to Mr. Skene, had been resident there—in what position is uncertain—when he issued thence on his career of conquest [1] Emerging from Galloway, well supported by his Pictish cousins, he had within a year regained his father's (Alpyn) throne of Scottish Dalriada; while the Norseman, who revelled in scenes of battle and plunder, taking the Northern Picts in the rear, opened his way to their easy conquest at Fortrenn, and beyond the Mounth; he was crowned king of the united Picts and Scots at Scone in 844. [2] Thence, with the help of the same allies, he extended his conquests to the Tweed. He now cemented the alliance which had proved so greatly to his advantage by giving his daughter to a Gallgaidhel or Norse chief, Olaf or Amlaiph. [3]

The services rendered by the Galwegians in this consolidation of the Scottish monarchy seem to account for the singular privilege they claimed in after times of leading the van of the Scottish armies. No reason has ever been advanced for their enjoyment of this "hardy pre-eminence," which moreover was undeniably admitted, even when its assertion was most inconvenient. We may with some confidence suggest that the right was conferred by Kenneth; and that in especial consideration of the assistance they then had rendered.

Voluminous records exist of the piratical operations of the

[1] *Celtic Scotland*, i. 319. The whole question of Kenneth's parentage, connections and exploits discussed.—*Ibid.* i. 313-332   Mr Skene conjectures him to have been at one time a kinglet in Galloway 832-839, King of Dalriada 839, King of the Picts 844.

[2] "We gather that Kenneth emerged from Galloway . . . If the appearance of the Norwegians on the scene had led the people of Galloway, as well as Scots from other quarters, to adopt the same piratical life under the name of Gallgaidhel, we can readily understand that Kenneth, taking advantage of the crushing blow inflicted on the Picts of Fortrenn by the Danes, would be readily joined by Scots from all quarters in regaining the kingdom of Dalriada and prosecuting his father's claim to the throne of the Picts"—*Ibid.* i. 319

[3] Pronounced Aulay. Kenneth's daughter was his second wife.   Olaf had previously married a daughter of a redoubtable viking, Caittil Finn   Caittil Finn is no doubt the same person as Ketill Flatnose.   His daughter Audur married Olaf the White, who became king of Dublin.—*Ibid* i. 312

His wife Audur the Wealthy, a son called Thorstein the red —*Ibid* i. 326

Kenneth had three daughters: one married to Run, King of Strathclyde, another to Olaf, King of Dublin; a third to Aedh Finnliath, King of Ireland.—*Ibid.* i. 313. *Pictish Chron., Irish Ann., Annals of Ulster.*

Norsemen, along with their Galwegian confederates, of which the shores of Galloway were the base, the story being much complicated by the internecine warfare which soon broke out between White Gall and Black. The most remarkable feature in the matter is the influence which these Norsemen (of whichever party) seem to have acquired over the Galloway Celts, this being the only period in their history in which they submitted to nautical discipline, as both before and after, their Celtic distaste for salt-water was a matter of notoriety.

They profited by their schooling, as their overlords, while teaching them the art of living at the expense of their neighbours, provided them also with rock-built citadels, which defied attempts at retaliation

The doings of the Galwegians during this period, in which the Norsemen, while supreme on the shores, appeared to have interfered little in the interior,—or meddled with the successions of Pictish chiefs or kinglets,—are frequently recorded in chronicles deemed authentic.[1] Along with their overlords, they were constantly involved in civil wars, of which it would be tedious to attempt to follow the fortunes and the changes. And without attempting to unravel the tangled skein, we shall simply glance at the more salient facts, as illustrative of these times.

Thus in 844, Olaf having -married Kenneth's daughter (presumedly a Galloway lass both by birth and kindred), the Galwegians assisted to elevate her to the rank of Queen by aiding her husband to gain the throne of Dublin. Again, in 852, they invaded Ulster, at first with success, but being attacked when retiring by the Irish king, they were totally defeated, and stripped of their plunder, many prisoners remaining in the hands of the victor, with whose heads he formed a ghastly ornament for the palisades of his stronghold.[2]

[1] *Annals of Ulster Icelandic Sagas. Wars of the Gaedhel with the Gaill,* Dr. J H Todd , published by Master of the Rolls in Ireland

[2] 852 A battle given by Aedh, King of Ailech, to the fleet of the Gallgael They were Scots, and foster children of the Northmen They were defeated by Aedh, and many of their heads carried off by Niall with him , and the Irish were

We next find them in Munster, with Mailsechnaill as their chief, but this time they were taken in rear by their former leader Olaf, who seems to have considered Munster an appanage of Dublin, upon which they turned furiously upon him.[1] But although Olaf's own father-in-law brought up reinforcements for the Galwegians, they were forced to retire.

Olaf now renounced all connexion with them, allying himself with Ivor (Imhair), a semi-Norse Galwegian, against Ketill Flatnose,[2] who came to their support

Meanwhile King Kenneth having died 860, was succeeded by his brother Aed, and he in turn by Kenneth's son Constantine.

Olaf and Imhair, after raiding both the Galloway and the Irish coasts, made a bold attempt to wrest the crown from Constantine. They attacked and took Alclyde (Dumbarton Castle), occupied all Pictavia, "from the Kalends of January to the Feast of St. Patrick",[3] retiring leisurely with their booty, they passed through Galloway, carrying along with them "a great prey of men as well as cattle," and returned to Dublin in triumph.[4]

We here see how little ties of blood restrained piratical instincts; Olaf unhesitatingly attacked his wife's nephew Constantine, whilst his own father-in-law, Ketill, was as ready to attack him   Both he himself and Ivor were connected with Galloway, yet the two conducted the only successful raiding expedition that is on record against the province. As for the Galwegians, they had helped Olaf to conquer Dublin, and it seems possible that notwithstanding their quarrel with

justified in committing this havoc, for these men were wont to act like Lochlanns. —*Fragments of Irish Annals* (Macfirbis)   *Chron of Picts and Scots*, p. 403.

[1] 856.   Great war between the Gentiles (Norsemen) and Mailsechnaill, with the Galwegians along with him.—*Annals of Ulster*

[2] 857   Victory by Imhair and Amlaibh against Caittil Finn, and the Galwegians along with him.—*Ibid.*

[3] Mr Skene remarks on this " His occupation of the country may have been in connection with some claim through his wife, daughter of Kenneth   On this occasion they attacked both the Picts of Galloway and the Angles of Bernicia "—*Celtic Scotland*, iii 324.

[4] 872   Amlaidh and Imhair sailed again to Alchath (Dublin) from Alban with 200 ships.

Imhair they yet assisted his son Sitruic to subdue Deira, the southern district of Northumbria.

The Norse chiefs extended their conquests in all directions, each fighting for his own hand, becoming by turns titular kings of Dublin and Bernicia (of which Bamborough was the capital), rivals being alternately sovereigns and fugitives, Galloway furnishing either party with a base for operations.

Among the most successful of these leaders, and whose rule was established on a firmer basis than that of most of his competitors, was a certain Ronald, variously styled Lord of Bamborough,—King of Northumbria,—Duke (rather military leader) of the Galwegians.[1]

He has left his name strongly impressed upon Galloway topography, and in conjunction with him we find mention of a younger Awlay, son of Sitruic, called, to distinguish him from his grandfather Anlaf the White, Anlaf Cuaran, that is, " of the brogues "[2]

Ronald, with his Galwegian legions, successfully arrested the advance of the Saxons under Edmund the Elder. The Saxon Chronicle classes him as an equal with the Kings of Alban and Strathclyde, all of the three entering into treaties of amity with Edmund himself, A.D. 924.[3] By this agreement Sitruic was acknowledged King of Deira; but Edmund had died A.D. 929, and Sitruic the year following. Whereupon Athelstane, who had succeeded his father Edmund the year before, seized upon it, to the exclusion of Anlaf Cuaran. He of the brogues was not so easily to be disposed of: hurrying to the court of Alban, he cemented an alliance with the greatest Scottish house by marrying King Constantine's daughter, and being consequently supported by the united forces of Scots, Britons, Galwegians, and Norsemen, made a desperate effort to

---

[1] Reginaldus Rex Northumbrorum ex natione Danorum et Dux Galwalensium —Flores. *Hist* Mr Skene suggests a connection with the family of Kenneth —*Celtic Scotland,* i. 373

[2] "Cuaran," a shoe, or brogue , apparently in opposition to " barefoot "

[3] 924. This year Edmund was chosen for Father and Lord by the King of the Scots, and by King Reginald, and also by the Strathclyde Britons.—*Saxon Chronicle.*

expel the English from his father's territory. They were defeated near the Humber at Brunnanbyrie in 937.[1] But four years later, another Edmund having succeeded Athelstane, Ronald and Anlaf Cuaran made terms with him.[2] In A.D. 943 the truce was broken Ronald and Anlaf marched southward, carrying all before them, "stormed Tamworth, and the Danes had the victory, and much booty they led away with them."[3] But in 944 the tide of war turned Deira was retaken from Anlaf, and Ronald stripped of his Northumbrian lordships; whilst Cumbria, taken from the Britons, was handed over to Malcolm, King of the Scots, on the sole condition of his occupying it, Edmund wishing to make this district a buffer between his own dominions and Galloway, to which Ronald had been driven[4]

Blood, notwithstanding, asserted itself as thicker than water. Malcolm proved unfaithful to the English king, and aided instead of resisting Ronald and Anlaf in recovering their possessions. In this they would most probably have been successful, had they not been taken in flank; and this not by Edmund's Saxons, but by one of their own race. This new pretender was Eric Bloody-axe, who, swooping down from the Orkneys and entering the Tees, drove both parties before him, appropriating the bone of contention to himself, Anlaf retiring for good and all to Dublin, and Reginald to Galloway.[5] The White Galls had expelled the Black! Duke Ronald's name is to be traced in

---

[1] *Celtic Scotland*, i 359. *Saxon Chronicle*, 937. Mr. Skene suggests Aldborough as the battle site

[2] 941. King Edmund received King Anlaf at baptism, and that same year he received King Reginald at the bishop's hands.

[3] 943. Anlaf stormed Tamworth, and the Danes had the victory. After that Anlaf acquired King Edmund's friendship, and after a good long time he received King Reginald

944 This year King Edmund subdued all Northumberland, and expelled two kings—Anlaf, son of Sitruic, and Reginald, son of Girthferth —*Saxon Chronicle.*

[4] *Saxon Chronicle,* 945

[5] The Saxon Chronicle gives the dates

949 Anlaf Cuaran came to Northumberland. 952, the Northumbrians expelled King Anlaf, and received Eric. 954, the Northumbrians expelled Eric, and Edred obtained the kingdom of Northumbria (henceforward it was English)

contemporary chronicles for over thirty years, 924-952, and his family maintained their position to the end of the century.[1] We presume that he was a Black Gall, but at the beginning of the following century we find that Sigurd the Stout, son of Thorfinn the Skullcleaver, an undoubted White Gall, married to a daughter of Malcolm II.[2] acquired the overlordship of Galloway, and named Malcolm (the Earl Melkoff of the sagas) as his lieutenant. He again was succeeded by his son, another and more mighty Thorfinn, who eventually possessed himself of nine "rikis" (provinces), of which Galloway was one, and there he frequently resided.[3] The somewhat contradictory chronicles of the period are independently confirmed as to this in the Nials Sagas, which state that Kari Solmundson, tax-gatherer to Sigurd, on his way to Ireland (Sigurd having gone there with an army to assist the Danes), hearing of the fatal result of the battle of Clontarf (1014), made for Burrow Head and "fared up into Whitherne," where he remained with Earl Melkoff or Malcolm for the rest of the winter.[4]

An old chronicle of Man states: "Earl Thorfinn resided long at Gaddgedlar, the place where England and Scotland meet" (Gadgedlar being the Norse for Galloway, and Gadgeddli for its people),[5] Ingiborg his wife having seemingly in her own blood some claims to rule in Galloway.

The next ruler we find is Šuibhne MacCinaeda (Sweeny, son of Kenneth), styled both by Tighernach, and in the Annals of Ulster, "King of Galloway";[6] the first appearance of a

The Danes of Northumberland were of the Dubh Gall branch or black strangers; the followers of Eric Bloody-axe were Norwegians, Finn Gall, white strangers — *Celtic Scotland*, i. 364.

[1] *Ibid.* i. 373.

[2] *Ibid.* i 386. As Thorfinn was only five years old when his father, Earl Sigurd, was killed in 1014, this places the marriage of King Malcolm's daughter in the year 1008 — *Ibid.* 390.

[3] *Orkneyana Saga*, and *Celtic Scotland*, i. 412.

[4] Mr Skene remarks on this, "Whose name (Malcolm) marks him out for a native chief"—*Celtic Scotland*, i. 390.

[5] *Chronicum Regum Manniæ*, Munck

[6] 1034. Suibhne MacCinaeda ri Gallgaidhel mortuus est.—*Ann. of Ulster*. Sinnyness, Old Luce, is Svein or Sweeny's point   Kilquhanidy, Kirkpatrick-Durham, is Cinaeda or Kennedy's grave.

Kennedy in Galloway. It is probable he was contemporary with Thorfinn, and a Celtic kinglet under him, as also may have been his successor, Dermot or Diarmid, who lived to ˙1072.[1] The Norsemen did not object to the co-existence of native chiefs with their own kings and "jarls."

Earl Thorfinn had died a few years before this, and his young widow Ingibiorg, a fair Galwegian[2] (probably of mixed blood), became Malcolm Canmore's queen. She bore him a son, Duncan, whom she did not long survive,[3] facts particularly to be noted, as it was through this marriage with Ingibiorg (often strangely overlooked) that Malcolm, in accordance with Pictish laws of succession, acquired claims to the throne of Galloway, which, according also to Pictish custom, held good in a less degree to the children of his second wife.[4]

The prestige of the Norsemen, weakened by their expulsion from Ireland, as the result of their defeat at Clontarf, was now waning on British shores as well; the simultaneous consolidation of the English and Scottish kingdoms having much narrowed their happy hunting grounds Moreover, their own rival factions were being gradually absorbed into one kingdom, the King of Norway being now acknowledged by all as sovereign, which checked the individual action of pirate chiefs. As a first result of this, these Norwegian monarchs, anxious to consolidate their power, occupied in force Caithness, Sutherland, and the Western Isles; resigning by treaty or exchange with the Scottish kings their more easily assailable positions in the south. Consequently their dragon-prowed galleys stood

[1] 1072. Diarmait MacMailnambo ri Breatan et insi Gall. Slain, and great slaughter of the Galls and Leinster men with him.—*Ann of Tighernach.*

Craigdermot, Stoneykirk, retains Diarmait's name.

[2] On Thorfinn's death, Malcolm appears to have endeavoured to conciliate the Norwegian element by making Ingibiorg his wife, by whom he had a son, Duncan.—*Celtic Scotland,* i. 414.

[3] The Galwegians rose to a man in favour of Ingibiorg's grandson, son of her son by Malcolm Duncan by Alice de Romilly, known as the Boy of Egremont, against Malcolm the Maiden.

[4] *Circ.* 1068. Malcolm married Margaret, sister of Edgar Atheling, heir to the Saxon crown of England. Her sons Edgar and David were in turn acknowledged king by the Galwegians, but Ingibiorg's grandson was preferred to hers.

out one by one to the north, no more to be seen in the tide-
ways of the Irish Channel or the Solway.

Strathclyde, whose Cymri alone had been too strong for the
Galloway Picts, was now united to the kingdom of Scotland.
The Galwegians therefore had now no choice but to turn for help
to the Saxons, weakened by civil war, or to become liegemen
of the Scottish king. They solved the dilemma by throwing themselves into the arms of Malcolm; and he, as a politic prince,
seems to have been careful that his yoke should not be galling.

Thus, as with the Northumbrian Saxons, the supremacy of
the Norsemen ended by a voluntary withdrawal; not, however,
without their leaving some impression on the soil.

The Olaves are characteristically remembered in Terally
Bay, a haven on the Bay of Luce, well fitted for a piratical
station; Tir (land) being suggestive of occupation—Macherally,
adjoining, was evidently a part of the same domain. Kirkcalla
in Penninghame is Olave's, or Anlaf's "Caer" (fort), not kirk.[1]
Blanivaird (Blean-a-bhaird), near it, is the "Bard's Creek";
the a in all three names pronounced aw. Imhair is reproduced in Emar's Isle near Corswall Point. The "Bloody
Rock" and "Bloody Slock," mapped beside it, translating
probably Sloc-na-folie and Craig-folly, are points on the Irish
Channel known to have been the scene of Anlaf's and Imhair's
sea-fights and depredations. Ketill, the first Anlaf's father-in-
law, and afterwards his foe, may give the prefix to Kelton,
sometimes written Kettleton. Kettleside in Cumberland is
held to have Ketill for its root.

Raonul, Duke Ronald, gives his name to the barony of
Loch Ronald. It is curious to find the neighbouring hills here
retaining the Norse "fell," whilst the Norse "inge," a coarse
pasture, appears in "Ink Moss." In the uplands behind
Loch Ronald is Somerton, where his herds were driven for
summer grazing, a name reproduced in the Celtic Belsavery,

---

[1] Even if it should rather be believed to be a dedication to a saint, we find
in King's Kalendar 30 March, "Siole (Anlaf), King of Norwege and martyr under
Henrie ye crowkit."

"Baile Samhraith," Summer Town.   Mailsechnall,[1] whose name the Norsemen wrote Malachy, appears strangely cor-rupted in "the Howe Hill of Haggamalag."[2]   "Hauga" being Norse for a barrow, a sepulchral mount, and "howe" its Saxon equivalent, "Howe Hill of Haggamalag" is a form doubly pleonastic.

The Teutonic Sweyn or Svein, on Celtic lips Suibhne (Sweeny), gives us Synniness, a headland on the Bay of Luce; at the entrance to which, moreover, two rocks preserve the exact old Norse form the Skares[3]

Of other test-words, byr appears in Corsbie, the dwelling by the cross; Sorby, probably from a proper name rather than sour,[4] Appleby, Busby (Byskeby), Bomby (anc. Bondeby), the husbandmen or churls.

Garth (gardr), a fenced place, as Fairgirth (faar),[5] Cogarth, Gadgirth (the sheep, cows, and goats enclosure); Applegarth, Mustardgarth.   Setr, a dwelling, as in Soulseat, Aldermanseat. The modern Norwegian "sæter"—a pasture and dairy place on the mountain side, a summer grazing, nearly an equivalent to Somerton (Sumar ton).[6]

Old Norse "oe" or "ey," primarily an island, signifying secondarily a green oasis in moorland, gives us in the first sense Ramsey (off the Isle of Whithorn), and Ailsa (Helsa or Eliza-beth's Island);[7] in the second, favoured spots innumerable in the 'Moors, often written down "the Eyes" alone, or appearing in

---

[1] Mailsechnall, originally servant of Secundinus, a pupil of St Patrick, rendered Malachy to suit weak Saxon capacity —Young, *Hist of Christian Names*, ii. 117

[2] It was the practice of the Norsemen to give the name of the departed chief to the mound where he was buried.   "Hauga," from which Howe is derived, is from the verb "hauga," primary meaning "to heap up," and the mean-ing of the word is "a sepulchral hill."—Ferguson, *Norsemen in Cumberland*, 56

[3] Norwegian "Skai," old Norse "Sker or Skjoer."—Worsaae, 262

[4] So Sowerby, Lake District.—*Norsemen in Cumberland*, 132

[5] So Fair Isle, north of Orkney, and the Faroe Islands (all sheep).

[6] Sumar lidi, or summer soldiers, was a name early applied to the Vikings, who as sea rovers usually marauded in summer time.   Whence the name Somerled, Celtic Somhairle, familiarly Sorley.

[7] By the Gaelic-speaking people of Arran Ailsa is still called "Ealdsaidh a' chuan" (Elizabeth of the sea) —Communicated to the author by the late Dr. M'Lauchlan of St Columba's Free Church, Edinburgh

such compounds as the "Eyes of Clendry," "Eyes of Kylfeddar," "Gleneyes," "Eyes Hill." "Saulsea" (Sol, a proper name), or "Rig of the Eyes," in which last we have the Norse "hryggr," Danish "ryg," the equivalent of the Celtic "drum" and the English "ridge."

In connection with pasturage, the Norse and Celtic meet in "cro," a fold or hut, the word being common to both languages, the frequent "Crows" with English plurals are probably Norse, but "Alticry," the burn of the cattle pen, is as plainly Celtic. "Croys" probably indicates a group of huts, "cro," rather than hard land, "cruadh"

"Gil," a small ravine, is a sure Norse test-word, as Physgill (anciently Fischegill), of the fish, Gilhow, of the sepulchral mound; the Gill on the Cree, Gillfoot on the Nith, Gategill, Borgue—"gate," here probably a proper name, as a "gil" often defined the boundary of a property.[1]

"Stone" also generally has the sense of a landmark, as Ravenstone (Rafn's),—Carlinstone (Carlinn's),—Gelston (Giles'), limit.

"Verke, wark," fortification, appears in Kemp's Wark, and Carlingwark, "borg" (glossed by "arx") is reproduced in Borgue and Borness, in modulated form in Burrow Head.

"Tun," in the Norse sense of a naval station, is the suffix of Wigtown (Vikinton), the viking's arsenal.

"Nes, naes," the nose, a headland, gives Borness, Eggerness, Almorness, Gowness, Synniness, severally Edgar's, Aymer's, Go's, and Sweyne's. [2]

"Vagr," a bay, is the affix of Solway, the prefix being "sulr," a sea swell (the same root as in Lough Swilly, Antrim). We have it also in Sulburn or Soleburn, a stream flowing into Lochryan, entered daily by the tide, and rightly named the burn of the tidal bore.

---

[1] Gatesgill, Gatescale, Gatesgarth, are referred to Geit.—Ferguson, *Norsemen in Cumberland*, 130.

[2] Auchness and Cardoness have nothing to do with capes, being corruptions of Each-iniss, Caer-donas (the first Horse Isle, or pasture, the second fort of bad luck, "donas").

Garthland, which seems Teutonic, is a corruption of the Celtic Gairachcloyne—Garbh cluain (rough meadows), a name frequent in Ireland as Garracloon.

Many proper names left by Norsemen in Cumberland are to be traced on our map; as Eigel, in Eagle's Cairn, Kirkmaiden; Go, in Gowness, Gill in Gellstone, Kott in Kidsdale (formerly Kittisdale), Rafn in Ravenstone, Sol in Soulseat, Geit in Gategill, Thor in Torhouse, Vere or Weir in Weirston [1] Celtic and Teutonic both meet in Neill, their descendants in Galloway being synonymously represented in M'Neill and Neilson.

After the death of Sweyne in 1034 and of Diarmait in 1072 (kinglets already mentioned), a hiatus occurs of thirty years; inasmuch as Fergus, the next lord of whom we read, was probably not born earlier than 1080,[2] nor in power much before the death of King Edgar in 1107. As to this interval, Galloway history is silent, and, strangely, all clue to the lineage of Fergus is lost.

We find Malcolm's family established in the suzerainty of Galloway at the close of the eleventh century, and as no force seems to have been employed, we infer that they ruled there with the acquiescence of its people.[3] The Norman conquest of England had indirectly strengthened Malcolm's position. He was individually no match for the Conqueror, and had to acknowledge himself "his man" for the Lothians; but this done, William's centralised authority in England had put a stop to private predatory incursions, and Malcolm's resources were largely increased by the immigration of Saxon Lords, and his ranks were efficiently recruited by a stream of Anglo-Normans pouring in, all eager for lands and employment, and ready to support the crown in whichever kingdom they could obtain a settlement.

[1] In Cumberland in Eaglesfield, Gobarrow, Gellstone, Kitt's Howe, Ravenside, Soulby, Thursgill, Weary Hall, Kelton. Hound Hill Cairn, Dalmellington, probably derives its name from a Norseman "Hundi," as in Hounds Howe in the Lake District.

[2] Fergus died very old, A.D. 1161, yet we can hardly place his birth before 1080. Again, his daughter Africa married Olave the Swarthy, King of Man, the date unrecorded; but his reign of forty years commenced 1102, and her son, well advanced in life (Godred), succeeded his father 1142. So that Fergus's marriage may be placed between 1107 and 1112

[3] "In the reign of Malcolm, the Bishop of Glasgow had several royal writs for enforcing the payment of tithes, especially in Galloway."— Cosmo Innes, *Early Scottish History*, 34.

A people these of different speech, and yet whose hands, if gloved in velvet, were as tenacious as those of the retiring Vikings, now took their places,—more polished in address, but quite as masterful Though indeed it is a mistake to term them of a different race, for what was a Norman but a Norseman, improved by centuries of cultivation in the sunnier clime of France !

Anglo-Normans did not settle in Galloway in any appreciable numbers till many years later; but already their society had been sought and their habits affected by the native chiefs. In the first decade of the twelfth century we find Fergus of Galloway a favoured guest at the English court, and accepted as a son-in-law by the English king , implying early association with the ruling race and knowledge of their language.

On the Conqueror's death Malcolm, thinking to recover the Cumbrian province between the Derwent and the Solway, took advantage of William Rufus's absence in Normandy in 1091 to let his mixed hosts — Highland, Lowland, and Galwegian—loose across the borders. Rufus hurried back, ordering an invasion of Scotland by land and sea; but as "almost all his ships were lost ere they reached Scotland," he was glad to come to terms, and "the kings separated in great friendship."[1] But the following year, Rufus ordering the erection of a fort at Carlisle to ˜curb the inroads of the Galwegians, Malcolm considered this an infringement of their treaty; crossed the Tweed, and endeavoured by a *coup de main* to possess himself of the Castle of Alnwick, to hold as a pledge for the discontinuance of the obnoxious work. Arrived before it, he was beguiled to the walls under pretence of a parley, and slain.[2]

Duncan, Malcolm's son by Ingibiorg, succeeded him, but was murdered soon after, his uncle Donald Bane and half-brother

---

[1] *Saxon Chronicle.*

[2] This is the Scottish account The *Saxon Chronicle*, 1093, says : "Robert, Earl of Northumberland, lay in wait for him, and slew him , he was killed by Morœl of Bamborough, the Earl's steward, and King Malcolm's own godfather."

Edmond becoming joint kings, but both were eventually dis-
placed by Edgar, Edmond's younger brother, in 1078.[1]

Taking advantage of the disorders of the times, Magnus
Barefoot appeared on the Irish Channel, when, according to the
Chronicles of Man, "Those of Galloway were so much awed by
him that at his command they cut down wood and brought it
to the shore to make his bulwarks withal." On this slender
foundation Chalmers asserts that he erected the fortlets of
Carghidown and Castlefeather, with a view to the permanent
possession of the country, adding, "Neither the chiefs of Galloway nor the feeble Edgar were able to oppose such power in
such hands,"[2] all which has been accepted as fact But not
only are the said castles built of stone, not wood, but their
immense size renders it impossible they could have been
reared in a few weeks; and the chronicle quoted allows no
longer time, as it relates Magnus's departure from Galloway
for Anglesea and Man, various campaigns there, an expedition
to Ireland, and return to the Western Isles, as all occurring
within the season. Nor is Chalmers happy in his epithet of
"feeble" as regards Edgar's reign in Galloway; for no sooner
was the accession of Edgar proclaimed than Magnus came
to a treaty with him, agreeing to leave Galloway and the
mainland of Scotland undisturbed, conditionally on his right
being guaranteed to all the isles between which and the shore
a helm-carrying ship could pass.[3]   Indeed, from a comparison
of all the authorities, it is to be gathered that the Galloway
chiefs supplied the Norsemen (with whom, be it remembered,

---

[1] Malcolm left by Ingibiorg (supposed Galloway born) Duncan (eighteen
years a hostage in England), and Donald, who predeceased him , by Margaret,
Edmund, Edgar, Alexander, and David, Eadgyth (renamed Matilda), Queen of
Henry I., and Mary, wife of Count Eustace of Boulogne An elder son,
Edward, was slain at Alnwick with his father. On Malcolm's death Rufus
released Duncan to fight for his own hand, who won the crown, but was
murdered next year. Donald Bane and Edmond were then joint kings till 1098,
when, with the assistance of Edgar Atheling and the concurrence of Rufus,
Edgar was declared king of all Scotland.

[2] *Caledonia*, iii 367.

[3] Magnus Barefoot's Saga. *Celtic Scotland*, i 442.

they were connected by blood) with such provisions as they required, out of friendship, not from fear.

In the year 1100 Edgar gave his beautiful sister Eadgyth, or Matilda (known to fame as Good Queen Mold), to Henry I., who had just succeeded his brother Rufus, and she took with her to the English court her young brother David, where, in the words of William of Malmesbury, "his manners were polished from the rust of Scottish barbarity," a circumstance destined to have no little bearing on the fortunes of Galloway.

For the seven years following Prince David, whilst being educated in a thoroughly feudal atmosphere, won the while, not only the brotherly regard of the king, but the personal attachment of the flower of the young Anglo-Norman nobility.   In the year 1107, Edgar dying unexpectedly, as unexpectedly bequeathed to him the Saxon districts of Scotland south of the Forth, and Galloway.   His elder brother, Alexander, protested against this dismemberment of the kingdom,[1] but the playmates of David's boyhood rising to a man to assist him, he made a triumphal progress through his newly acquired dominions,[2] and Alexander perforce had to acquiesce.   By the style of Earl, David kept regal court at Carlisle for thirteen years, recognising Fergus as overlord of Galloway, with whose entire acquiescence he introduced the Anglo-Norman element among the landowners.

Thus at a bound the new race, already predominating in the Saxonised Lothians and fertile valley of the Clyde, overleapt the barriers, social and physical, which had so long preserved the Celtic character of the land of the Novantæ, and within a generation effected a total change in the habits of the upper classes, as well as in the laws of the ancient province.

[1] Alexander at first disputed the validity of the donation, but, perceiving that David had won over the English barons to his interests, acquiesced.   Subsequently Henry I gave Alexander one of his natural daughters in marriage.—Hailes, *Annals*, 1 57.

[2] Thirty years later Bruce reminds him of this, when adjuring him not to break the peace with the Anglo-Norman barons at the Battle of the Standard. "Tu ipse rex cum portionem regni quam idem tibi frater moriens delegavit, a fratre Alexandro reposceres, nostro certe terrore, quidquid volueras sine sanguine impetrasti "—Ailred, *De Bello Stand.*, *Hist. of Scot* i. 445, Appendix.

It was a curious feature of this peaceable conquest that it was effected with such tact that the native chiefs, far from eying them askance, took the bold intruders for their models, affected their ways and manners, and eagerly competed for the hands of the daughters of the more accomplished race.

The social conditions of the period can only be gathered by inference. We know little of Edgar's administration of Galloway beyond his treaty for its evacuation with King Magnus, and his willing it away from the natural heir. Yet, how firmly must his power have been established when his dying wishes alone secured the alienation of the province; and David, with an alien bodyguard, was allowed to perambulate its difficult defiles without one organised attempt at resistance, and to take possession without shedding one drop of blood.

Next comes the fact of Fergus's marriage with the Lady Elizabeth, daughter of Henry I.,[1] whose sister Sibilla becoming Alexander's queen,[2] placed Fergus in the position of brother-in-law to the Scottish King. Now, though doubtless David promoted this union, either to secure, or in reward of, Fergus's assistance in his own settlement, we may certainly infer that Fergus could woo in French, as well as take his part in the knightly sports of the Anglo-Norman youth, and that he had acquired some polish from the association. Nor can we suppose that the king's daughter would have consented to follow him to his " Palace Isle " in his distant principality, unless assured she should have other persons about her with whom she could converse, and an understanding that her son was to enjoy all the feudal privileges of primogeniture. And if so, what a change must her arrival have inaugurated in the tone and usages of Galloway society as well as of its jurisprudence

[1] That Fergus was a prince of note even at the court of Henry I. is certain, as he took to wife the natural daughter of Henry I. In this transaction we see the original cause of the intimate connection between David I and Fergus.—*Caledonia*, iii 250 and 367

[2] It was the policy of Henry I to cultivate amity with Scotland. He bestowed his natural daughter Sibilla on Alexander I. Such an alliance was not dishonourable in these days.—Hailes, *Annals*, 1 56.

In 1124 David succeeded his brother Alexander, and Scotland again became a united kingdom, no more to be dismembered. His rule has been chronicled as firm and beneficent; and it is gratifying to find that in assuming his honours he justly esteemed Galloway as a precious jewel in his crown; significantly altering the official style adopted by his immediate predecessors in their charters, from "to all our adherents,— Anglo-Norman, English, and Scottish," to "all good men of my whole kingdom — Scottish, English, Anglo-Norman, and Gallovidians"[1]

On the accession of David, the Galwegians, of all his subjects, alone retained the name of Picts, the bulk of them being directly descended from the Novantæ of Agricola.   There doubtless had been a certain admixture of Welsh or Strathclyde Britons, a moderate immigration (though not nearly on such a scale as represented by Chalmers) from Ireland, both of Dalriads and Dalaradians; a small infusion of Northumbrian Saxons also, and a much greater one of Norsemen.   On these somewhat incongruous elements the Anglo-Norman "gentlemen" now poured in,[2] the peculiarity of their invasion being, as expressed by Cosmo Innes, that it was "all of what we should call the upper classes—men of the sword, above all servile and mechanical employment; they were fit for the society of a court, and many became the companions of our princes   The old native people gave way before them, or took service under the strong-handed strangers."[3]

With their introduction the racial element became complete, and as such practically subsists to the present day.   The wars of the succession two centuries later made sweeping changes in the personnel of the proprietors, through wholesale confiscations But the proportions of the races remained unchanged, Anglo-Norman blood largely preponderating among the landowners.

---

[1] Cosmo Innes, *Legal Antiquities*, 30.
[2] A new people was rapidly and steadily pouring over Scotland, apparently with the approbation of its rulers, and displacing or predominating over the nation or old inhabitants —Cosmo Innes, *Early History*, 9.
[3] *Ibid* 10.

CHAPTER III

FERGUS, LORD OF GALLOWAY

A D. 1124 to 1161

Eireas a Fhearghuis ann 'us deanas an iorghuill.
Go now, rouse thee up, Fergus, and mingle boldly in the fight.
Dean of Lismore's Book, 61.

FERGUS was a ruler of great force of character, and decidedly in
advance of his age; he carried out great changes, social and
political, all in the direction of sound progress, with a firm
hand and a princely liberality which well entitle him to be
remembered as enlightened and pātriotic. Feudalism, which
he may be said to have introduced, was much more calculated
to ensure strong and settled government than the customs
of Tanistry. His importation of foreign orders, which some
writers seem sentimentally to regret, as turning from Iona
to Rome, was no question of Protestantism or Popery, but a
much needed measure for the correction of abuses in the
Church, and for the instruction of the people at large, not
in religion only, but in the habits and rudimentary arts of
civilisation.[1]

The number, the size, and the beauty of the fabrics which he
reared, are equally matters of surprise; as, whether for grandeur

---

[1] Marriage, which is vaunted as the privilege of the Early Scottish Church,
had degenerated into the offices of the church becoming hereditary, and was
leading to the parish clergy becoming a mere caste. Birth—quite independent
of any course of study—being the only qualification for a cure.

of design or chasteness in execution, they cannot even now be surpassed, scarcely imitated.

This incidentally raises the question as to how he met the cost. Although he might have been able to command any amount of unskilled labour, skilled artisans had to be looked for beyond the province,—material had to be brought from a distance,—and as it was no question of conversion of the people, —who had long been nominally Christian,—the men of culture who were induced to reside in his newly reared abbeys must have had it made worth their while to do so. A Galloway overlord could have realised but little hard cash from the export of wool and hides and the sale of horses, hence, to account for his being able to find the means of supporting such a lavish expenditure, we must suppose him to have been able to draw revenues from England. His descendants held largely under English kings, and though there is no record as to any particular barony having been inherited from him, it may fairly be assumed that certain fiefs were granted to Fergus by Henry I. on his marriage with his daughter.

According to tradition, the Lady Elizabeth's favourite home was the Palace Isle in Lochfergus, and we may well believe that her settlement there was an influence for good in raising the tone of female society. The distinguished pair had other castles when disposed to change the air, such as Cruggleton, Long-caster, and Botel. Far more palatial, however, than any of these strong-houses were the edifices Fergus reared for his Prémon-stratensian and Cistercian canons   His prentice hand was tried on Soulseat (Monasterium Viridis Stagni),[1] to which he brought monks directly from Premontré in Burgundy; next he built the Priory of Whithorn, within a few miles of the classic Rosnat, to which St. Ninian's relics were transferred; Tungland followed, later St. Mary's Isle (Sancta Maria de Trayll), and Dundrennan, his *chef-d'œuvre*, to which the brotherhood were

---

[1] It stands on a peninsula of a small lake which has a greenish tint at certain seasons from the spores of an aquatic plant, whence " Monasterium Viridis Stagni "

brought from the Cistercian Abbey of Rievaux by Aildred, its abbot, the biographer of St. Ninian and personal friend of Fergus.[1]

In 1126, in concert with the king, Fergus restored the bishopric of Whithorn, Gilla Aldan being the first bishop under the new regime,[2] who was sent to York (to Archbishop Thurstan) for consecration. The fact of his being so sent proves the bishopric to have been a revival of the identical see founded by the Saxons (A.D. 730), which had seemingly been always (if somewhat irregularly) kept up; for it is inconceivable that David and Fergus should have originated the precedent had such a connection not already existed beyond all memory of man. Strange to say, this connection with York remained in force till 1359.

The formation of parishes in Galloway was commenced, and in a great measure carried out, under Fergus; which Anglo-Norman habits and laws greatly facilitated. An Anglo-Norman considered a chapel as necessary an appendage to his castle as his brew-house or his mill; he had been used to pay tithes for its minister, and continued cheerfully to do so when his barony constituted the parish, or a part of it. If he did not find an ancient "cell" upon his lands he built one. Many of the native proprietors had long habitually worshipped in such chapels, and if not, they too followed the fashion of the new-comers and reared them.

Up to 1130 Fergus's relations with King David were almost fraternal, but about this time we read that "Fergus, Earl and Great Lord of Galloway, failed in his duty to the King's Majesty, and incurred his serious displeasure."[3] His crime seems to have been one rather of omission than commission. The native lords throughout Scotland, who had made little objection to the king's first introduction of Anglo-Normans among them, became jealous on finding what a preponderating influence

---

[1] Founded by Feigus, Lord of Galloway, in 1142 The monks here were brought from Rievault Sylvanus was the first abbot of this place.— Keith, 255.

[2] Bishop Forbes's Preface to *Life of St. Ninian*, xlvii. *Celtic Scotland*, ii 376

[3] "Contigit Fergusium, comitem et magnum dominum Galwidie, regie majestati deliquisse et gravem incurrisse offensam "—*Service-Book of Holyrood, Bannatyne Mis.* ii. 19.

they were acquiring. And in 1130 Angus, Earl of Moray, raised
his standard to the cry of "Scottish land for the Scots." The
insurrection spread, and two circumstances threw Fergus into
communication with its abettors : his daughter Affrica had
married Olave, King of Man, closely connected with Somerled
of Argyle (a co-conspirator with Moray); and his Anglo-Norman
wife having died, he had re-married a lady of Celtic blood, the
mother of his younger son Gilbert, who sympathised with the malcontents. Thus circumstanced, Fergus had presumably a guilty
knowledge of what was going on, but the rebellion breaking out
prematurely, was suppressed, and many slain, before he could
have had time to have taken part in it, even had he meant to
do so. He fell, nevertheless, under suspicions so grave that he
found it prudent to fly for safety to the Abbey of Holyrood,
where he remained concealed until, by the complicity of its
abbot, he surreptitiously obtained from King David the "kiss
of peace" But this not till after the delay of many years.

Hence his absence from Galloway at its invasion by Malcolm
MacEth a few years later.

This adventurer, whatever his origin, had been a monk of
Furness, known there as brother Wymond, a man of great energy
and ability. Being sent on a mission to the Isle of Man, he so
charmed its people by his fine presence and address that they
sought to secure him for their bishop.[1] Their king and queen
were Olave and Affrica (son-in-law and daughter of Fergus), and
they interesting themselves in the matter, procured his consecration as such by the Archbishop of York.

Somerled, Regulus of Argyle, was closely allied by blood to
Olave, whence doubtless opportunities were afforded Wymond
for intercourse with his family; but however this may have
been, he very shortly renounced his monastic name and vows
of celibacy, declared himself to be the son of Angus Earl of
Moray (slain in 1130 at Strathcathro), married Somerled's

---

[1] "Ita barbaris placuit ut ab eis Episcopum peteretur."—*William of Newburgh*, bk. i. c 24.

MacEth the son of Aedh (Hugh) is the equivalent of the Galloway M'Kie,
the Highland M'Kay

daughter,[1] raised a band of followers, and with the direct assistance of Somerled and other Celtic chiefs ravaged the whole
northern coasts of Scotland.

Bold men of desperate fortunes flocking to his standard, he
soon became a power in the north, pillaging to his heart's content, if pressed by superior forces, leading them a long chase
to remote shores, and then embarking in the fleet which was
always at his back, he would turn up again at points where he
was least expected.

For long he met with no check, until once, having given the
go-by to David's army somewhere about the Moray Firth, he
transported his band to Wigtown Bay, landing there in full
hope of being able successfully to appeal to Celtic sympathisers,
having, moreover, Affrica's name to conjure with.

Far, however, from hailing him as a deliverer, the Galloway
Picts rose instantly to oppose him as a rebel to their king, and,
failing their overlord, followed their bishop to the attack.

This brave prelate, Gilla Aldan (termed by chroniclers
"Simplicissimus," to be translated ingenuous, for his conduct
proves him to have been anything but weak), not content to
beat the drum ecclesiastic, armed himself with a hatchet, the
only weapon he had at command, and marched at once, though
with a very unequal force, to meet the invader.

The showy Wymond,—the mock bishop as they called him,
—if disappointed as to support, laughed to scorn the rabble
led against him by a weaker "brother," and was in the act of
careering across a stream[2] which divided them, when Gilla
Aldan, little accustomed as he was to handling arms, hurled his

---

[1] Fordun terms him "a spurious bishop, who lied and said he was the Earl
of Moray's son" (bk v. c 41)   But what is final as to his being actually a
bishop, "Olave's letter (to the Archbishop of York) is preserved in the White
Book at York."—*Celtic Scotland*, i. 463.

For detailed account of his career see Hailes, *Annals*, i 97 *et seq*   He is not to
be confused with Malcolm, a bastard son of King Alexander, and a co-adjutor of
Moray in the rising of 1130, he claiming to be the son and earl of said Earl
Angus

[2] "The scene of this battle is fixed by local tradition in Galloway, and a
stream which flows into Wigtown Bay is said to have been crimson with blood "
—*Celtic Scotland*, 1. 464.

axe with such force and effect as to bring the intruder to his knees. Encouraged by the omen, the Galwegians pressed to the charge, and giving the foe no time to rally from a momentary panic, cut them down in such numbers that the rivulet ran red with blood, MacEth himself with difficulty escaping across the fords of Cree[1] with so few followers that he was shortly after tracked and taken prisoner by the king's vassals in the east, and lodged in the dungeon of Roxburgh Castle. The scene of the action has ever since been known as " the Bishop's Burn "

In 1138 the Galwegians received a welcome summons to take the field on King David's espousing the cause of his niece Matilda (Empress of Germany) as against Stephen   The lordship being still, as it were, in abeyance, they crossed the Borders under local chieftains,[2] whom they accepted as leaders in battle, though they paid them little deference in quarters   The only person who could exercise any real control over them, and to whom they yielded obedience as of inborn right, being William, son of Duncan (the king's nephew), and grandson of their well-remembered Ingibiorg   This William might have proved a formidable competitor for the crown, with Galwegians especially ; but happily for the uncle, David had no more loyal subject than this favourite nephew.

Stephen being detained in the south, the Scottish armies had it their own way in the north country, and committed

---

[1] This point on the Cree is mapped " Knockdown Ferry " An absurd idea obtains that it is so called because here MacEth was knocked down by the bishop's hatchet   Nothing is more obvious than that the word, if Celtic, is cnoc donn, " brown knoll."

[2] Without a shadow of authority Mackenzie thus writes "The vice-sovereignty of the province passed to Ulgric and Dovenald, probably brothers, and perhaps descendants of Olwen Galvus " (*History of Galloway*, i. 158) , and again, " Fergus succeeded Ulgric and Dovenald in the lordship of Galloway " (*ib* i 167) Ulrick and Dovenald are but *once* mentioned (and doubtless rightly) by Ailred as "duorum eorum ducibus," two of their "duces," or military leaders—this one occasion being the onslaught at the Battle of the Standard. Ailred in no way concerned himself in the provincial arrangements of Galloway , and whilst Mackenzie has been accepted without further inquiry, it has not been adverted to that by all the chroniclers *William son of Duncan* is the person mentioned as really controlling the Gallowidians, and that *constantly*, as at Hexham, Durham, Clitherow, and the eve of the Battle of the Standard

many excesses for which the chief blame is thrown on the
Galwegians, though we much doubt whether the other divisions
of "this impious host" ("nefandus exercitus," as Richard of
Hexham styles it) were gentler in their dealings with those
who lay at their mercy.   With all their savagery, the much
maligned Picts seem to have had purposelike arrangements
for amusement in their camp, carrying with them a troop of
actors and dancing men and women,[1] clowns and columbines,
these implying the presence also of musical performers, and
more appreciation of humour than might have been expected.

A charge is made against them of ransacking a chapel and
polluting the shrine of St. Michael at Hexham, also of
threatening to destroy its abbey, but the monk who chronicles
this naively prefixes an account of a wanton attack made upon
them, in which a chieftain was slain, which others might think
was quite sufficient provocation.[2]   Yet, enraged and excited as
they were, William Fitz-Duncan easily allayed the tumult and
saved the clerics and terrified townspeople from their fury.

Sacrilege, moreover, away from home, lay lightly on the
Galloway conscience, nor were sacred edifices within the Scottish
Borders more respected by Englishmen with much greater pre-
tentions to civilisation at a much later date

The Scottish armies marched southwards, plundering and
desolating the country, until when near Durham they were
brought to a standstill by open mutiny in the Galwegian camp.

The king had interposed (not unreasonably, we may be sure)
in favour of a female, probably of rank, whom they had made

---

[1] "Histriones, saltatores et saltatrices "—Ailred, *De Bello Stand*.
Lord Hailes translates this· "Jesters or buffoons, and dancers both male
and female "—*Annals*, i 825
[2] David had granted a protection to the Abbey of Hexham   The youth of
Hexham rashly attacked a party of Scots and slew their leader   The Scots,
inflamed with revenge, ran to destroy the Abbey and massacre its inhabitants.
William, the son of Duncan, interposed and stayed their fury —Hailes,
Annals, i. 79.
This is abridged from John of Hexham, 259, 260.
Lord Hailes points out that John of Hexham always calls the Galwegians
Scots, and Richard of Hexham calls them Picts, adding, English historians call
these (same) men "Picti, Scoti, Galwenses, Loenenses.—*Annals*, i. 86.

captive; but not only did they absolutely refuse to comply or even discuss the question, but on the king going in person to enforce his desire, they roughly handled the members of his suite and even threatened his own life.[1]

Alarm and confusion were general when William, attracted by the noise, appeared upon the scene and instantly produced a calm

A rumour, probably spread by himself, that the English were approaching, caused all the divisions to close their ranks, William tactfully detaching the Galwegians from the main body of the army; and when this new alarm proved to be groundless, and David moved to the siege of Norham, he, with the king's concurrence, led them westward, finding them congenial occupation in a raid through Craven.[2]

Advanced as far as Clitheroe, which they expected to surprise, they found an English division drawn up in battle array beneath its walls, whose men-at-arms, from their tall horses, smiled at the disorderly rabble of riders and walkers interspersed

But no sooner did the wild Scots realise the position than, disengaging themselves from ponies, impedimenta, and plunder, they assumed their normal fighting formation (wedgelike, much like a gaggle of geese), and, filling the air with cries, they threw themselves against the hostile ranks with such force that the horsemen falling into confusion, their formation was broken

The agile Picts gave them no time to rally; their victory was complete, numbers were slain, many knights were made prisoners, and an immense booty of every sort secured.[3]

Purged of their delinquencies, William led back his Galwegians in high feather to the royal headquarters, now near

---

[1] Picti ipsum Regem cum suis extinguere minabantur.—Richard of Hexham.

[2] He laid siege to Norham with the more orderly part of his army, and sent *these barbarians*, under the conduct of William, a son of his nephew (brother) Duncan, to penetrate into Yorkshire —Lord Lyttelton, *Henry II.*, i 268.

[3] Hailes, *Ann* i 81 *et seq.*: "Multamque prædam et multitudinem captivitatis adduxit Hoc bellum factum est inter Anglos Pictos et Scotos apud Clitherow feriâ 6tâ, die xv. ante nativitatem Sancti Johannis Baptistæ, an. 1138."—J. Hagustald, 261.

Northallerton, where the king was only waiting their return to attack the English.

These, under Walter l'Espec, had erected their standard [1] on Cutton Moor. Such English barons as had feudal holdings in Scotland and declared for Stephen were now in an uncomfortable position, as David had a right to claim their military services, and with all the more grace when in favour of the daughter and chosen heir of their late king. Foremost among these men of double allegiance were Baliol and Bruce. great Yorkshire barons—names well known in Galloway.

Bruce sought out the Scottish camp, and in the name of both besought the king to allow them to make terms for him with Stephen and to end the war He expatiated on the services and attachment of his English feudatories, and implored him not to put a too severe strain upon their allegiance.

"Which expressions," we read, "so wrought upon the king that he forthwith broke out into tears, and had condescended to a peaceable accord, but that *William his nephew* came in, and in great fury charging Robert de Brus with treachery, dissuaded the king from hearkening to him." [2]

This fury is partly to be accounted for by the exaggerated language in which Bruce is represented to have denounced the Galwegians as "not men but brute beasts, devoid of every spark of piety or humanity," laying every outrage committed at their door Fitz-Duncan naturally resented this, and seeing he was to gain the day, Bruce further sarcastically taunted the king with "his new-found confidence in these Galwegians," whom English barons had helped him to conquer, and whom he in turn ruled rather by fear than love [3]

He then formally renounced his fealty and retired weeping. A grand oration is put in his mouth by Ailred, but the dignity

---

[1] The standard was the mast of a ship fitted on the perch of a carriage, from it were displayed the banners of St Peter of York, St John of Beverley, and St Wilfrid of Ripon ; on the top was a casket containing the consecrated host

[2] Dugdale's *Baronage*, i. 448.

[3] "Nova est in Walensibus ista securitas, qui eos hodie armis petis per quos hactenus amabilis Scottis terribilis Galwensibus imperasti "—Ailred, *De Bello Stand*

of his conduct is somewhat impaired when we find it elsewhere
related that he left a son, a boy of sixteen, in the Scottish camp
to perform the military service which he owed for Annandale.

David now prepared for battle. The great temptation not
to treat with Stephen (which would have been the safer policy)
was that his army for the moment was numerically superior.
He had, however, fewer mounted men, and fewer archers, and
obviously good generalship required that he should begin the
attack with his archers and men-at-arms, and when the enemy's
ranks were broken or loosened then hurl in the Gallovidian
phalanx upon them. But no sooner had he so arranged it than
ominous murmurs rose from the Galwegian lines, and it was
understood that they insisted on leading the van as their ancient
and unalienable right. Their triumph so lately over mailed
squadrons being notorious, they scoffed at the idea of its being
a military necessity to keep them in reserve, and refused to
move if their privilege was ignored — " kittle cowts " at all
times to deal with !

A warm discussion ensued, and though the speakers who
vigorously pressed their claims upon the king are unnamed, in
the closing sentences we seem unmistakably to recognise the
tone of William, their late leader in their raid.

" Be well advised, sire, and trust rather to the iron breasts
of your Galwegians than to those whose trappings, however
formidable they look in the distance, are mere encumbrances
at close quarters." [1]

Nothing is more remarkable than that the bulk of the
Scottish army should not have demurred at the Galwegians
being humoured in this matter, contrary to the judgment of the
king and his councillors ; but these were principally Anglo-
Normans, and jealousy was probably the ruling influence of the
moment.[2]

---

[1] More at length . "Nobis certe sunt latera ferrea, pectus aereum, mens
timoris vacua. Quid Gallis apud Clitherou profuere loricæ ? Videat igitur
prudentia vestra, O rex, quale sit in his habere fiduciam, quæ in necessitate
magis sunt oneri quam consolationi "—Ailred, *De Bello Stand*

[2] As to this privilege. we have distinctly stated . (1) *its assertion*—' Galwenses

Whilst the king still hesitated to disregard rules of military prudence, Malise, Earl of Strathern, a great magnate of the North, darting looks of defiance at the king's *entourage*, exclaimed, "Whence this mighty confidence in these Normans I wear no armour, yet not one of those here who do will go farther than me amongst the enemy to-day."

The hands of those addressed grasped instinctively their sword-hilt, and the king, with difficulty repressing an outbreak, acceded to the demands of the Galwegians.

The order of battle was then formed as follows .—First marched the Galwegians. Next followed the men-at-arms and archers under Prince Henry, and the men of Cumberland and Teviotdale. The third division were from the Lothians, and Lennox with the Western Highlanders.[1] The fourth, commanded by the king in person, consisted of the Scots proper of the period, dwellers betwixt the Forth and Spey, the men of Moray, and a bodyguard of Anglo-Normans.

Profiting by their experience at Clitheroe, the English men-at-arms dismounted, and, standing shoulder to shoulder, presented a front of solid steel to their assailants.

With terrific yells and shouts of "Albanaid !" the Galwegian phalanx dashed against the iron barrier, whence issued Saxon voices scornfully retorting, "Yry ! Yry !"[2] Spear after spear was uselessly shattered on proof coats of mail, but here and there a lithe Pict forced an entrance through an interstice inside the square, and hacked away as determinately with his short battle-sword, until gradually the dismounted squadrons fell somewhat into disorder. Their archers now advanced, riddling them with

dicentes sui esse juris primam construere aciem " , (2) *their insistence*, in spite of the commands of the king and the reasons against it by his generals—"Restitere Galwenses !" "Galwenses nichilominus insistebant ;" (3) *its concession*, against the king's judgment—"Rex, ne tumultus nasceretur, Galwensium cessit voluntati." Yet for its origin we are thrown back on conjecture, although their helping to place Kenneth on the throne seems the probable cause.—See p 28, *ante*

[1] Galwensium cuneus more suo ter ululatum diræ vocis emittens.—Ailred

[2] Equivalent to Irish. Lambardi records that at the Battle of the Standard, when the Scots shouted "Albanaid ! Albanaid !" the English retorted, "Yry ! Yry !" (Erse), a term of great reproach in those days.—Dean of Lismore's Book, Int xiii.

arrows. Two of their leaders, Ulrick and Dovenald, had already fallen, the former wounded mortally, when Prince Henry charged and dispersed the mass of archers and dismounted horsemen "as if it had been a cobweb," then fell upon the troops who were guarding the horses in their rear, and followed far (alas too far) in pursuit.[1]

The Galwegians rallied, and prepared to renew the combat, when an Englishman, cutting off the head of one of the slain, cried, "The head of the king of Scots." Confusion ensued ; the Galwegians looked for support from the other divisions, but these unaccountably stood still.

The king vainly ran hither and thither to prove he was not slain , panic seized upon the third division, their hesitation proved fatal, and the Galwegians were driven from the field.

If the Galwegians had been perverse as to the order of the battle, still they were not responsible for its loss. They had gallantly shown the way, they had paid the penalty of their waywardness in blood, but had effectually stormed the key of the position, and it was entirely owing to the inertness of the reserves that their excess of spirit was proved to have been expended in vain. The disaster was intensified by its attendant circumstances, as, instead of holding closely together, the divisions separated with mutual recriminations, suffering in their retreat not only from the hostility of the English peasantry, but recriminations leading to bloody collisions among themselves.

At last the Galwegians reached Carlisle with greatly diminished numbers, but yet (whether accompanied by William or not) in tolerable order; for we have it from an English chronicler that here they were overtaken by Alberic, Bishop of Ostia, the Papal legate, who persuaded them to restore all the women they had driven into captivity a fact as creditable to themselves as to the prelate.[2]

---

[1] "Videres ut *hericium spinis* ita Galwensem sagittis undique circumseptum, nichilominus vibrare gladium et cæca quadam amentia proruentem, nunc hostem cædere, nunc inanem aerem cassis ictibus verberare."—Ailred, *De Bello Stand*

[2] Hailes, *Annals,* i 89 *et seq* —Ailred

After this David, satisfying himself with taking the castle of Werk, which belonged to Walter l'Espec who had commanded at the Battle of the Standard, concluded peace with Stephen, whose wife was his niece as well as the Empress Matilda.

A rather amusing story forms a sequel to these dismal tales of ravaging and rout. The younger Bruce, the hobbledehoy of seventeen whom David had so easily accepted as an equivalent for the knight's service due to him from Annandale, was taken prisoner by his own father at the Battle of the Standard, by whom he was delivered to Stephen, the elder Bruce gravely asking to what person he would have him committed. "Pooh, take him to his nurse,"[1] the king good-humouredly answered.

Soon after this Fergus emerged from his hiding-place. As for the necessity of his concealment, there must always be some mystery, but we have authentic details from church history as to how he made his peace with his sovereign.

An ancient service-book of Holyrood tells us that "Fergus, being much devoted to God, and, notwithstanding his accidental fault, always faithful to the king, by various means was endeavouring to regain the king's favour, and at length in most secret manner repaired to Alwyn, Abbot of the Monastery of Holyrood, the king's confessor, for advice and assistance. The abbot compassionating the aforesaid penitent, Lord Fergus prayed to God to obtain the king's favour; and at last, by the ingenuity of both Fergus and the abbot, it was contrived that the said Fergus should assume the cloister habit of a canon regular, and thus, God directing, should obtain along with his brethren the king's favour and pardon of his offence"

"Leaving to God their purpose, they wait for a convenient hour and day." An occasion occurred thus: Some repairs being

---

[1] Dugdale gives us a more courtly phrase. "By reason of Annandale, Robert the younger being liegeman to the King of Scotland, and war happening between the English and the Scots, it was his fortune to be taken by his father, fighting valiantly for that nation, and sent prisoner to the king of England, whose courtesie was such, when he had him so in his power, as that he delivered him back into the hands of his mother."—Dugdale, *Baronage*, i 448.

carried on, the king came to inspect them. The brethren were
hastily summoned to the chapter-house, Fergus among them
And while the king was visiting the builders the abbot at
a seasonable moment thus addresses him . "We, though un-
worthy petitioners, beg to have the presence of your highness
in chapter" The king, highly pleased, enters The abbot continues "Most gracious prince, we, the petitioners of your highness, confessing our faults, that we are faulty and transgressors,
most humbly beseech thee, in the bowels of Jesus Christ, to pardon
us, *and every one of us, every fault and offence committed against
your majesty, with a single and unfeigned heart* ; and that in
token of this gracious pardon to bestow upon every one of us
the kiss of peace"

The king, with most placid countenance, replied . "Dear
brethren, *I forgive you all*—I commend myself to your prayers,"
and rising and taking the abbot by the hand, kissed him.

Of the interview and explanations with Fergus that followed
no record remains; indeed, it was hardly to be expected. The
relation is made in connection with the building of the Priory
of St. Mary's Isle (or Trayle), which was raised and handed over
to the monastery of Holyrood by Fergus as a lasting memorial
of his gratitude to God for his restoration to the king's favour
and the enjoyment of his offices, as also in grateful recollection
of the hospitality of the convent.[1]

Of the entire cordiality accompanying the reconciliation
there can be no doubt, as hereafter we find him in constant
attendance upon the king, his name appearing as a frequent
witness to royal charters [2]

---

[1] "Hec est hysioria fundacionis Prioratus Insule de Traile et quo-
modo Fergusius Magnus Dominus Galwidie, fundatoi ejusdem, optinuit pacem
Regis "—"Service-Book of Holyrood," printed in Bannatyne's *Miscellany*, ii 19.

[2] In the chartulary of the Bishopric of Glasgow are two charters, "Apud
Castium Nostrum de Cadhow," dated approximately 1139.

The one a grant of Perdeye (Partick) "Testibus Herberto, Abbate de
Rochesburc, Willelmo cancellario, *Willelmo filio Dunecan*, Malis comite, Dunecano
comite, *Fergusio de Galueia*, Æd. cum barba, Malduuem, MacMurdac, Maloderi
de Scona, Malodeni marescal, Radulpho filio Donegal, *Duvenald fratre ejus*,
Uchtred filio Fergus, Hugoni Britoni, Herberto Camerario, *Giliberto fimboga*
Giliberto de Strivelin, Dufoter de Calateria "

Within a very short time of his receiving the kiss of peace we find him in the royal circle along with William Fitz-Duncan, who had led his Galwegians in his absence; Hugh de Moreville, Constable of Scotland, to whose office and possessions his descendants fell heirs; the gallant Malise of Strathern, who had so lately supported the claims of the Galwegians to the right of the line, and Dovenald, recovered from his wounds in the late battle. Walter, the son of Alan, High Steward, ancestor of the Earls of Galloway, and his own son Uchtred, never arrived at man's estate.

A church legend of the period seems referable to the very date of the signature of these charters. St. Malachi O'Morgair, visiting King David in a certain castle,[1] found Prince Henry his son dangerously ill; whereupon, sprinkling him with holy water, he assured him he should recover, and next day he was well.[2]

Thence going, probably accompanying Fergus, to his "country seat of Cruggleton,"[1] he there miraculously loosed the tongue of a girl who had been born dumb; whence, travelling westward, he arrived at last at Cairngarroch (Lapasper),[1] where, finding no vessel in port, retiring a little inland, he raised an oratory, surrounding it with a rath; consecrating also near it a burying-ground. Here he watched for the arrival of a ship, and one coming in due time he embarked, and a fair wind wafted him to Bangor.[1] Topography verifies the outline of the story.

In the second David makes known "omnibus fidelibus tam Gawensibus quam Anglis et Scoticis" that he gives the tithe of cane, animals, and pigs of Renfrew, Cunningham, Kyle, and Carrick, to the Church of St. Kentigern   Testibus Will Cumino cancellario, Hugo de Moreville, Fergus de Galweia, Hugo Britom, Waltero fil Alane, Alano MacArchel, Rad fil. Dunegal, Duvenald fre sui.

[1] "Quodam castello suo "   . "Villam nomini Crugeldum ad portum Lapasperi "   "Constructor in oratorium, consummatum circumdedit vallo "   .   "Prospere navigavit applicuit monasterio suo Benchorensi "—*Vita S. Malachi*, Auctore Barnardo, c 6.

Dr. Reeves first called the author's attention to the identification of Rough Cairn, or Cairngarroch, with Lapasper. There are no less than three Cairngarrochs on the Galloway coast   Bishop Forbes rightly puts it "Laperasperi or Lepasper, probably some bay opposite Ireland, near Portpatrick "   He mistakes grievously, however, supposing that St. Malachi went hence and founded Soulseat, which had been built by Fergus twenty years before.—See Keith, *Scotch Bishops.*

[2] Lord Hailes sarcastically remarks : "It is remarkable that the cure was not instantly effected."—Hailes, *Ann.* i. 103

Cairngarroch, anglified in recent maps to Roughcairn, overlooks
Caer Ochtree (named from Fergus's son), at the southern
extremity of Larbrax Bay.   The saint has left his name on
Taphmalloch, Malloch's hillside (taebh), whence Copeland
Island, at the entrance of Belfast Loch, just opposite the old
monastery of Bangor, is visible to the naked eye.   The Ghaists'
Ha', Taphmalloch, preserves possibly a recollection of the
burying-ground.

In 1142 Fergus's magnificent Abbey of Dundrennan being
finished, was peopled by a band of Cistercians from Rievaux,
Yorkshire, with Sylvanus, a man of considerable eminence,[1] as
their first abbot.

Fergus had doubtless been assisted by Ailred in recruiting
for his religious colonies, the latter being intimate with all the
magnates of David's court, where he was a frequent and
honoured guest, and a visitor at that of Fergus as well as his
son.   His own connection with Rievaux suggests the probability of his having introduced the members of his fraternity to
Dundrennan and taken part in the dedication services, and we
may with some confidence refer his first intercourse with the
Bishop of Whithorn to this date, who then and there "imposed
upon him," as he tells us, "the task of bringing into the light
of clear Latin diction the life of the most renowned Ninian—told
already, truly, by those who had gone before him, but in too
barbarous a style"[2]

This book owes its value entirely to the date at which it
was written.   The elegance of its Latin proves Ailred to have
been a man of culture, but as to historic facts it gives us really
no more than those already succinctly told by Bede   In the

---

[1] In 1167 he became himself Abbot of Rievaux

[2] Ailred, or Ethelred, was born 1109   In 1133 took vows as a Cistercian monk
at Rievaux, 1142 was Abbot of Revesby; 1143 Abbot of Rievaux.   Bishop
Forbes *conjectures* Ailred's prologue to the life of Ninian to be addressed to
Bishop Christianus after 1134.   But a considerably earlier date is probable, no
date being given in the prologue, Ailred himself introducing the members of his
fraternity to Dundrennan would be a more appropriate occasion for a meeting
with the bishop, who must undoubtedly have been present at the consecration,
their bishop being Gilla Aldan, who was succeeded by Christianus in 1154

relation of miracles, however, which in themselves are worthy
only of a place in the Breviary of Aberdeen, glimpses of real
life evidently take their colouring from the light in which the
author saw the province ; and such scenes as the convent
garden abounding in leeks and potherbs of every sort, the
shielings for the flocks, and more especially the division of the
whole land into parishes, if not appropriate to the fourth
century, yet as not being later than the twelfth, rank as the
earliest local sketches we possess.

William Fitz-Duncan had long previously married Alice de
Romellie, heiress of Skipton and Craven, and by her had, with
three daughters, a son, also William, generally known, from
being put into possession of one of his father's fiefs, as the Boy
of Egremont[1] Owing to the disorders in England his enjoyment of these lands seems to have been interfered with, and
David, again letting loose the Galwegians across the borders,
put him forcibly in possession.   When at Carlisle the King
had an interview with his grand-nephew, son of the Empress
Matilda, and afterwards Henry II, who then receiving knighthood from his father, swore solemnly that on receiving the
English Crown he would restore to him Newcastle, and cede to
him and his heirs for ever the whole territory between the
Tyne and the Tweed   Within a year of this William died, as
in 1151 we find his mother granting charters in her widowhood[2]

The year following Prince Henry died ; Malcolm, his eldest
son, being a boy but ten years old.[3] King David, too infirm to
accompany him, sent him on a progress through the kingdom.

---

[1] "David *conferred* the honours of Skipton and Craven on William, the
son of Duncan, and with an armed force put him in possession" (Hailes, *Annals*,
i 102). William, however, had previously *possessed* these in right of his wife
"The Scots again pillaged the places sacred to religion. David bestowed a piece
of plate on every church that had suffered from these depredations."—*Ib* and
J Hazalsted, 279

[2] In 1151, among the witnesses to a charter by Adeliza de Rumelli is "Willelmo filio meo de Egremont "

[3] By his wife Ada, daughter of the English Earl of Warrenne and Surrey,
Prince Henry left Malcolm (the Maiden), b. 1142 , William (the Lion), b. 1143 ;
David, afterwards Earl of Huntingdon, b 1144

In Galloway he was received and escorted by Fergus, and proclaimed to the people at large as heir to the throne, and his succession actually took place 24th May 1153.

Donald, a son of Wymond, or Macolm MacEth, was set forward as a pretender to the throne, strongly supported by Somerled and other Celtic chiefs ; but Fergus would not, either by threats or blandishments, connect himself with the insurrection, and even refused to allow Donald to obtain an asylum in his province when, as a hunted rebel, he sought refuge from his pursuers at Whithorn.[1]

Thus far Fergus was strong in his allegiance to the boy king; but Malcolm, as he grew in years, did little to retain the affection of his adherents, and in place of leaning upon them for council in the art of government, tried fawningly to ingratiate himself with the English king.

This was Henry II., who, on succeeding Stephen in 1154, instead of making the cession he had promised to his uncle, laid claim to all lands in the northern counties held absolutely by Scottish subjects; his only action in the north being to bribe some of Malcolm's ministers, by whose advice he went to meet Henry at Chester, and there, with no consultation with his own great lords, surrendered all their rights

Fergus, with many others of these, was deeply aggrieved, nor was their displeasure lessened when, utterly neglecting his home duties, Malcolm was only heard of as dancing attendance on the King of England, with a puerile desire for knighthood, which the King dangled before him but delayed to give, till at last Malcolm crowned his folly by passing with Henry into France, and there (that nation being at peace with the Scots) fighting under the banner of Henry, who then contemptuously

---

[1] He was taken by Fergus's orders and conveyed to the dungeon of Roxburgh —*Chron. Sax. Con* ; Hailes, *Annals*, i 114

Somerled kept up the civil war, but his nephew Donald, one of Malcolm MacEth's sons, was taken prisoner at Whiterne by King Malcolm's friends, and was imprisoned in that same keep of Marchmont with his father.--Fordun, *Annals*, i.

invested him with the honours he had won at the expense, as it proved, nearly of his crown.[1]

Living in a fool's paradise, he was roused from his day-dreams by ominous murmurs at last re-echoing from Scotland, "We will not have Henry to reign over us." [2]

Hurrying back, he found himself all but too late, his great lords holding aloof from him, and the Galwegians irrevocably committed to a rising in favour of William, great-grandson of Ingibiorg

Some mystery hangs over the state of affairs at this crisis, history is not explicit as to whether there was any organised insurrection in Scotland generally in favour of any individual, and more especially as to whether William himself was any party to it, or would under any circumstances have accepted the position Fergus seems to have wished to thrust upon him.

All that we know historically of this is that Malcolm, having trysted his estates to meet him at Perth, they not only failed to appear, but six out of seven of his great earls closely besieged him there; Wyntoun hinting that the "Boy of Egremont" was among them,[3] and the Orkneyan Sagas relating as notorious that all the Scots wished to make him king.[4]

Next we read that the earls failed to take Malcolm prisoner, and that the clergy intervening, restored them to their allegiance. No reason is given for the collapse, but modern research has

[1] Henry invested him with the honours which his military service had merited in an enterprise undertaken against the judgment of his nobles.—Hailes, *Annals*, 1 118

[2] Nolumus Anglorum regem Henricum regnare super nos —Fordun, *Annals*, 111.

[3]   A mayster-man cald Fevetawche,
    With Gyllandrys, Ergemawche,
    And other mayster-men there fyve,
    Agayne the Kyng that ras belywe
    For cants that he past till Inlows "
                  Wyntoun, bk. vii c. 7

Fevetawche is of course Ferquhar, Earl of Stratherne, but it required Mr. Skene's eagle eye to detect the Boy of Egremont

"Wynton's barbarous name Ergemawche may have been intended for Egremont."—*Celtic Scotland*, i. 472.

[4] "William Fitz-Duncan was a good man , his son was William the Noble, whom all the Scots wished to take for their king."

recovered a fact which goes far to account for it. "William the Noble" died at this very conjuncture, being still under age. Providence thus removing his rival (whether William was such willingly or unwillingly) from Malcolm's path.

Fergus, who had been so slow to rise, now alone proved irreconcilable ; and the great moral power he wielded, and his tactical skill, are evidenced by the fact that, although immediately invaded by the whole royal forces,—backed by the seven great earls of the kingdom,—he discomfited them at every point, and drove them with great loss out of the province.[1]

Again a greatly superior army descended upon Galloway, which Fergus, unaided, drove back ignominiously.   But on learning that the king was mustering for a third expedition, feeling that his resources were inadequate to compete with those of the whole kingdom, he made his submission, in accepting which the king made it a significant condition "that he should not be molested on retiring."[2]

Almost immediately after, Fergus, resigning his lordship to his son, entered the monastery of Holyrood as a canon regular.

The reasons given for his doing so are somewhat conflicting. One version, as epitomised by Chalmers, being that "Malcolm obliged him to retire to the abbey of Holyrood House, where he died of grief and disappointment the following year."[3] The other that Fergus sent his son Uchtred as a hostage, retaining his vice-royalty,[4] but that his life being embittered by family dissensions, his old friend Ailred came to his assistance, and advised him to withdraw from the world : advice which he followed.[5]   He certainly died as a monk of Holyrood in 1161, at

[1] Lord Hailes suggests that Fergus's solitary defection was an advantage to Malcolm   "The insurrection in Galloway at this critical moment enabled Malcolm to employ his factious nobles, and to concentrate the affections of his people by personal valour   Twice he invaded Galloway, and was twice repulsed. —Hailes, *Annals*, 1. 119

[2] Rex Malcolmus duxit exercitum in Galweiam, ter et ibidem inimicis suis devictis, *fœderatus est in pace*, et sine damno remeavit —*Chron. S Crucis*

[3] *Caledonia*, iii 251, and *ibid* 368   [4] Fordun, *Annals*, 3.

[5] Descendens in Galwediam Alredus invenit regulam terræ illius contra filios suos iratum filios in patrem sævientes et in se invicem fratres   Alreedus patrem filiorum habitum religionis suscipere inflexit, et qui multa millia hominum

a great age,[1] having during his long life done much to elevate the tone of those he ruled, and leaving his native province adorned with imperishable monuments of his beneficence and taste.

He has left his name directly on "Loch Fergus," and Drumargus (Fheargus) Minigaff; Ben Ailsa (ealasaidh), which over-looks it, bearing that of his wife. Knockeffrick, near one of his residences, is supposed to be named from his daughter, the Queen of Man; and an outpost he held beyond the Irvine (in his days the boundary of Galloway) is still mapped Fergushill.

Besides Affrica, he had another daughter, Margaret, married to Alan, son of Walter, second High Steward of Scotland.

vita privaverat vitæ participem eternæ fieri docent.—Capgiavi, *Nova Legenda,* fol. xii

[1] 1161.   Obiit Fergus, Princeps Galwaiæ quarto Idus maii. — *Chron S. Crucis.*

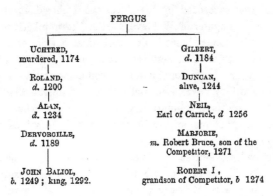

FERGUS
|
UCHTRED, murdered, 1174 — GILBERT, *d.* 1184

UCHTRED,
murdered, 1174
|
ROLAND,
d. 1200
|
ALAN,
d. 1234
|
DERVORGILLE,
d. 1189
|
JOHN BALIOL,
b. 1249; king, 1292.

GILBERT,
d. 1184
|
DUNCAN,
alive, 1244
|
NEIL,
Earl of Carrick, *d* 1256
|
MARJORIE,
m. Robert Bruce, son of the Competitor, 1271
|
ROBERT I ,
grandson of Competitor, *b* 1274

CHAPTER IV

LORDS OF THE LINE OF FERGUS

A.D. 1161 to 1234

Francia Pepinis — Brabantia milite signi
Anglia Richardo — Galwidia gaudet Alano.

HENRY DE AUBLAY
(*A Monk of Dundrennan*)

FERGUS was succeeded by his eldest son Uchtred, married to
Greynolda, daughter of Waldeve, Earl of Northumberland, who
brought him sundry lands in Cumberland as her dower.

It has been usual to designate Uchtred and Gilbert as joint-
heirs of Fergus,[1] but examination of contemporary writs prove
the lordship to have been indivisible. Gilbert's claims to
equality were the mere mutterings of treason, and when he did
get the better of his brother, it was to rule the province alone,
not to share its government with him.

For at least fourteen years after his father's retirement, we
find Uchtred making grants of land, and solely exercising
sovereign powers at every point of the compass within the
province, Gilbert's consent not being required, nor he even pre-
tending that it was so.

---

[1] Lord Hailes states this on the authority of Roger de Hoveden, who was
deceived by the petition of Gilbert to be allowed, *jointly with his brother*, to do
homage to the English king, his brother having been murdered with his con-
nivance. Mackenzie intensifies the mistake, "Fergus was succeeded by his
sons Uchtred and Gilbert," by adding "between whom, according to the ancient
Celtic law, his dominions had been *equally divided*" (I. 172). Galloway was then
not under Celtic but under feudal law, of which primogeniture was the leading
feature, the feudal law having been introduced by Fergus himself.

Thus, from the chartulary of Holyrood,[1] we find him confirming to that abbey lands and livings given by his father in various parts of Galloway, adding, as his own gift, the church of Colmonell.

To the monks of Holmcultram, across the Solway, he granted in fee-farm the lands of Kirkgunzean.[2]

He bestowed "a carucate and a croft" in Troqueer upon the hospital of St. Peter's at York;[3] and (as every Galloway archæologist ought to be aware of) "he conceded in perpetual alms the church of St. Bride, in Kirkmaiden," with "a carucate of land, and all its rights in fisheries, wood, water, and common pasture," "to the church of Holyrood and the canons there serving God," for the safety of the soul of King David, his son Henry, King Malcolm, "and my father Fergus."[4]

These are but a few of his gifts.

Further, we find his position as first subject in the province recognised by the sovereign. Malcolm addresses him as such in a letter granting protection to all settlers on the lands of Dunrod (which Fergus had given to the church of Holyrood), with full confirmation of Uchtred's charters, implying his right to grant them.[5] And Uchtred himself, in attendance upon royal progressions, led the king near his marches.

---

[1] Munimenta Sancta Crucis.—*Reg. Malc.*

Uchtredus, filius Fergusi, grants "Ecclesia de Calmaneli" to God and the Abbey and Convent of Holyrood   Witnesses — Macmares Judice, Gillecatfai Collactaneo Uchtredi (foster-brother), Gilliechrist MacGillewinne Mectheuel, Daniel fil. Erlemine

[2] Roland confirmed his father's grant, and added Saltcoats.—Dugdale's *Monasticon*

[3] *Grants by Scottish Kings and Nobles to the Hospital of St Peter at York*— Troqueer is there written Crevequer. Bain's *Calendar*, ii. 422 —The gift is in "frank almoine for the soul of King David, Fergus his father, his mother, and all his ancestors."

[4] This, known as the "Logan Charter," is published in facsimile in the *Archæological Collections of Ayr and Wigtown* (vol. iv p. 52). Witnesses—Robert, the Archdeacon, Salomon, the Dean, Malbec, the Dean; Helias, clerk to the Bishop; Ingerannus, chaplain to the Bishop; Ralph, priest of Lertune, Gillecharfar, Gilliechrist, MacGilliwinne, Daniel, son of Herlewine.

[5] Malcolmes R., Uchtredo filio Fergus, et Gileberto fratri ejus, et Radulpho filio Dunegal, et Duvenaldo fratri ejus, universisque aliis probis suis hominibus totius Galweie, etc.   "Quam Fergus dedit quam etiam Uchtredus filius ejus sua carta confirmavit, quorum etiam cartas ego ipse carta mea confirmavi."

Malcolm having died in 1165, we find Uchtred immediately after in attendance on William the Lion, and witnessing a Crown charter in favour of Robert de Brus, sealed by William at Lochmaben, and addressed "to all good men—French, English, Scots, and Galwegians."[1]

The names we thus find grouped together in the court circle are of genealogical interest.

Subscribing first after the bishop is Richard de Moreville, Constable of Scotland, feudal superior of the whole of Cunninghame, owning also wide tracts of forest on the Gala Water.

His daughter Elena had married Rolland, Uchtred's eldest son (whose signature we find here for the first time), and who through her eventually fell heir to his father-in-law's offices and estates[2]

Next to the Constable signs Alan, High Steward, and brother-in-law to Uchtred, by whose sister Margaret he had a fair-haired son Simon, ancestor of the Earls of Kilmarnock;[3] Alan himself being the progenitor of a long line of kings, of the Dukes of Lennox, the Earls of Angus, Atholl, Buchan, and Traquair, Lords Blantyre, and (the title still surviving in direct descent) the Earls of Galloway.

William de Haia was the common ancestor of the Earls of Errol and Kinnoul, and the Marquises of Tweeddale.

Simon Locard held lands in Kyle under Alan the Steward, and names the parish of Symington there, as also another Symington in Lanark   He was ancestor of the Lockharts of Lee.

[1] Witnesses—Engelram, Bishop of Glasgow , Christian, Bishop of Whithorn , Richard de Moreville, Constable , Walter Fitz-Alan, dapifer , Odenell de Umfranville ; Huctred, son of Fergus ; Gilebert, son of Fergus ; Gilebert, son of Richard , Rolland, son of Huctred , William de Hara , Simon Locard ; Robert de Chartres, etc , at Locmaben —*National MSS. of Scotland,* vol 1 No 39

[2] Hugh Morvill, under David I , became Constable of Scotland, and acquired a grant of Cunninghame   Under him settled as vassals many from England. The progenitor of the Loudons was a vassal of Morvill's, the Cunninghams also, whose name was local   The numerous family of the Rosses settled here in a similar manner —*Caledonia,* iii 457

[3] By Margaret, daughter of Fergus, Lord of Galloway, Alan had three sons Walter, Adam, and Simon, whose son is allowed to be ancestor of the Boyds Earls of Kilmarnock —Noble's *Genealogy of the Stuarts,* 5.
Boyd is a hardening of the Celtic Buidhe, yellow or fair (haired)

Richard de Charteris (oddly often latinised De Cornoto)[1] was of Amesfield, now represented in the female line by the Earls of Wemyss.

Before Malcolm's death Uchtred had built the comparatively small but very beautiful abbey of Lincluden,[2] and had it not been for intestine feuds, there is little doubt he would have followed further in his father's footsteps as to church-building.

This house, in the first instance a nunnery, peopled by a sisterhood from Clugny in Marmoutier in France, lay in a sequestered dell near the junction of the Cluden with the Nith. Above it a hillock, artificially scarped as a mount of defence in prehistoric times, served monks of a later period for a Calvary, · still attractive from its fine views ; such of the ruins below it as are of the original erection being peculiarly interesting as specimens of the architectural transition from the severer Norman to the Gothic. Early English as yet entirely undeveloped into the "Decorated" of the two following centuries.

From his father's retreat until 1174 Uchtred kept his court at the Palace Isle. Kerroughtry, believed to have been a strong house of his building, may probably have been occupied by his son; and Rolland Hill, on the opposite side of the Cree, may have been given from some adventure of his in the chase or war.[3]

Church records give us a glimpse of Galloway life of the period in a little more than usual of details

Ailred, the Abbot of Rievaux, appears to have been on a visit to Uchtred in 1164, and at the date of the feast of St. Cuthbert, the 20th March, a great gala day in the neighbourhood of the saint's especial mother church.

· Services having been celebrated with great pomp, a penitent

---

[1] Sir Robert Charteris, probably grandson of the above, gave to the monastery of Kelso the patronages of the churches of Traverflat (now Trailflat) and Dumerinoch, in the shire of Dumfries, in which he is designed Robertus de Cornoto, miles.—Douglas's *Baronage*, 1. 150.

[2] Lincluden was founded in the reign of Malcolm IV. by Uthred, father to Rolland, Lord of Galloway.—Keith, 280.

Cludan, dim of Clud (Clyde), Cledfein, and Cleddyfein—Sixth century bards.

[3] Reginald of Durham, Surtees's edition, 178

was " miraculously freed from an iron belt " before all the congregation ; without was tethered a bull, " offered in oblation to
St. Cuthbert," by which we understand intended as a provision
for his votaries, when butcher and cooks had duly performed
their offices.

But before they had taken him in hand, Ailred, on leaving
the church, was greatly scandalised at finding a party of
" scologs " [1] most unclerically engaged in baiting this bull ; he
remonstrated warmly, when one of them " mocked the saint,"
and was instantly gored by the bull

The point the monkish chronicler seems principally intent
in making is that the animal was miraculously impelled to
avenge the embryo saint,[2] and instinctively to pick out the
principal offender; but historically it is of greater interest to
gather from the tenor of the relation that there was still proper
tranquillity near Uchtred's headquarters, and that the gatherings
were for merrymaking and fun, as there is nothing in the narra-
tive inconsistent with the belief that the saucy boy was more
frightened than hurt.

Indeed the general repose of the province seems to have
remained unbroken until 1173   In this year the Scottish king
most unhappily allowed himself to be bribed by a promise of
the Earldom of Northumberland to assist a rising in England
against Henry II. in favour of his own son.

The summons to arms went forth, and being responded to
enthusiastically by the Galwegians,[3] they were at once hurried
across the borders, and masking such fortresses as Werk and

---

[1] Scolog, Lat. scholasticus, the lowest order of the ecclesiastical community ;
root, sgol ; Celtic, ysgol, a school.   In early Columban monasteries the Toiseach-
na-Scolog (chief of the scologs) was an office   Scolog in Ireland, scallag in
the Western Highlands, is now applied to tacksmen, small crofters, and in a
contemptuous sense

[2] So early as 1250 Ailred was regarded as a saint, his canonisation following
his death unusually quick   For the legend see Reginald of Durham, Surtees's
edition, p 178.

[3] The King of Scotland's " army being chiefly composed of Galwegians "
(Lord Lyttelton, *Henry II.*, book iv vol. v. 165), " who having no pay but
plunder could be under no restraint " (*Ibid* p 175, based on Abbas Benedic.
and Hoveden).

Carlisle, which they had not means of reducing, they were let
loose on the unguarded lands beyond, and devastated the whole
countryside as far as the Humber.

Remorseless forays were continued uninterruptedly, saving
a few weeks' time, until the following summer, when, riding
in the early morning (13th July 1174) insufficiently attended,
William the Lion was surprised by a band of horse under
Barnard Baliol, and hurried off ignominiously into captivity.

Dire was the confusion in the Scottish camp as the maraud-
ing bands dropped in one by one with their ill-gotten booty,
their rage and resentment venting itself perversely in murderous
assaults on Anglo-Norman gentlemen in their own ranks, on
the pretext of their affinity to the captors of their king.

Gilbert—whose name, be it noted, never appears before, except
as an occasional witness in his brother's suite—was not slow to
turn the momentary madness to account,[1] and denouncing his
brother as a favourer of foreigners, roused race jealousies to such
purpose that Uchtred had to fly from the camp, and was afterwards driven from his home ; and, wandering as a fugitive, was
finally tracked to a cave on the Leswalt shores, dragged out, and
murdered with circumstances of revolting barbarity, Gilbert
inaugurating his succession by a general massacre of Anglo-
Normans.[2]

This savage exultation, however, was succeeded by some
alarm lest William the Lion should be released and call him to
account ;[3] and, anxious to secure support, he sent ambassadors
craftily, in the joint names of his brother and himself, offering

[1] Just after the king's capture, the Galwegians, led by Gilbert, treacherously
made a conspiracy, separating themselves from Scotland —Fordun, *Annals*, 14

[2] Abscissis testiculis et oculis evulsis.—Benedic. Abbas, 92.

Ochtred, who was a true Scot and could not be shaken, was taken prisoner
by his brother Gilbert on the 22d September, given over unto bonds, and at
length his tongue was cut off, his eyes torn out, and he was ruthlessly murdered
—Fordun, *Annals*, 14.

Lord Hailes says · "Gilbert, by the ministry of his son Malcolm, cruelly
murdered Uchtred."—*Annals*, 1 142

[3] William of Newburgh, 216. "After William's captivity the natives of
Galloway murdered many subjects of Scotland who were settled in their territory,
and expelled the king's officers."—Hailes, *Annals*, i. 14.

to transfer their allegiance to England, trusting to be able to give his own colour to the circumstances of his brother's death. Henry II. desired nothing better; and, pleased at the idea that consanguinity should so readily aid in the extension of his influence, he sent Roger Hoveden and Robert de Val forthwith to accept the homage of the two brothers,[1] and to assure Uchtred of his cousinly regard.

On arriving, however, the envoys found but one to treat with; and however Gilbert may have prevaricated as to the cause, the true story leaked out in all its ghastly details, and they left, refusing to have any dealings with "the murderer of the king's cousin."[2]

Gilbert, unabashed, renewed negotiations, offering to pay a price of 2000 marks of silver, a tribute in money, as well as of 500 cows and 500 swine in kind. This Henry could not so soon, with any decency, accept; the more especially as he, having given William his liberty, but as his vassal, and thus all Scotland being practically at his feet, preferred to allow the Scottish king to be the avenger of his kinsman, and so let matters drift

William, as he had expected, instantly invaded Galloway, but soon found that Gilbert was too strong for him, and was fain to accept a moderate fine and a nominal submission, with a further promise to submit himself to Henry II. also.

The next year, consequently, Gilbert accompanying his own king to York, both did homage to the English king as suzerain, Gilbert's delinquency being condoned for a fine of £1000,[3]

---

[1] Ut alliecerent eos ad servitium suum —Benedict. Abbas

[2] Consanguineam Henrici Regis.—*Ibid.*
Henry, being informed of the murder of his kinsman, . . . knowing too that the Galwegians had murdered many English and Normans whom they found in the country, refused to make any treaty with them —Lord Lyttleton, *Henry II*, bk. iv vol. v 237.

[3] Henry made little by this dishonourable transaction. He had the power of punishing Gilbert, but was put off by the promise of the gold We find that in 1179 Gilbert, son of Fergus, accounts for £1000 for "having the king's benevolence." One payment into the Exchequer "camera curie" of £80 : 11s. by the hands of Robert de Vallebus is noted. He further reduced it by the merest trifles, as at his death in 1184 £917 : 19s. remained unpaid —Bain's *Calendars*, i. 23, 24
"Gilbart, son of Fergus, charged £917 19s. for the king's good-will."—Madox, *Exchequer*, i 437

he also giving up his son Duncan as a hostage for his good
behaviour

Gilbert's rule, based on the murder of his brother and all of
Anglo-Norman proclivities, was ruinous to the province, and a
curse to the shires bordering on it. A tyrant at home, " at odds
with his neighbours," perpetually engaged in raids conducted
with fiendish slaughter, it was a general relief when " *that
lover and wager of civil war*," as Fordun terms him, through the
kindness of Providence, was removed from the scenes of his
crime in 1185 [1]

Roland now appeared upon the scene, and, backed by his
father's friends, asserted his lordship. A certain " Gilpatrick
and Henry Kennedy and Samuel" rose in support of Duncan's
claims (Gilbert's son, a hostage in England); but in a battle,
" sare, scharpe, and snell,[2] fought on " Thursday, the 14th of
July," were utterly defeated, and themselves slain He next
turned upon a robber chief, Gilcolm, who had wrested a part of
the province, from Gilbert, conquered, and slew him,[3] thus constituting himself (and with the king's good will) sole lord of
Galloway.

But now the difficulties attendant on the strange state of
double allegiance owed by Scottish magnates began to develop.

Henry II. had not been consulted, and was furious at
Roland's success. Under pretext that he was honourably bound
to defend Duncan's rights, he ordered Roland to quit the field ;
and he, naturally refusing to relinquish the advantages he had
just gained, refused, on which Henry, assembling a mighty
army, advanced to the Borders. Roland fortified his passes, but,
by William's mediation, procuring a safe conduct, he presented
himself before the angry potentate at Carlisle. Here, his own
king becoming answerable for him that he would submit to
Henry's judgment, it was finally arranged that Roland should
retain all Galloway in its ancient boundaries up to the Deil's
Dyke, giving up Carrick to Duncan [4]

---

[1] Fordun, *Annals*, 17.   [2] Wyntoun, bk. vii. c. 8, l. 1980.
[3] Hailes, *Annals*, i 142.   [4] *Ibid.*, and Fordun, *Annals*, 18.

Duncan proved an amiable and able man ; the treaty was honourably observed by both parties; friendly relations were ever after maintained between the two cousins; and Roland himself rose almost as high in favour with Henry II. as with his own king.

In the year 1187 there was a rising in the north in favour of Donald Bane, calling himself also MacWilliam, as claiming to be a son of William, son of Duncan. This was almost certainly an imposture, as the said William had no legitimate son but the Boy of Egremont, long since deceased ; and King William would hardly have trusted a Galloway force alone to oppose even an illegitimate son of their favourite chief.

Roland was sent to encounter him, and falling· in with the rebels on the moor of Mongarvey, near Inverness, entirely dispersed them, and slew Donald.[1]

He was now in such high repute as a commander that we find him summoned by the King of England to quell an insurrection on the west marches. It was probably in reward of his services there that Henry II. bestowed upon him the large estates in Northamptonshire and Leicester which we know him to have enjoyed.[2]

Having now more leisure, and his affairs prospering, in 1190 we find him founding the Abbey of Glenluce, peopling it with Cistercians from Melrose. The building in its day must have been both beautiful and imposing ; its ruins cover a full acre of ground, and the few arches of white freestone yet remaining are artistically sculptured in quaint designs. Attached to it was a garden more than fifteen acres in extent, the names still mapped upon its site being Auchenmanister and Balmesh—the "field" and "orchard" of the monastery[3]

On the death of Richard de Moreville in 1196, Roland, in right of his wife, succeeded him as Constable of Scotland, inherit-

---

[1] *Chron. Melrose*, Hailes, *Annals*, 1. 144

[2] 1186   Paid to the army of Galloway at Chester, £119 10.7 (a very large sum in those days) —*Exchequer Rolls*

[3] In early charters always written Glenlus ; lus, a herb, plant, or leek   Balmesh, Baile-meas, the townland of the fruit.

ing also his vast estates, for which he paid to the Crown, as a relief, 700 marks.

A grant of a salt-work to the monks of Kelso proves Loch Kendelach to have been still the name of the parish of New Abbey,[1] and the Viponts (Veteriponti), who had feudal holdings under him, near Whithorn, seem to have left their name translated in Auldbrick.[2]

In 1199 Roland, as High Constable of Scotland, accompanied King William to Lincoln, who there did homage to King John, who had just succeeded, for his earldom of Huntingdon. A few weeks afterwards he died, apparently in his English domain, he being buried in the church of St Andrew at Northampton. His reputation stands high as a statesman and a military commander, and in his native province he was esteemed a king, and such, indeed, he is styled by contemporary chroniclers[3] He left Alan, his heir; Thomas, who in right of Isabel his wife became Earl of Athol; and a daughter, Ada, married to Sir Walter Bisset.

The prestige of Alan even exceeded that of his father and grandfather, he is styled by Chalmers "one of the greatest nobles of his age," and by Buchanan, "by far the most powerful of Scotsmen."[4] In Scotland he was the highest court official; south of the border he was recognised as one of the guardians of the British Constitution, in Galloway he was supreme; and his dealings with both the sovereigns, to whom he owed fealty, were rather those of an ally than of a subject; more especially in the case of the unpopular King John, who set great store on his support, whilst in 1209 his marriage with Margaret, daughter of the Earl of Huntingdon, the king's brother, brought him into the most intimate social as well as official relations with William the Lion.[5]

---

[1] *Chart Kelso*, 253   Grant by Roland of Galloway of a salt-work

[2] Roland confirms the grant by Ivo de Veteriponti of the church of Great Sorby.—*Chart. Dryburgh*

[3] 1199, Kal. January   Rollant, MacUchtraigh-ri-gallgaidhel, in pace, qui ævit.—*Annals of Ulster*.

[4] Scotorum longe potentissimus.

[5] Margaret's sister, Isabella, married Robert de Brus

On Candlemas Day 1212, he was present at Durham at a meeting between the English and Scottish kings, at which the delicate matter of the latter doing homage for his English estates was compromised by arranging they should be vested in Prince Alexander, and that he should do the homage to King John.[1]

Alan afterwards accompanied the king to Norham, where, in presence of the ministers of both sovereigns, his seal as High Constable was attached to deeds professing to secure "peace and love" between England and Scotland for ever,[2] and "by leave and license of his royal master" Alan did homage for himself[3] for large possessions which the English king further heaped on this Galloway magnate. King John had previously granted him many lands in Ireland for services in 1207, when he had assisted him with an army and a fleet, and five years later he bestowed upon him in fee the whole of Dalriada,[4] consisting of one hundred and forty knights' fees, of which his brother Thomas, Earl of Athol, took seizure forthwith

Alan succeeded in resuscitating the buccaneering tastes of the Galwegians, which had slumbered since the departure of the Vikings; his fleets, under his brother Thomas, becoming the terror of the whole countryside, from Bangor to Innishowan.[5] And although his ships and men in great force were thus engaged plundering the Irish, he was able to raise a second army to support King John on the Welsh marches. He had previously sent twenty men-at-arms with their attendants, but these proved insufficient, as the following letter shows:

[1] Fordun, *Annals*, 26

[2] Kalendars in Record Office

[3] "Alan, Lord of Galloway, Constable of Scotland, did homage to John, King of England, by his lord's will and leave, for some broad lands which the latter bestowed upon him."—Fordun, *Annals*, 27

[4] Dalriada, Riada's portion or tribe, that part of Antrim extending from the Ravel Water northwards. Riada, corrupted in Latin to Ruta, was anglified "the route."

[5] 1212. Thomas (grand)son of Uchtred, came to Derry Columcille with seventy-six ships, the town was spoiled by them very much, and Inisowen altogether was spoiled by them.

1213. Thomas, son of Uchtred, and Roderick, son of Ronald (of the Isles), plundered Derry altogether, and carried away the goods of the men of Derry and the north of Erin out of the temple and the monastery.—*Annals of Ulster*

" The king to his faithful cousin Alan de Galweia, and requests him for the great business regarding which he lately asked him, and, as he loves him, to send 1000 of his best and most active Galwegians so as to be at Chester on Sunday next after the Assumption of the Blessed Virgin ; Alan to place over them a constable who knows how to keep peace in the king's army, and to harass the enemy. The king will provide their pay"

Thither, accordingly, Alan led his men in person, and so efficiently handled them that a month later we find an entry in the Exchequer of a largesse given in excess of the stipulated pay[1] " At Nottingham, 16th August 1212, To Alan of Galloway, by way of gift, 500 merks, to pay his squires, who had come with him to the king's service in the army of Wales."

Notwithstanding John's blandishments, however, three years later Alan sided with the English lords, who at the point of the sword demanded attention to their complaints. He appears to have joined his fellow barons, of whom Saier de Quinci was a leading spirit, in the spring of 1215, their first overt act of rebellion being the siege of Northampton, near which Alan owned many manors. He advanceed in their company to London, and was with them on the memorable 15th of June 1215 at Runnymede, where the signing of Magna Charta[2] verified their success and John's discomfiture. Entries both before and after that date in the English kalendars throw a curious light on the dealings of King John with this great Galloway lord of double allegiance. Early in 1215 Alan not

[1] 8th July 1212. 55s allowed for expenses of twenty horsemen sent from Galloway

15th July   Ralf de Cambray going to Alan of Galloway with a letter

At Nottingham, 16th August 1212   To Alan of Galloway, by way of gift, 500 merks —*Kalendars*, Record Office.

1211 Alan paid 600 merks and 6 palfreys for recognition of his mother's right to Whissendine and other lands.

[2] Alan had the honour of being one of the illustrious barons to whom the great charter of King John was addressed. He was one of the Magnates Scotiae who witnessed the marriage of Alexander II with Joanna (John's daughter) He was the witness of many charters of William and Alexander II , as his rank and office led him to be much at court —*Caledonia*, ii 257

only detained an English ship at Kirkcudbright, but sent it to
Dublin, there to be laden with merchandise for himself. Yet
on the 2d of April, when Alan was then actually in the field
against him, King John signed a mandate to the Justicier of
Ireland ordering "him to permit Alan to traffic, to allow the
very ship he had seized to go back to Kirkcudbright. The
case to stand over for the king's investigation "[1]

On the 5th of May the king signed orders for the payment
of 330 merks respectively to Alexander of Galloway and Thomas
Galloway, Earl of Athol. Only a fortnight before the king's
capitulation at Runnymede, Alan sends a present of "a fine
hound to the king," receiving from his majesty in return "two
geese"—the latter reading almost like a joke And just a fortnight after that event John makes further grants of Irish lands
to Alan, and signs his brother Thomas's commission as Keeper
of the Castle of Antrim.[2]

The previous December William the Lion had died, and
the first Parliament of Alexander II. (his successor, a youth
of seventeen) was held in Edinburgh the same year, in which
the Constableship of Scotland was ratified to Alan. King
John died 17th October 1216, and so great was the influence of
Alan supposed to be by the English Council, that they addressed
a letter to him in the name of the boy king, Henry III.,
entreating that "his councils may be used in the interests of
peace, and for the restoration to the English of the Castle of
Carlisle" Alan seems to have complied with both requests,
as an order was made forthwith for the delivery of the castle,
with all English prisoners therein, to Richard de Vetereponte.
After this, Alan delaying an unreasonable time to do homage
for his English and Irish estates, a threat of forfeiture was made

[1] The king commands the Archbishop of Dublin, Justicier of Ireland, to
allow the men of Alan of Galloway to come to Dublin, and to return with the
ship that Alan took at Kirkcudbright, and allow Alan to have his merchandise
in the said ship, till the owner of the vessel shall come over to speak to the
king. At Lichfield, 2d April 1215 —*Kalendars*, Record Office.
[2] Grant of lands to Alan from Winchester, 27th June

To Thomas of Galloway, Keeper of the Castle of Antrim, 30th June 1215.—
Kalendars, Record Office.

in King Henry's name, which occasioned a voluminous correspondence ; and in 1218 a safe-conduct was offered him for
the purpose, but of this he neglected to avail himself, and
even under further pressure, only made his submission in writing. With even this, however, the English Council appear to
have been satisfied, writing : " The king takes into consideration
that Alan of Galloway is at a distance, and unable, without great
trouble and expense, to come and do homage to the king, and
he gives orders accordingly."

The following letter also passed as to his Irish holdings.
" Alan, son of Roland, Constable of Scotland, to the king —
He believes that the king is not ignorant that he and his
brother are his relatives in the line of consanguinity . . . .
For the goods and lands conferred on them by the king's
father, they embrace him with warm affection Seeing, however, that they have had little use of the lands granted them
in Ireland, he sends messengers to speak to the king on
the writer's behalf, who is ever ready to go by sea and land
on his service." To which Henry III., dating from Westminster 18th April 1220, replies : " Harriz of Galloway, clerk,
having come to the king and council, seeking in Alan's
behalf restoration of his lands, and assuring them of his
devotion to the king, the king has ordered that his lands in
Ireland shall be restored. The king is to meet Alexander, King
of Scotland, at York to discuss matters relating to their kingdoms,
and he invites Alan to come there and do homage for his lands
in England " [1]

Alan was present at York at this meeting of the two
sovereigns, and accordingly shortly after assisted at the
marriage of King Henry's sister with the Scottish king, signing
as a witness to the settlements, by which the young queen's
jointure of £1000 a year was secured over the lands of " Jedd-

---

[1] The letter further adds " The Jucticier of Ireland is also ordered to allow
Thomas de Galweia to hold the lands given him by King John in peace."—
Kalendars, Record Office

Thomas was now recognised as fifth Earl of Athol in right of his wife Isabel,
daughter of Alan, fourth and last Earl of Athol of that line.

worth, Kyngor, and Carel."[1]   Alan becoming a second time
a widower, crossed the Irish Channel as a wooer, and married
a daughter of Hugh de Lacy, Lord of Ulster. In returning,
his gay flotilla was overtaken by a storm, many of his vessels
being lost, he and his young wife with difficulty effecting a landing in a creek, believed to have been that about a mile westward of Cruggleton Castle, which bears the name Port Alan.[2]

On the 26th October 1229 a mandate, dated from London,
peremptorily orders Alan to appear there personally "on Palm
Sunday next, with horses and arms, prepared to go abroad with
the king." Whether this order was a matter of form or not, it
was not obeyed; we find him otherwise engaged at that time.

For some years he had been actively intervening in disputes
between two brothers, his distant relatives, Reginald and Olave,
for the sovereignty of Man.

Reginald having been worsted, passed in the winter of 1224
to Alan's court, taking a daughter with him, who there won the
heart of Thomas, Alan's illegitimate son, who married her, and
induced his father to support Reginald. A pitiless war, its area
extending from the Hebrides to Anglesea, dragged its desolating course for years. Its results in Man are thus described in
the chronicles of the island : "In 1228 Alan Lord of Galloway,
Thomas Earl of Athol his brother, and King Reginald, came
into Man with a great army, and wasted all the south of the
island, and spoiled the churches, and put all the people they
could meet with to the sword . . . After this Alan returned
with his army, leaving his bailiffs in Man to collect the tribute
of the country.   . . King Olave, coming on them unawares, put
them to flight and recovered his kingdom. But the same year
King Reginald came by surprise in the dead of night with five
ships from Galloway, and burned all the ships that belonged
to his brother Olave."[3]   Being thus worsted, Olave appealed to

[1] Rymer's *Fœdera*. Jeddworth (Jedburgh), Kyngor (Kinghorn), Carel (Crail)
[2] 1228 This yeare Allane, Earl of Galloway, went to Ireland, and thar
married the daughter of Henry de Lacy, and in his returne had many of servands
drowned, himself and his ladey verey narrowly escaping —Balfour, i 46.
[3] *Chronicles of Man.*

Haco, King of Norway, who, styling himself Lord Paramount of
the Western Isles, sent a message to Alan, desiring him at his
peril not further to molest Olave.   To this Alan with becoming
spirit responded that the voyage from Galloway to Norway
was quite as easy as that from Norway to Galloway, and if
Haco felt inclined to try issues he should see whether Galwegians could not find their way as easily through the fjords
of Norway as his Norwegians among the creeks of the Solway.

If an Icelandic legend may be believed, this proved no idle
boast.   It relates that Haco furnished Olave with an army and
a fleet of 80 ships, which, having desolated the Hebrides,
Cantyre, and Bute, were sailing merrily southward, when they
learned that 150 ships of the Lord of Galloway were lying in
ambush for them inside the Mull ; on hearing which, they put
about without attempting a landing in Galloway, and entirely
gave up their purpose of going to the Isle of Man [1]

In 1234 the great Alan died , he was buried in the Abbey
of Dundrennan, where his tomb is still preserved.   He left no
legitimate son , the Lordship of Galloway by feudal law passing
jointly to his daughters, and the Constableship of Scotland to
the husband of the eldest.

These ladies were all married to Anglo-Norman barons, holders
of English fiefs ; the eldest, Helena, to Roger de Quenci, Earl of
Winchester; the second (the elder by his second marriage), Dervorgille, to John Baliol of Barnard Castle ; the third, Christian, to
William de Fortibus, Earl of Albemarle. To anticipate a few years,
we may mention that Christian dying in 1246 without issue,
her Galloway inheritance was shared by the surviving sisters.

The prestige of these joint Lords of Galloway necessarily
fell below that of their father and grandfather; Alan being the
last of those rulers of Galloway who in contemporary records
are chronicled as kings.[2]

[1] The " Black King of Man "   A legend, translated from the Icelandic, p 16.
Alan, Lord of Galloway, is said to have driven Olave, King of Man, from his
dominions, having collected for that purpose 150 vessels at the Rhynns of
Galloway.—Macpherson, *Ann of Commerce*, i. 387.

[2] 1234   Kal Jan   Ailin MacUchtraigh Ri Galgaidhel mortuus est.—*Annals
fn Ulster.*

CHAPTER V

ALAN'S HEIRS TO THE BRUCIAN SETTLEMENT

A.D. 1234 to 1360

> Bot in Karryk John Kennedy
> Warrayid Gallwey sturdely
> He and Alane Stewart tha twa
> Oft dyd Galluays mekill wa
> Yhit the Balholl all that qwhill
> In Gallwa wes at the Brynt-yle.[1]
>
> WYNTOUN, bk. 3, c. xl.

FEMALE succession was opposed to Celtic customs, and this, aggravated, as in the case of Alan's daughters, by the passing of the province to three alien overlords, occasioned a strain on the loyalty of its inhabitants which it could hardly bear. The Galloway Picts entreated the king to assume their lordship himself, but Alan's settlement was in perfect accord with feudal law, and the king "preferring justice to ambition"[2] declined the offer. They next implored him, failing this, to allow Thomas, Alan's illegitimate son to be their lord, but this request Alexander absolutely refused to grant, whereupon they rose as one man in favour of the said Thomas, receiving active support from Gilrodh, a native Irish chief, and Hugh de Lacy, father of Alan's widow.[3]

Alexander II. invaded the province to quell this rebellion;

---

[1] It requires local knowledge to recognise Botel in Brynt-yle !

[2] Hailes, *Annals*, 167.

[3] Hugh de Lacy, Lord of Ulster, in anno 1235 entered Scotland, endeavouring to restore Galloway to the bastard son of Alan of Galloway, which country the King of Scotland had given to the three daughters of Alan as their rightful inheritance but in this attempt he prevailed not —Dugdale's *Baronage* i 98

but his troops getting entangled in the mazes of the forests and
"flows," which the initiated alone could thread, became demor-
alised, and were surrounded by the natives, who would probably
have overpowered them had not the Earl of Ross burst unexpectedly "with furious might upon their rear,"[1] and restored
the fortunes of the king.

Thomas fled, and next day the chiefs of the Galloway Picts
appeared, and with ropes round their necks humbly entreated
for, and obtained, the king's pardon.

The following year Thomas, having raised a band of despera-
does in Ireland, landed with them in the Rhynns, and burnt his
boats, to show his determination to do or die.   The Galwegians,
however, kept entirely aloof, and he, finding his ragged regiment
quite unable to cope with the royal troops, made his own peace
with the king, leaving his wretched kerns to their fate.   Few, if
any, succeeded in escaping   The conduct of the king's army,
especially considering that the native population had declined
to rise, was disgraceful.   They not only despoiled the land, but
robbed the churches, the larger abbeys even being unable to bar
them out.   The Prior of Tungland and other ecclesiastics were
murdered, and a dying monk at Glenluce robbed of his covering
upon his death-bed.[2]

---

[1] The natives unexpectedly started out of the hills and woods, and assailed
the king and his army, who were resting in their tents, for that spot, full as it
was of marshes and goodly with green grass, gave them no little confidence
But MacIntaggart, Earl of Ross, burst with furious might upon the rear of the
natives, swept down many, and forced many to flee.—Fordun, *Annals*, 43

The Earl is styled Comes Rossensis Macintaggart by Fordun, Comes Rossensis
Mackintagard by the Melrose Chronicle   Peerage writers give Ferquard as the
name of the Earl of Ross of the name.   Mackintagard is "son of the priest."

[2] Seeing his own men could not withstand the king's majesty, Thomas, Alan's
bastard son, by the advice of the Bishop of Whithorn, besought the king for
peace, so the king kept him a little while in the Castle of the Maidens, and then
let him go   The rest of the Irish were slain by the citizens of Glasgow—two
of the chiefs, however, the king ordered to be torn by horses.   At that time the
Scots of the king's army despoiled the lands and churches of Galloway with un-
heard of cruelty, so much so that a monk of Glenluce who was at his last gasp
was left naked but for his hair shirt, and at Tongueland the prior and sacristan
were slain in the church.—Fordun, *Annals*, 43

Particularly note that in the original these place-names are written "Glen-
lusse" and "Tungland."

The province was now formally divided between De Quenci and Baliol, the river Cree being their march.

Northward Carrick was still ruled by Duncan, the good son of the hateful Gilbert, who in a green old age, with energy and taste worthy of a grandson of Fergus, reared the beautiful Abbey of Crossregal.[1] This was completed about 1244, and shortly after he was succeeded as third Earl of Carrick by his son Neil, married to Margaret, daughter of Walter, the High Steward of Scotland.[2]

In 1247 De Quenci somehow provoked a rising so serious that he had to fly to his own castle, whence, finding his defences likely to be forced, in which case the rebels would have allowed him but short shrift, he made a desperate sally, and with a few men-at-arms cutting his way through the unarmoured crowd, rode straight to the Court, and laid his complaint before the king, who re-established him in his rights.[3]

Before this he had remarried,—his second wife being a Bohun, widow of Anselme le Mareschal, Earl of Pembroke.[4] The re-bellion of the native Galwegians, with which he had been hardly

[1] A Cluniac monastery in Kirkoswald Parish, near Maybole Chalmers, giving no authority, suggests its date as before 1240 Keith gives 1244, quoting the Chartulary of Paisley.—Keith, *Scotch Bishops*, 253

The name is a puzzle to etymologists It has been variously written Croce-regal, Crossraguel, Crossragmal, and Crossragwell.

[2] This was Walter, fifth High Stewart, styled in genealogies "of Dundonald." He gave active assistance to Alan's heirs when hard pressed by Thomas (the Bastard) and Gilrodh. He is said to be the first of the family who used "Stuart" as a family name. "His father was styled Dapifer, as were his ancestors, but he changed it into Senechallus, whence came the surname Stewart, Stuart, or Steward, in the same manner as we have Boteler and Chamberlain."—Noble, *Genealogy of the Stuarts*, p. 7

The Neilsons of Craigcaffie claimed descent from this Neil of Carrick, husband of Margaret Stewart

[3] In 31 Henry III. de Quenci, being in Galloway, and exercising more severity to the people of that country than becom'd him, he was besieged by them in a castle there, and being apprehensive of his danger, mounted his horse well armed, and with some followers broke through them Whence he came to the King of Scotland, to whom he made his complaint, who punished them for their rebellious insurrection, and re-established him in the possession of his rights —Dugdale, *Baronage*, i 688 ; *Matthew of Paris*, 496.

[4] Maud, Countess of Pembroke, was daughter of Humphrey de Bohun, Earl of Hereford. The title becoming extinct in the head branch of the Mareschals, was bestowed upon the family of Valence.

able to cope, made him doubly anxious to surround himself with powerful vassals on whom he could rely, and he availed himself of this new connection to induce a Mareschal to settle on the important fief of Toskerton in the Rhynns.[1] The Champaignes also, who had already some holdings east of the Cree,[2] accepted other baronies under him in the west.   But by far the most important of new comers to his lordship were the Comyns

In 1249 King Alexander II. died, and was succeeded by a third Alexander, a child of eight years old   During the long minority ensuing, the Comyns gained a preponderating influence in the regency . of their clan, Alexander, Earl of Buchan, William, Earl of Menteith, and their nephew, Lord of Badenoch, held prominent offices in the state.[3]

In 1251 the Earl of Buchan being Justiciary of Scotland, the new office of Justiciary of Galloway was created at his instance, and John Comyn of Badenoch named as first holder.

Very early in the reign, Alexander Comyn established intimate relations with De Quenci, whose second daughter, Elizabeth,[4] he eventually married.   His frequent residence in Galloway led to his acquiring many lands in addition to those to which he afterwards fell heir through his-wife, among which was that lordly chase on the marches of Carrick which still retains his name—the Forest of Buchan.

[1] The Mareschals of Toskerton were of direct descent from John, nephew of William, Earl of Pembroke, who in 8 John (1208) obtained a grant in fee of the office of Marshal of Ireland —Dugdale's *Baronage*, i 599.

[2] In 1253 Sir Rauf de Campania granted the church of Warg (Borgue) in Frankalmoigne to the Canons of Dryburgh.—*Chart. of Dryburgh*, f 22

[3] "At this period the Comyns held the principal sway in Scotland "—Hailes, *Annals*, i. 181.

They were obnoxious to Edward III., to whose daughter the boy king was married   By his influence they were removed from the King's Council in 1255, but two years after they overpowered their opponents and obtained possession of the persons of the king and queen   Fordun tells us there were thirty-two knights of the name of Comyn in Scotland

[4] "The date of that marriage formed the epoch of the connection of the Comyns with Galloway, where they bore sway for many a day.—*Caledonia*, iii 262

Fordun writes of the Justiciary as "prone to robbery and rashness " (ad rapinam et temeritatem expeditus).—*Annals*, 52.

Notwithstanding, it is a historic fact that Galloway flourished especially under the rule of the Comyns and Baliols

The Stewarts also first acquired their baronial status in Galloway in De Quenci's lifetime.   Alexander, the sixth Steward, commanded the right wing of the royal army at the great victory of "the Larkis,"[1] and received in reward of his services the Barony of Garlies.

About 1250 De Quenci's eldest daughter, Margaret, married William de Ferrers, Earl of Derby, as his second wife, and after this, as his third wife, De Quenci married[2] Alianore, widow of William de Vaux, and daughter of the said Earl of Derby by his wife Sybil, a De Mareschal.   Thus placing Margaret in the amusing position of mother-in-law to her father.

Ela, De Quenci's third daughter, married Alan de la Zouche; and he himself dying in 1264, by law and custom the Constable-ship of Scotland should have passed to his eldest daughter, the privileges attached to the overlordship, as well as his lands, being equally divided among the three.   But these were days when might was an essential factor in questions of right, and Margaret's husband being dead, her claims were either prudently resigned or set aside, and in place of her son, the young Earl of Derby, the Earl of Buchan was installed as High Constable of Scotland.   Alan de la Zouche, moreover, content to draw the revenues from his wife's portion of the estates, renounced all claim to rule, and the Earl of Buchan assumed the overlordship undivided as it had been enjoyed by De Quenci.

John Baliol and Alexander Comyn were thus sole, and in the circumstances irresponsible, potentates west of the Nith, in right of their wives, who stood to each other in the relation of aunt and niece, the family ties being further strengthened by the marriage of Baliol and Dervorgille's only daughter Marjory with Buchan's kinsman, the young lord of Badenoch (the Black Comyn), son of the Justiciary.   Happily for the people, the heads of the two families were men of vigour, and of a culture

---

[1] Largs, fought 2d October 1263, Haco's fleet and army being utterly defeated and dispersed.   The gift of the Barony of Garlies is dated 30th November 1263 —Noble, *History of the Stewarts*, 9.

[2] William, Earl of Derby, died in 1254 ; William de Vallibus (Vaux), *before* 1153.—Dugdale's *Baronage*, i. 258, 526

unusual at the period—lovers of justice and progress, able to keep the peace—and under their paternal rule Galloway enjoyed a period of prosperity for many a long year looked back to with regret.

Baliol from the first succeeded in gaining the affections of the Galwegians, the secret of which seems to have been that he loved Galloway himself; for though, like Comyn, he had English manors,[1]—among them such princely possessions as Barnard Castle and Fotheringay,—his favourite residence is said to have been Botel, on the banks of the Urr, where he liberally expended his ample revenues on his estates, as Comyn did at Cruggleton[2]

It was at Botel that Dervorgille gave birth in 1249 to the future Competitor.[3]   Her husband died in 1269, and it was from Botel that she dated and signed the statutes of Baliol College, founded and endowed in accordance with the wishes of her husband,[4] to whose memory she reared at once a splendid memorial and fitting resting-place—the Abbey of Sweetheart.[5]

[1] From English sources we gather that he had manors in Hitchen, county Hertford, Wightwicke in Leicester, and others ; whilst, "having married Elizabeth, daughter of Roger de Quenci, in 51 Henry III , he had living of her inheritance, whilst again, 3 Edward I (1275), he obtained renewed living of the inheritance of the said Elizabeth, his wife, though she could not at the time come to the king in person, being great with child."—Dugdale, *Baronage*, 1. 685

[2] Chalmers, not much given to eulogy, thus writes of the two Comyns who occupied Cruggleton for more than half a century   "Alexander Comyn, Earl of Buchan, acted a distinguished part in the government of Scotland during half a century , he became a councillor to the king before 1240, was made justiciary 1251, obtained the office of High Constable 1270, and died full of years and honours 1289, at the end of a long civil war which ended in the ruin of his illustrious family.   His son John succeeded him, and acted a still more distinguished part in the busy scene of a disastrous period "—*Caledonia*, iii 262

[3] Dervorgille had four sons   Hugh, married Anne, daughter of William de Valence, Earl of Pembroke, sister to Joan, who married her grandson the Red Comyn, and died without issue in 1272.   Alan, died young.   Alexander, died 1279, and John, born at Botel in 1249   Her name is variously written Devorgilla, Dornagelle, Dervorgille   Edward I , summoning her as a vassal to the Welsh wars, styles her Dervergoyle de Baliol

[4] She writes herself S. Dervorguil de Baliol in the foundation grants dated "Apud Botel, 1282 "

[5] So called from her husband's embalmed heart in an ivory casket built in over the high altar, after her death placed on her bosom in her coffin   Latinised Dulce Cor, Suavecordium ; French, Duize-cœur, Duzquer

With much acceptance she reigned as queen of the hearts of all her subjects for twenty years, devoting her energies to the establishment and development of the resources of the province;—her rule and her works equally evidencing her tact, her taste, and her sense of responsibility   In her architecture beauty is happily combined with utility.   She built a bridge of nine arches over the Nith, a model and a marvel in its day, which still spans the stream; and besides the splendid new Abbey of Sweetheart, she built and endowed a monastery for Black Friars at Wigtown, and for Gray Friars at Dumfries, another monastery at Dundee, and no doubt she added largely to Botel, and according to tradition built Kenmure Castle, though of her handiwork on these houses no traces remain.[1]

She died at Barnard Castle in 1289, but by her desire her remains were brought to Sweetheart.   Wyntoun, who says, as we may well believe, that she was " right pleasand of bewté," adds :

> A bettyr lady than scho wes nane
> In all the yle of Mare Britane [2]

Meanwhile Neil, Earl of Carrick, had died in 1256, leaving, by a daughter of Walter the Steward, an only daughter Margaret,[3] who, when a young widow, meeting, returning from the chase, Robert Bruce, son of the Lord of Annandale (by Isabel, an aunt of Dervorgille), forcibly carried him off to her Castle of Turnberry, and married him ; of which abduction the birth of Robert, future King of Scotland, was the result.

The death of Alexander III. in 1285, followed by that of his infant grandchild Margaret, the Maid of Norway, plunged the whole of Scotland into all the embarrassments of a disputed succession.   Many claimed the crown, on pretences more or less plausible ; but eventually the competition was narrowed

---

[1] According to Kirk, the Dominican Abbey at Wigtown was built 1267, that of the Cistercians at Sweetheart in 1275 ; and that of the Franciscans at Dumfries a few years later   She granted the monks the toll of the bridge that she had built there

[2] Wyntoun, b viii. c 8. *Mare* is great, from Celtic *mor* ; should be written " mare "

[3] Her first husband was Adam de Kilconcath, who, going on a crusade in 1268, died in Palestine in 1270.   Her adventure with Bruce occurred in 1271.

to the descendants of David, Earl of Huntingdon, brother of
William the Lion, and that again to the heirs of his two eldest
daughters : Margaret, who had married Alan of Galloway, and
Isabella, who had married Robert Bruce These were John
Baliol, son of Margaret's daughter Dervorgille, and Robert
Bruce,[1] the son of Isabella

Baliol claimed as grandson of the eldest daughter, Bruce, as
son of the second, therefore one degree nearer in blood than
Baliol. This latter plea was fairly overruled by Edward I, to
whose arbitration it was submitted, it being absolutely inconsistent with feudal law.

The candidates both had a common ancestor in Fergus, and
a blood connection with all the descendants of his line.   There
was an interregnum of nearly two years whilst the matter was
in abeyance   The attitude of the Galwegians towards the
competitors was not for a moment doubtful—Baliol, the son
of their own gracious Dervorgille, being a favourite with them
as well as their hereditary lord.

Previous to acting as umpire, Edward I. had required that
all the strong castles of the kingdom should be surrendered to
him, and had given the keeping of those of Wigtown and Kirkcudbright to William de Boyville[2] and Walter de Curry, both
Galloway landowners (De Curry was succeeded by Richard
Steward), to whom Edward addressed a mandate in 1292 to
deliver both to Baliol.

In 1294 Benimundus di Vicci, sent by the Pope to Scotland
to ascertain the value of ecclesiastical benefices and the inci-
dence of tithes, explored Galloway from end to end.   The rent-

---

[1] The competitor was father of Robert Bruce, who, from his marriage with
Marjorie, Duncan of Galloway's granddaughter, became titular Earl of Carrick. He
resigned his pretensions, and died at his castle of Lochmaben in 1295, aged 85.

His son, Earl of Carrick, had by Marjorie, Robert—eventually king; born
1274, he himself dying 1304   The famous Robert Bruce was therefore the grandson of the original competitor

[2] 15 Aug. 1291. William de Boyville, keeper of the castles of Dumfries,
Kirkcudbright, and Wigtown, had 1 mark per day.   1291. Sir Walter de Currey
summoned to be castellan in room of Boyville deceased   24 March 1292 A
payment of 40 marks to Richard Steward, knight, as keeper of the castles of
Galloway and Dumfries

roll by which these dues were levied is well known by the curious corruption of "Bagimont's Roll."

Alexander Comyn, dying in 1289, was succeeded by his son John, as third Earl of Buchan; and it being on record that he had licence from the English king to dig for lead in the Calf of Man, to cover eight towers of his Castle of Cruggleton,[1] we may presume his occupation was not interfered with. These were difficult days for those of divided allegiance. When Baliol finally broke with Edward, he turned especially to Galloway for assistance, and had a willing response ; the Earl of Buchan heading "a mighty force," his kinsmen the Red Comyn and Richard Siward being forward amongst his partisans, and carried the war across the Borders, burning Carlisle and sacking the neighbouring monasteries

Nimble and daring as may have been Baliol's Galloway levies, they were no match for the armed and well-appointed forces which Edward had called out and ordered to muster at Newcastle-upon-Tyne, citing Baliol also to appear there.

Baliol declined ; but soon 30,000 soldiers, of whom 4000 were horse, answered to Edward's roll-call, with whom he crossed the Tweed, and, taking Berwick, marched northward in search of King John.

Fortress after fortress fell before him, and Baliol was fain to implore mercy and resign his crown. Returning southward, Edward held a Parliament at Berwick, and the Scottish lords and barons flocked in there to make their submission. The lists of the clergy and laity who then did homage constitute the paper known as the "Ragman's Roll," useful as preserving the names of many of the actual proprietors of that day.

From English writs we find that in the king's train, a spectator of the pageant, was a John de Aignell, summoned to perform knight's service against the Scots in virtue of an English fief,[2] little aware how closely his descendants were

---

[1] The words used in the royal mandate are. "To cover eight towers on his Castles of Crigelton and Galwey in Scotland," obviously a clerical error for Cruggleton in Galloway.—Dugdale's *Baronage*, i 685.

[2] Johannes de Aygnell, returned by the Sheriff of Hertford as having been

soon to be connected with the baronage of "Dunfres and Wyggeton," as they swept past the royal presence.

Of these Comyn now made his peace with Edward, and the earl remained unmolested in his forest of Buchan His name appears prominently on the "Ragman's Roll," while that of Thomas of Galloway is absolutely wanting. Just previous to the Comyns making their submission, Thomas had tried to profit by the occasion, and to stir up an agitation in favour of his own claims, which, he hoped, the English king might find it politic to encourage.

When Edward issued a proclamation addressed to the "good men of Galloway," setting forth his complaints against Baliol, Thomas took upon himself to answer for the community, suggesting certain grievances, the redress of which might incline them to the English. To which the king at once replied by letters patent, "that, at the request of Thomas of Galloway, he has granted to the whole community of Galloway all their liberties and customs, as they and their ancestors held them in the time of King David, and of Alan, the said Thomas's father,[1] and will consider as to the relaxation of such amounts of their rents as they have asked by the said Thomas." But the ink was hardly dry when the king seems to have realised that Thomas was an impostor, and sent an order to the Sheriff of Westmoreland "to take the said Thomas and keep him in close custody in the castle of Carlisle"[2]

We hear no more of Thomas of Galloway.

All traditions respecting Wallace, and especially those in which Galloway matrons are described as rearing their children

summoned to perform military service in person against the Scots. Muster at Newcastle-upon-Tyne, 1 March 24, Edward I Two years later we find Johannes Aygnel Knight of the Shire for Hertford, Parliament of York, 25 May, 26 Edward I.—*Parl Writs*, p 276, No. 7 , p 70, No. 16.

[1] It is impossible to conceive that the Thomas who was an active warrior years before Alan's death in 1234 could have been an efficient commander in the field in 1296. For "father" it seems evident we should read "grandfather."

[2] 7 March 1296. The King commands the Sheriff of Westmoreland to receive Thomas of Galloway from William de Heck, and conduct him to the castle of Carlisle, and keep him in safe custody, as Antony, Bishop of Durham, will instruct —*Kalendar of State Documents* Reg. Edw I.

iń undying loyalty to Bruce, must be ranked as spurious, being opposed to the whole tenor of authentic history. In one of these Cruggleton Castle is stated to have hereditarily belonged to Kerlé, Wallace's lieutenant, and to have been taken from him treacherously by Lord Soulis. Wallace thereupon marched into Galloway, took every strength from the Water of Urr westward, the garrison of Wigtown flying at his approach, and Cruggleton, which held out, he demolished. Trustworthy records oppose this story at every point. Cruggleton was not the patrimonial domain of the Kerlés, but of the Galloway petty kings and their descendants.

Comyn, we know, held Cruggleton in 1292, and continuously until 1308, when his lands were forfeited and given to Lord Soulis by Bruce, who in his turn being forfeited for conspiracy, the castle passed to the monks of Whithorn. The strengths westward of the Water of Urr were never taken by Wallace, but held by English partisans till wrested from them many years later by Edward Bruce

Indeed, it seems a stretch of fancy to identify Cruggleton Castle with a "strength on the Water of Cree" The Bladenoch intervenes between Cruggleton and the Cree Moreover, on the Water of Cree itself a spot is still mapped "Wallace's Camp," which, if rightly named, was no doubt palisaded Blind Harry's epithet, "built of tree," is certainly more applicable to such a structure than to a stone castle on the sea-cliff.[1]

The incursion of Edward I. into the province in the summer of 1300 stands on very different authority. The official entries in his accounts and state papers are of the highest value as accurate records of the agricultural prosperity which the

[1] We cannot trace the tradition beyond Captain Denniston's introduction to certain novelettes styled *Legends of Galloway*, published in 1825, in which he affects to quote from a certain volume styled "Buke of me Wanderins in the Weste, be Father Stewart, ane Moncke o' Crossraguel," "written partly in Latin and partly in English, sometime about the middle of the sixteenth century." But besides the obvious objection that a mendicant friar of Crossraguel would be little authority for domestic matters in Wigtownshire, much less for the history of two centuries earlier,—the book is absolutely unknown to the learned Nor do we believe that, from the nature of the context, Captain Denniston intended his statement to be taken seriously.

Galwegians enjoyed as a result of the mild rule of the Baliols. Having taken Caerlaverock on the 17th July, his queen riding by his side, he defiled over Dervorgille's Bridge across the Nith. Entering Galloway, "mountains and valleys seemed suddenly alive with sumpter horses, wagons with provisions, tents, and pavilions. Afar off was heard the neighing of his horses, many a beautiful pennon fluttering over lances, many a banner displayed, and the days being fine and long, he rode leisurely to Kirkcudbright."[1]

Here the king occupied the old castle, requisitioning provisions of all sorts, for which he paid, the prices minutely entered. Beans as well as oats were used for the cavalry horses, the soldiers being supplied with wheaten bread and peas for the kitchen, butcher-meat in unlimited quantities being washed down by strong ale and beer. Malt made from both oats and barley was bought in large quantities, and wines of various sorts were procurable at Kirkcudbright. The best (Vinum Clarum, whence claret) at 30s. a hogshead, and Ordinaire at 1s. 6d.[2]   What is especially worthy of remark is that the agricultural produce of this part of Galloway sufficed not only to maintain an army in the field and the royal retinue, but that Edward despatched thence supplies to another army in the north, besides provisioning his castles of Ayr, Caerlaverock, Dumfries, and Lochmaben. Within a narrow radius from Kirkcudbright he collected more wheat than the mills of the country could grind, and many cargoes were shipped to ports in Cumberland and Ireland, there to be made into flour and re-exported to his garrisons.[3]

[1] Walter of Exeter, who accompanied the army and wrote a poem on the campaign in old Norman French

[2] Large purchases were made at the undermentioned rates.—

"A whole ox, 5s to 6s 8d., fat pigs (bacones), 2s 2d to 3s. 9d., barley malt, 4s. 4d the qr.; oat malt, 2s 9d , wheat flour, 7s.; beans, 5s , peas, 2s. 9d., salt, 2s 6d to 3s. 2d., strong ale, 18s., 16s , 12s. the butt; small beer, 8s. , vinum clarum, £1:10s per hogshead; vinum expensabile, 1s. 10d. ; 40 hogsheads, £3 : 18 : 4 "—*Wardrobe Accts. Edward I.*

[3] Simon Kingsman, master of the *Margaret*, was paid £2 . 9s. for carrying 30 qrs. of wheat from Kirkcudbright to Dublin to be ground, thence to Ayr for the king's army. Wymond Gegge of the *Sauveye*, £1 : 7 6 for carrying 143

From Kirkcudbright the king presently advanced to the Fleet, encamping in the glades of Cally.[1] Here he held courts for the administration of justice, and pushed on detachments to Wigtown, whence, having there obtained the adhesion of the MacDowall's, he opened up communication with Ayr[2] He then retraced his steps, and sleeping on the 24th of August at the Abbey of Sweetheart, written in his journals "Douzquer," he recrossed the Nith

Robert Bruce, Earl of Carrick, and John Comyn were now styled Guardians of Scotland,[3] and meanwhile had taken Stirling Castle.

Edward I. having secured the ground behind him, advanced in person against them, and the capture of Stirling early in 1303 left him undisputed master of Scotland.

Galloway remained perfectly quiet, enjoying her "ale and bread," and continuing her superior cultivation for several years, until the impious if unpremeditated murder of her Justiciary, the Red Comyn, in 1386 sent a thrill of horror through the province, and lighted up the flames of war farther north. No one knew better than Bruce himself that he had hopelessly alienated the affections of the Galwegians by his rash act, and he gave a wide berth to the province whilst reeking with the blood of the grandchild of Dervorgille, in connection with which is a strange episode. The Earl of Buchan having all along been a consistent opponent of Bruce, had now, with all his clan, a blood feud with him. Bruce, moreover, driven to

qrs of wheat from Kirkcudbright to Whitehaven to be ground, thence to Ayr, etc When retiring, Edward paid to William de Carlisle £20 for 40 acres of oats damaged by his army, adding two hogsheads of wine as a royal present

A similar present was made to Ada, widow of Robert de la Fierti, for injury to her crops at Dornoch —*Wardrobe Accts Edward I*

[1] Heningford calls the Fleet "the Swim," catching the radical meaning of the word   Near Cally, on the lands of Enrick, a spot is mapped "Palace Yard," where, doubtless, Edward held his courts, amercing the authorities, among other misdoers, for habitually using false weights, and Henry le Mounier for short measure from his mill

[2] Expenses of Sir John Walleys and two men-at-arms and twenty foot, from the toun of Are to Wygeton in Galloway, 60s —*Wardrobe Accts Edward I.*

[3] Lord Hailes remarks " Bruce, Guardian of Scotland in the name of Baliol, is one of those historical phenomena which are inexplicable."

fight, knowing that the alternative was a scaffold or a throne, well knew also that he had to count upon the *deadly* hate of the Comyns. Great, therefore, must have been the surprise and rage of the head of the house on finding that his *own wife* had stolen secretly away from Cruggleton, and repairing to Scone, had with her own hands placed the Scottish crown upon his foe, her pretensions as a descendant of Macduff giving a colour of legality to the act. Though historians call it high-spirited, and Bruce proved worthy of the crown, thus to have scandalised at once her father's, her husband's, and her adopted family, cannot be called a wifely proceeding.

In great wrath Edward I. appointed Aymer de Valence, brother-in-law of the murdered Comyn, to be guardian of Scotland; and Isabel, Countess of Buchan, he committed to close confinement in the Castle of Berwick. She and her justly incensed husband met no more.[1]

So embittered were the Galwegians generally, that when Thomas and Alexander Bruce, bringing succours to their brother, landed shortly after in Lochryan, they were pounced upon instinctively as enemies by the people, their followers receiving no quarter, and they themselves, bleeding from the blows of their captors, were led off at once by Duncan Mac-Dowall to the King of England at Carlisle, who ordered them to immediate execution, bestowing the hand of a wealthy heiress upon MacDowall's son, in reward of his energy.[2]

To this period may be referred that series of Bruce adventures in woods and wilds on the Galloway marshes narrated with

[1] The second Earl of Buchan had married Isabel, daughter of Duncan, Earl of Fife. Her brother, also Duncan, Earl of Fife, favoured the English interest. Matthew of Westminster accuses her of a criminal partiality for Robert Bruce (p 454). The unfortunate woman was confined in a cage strongly latticed and barred in the Castle of Berwick, as to this Hemingford says, "The Earl of Buchan, her husband, sought to kill her for her treason, but Edward restrained him, and ordered her to be confined in a wooden cage." She was not released until April 1313, before which her husband had died.—Wood, i. 263; Hailes, *Annals*, ii 11; Matthew of Westminster, *Fœdera*.

[2] The king, at the request of Dungall MacDowyl senior, for the good services which he and Dungall his son both have done, grants to Dungall junior the marriage of the daughter and heir of Hugh de Chaumpaigne deceased. Dated from Lanercost, March 1307.

poetical license by Barbour, and of such hairbreadth escapes as
are quaintly indicated by such lines as—

> Quhen the Gallowaiss wyst suthli
> That he was with sa few menye
> Thai maid a priwé assemblé
> Off wele twa hundir men, and ma,
> And slewth hundis with thaim gan ta.
>
> Book iv. 688.

A considerable English force, commanded by Aymer de
Valence, Earl of Pembroke, closely searched the borders of
Galloway, determined to take him dead or alive. No local tradition is more current than that of Bruce taking refuge with the
Dame of Craigencally, and assisted by her three sons with a
handful of followers defeating the English with great slaughter
at Glentrool. That the English cavalry fought at a disadvantage
owing to the nature of the ground, and were obliged to retire
without inflicting any loss upon their nimble opponents, is
probable enough; and that Bruce himself, seated on a boulder
at Moss Raploch (still called the King's Stone), watched with
satisfaction their retreat, is as likely, but we are as incredulous
as to the heavy losses inflicted by a handful of peasants upon
the men-at-arms, as to the feats in archery eclipsing those
of William Tell[1] which are popularly ascribed to the widow's
sons. It is preposterous to suppose that Sir Aymer and his
veteran cavalry were frightened out of their wits by herds of
deer and goats driven down upon them from the heights by
the happy thought of these striplings!

The simple fact, disguised under much embellishment, is,
that Pembroke gave up his search as hopeless, driven from the
district by want of subsistence.

On the 6th of July 1307 Edward I. died; his son Edward
II advanced immediately after into Ayrshire, but somewhat

---

[1] Annabel, his hostess, had had three sons by different husbands,—MacKie,
Murdoch, and Maclurg Bruce expressed a wish to test their skill in archery,
and two accompanied him forthwith MacKie called his attention to two carrion-
crows seated side by side on a rock, and drawing his bow its full stretch,
skewered both birds together through the head. A raven croaked high above
them in mid-air, Murdoch, aiming his shaft, struck it in the very heart, and it
fell quivering at their feet.

ingloriously retreated. Bruce thereupon re-entered Galloway, and summoned the inhabitants to his standard; but they failing to comply, he ravaged the country with fire and sword. Sir Aymer de Valence came to their relief, put Bruce to flight, who, retreating northward, was followed by the Earl of Buchan at the head of the Galwegians. The north country people rallying to Bruce, he turned upon the Galwegians and drove them back again.

The fortunes of Bruce now began to turn. Being now opposed to one of the weakest, as formerly to one of the strongest of the kings of England, his own superior talents became apparent, and many Scotsmen who had sided with Edward I. deserted the cause of Edward II.

The Galwegians, however, were irreconcilable,[1] and the king's brother, Edward Bruce, was despatched against them. He defeated them in a sanguinary battle near the Dee, where many of their chiefs and a "certain knight named Roland" were slain[2] This was followed by a series of victories terminating in a *coup de main* at Kerrouchtree, near the Cree, in which it is asserted that Edward, under cover of a thick mist, with only fifty horsemen, surprised and almost annihilated 1500 Englishmen under John de St. John. The result of this campaign was the reduction of thirteen fortlets for his brother; Fordun preserving a rhyming legend—"Insula combusta semper Scotis inimici"[3]—which seems to point to the fortlet which gives its name to the parish of Inch. Botel was now the only garrison which held out against King Robert, which he took himself in

[1] The *Fœdera* mentions Comyn, "Donegal, etc.; et tota communitas majorum et hominum Galewydiæ," as being faithful to England —*Fœdera*, t iii. 14.

[2] Quondam militem nomine Rolandam cum multis nobilibus Galwidæi interfecit, ac dictum Donaldum, ducem eorum, fugientem comprehendit, et post hæc *Insulam* combussit —Fordun, *Annals*, 125

[3] Quoting this, Lord Hailes says "By Insula I understand interior Galloway, or that part of the country which lies next to Ireland —Hailes, *Annals*, 231

Lord Hailes was probably unaware that *Insula* was the old charter name, as the Inch was the later one for the strength on Loch Inch, which lies close to Lochryan, and gives its name to the parish. From its position it was impregnable in those days if well provisioned It afterwards fell into the hands of the Bishops of Galloway.

person in 1312, thus completing the conquest of the province.
From Botel he crossed to the Isle of Man, which he subdued,
taking prisoner his inveterate enemy Duncan MacDowall, the
governor of its chief castle.   A year later the crowning victory
of Bannockburn—in which, sentiment notwithstanding, we
suspect as few Gallovidians were "led" by Bruce as had "bled"
for Wallace—enabled him to deal as he chose with the un-
friendly province   in other words, to escheat its proprietors
wholesale, resettling their lands on his own partisans, retaining
a few of the old landowners, who accepted such conditions as
he chose to grant them.[1]   The private property of the old lords
was divided between Edward Bruce and Isabele, Countess of
Athol; Thomas Randolph, her husband; and Margaret, wife of
William Karlo, his sister; whilst the disappearance of all
the Mareschalls, De Buskebys, Champagnes, Percys, De Ferrers,
De Roos, and other Anglo-Normans, left wide lands at his
disposal.

To the "good Sir James Douglas" he gave Percy's Barony
of Urr, to Lord Soulis Comyn's Castle of Cruggleton, to Sir Alan
Stewart the Barony of Corswell, and to De Mande Vella
(Mandeville) the site of the modern burgh of Stranraer.[2]

Edward Bruce was now titular Lord of Galloway, but the
sphere was not wide enough for his restless ambition.   He
eagerly accepted an offer of certain discontented lords in Ulster
to make him their king, and early in 1315 sailed for Ireland
with a following, among whom we recognise Galloway
barons in—

> Sir John the Soulis, ane guid knycht,
> And Schyr John Stewart that wes wyght,
> And Schyr Alane Stewart alsua.

---

[1] The third Earl of Buchan was probably the last of his line , he left two
daughters Alice, who married Henry de Beaumont, who had in her right the
manor of Whitwicke in Leicestershire, and assumed the title of Earl of Buchan,
and was one of the descendants who rose in favour of Edward Baliol , and Margaret,
who married Sir John, son of the fourth Earl of Ross, and got eventually as her
tocher the half of her father's lands allowed her by King Robert

[2] To Fergus de Mondo Villa, the lands of Stranrever in vice de Wigton—
Robertson's *Index*

With these he landed at Carrickfergus on the 25th of May and ravaged mercilessly the possessions of the English settlers in the north

Meeting with no encouragement in the west or south, he was brought to a standstill, till King Robert, his brother, bringing him succours by way of Loch Ryan, the two advanced as far as Dublin, which they failed to take. Edward nevertheless allowed himself to be crowned King of Ireland by his Ulster friends on the 2d of May 1316, although he hardly possessed a stronghold but Carrickfergus, and on the 5th of October 1318 he was killed at the Battle of Fagher, near Dundalk, Lord Souls and one of the Stewarts being among the slain. Thus the rash enterprise collapsed. On Edward Bruce's death it was enacted by Parliament that, if King Robert died without male issue, the succession should lie in the son of his daughter Margaret by Robert the Steward. The king did, however, leave an heir, David II., but he being childless, Margaret's son eventually succeeded in virtue of that Act.

The lordship of Galloway was now given to Edward's natural son, Alexander.

In 1320 a plot against the king was discovered, and William, Lord Souls, heir presumedly of John, who had fallen at Fagher, forfeited his lands and liberty, and his Castle of Cruggleton was given to the monks of Whithorn.[1] Sir Eustace de Maxwell was tried for complicity in the same plot, but had the rare good fortune, for one lying under such a charge, to be acquitted.

In 1322 Edward II. invaded the Lothians, and King Robert found congenial employment for his Galloway lieges by letting them loose upon his flank. The wild Scots ravaged Lancashire from end to end, laying homesteads and abbeys alike under contribution, and having joined hands with the column led by the king in person at Stanemore, near the Yorkshire marches,

We identify Stranrever with Stronrawer in a writ in the Lochnaw charter-chest dated 1484

[1] Carta Candida Casa, of Craigiltoun, quhilks pertenit to Lord Souls.—Robertson's *Index*

they returned home in triumph with an extraordinary booty, having suffered hardly any loss.

Scottish historians wrote of this affair rather vaguely, but Knighton, the English contemporary chronicler, whom all later ones follow, distinctly states that these successful raiders came by way of Furness, necessitating the conclusion that the Galwegians operated in a separate column, as they evidently went by sea Furness was easily accessible from Galloway, and a sea route especially convenient for bringing back plunder, but to suppose that the army from Lothian, Fife, or the eastern borders marched to Galloway to embark is preposterous.[1]

King Robert I., prematurely aged at fifty-five, is believed to have visited Whithorn a few months before his death to plead at St. Ninian's shrine for his recovery.[2]

He, dying the 7th June 1329, Randolph, Earl of Moray, immediately assumed the Regency. He made frequent progresses through Galloway. Two standing-stones on the moor of Dranandow, mapped "The Thieves," are the grim monuments of a band of robbers who, daring to assault persons on their way to attend his courts, were justified on the scene of their misdeeds

The reins of government falling from the strong hands of Randolph—who succumbed to disease in 1332—into the feeble ones of the Earl of Mar, Edward Baliol profited by the occasion to effect a landing in the Forth.

His principal lieutenant was Henry de Beaumont, married to the Earl of Buchan's daughter, his leading partizans being "disinherited" Anglo-Normans and other claimants, quaintly

---

[1] "Intraverunt Scoti in Angliam *per medium Forneficæ*, et comitatum Lancastriæ devastaverunt undique, absque aliquo damno suorum, colligentes immensam prædam auri et argenti, animalium, ornamentorum ecclesiasticorum, lectualium, mensalium, abducentes onustas carrectas omnibus bonis patriæ ad suum placitum."—Knighton, p. 2542. "Furness, the furthest point of Lancashire north of the sands, derived from *fur* or *fyr*, a light."—*Norsemen in Cumberland*, 108

"Furness, a Norse name indicating the antiquity of the lighthouse."—Taylor, *Words and Places*

[2] A royal charter to the city of Aberdeen is dated from Galloway 16th March 1329.

styled by old chroniclers " Les Querrelleurs " — quarrellers
with the Brucian settlement. Of these connected with Galloway, besides De Beaumont, there were John, son of the Red
Comyn; Henry de Ferrars; William de la Zouche; Sir John
le Mareschal; Henry de Percy; John de Mowbray, Thomas
Bisset, and his younger brother Henry Baliol, and of native
Galloway family Sir Patrick M'Culloch, and many more.[1]

Thus supported, Edward Baliol joined issue with the Regent
Mar on Dupplin Moor, gained a complete victory, and on the
29th September 1332 was crowned king at Scone, immediately
after which he turned his footsteps southward, eager apparently
to revisit the scenes of his youth

The eastern shires remained true to David, but so great was
the attachment to the name of Baliol in the west that the
Galwegians rose *en masse* to receive him; and, carried away
by the general enthusiasm, the first to interpret their feelings
and place his own services at Edward's disposal was Alexander
Bruce, the especial representative of the rival house.

Among the leaders of the Brucian party were the Earl of
March and Archibald Douglas, whose estates lay especially
exposed to Baliol's attack; and they, despairing of immediate
succour, and knowing that they could not hold their own
unaided, asked and obtained from him a truce until the 2nd of
February following, on the specious suggestion that before that
time all controversies ought to be settled by a national convention.

This treaty signed, Baliol moved about freely, often slenderly
attended; this coming to Archibald Douglas's ears, he raised a
a body of horse, and on Christmas eve treacherously attacked
him at Annan, at dead of night. Both Baliols had already
retired to bed, and their followers were indulging in noisy
revelry. The king escaped to Carlisle with difficulty, on a
sorry steed, literally in his nightdress. His brother Henry and

[1] Henry de Beaumont claiming the earldom of Buchan and the Castle of
Cruggleton, Forest of Buchan, and other lands, guided by the counsels of Henry de
Beaumont, the disinherited barons assembled 400 men-at-arms and 3000 infantry.
—Hailes, *Annals*, ii 258

Walter Comyn offered a stout resistance, but both were slain, and Alexander Bruce was taken prisoner.   As Wyntoun has it—

> Alysawndyre the Brws wes tane,
> Bot the Ballyoll his gat is gane
> On a barme horse wyth legys bare.[1]

For this feat Archibald Douglas was now named Regent, but the first effect of his sharp practice proved in every way disastrous, as it brought Edward III. forthwith upon the scene, furnishing him, moreover, with an excuse for further claims on the Scotch exchequer, for settling its affairs against his will.

Baliol being soon rejoined by his followers at Carlisle, recrossed the Borders, and faced his foes, and on the arrival of the advanced guard of the English gained a decisive victory in a sanguinary battle at Halidon, near Berwick, in which both the Regent and Alexander Bruce (who had again changed sides) were slain

But now, as a serious drawback to his triumph, Baliol had to reckon with his protector, who exacted for his assistance the castle and town of Berwick, the Ettrick Forest, the shires of Edinburgh, Roxburgh, Peebles, and Dumfries, this last including the whole modern stewartry of Kirkcudbright; and so determined was the demand, and so precipitate the surrender, that Baliol found he had inadvertently signed away the possession of his private property, which was only restored to him as an act of grace[2]

Disgraceful as this surrender may have been considered elsewhere, as a matter of fact in Galloway it was not unpopular There all classes profited by free intercourse with England; an intercourse long established, and which it was necessarily the policy of all English kings to encourage, whilst it was the

---

[1] Wyntoun, bk 8, c. 26, l. 3725.

[2] Parliament at Edinburgh made the surrender 12th February 1334, ratified by Edward III 12th June and 18th June 1334.   Asserting that he had too much reverence for God, justice, and good faith, to allow the cession to be prejudicial to Baliol's private interests, the King of England issued a declaration that the lands of Botel, Kirk Andrewes, and Kenmure, were Baliol's private property, and not included in the resignation —*Fœdera*, iv. 590-618

avowed if benighted policy and constant practice of Scottish kings and parliaments to prevent.

The leading families of the province had been reared under a system of double allegiance tending to relax strong feelings of nationality, and although the successes of Bruce had put an end to such a state of things, yet the very circumstances attending the struggle had tended rather further to alienate the affections of Galwegians from his family, and many would have been glad to accept English protection if ensuring them free trade.

Galloway was at this moment completely isolated from the rest of Scotland. David II. had command of all the approaches to the province, and advancing in person to Ayr, there signed, 9th November 1342, a patent to Sir Malcolm Fleming of the Earldom of Wigtown, granting him extraordinary jurisdiction, and all the Crown lands of the shire on fee.

He thus practically threw down the gauntlet to Edward III, who was not slow to take it up, and at once liberally supplied his partizans with the sinews of war, such military stores being usually consigned to Dugald MacDowall as their chief.

MacDowall was summoned to the English Court, and there renewing vows of allegiance, received promises of assistance which were loyally redeemed; and by aid of the *Rotuli Scotiæ*, in which all such subsidies and presents are minutely accounted for, we are able to follow his fortunes in all their twists and turnings, which we shortly glance at as a typical illustration of the vicissitudes incident to the position of a Galloway baron during the quarter of a century succeeding 1332.

MacDowall, originally a strong partisan of John Baliol, afterwards supported Edward I. in preference to Bruce. After Bannockburn he made his peace with King Robert, kept aloof from Edward Baliol in 1332, and rejected the advances of Edward III. when claiming the sovereignty of Galloway. When, however, Baliol took up his residence at Botel, personal intercourse revived hereditary leanings and overcame all scruples. An entry in the rolls of August 1339 attests that "Edward III then received the fealty of Duncan MacDowall, and pardoned him for his late adherence to the Scots and all his political crimes." He was now received into that sovereign's full confidence, summoned to a personal interview in 1342, his lieutenants subsidised, and arrangements made for a campaign.[1]

In April Edward III. ordered his "admiral to furnish a large ship and take MacDowall to Galloway, as had been agreed on by the king and his council," issuing at the same time a precept to the Treasurer of Ireland, "to provide 100 quarters of corn and 18 tons of wine for the furnishing of the said ship." He granted safe-conducts "to all merchants to carry provisions and merchandise to MacDowall's fortalice in Galloway", and by the king's command wines were furnished to him "gratis" from the royal stores at Carlisle.

Mandates were addressed to De Lacy, the warden of the marches, and to the sheriffs of Cumberland, Westmoreland, and Lancashire, commanding them to give MacDowall prompt assistance if his fortalice should be besieged, and to "collect provisions and furnish archers to be sent to the sea-board, thence to be transported to the Pele of MacDowall in Galloway."[2]

Sir Patrick Maculloch, his son Patrick, and John Gilbert and Michael Maculloch, John le Marechal, and Thomas Bisset, are among the landowners mentioned who were largely subsidised. And in December of the same year, 1342, precepts were issued to six merchants in Bristol, commanding them to convey 10 tons of wine, 100 quarters of corn, and 2 barrels of

---

[1] All from *Rotuli Scotiæ*. The following are but a few of the entries alluded to.—

Sirs Patrick MacCulloch, John le Mareschal, and Thomas Bisset each received £10 for outfit. 15 August 1341

Patrick MacCulloch has £20 to account, and a quarter of a year's wages for the men at arms, besides a yearly pension of £20.

Patrick, son of Patrick, John, and Michael MacCulloch, five marks each, Gilbert MacCulloch, £4 : 11s , a year's wages for himself and a man-at-arms, and £5 as a gift from the wool-money   June 1342 —*Rotuli Scotiæ*

Previous to this Edward III had lent Baliol £300 sterling, and 27th January 1336 bestowed upon him a pension of five marks a day. Given him in three sums, £500 in 1335, and 6 ten dolia (tons ?) of flour, besides loose quantities of wine and provisions.—*Fœdera*, IV. 674-710

[2] The passages within inverted commas are quotations from *Rotuli Scotiæ*

salt to the Island of Eastholm (Hestan) in Galloway, in aid of MacDowall and his men

All this time, however, the national party in Scotland were increasing in strength, and Edward III. being involved in war with France, David II. might have easily overcome Baliol had he not imprudently resolved to take advantage of Edward's absence to reannex Northumberland to Scotland. He crossed the Borders in the autumn of 1346, and carried all before him to the Tyne, where the English, commanded by William de la Zouche, Archbishop of York, Metropolitan of Galloway, joined issue with him near Durham, gained a complete victory, and led away both David himself and the Earl of Wigtown to a long captivity, Baliol being thus left to keep his little court undisturbed a little longer on the Urr. Here he was joined by Henry Percy and Sir Ralph Nevil with a goodly following.[1]

An entry of Duncan MacDowall's name in the English Exchequer Rolls, as a prisoner at Rochester the following year, is somewhat mysterious. It has been erroneously inferred from this that his "Pele" at Hestan had been reduced before the battle, and that he had thereupon transferred his allegiance to David II., and was one of the Scotch prisoners taken at the battle But for this there is no authority whatever, and though the cause of his detention is not stated, it is further mentioned that (unlike the Scottish prisoners taken at Durham) he was released the following year, having been first conducted to York, where his wife and sons met him and surrendered themselves as hostages for his good behaviour, upon which he returned to Galloway as warm a partisan of Baliol as before Six years later, however, Sir William Douglas, gaining advantages over the English, and expelling them from Teviotdale and the Ettrick Forest, penetrated to Galloway, and induced MacDowall to come to a parley—when, whether through fear or persuasion, he persuaded him to detach himself from the English party and

---

[1] Henry de Percy had 100 men-at-arms and 100 archers on horseback ; Ralph Nevil 80 men-at-arms and 80 mounted archers —Hailes, *Annals*, i 243.

to swear fealty to David II. in the church of Cumnock, an oath which he faithfully observed.[1]

The defection of MacDowall doubtless hurried on the closing scene of Baliol's reign; although, by the irony of fate, the victory of his own partisans at Durham had at least an equal share in his final eclipse

He had only been King of Scotland by favour of Edward, and Edward having the rival king of the Scots in his power, conceived he might best further his own interests by making terms with David, the chosen king of the nation, which the Scots would readily endorse to effect his restoration. Negotiations for his release were entered upon, that he was to be acknowledged by Edward as sole King of Scotland. Baliol protested, but in vain, the only voice he was allowed to have in the matter being that three of his partisans—Patrick M'Culloch, John of Wygginton, and William of Aldeburgh[2] —were allowed to be present at the conferences to protect his private rights, the final results of which were that Edward Baliol surrendered all claims, whether to the throne or his estates, to Edward III for 5000 marks in gold, paid down, in addition to a pension of 2000 marks a year This absolute surrender having been made by delivery of a portion of the earth of Scotland, and also by the upgiving of his golden crown. On the 20th January 1356 Baliol left Scotland never to return,[3] and Edward III, after some dallying, released David from his captivity the following year, and summoned a parliament, which ratified the conditions of his release at Scone on the 6th November.

[1] Fordun seems to place the event in 1356, but I have placed it in 1353 on the authority of an instrument in *Fœdera*, v 759 —Hailes, *Annals*, i. 250

[2] Aldeburgh, Saxon eald byrnc, the old fort, a strong position so mapped between Port Alan and Port Yerioch. The present lands of Auldbreck lie inland.

[3] The fate of Edward Baliol was singular. On his invasion of Scotland he displayed a bold spirit of enterprise and a courage superior to all difficulties By the victory of Dupplin he won a crown ; some few weeks after he was surprised at Annan and lost it The overthrow of the Scots at Halidon, to which he signally contributed, availed not to his re-establishment Year after year he saw his partisans fall away He became the pensioner of Edward and the tool of his policy He died childless in 1363 —Hailes, *Annals*, i. 255

So undoubted, however, were the territorial rights of Baliol held to be, that the Scottish estates were inclined to admit the justice, if not the expediency, of recognising Edward's III.'s claim to Galloway estates, based on Baliol's resignation, and entertained proposals for settling them on the King of England's son, which, however, came to nothing.

No sooner had Baliol and his partisans disappeared than Fleming asserted his chartered privileges in his Earldom of Wigtown, whilst Sir William Douglas (younger brother of the "good Sir James"), also created an earl, exercised similar powers east of Cree.   So great did the power of the Douglases speedily become, that the person whom they entrusted with the administration of justice between the Nith and Cree (inter aquam de Creth et aquam de Nyth), they considered their own personal officer, and designed him Steward, Western Galloway continuing under the jurisdiction of the king's sheriff; hence, until the other day, it was considered a *lapsus lingua* to speak of the "Shire" of Kirkcudbright, Wigtown and Kirkcudbright being popularly known as the "Shire" and "Stewartry" of Galloway.

Following the re-establishment of David II.'s power came the tale of forfeitures, offices and lands innumerable falling to the Crown.   The lion's share fell to Fleming and Douglas. Almost all the descendants of Anglo-Normans introduced by Roland and Alan were proscribed, others of the same race taking their places, many of whom took deep root in the soil.

Fleming soon ousted John of Wigtown.   William of Auldbreck, as well as Henry de Beaumont, were succeeded in their lands by Sir Gilbert Kennedy, who had been one of the hostages for King David on his return in 1353.   Percy's lands were all taken by Douglas   Lauchlan Adair (Edzear) received Bomby, "qwhilk was Lyndsay's."   Fergus MacDowall, now in favour, got the barony of Borgue, which "Mowbray forfeited"; and an Aygnell or Agnew was given a share of Crown lands untenanted in the Rhynns, with the keeping of the Castle of Lochnaw.

CHAPTER VI

THE RAGMAN ROLL

My ladyes and my maistresses echone
.   .   .
Resave in gré of my sympille persone
This rolle which withouten any drede
Kynge Ragman me bad mesoure in brede.

On a Ragman Roll, 15th Century.

THE word " Ragman Roll," which has much mystified philologists,[1] admits of the simplest explanation, having had its
origin in good-humoured banter, and far from being intended in
any way to wound Scottish susceptibility, was a merry allusion
to a favourite diversion of the Ladies' Bower.

Ragman or King Rageman was a game much affected in
Anglo-Norman society in the thirteenth century. A number of
characters, good, bad, and indifferent, were written in couplets
consecutively on a sheet of parchment. To each character a
string was attached, having a piece of wax or metal at the tip.
This sheet when rolled up was called a Ragman Roll; each
person playing drew a character by pulling a string, which he
or she maintained for the rest of the evening.

When the Scottish Baronage swore fealty to Edward I. at
Berwick, their names were written down, and the seals of
such as had them attached to the sheet by small strips of
parchment. The rolls containing the signatures, when made up,

---

[1] In Brewer's *Dictionary of Phrase and Fable* (a really useful work) the
Ragman Roll is explained to be a corruption of "Ragimund's Roll"—an absurd
confusion, Bagimont (Baimundi's), which is obviously intended, being a list of
benefices and church dues, and has no connection whatever with the Ragman
Roll.

with a mass of seals dependent from them, had each much the appearance of a huge roll[1] of this game of Ragman, and that name being jokingly given to it by some of the young courtiers in attendance, has stuck to this important state paper ever since.

The roll for Wigtownshire is drawn up separately, but that of Kirkcudbright is included in Dumfries, with no territorial arrangement, and it is impossible to decide what names, and even what holdings, are to be set down exclusively to Galloway.

DEL COUNTE DE WYGGETON

Johan Comyn, Comte de Bouchan.
Thomas, Euesqe de Candida Casa [2]
Morice, Priour de Whiterne.
Johan le Mareschal de Toskerton.[3]
Thomas de Torthorald
Fergus MakDowylt.
Roland MacGaghen [4]
Thomas MacUlagh [5]
William Polmalot.[6]
Andreu de Logan

Johan de Meynreth.
William de Champaigne.
Dougal MacDowyl
Rauf de Champaigne
Hectur Askelot.[7]
Arthur de Galbrath
Gilbert de Hannethe
Fergus Askolo.
Thomas de Kithehilt
William de Byskeby

---

[1] The Ragman Roll, when rolled up for use, would present a confused mass of strings hanging from it, with bits of wax at the end, from which the drawer had to select one This game possesses a peculiar historical interest   When the Scottish nobles and chieftains acknowledged their dependence on the English crown in the reign of Edward I., the deed by which they made this acknowledgment, having all their seals hung to it, presented when rolled up much the appearance of the roll used in this game, and hence, no doubt, they gave it in derision the name of Ragman's Roll.—Wright, *Domestic Manners of the Middle Ages*, 233

[2] Succeeded "Henry" as Bishop before 1296 , succeeded by Simon before 1321 —Keith

[3] Elsewhere described as Johan le Mareschal de Toskerton, Chevalier. His barony was also a parish, afterwards called Kirkmadrine, now absorbed in Kirkmaiden Tuaiscairt with the formative particle *an* · the northerly place, *i e.* north of Kirkmaiden

[4] Fergus MacGachan (addressed by George Douglas as cousin) is described as of "Corsmagachan in Glenluce," an. 1455 —*Lochnaw Charters.*

[5] Sheriff of Wigtown 1296.—Ryley, *Placita.*

[6] Now Polmallet May have its name from a deep pool, once much larger than now, Pol-mallacht (the cursed pool), whether as a scene of massacre or strife, or even a want of fish ' such a meaning for the suffix being recognised in Irish place-names.—Joyce, ii 448

[7] We find the name elsewhere written Ector Ascelog, suggestive of ap-or-ui scolog, the son of the scholar or crofter

William MacUlagh.
Dougal Gotheriksone
Michel MacUlagh
James Seneschal Descoie.

Johan Seneschal frère mon sire
James Seneschal.[1]
Marie la Regne de Man.[2]

DEL COUNTE DE DUNFRES [3]

Johan, Abbé de Douçquer [4]
Alisaundre, Abbé de Tungeland.
Wautier, Abbé de Dundrennan.
Dungald, Abbé de Saint Boiz.[5]
William, Prior de Canonby.
Henry de Mundeawill.
Thomas de Colewill.[6]
Andreau de Chartres [7]
David le Mareschal
Umfrey du Gardin (Jardine)
Mariot de Sutton
Patrik de Botle.
Dovenald fiz Can
Wautier de Twynham
Wilham de la Chaumbre
Johan de Geueleston.
Wautier fiz Richard de Twynham
Steuene de Kilpatrick.[8]
Wautier Durant
Mathew de Legh.
Thomas de Kirconnel

Thomas de Bardonan.
Robert de Moffet.
Rogier de Fauhside.[9]
Dunkan de Coningesburgh.
Gilmyhel MacEth [10]
Macrath ap Molegan.[11]
Johan Murthoe
Robert de Chartres.
Alisaundre de Keth
Johan de Joneston, Chevalier.
Johan le Blunt de Eskeby
Henry de Graham
Johan de la Leyle
Johan de Seton.
Piers de Graham.
Beatrice de Carleal
Adam de Holm.
Eustace de Boyuill.
Tue le Messager
Richarde de Seton.
James de Tortherald.

---

[1] Sir James Stewart, seventh High Steward of Scotland, his brother, Sir John, married the daughter and heiress of Sir John de Bonkil, and by her was progenitor of the Darnley or Lennox branch

[2] Widow of Mahse, fifth Earl of Stratherne, "daughter of Eugene of Ergadia," previously "relict of the King of Man."—*Fœdera*, ii. 571; Wood, ii 557

[3] The following names are in the published edition Eufemme qui fut la femme, William de Hornden, William de Weston, Johan de Mundeuill, persone de Moffat, William de Striulyn (Stirling), Nicol de Swafham, persone de Grant Dalton—but not followed with any indication of being connected with "Wyggeton," obviously out of their proper place

[4] New Abbey—Douzquer in the *Wardrobe Accounts.*

[5] De Sacro Nemoris, Celtic Dercongal, doire conghbhail, church wood; not St Connal or Congal.

[6] Ancestor of Lords Colville of Culross, and of Ochiltree

[7] Of Amisfield, represented by the Earl of Wemyss.

[8] Kirkpatrick of Closeburn, reputed ancestor of Eugénie, Empress of the French

[9] "Faugh," a part of the outfield never dunged —Jamieson. "Farmers' faugh gars lairds laugh"—Proverb, whence name Fawcett, and probably Forsyth.

[10] Represents equally Mackie, Macghie, and Mackay

[11] Fergus Amulligan acquired Dempstertown, Dunscrore, his descendants are Milligans

Hughe de Urre.

Johan de Seton.

Nicol de Corry

Johan de Dordof

Rauf de Erington.

Symond de la Chaumbre

Robert de Dunbretan.

Robert Freser [1]

William de Hellebeck.

Henry de Gillonby.

Gyles persone del Eglise de Egglesfeyan

Robert de Perressar [2]

Johan de Kirke Patrik.

Thomas Moffet.

Maucolum MacCuffoc

Bathelmea de Egglesham Chopelyn.

Gardein de Nouel leu de Seneware [3]

William le Tailleur.

Patrik fiz Mathieu de Parton

Henry Vicaire del Eglise de Laurineton

Robert de Tyndale persone del Eglise de Grant Dalton.

Wautier Curry.

Henry Crak

Johan de Normanwill

Johan de Araz.[4]

Patrik de Bardonan

Morice MacSalny.

Humfrey de Boys, Chivaler.

Rogier de Kirkepatrick [5]

Hugh Manleurer

Gilberd de Joneston

Huue de Orre.

Cuthbert Makelemwyn.[6]

Gilbert Makenight

Johan de Bundeby [7]

Fergus le Mareschal.

Roulande le Maieschal.

Morice de Esttubbille

Gilbert de Southeyck.

Gilbert de Karlel.[8]

Wautier fiz Wautier de Gummeston

Thomas de Coleuile.

Adam de Colwenne

Thomas de Southayk (Southwick)

Michel de Cardelnesse (Kirkdale)

Duncan fiz Andreu.

Dougal fiz Gothrik

Aleyn de Rossa

Robert de Drusquem [9]

William de Heriz.

Thurbrandes de Logan.

Johan de Kerdernesse (Cardoness) [10]

Piers de Jarum, persone de Kelles.

Johan Vicaire de Urres

Sire Herbert de Makeswell.

Sire Richard Freser

Wautier de Deinington, persone de Parton

Mestre William de Goseford person de Castelmilke

Robert de Carsan, persone de Kirkandres

Alianore Prioresse de Lincluden.

Johan de Hayton.

Wautier, persone de Morton, emestre de Caldestreme.

Gordon (Adam de Miles) chevalier [11]

---

[1] The Frasers carried originally three strawberry leaves for arms, now registered cinquefoils   In Galloway they were " Frisells "

[2] A clerical blunder for Pennersax, anciently a parish, now absorbed in Middlebye.

[3] In Galloway, Newall; in England, Noel   [4] Herries.

[5] Kirkpatrick made siccar the Red Comyn's death.

[6] MacClellan, MacGille; Fhaolain, son of the servant of St Fillan

[7] Bomby

[8] Father of William, who married King Robert I 's sister, ancestor of Lords Carlyle.   [9] Rusco.

[10] Caerdonas, Cardoness, cyrc dael (Saxon), Kirkdale.

[11] Son of Alicia, heiress of Thomas, son of Richard de Gordon   Alicia married her cousin Adam, grandson of the foresaid Richard, brought him the lands of Gordon in Berwickshire, and had a son Adam, the above, who died the year of

William de Soulis Dominus de Gilbert Maccoignache
Lydisdale Hwe de Deresdere.

As the earldom of Carrick represented the portion of Galloway allotted to Duncan (Fergus's grandson) in 1186, we give
such of the names of Ayrshire as have connection with our
history.

DEL COUNTE DE ARE

Renaud de Craufurd.[1]
Andrew fiz Godefrei de Ros [2]
Gilbert fiz Roland.[3]
Mestre Neil Cambel [4]
Johan de Knoudolyan.
Adam de Waleys [5]
William de Kathkerk.[6]
Robert de Boynill.[7]
Aylmere le Huntere [8]
Thomas de Cregayn.[9]

Gilmor fiz Edward [10]
Wautier de Lynne.[11]
Michel de Mohaut, Chivaler.[12]
Gilchrist More.[13]
Alisandie de la Boutelerie.
Ingram de Umgrauile.[14]
Rogier de Crauford (and five other
Craufords)
Wautier (James and Robert) de Ros
Johan fiz Roland.

---

his signing the Ragman Roll, Marjory, his widow, having restitution of his
estates, 3d September 1296 , in consequence, his son Adam, by this Marjory, was
the common ancestor of the Dukes of Gordon and Viscounts Kenmure.

[1] Sir Reginald Crawford of Londoun, Sheriff of Ayr, murdered there by
English garrison 1297. His son, Sir Reginald, was taken prisoner in Lochryan
along with Thomas and Alexander Blair in 1307, sent to Carlisle, and executed
His only daughter, Susannah, married Sir Duncan, son of Sir Donald, second
son of Sir Colin Campbell of Lochow, ancestor of Dukes of Argyle.

[2] Godfrey de Ros was appointed Sheriff of Ayr by Edward I 1305 He
was ancestor of the Lords Ross of Halkhead Roos and Rose are forms of same
name

[3] Roland is held to be Roland of Carnek, and (Sir) Gilbert de Carrick
to have been the person recorded as submitting a difference between himself
and the nuns of North Berwick in 1285 to the arbitration of Robert Bruce and
Robert (Henry ?), Bishop of Galloway. He is believed to be ancestor of the Earls
of Cassilis

[4] Either Sir Neil Campbell of Lochow or a near relative.

[5] Wallace of Riccarton—the name meaning the Welshman or Briton

[6] Ancestor of Earl Cathcart

[7] Boyle of Kelburn, ancestor of Earls of Glasgow

[8] Hunter of Arnul, afterwards of Hunterston , on an ancient boundary charter
his neighbour's lands are described as marching "terris Normani venatoris"

[9] Craigy was carried by an heiress to Wallace of Riccarton

[10] Head of the Cunninghams of Kilmaurs, ancestor to the Earls of Glencairn

[11] Probably ancestors of Lynnes of Larg

[12] De Monte Alto, Scotticised Mouatt

[13] "Rowallan Mures," Nisbet Mure of Polkelly

[14] Appointed by Edward II. in 1310 to receive submission of Galloway men ;
an English baronet possessed of great estates in Angus as well as Ayr.

Johan fiz Neel de Karrik [1]
Duncan de Carleton.
Nicol de Waleys.
Hawe of the Blare. [2]
Richard de Boyuill.
Rauf de Eglynton. [3]
Neel fiz Robert de Dullop.

Rauf Faireye. [4]
Murthauch de Montgomery. [5]
Symund de Spalding, persone del
    Egliss Ogheltre (Ochiltree)
Renaud de la More and Adam.
Aleyn le Barbour.
Maucolum Lockare. [6]

---

[1] Believed to be the ancestor, and to have given his name to the Neilsons of
Craigcaffie.   [2] Whence perhaps Blair of Blair.

[3] Eglinton of that ilk.   His line ended in a daughter, married to Sir John
Montgomery, ancestor of the Earls of Eglinton.

[4] Fairly of that ilk.   Root of name apparently Norse: faareye, "sheep
pastures."—Nisbet, *Remarks on Ragman Roll*, ii. 41.

[5] Second son of John Montgomery, whose great-grandson married the daughter
of the Lord of Eglinton.

[6] Malcolm Lockhart of Barr.

CHAPTER VII

PLACE-NAMES ILLUSTRATING OLD GALLOWAY PURSUITS

Æternumque tenet per sæcula nomen.
VIRGIL, *Æneid*, vi. 231.

THE ancient language of Galloway is so indelibly impressed upon its soil, that in default of any Pictish literature, its old place-names, if read aright, may largely supplement the meagre chronicles of the middle ages.

They retain memories of its mighty men, many mythic, "carent quia vate sacro"; of its princes, of its warriors, of its saints, of its pirate chiefs, of the callings of its people, lay and cleric—friar, artificer, robber, herd, hunter, or beadsman; they specify the very trees of which the primeval forest was composed, they name its denizens, and enable us in a measure to judge of the progress made in arts and agriculture by its people previous to their speech being assimilated to that of Lowland Scotland.

A certain mystery attaches to the "Pictish" tongue; but for our purposes it is sufficient to know that "Pictish is a Gaelic dialect partaking largely of Welsh forms."[1] And this, qualified by the fact that prior to the fifth century, before which the bulk of old Galloway place-names had been probably given, the various dialects of Celtic differed very much less from one another than they do at present. And whatever inflections may

[1] *Four Ancient Books of Wales*, i. 188. "There are seven Celtic dialects—Irish, Scotch-Gaelic, Manx, Pictish, Welsh, Cornish, British or Armoric.
"Cymric and Gaelic had each a high and low variety, Scotch-Gaelic, Irish, and Manx are high Pictish low, Cornish and Breton, high Welsh low"

have been peculiar to the Pictish, two broad facts are capable of historic proof.

First, That in its application to places the Pictish differs immaterially from names imposed by Dalriad Scots or Strathclyde Britons.

Second, That as to its colloquial use, the youth of both sexes in all the neighbouring kingdoms, as the clerics of all the three nationalities, had a common meeting-place at once for intercourse and instruction at the "Magnum Monasterium," the great Galloway *Pictish* College at Rosnat.

As to the first, just opposite Galloway, lay Dalaradia and Dalriada, their inhabitants respectively Picts and Scots. Now, not only is there no radical difference in the place-names of these two peoples, but those of *both* closely resemble those of Galloway.[1] Again, north and east the Pictish Novantæ were closely pressed upon by the powerful septs of British race, known to the Romans as the Damnii and Selgovæ. Yet, as a matter of fact, there is no radical difference between the old Celtic place-names of Dumfriesshire and Ayrshire, and those of Galloway. In the three districts the great majority of names are alike to be explained by Gaelic and Irish dictionaries, and of the very few referable to the Welsh, there are as many to the south of the Deil's Dyke as to the north of it.

Of such exceptional instances we may name Cumloden, Minigaff (the cwm especially Cymric), as also Ochiltree (Penninghame), Galtway, Trayl, and Threave.[2]

As to the second, the whole tenor of early Irish history and its church legends point to the constant interchange of visits between Irish saints and the brethren of Candida Casa, Cymric

---

[1] "The Irish annals do not contain a hint that the Dalaradians spoke a language different from the rest of Scotland."

"Nor is there the slightest hint of any diversity of language between the Cruithne (the Dalaradians) and the Scots "—*Celtic Scotland,* i 198.

[2] Cwm-llydan, "the broad hollow between hills," which exactly describes it Uchel-tre, "high house", Galtway (pronounced Gatah), Gallt-gwy, "the ascent from the water"; Trahel or Trayle (now St. Mary's Isle), Tre-hel, "the house and the river holm" (a living Cornish name); Threave, Tref, "a homestead"

kinglets and chieftains sending their children to the famous seminary,[1] from which the inference fairly to be drawn is that Strathclyde Britons could then freely converse with Galloway Picts, and both races alike with Irish Dalriads and Dalaradians.

As a rule, all over Scotland names given by the Picts are indistinguishable from those given by the Scots, both having an occasional mixture of what is called the Cymric element, but which may really be an unrecognised trace of the ancient Pictish [2]

The intermarriage of Pictish chiefs with Anglo-Norman ladies led to their children learning to lisp in their mother's tongue. The monks first introduced as the schoolmasters of the province were mostly Frenchmen, and though these were followed by English-speaking friars, few if any of these clerics attempted to acquire, much less to commit to writing, the Pictish speech, rather teaching Latin as the common medium of communication. Consequently, on the accession of Alan's heirs A.D. 1234, French was the language of the "classes," Pictish of the "masses"

A great change was, however, in the air. Saxon had been adopted, both in the palace and at the courts of law, earlier in Scotland than in England; in the counties of Ayr and Dumfries it had even then superseded the Cymric. All classes in Galloway soon found it most convenient to adopt the language of their neighbours

The flight of Baliol severed the connection of the baronage with the English court, the forfeitures incident to the Brucian settlement largely introduced a Saxon-speaking proprietary, even

[1] "As a daughter of the king of the Picts received her secular education here, so we learn that the king of the Britons also sent his children to the school "—Forbes, *Life of St. Ninian*, Introduction, 42.

[2] Having submitted a list of Galloway names to Dr. Joyce, he made the initiatory remark, "When I plunge into your names, I fancy myself walking in a quagmire guided by a rushlight", and on a subsequent occasion, "In dealing with your local names I feel somewhat as we may suppose a good billiard-player would feel if asked to play a game with cubical pieces instead of familiar balls The Scottish names don't suit my hand at all." Why so? Obviously because Galloway names, though to the uninitiated resembling the Irish, have Pictish as their root.

of Anglo-Norman blood, all of whom brought with them followers who knew no Celtic.

Hence the double change. The upper classes ceased to speak French, whilst the lower classes gradually dropped their Pictish, which, never having been a written language, was soon absolutely forgotten, surviving only for a while in isolated hamlets on the moors.

We are therefore entitled with some confidence to assert that all Celtic place-names date at latest before the close of the thirteenth century : many of them before the Christian era. Genuine Norse names carry us back to the ninth and tenth centuries, and Northumbrian Saxon two hundred years earlier.

Of the first the Moat of Innermessan stands a stable and imposing relic of a station visited by Phœnician mariners in prehistoric times. All other buildings have disappeared, but the bay in which their galleys rode retains its name phonetically almost unaltered, whether in its Celtic or Cymric form (Loch-riaghan or Llwch Rheon),[1] as known to Strabo or Pliny Whilst among last of Celtic names we have Auchmanister, Old Luce, which could not have been so named for fourteen centuries later, and being so called as the field of the monastery founded by Roland a little previous to A.D 1200.

The Saxon and the Celtic name-giving period seems to over-lap on the moors of Minigaff, where Craigencally (cailleach, old wife, witch) is so called as the site of the cothouse where an old dame sheltered Robert Bruce on the eve of the battle of Moss Raploch, whilst "the King's Stone" near it is the boulder against which he leaned while watching the issue of the fight.

No one can carefully study place-names without observing how old they generally are, and that many which seem modern

[1] Caer Rheon (Cymric) and Rath riaghan were the synonyms, whence the Romish corruption Rerigonium

Pytheas, a Massilian, reaching the Land's End (Belerium) about three centuries B C , sailed northward through the Irish Channel, passed Loch Ryan, reaching Orkney, whence he made a six days' voyage to Thule (probably Shetland), and returning by Cantium (the North Foreland), proved Britain to be an island. From him Strabo, Diodorus Siculus, and Pliny derived their information of the British Isles —Lemprière, art "Pytheas ," *Celtic Scotland*, i. 30.

are merely translations of the original Celtic. A difficulty to the inquirer lies in finding a genuine and if possible ancient form of the word with which he has to deal. But having satisfied himself as to this, if Celtic, he must master certain rules before he can explain it, as the Celtic root-words are often almost unrecognisable owing to the disguises they assume. Consonants are changed in sound or altogether disappear by aspiration (expressed in writing by being followed by an *h*), whilst one consonant often takes the place of another by eclipse. There are also various recognised interchanges of letters · the addition of *d* after *l*, *n*, and *r*, the addition or attraction of the article, the insertion of *t* between *s* and *r*, and various others more or less systematic.

As examples, aspirated *b* becomes *v* in Culvenna (bheanan), "back of the peak"; *w* in Laniwee (leana bhuidhe), "yellow mead"; *f* in Dinduff (damph), "ox fort", *ch* is changed into *wh* in Ringanwhey (rinn-an-chaedh), "point of the marsh"; *c* is eclipsed by *g* in Altygunnoch (g-cuinneag), "the glen of the churns"; *b* is eclipsed by *m* in Lignaman (leac-nambam), "the witches' stone"; *s* by *t* in Baltier (baile-an-t'saier), "carpenter's town" We have the addition of *d* after *n* in Landberrick, "St. Berach's Church" (lann); and the insertion of *t* between *s* and *r* in Stranraer (sron reamhar), "the bluff point"

A source of error in dealing with place-names arises from ignoring "the growth of words," *i.e.* treating idiomatic particles as substantive roots.[1] Of these, ach, lach, trach, seach, and others, have the simple force of "abounding in"; en, nat, can, gan, nan, og, etc, are diminutives, an, common to both, is sometimes

---

[1] A good example of such an error exposed is the case of Clogher, Tyrone, long confidently asserted to represent cloch oir, the golden stone. A tradition being adapted to the translation—namely, that "Clogher takes its name from a golden stone, from which in times of paganism the devil used to pronounce juggling answers like the oracles of old."

The derivation and story Dr Reeves (now Bishop of Down and Connor) annihilates in a sentence: "The prevalence of the name of Clogher in various parts of Ireland with the same general meaning of 'stony place' is rather damaging to such an etymon."—Joyce, i 414

merely ornate or formative. Thus smeurach is not " blackberry
field," but a place abounding in blackberries Brockloch is not
necessarily a " badger's lake," but a " badger warren." Rashnock
has no connection with cnoc, " a hill," but is a place abounding in
briars or roses. Toskerton, the suffix, is not a diminutive, but
primitive tuaise-art-an, " the northerly place."

It is the *rule* in Celtic names that the qualifying term comes
last, it being the reverse in Teutonic ; but there are numerous
exceptions, as Shinvolley, Kirkcowan, old dairy-place (and
sean is almost always prefixed) ; Fennart (feonn ard), white
height

It is impossible here to enter on the wide subject of changes
in the names of saints to which have been prefixed or added
terms of reverence or endearment, such as Moinean for Ninian,
Maccuddican for Cuthbert.[1]

Connected with personal as apart from place-names, it seems
worthy of notice that four Galloway landowners, presumably of
native stock,—Hannay, Carson, Shennan, and Milligan,—were
anciently written, Ahannay, Akersane or Accarson, Aschen-
nan, and Amulligan — the latter Ap Molegan in the Ragman Roll, suggestive rather of the Cymric ap than the Irish
ui, o'.

We shall now proceed to group certain place-names as
examples.

First, As to FORTIFICATIONS ; RESIDENCES generally ; HOS-
PITALS and CHURCHES.

The terms we find in use for forts of any sort are dun,
cathair (C. caer), caiseal, mur, rath, lios, aileach, teamhair,
longphort. Northumbrian Saxon, burh and byric, Norse, borg
and wark (verke).

By far the most common is dun, C. don, Latinised dunurn,
a stronghold Whence Dunikellie, Kirkmaiden (Ui Cheallagh),
O'Kelly's fort, Dunmurchie, Kirkcolm, and Dinmurchie, Barr,

---

[1] More singular is it to find ai classed as an equivalent for morgue from the
same cause. "Aedh (Hugh) is the same name as Maedhog (mo-aedh-og), my
little aedh , though when pronounced they are quite unlike, aedh being ai, and
maedhog morgue."—Joyce, 1. 147.

Murchad's or Murdock's;[1] Dunorrock, Kirkmaiden, Orry's or
Eric's,[2] Dunharberry, Girthon, Cairbre's or Carberry's, Dun-
ragit, Old Luce, Ragat's; Dunahaskel, Kirkmaiden, Macaskill's;
Dunerrun, Inch, and Dunrod, Borgue (din-y-Run, din-Rhudd),
Rhun and Rhudd, of Bardic fame;[3] Dunottrie, Minigaff, Uch-
tred's; Dundonald, Girvan, Domhall's, Dinvin, Portpatrick and
Girvan (as also Dinfionn, Arran), Fingall's; Dumfries (Doun-
fres), of the Frisians.

Connected with animals we find Dunnanee, Minigaff, fort
of the red deer, Dunmuck, Kirkmaiden and Colvend, and Duni-
muck, Girvan, of the wild swine; Dinduff, Leswalt, of the oxen,
Dunagarroch and Dunanrae, Stoneykirk, of the sheep and
ram; Dinveoch, Kells, of the ravens; Dunkirk, Kells, of the
moorfowl, Dunannane, Kirkmaiden, of the birds; Dunman,
Kirkmaiden, Gaelic, phonetically Dum-Meadhon, central fort—as
probably the suffix is the Cymric *maen*, stone fort.

Connected with bale - fires we have Dinniehinney, Kirkmaiden; Dindinnie,[4] Leswalt; Dunniechinie, Inch (all Dunteine),
fort of the fire. "Doon" alone occurs in Glasserton, Penninghame, Mochrum, Kirkcowan, Kirkinner; we have also the
Doon of May, the Doon of Borland, and Doon Castle (pleonastic); Baldoon, Wigtown, is the townland of the fort, and
Dinnan, Dunan, and Dunnance, are diminutives of frequent
occurrence. Duncow, Kirkmahoe, anciently Duncoll, in Robertson's *Index* Duncole, is Coyl's.[5] Dunanskail, Kirkmaiden, was
presumedly haunted by some sea-king's ghost, scal meaning a
spectre or apparition[6]

[1] Muireadhach, sea protector, whence the family name of Murray, though
generally Murdoch in Scotland, Morough in Ireland, Meredith in Wales

[2] Orry or Eric, Danish King of Man in the tenth century (*Worsaae*, 295), also
Eric Bloody-axe, a Norwegian rover of later date, harried the very sea-boards

[3] The grave of Llacher, son of Rhun, is in the valley of the Ken (clun kein) —
Taliessin. "The grave of Rhudd is not covered with sods "—*Ibid*
There were three Runs son of Maelgwn, son of Artgal, and Rhun Drum-
rudd, son of Brychan, from whom Loch Roan has its name; his sister was mother
of Llywarch Hen

[4] It might be Din duine, of the men, but inspection proves it to be a fire-hill

[5] There is a Duncow on Loch Doon more certainly connected with Coyl Hen
—the old King Cole.

[6] A spectre, a hero is a secondary meaning (Joyce, ii. 103) O'Donovan

Cathair or caer gives the Roman Corda, afterwards Sean Caer (Sanquhar), the old fort , and is the prefix of Carbantium, probably Kirkbean, synonymous with Castle Bann, white, that is of stone.   Cardoness (the second *s* corrupt) is the devil's fort; Cardrine, the fort of the blackthorn.   Caer runs easily into kirk, as Kirkmagill and Kirklauchlane, Stoneykirk, Magill's and Lauchlann's forts.   Craigcaffie (Karcophy, Pont) is a corruption, being Cathbhodh's or Coffey's fort[1]   In Ireland Cathair takes the form of Caher.

Caiseal, which in Ireland indicates a circular stone fort, and is usually called a cashel, has in Galloway a more general application to any strong house of stone, and pronounced castle, as Castle Ayne (Aine's, or of joy) , Castlecravie, Rerwick, the wooded , Castlenaught, Kirkmaiden, the bare; Shancastle, Parton, the old, or Nectan's ; Castle Maddy, the wolf's; Castle Feather, Peter's, or the piper's (fhiobaire's) ; Castle Shell, Sheil's, or of the hunting ; Castle Gower, Buittle, Guaire's,[2] possibly the vitrified ; Castle Donnell, Penninghame; Castle Larrick, Inch, Leurig's (or the *castle site*) ;[3] Castle Bann, Kirkcolm, the stone.   As a suffix we have Auchengashel (Twynham), Poulnagashel, Stragashel, Craigengashel (Minigaff), the field, pool, river, holm, and rock of the stone fort.

Mur is a rampart, a bulwark, a fortified place; mothar (*t* mute), not unlike it in pronunciation, denotes a ruined fort, and in the form of mōher is applied in Ireland to the remains of any old rath or castle.   Murdonachie, New Luce, is Duncan's

---

gives a hero; O'Reilly (besides), a noise, a rumbling, the cry of a hound in chase

[1] "Obviously the great Celtic historical name Cathbhadh, which in the genitive form is pronounced Caffie. The oldest form is Cathbie , it has descended to Coffey."—Dr. Joyce's Letter to the Author

[2] Gwawr, a Cymric name. Dunguaire was the Celtic name for Bamborough. Castle Gower is one of our few vitrified forts , Caer Gwydr is named as if in Galloway by Taliessin ; Gwydr, Cymric for glass, might imply vitrification , Caer Gwydr might easily turn to Castle Gower.

[3] Larrack has many meanings · it represents Leath Rath, half rath; Lathrach, a house site , Larach, a mare. There was a Leurig kinglet at Whithorn (*Chron. Picts and Scots*, p 52). Laraig, a Norse chieftain, who from Galloway plundered Waterford A.D. 951.

fort; Monreith is corrupted from Murrith, the gray tower. The name has travelled with the family from their original location in Glasserton to Mochrum. The tower house in which they first settled they called "the mouri," built probably on the site of, or adjoining, the older gray moher, which gave its name to their lands [1]

Rath and lios, denoting circular entrenchments, are terms less used in Galloway than in Ireland. Of the former, we have Rattra, probably Ram's fort, Borgue, Coolraw, Buittle, the back or angle of the rath; perhaps Wraiths, Kirkbean. A well-defined camp gives its name, with hardly the change of a letter, to the parish of Leswalt (Lios uilt), the fort of the glen; Lashandarroch, the old fort of the oaks, is in the same parish, Garlies, Minigaff, is the rough fort; and Drumlass, Rerwick, the ridge of the fort, Airless, Kirkinner, the height of the fort.[2] Aileach (Ailthach, literally stone-house), indicates a stone fort, whence Craigenellie in Crossmichael and Balmaghie, Drumanelly, and Craignellie in Kirkcolm, and Craigenally, Mochrum (rock, townland, and ridge of the stone tower), whilst Eilah Hill, New Luce, is a half translation

"Teamhair," genitive "teamhrach," pronounced tawer and tara, indicates an elevated entrenchment which commands a wide view. Of this a notable example is the "Kirkland Tawer," as it is generally termed, in Leswalt, or, as Chalmers writes it, "the Tower of Craigoch," Craigauch, as it should be written, the suffix representing King Eoch or Eocheidh, the Norseman. Glenterra in Inch (the word taking exactly the same form as the famous Tara in Meath) is the scene of one of Gwallauc's battles, as told by Taliessin, the standing-stones of Glenterra being monuments of the slain.

Longphort is another term for a fortress, whence Drumlamford, Colmonell; Dallamford, Dailly; Lamford, Carsphairn,

---

[1] Symson says: "The mower," together with the whole parish of Kirkmaiden (in Fernes) belongs to Sir William Maxwell Kirkmaiden is absorbed in Glasserton.

[2] Possibly the name is Dhurlas, strong fort. Thurles, Tipperary, is a corruption of Durlas.—Joyce, 1 273

and Longford, New Luce. Cannphort suggestive of a chief's principal residence, gives us Camford on Loncaster Loch.[1]

The Northumbrian Saxon burh and byric appear in Burrowhead and Auldbreck (eald byric); the Norse borg and wark (verke) in Borgue, Borness, Carlingwark and Kemp's walks (wark), Leswalt, and Burnswark beyond the Nith.

Of residentiary structures, not necessarily fortified, the most imposing in name was the grianan, literally a sunny spot, conventionally a palace, whatever meaning we may attach to the word.[2] "Grennan" stands as a name alone in Stoneykirk, Kirkmaiden, Glasserton, and Old Luce. We have Argrennan, Tongland, and Bargrennan, Penninghame, both meaning the palace height

Lucairt, used in the sense of a palace in the Highlands, gives us Drumloccart, Leswalt, Barlockhart, Old Luce.

Baile, the word for dwellings most in use, means not merely a town or townland, but often a single homestead, like the vernacular "farm toun."

Celtic and Norse meet in suidh, and seat, Sheuchan (Suiddeachan), Inch, is a diminutive of the former, and Sheuchanowre, Minigaff, the gray seat; Soulseat, Inch, and Aldermanseat, Gretna, are examples of the latter.

Teach and tigh, cognate with Cymric tref and tre, mean "house," as Nashantee (na sean teach), the old houses, Tannielaggie (tynalagach, Pont), the hollow of the house[3] Threave, Balmaghie, and Penninghame ; Ochiltree, Penninghame.

[1] In a Monreith estate map, 1777, a rectangular fort is marked "Roman Camp," all traces of which have disappeared under the plough. Ceann-phoit, lit. head-fort. Longphort has a more general meaning, applied alike to circular raths and entrenched forts of any sort, all the Longfords in Ireland (of which Joyce says there are twenty) are Longphorts . "a further softening is in Ath-lunkard, Lemerick, the ford of encampment."—Joyce, i. 300.

[2] O'Brien explains Grennan as "a royal seat," in which sense it is used by the best Irish writers ; and *this is unquestionably its general meaning when it occurs in topography.*—Joyce, i 290.

[3] Tamhnach, a meadow, often confuses with "Tigh na", *e.g* Tannie flux, Tamnach fluch, the wet meadow, not the house in the swamp.

Arost appears frequently in airies, "the house." [1]

The Saxon ton appears in Myreton and Broughton, the dwelling by the lake and fort We have in Cauldhame and Cuningham, the cold and cuning's home.

Botl, a house, is the same in Norse and Saxon, whence Buittle; and by is a Norse test-word, appearing in Appleby, Corsbie, Busby, Sorbie.

Cil is the most frequent root for church, as Kilpatrick, Kilfillan, Killantringan (Ninian's), but it is so prolific and well known that we shall rather try to trace it in its corruptions. Thus Culcaldie, Inch, should be (as written in the curates' lists of 1684) Kilcaldie, the Culdees' church (cil celide), Culmore, Stoneykirk, is not the great back or angle, but great church, cil being the head or parish church of Clayshant (clach seanta, holy stone), now absorbed in Stoneykirk , so Culmalzie is St. Malie's church, and should be written Kilmalzie, as in Argyle ; Gillespie, Old Luce, is Killespie, the Bishop's church ; we have a pleonasm in Kirklebride (the Saxon cyrc before the Celtic cil), St. Bride's church church.[2] Lann (Cymric), "land" (old Irish), appears in its ecclesiastical application in Landberrick, Mochrum, St. Berach's church.

Domhnach, a term of frequent application in Ireland, is held to imply that a church so-called had been personally founded by St Patrick [3]—a ceremony he performed invariably on a Sunday.

In Ballantrae we have Kildomine, locally corrupted to Kirkdamnie, a name which has puzzled philologists, unaware of the fact recognised by the Bishop of Down, and other high ecclesiastical authorities.

Eaglais, a Celtic adaptation of the Latin, appears in Terregles,

---

[1] Trehel or Trayle (now St Mary's Isle), Kirkcudbright, synonymous with Trehal, Cornwall, given by Bannister as house on the saltwater estuary. Dreghorn, Parton, seems Celtic tregwern, house on the marsh or alders. Ochiltree (Uchel-tre) is Welsh as spoken, high house.

[2] Joyce estimates that 2700 names in Ireland are derived from cill , 700 more beginning with kel or kyle represent coill, a wood

[3] Domhnach, from Domenica "All the churches that have the name of Domhnach were originally founded by St. Patrick."—Joyce, i 318.

originally Traveregles, the church lands; Slewnagles (s omitted in Ordnance Survey), Leswalt, the church hill. In Clashmahew, Inch, clash is a clerical error for eaglais, St. Machute's church. Caipeal, from the Latin capella, appears in Chapel Donan, Kirkcolm; Chapel Finian, Mochrum; and Chapelrossan, Kirkmaiden—the two former from well known saints, the latter the chapel of the little point; the said chapel being probably the dedication to St. Lassair, mother of Finian of Moville, whence the lands of Killeser are named, her church being a place of peculiar sanctity, overlooked by Hermon Hill (Tearmann), suggesting the existence of a sanctuary.[1]

Annoid means "a parent church" (a church of a patron saint), whence Annat, Kirkinner; Annatland, New Abbey; Penhannat, Barr—the lands of the Annat.

Spital (spideal) in the early times meant rather a place for entertainment than for cure—a hospice So Portesspital, Stoneykirk, below the Roman camp of Kildonan; "Spital" frequently alone, as in Kirkcowan and Kirkmabreck; and "Spital Crofts" in various places; many of these were once possessed by the Knights Hospitallers of St. John of Jerusalem.[2]

From very early times there seem to have been places for the isolation of lepers, such were Killielour, Kirkpatrick-Irongray, the leper's wood, Barlour, New Luce, the leper's height. Ochtralure, by Stranraer; Farrenlure, Inch; Craiglure, Straiton; Carlure, New Luce. This last translated by "Liberland" near it.[3]

Second, As to OCCUPATIONS The oldest industries were the

[1] Termon and Tarmon are the names of several places, indicating in every case the former existence of a sanctuary —Joyce, ii. 210.

[2] In the Lochnaw charter chest there is a conveyance of the spital croft of Craichmore, dated from the Preceptory of Torphichen, the headquarters of the Knights of St John. The Hospitallers fell heirs to the Knights Templar on the suppression of that order, whose occupation is proved by the existence of various Templelands and Crofts

[3] Lobar is glossed in the oldest Irish writings by "infurmis" and "debilis," and was not confined in its application to leprosy Dr Reeves translates lobar by sick. The usual anglicised forms being lour, lower, and lure "Whenever we find a name containing this word, we may generally infer that some kind of hospital or asylum was formerly established there "—Joyce, ii 79

The parish of Liberton, Midlothian, is supposed to take its name from lepers.

pastoral , horses, hides, and wool being the principal exports from which the lords of the land derived their revenues of old

Of the structures required for such purposes, we find the Celtic and Norse languages meeting in the word " cro," a cattle pen ; the former in Craigencroy, Stoneykirk , Alticry, Mochrum ; Dyrnagrow (na-gcroithe) obsolete   The frequent " crows " and " croys " may be as possibly Norse as Celtic, with English plurals

Airidh, and its diminutive aroch, a mountain booth, is equivalent to the Norwegian saeter.   In nomenclature aroch is hardly distinguishable from earrach, spring ; but in connection with herding the terms are cognate, both alike indicating haunts resorted to in spring.   Clashnarroch, Leswalt ; Knockanarroch, Stoneykirk ; Lochnarroch, Minigaff, are the hollow, knoll, and lake of spring sheilings.   Bellsavory and Fellsavory, Inch, the root of both samhraidh, indicate summer grazings.[1]

Of airidh itself we have examples innumerable : as Airieglassan, the green ; Shannarie Urr, the old ; Savery, the summer ; Airieguilshie, among the broom ; Airieolland (twice), of the wool , Airiequhillart, of the orchard ; Airiewiggle (bhuachaile),[2] of the herdsmen.

Mr Joyce does not give a single example of airidh in his *Irish Names of Places*.   Bo teach, a cow-house, appears in Buyoch, Whithorn , and aspirated, Wayoch, in Mochrum.   Traboyach, Barr, is the three byres ;[3] Craigwoughie, Stoneykirk, is a corruption of bho tigh, and we find " bo " impressed into the

---

[1] Bellsavory is baile samhradh, exactly translated by Somerton in Norse form across the Tarf   Fellsavory, Inch, translated by Sommerhill in Balmaclellan, Balmaghie, and Holywood.   All these indicate summer pasturages , whilst, on the contrary, Minigaff (gauf, Gaelic , gauaf, Cymric), means the wintry moorland

Ceitein is another Gaelic word for spring, whence Glenkitten, New Luce, the glen of springtime , whilst Samaria, Mochrum, if a genuine name, is the summer sheiling   Aroch is glossed by O'Reilly as " a hamlet, a little *sheilding* "

[2] Bhuachaile (Cymric, bugail ; Cornish, bigel).

[3] Other numerical combinations are Traloddan, Barr, three pools , Tryach, New Luce, three fields ; Tregallan, Troqueer, three pillar-stones , Trolane (lánn) Dalry, three enclosures or churches , Lanedripple, Inch stream of the three pools ; Troqueer, is perhaps three forts.

vernacular in Akebusbowhouse, Teriegles, the byre by the pollard oak.

Badhun, pronounced bawn, is a cow fort, whence Drumbawn, Stoneykirk; Millbawn, Portpatrick; Knockbawn, Stoneykirk; it is aspirated in Drumawan, Kirkcowan. Buaille (angliceised in Ireland, booley) is a dairy-place, whence Shanvoley, Kirkcowan; Altivolie, Stoneykirk, Craigenvolie, Balmaclellan; Craigenvolie, Carsphairn, the old dairy place, and the booley of the glen and rock The Ox-fort, Dinduff or Dundaff, has been already mentioned.

Cuinneag, Cymric cunnoch and cunnog, a milk-pail or churn, is equally suggestive of a dairy-place. Cunninghame, "Canawon" of the Bards, was the churn country,[1] abounding in butter and cheese Drumcunnoch, Minigaff; Altigunnoch, Ballantrae; Glengunnoch, Parton, Knockcunnoch, Carsphairn, are the ridge, stream, glen, and knoll of the milk-pails or churns, the c being eclipsed in the three latter by g [2]

Eachlann and stabull [3] stand for stable, whence Auchlane, Kelton, long celebrated for its breeding studs and horse fair, Auchlannochy, Minigaff (Eochy's stable); Drumstable, Penninghame; and Stable Alan, Kirkmaiden [4] (Alan's).

Turning to the animals themselves, the cow is bo, plural ba, Cymric bewch, whence playfully Bilnavoe (beul), the cow's snout, a rock in Kirkmaiden; Slocknaba and Sloganaba, the cow's gullies (on the sea coast), Drumawa, New Luce, and Kirkcowan; bo is eclipsed in Darnemow,[5] New Luce, and Ringimow, Kirkmabreck, the oak wood and point of the cows.

A milking cow with a year old calf (in Ireland a stripper) was gamnach (gaunie), whence Pulgawny, Kirkcowan, and Knockagawny, Kirkmaiden, the stripper's pool and knoll

[1] Cunningham, topographised by Pont, 31.

[2] Joyce, ii 186.

[3] Auchland, near Wigtown, properly Auchleand, is the broad field (leathan). Auchland in England means oakland.

[4] Stable appears in the Cornish as well as the Irish and Gaelic dictionary. In Cornwall we find Park and Stable as a place-name, the Gaelic and Irish form is Stabul

[5] Daire-nam-bho.

Odhar, genitive huidrie, dun, in old legends is applied in a substantive sense to dun cows. The famous " Lebor-na-huidre," book of the dun cow, was made from the hide of St. Kieran's favourite dun cow. Barnhourie, a dangerous sandbank in the Solway, and Glenowrie, Minigaff, may derive their names from dun cows, real or legendary [1]

Earc is glossed by O'Reilly and Armstrong as "a beast of the cow kind," whence Dirneark; but as they add that it also signifies honey, a salmon, a bee, a tax, heaven, speckled, and red, the explanation is somewhat vague.

Damh is an ox, its force in names variously daw, daff, duff,[2] and dam. Thus Knockdaw, Girvan, knoll of the ox; Daffin, Rerwick, a place of oxen; Dinduff, Leswalt, the ox fort; Damlach, New Luce, abounding in oxen. The ancient name for the site of the town of Ayr was Monadamdarg, moss of the red ox, and for its people, Damnii, the breeders of oxen

A bull is tarbh. Clontarf, Kirkcowan, is the meadow of the Water of Tarf, the stream being so named from a belief in its being haunted by a bull spirit, the mate of the Highlanders' " water cow," the legendary " Tarroo ushley " of the Manxmen. Cairnharrow, Anwoth, Barharrow, Borgue; Lochharrow and Pulharrow, Kells, are the hill, lake, and pool of the bull [3]

A calf is loogh or laech (low and lee), whence we have Bennylow, Kirkcowan, Linnielow, Kirkmaiden, Loddenlaw, Portpatrick, the hill, meadow, and pool of the calves Carslae, Wigtown; Barlae, Old Luce; Slocklaw and Slockalew, on the sea-shore, are the carse, hill-top, and gulley of the calves. Ballochalee, Stoneykirk, is the calves' road; Bellowe, a cave in Portpatrick, the calves' mouth.

Milk was bainne, whence Acanabaine (obsolete) in Inch, Auchanbainzie, Penpont, Lagabaine, New Luce; Knockvenie in Parton and Kirkpatrick-Durham, Kirvenie, Wigtown, the field, hollow, and knoll of the milk. Whilst whey was meag,

---

[1] Monahoora, County Down, is the bog of the dun cow.—Joyce, ii. 280

[2] In the end of a word damh often changes to duff, as Clouduff, Down, meadow of the oxen

[3] Harry as a suffix is usually "fhaire," a watcher

whence Balmeg, Wigtown, Slewmeg, Kirkmaiden; Altimeg, Ballantrae, townland, knoll, and stream of the whey.

Caora (gen. singular and plural caorach) is a sheep, whence Drumacarie, Kirkcowan; Culgarie, Glasserton, Slocnagarry, Kirkcolm, ridge, corner, and gulley of the sheep; plural Darngarroch and Knockingarroch, Carsphairn; Craignaquarroch, Portpatrick, wood, knoll, and rock of the sheep. The Cymric hespin, a year old ewe, appears in Garrahaspin, Stoneykirk.

We trace the Norse faar (a sheep) in Fairgirth.

Lumagarie, Glasserton, is the sheep's leap (leum); Sloclomairt, Kirkmaiden, is the shearing pit; Ariolland, in Mochrum and Stoneykirk, is sheilings of the wool, olann.[1]

Reithe, a ram, is often undistinguishable from reidh, smooth. Dunanrae, Stoneykirk, is probably ram's fort; Loddanrae, Old Luce, the ram's pool; Ramsey, Whithorn, is pure Norse, ram's isle; and Ramshawwood, a Teutonic form old enough to have a pleonastic addition.[2] Drumrae, in several places, may either be the ram's or the smooth ridge

Mult is a wether; whence Knockmult, Rerwick; Wetherhill, in Kelton and Dalry, are probably translations, taking a Norse form in "Wedderdod," Sanquhar.

A lamb is luan and uan, Cymric oen, plural wyn, giving the suffixes Drumalone, Dalry; Drumanoon, Penninghame; Lagwine, Carsphairn.

Gabhar (gower) is a goat, as in Knockgower, Leswalt; Inchnagower, Kirkmaiden; Lannigore, Old Luce, the goats' meadow, (leona); Altigober, Ballantrae; and very many others. Castle Gower, as before said, is from a proper name, or vitrification.

A horse has many names, as each, capall, mark, peall, gearran;[3] a mare is laer, a foal searrach. Whence we have

---

[1] Leffnoll, Inch, is a modern contraction for Leffin olla, the halfpenny land of the wool.

[2] Shaw is both old Saxon and Norse; the former sceaga, the latter skogr.

[3] Gearran is not from gearr, to cut, but is a diminutive of gobhar, a goat, anciently a horse. It is often translated "gelding" from misapprehension. O'Reilly renders it work-horse, hack

Craigeach and Craiglarie, Mochrum, the horse and the mare's rock; Clashneach, Kirkmaiden; Auchness (a very frequent form, "eachinis"), horse isles , Cassandeoch (da each), the path of the two horses, Slocklaurie, Kirkmaiden; Glenlair, Parton ; Auchenlary, Anwoth. Mark in topography is often a march, as well as indicating the duty of a mark (coin) to a superior; but considering Ochley, a sea rock, is undoubtedly the gray horse, a similar rock being mapped "the yellow horse" near it ; we conceive Markbain, Kirkcowan, and Markdow, New Luce, to indicate white and black horses, whether real or representative. Marklach, New Luce, abounding in horses ; Barmark, Millmark, and Portmark, being as likely to be horse hills and port as marches. Peall we find only in Drumpail, Old Luce, translated in "horse hill" opposite , and peall again explained in the " moss of the horse hill," lying between the two ridges.

Capall appears in Barcaple, Tongland ; Barhapple (twice); Glenhapple (twice); Cairnhapple, Leswalt ; Portwhapple, Mochrum, and Sorbie, the summit, glen, hill, and harbour of the horse ; Craignagapple, Mochrum, Lodnagapple, Old Luce, Fannygapple, Kirkinner, the rock, pool, and slope of the horses.

Searrach, a foal, is the root of Balsarroch, and Dalsharroch, Kirkcolm; Laggansarroch, Colmonell, Barsherry, Alcherry (allt); Falincherry, Kells—the town, field, hollow, hilltop, glen, and rock (faill) of the foals (an t'searraich).

The Norse hest appears in Hestan,[1] Horse Isles being mapped opposite to it. Gearran has been adopted into the vernacular as Garron, for the Galloway nag, as the modern Garranton, Carsphairn, is equivalent to the Celtic Balgarron, Crossmichael the latter the site of Kelton Hill horsefair ; Dalzerran, Inch , Knockgarran, Girvan ; Glengarron, Minigaff.

Madadh is the dictionary word for dog, but in topography allaedh, wild, is usually assumed to follow it when it denotes a wolf; and in place-names it is generally so translated. Domesticated dogs are cu, genitive con; and gadhair, the latter a

---

[1] As it does across the Solway. "We have hestr, a horse, in Hest Bank, Hest Fell, Hest Holme "—*Norsemen in Cumberland*, p. 123.

greyhound or mastiff, as in Ossian's line, "gath-gadhar-a-cnoc-gu-cnoc," the voice of hounds from hill to hill.[1]

Carrickcune, Kirkmaiden, and Carrickcundie, are respectively the rock of the dog and of the black dog. Many names ending in quhan or whan, as Glenwhan, Old Luce; Drumquhan, Penninghame; Torquhan, Craiglewhan, we suspect to have con for their root. Attiquin is undoubtedly Con's house site, con there being a proper name; and Dernoconner, Colmonell, by Irish analogy, should be the oaks of the dog's wood; Glengyre, Leswalt, is the hound's glen; "Dogstone Hill," overlooking it, and Balingair, Dalry, the townland of the hounds. Such names mapped as "Dogtail Hill," Mochrum, "Hound Hill," Carsphairn; "Doghead," Urr; "Hound's Loup," Portpatrick, seem translations.

Of swine, which ran wild, and were followed by hound and horn, we shall speak further on.

Turning to agricultural processes, "ar" is ploughing, but the same word means slaughter, and although with some confidence we suggest that Falhar, Mahaar, Macherhaar, indicate ploughed lands, "Craignair," which appears four times in the map, may as probably refer to the battle-field.

Ceapach is a tillage plot, whence Capenach, Kirkinner, Knockcappy, Kirkmaiden; Glengappach, Crossmichael.

Losaid, a kneading trough, is used in Ireland to denote a rich, well-tilled field. We find "Lossit" in Kirkcolm, and "the trencher" in Kirkmaiden may be accepted as representing another Lossaid.

Garradh, Norse gardr, modernised garth, was an enclosure. From the Celtic root we have Garryharry, Stoneykirk, Garryhorn, Colvend, respectively the bulls and the barley enclosure; whilst the Norse is instanced in Fairgarth, Cogarth, Gadgarth, and Applegarth, the enclosures of sheep, cattle, goats, and apple trees.

Fal, a penfold, hedge, or fence, separating holdings, as Fal-

---

[1] Dean of Lismore's Book, p 6.

Clooseguire, Kerry, is the dog's ear.—Joyce, ii 402

Phonetically, Glengyre might be rendered short glen, but it is particularly long and shallow. Dogstone Hill above it seems conclusive.

shawn, Falkeown, Kirkmaiden; Falhar, for ploughed enclosures; Falbae, by the birches; Faldarroch, among the oaks, Fallincherry, ant'seanach, of the foals; and probably Ardwall, Anwoth, Borgue, New Abbey (Ard bhfal)[1]

Grabh is to grub, whence graffans, a grubbing axe, gives Glengruff, Whithorn; Culgruff, Crossmichael; Glengrubboch, Minigaff—the grubbed glen and angle.[2]

Winnowing-places are indicated by Cathia, chaff; slight elevations were desirable for the process, so Knockricaw, Colmonell, means the knoll of the winnowing. Urlar, is a threshing-floor, of which the Airlour, Mochrum, furnishes an example.

Celtic words for structures connected with agriculture are ith-teach and lann-ith, synonymously cornhouse; and sab-hall (soul) a barn. The first we find in Lagatie, Dailly; Knocketie, New Luce, and Kirkmaiden, Drumatye, Glasserton; Ernanity, Crossmichael—the hollow, hill, and portion of the cornhouse.[3]

"Island Buoy," Stoneykirk, is an amusing instance of the tendency to force Celtic words into English forms The place is neither an island nor near any channel requiring to be marked by a buoy, but the English-sounding word closely reproduces the Gaelic original, "Ithlann-buidhe"[4] (i and d mute), the yellow barn, or perhaps Boyds, a proper name. Lann-ith appears in Knockalanny, Kirkcowan, equivalent to "Barnhill," in constant use. And "Linney" (Lann-ith) has been pretty generally accepted in the vernacular as a synonym for a corn-barn[5] Sabhall (soul) appears in Drumsoul, Old Luce; Auchensoul, Barr; and eclipsed in Knockatoul, Portpatrick—the ridge, field, and knoll of the barn.

[1] In the genitive plural fal is usually represented by wall or vaul, as Cornawall Moneghan, round hill of the hedges.—Joyce, ii 212
[2] Graf, primarily to write, secondarily to grub; grafan, a grubbing axe — O'Reilly.
[3] Atty, as a prefix, represents eth-teach, a house site, as Attiquin, Con's house, as a suffix, a cornhouse or granary, as Knocketie.
[4] The Brehon laws explain "Idhlann" (d mute), "Frumenti Repositorium"
[5] Ithlann and lannioth (ihlan and laniha), Cymric ydlan, all signify a granary, literally "house of corn" The English-speaking people of some counties call a barn a "linney"—Joyce, i. 321.

" Aith," a kiln, whether for malting or drying corn, is usually distinguished from ath, a ford, by having the *h* of the genitive prefixed. Thus Auchenhay in Borgue and New Abbey; Knockenhay, Old Luce, are the field and knoll of the kiln[1] The "Auld Kilns," a little south of the Dunman in Kirkmaiden, was supposed to be the great distillery where the Picts prepared the heather crop. The tradition has taken a hopelessly unhistoric form, but it is worthy of note that the fifth century bards apply as an epithet to the Galwegians the name "kiln distillers."

Bro was a quern (genitive broin, plural brointe) Lignabrawn, Kirkmaiden, is the hollow of the quern; Craignabronchie, Penninghame, is equal to "Knocking-stone Hill," in Kirkmaiden and New Luce.

Muilenn, Cymric melin, a mill, enters largely into our topography.

The quern, if humbler as a utensil, was hardly a more primitive one than the mill.

The use of water-mills in Galloway is to be traced back to archaic times : indeed, in past ages they seem to have been more numerous than now This is moreover attested by Irish Annals. It is there a historical tradition that Cormac M'Art, monarch of the third century, sent across the channel for a millwright ; and as the man so sent was probably a Niduari Pict, it is a curious coincidence that the mill then erected was placed upon an Irish Nith, a stream which flowed from the well of Tara.[2]

From Church History we learn that the founders of the earliest Irish sixth century monasteries received instruction in the arts of secular as well as of religious life at Whithorn,— notoriously founded their respective houses on the model of Candida Casa,—and that their names are usually expressly connected with the construction of mills at the said monasteries.

The Ordnance Map marks a mill dam as still existing by the

[1] Not to speak of the mythic Picts' kilns (Cymric or Ydlan) which every one has heard about, but few have seen.

[2] This tradition is still vividly preserved, not only in the neighbourhood, where a mill still occupies its site, but also in most parts of Ireland —Joyce i 374 ; *Ordnance Memoir of the Parish of Tenyslemore.*

site of St. Ninian's famous monastery; Drummullin Hill, which overlooks it, having its suffix from the very mill used by the fraternity at Rosnat. We find Molland Hill (anciently Drummollin), Penninghame, Ballymellan, Mochrum; Knockmullin, Stoneykirk; Drumwhillan (Mhuilinn), Kirkcowan; Carnywillan, Kirkmaiden, Tormollen; Drummullins without number; several Barmullins, also Milton, Millisle, Millhill, in every direction.

The antiquity, number, and ubiquity of these mills prove that from a very early date crops were produced which they were required to grind.

Ith, or iotha, Cymric yd, and arbha (arrow), both mean corn in general The former appears in Ballyett, Inch; the latter in Arrow, Glasserton; Ervie, Kirkcolm; Arvie, Parton; Arbrack, (Arbharack), Whithorn. Coirce (kirke) for oats, whence Culquhirk, Wigtown, Awhirk, Stoneykirk—the angle and field of the oats Eorna for barley; whence Culhorn, Inch; Tallowhorn, Kirkbean, Horney, Stoneykirk; Knockhornan—enclosures and hills of barley. "Berefeys" are mapped in every parish;[1] Berehill and Bereholm are connected with barley, but "Barley Hill," Mochrum, is probably Celtic Barleath, gray hilltop, "hill" being pleonastic.

Seagal, Cymric rhygen, is rye, somewhat oddly we find our only Cymric example in Pictish territory—Carseriggan, Penninghame; whilst in Cymric Kyle we have the Scottish Gaelic in Knockshoggle. Under Norse rule rye seems to have been cultivated in Rydale, Troqueer. Lin, flax, an important factor in Celtic economy, appears in Glenling, Mochrum; Auchteralinachin (upper flax pool), Leswalt, Lochanaling (the lakelet in which it was steeped), and Portleen, Kirkcolm (whence it was exported).

Abhall (having the force of owl and howl in composition) is the apple. The sixth century bards sang of the "sweet apple trees of the woods of Celyddon," which

[1] Bere (Hordeum vulgare, Linnæus)—a coarser sort of barley, having four rows of grains.—Jamieson.
Pese and atys, bere and qwhet.—Wyntoun Bere means barley of any sort.

could hardly have roused poetic enthusiasm had they been uncultivated crabs. We find "Glenhowl" in Glenluce, Kirk-' cowan, and twice in Dalry ; Knockhooly in Kelton and Colvend , Marnhoul, Parton—the glen, knoll, and plain of the apple trees. Abhalgort, pronounced Oulart, is an orchard, whence Balnowlart, Ballantrae ; Airiequhillart (anciently Arywhollart), Mochrum— the townland and sheiling of the orchard [1] Orchard hill and "the orchard " are common place-names, which, if translations, from the Celtic, are sites of fruit orchards, if Old Saxon, vege- table gardens [2] Orchardton is from a man's name,—Archar, Orchar,—strangely accepted in Galloway as an equivalent for Urquhart. Appleby, Glasserton, Norse, seems to refer to the fruit, and exactly to translate Balnowlast

Meacan signified any taprooted plant, the usual translation of the word connected with garden produce being parsnip , thence Lagnamekan ; Blairmakin, Kirkcowan ; and Barnamachan, Pen- ninghame—the hollow, field, and hill-top of the roots.

Meas, a general term for fruit and acorns, appears in Tannymaws (Tigh-na-meas or Tamhnat), Borgue, and Balmesh, adjoining the garden of Glenluce Abbey, house or field and town of the fruit.

In the life of St. Ninian, written in 1142, we read of the saint inquiring why there were neither leeks, other vegetables, or garden herbs upon the table , and even if we doubt Ailred having obtained any such particulars as to the fifth century from an older life of the saint, yet had a garden of some sort not been attached to the monastery when he wrote, the mention of the unexpected failure of leeks and potherbs would have fallen rather flat if they had been then unknown in the convent garden.

Achadh [3] (auch), tamhnach, is a field , as Auchencleish,

---

[1] Agowle, Wicklow , Aghywle, Fermanagh ; Ballyhooley, below Mallow, are the field and the ford of the apples   Ballynowlart, Wexford ; Ballywhollart, Down, signify the town of the orchard —Joyce i. 515.

[2] Saxon "ooit-yeard," vegetable or wort garden

[3] Eilean dubh is the exact equivalent of the constantly repeated "Black Isle "—a moory meadow.

Kirkmaiden, the field of the hollow, Auchenfranco, Lochrutton, of the Anglo-Norman. We also have Tannul Pen, New Abbey, later Tonneshree, Irish ailean, a meadow, as Allanbey, Kells; Allandoo, Leswalt, the yellow and black meadow, cluain, very similar in meaning to the Norse "eyes," a green or arable spot in bog or marsh, as Clonidder (eadar), Penninghame; cashel, the meadow, and in the plural Clantibuies, Kirkcowan, the yellow meadows; a very wet meadow is leana, as Lanigore, Old Luce, the goats, and Laniwee, Minigaff, the translation mapped beside it "yellow bogs."

The chase was as much a source of subsistence to the Celtic chief as cultivation. The larger game, such as the hart and hind, the roebuck and the boar, were sought for the pot, whilst the wolf and fox, the wild cat, and otter, were hunted in defence of the breeding lairs and fish weirs. Sealg (shalloch), hunting, appears constantly in names. Barn-shalloch, Kirkpatrick - Irongray, and Barnchalloch[1] (the c a corruption for s), Stoneykirk, are the ridge of the hunting. Kittyshalloch (ceide), the hillock of the hunting. Castle Shell, Kirkmaiden, is from its name still pointed to as the "hunting seat" of a laird of olden time. Slewnark,[2] Portpatrick, and Mulwharker in Barr and Minigaff, from Irish analogy, are to be explained as "the hills of the hunting horn," and still re-echo the wild music of the chase: most appropriately so in the latter example, as Mulwharker, Minigaff, overlooks "Hunt Ha'," a favourite rendezvous for the Earl of Cassilis's hounds in the forest of Buchan. Assemblies of any sort, fairs, and cattle markets, were called aenach, and coinne (from verb connich). The site of a cattle fair is to be recognised at least five times absolutely unchanged phonetically; as Enoch or New

---

[1] c is often corruptly interchanged with s, and vice versa. Whilst Barn-challoch, Stoneykirk, should be written Barnshalloch, Shalloch O'Minnoch and Shalloch O'Tig in Carrick should both be Challochs—i.e. Tulach—conical hills overlooking the streams, whence their names.

[2] The very spot where the huntsman wound his horn to collect his dogs and companions is identified by such names as Killinerk, West Meath, Drumna-heark, Donegal, Tullynaherka, Roscommon—the little hill, ridge, and knoll of the hunting horn (adharc, genitive, adhairce, a hunting horn).—Joyce, i 21

Cumnoch, Maybole, Whithorn, Glasserton, and Portpatrick.
The approach to Enoch in the latter case is across the Pinminnoch Burn at Ashendram, the ford of the old ridge (Alti-
sean-druim). Why *old*? the obvious answer being, " Because
a place of assembly from the earliest times.".[1] Examples of
comnich as a meeting-place are to be found in Barquhanny
(anciently Barwhinny), Kirkinner; Barwhinny, Buittle; Craig-
whinny, Girthon and, Kirkmaiden; Lochwhinny, Dalry.[2]
Farrach was also a meeting-place, as Farrach Bay, Minigaff,
the meeting-place at the birches, and Loch Farroch, Colmonell. Mordhail, glossed an assembly.

The cattle herdsmen was buachile, Cymric bugel, Cornish
bigel: whence we have Barnbauchle, Loch Rulton; Porto-
beagle,[3] Colvend; Airiewiggle, Old Luce. A shepherd was
aodhaire, not easily distinguished from airidh in composition, but in Drumanairy, Portpatrick, the use of the masculine
genitive article points rather to the shepherd than the
sheiling.

In early days no duty was more important than the keeping
of watch and ward. Faire, a watcher, sentinel, a watching,
occurs frequently in our topography.

At the entrance to the Isle of Whithorn, the great sailing resort, is Knockenharry, exactly translated by the name
" watch crag" on an opposite rock.[4] At the entrance to the
roadstead of the ancient Rerigonium is another Knockenharry,
with a similar translation, " watch knowe," Kirkcolm. At
the foot of Harry's Hill, Inch, we find in ancient charters
Ballyferry, the townland of the watchers. Kilfairy, near
Killgallioch, is the watcher's grave; Drumferry, Parton, the

---

[1] An assembly of people for any purpose was anciently called aenach, in
modern times the word is always applied to a cattle fair.—Joyce, i 203.
    Aenach, hardly distinguishable in sound, is a marsh   Loch Enoch,
Minigaff, may have been a place of assembly, but as probably its name indicates a marsh.

[2] So Dalwhinnie, Blair Athole, which any of the recognised guides will
translate to the traveller the field of meeting

[3] Rose-au-beagle, Cornwall, the shepherd's moor —Banister's *Cornish Names.*

[4] Clachnaharry, Inverness, is recognised as the stone of the watchers. Dr.
Reeves translates Cnocnafaire, Iona, hill of the watchers —Reeves's *Adamnan.*

watcher's ridge, whilst "The Look Out," Troqueer, and "Ward Hill," New Luce, are translations.

Connected with watching were bale-fires, usually denoted by teine, plural teinte and tendal, whence Tintoch, Kirkinner, which (as also the well-known hill in Lanarkshire) is the place of fires; Dumchinnie, Inch, Dindinnie, Leswalt; Dinmehinney, Kirkmaiden; Drumhinnie, Old Luce; Knockytinnie, Kirkcowan, are all named from bale-fires; but when the term is applied to hollows and waters, fish-spearing seems rather to be indicated. Piltanton (although apparently St. Antony's water) was probably so called from sea trout being habitually speared in its pools by torchlight. Aldinna, Barr, and Lochnahinnie, Colmonell, are the stream and lake where fishermen pursued their trade by "burning the water." Culchintee, Kirkcolm, the angle of the fire, is the scene of a legendary adventure of St. Cuthbert. Knocktentol is the hill of the bale-fire.[1]

Of professions, there was one not of the Church that might be called learned, that of the sennach or the bard: whence Blanivaird, Penninghame, near Castle Donnell; Dervaird, Old Luce, near Barlochart (Lucairt); Dalvaird, Minigaff, near Uchtred's fort; Milvaird, Leswalt, by a rock-built fort, Drumavaird, Colmonell; Barneboard, Balmaghie—the first the bard's creek "in Loch Ochiltree, Bleau," the others bards' woods and hills. The bards were poets and genealogists; lower in the scale were musicians, feadaire (piob fhear), in short, whistling men or pipers: whence Allanfedder, Kells, the piper's hill, and it is quite as probable that Kilfeather, New Luce, is the piper's grave, rather than Peter's; indeed this may be the case with Castle Feather, a ruined stronghold in Glasserton. The Piper's Cove, Colvend; Piper's Hill, Inch, all represent this "piob air."

Those names indicative of clerical functions in the Scoto-

---

[1] It is curious to note the change in the position of the site of these beacons after the Brucian settlement. They lay largely to the westward, and especially on the Irish Channel, whereas in the Douglas's laws of march not one is detected on the western seaboard, those being all to the eastward, and mostly inland.

Irish Church are many of them very old , such as easpuig, bishop, whence Ernespie and Gillespie, the bishop's share and "cil."

Abbot (ab), as Balnab, Craignab.   Culdee (Ceile-de), Knockaldy, Leswalt (the old Culdees' well, "fors Colidee," bubbling up before it); Culcalday, Inch, the "cul," probably a corruption for the Culdee's chapel or cell ; his glebe indicated by the name " Garclearie," the cleric's enclosure.   Priest (sagart), Altaggart, New Luce ; Drumataggart, Minigaff.   Monk appears in Dalmannoch, Inch ;   Ernmannoch, Parton ; Kirminnoch, Kirriemannoch, and many others.   Friar (brathair), Altibraiar, New Luce ; Portbraiar, Whithorn.   Scholars (scolog), Balscalloch, Kirkcolm; Craigenskulk, Minigaff.

Clerics generally (cleireach), Barneycleary, Penninghame , Portacleary, Kirkcolm ; Garthleary, Inch (which old charters prove to have been anciently Garclearie), keeper of the relics. The Jore, Dewar, keeper of the relics, names Glenjorie,[1] near the monastery of Luce.

A nun was caileach, "a veiled person," but indistinguishable from a witch in nomenclature.   Of Portencailzie, Kirkcolm, believed to be named from St Cuthbert's mother, an outraged princess and nun, however, we have a clue from its translation upon the map, " Lady Bay."

Of ranks we find king (righ), Portree, Portpatrick; Kilroy (king's grave), Dunscrore ; King's Laggan, Anwoth, seemingly a translation.   Queen (rioghan, genitive riogna), Kilrhiny (a queen's cell or tomb), Ballantrae.   Chiefs (toisech) in Cairntosh, Girthon, and Barhoise (pronounced bar-hosh) in Kirkcowan and Minigaff.

Earlston, Dalry, has its name from James, Earl of Boswell. Each Mhilidh, the horse knight, of which Agholy is reduced by aspiration, may be represented by the suffix of Cairnholy. Knight (riddere) is half translated in Ridersknowe, Carsphairn,

---

[1] Deoraidh, a pilgrim.   The word assumed a religious limitation, an official keeper of the relics, and became a family name, Dewar , thus we find "lator de Coygerach qui Jore vulgariter dicitur."   These Deorays or Dewars were probably descended from some Irish families whose proper names merged in their officia title —Reeves's *Adamnan*.

and may appear in Glenruther, Penninghame, though that is
probably from riderel.

Of tradesmen, the foremost was the armourer, — gobha
(gow), genitive gobhan (gown), of a very different position from
the modern smith, as the word is translated, the ancient "gow"
indicating a man of high position, often a chieftain, and armourer
by profession. Places named from them are innumerable, as
Calgow, Minigaff; Balgown (numerous), Killiegown, Anwoth.

Ceard was an artificer of any kind. Cerdach was his workshop; whence Cloncaird, Glencaird, Slewcart, Carty, Penninghame; Drumicarty, Old Luce, Polcardoch, Ballantrae; Knock-
kerdoch—the meadow, glen, hill, pools, and knoll of the artificer
and workshop. Caird has now sunk to tinker.

Greusach, of which a most undignified modern rendering is
cobbler, is from Greis, and meant originally an embroiderer
and ornamental worker in leather; whence Glengroosy, Stoneykirk; Balgracie, Leswalt.

Sudaire was a tanner—a term which, always eclipsed,
appears in Bentudor, Rerwick, Drumtooter, Dalry; and Cairn-
tooter, Old Luce.

Saor or saer was a builder or architect, usually translated
carpenter, whence the name M'Intyre (Mhic-an-t'saoir), son
of the carpenter. We have both Balsier and Baltier, Sorbie,
Drumasor, Kirkcowan; Drumatier, Penninghame; Drumashore,
Colvend; Dunsour, Kirkcolm, and Lochintyre, Anwoth—all
townlands, hillsides, and lake of the carpenter.

Ceannighe, a chapman, a merchant in modern Irish, a pedlar,
appears in Barneconachie, Old Luce, Cairnkenny, Inch and New
Luce; Cairnkennagh and Cairnkinna, Minigaff; Cairnhandy,
Stoneykirk—numerously translated, as in Chapman's Craig, Chap-
man's Stone, Chapman's Cleugh, Chapman's Lees, and with a
Norse ring in Copinknowes, Minigaff, as also in Copeland Island,
opposite the entrance of Belfast Lough, and in vulgar form in
Cadger's Loup, Kells.

In forging iron weapons charcoal was required more than
for culinary purposes, in Celtic "gual," coal, it being the coal

of the Galloway Picts; more fully fiodh-ghual, whence Dargoals, Old Luce, now a flow moss, but where once the charcoal-burner pursued his trade in a dry clearing amidst umbrageous oaks. So Auchengool, Rerwick, whilst Gool-hill, Kirkcowan, is a half translation. Dernafuel is daere-na-fiodh-ghual, the oak wood of the charcoal; fiodh-ghual (fewal) having the definite sense of *wood coal.*

Fighting and tuilzying are certainly to be counted among Pictish occupations Tachor (strife), a skirmish, appears in Drumteacher, Old Luce, half translated in Tacher Hill, Sorbie, Tacher Burn, Rerwick; and wholly translated in our frequent Strife Hills, Strife Knolls, Strife Land.

Fuel, genitive fola, blood, in nomenclature refers to its effusion, as Loch-na-folie, Leswalt, Craigfolly, New Luce; Damnaholly, Kirkmaiden, are all allied to a class of names —bloody wheel, bloody rocks, bloody burn, bloody neuk—into which the genitive fola enters and has been translated. Balloch-jargon (dearg, the red), may mean the bloody pass. A quarrel is trodan, whence Drumtroddan, Mochrum; here three large stand-ing stones perpetuate the memory of a tuilzie, the actors in which have been long forgotten. Where quarrel appears in the vernacular,—as Quarrelknowe, Balmaclellan; Quarrelend, Carsphairn,—it is not a translation of trodan, but simply Scottice for stone-quarry.

Piracy and brigandage were recognised, indeed honourable, vocations during the early name-giving period of Galloway history. In Ireland " places where bands of robbers fixed their lair and hid their plunder are to this day known by the word ' Bradach,' "[1] a word figuring largely in maps of the Rhynns. East and west of Corswall Point we have " Braddoch " as " Braidport "; between Salt Pans Bay and Portslogan, the Ordnance map has Broadsea Bay, a name as absolutely unmeaning as unknown to " residenters." As in the case of Kemp's Wark, which the English surveyor changed to Kemp's

---

[1] Bannister translates Braddoch, Cornwall, " a place of treachery," and Dinny-road as the " castle of treason or plotters "—Joyce, ii. 108.

Walk, so the sapper employed on the Ordnance Survey considered Broadsea[1] a happy modernisation of Brodseach, utterly unaware that it conveyed the idea of a pirate's cove. Near the Mull of Galloway, again, we find "Breddoch" and "Breddoch Cave," all dens of sea robbers, exactly where we might expect to find them. Bradach and Braid occur in the hills overlooking the eastern shore of Lochryan; the last in connection with Shinraggie, where the ancient floors of what may be supposed to have been a thieves' village are to be traced within an angle of the Deil's Dyke. The prefix evidently "old," the suffix a corruption of entrenchment or rogue's place ; whilst Braidenoch and Braiden[2] Knowe point to haunts of the same fraternity in Carsphairn. Sladaighe and Sleidear are also synonyms for robbers and robbery, whence Barnsladie, Kirkinner ; Garasladoch, a charter name in Penninghame. Near Sliddery, Sorbie, is mapped "Reifer Park," which seems so obvious an attempt at translation that we are inclined to think that Inchsliddery, and more especially Slidderich in Kirkmaiden, are not slippery places as representing the vernacular, but rather derivatives of the Celtic "sleiderach," the resort of thieves.

Meirleach, genitive Meirlech, was another term for a robber, whence Knockamairly, the thief's knoll, in Stoneykirk. Bradach and meirlech figure side by side in the proverbs. "Ghoid am *meirleach air braideen* e," "The thief stole it from the robber."[3]

Little dishonourable as may have been esteemed the profession of a thief, the "reifer" carried his life in his hand, and if taken redhanded was dealt with by a man of a calling as legitimate—crochaire, the hangman. This official's name appears in

---

[1] Similarly, just above this very "Bradseach," we find "Light of the Maze," another amusing simulation of English forms, the sapper apparently supposing this to be the ruins of a lighthouse, whereas the true name, which he failed to catch, was "Lacht o' Maize," the "lacht" being the monument of some robber chief, and the word pure Celtic.

[2] Braidein, a thievish fellow, fined for braid theft. Braidenoch, a hill of some height near the eastern end of the Deil's Dyke. Brady, as a family, derives from this once honourable calling

[3] Sheriff Nicolson's *Proverbs*, p. 204.

Knockrocher, Dailly, and Auchrocher,[1] Inch—the hangman's knoll and field, and the instrument of his trade, croiche, in Belcrosh, Sorbie; Culcruchie, Penninghame—the townland and back of the gallows. The Gallow-hills, in every part of the province, when used for executions before the Brucian settlement, are probably translations "The Thieves," two standing-stones on the moor of Drennandow, are said to mark the spot where a gang of robbers were "justified" by orders of Randolph, Earl of Murray, in 1330.

As to divisions of land: "tir" is land generally, territory, as Terawly, Awlay, or Amlaph's land.

"Earrann" (ern or iron in names) is a share or portion, district or division, as Ernmenzie, Aarnmacnillie—Menzies's[2] and Macnillie's portion; Irongrey and Ironmacannie, Grey's and M'Kenna's; Ernespie, the Bishop's; Ernfellan, St. Fillan's; Ironlost, the burnt portion; Arnmannoch, the monk's portion; Arndarroch, the oak-wood district. Baille is a town, townland, residence, or holding, a "very vague" term, but very common, entering into 6400 place-names in Ireland as Balgreddan, Kirkcudbright, the townland of the greaddan, corn parched, or rather burned, out of the ear. Balquhirry, of the Corrie; Balgoun, the smith's townland. Leath is a half, as Cockleath, Halkett's Leath, the red, and Halkett's half. Lucarron, again, is the half of a quarter.

Ceathramhaidh (Carhoo) gives us Kerrone, Minigaff, and Carhowe, Twynholm and Mochrum; Kerronrae, Kirkcolm, and Kirminnoch, Inch, the gray and the monk's quarterland, besides many others.[3] It is translated quarter in a place-name in New Luce

The davoch explained is land capable of pasturing 320 cows, or as containing four ploughgates of 104 acres arable

---

[1] In a charter of the Bishop of Galloway to Sir Patrick Agnew the name is written Ardcroquhart

[2] Ardmynnies, Pont, precisely as Highlanders pronounce Menzies.

[3] Carron begins the names of more than 700 townlands in Ireland, and Carhoo of about thirty. Lecarrow, half quarter, gives names to about sixty —Joyce, i 243

each, or as equal to twenty pennylands[1] Whence Ardoch, Dalry (an old holding of the Agnews) And Ardoch in Cunningham which Pont translates "a high plot or daach of land lying upon a knowe." Duchrae (Dochray Pont), the smooth[2] davoch, appears in Buittle, Dalry, Colmonell, and Inch. Dochroyle, Barr, is the royal davoch (rioghail); Culindaich, Girthon, is the back of the davoch (but Culdoch, Twynholm, is the back of the doach, cruive, or weir)[3]

"Mark," "Half Mark," "Two Mark," "Three Mark," as place-names, all have reference to Crown dues. Pen-peighin and Leffin (Leath-peighin) mean penny and halfpenny The markland had no uniform relation to the pennyland, the old Norse measure; but an approximation is suggested by the statement that "five-pennylands were equal to a forty-shilling-land, which equalled a three-markland." The penny was the Norse expression of this measurement, because under Norwegian rule each homestead paid a penny as "scat." The Wigtownshire Pens are not the Cymric equivalent for Ben, but the Celtic peighin, the penny, and the halfpenny, Leathpeighin (Leffin),[4] whence Pennymuir, Borgue, Muir's pennyland; Penverrains, anciently Pennyveran (gwern), penny alderland; Penninghame, nearly Teutonic. Pinminnoch, Portpatrick, in old retours is always Pigmoinoch, the monk's pennyland. Penkiln, Sorbie, is an instance of the proneness for simulating English forms, the n being corruptly added by a person ignorant of Gaelic supposing it had been a kiln, whereas the true meaning is the pennyland of the church (cil.). Dupen, Ballantrae, is probably Dapeighin, the two-pennyland.

[1] Davoch is sometimes translated oxgang, which Mr. Skene shows to be incorrect. "The oxgang contained only thirteen acres, two oxgangs made a husbandland, eight oxgangs a ploughgate."—*Celtic Scotland*, iii 221.

[2] The force of the word is prepared for cultivation. O'Reilly gives under reidh, "level, smooth, prepared." Armstrong has the significant addition, "freed of obstructions"

[3] This name is from dabhach, primarily a tub, secondly a cruive. The Doachs of Tongland are now well-known as a salmon weir

[4] In the western districts we find pennylands entering into topography in the form of Pen or Penny; while the halfpenny becomes Leffin.—*Celtic Scotland*, iii 226

Leffin appears in Leffinolla, Ballantrae; Leffinclery, the clerics'; Garleffin, both in Barr and Dalry, the rough halfpenny-lands, or the enclosed pennylands (garadh); Leffnoll, Inch, anciently Leffindlea, the halfpenny wool - land. Valuation descended to the eighth of a farthing (clietach), which appears in Clutag, Mochrum,[1] which might be freely translated the pendicle.

Third, FAUNA and FLORA.—The most formidable of the animals indigenous in Galloway was the wild boar, torc; whence Glenturk, Wigtown; Mindork, Kirkcowan; Craigork, New Luce; probably Glen Orchy, Mochrum. Muc, wild swine in general, appear unmistakably in Slewmuck, Kirkcolm; Killymuck, Kirkcowan, Knocknamuck, Barr; Lochmuick, Carsphairn, Drummuckloch, Inch, abounding in swine, and very many others. Litters of piglings, bambh or Bonibh, named such places as Auchnabony, Rerwick; Craigbonny, Balmaclellan.

The red deer, hart and hind, were respectively fiadh (the *f* almost always aspirated) and eiled, genitive eilte, whence Drumannee, New Luce and Kirkinner; Craiganie, Dervananie, Larochanea,[2] New Luce; Pulnee, Kirkcudbright, the Gairy of Pulnee, Minigaff—all hills, pools, woods, and sites frequented by the red deer.[3]

Kinhilt, Portpatrick; Craignaltie, Inch; Craignalty, Mini-gaff; Craigneltoch, Kells, are exact equivalents of " Hind Hill "

---

[1] The common computation of land in these countries (Western Highlands) is by pennies, halfpennies, farthings, half-farthings, and clitighs.—*Old Stat. Account* (Harris), x. 366.

[2] So Gortnavargh, Tipperary, and Gortnavea, Galway.—Joyce, 1 477.

[3] The Galloway poet Montgomery, thus describes the fauna which might be seen in a morning's walk from Cumston Castle on the Dee, *circum* 1580

> I saw the hurcheon and the hare
> In hidlings hirpling here and there
>   To make their morning mange:
> The con,[1] the coney, and the cat,
> Whase dainty downs with dew were wat,
> With stiff mustachis strange,
> The hart, the hind, the dae, the rae,
>   The fulmait, and false fox,
> The bearded buck clamb up the brae,
> With birsie[2] boars and brocks
>   *The Cherrie and the Slae*

---

[1] *Con*, squirrel   [2] *Birsie*, bristly.

and "Hind Craig," frequently mapped, as also is Hart Burn, Kirkcudbright, Hartthorn, Terregles; "Deer's Den," mapped five times in Minigaff and Carsphairn; Deerhow, Ballantrae; and Bucksloup, Minigaff.

From the roe-deer, carbag, are Drumnarbuck, New Luce; Craignarbie, Kirkcowan, both translated in "Rae Hill," Parton; "Raeford," in Dalry; and Raeberry, Kirkcudbright, suggestive of earliest Saxon occupation.

The hare was gearrfiadh (geary), literally small deer,[1] whence Craigengeary, Carsphairn, Craigengearoch, Kirkcolm; Knockengearoch, Carsphairn; and in the vernacular, "Harecleugh," Carsphairn, translates the three. We also find "Haremoss," Rerwick, Mawkenhole, Loch Ken.

The badger, which once greatly abounded, was in olden days much esteemed for food (as was also the seal). Cairnbrock, Carsnabrock, Kilbrock, represent a large class of names. In Brockloch, occurring seven times, "loch" is not a lake, but the "lach of abundance," and the word should be translated Badger Warren; as also Brocklan Braes, Kirkmaiden, Brockennie Braes, Parton.

Ronan is a seal, whence Gobaronning, a sea rock in Kirkmaiden, "the seal's snout," and near it Knocknossan,[2] literally the "Whelp's Rock," probably indicating the haunt of the young seal.

Madadh, as said before, is supposed to be used in nomenclature for wolf; Slocamaddy, Kirkmaiden, is exactly translated by "Wolf's Slock," Carsphairn, where we also have Castle Maddie. Claymoddie, Glasserton, is equally matched by "Wolfstane," east of the Nith. We have Strathmaddie, Minigaff, Pulmaddie Gairy, Kells, Poomaddy, in the Forest of Buchan,[3] and Lochmaddy, on the marches of Carrick, all of which

[1] The hare would appear to be the smallest animal to which fiadh (originally any wild animal) was applied, if we may judge from the composition of the name gaarr, fiadh (gerree), short or small fiadh —Joyce, ii 393.

[2] "Ossin, usually a fawn, is also a seal or sea-calf, and so used on the seashores of Cork "—O'Donovan.

[3] Joyce gives mactire as a term for wolf, signifying literally "son of the country," as also, breach. Sir Herbert Maxwell suggests that this last word may

we should be disposed to explain as connected with the wolf, which the sheriffs were enjoined to hunt, and more especially "in the gang and time of year when they have thar quhelps," as late as 1427

The polecat (feocalan, foclan) appears in Cornefech Loch (feoclan ent), Minigaff; Drumvogal, New Luce, translated in Fumart Glen and Fumart Liggat.

The fox, sionnach, looms largely in Galloway nomenclature (although we find *no* mention of the "varmint" in Joyce's names of places in Ireland) Knockshinnoch, Kirkcowan and Kirkpatrick-Irongray; Kirshinnoch, Minigaff, Inchshaennoch, Kirkmaiden, practically translated by "Fox's Rattle" close by; Auchenshinnoch, Dalry; Benshinny, Parton; Craigshinny, Kells; Dalshinnie, Troqueer, are examples.

Another troublesome poacher, the native wild cat, expressed by the same monosyllable in Cymric, Norse, and Anglo-Saxon, gives us Allwhat in Dalry, Carsphairn, and Cumnock—"the rock (aill) of the wild cats,"—"Cat Craigs", Altiwhat, Girthon and Carsphairn; Dalwhat, Kirkoswald; Drumwhat, Mochrum and Minigaff; Macherquhat, Colmonell; Magherawhat, Old Luce, are the "glen, ridge, and fields of the wild cat."

Lagnagatchie, Kirkmaiden, Pulhatchie, New Luce, are "hollows and holes abounding in wild cats." Craighet, New Luce, Dalhet, Kirkcowan, are the "rock and field of the wildcat" We also have in the vernacular "Wild Cat Knowe," Kells, "Wild Cat Wood," Rerwick; "Wild Cat Craigs," Southwick; and the "Cat Craigs" of Auchencloy, Girthon.

The otter, doran, literally "the water-beast," names Aldouran, Leswalt; Puldouran, Glasserton, Bardouran, Stair

There is a remarkable cavern on the Galdenoch shore known as "The Otters' Cave," which, arched lightly over with rock, running far under the cliff, is divided from the ending of the den by a deep pool, almost a lakelet. To this otters resort, and in former times were sometimes trapped by gamekeepers, their fur

be preserved in some of our numerous names ending in brake or breck.—*Galloway Topography*, 32.

being valuable. The cliff above it is "Drumahowan," a name which local knowledge confirms as truly descriptive (druim-an-uamhaim, the ridge of the cave).[1]

Of Luchog (dim., a mouse), we find an example in Glen-luchoch, Penninghame.

Of birds, we have the eagle, iolaire, presented in Pictish form in Petillery,[2] Carsphairn; also Benyellary, in the same parish, reproduced exactly in the vernacular as "Earnscraig," New Abbey.

A hawk is seabhach; its force in names shouk or habback, when aspirated, and eclipsed touk   The Cymric is gwalc (whence Gwallauc, "the hawk of battle") and hebog The four examples are Slewsack, Kirkcolm, Pulsack, Balmaghie: Balshaig and Garnshog, Mochrum—the hill, pool, townland, and cairn of the hawks.   Eclipsed we have Bartyke, Kirkcowan; and aspirated or affecting the Cymric, Dalhabboch, Inch; Poulhabbock, Stoneykirk, Barnhabbock (obsolete) Pont;[3] whilst "Hawk Hill," "Hawk's Hole," "Gledknowes," "Gledcraig," "Gledebog," "Gledsmuir," and many others, are reproductions in the vernacular.

To kill a hawk or destroy its nest in feudal times was as great a social crime, more serious for the perpetrator, than shooting a fox would now be thought to be in Leicestershire

For aristocratic hawkers the favourite quarry was the heron, "corr" (in dictionaries translated a heron, crane, or stork).   Knockencurr, Kirkinner; Craigencorr, Leswalt, New Luce, Dailly, and Dalry; Knockcorr, Kirkcudbright; and Knockcore, Stoneykirk, all mean the heron's rock

Bunnan, the bittern, does not show in Celtic form, except

[1] Uaimh, gen. uamhain, so Muill'enn-ia-huamhain Mullinahome, Tipperary, Athhowen, Cork, mill of the cave, Knocknahooan, Clare, cave hill —Joyce i. 440.

[2] Pet occurs frequently in the Pictish nomenclature of the east of Scotland, and is understood to have meant a portion or place, as Pitlochrie, Pitancleiroch, a portion of the clerics.

[3] Habbock has been supposed by dabblers in nomenclature to be kebbock, the Lowland Scotch for a large cheese, but seems certainly Celtic. So tyke is Galloway vernacular for a dog or cur, but Irish examples show that it is rather tseabhaic, as is Craigatuke, Tyrone, the hawk's crag —Joyce, i 485

perhaps in Barbunny, Kirkcowan, though often translated in
its old Scotch name *butter*, as Butterburn, Minigaff, Butter-
cairn, Penninghame ; Butterhole, Dalry, Kirgunzeon, Buittle,
and Terregles—all marshy spots resorted to by the bittern,
utterly unsuitable for the dairy or manufacture of butter.
To both bittern and heron was extended the especial
protection of the law. So late as 1600, among the Acts of
James VI., Parliament "discharges any person whatsoever,
within this realm, in any ways to sell or buy skeldraikis,
herroun, butter, or ony sic kynd of fowllis, commonly usit to be
chasit with hawkes."

The raven (fiach and fitheach) appears in Craigenveoch,[1]
Old Luce ; Benaveoch, Kirkmaiden , Dinveoch, Kells ; Minny-
wick, Minigaff (a corruption of Minnyveoch). We have also
" Ravencrags," Kirkpatrick-Durham ; " Ravenshall," Kirkmabreck ; " Ra'ennest Haugh," Minigaff , " Ravenstone," Glasserton
(though the raven (rafn) here was probably a Viking name)

Coileach and ceare, genitive circe, in the dictionaries cock and
hen, in our topography represent black-game and moorfowl.
Thus Barnecullach, Kirkcowan; Cornhulloch, Mochrum ;
Rasnagulloch, Colmonell ; Clashgulloch, Barr, represent the
ridge, hill, thicket, and hollow of the grouse or blackcocks ;
and Barnkirk, Penninghame, and elsewhere, three times ;
Barnkirky, Girthon , Millwhirk, Inch ; Dunkirk, Kells ; Loch-
kirky, Colmonell, are the hills, fort, and lake of the moorhens,
the latter matched by " Grayhen Bay," Stoneykirk.

Partridge and quail seem to have been included under the
general term of birds, enn, whence Dunanain, Kirkmaiden ;
Slewnain, Leswalt ; Barnean, Penninghame ; Knockneen, Kirkcolm.[2]

Creabhar (crower) is a woodcock, and naosg a snipe, whence
Knockcaars, with the half translation, " Crowarstone," adjacent,
as well as " Crowarhill," and the full one of " Cock Hill" in

---

[1] Craigenveoch was the war-cry of the Glengarry Macdonalds

[2] Nighean, a girl, pronounced nyen, was applied to the " little folk," i e.
fairies. There are here a group of three remarkable knolls, which were probably
called Knocknain, as haunts of the girls, i.e fairies

Kirkmaiden, where, as of old, woodcock still abound. Pulnasky, Mochrum; Lochnisky, Colmonell, Knochenausk, Stoneykirk, Lagganausk, Kirkmaiden; Knochnaskrie, Portpatrick, all point to spots abounding in snipe, "naosg." [1]

Lacha, genitive lachan, was a duck, whence Craiglauchie, Kirkmaiden; Craiglochan, Inch; Portlochan, Kirkinner; Benlochan, on the sea cliffs of Kirkmaiden, seem rather to mean bays and cliffs of ducks than of the lakelets, which would be colourless [2]

Gadh was the goose. In composition the word is indistinguishable from gaoth, wind; but Ilan-na-guy, Kirkcolm, Lochanghie, Girthon, Craugie, Penninghame; Glenghie, Dailly, Derhagie, Old Luce,[3] seem certainly to denote wild geese (rather than gulls), which notoriously abounded on Galloway shores, as Goose Isles, Crossmichael, in the vernacular. Gayfield, Leswalt, and elsewhere, means "goose field," but the birds were of the domestic sort

Eala is the wild swan, a frequent winter visitor to Galloway, whence Craignell, Minigaff; Craiganelly, Crossmichael and Balmaghie; Craignallie, Kirkcolm.

Allanfaichie, Kirkmaiden, is the rock of the puffins (fachach), nearly equivalent to "Gull Craig," Leswalt.

Gairg is the cormorant, and Gargrie (gairgreach), abounding in cormorants, is the appropriate name of the mossy meadow adjoining the Castle Loch of Mochrum, where to this day "scarts" breed in thousands. The throne of Gargrie is an elevation overlooking the spot. We have "Scart Island" in Mochrum Loch itself, "Scart Craig" is frequent on the sea coast; and we have native authority for saying that "Dooker's

[1] Naosg, naosga, a snipe "The word is generally easy to recognise in names, as Tullynesky, Cork, the little hill of the snipes "—Joyce, ii. 288

[2] Cadhan (coin) is a barnacle goose, the word used much in Ireland; as Gort-na-goyne, Galway, the field of the barnacle goose So Carrickeune, Kirkmaiden, may very probably be the rock of the barnacles, although phonetically it may be equally rendered of the dog.

[3] This agrees with Irish examples. Monagay, Limerick, Morn-a-ghedh, bog of the goose; and Inis-na-gedh, Fermanagh, is the counterpart of Ilan-na-guy goose island —Joyce, i 488

Byng," Colvend, denotes the cormorant and not the northern diver.[1]

Feannog is the hoodie crow, and appears in Barnvannoch, Ballantrae, Barwhinnoch, Glasserton ; Knockenfinnoch, Ballantrae ; Ringvinaghan, Stoneykirk ; Slannievannach, Minigaff—all ridges, points, and hills of carrion crows.

We have the cuckoo (cuach) in Altigowkie, New Luce ; Barnegowk, Kirkcowan ; translated "Gowk Hill" in Whithorn and Leswalt.

Traona, or more correctly tradhnach, the corncrake, appears in Clontrainnaight, Mochrum (now contracted to Clone), and Drummatrane, Kirkcowan , and snag, the woodpecker, is unmistakable in Darssnag, Mochrum.

The thrush, smeorach, appears in Slewsmirroch, Stoneykirk. "Cha dean aon *smeorach* sambhradh," as Sheriff Nicolson tells us, was proverbial : "One mavis makes not summer." The song-thrush in Scotland did duty for the nightingale.[2]   Once only do we find the wren, dicalan, in Drumadryland,[3] Inch, the

---

[1] Scarts, a name for the black cormorant. Its common name is Dooker, also Mochrum Lairds, because they have been, as it were, proprietors there for an unknown length of time. They are also called "Elders o' Cowend," from their black, grave, and greedy appearance, being common on Colvend shores. —M'Taggart, *Gal Encyclopædia.*

Byng, a heap or lump

[2] Montgomery describes himself as walking near the old Bridge of Tungland—

> About a bank with balmy bews,
> Where nightingales their notes renews,
> With gallant gowdspinks gay.

And adds—

> To hear her sae near her,
> I doubted if I dreamed.

The idea in Scotland that a song full, clear, and of great variety, heard after dark, as it constantly was in the very early spring, must be that of the nightingale. It was, however, certainly that of a throstle or mavis, as there is no reason, as in the case of red-deer, black-game, or snipe, that the nightingale should have changed its habits   As natural history became a science, it was accepted by the Scots that they had no nightingales , but this seems to have been a sore subject.   A Galloway laird visiting English friends was awakened in the middle of the night to hear a nightingale sing.   Cross at being disturbed, and offended at the air of superiority his hosts seemed to be assuming, when pressed by a lady to say if the song was not exquisite, he bluntly exclaimed, "Ma'am, I wadna gie the wheeple o' a Galloway whaup for a' the English nightingales that ever sang."

[3] The dryland might, and may, mean the three enclosures (lann), or three churches.

ridge of wrens; a nest (nead) in Knockaneed, Stoneykirk, and Knocknidi, Cumnock; and eggs (ubh) in Dirnow, Kirkcowan.

Of fish, a salmon was "bradan," whence Loch Bradan, Straiton, Lanebreddan, Minigaff; and it is probable that Drumbreddan, Stoneykirk, is the salmon-shaped ridge, or salmon may have been caught on the shore adjacent, just as Knockscadan, Stoneykirk, is the *hill* of the herring. Breac stands for trout, to be so translated with discretion, as the word means simply speckled. Lochinbreck, Balmaghie; Lochbrack, Balmaclellan; Altibreck, Kells, are the trout lake and trout stream; Lochbreckbowie, Straiton, being the lake of the yellow trout [1]

Culscaddan, Lochanscaddan, Glasserton; Knockscaddan, Stoneykirk, are respectively the corner, bay, and knoll of the herrings (scadan), the latter overlooking a place of their resort

A fish-weir is coradh, and towards the mouth of the Cree we find twice on opposite shores (Cassencarie-cos-an-coradh), foot of the weir—a familiar name (we believe) near the confluence of the Luce and Piltanton, and a weir seems to have for this purpose been used where the tide enters the Soleburn, Lochryan, the present lands of Salchrie being written in all old charters Salachquharry, the dirty or salt-water weir.

Giol is the leech, and one or two lakelets bearing this name— as Loch Gill, Penninghame, and "Gill's Loch," Kells—are not to be rendered "Lochs of the Brightness," as they might be in Ireland,[2] but "Lakes of the Leeches." Indeed "gill" has been adopted into the Galloway vernacular, *gill-gathering* being long a recognised occupation for old women of a certain class, who, armed with a long stick cut for the purpose, called the "gill-rung," and a bottle suspended by a string from their waists, waded into such lochlets courting the attack of the said leeches, which no sooner fixed themselves upon their legs than they were transferred to the bottle and thence to the apothecary's shop.[3]

---

[1] We have many small lakes called Lough Nabrackboy, the lake of the yellow trouts   What these are I cannot venture to conjecture

[2] Joyce, ii. 298.

[3] Music was supposed to allure them   M'Taggart writes: "These old women

The ant, seangan, plays a prominent part in topography, it is difficult to say why. Dalshangan, Carsphairn, Minigaff, and New Luce ; Barnshangan, Stoneykirk, and Barnshannon, New Luce (which, as written, seems to represent sean dun, old fort), is mapped by Pont Barnshangan, and consequently, along with others named, is the gap, summit, and field of the ants.[1]

The reliability as well as the extreme antiquity of many of our place-names is especially illustrated by those which, whilst suggestive of umbrageous forests, are now attached to our deepest and dreariest mosses. Their correctness can be easily tested by the spade. The bleak tract from Killiemore to Darvaird, impassable in a bee-line from the frequent "flow," is studded with names recalling oaks and golden birches, with copses of hazel and holly interspersed. And these names not only rightly indicate the position of woods, but retain the exact description of the species of trees which grew on them Their names are so numerous, and their correctness so well authenticated, that we shall only give one or two specimens of each.

Coill and coillidh, plural coile (Cymric coed), are wood and woodland, represented by kil and killy,[2] whence Killiemore, Penninghame, great wood; Glenwhilly, New Luce and elsewhere, wood of the glen ; the Celtic plural in Cultiemore, Minigaff ; and with the English plural frequently in Cults, notably as Inch and wade about with their coats kilted high , when they come to a deep hole they plunge the gill-rung into it and start the leeches, singing a strange song at the same time " We give a few lines as a specimen

> My under-cotie's hie now,
> Gif ony bodies see now ,
> The water's boon my knee now,
> Aye faith, aboon o' thee now ,
> Among my yellow spawlies,
> There ye come and crawlies ,
> Now thou sticks, my gilly,
> Scok thy filly, filly
> Bonnie's the moss lily,
> But bonnier far my gilly "
>
> *Gallovidian Encyclopædia*, 228.

[1] Seangan, the Irish word for pismire or ant, is a diminutive from seang, slender, and means a slender little fellow —Joyce, ii 284.

[2] I have conjectured that about a fifth of the kils that begin names are woods. Kilmore, Cork, is great wood, but the vast majority of Kilmores are great church. —Joyce, i. 491.

Killy is always wood

Sorbie; Kelton, Kells, being the diminutive, a little wood. Doire is a grove, strictly of oaks, hence the frequent Derry, as in Kirkcowan, Old Luce, Mochrum, Penninghame, Kelton. The Cymric coed seems to appear in Cuttiemore, Minigaff, Cutfad, Kirkpatrick-Durham; Cotreoch, (Rioco) and Cutcloy, Whithorn, and we have an example of the Norse holt in Chapelshot, Buittle.

Ras was brushwood, smaller bushes, briars and roses, as Rasnygulloch, Colmonell; Drumrash, Parton; Glenrazie, Penninghame, Rashnoch, Mochrum—"the brake of the moorfowl," the "ridge," and "glen," and "the place abounding in bramble," and wild rose.

A small tuft or copse was gas, as Gass in New Luce and Kirkinner

Ceap was a tree-stump, frequent objects when wanton waste of woodland was the order of the day. Thence Dalnagap, Inch, Glengap, Barr and Twynham; Pulgap, Minigaff; Kipple, Urr—the field, glen, pool, and place of stumps; and Balloch o'Kip, Kirkcolm, the road through the tree-stumps."

A single tree was "crann," "craobh," and "bile," whence Slewcreen, Kirkmaiden; Crancree, Inch—"the mill of the tree," and the "march tree"; and Lochchranochy, Mochrum, the tree trunks at its bottom; Castlecraivie, Rerwick; Corncraivie, Stoneykirk; Knockravie, Kirkcowan. Bile gives us Knockville, Penninghame; Billyshill, Portpatrick, as a half translation.

Tom, genitive tuim, was a bush, and tomach, adjective, bushy; whence Knocktim, Kirkcolm, Milltim, New Luce—the knoll and hill of the bush; Knocktammoch, Stoneykirk, Lochnatammoch, Penninghame—the bushy knoll and loch.

Dreas means briar and bramble, adjective dresach, whence Glendrissoch, Ballantrae.[1]

---

[1] Dumfries is usually explained by dun phreas, the fort of the shrubs, equivalent to the English Shrewsbury, (scrobbea byric). Mr. Skene, however, usually a safe guide to follow, considers the suffix to be derived from the Frisians (the Frisia or Frissonco), whence also the term "Frisian shore," or the south of the Firth of Forth.[1] The spellings are very various: Dounfres, Cottonian MSS.,

[1] *Celtic Scotland*, i 231

Of generic names, dair, genitive darroch, Cymric dar, is oak; whence names innumerable, as Kildarroch, the chapel of the oaks, Dirnow (n'ubh), "oak wood of the eggs," Kirkcowan; Darachans, Minigaff, "abounding in oaks", Pinderry, Ballantrae, the pennyland of the oak wood

Uinnseann and Uinnseog, is ash; whence Inshanks in Kirkmaiden and Kirkcowan; Drumnaminshog, Minigaff; Knockninshock, Kirkmabreck.

Leamhan, longhill, and sleamhan, are elms; whence Auchlewan, Barr; Barluell, Old Luce; Ringielawn, Mochrum; Craigslonn, New Luce—the height, field, and rock of the elm; and Lowran, Kells, "abounding in elms."

The birch was beith, whence the numerous "Beochs"; Dalbeattie, Knockibay, New Luce; and Cassanvey, Balmaclellan, "the pathway through the birches."

The alder was fearn, Cymric gwern. Examples are numerous, as Balfern, Kirkinner; Drumfarnachan, Kirkcolm, "ridge abounding in alders" The parish of Carsphairn, is the alder cairn; and Glashverains, on the Carrick marches, "the hollow of the alders," has a Cymric ring.

Willow, seileach, confuses in nomenclature with salach, dirty; Balsalloch may either be the "miry townland," or "of the osiers" We can point to the willow with some confidence in Glenselley and Barnsallie, Old Luce, and Mountsallie, Kirkmaiden, is probably not Sally's hill, but of the willows, a half translation.

The yew tree, once much prized and commoner than now, "iubhar" (yure), appears in Glenour, Ballantrae, Glenowrie, Minigaff; Palnure, Kirkmabreck Uroch; Balmaghie, means "abounding in yews", and Ballochanure, Kirkmabreck, the "pass of the yew tree"

The holly is coinleann, whence Collin, Rerwick, Collindoch, Girthon and Kirkmabreck, and Cullindeugh, New Abbey—as

---

1292, Dunfreze, Harding; Dunfres, 1305; Drumfreiss, 1395, Charter of Robert III, Drumfrees, Pont, Dunfreys, Camden. Preas is synonymous, indeed only another form of dreas.

wrtten, all the "davoch of the hollies," unless indeed the *d* is intrusive, in which case the "nach" is of abundance, and the name is synonymous with Cullenoch, Balmaghie, "a place abounding in hollies "[1]

The hazel is coll (its force when aspirated quill), a hazel copse calduinn, whence Barwhill, frequent; Auchenquill, Rerwick, Knockenquill, Kirkmaiden, refer to bushes, and Caldons, English plural added, in Stoneykirk and Minigaff, represent larger copses. Though we can hardly doubt that the Scotch fir abounded, strange to say we can trace it but once in a Pictish name, viz Lochgoosy (guisach), Kells.

The rowan tree was carthainn (kearan), whence Barwhirren, Penninghame; Drumconran, Kirgunzeon, and Cooranlane, Minigaff, which seems translated in "Rowantree Burn," Barr.

The white-thorn was sceach, as Scaith, Penninghame; Skeock, Kirkpatrick-Durham, Skeog, Whithorn, with Drum-skeochs, and Knocksceochs innumerable.

The blackthorn was draighean, Cymric draen; whence Knock-dronnan, Parton; Cardryne, Kirkmaiden; Auchendrane, the knoll, fort, and field of the blackthorn; Drannigower, New Luce, the goats' thorn, Lanedriggane, Leswalt, the thorny meadow; and Dronnan, Penninghame; and Drangans numerous; Drungan, Kelton; and Drongan—all meaning brakes of blackthorn. The sloe (airne) is even distinguished from the blackthorn: Clachanarnie, Mochrum; Barnarnie, Kirkcowan—the stone and summit of the sloe-bush.

Muine (difficult to distinguish from moin, a peat-moss, in composition) means a brake or thicket a compound leath-mhuine, pronounced leewinny, is often used in Ireland, glossed as gray brake Drumlawhinnie, Minigaff, seems to be the ridge of the gray brake[2] Dalmoney, Urr, may either be the field of the thicket or the peat-moss.

Conadh is firewood (force, conny; when aspirated, honey).[3]

[1] Calenick, Cornwall, a place of hollies.—Bannister
[2] Joyce, 1. 496
[3] The Irish examples are severally, Killconny, Westmeath, Kilconny, Cavan; and Drumhoney, Fermanagh.—Joyce, 11. 331.

Alwhenny, Carsphairn; Barwhanny, Kirkinner, Drumhoney, Old Luce, seem to be the glen, hill, and ridge of the firewood.

Heather is fraoch, reproduced simple in Freugh. The *f* often disappears by aspiration, so that Knockenree, Kirkmaiden; Auchenree, Portpatrick, by Irish analogy when naming small moors, should rather be translated "heathery hills" or "places," than of "the king's."

The whortleberry, Scottice blaeberry, was fraochan, whence Stronfreggan, Dalry, and Barfreggan, Kelton, "the point of the blaeberries."

Samhadh, having the force of sow, appears in Pulsow, Carsphairn; Arnsow, Kirkmichael; Auchensough, Sanquhar; and Sowiehill, Minigaff, exactly corresponding to Sooey, Sligo, explained by Joyce as sorrel-bearing land. Smirle, Glasserton, and Smeurach, Ballantrae, are spots abounding in blackberries (smeur, Scottice blackbides), and Smyrton, Ballantrae (the suffix "ton" dim. of abundance).

Creamh is wild garlic, and, combined with coill, forms a compound well known in Ireland. Creamhchoill (cramuhill), wild garlic wood.[1] The word, almost identical, appears in Tongueland—Cramuhill. We may suspect Crow Hill, Parton and Old Luce, both rather represent hillsides abounding in wild garlic than hills of either rook or crow.

Four Celtic words are used for ships and boats in our place-names—long, bad, corrach, and cot.

Long indicates shipping generally. Port Long, Kirkcolm, Portlung, Inch—ship port. Cumlongan, Holywood—the ship's nook. Killylung, Holywood, and Derlongan, Old Luce—the wood of the ships, that is, whence the oaks of which they were formed were taken.

Bad, is a boat. We have very early particulars as to Galloway boat-building. Writing of Whithorn, Ailred says: "It is the custom in that neighbourhood to frame of twigs a certain vessel in the form of a cup, of such a size that it can contain three men sitting close together. By stretching an ox-hide

[1] In Sligo the name becomes "Crawhill."—Joyce, ii 328

over it, they render it not only buoyant, but impervious to water." It was the middle of the twelfth century that he was there himself, and referring to the days of Ninian, with which he is dealing, he adds "Probably at that time vessels of immense size were so built" Possible enough, for, however constructed, regular passages were made, and generally safely, from Bangor and Rosnat to Mantes

Moreover, sails as well as oars were in general use ; as, in proceeding to describe a miracle worked by Ninian's staff, he tells us that this " staff, acting for sail, caught the wind, acting as helm, directed the vessel"; and that, as it unexpectedly entered a distant port, the people gazed amazed at the little vessel moving swiftly and directly thence, neither propelled by sail nor moved by oars,[1] both which methods of propulsion they had been accustomed to see.

Portavaddie (bhada), at both Kirkmaiden and Portpatrick, are boat ports. Craigavad, opposite entrance to Belfast Loch, is translated by Boat-rock, Whithorn. The word appears also in Portvad, Ballantrae.

Ailred's description of the little vessel exactly coincides with that usually given of the Welsh coracle.

Corrach, Cymric cwrwyg, in the construction of the word implies a hide, as we have the name in Glencurroch, Kirkcolm.

Cot, or coit, a boat hollowed out of a tree-stem,[2] is more generally used in our nomenclature , having coiteen for a diminutive A few such boats, made from monarchs of the forest, were long and large ; the majority, little canoes, of which the shells are yet often to be found deep in the mud of river bottoms.

Cottach, Troqueer, means a place where such little boats were made or lay , so is Cattar, Kirkmaiden

[1] Ailred's *Life of Ninian*, ch x.
[2] "A boat formed out of a single oak wrought hollow is called in Irish coiti" (Harris). The correct word is cot, of which coite is the genitive , it is still in constant use, whence Ath-na-coite, Annacotty, Limerick.
Carrickcottia indicates that the cot used to be moored to the carrock or rock a diminutive the people pronounce Loch Coiteain—the lake of the little cot Lough Cullein, Tipperary, shows a different diminutive —Joyce, i 225

Cutbraid, Portpatrick, is the gulley of the little boat

Cutcloy, Whithorn, Cothg, Portpatrick; and Cotvennane [1] —the stone or little peak to which the boats were moored.

When the meaning of individual names has been entirely lost by the residents, the pronunciation gradually becomes confused, and the spelling hopelessly corrupt. It then becomes difficult to ascertain the true roots, as syllables phonetically alike represent very different words, and, as a further complication, the same word is sometimes used in very different senses.

Thus riabhach, brindled or gray; reidh, smooth, and reith, a ram, have on Saxon lips alike the force of ray Whilst breac, brindled or spotted, generally used adjectively, sometimes as certainly represents a trout (the spotted fish), and also speckled land, in a substantive sense, as Brochdoo Leswalt, of which the unusual neighbouring name, Blackspots Hill, is an evident translation

In such cases much assistance may, as in the case first mentioned, be derived from old maps, on which translations, even if seemingly unintended, suggest the probability of the name having the sense thus shown

Drumrae, which might be "the gray ridge," or "the smooth" one, yet, from the frequent recurrence of "Ram's Hill," was as probably connected with the "ram."

Again, whilst Benbrake is certainly "the spotted peak," that is, heath interspersed with mountain grasses, Lochbrack and Lochenbreck should be translated "lake of the trout."

Madadh is a dog, but in topography is generally applied to the "wolf" or "wild dog"; and we feel some confidence in rendering Slocamaddy on the Kirkcolm shore "the wolf's pit," or "gully," from finding "the wolf's slock" a place-name in Minigaff.

Auchness, which at first sight has a Norse ring, is pure

[1] The Ordnance Survey alters the local *o* or *u*, coat or cut, to *cat*, which, though immaterial, is radically wrong. The Catevennan as mapped is from cot or coatvennan, not as in the Christian name Kate.

Celtic, "each inis"; and we are confirmed in the correctness of the assumption by the frequent recurrence of Horse Isles upon our maps.

We are disposed to believe that Allanfedder, Kells, refers rather to a musician than to Peter, or to the "whistling plover," by the closeness of the translation in "Fiddler's Bog" close by.

To give a few more examples of translations intentionally or unintentionally mapped down:

Craigengeaviach, Kirkcolm	Hare Cleuch, Carsphairn
Mulnigarroch, New Luce.	Sheep Hill, Kirkinner.
Knockmuck (frequent).	Hoghill (as common).
Drumancon, Penninghame	Lamb Hill, Inch.
Benyellary, Minigaff.	Earn's Craig, New Abbey
Cornefeckloch (feocalach), Minigaff	Fumart Glen, Kells
Craigenveoch, Old Luce	Corbie Crags, Inch
Kinhilt, Portpatrick.	Hind Hill, Leswalt.
Knockmult, Reiwick	Wether Hill, Dalry.
Barnsoul, Kirkpatrick-Irongray	High Barns, Inch
Knockalanny (lannith), Kirkcowan.	Barn Hill
Boothnaw, Dalry.	Ford House, Penninghame.
Craigencroy, Stoneykirk	Sheil Hill (frequent)
Drumanazy, Portpatrick	Shepherd's Hill, Leswalt.
Auchenhay, Borgue, etc.	Kiln Park (Scottice, field), Kirkcolm.
Farrenlure, Inch.	Libberland, Kirkcowan
Craignargit, Mochrum.	Silver Hill, Kirkcudbright
Craigfolly, New Luce.	Bloody Brae, Kirkcolm
Knockormal, Colmonell.	Blue Hill, Rerwick
Portancorkrie, Kirkmaiden	Redstone Cove, Leswalt.
Balgracie, Leswalt.	Souter's Croft, Kirkmabreck
Knockwhasen, Portpatrick.	Path Brae, Kirkcolm.
Auchenquil, Rerwick	Hazelfield (frequent).
Drumfleuch, New Luce	Rig of the Jarkness,[1] Minigaff.
Curghie, Kirkmaiden.	Wondy Hill, Wigtown.
Belsavery, Inch.	Somerton, New Luce
Allwhat (three times), Carsphairn, Dalry, Cumnock	Wild Cat Craigs.
Knockeen, Kirkcolm	Bonnyknowes (adjectives).

In others the same idea runs in the two tongues thus: Ochley (each liath), the gray horse, Kirkcolm, is matched by "Yellow Horse," a rock on the same shore. Cunnoch, a churn or barrel, Kirkcolm; Beef Barrel, on the same shore. Bilnavoe,

[1] Jarkness, Galloway vernacular, same as Jarness, Lowland Scotch, "any place so wet as to resemble a marsh"

Kirkmaiden; Cow's Snout, Colvend. Gobawhilkin (choilchean), Kirkmaiden; Cock's Comb, an adjacent rock. And Tondoo, also on the Irish Channel, seems freely translated by "Dutchman's stern."

Fourth, Under MISCELLANEOUS we shall treat of roots generally, commencing with adjectives, endeavouring to throw these as much in apposition as possible.

Big—mor; as Kenmure, Barmore, all frequent.

Little—beg, Cymric bychan, whence Barbeg, Portpatrick, "the little hilltop"; and we suspect Barbuchany, Penninghame, to be synonymous with the Cymric bychanig. The adjective takes a funny form in Cash Bay, Kirkmaiden, little fissure, cos being a cave or crevice as well as a foot.

Long—fad, as Drumfad, Minigaff and Terregles.

Short—gearr; as Gairloch, Kells, Garlakin (leacan), "the short hill" and hillside. It is often impossible to distinguish it from garbh, rough.

Broad—leathan, Cymric llydan, whence Auchleand, Wigtown, "the broad field"; and we seem to have pure Cymric in Cumloden, Minigaff, Cwmlwydan, "the broad hollow between hills."

Narrow—caol; so Portkale, Portpatrick; Killiness (caolinnes), "narrow isle or pasture," Kirkmaiden.

High—ard, Cymric uchel; whence Ardoch, Dalry, "the high davoch"; Ardrie and Airdrie, frequent "high places" or "sheilings", and Ochiltree, Penninghame, "the high dwelling."

Low—iosal; Falwhistle, Kirkinner; Craigeazle, Inch; Corvisel, Peninghame, "the low dyke, rock, and corrie."

Upper—uachdar; as Corrochtrie, Kirkmaiden; Barnywater, Girthon, "the upper hill and quarter."

Bare—maol; whence the Mull (of Galloway) in the sense of bald. Lom (sheared), as in Kenlum, Anwoth. Nochd (naked), in Auchnaught, Kirkmaiden; and the ancient Ros-nat (Rosnaught), Whithorn

Bushy — creabhach, as Corncravie, "the bushy hill," Stoneykirk; tomach, as Knockantomachie, "the bushy knoll,"

Kirkmaiden; and rasanach, "abounding in briars and roses," as Rashnoch, Mochrum.

Crooked—crom; as Cromoch, Kirkmaiden.

Round—cruin; as Slewcroan, Leswalt, "round hill"; Mill-croon, Ballantrae.

Rough—garbh; as Garvallock, Inch, "rough road"; Gar-rarie, Kells and Mochrum, "a rough place"; Garleffin, Barr, "rough halfpenny land."

Also carrach; as Cairngarroch, Leswalt, and Drumcarrick, Inch, "the rough cairn and ridge."

Smooth—reidh; as Ballochrae, Kirkcowan, "the smooth pass."

Mid—meadhan; as Balminnoch, Kirkcowan, "mid town-land."

Between—eadar; as Adderhall, Penninghame; Clonidder, Penninghame, "the centre fence" (fhal) and "meadow."

Across—tarsuinn; as Craigentarsie, New Luce; Kilterson, Kirkcowan, "the rock and wood lying athwart."

Dirty—salach; as Barsalloch, Penninghame and Wigtown.

Beautiful — caoin; as Knockeen, Alticane, Colmonell, "bonny braes" and "glen."

Cold—fuar; as Milfore, Minigaff; and Cairnfore, translated by "cold-craig," Balmaclellan.

Sunny—grianach; as Milgrane, Penninghame.

Warm—teth (pr. tya); Pultayan, Kirkcowan.

Windy (see gaoth afterwards)—saideach; Sheddoch (sched-ack Pont), Whithorn, "a stormy place."

Sloping—claen; as Clenarie or Clendry, Inch, Old Luce, and Kirkcolm; Clennoch, Carsphairn and Inch—all "sloping places." And staonach; as Stenoch, Whithorn, and Knock-sting.

Wet—fluish; as Drumfluich, and Fleuchlarg, Penning-hame—"wet ridge" and "hillside."

Rocky—sceileach (from sceilig, a sea rock), as Dunskirloch, Kirkcolm.

Sandy—gaineach; as Gainoch, Genoch (very common)

Mullachgany, Minigaff; Bargany, Girvan; and Ringuinea, Stoneykirk, equal to sandhead.

Spotted—Breac, as Benbrack, Carsphairn; Kells, Dalry, Benbrake (the highest hill in Wigtonshire), Kirkcowan; Larbrax, Leswalt; Learg-breac, the spotted hillside.

Of colours in an adjective sense we have fin, Cymric gwyn; whence Finloch, Stoneykirk; Fintloch, Kells—not "white lakes," but "white land"; Fyntalloch, Penninghame, "white knoll"; Finnart, white headland.

There is a derivative of fin, Ceinnfhionn (pr cannon), literally "white head," but applied to any objects speckled with white spots. Whence Slewkennan, Kirkcolm; Knockcannon, Balmaghie—both meaning "the speckled hill." [1]

Geal, also white; whence Ringheal, Mochrum, "the white point"; Port Gill, Kirkmaiden, suggestive of white sand in the little creek; Loch Gill, if clear (but also giol, *leech* lake), Ban, C. can; whence Inchbane, Kirkcolm, "white pasture"; Torbain, Parton and Minigaff, "white knolls"; Markbain, Kirkcowan, "white mark" or "horse" [2]

It is probable that the Cymric "can" names the river Ken, the "White," in opposition to Dee, the "Black." The namegivers did not consider the Ken to be the head water (ceann), because when the combined streams issue from Loch Ken, the name for the river formed by both is Dee. Dee, moreover, is more in Cymric form than Gaelic; and, as if especially to point to the distinction in colour, the Dee above Loch Ken is mapped the "*Black* water of Dee."

Black—dubh. C. du. pr. dee; as Faldoo, Kirkmaiden; Inchdow, Kirkcolm, "black enclosure or meadow"; Craigdhu,

---

[1] The word Ceinnfhion is now applied to a cow with a white spot on the middle of her forehead. It is, however, extended to designate anything speckled with white spots, as Lettercannon, Kerry, "speckled hillside"; Clooncannon, Galway, "speckled meadow"—Joyce, ii 268

[2] Mark, C march, is in all Gaelic dictionaries glossed "a horse," though in Galloway names it usually signifies a march or a markland. We find, however, a "Markbain" and a "Markdow" in New Luce, and as several translated names are "white" or "yellow horse," it seems very probable that there were hills which were so fancifully called.

Glasserton, "black rock", and on the river Dee, Ballochadee, Kirkcowan, is "the black pass." Black topographically denotes peaty soil, in opposition to sandy, loamy, or hard till.

Brown—doun, as Knockdown, five times; Milldown, four; Slewdown, Leswalt, all "brown hills."

Gray — riabhach, brindled (force ray); as Monreith (murrith), "gray tower"; Culreoch, Inch, "gray corner"; Kirrereoch, Minigaff, "gray corrie", Lochree, Inch, "gray loch."

Liath (pale); as Craiglaw (anciently Craigley), Kirkcowan, and Craigley, Urr and Kirkgunzeon, "gray rock."

Dunis-odher, gen. uidhre; whence Bennour, Girthon; Dunower, Balmaclellan; Milleur in Kirkcolm, Kirkbean, and Girthon; Knockodher (hardened) in Barr; and genitive form Barnhourie—all "dun hills."

Green—glas; as Knockglas, four times This is really equivalent to "white hill"; in Galloway topography "glas" is always "green" (implying good soil), whereas in the north "glas" means gray. Muirglas, New Luce, is "the green tower"; Barglas, Kirkinner, "the green top", Challochglas" (pr. Challass), Mochrum, "the green knoll." The Glaster, New Luce, and the Glaisters, both mean "green land" (tir).

Pale green is uaine (wan), as Caimwanie, Kirkmaiden.

Blue is gorm; as Gormal, with the pleonastic hill, in Girthon and Minigaff (Gormaill); Craighorn, Carsphairn; Knockormal, Colmonell; Drumgorman, Dalry, translated by "Blue Hill" in Rerwick and Balmaclellan.

Yellow is buidhe; as Kilbuie, Kirkmaiden, "yellow wood" or "cell"; Blairbuie, Glasserton, "yellow field"; Drumbuie, Kirkcolm and Kells, "yellow field" and "ridge;"[1] Lanniwee, Minigaff, "yellow meadow."

Red is dearg, as Barjarg, Penninghame, Leswalt, and Colmonell, "red top"; Benjarg,[2] Girthon, Drumjargon,[2] Kirkinner, "red hills"; Daljarroch, Colmonell, "red field", Baryerroch,

[1] Yellow applied to objects above the soil; as Milkbuie, Kirkmaiden, "yellow hill," to gorse and broom; in woods, to golden birch in autumn, in fields, to cornflowers, in mosses and wet meadows, as Mimburn, Minigaff, to the bog asphodel

[2] In these cases the dearg, red, applies to red clay or reddish till

Kirkinner ; Glenzerroch, Kelton ; Poolzerroch, Anwoth, " red top, glen, and pool."

Ruadh, C. rhudd , whence Rouchan, Glasserton, " reddish land " ; Milhow, Kirkoswald, " red hill "

Rod (but this last also means road) signifies " red " in the sense of soil impregnated with iron scum ,[1] whence Knock-arod in Leswalt, Portpatrick, Stoneykirk, and Kirkcolm , Rud-doch Hill, Leswalt (Drumerand, New Luce, means "the ridge of the road ").

Red, or rather crimson, is corcur. Portencorkrie and Barn-corkrie are respectively an-corcur, " of the crimson," as here a mass of red granite crops up above the bay.

The Cymric coch appears unmistakably in Cochlick, Kirk-gunzeon ; Cochllech, pure Cymric for red flagstone, as also in Cochrossan, " the red point ", and Cochleaths, the Celtic leth, a " half portion "

Two adjective forms of gall, literally a stranger, but in their local application meaning Anglo-Norman, are masculine

Gallda, whence Galdanoch or Galdenoch (four times) in Wigtownshire, Leswalt, Inch, Stoneykirk, and New Luce, means the place of the Anglo-Norman Gaillseach (fem.); as Arriegilshie, Kirkinner , Gilshi Feys and Knockgilsie, Kirkcolm—the sheil-ing and hill of the English, that is Anglo-Norman, lady.[2]

The cardinal points, the elements, and seasons, are all frequently used adjectively.

North—Tuaith and Tuaiscairt , whence Slewintoo, Leswalt,

---

[1] Knockarod occurs in frequent cases where local knowledge points clearly to such red oozings which so often choke our drain-tiles, and also not on any line of road.   Dunrod, Kirkcudbright, is believed by its inhabitants to mean a reddish hill.   It might have been so called from a fort above a road —Joyce, ii. 350

[2] From gall foreigner, we have Gaillseach, constantly used in Irish writings for an Englishwoman ; so Ballynagalshy, Meath —Joyce, ii 9

The author referred the name, remarking that other interpretations had been offered, to Dr Joyce himself, *facile princeps* in this field ; he replied from Rathgar, Dublin, " I am quite in favour of English Lady."

On paper guilshie is not unlike Guileach, rushing or abounding in broom, but again Dr Joyce remarks, "grollach pronounced *gelka*, g hard, which is fatal to the rendering " and Drumatoo, Barr, northerly hills ; and Toskerton, Stoney-kirk, " the northerly place."

South—deas ; whence Ringdoss, Inch, and Torindoos, Les-walt, " the southern point" and " hillock."

East is oir, and has usually s prefixed; whence Druma-shure, Colmonell, " the easterly ridge."

West is iar, which, with the usual s, gives us Balshere, Kirkmaiden, " the westerly townland." [1]

Wind is gaoth, and appears three times in that singular compound Ton-re-gaeith, " backside to the wind "; in Tonderghie, Whithorn ; Tandragee, Stoneykirk ; Tonerahie, Minigaff. Ben-ghie, Girthon ; Curghie, Kirkmaiden, are both " windy hills."

As respects the seasons, names connected with spring and summer do not imply warm or sheltered places, but rather the reverse, too exposed for occupation in winter.

Spring is earrach ; whence Knockannarroch, Stoneykirk ; Lochnarroch, Minigaff; Clashnarroch,[2] Leswalt; Clachanarrie, Mochrum, are respectively the knoll, lake, hollow, and stones of spring.

Ceiteiun is also spring, and has probably the same meaning in Glenkitten, New Luce.

Summer is samhradh (savry), which appears little altered in Bellsavery, Inch ; and Fellsavery. Savery is also a place-name in Inch, evidently conveying the idea of summer pasturage.

Winter is gamh (gav), whence Bellgavery, Kirkmaiden, and probably the parish name of Minigaff, anciently written Money*goof* and Monigov ; the suffix, having exactly the force of the Cymric gauaf, is winter and cold.

---

[1] Oir, soir, and thoir, are used for east. So iar, west, is quite common in the form of siar. The most eastern of the Aran Islands is now Inisheer, which is very puzzling, for it exactly represents the pronunciation of Inissiar, Western Island.—Joyce, ii. 423.

If it is difficult to distinguish between soir and siar in Ireland, where Celtic is spoken and the language written ; it is doubly so in Galloway, in which this is not the case.

[2] Aroch, as before said, is a dim. of aros, and is glossed a little hamlet, sheil-ing ; where not summer pasturages, this may be the root of some narrochs.

Almost every part of the body has its counterpart in some of the features of the country

The head—ceann, C. pen; as Kindee, Mochrum, "black head"; Kinilaer, Barr, " head of the plank," *i.e.* plain ; Kenlum, Anwoth, " bare head "; Cymric Pinwherry, Inch and Colmonell, " head of the corrie."

It is to be remarked that in the West pen is not Cymric, but Gaelic peighin, and refers to " pennyland ", so Pinminnoch, not central head, but " peighin manach," monk's pennyland.

Hair of the head was urla; whence Urrall, anc. Urle, Kirkcowan, indicating a place with long hairlike grass.

Mong, C. mwng (meaning also a horse's mane), indicates places with long sedgy grass, as Balmangan, at the mouth of the Dee.

The breast is ucht ; whence Auchneight, Kirkmaiden   Dim. Uchtdan; whence Auchten (a rock), Portpatrick.

The back is drum, a word adopted into the vernacular in "The Drums," Leswalt ; "The Little Drums," Kirkcolm ; "the Drums of Carsebuie," Kirkcowan   *Cul* is also the back of anything.

Humpbacked is cruit (literally gibbous), and is applied to humpy-looking mounds.   So Crotteach, Kirkcowan, and Culgroat, Stoneykirk, "the back of the humps "; closely allied to Crottees, and Barnagrotty, given as Irish examples [1]

The shoulder of a hill—guala, as Slewgulie, Kirkmaiden

Pap—ciche, whence Carrickkee, Kirkmaiden, equivalent to Maiden Pap, Colvend.

The throat, braghad, is applied to a gully, as Braid, Inch, Powbrade, Colvend.

The tongue is teanga ; Norse, tang. We have Tongue, Inch ; Longthang, Kirkcowan, and the curious corruption Chang in Mochrum and Barr.

The nose—sron, Celtic trwyn ; whence Strone, Kirkmaiden, Troon, Ayrshire ; Stronfreggan, Dalry (Fraochan), point of the bilberries.

[1] Joyce, ii. 398.

The mouth—beul; whence Beliavo, "the cow's mouth," Kirkmaiden.

Snout—gob; Gobaronning, Kirkmaiden, "the seal's snout."

The palm of the hand—glac; whence Core of the Glaik, Leswalt.

The finger is meur, adj. meurach; as the well-known Merrick, Minigaff, the "centre of finger in the group"; Tulmerrick, Old Luce, "fingerlike knoll."

The groin is blean; in topography means a "creek," as Blanivaird on Loch Ochiltree, "the bard's creek."

The thigh is mas; whence Masmore and Knockmassan (the latter dim.), Leswalt.

The rump is ton; whence Tandoo, Portpatrick; and Tonderghie.

The foot is cos; as Cushiemay, Buittle; and Cassancarry, "the foot of the meadow," and "of the weir."

The side is taebh; as Taphmalloch, Leswalt, "Malloch's hillside."

The knee—glun; as Rig of Gloon, Minigaff; and the translation near it the "Knee of Cairnsmore."

The fist is dorn, and is generally accepted as the root of Dornoch, Sutherland,[1] whence it seems possible that the two lakes Dornal, Penninghame and Balmaghie, may be the "fist-shaped lakes."

The tail is earball, and applied to the extremities of any natural features; as Darnarble, Minigaff; and Drummienarble, Kirkcowan, "the oak wood" and "ridge of the tail."[2]

Of other hill roots, barr is the top of anything; Lochinvar, "lake of the summit."

[1] Dorn-eich, the horse's fist, i.e. hoof. This, which is the name, as well as the arms, of the borough, was given because a thane of Sutherland being disarmed in a battle here with the Danes, picking up a horse's foot which lay by chance on the ground, laid about him with such a will that, like Samson with the jaw-bone of an ass, he slew "heaps upon heaps" of the foe, as well as the Danish general.

[2] Though our other examples have been from parts of the human body, no confirmation of the Darwinian theory can be founded on the tail in this place-name, however old, as the translation is recoverable within measurable distance, "Dog-tail hill."

Barrachan, a common name, "the uplands"

Sliabh (slew), in Galloway, as in Ireland, is generally used for a hill, not a moor or marsh, as is often supposed; as Slewfad, Leswalt, "broad hill," one of a group of ten "slews" rising out of the contiguous levels of the Galdenoch or Garthrie mosses.

Beinn, dim. beannan, is also used as in Ireland, applying here rather to a small pointed hill than to a mountain. It takes the curious form of "Bine" alone in Portpatrick and Kirkcolm, both remarkable sugar-loaf hillocks Bennane alone is frequent, Culvennane is "the back of the peaks"

Cnoc is our commonest name for a hill, dim. cnocan, Cnockynocking, Stoneykirk, and Cnockanicken, Kirkcowan, being curious reduplications.

Meall, lit a lump, is also a hill. As Barmeal, Glasserton, "top of the hill", Millgrane, Penninghame, "sunny hill."

Cruach, lit. a stack, means a stacklike hill, as Craichmore, which is often corrupted to Craighmore, but which is "the large stack" The word appears alone in Croach. It is sometimes corruptly spelt Craig.

Cnap is a hillock; whence Knapps, Barr; and with an *s* prefixed, "the Snap," Penninghame.

The Norse dodd appears twice in Carsphairn. We also find the "Dodd of Troquhair, Balmaclellan, and the corrupt Dogtummock, probably meaning the bushy (tamach) dodd. We find also Mickle and Little Dodd, as well as "Wedder dodd" (wether), Sanquhar.

Ceide, a hillock level at the top, appears in Kittyshalloch, "the hill of the hunting," Minigaff. Leiter, a hillside, in Letterfin, Girvan. Tulach,[1] a knoll, takes in Galloway the peculiar form of Challoch The word alone occurs seven times in Wigtownshire, besides Challochglass, Challochmunn, Old Luce, it is possible it indicates tallach, "a forge," but generally a remarkable hillock can be discovered. We believe the *tch*

---

[1] We have two words which mix a good deal: tulach, a hill, sometimes spelt tealach; and tealach a hearth properly spelt teaglach, as derived from tech, a house I would hesitate, unless I were aware from other sources that tealach was used elsewhere for a forge, so to designate it."—Dr Joyce to the author

to be peculiar to Galloway ; we also find Laggantalloch, Kirk-maiden, Fintalloch, Penninghame ; and Shalloch o' Minnoch and Shalloch o' Tig are respectively "the hills" of those two said streams Shallochwrack, Ballantrae, is a corruption of tulach-bhreac, "the spotted hill"; whilst again Barnchalloh, Stoneykirk, is a corruption for Barnshalloch, "the gap of the hunting."

Torr also is a hill, as Tordoo, Tormollen, Tarbreoch, Torbay, Colvend—"the black hill, or rather round knoll, of the mill," "the spotted hill," and "of the birches."

Of roots for plains and hollows. A plain is magh, Cymric maes. We find it as May in Mochrum, "the Doon of May", and Mye, Stoneykirk.

The Cymric appears in "The Maize," Leswalt (a wet meadow) Machair,[1] a derivation from magh, is extensively used, as "the Machars," generally denoting arable, or at the least "white" land, sometimes a field Blair is a green field There is no reason to suppose that here the term (as it is said elsewhere) applies only to battlefields. Reidh is a flat; as Rephad, Inch, "the broad flat." Cluain is a meadow, gener-ally supposed to be an insulated one ; as Clone, Mochrum, Cloncaird, "the tinker's meadow"; and Gairachcloyne (the old name for Garthland), "the rough meadow."

Glac, literally "the palm of the hand," is a narrow glen Sloc, a hole or gully. Coire, literally a caldron, a narrow glen ; generally a *cul de sac*.

Amar, literally a trough, is also a hollow; as Slocanamar, Kirkmaiden; Laganamour, New Luce; Ballochanamour, Kirk-mabreck—the pit, hollow, and pass through the hollow.

Bearna, a gap, a common affix, difficult to distinguish from "bar-na"; thus Barncalzie and Barnbauchlie, Loch Rutton, might be either the summit of, or the gap of, the witch and the herdsman, though most probably "the gap."

---

[1] Machair is in Galloway often corrupted to mar, as Marbrack, Carsphairn, Marscalloch, the spotted field, and of the scolog (scholar and crofter); it is obviously not *mor*, great.

As a suffix it is unmistakable ; as Craigbernoch, New Luce ; Glenvernoch, Penninghame—"the gapped rock" and "glen"

Passing over roots readily understood, as pol, port, gleann, laggan, etc.,—traigh is "a strand," generally applied to a sandy beach ; as Killantrae, Mochrum ; Ballantrae, "the chapel" and "town upon the shore."

Cladach, in apposition to traigh, indicates a stony beach ; as Cladiochdow, Kirkcolm, "the black stony beach"; whilst across Loch Ryan we find the word used in the vernacular in Cladyhouse.

Murbhach is a sea plain, a flat piece of land extending along the shore, whence Morroch, Stoneykirk, Morrach, Whithorn ; and Myroch, Kirkmaiden, all meaning "sea plains."

Several roots for bogs and swampy places are curious. Leana, a meadow, indicating "grassy land with a soft spongy bottom," appears in Laniwee, Minigaff, Lanigore, Old Luce, "the yellow swampy meadow" and "of the goats." Laindriggan, Leswalt, is the "thorny meadow."

It is obviously the root of the Galloway "lane," explained as "the hollow course of a stream in meadow ground," applied "to brooks of which the motion is so slow as to be barely preceptible."

Leoghuis, an adjective form of leog-a-marsh, gives us Loch of the Lowes.[1]

Muchan, a derivation from Much, smoke, is applied to a morass, as a place in which people are liable to be suffocated. Loch Moan, Minigaff, Drumanmoan, Ballantrae.

Maothail, spongy ground, gives us Moile in three or four places; Meowl also four times in Wigtownshire ; Mahoul, Glasserton, Meehools, Old Luce ; Moine, C. Mawn, is a peat bog, as Monjorie, Kirkcowan, red bog; Portmona, Kirkmaiden, "port of the bog."

Munloch is a puddle, "dirty water, mire"; whence Menloch, Penninghame ; Muntloch, Kirkmaiden.

---

[1] Leoghas, the Isle of Lewis   This name given because Lewis abounds in swampy grounds —Armstrong.

Bog, which is really a Celtic (not an English) word adopted by Saxons, gives Bogue, Minigaff, Glenvogie, Penninghame; with derivatives Boggrie, Girthon, and Annaboglish, Mochrum. Ath-na-boglish, "the ford of the flow."

Turlach is explained as a spot marshy in winter, dry in summer, whence Drumtarlie, Penninghame. The root, "tur," dry.

Corcagh,[1] C. cors, a marsh, whence Carcow, Cumnock, Trevercarcow, an absorbed parish in Kirkcudbright. Whilst to the Cymric we must refer Corsoch, Parton; Corsglass, Dalry; Corsmalzie, Mochrum.

Crith, a verb, "to shake," with the particle lach, is used for a shaking bog; as in Crailloch, Portpatrick, and Creloch, Mochrum, in both which names the suffix has no reference to a lake, but has the force of *very*—very shaky.

Riasg is a marsh, whence Risk, Minigaff, Kirkoswald, and Balmaghie, Rusco, Anwoth.

Eanach is also a marsh, and probably gives us Loch Enoch, Minigaff, but it is difficult to distinguish the word from Aenach, a market or fair, which is in more general use.

Caedh, a marsh (whence the vernacular Quaw), appears in Culquha, Twynham; Culkae, Sorbie, and Lochquie, Penninghame.

Caladh also is a marsh, but it has a secondary meaning, Cala or caladh, a port or ferry, whence Cally, Girthon, anc. Kalecht, the landing-place or ferry. Its primary meaning, a low marshy meadow along a river or lake, we find in Brackenicallie (New Luce) on the Tarf.

Breaenach Caladh, the spotted land of the marshy meadow; or, as it would be expressed in Ireland, of the callow.[2]

Of roots relating to the supernatural—

---

[1] Corcagh names the city of Cork. Its marshy site was known for many hundred years as Corcach-mor-munhan, the great marsh of Munster

[2] Callow, as an English word, is quite current in Ireland. For both meanings see Joyce, i. 464. We are much disposed to think the prefix should be Bruckene, the callow frequented by badgers—broken, rocky ground, very much interspersed with meadow.

Sidh (pronounced shee) is a fairy, with a diminutive sidhean (sheen), meaning more especially a fairy hill. Knock-nishy, Whithorn; Brishie, Minigaff; Auchansheen, Colvend; Arnsheen, Ballantrae, Barnshean, Kirkmichael; Shawn, Stoney-kirk, and very many more, all denoting "haunts of the 'Little Folk'"

Bruigheen, a diminutive of brugh, a distinguished residence or fort, now generally applied to ruined forts or palaces, as these are always supposed to be inhabited by fairies; whence Kil-breen, Stoneykirk; Kirbrean, Kirkinner, and Loch Braen, Mochrum, uninviting as its site appears for a palace, represent the wood, quarters, and lake of fairy residence [1]

Ban, a woman, when used in the supernatural sense, applies rather to malevolent old crones than the elves of the fairy hills. Thus Barnamon, Stoneykirk (Barr-nam-ban), and Cairnmon, may properly be rendered "the gap or round hill of the witches"

Seanta is fortunate—having a charm or protection in the superstitious sense; whence Clayshant, Stoneykirk, "the holy" or "fortunate," or as glossed by O'Reilly, "enchanted stone."

Donas was misfortune, bad luck; applied also to the devil himself; whence Cardoness and Miltonise, New Luce, respect-ively "the devil's fort and hill of bad luck."

Diabhal, Celtic diawl, is the devil; whence Drochdhuil, Old Luce, "the devil's bridge"; Whithorn, Knockatonal, Kirk-cowan and Ballantrae, "the devil's hill."

Mallacht, a curse, appears perhaps in Polmallet, Sorbie.

The following in modern garb are probably reproductions of ancestral humour. Lot's Wife, Colvend; Adam's Chair, Rerwick Goleach (the witch), Kirkcolm, a sea rock having the contour of an old woman; so Monachan (the monk), Whithorn Shore, Yellow Horse, Kirkmaiden; Green Saddle, same shore. The Celtic Cunnoch (the milk-stoup), Whithorn, is matched by Beef Barrel, Kirkcolm   The Dooker's Bing,[2] Colvend; the

[1] Joyce, 1 288.
[2] Bing, a rude lump or heap of anything. Dooker, here the cormorant.—M'Taggart.

Scutching Stock,[1] Kirkmaiden. Throne of Gargrie, Mochrum, Pharaoh's Throne, Twynham, neither of which we can explain Three Brethren (rocks), Borgue; Old Man, Rerwick, Nick of the Dead Man's Banes, Girthon.

Two or three words are peculiar to Galloway, as gairy, in such composite forms as "North Garry," "the Garry of Pulnee," Minigaff, "Poomaddygarry," and the "Black Garry," Kells; Dougaries in Glenluce. The word seems to convey the idea of a piece of land cut off either for pasturage or cultivation.

Knoits is such another; as "the Knoits of Bentudor," "the Knoits of Linkens"; the word meaning rocky knobs, "little rocky hillocks."

Nearly allied to knoits are clints: the "Clints of Clendrie," Kells; "Clints of Dromore," Kirkmabreck; "Clints of the Bus," Minigaff. Clints glossed by M'Taggart "little awkward-lying rocks"; by Jamieson, "hard flinty rocks."

Elrich has undoubtedly the meaning of eerie, whether as expressing relation to evil spirits, or to a wild, lonely, frightful place; as such we believe the place-name to apply in remote-lying spots where no cultivation can have ever taken place, such as Loch Eldrig, far away on the moors The name is interchangeably written Elrig, Elrich, Eldrig; and Oldrig may of course frequently, but not always, apply to old cultivation.

Gurlie, a bleak spot given to squalls, appears in Gurlie-hawes,[2] Kirkcolm, anglice a bleak-lying narrow gorge. The word is rendered unintelligible in the Ordnance Map as spelt Garlehawise.

Pasper is a living Galloway word for samphire,[3] whence Pasperrie Rock is on the Leswalt seashore. This has been mis-printed in the same map as Pasbuery.

In these, as in other instances innumerable, it will be found

[1] A stick to beat out flax or hemp. M'Taggart calls it a scutching spurkle.
[2] Hals Hawse —(1) the neck; (2) any narrow entry or passage — Jamieson
[3] M'Taggart, under Pasper.

that local knowledge is absolutely required for the discovery of the true forms of place-names, which is essential to their interpretation.

As these have never been written in their original form, and are not understood by the people, local pronunciation is by no means the same sure guide as it is in Ireland to the real roots.

Dr. Joyce[1] tells us that " whether the syllables kill and kyle mean church or wood, we can ascertain only by hearing the names pronounced in Irish, for the sounds of cill and coile are quite distinct."

No such nicety of inflection is to be looked for from a Galloway resident; even upon the spot the inquirer will often be baffled by the interchange of "achs" and "ochs" *ad lib.*, and the different intonation given in the same words by every one he applies to in succession.

True, an old residenter may set a stranger right in some such ridiculous blunder as light (suggestive of a beacon) for lacht (indicating a commemorative standing-stone); but in such a common case as "Cos-an-coradh," few local persons would so pronounce it as to make its recognition inevitable. Some might rightly call it Cussencorry, but at least as many would adopt the form of the Ordnance Map, "Cass-en-carie"; even this being an improvement on a former survey, in which it was mapped "Castle Cary," though the true meaning is "cos," the foot, whereas "casan" is a footpath.

Within the recollection of many living, Auchleand, Wigtown, has been changed to Auchland. Old people rightly pronounced the word Auchlawin (achadh-leathen), a *d* added made it Auchleand; as a further corruption *e* has disappeared, and probably the next generation will change *h* into *k*, the radical meaning thus apparently shifting from a "broad field" to "oakland."

Croft-an-righ, pronounced as written, to the author, by no less an authority than Sir James Caird, when giving him

[1] Joyce, i. 491.

interesting particulars as to an excellent apple once cultivated here, which bore its name, has recently been changed to Croft-angry, also pronounced as written, a name which will puzzle future philologists.

Two suggestions may be offered in conclusion. The same name may in different places have an entirely different meaning. Interpretations must always depend upon circumstances and facts.

We are authoritatively told that Lisnegarvie (now Lisburne) means "the fort of the gamblers." [1] But it would be absurd so to translate Belgarvie on the Tarf, which probably simply means "a rough townland," as the suffix usually implies in other places.

Secondly, it does not follow that we have ascertained a true root because the word we are in search of is found in the dictionary. The author of *The Gaelic Topography of Scotland* confidently asserts that Glenapp means the "glen of the ape," simply because the suffix is so glossed in the dictionaries; naively adding, "At some very remote period these animals, therefore, must have existed in the south of Scotland, though they are long since extinct." [2]

Had the writer of this sentence ever visited the locality, he might have observed a remarkable pillar-stone overlooking the entrance to Glenapp, the name of which, well known in the locality (Laight Alpyn), as pronounced by any herd boy, must have suggested a more likely origin for the word than dictionaries could give him.

The following places retain the names of saints who either frequented, or were held in honour, in the several localities :—

---

[1] A gambler is designated in Irish by the word Cearrbhach, which is still in common use. One of the best illustrations of this word is Lisne-garvie We read in a pamphlet published in 1691 · "We marched towards Lisburne, one of the prettiest towns in the north of Ireland ; the Irish name is Lisnegarvah, which, they tell me, signifies 'gamester's mount '"—Joyce, ii 118

[2] Robertson, *Gaelic Topography of Scotland*, p. 342

They are generally to be identified in the Kalendars[1] Their "days" are those of their death.[2]

From Ninian, 16th September 432 (437, Adam King). Killantringan, Portpatrick, Leswalt, Ballantrae; Killanringan, Colmonell; St. Ringan's Well, Kelton; Tringan (the attraction of the *t* of the Saint), Leswalt, etc.

Patrick, 17th March 432 (the saint is, however, tripartite). Kilpatrick, Kirkpatrick (1) Irongray, and (2) Durham, Portpatrick, Patrick's Well; Cullenpattie, Inch, etc.

Malidh, Mallie Mell, son of Patrick's sister Darerca, 6th February 487; Culmalzie (Kilmalzie), Water of Malzie (Malzie Symson), Malzie Well, Crossmichael. Egilsmalzie, a dedication to him in Fife, is corrupted to Egsmalee.

Medana, 18th November, contemporary with Ninian. Three Kirkmaidens, Medana's, chapel and well of the Co., Kirkmaiden.

Brioc, Briocus, 29th and 30th April 500.

Kirkmabreck parish, which Symson says is "so called from some saint or other whose name was M'Breck"—the worthy curate did not understand the mo of endearment (maith, holy), also Kirkmabreck, Stoneykirk; Kilbrocks, Inch.

Bridget, 11th February 523. Kilbride (1) Kirkcolm, (2) Kirkmaiden; Kirklebride, Kirkpatrick-Durham.

Machute, 15th November 565, patron saint of Wigtown Parish Church. Kirkmahoe parish, Clashmahew, Eglaismahew, Inch.

Columba, 9th June 597 Kirkcolm Parish Church, St. Columba's Well.

Finian of Moville, Wynnen (white and fair men), 10th September, M.D.;[3] 24th January 379, K.S. Chapel Finian, Mochrum, and holy well, Kirkgunzeon parish; Loch Whinzean, Girthon; Kilwinning, Ayrshire.

---

[1] The *Felire of Aengus*, O'Clery's "Kalendar" (embodied in *Martyrology of Donegal*), Keith's *Scotch Bishops*; King's *Kalendar, Breviary of Aberdeen*, Bishop Forbes's *Kalendars of Scottish Saints*.

[2] Where two dates are given, M.D. is *Martyrology of Donegal*; K S. Bishop Forbes's *Kalendars*

[3] According also to Tighernae and *Annals of Ulster*

Lassair, "flash of fire" (so named in the Kalendars), mother of Finian of Moville.[1] Killeser, Stoneykirk.

Fintan (the generous), the little fair man, 17th February 973. Knockiefountain, New Luce.[2]

Barr or Finbar (white head), 25th September, named Parish of Barr, as well as Island of Barra. Landberrick (Llanila), Mochrum, probably Barrbarrons, also probably Lochmaberry (Maith Berarch), and may, however, confuse with Berach, Abbot of Kilbarry, Roscommon, 18th February, from whom Kilberry, Argyle, has its name

Colman Eala (of Llanila), 26th September 610. Colmonell Parish.

Kentigern (Munghen, the wild man), 13th November 603. St. Mungo's Well, Dalry.

Donan (of Eigg), 17th April 616, names six church sites: Kildonan, Kirkmaiden (Stoneykirk), Kircolm (Colmonell), Chapel-donan, Kirkcolm, and Girvan

Medhren or Merimus, 16th September (and two Medhrans, Mart. Donl., 6th and 8th June). Kirkmirren, Kelton; Kirk-madrine, absorbed parish, Stoneykirk.

Begha, 31st October 660 Culbee, Kirkcolm (near Kirk-bride); Culbee, Kirkinner; St. Bees', opposite Whithorn in Cumberland.

Cuthbert, 20th March 687. District and Church, Kirkcud-bright, Kirkcudbright, Invergavane (Girvan), Kirkcudbright, Innertig (Ballantrae); Killie-me-cuddican, Leswalt.

Sabina, his mother, may possibly have had a dedication in Mochrum, Culshabbin (Cil Sabina).

Kennera—a virgin martyr, one of the companions of St. Ursule, names Kirkinner, her day, 29th October 450.

Catherine, martyred in the fourth century, had dedications, near one of which in Kirkmaiden is the curiously corrupt name Kibbertic Kite. On referring this to the accomplished scholar

[1] On authority of Capgrave See letter of Dr. Reeves to Bishop Forbes, *Kalendars*, p. 465

[2] "To your Knockiefountain our Kilfountain in Kerry is a parallel."—Letter of Dr Reeves to Author, 13th March 1876.

Dr. Thomas M'Lauchlan of St. Columba's, an answer came by return that the explanation was easy *t* corrupted to *k*, Tiobar-tighe-chert, the well of Kate's horse.   There are St. Catherine's Wells in Stoneykirk and Glenluce.[1]

Lawrence, 2d February 617, a Bishop of Canterbury, is named in St. Lawrence's Well, Colvend.

Comhghain, or Cowan, 23d October 527, uncle of one of the St. Fillans, appears in Kirkcowan parish and Tencowan.

Fillan ("faelan," the little wolf), 9th January 703.   There are nineteen saints of the name, but we presume the dedications to be to him whose arm bone wrought wonders for the Scots at Bannockburn   Kilfillan, old Luce; Kilfillan, Sorbie.

Molor, Molonache of Lismore, 25th June 592, seems to have his name in the singular Norse corrupted and pleonastic place-name, the Howe Hill of Haggamalag, Whithorn ; his name is joined with St. Ninian's in Kilmaluag and Kilmorie in Mull.

Malachi O'Morgair (really the same name), a much later saint, who died 3d November 1148, and was not canonised till many years after, names Taphmalloch, a hillside, where he built a chapel without a rath in Leswalt parish ; and to Kilmalloch, New Luce.

Enan of Eigg, 29th April M D, 18th August (King's Kal-endar), 839, leaves his name in two Kirkennans, Buittle and Parton ; Fellyennan, Mochrum ; St. Inan's Well, Beith.

Glas, Glasvanus, is mirrored in St. Glas's Well, Rerwick , he was similarly invoked in wells in Argyle and Fife.

Galgacus, classic Latin Volocus, Saxonised or Low Latin for Wallach, Cymric Gwallawc, "hawk" of battle, was a name known to the early church militant ; Woloch or Voluen's day standing 29th January 720 in the Kalendars   It appears also in our topography in Carsewalloch, Kirkmabreck ; Knockwal-loch, Kirkpatrick-Durham , Ulloch Cairn, Balmaghie ; but we cannot tell whether they refer to a warrior or a cleric.

[1] It is impossible the old Celtic name could refer to St. Catherine of Sunric, who was of a much later date

Maure, a virgin, 2d November 899, who names Kilmaurs parish in Cunninghame, is probably remembered in Maurs Cairn, Kirkcowan ; Maurs Craig, New Luce.[1]

[1] Two Christian names common in Galloway have derived their origin from saints :

Quentin, which does not, as elsewhere, mean the fifth, but is an abbreviation of the Gaelic Ceam tighearn = Kentigern, a clear proof of which is that the saint's honorific title—Munghu, the mild or gracious one, is always accepted as its diminutive.

Gilbert is not the Teutonic "bright pledge," but Gille Brighd, "servant of St. Bride."

CHAPTER VIII

THE AGNEAUX IN FRANCE

A.D. 1000 to 1460

Le premiere jour de mai par permission divine
Saint Lo fut assailli a coups de couleuvrone
Matignon y etoit la et sa gendarmerie
Rampon-Cleret, aussi, Agneaux Sainte Marie.

THE Agnews of Lochnaw are a branch of a family which
take their name from a district in the Bocages of Normandy,[1]
which for many centuries they owned.[2] Their name figures
frequently on the early rolls of the chivalry of France, and
notwithstanding all the vicissitudes of time, — outlawries as
Huguenots, proscriptions as aristocrats,—a Marquis d'Agneaux
still owns portions of the ancestral fiefs, and the Château
d'Agneaux still overlooks the valley of the Vire.[3] Popularly
the origin of the name is ascribed to a miracle wrought at
Les Deux Jumeaux, near Bayeux, which, notwithstanding anachronisms common to all early legends, deserves mention as a
really old and genuine tradition, supported by the well-authen-
ticated coincidence that Les Deux Jumeaux have been possessed

[1] La famille d'Agneaux a ou donner son nom à la paroisse d'Agneaux ou le
recevoir de ce lieu.—Le Claude d'Anesy, *Recherches sur le Domesday*, 258.

[2] La famille possédait la Baronie d'Agneaux depuis un temps immémorial,
et un grand nombre de fiefs nobles. Deux Jumeaux, De Soucelles, De Putot, De
Sainte Croix d'Ardennes, De St. Contest, De Buron, Du Holme, De l'Ile Marie,
De Carneville, De Formigny, etc.—De Magny, *Nobiliaire de Normandie*, Part
2me p 5.

[3] Les Seigneurs d'Agneaux possédaient de vastes domains dans le Cotentin,
ses donations de l'année 1066 prouvent qu'ils existent depuis longtemps.—Le
Claude d'Anesy, *Recherches sur le Domesday*.

1. Seal of Helié d'Agneaux, 1190.
2. Seal of Andrieu l'Aignell, end of thirteenth century.
3. Seal of Herbert d'Aigneaux, Seigneur de Tocqueville, 1224.
4. Seal of Richard d'Aguellis, 1269.

by the Agneauxs since the days of Duke Rollo[1]   It runs
thus .

Among the earliest of the Norsemen who took seizure of
lands in France, was a viking settled near Bayeux. Things
went well with him, and he and his buxom wife had but one
unsatisfied desire,—they were childless,—but long after they
had ceased to hope, the lady presented him with two fine twin
boys. Their happiness seemed now complete, when suddenly
their darlings sickened, drooped, and died. Hardly had the
cry of agony broken from the mother's lips when a knock was
heard at their gate, and St Martin of Tours, whose name and
fame were equally unknown to the heathen Dane, stood without
and humbly begged for shelter. Even in this, the darkest hour
of grief, the claims of hospitality were paramount with the
worthy pair ; he was at once admitted and his wants carefully
attended to. When shown to his bed the saint could not sleep,
his feelings harrowed by his entertainers' sorrow, intensified to
himself by the thought that the unburied babes were unbaptized.
He rose in the night, hastily consecrated water, and stealing to
the silent chamber sprinkled it, mingled with his own tears, on
the faces of the little ones as they lay beautiful in death; he
breathed a prayer for their eternal welfare, and for that of his
hosts, and left their dwelling unperceived.

Early next morning the bearers arrived to carry the corpses
to the grave; the weeping friends were following, when a shout
was raised, "the children breathe !" It was no illusion : the
parents had entertained an angel unawares—the lost ones were
restored to the maternal embrace.

The news spread, crowds came from afar to verify for themselves the story, the most incredulous were convinced of the
completeness of the miracle, and as they watched the merry
gambols of the twins—snatched but a few hours before from the

---

[1] Une ancienne tradition bien connue dans la province, fait remonter la
Maison d'Aigneaux aux premiers invasions des Normands

Le nom de cet famille est ecrit dans les anciennes chartres, Agnus, Agnes,
Agnelles, d'Aigniaus, d'Agneaux ou d'Aigneaux et Aigneaulx. — De Magny,
Nobiliaire de Normandie, article "d'Aigneaux."

brink of the grave—the words "Agneaux de St Martin" rose spontaneously from their lips. And the name clung to the pair as they developed into manhood.

Topography enhances the antiquity of the legend, as from the date of the earliest records this scene has been known as "Les Deux Jumeaux," the owners of which were lords also of the district of Agneaux. Heraldry also associates the story with the name, as from the time when armorial bearings and surnames went together, the d'Agneaux or De Agnellis carried what are known as canting arms, or *armes parlantes*, which were lambs.

Simple, however, as was the name, and obvious as is its meaning, the perverse ingenuity of scribes made many changes on its form, which was originally plural. De Agnellis and De Agnis in Latin, d'Agneaux and d'Agnels in French; an *i* was early introduced before the *g*, when d'Aigneaux and d'Aignells, usually written in English *y*, Aygnell, and an *l* was sometimes introduced before the final *x*, Aigneaulx. The Galloway and least euphoneous form Agnew is not an attempt to return to the original Agneau, but from the Scottish custom of considering *ll* and *w* interchangeable; and the first Agnew arriving from England when his name was written Agnell, the equivalent *w*, used accidentally, seems to have become the settled form [1]

The blessing of St. Martin followed the progeny of his "Lambs." When the Norse chief Hrolf received investiture of Normandy as Duke Rollo from the King of France as his suzerain, he in turn gave feudal investiture to the Agneaux of the lands connected with their name, on which they flourished, and to which they added during the reigns of three successive Dukes Richard who followed Rollo.

The first scion of the house who acquired any distinction individually, and, what was then rare with his race, acquired some literary fame, was Andrew De Agnellis, who in pursuit of letters travelled to Italy, studied in its universities, took

[1] In many of the earliest charters at Lochnaw it is impossible to say whether *ll* or *w* is intended.

orders, and at his consecration assuming, with curious agreement with the after traditions of the family, the name of Andrew, rose eventually to be Archbishop of Ravenna, and wrote many works considered of great value in their day, and which have been frequently republished : in particular a history of his own see, characterised by an independence of thought unusual for the period.[1]

The next whose name appears in writing is Herbert d'Agneaux, who, at the accession of Duke Robert in 1028, was safely housed in his almost impregnable fortalice upon the Vire, and so well landed that it is said he could mount his horse and ride uninterruptedly from his gate over seven leagues upon his own estates.[2]   And this Herbert, on Robert's death, was a leading spirit in the confederation of nobles who refused to acknowledge William (the future conqueror of England) as their sovereign, on the ground of his illegitimacy.

For years these Lords of the Cotentin successfully defied him, till William, sorely against the grain, called on the help of his feudal superior.   Even then the malcontents faced the united forces of the king and duke, and victory long hung in the balance, and slipped almost accidentally from their hands.

The deciding conflict occurred at Val des Dunes, A D 1047, and was all but won by the chivalry of the Bocages.   So fierce was their charge, though against superior numbers, that they broke the imperial ranks, unhorsed the King of France, and held him as their prisoner.   The battle was won, their opponents fled, but in the excitement of success, and guarding their prisoner, they neglected the pursuit.   William, with eagle glances took in

[1] His entire works were published by P. Bacchino in 2 vols. 4to, in 1708. His name written " Agnelli qui est Andreas

His *Liber Pontificalis sive Vitæ Pontificum Ravennatum*, is reprinted by Muratori in his Italian historians

[2] Le premier propriétaire de ce château qui nous soit bien connu est Herbert d'Agneaux qui vivait au milieu de XIme siècle   Outre le fief d'Agneaux, il possédait les terres de Loncelles, Putot et Sante Croce.—Dubosc, *Notes Historiques*

Les Seigneurs d'Agneaux possédaient de vastes domains dans les environs de Caen et une baronie plus importante séparée par la rivière de la Vire pendant sept lieues du cours de cette rivière.—*Recherches sur le Domesday*, Le Claude d'Anesy

the situation, galloped after the flying squadrons, rallied, brought them back, fought another action, and snatched from the barons the honours of the day.

Henceforth he ruled supreme; the malcontents were at his mercy. Short shrift for those first clutched in that iron grasp. Happily for Herbert d'Agneaux, his castle offered a retreat almost impregnable until the "Conqueror's" anger had time to cool.[1] Whilst there he had a foretaste of how heavy his hand could be On hearing that three of his manors were gifted irretrievably to the Church as a thank-offering for the victory gained over the Lords of the Cotentin,[2] and happily for himself taking his punishment with a good grace, he appealed to the victor's clemency. William was a born ruler of men. Appreciating the courage he had found it so hard to daunt, he accepted the submission of such of these lords as offered it. Herbert d'Agneaux was confirmed in his principal fief, received into especial favour, and henceforward William had no more loyal subject.

The unhorsing of King Henry of France is a favourite tradition at St. Lo, with which the name of Herbert d'Agneaux is always connected. And the visitors to the picturesque entourage of his ancient keep are often reminded by the sturdy peasants, who like to serve themselves heirs to the glories of their forbears under their ancient chiefs, that

> Du Cotentin sortit la lance
> Qui abattit le Roi de France.

Herbert d'Agneaux is the common ancestor of several branches of the family once powerful in France: of the Agneaux or Aygnells of Redenhall in Norfolk, and Aignells of Pentlai in Hertfordshire; of the Lords of Larne, if they had any exist-

---

[1] Assis sur un rocher escarpé a 60 pieds au dessus de la rivière le Château d'Agneaux était imprenable de ce côté, et la disposition du terrein devait rendre presque inutile une tour avancée dont on voit encore les ruines de l'autre côté ; il était défendu des murs, un pont levis, des tours et autres ouvrages.—*Archæological Journal of Le Manche*, vol 1 p 2

[2] In 1056 William confirmed by charter to the cathedral of Coutances their fiefs: "De Loncellis, et Putot et Sancta Cruce, quam Herbertus de Agnellis tenebat. —*Abbé de Rouen*

ence excepting in scrolls of genealogists; of the Marquis d'Aigneaux and L'Isle Marie and Les Deux Jumeaux, of the Marquis St. Marie d'Aigneaux, still owning the Château d'Agneaux, and of the Agnews of Lochnaw.[1]

Herbert died before the conquest of England, leaving three sons, Herbert, Pierre, and Fulque, minors,[2] who all had issue.

The second Herbert was early taken into the royal household, and was frequently with the Court in England, where he acquired large estates in Norfolk and Suffolk, but not until after the Domesday Survey, at which date he only had some eighty acres.   He is a witness to several charters of the Conqueror's reign, one of which is reckoned among the treasures of the Museum of St. Lo,[3] and in another charter the king and queen are themselves witnesses to a purchase of a plot of ground from Herbert d'Agneau by Odo, Bishop of Bayeux, the king's turbulent brother.[4]

Herbert—identified by Norman genealogists with the Agneli of the Domesday—had three sons, Corbin, Henry, and Robert, all to be traced in official writs, and a nephew Fulque, who, in

[1] MM. les Barons Athanase, et Frederick Agneaux à Bayeux, et M. Paul d'Aigneaux, à L'Isle Marie (Marquis) possédent la terre qu'y possédaient ses ancestres il y a huit cent ans   Il existe en Grand Bretagne de la même souche une famille d'Agnew qui habite le Comté de Wigton —Dubosc, *Paroisse d'Agneaux*, 7, 8

[2] Various "corrected lists of the Battel Roll" have been published in which Herbert d'Agneaux is confidently introduced.   In a recent work, *Les Conquerants d'Angleterre*, there are three Agneaux, which seem all without sufficient authority.   Moreover, a comparison of dates renders it certain that the Herbert who was in possession at Duke Robert's accession, a witness at the Val des Dunes, could not be the Agneli of the Domesday.   The second Herbert was almost certainly under age in 1066

[3] In the charter shown at St. Lo the witnesses' names are entered after their crosses, as below ·—

(Signum)	+ Willmi Reges	+ Gaufredo de Saie.
	+ Odonis de Baiocenci.	+ Herberti de Agnellis.
	+ Henrici filii Rego.	+ Gaufredi de Carbonell.
	+ Rogeris de Albineis	

[4] Ego Odo d g Baiesis Epis frater Guillelmi Normanorum Ducis Anglorum reges, emi quondam terris qui vocatur Chernetville a Herberto de Agnellis Subscript + Gillelmo Rex, + Mathilda Regine, + Johan Archiepiscopus, + Herbertus de Agnellis, + Corbin filius ejus.—*Cartulars of Bayeux*.

company with their neighbour Robert de Couvey, attended Duke Robert in the first Crusade.[1]

On the second Herbert's death the fief of Agneaux was inherited by Corbin; Les Deux Jumeaux and L'Isle Marie fell to Robert, the third son; and his English lands he bequeathed to Henry,[2] who retained possession of the lands and castle of La Roque, in the neighbourhood of Caen.[3]

The three brothers all survived the reign of William Rufus. When Henry I., not satisfied with securing the English crown, had ousted his brother from his rights in France, he appointed commissioners to ascertain what these Norman rights actually were, and from their recorded report we gather that "Corbin d'Agneaux, Baron of Agneaux, owed a knight's fee for Carneville, Henri d'Aignel, Baron d'Angleterre, a knight's fee for his Norman lands; and Robert d'Agneaux, chevalier, a knight's fee for the Houlme."

Corbin we find married a De Bohun; Robert's eldest son Helie married Adeliza, daughter of an Earl of Albemarle; and we trace family connections with the De Hommets, Saies, Beaumont, and the lordly rhymer Gace de la Bigne, who introduces the name in vaunting his quarterings—

> La poete est né en Normandie
> De quatre costes de lignée
> Que moult on aimez les oiseaux
> De ceux de La Bigne et d'Aigneaux
> Et de Clinchamp, et de Burm [4]

The Agneaux continued their connection with the Court,

---

[1] In lists of first Crusade, Foulques d'Aigneaux, Normandie —*La Noblesse de France aux Croisades*, P. Roye, from MSS. Bibliothèque Royale.

[2] Herbert d'Agneaux eut trois fils, dont l'un Henri herita les possessions en Angleterre; à Corbin échurent les terres d'Agneaux, de Carneville, de Tocqueville, et Lieville, en Cotentin; de Loncelles, Purtot, et autres en Basson, à Robert, Deux Jumeaux et Vierville, diocèse de Bayeux, L'Isle Marie ou le Houlme Bolleville, et autres fiefs dans le diocèse de Coutance —Dubosc, *Paroisse d'Agneaux*, v 94

[3] "Le Manoir et Motte de la Roque ou demeuraient Henri d'Agneux et Jehan son fils, chevaliers"—Hozier, *Armorial Général de France.*

[4] Gace de la Bigne attended King John of France when a prisoner in England in the reign of Edward III. "Que moult on aimez les oiseaux," is the refrain or burden introduced by the troubadours, much affected at the period

and it is a Norman tradition that when the *Blanche Nef* foundered within sight of land with Henry I.'s only son and the flower of the young Anglo-Norman nobility, a son of Robert d'Agneaux was of the number.

On Henry I.'s death, hastened by this catastrophe, happily for themselves all the Agneaux were ranged on the side of his daughter Mathilda; and as her cause triumphed in Normandy, they remained in high power there, and stood well in England on the accession of her son Henry II.

In the next generation Henry d'Agneaux, now of English domicile, having attended Henry II. in a progress in Normandy, was drowned with other officials by the foundering of a ship of the royal squadron on their return voyage.[1]

Of this generation the sons of the two lords of Agneaux and L'Isle Marie were both Helie, a name which, with those of Herbert and Henry, in a prolific race, is so often repeated as to produce some confusion[2] when no date is given.

The seal of the former Helie, attached to a charter, *circum* 1190, preserved among the archives of St. Lo, is noticeable as the oldest impression extant of the family arms: three lambs passant (but somewhat wolf-like in their bearing). It is docketed "Chartre de Helie d'Agneaux fils de Herbert le vieux, partant pour Jerusalem et donnant aux religieux de Cherbourg quatres quartiers de froment de rent a prendre dans son moulin du Val de Saire."

A gift by the widow of the other Helie is amongst the charters at L'Isle Marie (she styling herself "Adeliza Cometis Albemaris) in favour of the Abbey of St Sauveur, "for prayers for her husband's soul." This witnessed by Engler de Bohun.

The crusader Helie married another Bohun, a cousin, his father Corbin having married Engler's aunt, as proved by his

---

[1] Quatre cent personnes furent submergés, dans le nombre Henri d'Aignel, Baron d'Angleterre.—Depping, *Hist de Normandie,* ii 80   In the English account he is written "de Agnis."

[2] On rencontre pendant 300 ans un grand nombre de seigneurs du nom d'Agneaux portant les prenoms d'Helie, Henri, et Herbert, hereditaires dans les diverses branches de cette grande famille ce qui rend assez difficile l'établissement d'une généalogie exacte.—Dubosc.

son Walter, who, when appearing as a witness in a record of an
action raised by the de Bohuns in vindication of their manorial
rights, is there described as "Walterris de Agnellis," nephew to
Willelmus de Bohun.

The said Walter is credited in the Exchequer Rolls with a
payment of 20s. towards the ransom of Richard Cœur de Lion.
And in 1206 there is record of his taking a solemn oath on
the high altar at St. Lo to defend and maintain the Abbey in
its dues, various deeds existing connected with his gifts, in
which his position in the family tree is rendered unmistakable
by such descriptions as "Walteras de Agnellis Miles" and
" arrière petit fils de Herbert Agneas."

To Walter succeeded Philip, whose memory is especially
fragrant at St Lo, as he added to the previous dotations of his
family the beautiful wood of Falaise for the benefit of the poor
of St. Lo, which, besides yielding a handsome revenue, is to this
day a much enjoyed recreation ground   When the Emperor
Napoleon inaugurated the Hall of the Crusaders at Versailles,
the Archæological Society of La Manche brought Philip
d'Agneau's claims under the notice of the Government, which
were admitted,[1] and his name and achievements consequently
appears upon its walls.

[1] The official reply of the minister is as follows .—

"M. LE PRÉSIDENT—L'examen par le Conservateur de Chartres ne laisse
aucun doute sur les droits qu'a le nom d'Agneaux d'être admis dans la Salle
des Croisades

"Connu dès le XIe siècle comme celui d'une famille bienfaitrice de l'église
de Bayeux, des Abbayes d'Ardennes, de Lorgues, Saint Sauveur, le nom d'Aigneaux
c'est perpétué en Normandie jusqu'à nos jours par une filiation non in-
terrompue

"Les armes de la famille d'Agneaux ont été tout d'azur à trois agneaux
argent.   Quand au fait de Croisade il resulte d'un passage d'un registre de
l'Échiquier de Normandie de l'année 1221.

"Les trois conditions—ancienneté, armes, et fait de Croisade—se trouvent ici
complètement remplies

"Il est donc de toute justice de placer dans la salle des Croisades :

"Philippe d'Agneaux, 1221.

"D'azur à trois agneaux d'argent.

"Le Directeur-Général des Musées Imperiaux

(Signé)   "COMTE DE NEUERKERKE.

"M. le Président de la Société d'Archéologie de la Manche."

During the thirteenth century the family multiplied and throve, as is evidenced by numerous charters in the archives of St. Lo, relating to benefactions to the Church and charities, with seals attached, and the frequent names of Herbert, Henry, and the still older one of Andrew. This latter is remarkable, as being somewhat unusual in France, a facsimile of such a seal which we possess being different from that of the head of the house by the substitution of one lamb for three, the lamb carrying a staff and a banner with a St. Andrew's cross.

Another seal, having Andrew D'Aignell for its legend, was found among the charters of the Abbé Blanche, near Mortain.[1]

The Ban Rolls of France—King Philip Augustus having summoned the Norman nobility to Tours in 1272—show that then a Henry and a Herbert d'Agnew there presented themselves.[2]

Towards the middle of the fourteenth century the fief and château of Agneaux passed by an heiress to the Paynells, and from them consecutively through the De la Hayes and D'Esquays, to the St. Marie. Rudolphus or Raoull St. Marie, who married Gillette D'Esquay, being previously a near kinsman of the Agneaux,[3] whose name he assumed. And his direct descendant, the Marquis Theobald St. Marie Agneaux, owns and inhabits the Château d'Agneaux at the present day.[4]

Les Deux Jumeaux remained with the representatives of the second branch. In 1459 we find Jean d'Agneaux, chevalier, in possession, and marrying " la noble demoiselle Elizabeth de

[1] The courteous Archiviste of St. Lo thus writes to the author   "J'ai l'honneur de vous adresser une représentation, obtenue par moyen du moulage, d'un sceau de la fin du 13ᵉ siècle, le champ occupé par un Agneau et qui a pour legende + S Andrieu D'Aignel (Andrieu est la vieille forme du nom Andre) —DUBOSC FRANCOIS NICOLAS, Archiviste, St. Lo, 25 Avril 1874."

[2] Herbertus de Agneaus, in Vicecomiti Barocenci,
Henricus de Aignaus, Miles in Vicecomiti Cadomaner.
    Anciens Rolles du Bans et Arrière-Bans en 1272.

[3] In the next generation the connection was renewed.   In the Marquis d'Agneaux pedigree we find, " 1473, Pierre d'Agneaux épousa en 1473 sa *cousine* N. de St. Marie d'Agneaux "

[4] The governorship of Granville and the Isles Champees was long hereditary in his family , his arms are écartelé d'or et azur —Hozier, *Armorial Général de France et de Mayence.*

Beauqendre ", [1] the following year being in every sense an eventful one for the family. Formigny formed a part of his estates ; here, on 15th of April, the Constable de Richemont gained the victory which finally severed Normandy from England. It is a strong family tradition that the two brothers Agneaux took different sides in the civil war, John, happily for his heirs, siding with the victors ; both brothers falling on the field almost in sight of the young wife, who, widowed, gave birth to a posthumous heir, Pierre, who married his cousin, daughter of Agneaux Sainte Marie.

Relations embittered by the fratricidal strife, all intercourse now ceased between the branches of the family on the two sides of the channel.

But although England was no longer open to their enterprise, members of the family prospered on other fields in France. Doubtless particulars as to their names and holdings might be obtained from the Departmental Records, which we have not the energy to explore.

We have ascertained, however, that there was a branch of the Agneaux in Burgundy, another in the Isle of France, where a château and a smiling village still bear their name; as also it has undoubtedly been left in Agnehers in Provence. The heads of all these branches being enrolled in the lists of the noblesse, and their arms differenced in heraldic visitations.

To revert to the Norman line, we may briefly state that they all embraced the reformed doctrines, and arrayed themselves under the banner of Coligny against the Guises. During the brief hour of Huguenot success an Agneaux led the assault at the capture of Bayeux, and this leading to the surrender of St. Lo, the Lord of Agneaux, by his influence with Montgomery and Columbières, saved the old Cathedral of St. Lo and its religious houses from the iconoclastic grasp of the eager Protestants—a moderation he (much to his disgust) failed to induce other commanders of the division before Caen to imitate.[2]

[1] *Nobiliare de Normandie*
[2] Agneaux en Normandie ancienne noblesse.   Parte d'azur à trois d'Agneaux d'argent 2 en chef, 1 en point

As the superiority of the Roman Catholic party in the field became pronounced, the strong defences of the Château d'Agneaux afforded the provisional leaders of the Huguenots a rendezvous for consultation, and their pastors a safe meeting-place with their flocks.

The gnarled trunk of a pollard within bow-shot of the out-works, where these proscribed ministers used to preach when the coast was clear to the assembled faithful, still remains, retaining the name given by the clerics when in the ascendant, of "the Devil's Pulpit",[1] whilst a grotto, the entrance to which was carefully guarded, where the Communion was at times administered, was called in the same spirit "the Serpent's Cave." Happily to-day the priests of St Lo can point out both to the Protestant visitor and explain the terms with perfect good humour,[2] but there was no joking on such matters in days when neither party regarded toleration as a virtue.

Heavily fined, excluded from Court and military employ-ment, the Agneaux, though not absolutely disturbed in the pos-session of their lands, for several generations passed through evil times.[3]

Agneaux de Provence, parte d'azur au chevron d'or accompagné en point d'un Agneau d'argent

Agneaux de Bourgogne, parte d'azur au chevron d'or accompagné de trois roses de même.

Agneaux, Sainte Marie, écartelé d'or et d'azur —*Dict. Généalogique et Hér-aldique, Armorial Général de France.*

[1] *Histoire de St. Lo*, Jonstain de Bilby, and *Histoire de Bayeux*, l'Abbé Beziers

[2] On remarque particulièrement trois lieux ou cis premiers Protestants faisaient leur assemblées pour leur Cêne :

1 La Maison d'Agneaux, dont le Seigneur était perverti

2 Une caverne à l'autré côté de cette maison dans un rocher, a laquelle pour cette raison on a donné le nom de Caverne au Serpents.

3. Au coin du bois de Soulles, prêche d'une arbre qu'on appelle La Chaire du Diable —Dubosc, *Parousse d'Agneaux*, Delalande, *Hist des Guerres de Religion dans la Manche.*

[3] Devenue protestante cette famille suivit le parti de L'Amiral de Coligny, Agneaux, et de Piriqueville Columbières, chefs des protestants, prisent le Château de Bayeux.   Eloignée de la Cour elle n'abbandonna la religion réformée que vers la fin du règne du Louis XIV   Le Roi Louis XV fit enlever un des derniers protestants de cette famille pour le faire élever aux nouvelles Catho-liques.—De Magny, *Nob de Normandie*, ii. 8.

The youths, however, of the house, debarred from winning their spurs upon the field, seem to have been brought up with unusual refinement, Robert and Antoine d'Agneaux courting the muses with success, made themselves a name as scholars and poets which was recognised even by Henry III., bigoted as he was against the name of Huguenot.

Their translations of Virgil and Horace, the first then attempted in French verse, were read by themselves by royal command before the assembled Court, on which they were publicly complimented by the King.[1]

With the revocation of the Edict of Nantes difficulties thickened for the family, till Louis XV. accomplished the conversion of the head of the house in a characteristic manner, by forcibly abducting the young heir from a widowed mother and having him educated to order in the Catholic faith.

Notwithstanding religious disabilities, many branches of the family figure on the rolls of the provincial nobility and landowners during the sixteenth and following century,[2] as for example on the Register of Nobles for the Generality of Caen, marked "an. 1592, maintenu,"—which has the force of having been made good after official inquiry,—are inscribed " Charles et Adrien d'Aigneaux, Seigneurs des Deux Jumeaux ; Gilles d'Agneaux, Seigneur de la Perille , Michel d'Agneaux, Seigneur de la Pionière."

And on a similar visitation, 1667, an Agneaux des Deux Jumeaux de la Rivière et de L'Isle d'Auval ; and as individuals ("nobles qui ont bien justifié leur quatre degrés") who

---

[1] Virgil and Horace in French verse were published respectively in 1582 and 1588, and dedicated to the king by Robert and Antoine d'Agneaux, chevaliers " Ces productions furent très goûtées à l'époque où elles parurent "—Jourigny et du Gouget,—*Hist Biog*   A fellow poet, Lonceur, thus apostrophises them —
> En l'âme de Maron des Agneaux transformes,
> Des neuf muses leurs sœurs

[2] The Protestant successions are given as follow .—
> Charles d'Aigneaux a embrassé la religion pretendue reformée.
> Guillaume d'Agneaux marié a une noble demoiselle et auteur de la Granberge.
> Guillaume d'Agneaux (IIe du nom) eut pour fils
> Jean Philippe d'Agneaux, de la religion protestante, enlevé par les ordres du Roi Louis XV. et élevé aux nouvelles Catholiques.

had proved their four quarterings, Guillaume, Jacob, Robert, Jean, Guillaume Jean, Christophe d'Agneaux, Electors de Bayeux [1]

Shortly before the great revolution effectually broke up their old family estates, a visit of a Scottish kinsman of the old house is thus recorded :

" Lors de la guerre d'Amerique, un membre de cet famille (Baron de Luknow), officier supérieur dans le Regiment de la Reine fut fait prisonnier et est venu passer plusieurs mois dans la famille Normande établie près de Bayeux "

The Baron de Luknow, it is hardly necessary to explain, represents the Baronet of Lochnaw, and the superior officer, as nearly as we can judge, is Colonel Montgomery Agnew, nephew of Sir James Agnew of Lochnaw, distinguished at the capture of Louisburg, an aide-de-camp to the king, and who served in the American war This was probably the first meeting of scions of Saint Martin Lambs since the battle of Formigny, though happily, now, intimate relations are re-established between both houses.

When on a visit to the late Marquis d'Agneaux at his hospitable château of L'Isle Marie, he mentioned to the author that amongst his earliest recollections was that of Colonel Agnew being brought to their home by his grandfather, who, recognising his name in the lists of prisoners, had sought him, claimed him as a kinsman, become answerable for his security, and entertained him until regularly exchanged.

We have only to add that the late Marquis paid a visit to Lochnaw in 1875, and was a witness to the marriage of a daughter of the house, leaving very agreeable impressions, and that his grandson has inherited " les Deux Jumeaux," his usual residence being the Château L'Isle Marie, identical with the Holme or Houlme, the Castel æt Hulme of the Saxon Chronicle.

The Marquis St. Marie d'Agneaux occupies the Château d'Agneaux, and has also kindly given the author much family information.

[1] Harleian MSS 4581 —*Nobiliare de Normandie*

CHAPTER IX

THE AGNEWS IN ENGLAND

A.D. 1084 to 1360

And heralds stickle who got who
So many thousand years ago.

AT the date of the Domesday survey Herbert d'Agneaux owned eighty acres of Redenhall in Norfolk,[1] and a few years later had acquired the entire manor "Redenhall Manor," says Bloomfield, "was so called from Rada the Dane, lord hereof in the time of Edward the Confessor. It was a mile and a half long and a mile and three perches wide, and paid ten pence to the Dane geld. It extended into Aldborough and Stanton. In the former were fifteen freemen, in the latter nine"[2] It was owned by Henry de Agneux in Henry II's time. This Henry was son of Walter, grandson of that Agneli who held eighty acres at the Conqueror's survey.

Redenhall was on the banks of the river Waveney, which divides Norfolk from Suffolk, and in this latter county his descendants, if not he himself, had considerable possessions.

His brother Peter d'Agneaux is entered in the *Liber Wintonensis* as a householder in Winchester, then the royal residence; and, curiously enough, another Norman (also hailing

---

[1] In Radanahalla Agneli tenet LXXX Acr —*Domesday*, fol 80.
Agneli, de Agnellis, ici nous retrouvons une noble et ancienne famille Normande ; plus tard ils devinrent puissants en Angleterre.—*Recherches sur le Domesday*, Le Claude d'Anesy

[2] In connection with their tenure of Redenhall we find five different spellings of the family name De Agnis, De Agneux, Agneus, Agnells, Agneli.—Bloomfield, *Norfolk*, iii 248.

1.   2.

3.   4.   5.

6.   7.

1. Aigneaux en Normandie.   4. Agneaux en Bourgogne.
2. Agnew of Lochnaw—Scotland.   5. Agneaux en Provence.
3. Agneaux de l'Isle.   6. Agneaux (early English), date 1298.
          7. Sir John Aygnell, Hertfordshire.

from St. Lo), Lupus, is named as his next-door neighbour; the wolf and the lamb living peaceably together in this paradise of courtiers.[1]

Another brother, Robert, is said to have founded a third English branch, though whether in Suffolk or Hertfordshire is uncertain[2]

Herbert himself was only a visitor in England, residing principally at his Château d'Agneaux on the Vire, but we learn from both French and English authority he bequeathed his English possessions to his second son Henry, who thenceforward may be looked upon as a naturalised Englishman.

We infer a very early date for the establishment of a branch in Hertfordshire, as their name still clings to two manors which they once possessed— Aignell in Hemel Hempstead, and Aignell or St Aignells in Redbourn.[3]

The Norfolk branch we can trace with the greatest certainty as to name or date up to the reign of Richard Cœur de Lion. Herbert d'Agneaux bequeathed Redenhall Manor to his son Henry, and his son or grandson, also Henry, is mentioned by contemporary chronicles as a man of considerable position, whose death by drowning caused much sensation at the period.

As members of the royal household, Henry de Agneaux and William de Courcy attended Henry II. in a progress through Normandy[4] in 1169, the king holding his Christmas court at

[1]   In Wunegre Stret, Petrus Agnellus, Radulphus Lupus,
        In Sildworden Stret uxor Gaudfredi de Sancto Laude
                                    Liber Winton viii 55.

[2] Herbert d'Aigneaux returned to Normandy, where his descendants still subsist   Robert d'Agneaux founded a second branch, extinct about 1289, and Peter a third —Gabriel Ogilvy, *Les Conquerants d'Angleterre* (a painstaking Norman genealogist, but often incorrect)

[3] Of the latter Chauncy writes "The Manor of Aignell undoubtedly borrowed its name from John de Aignel, lord hereof.—Chauncy's *Hertfordshire*, 593.

[4] The Abbot Benedict, who gives a circumstantial account of the progress, thus narrates the catastrophe "Una illarum (navium) quæ recentior et ceteris splendidior videbatur et melior, onusta ditioribus et nobilioribus familiæ Regis, proh dolor ! in ipso diei diluculo fluctibus maris obruta submersa est. Submersi autem in ea sunt Henricus de Agnis nobilissimus Baronum Angliæ, et uxor ejus.
. .   et multi alii de nobilioribus Angliæ."—*Benedict Abbas*, i 2

Nantes, where Agneaux was joined by his wife with two of his children. When recrossing the Channel the following March a hurricane scattered the royal squadron, and one of the largest and best found ships, in which were Agneaux, his wife and children, and other passengers of distinction, foundered.

His successor, also Henry, was presumedly an infant at the time of the catastrophe. That he lived at Redenhall we know, and that in due time he married, our knowledge being derived from the rather startling record that his lands were seized,—he being a rebel to King Richard,—reserving, however, to the Lady Mabel, his wife, her dower.[1]

This forfeiture, as to its date and attendant circumstances, certainly fits in, if it does not actually substantiate, with the Ulster tradition that Henry de Agneux accompanied Sir John de Courcy, the son of his father's comrade William de Courcy, in his conquest of that province ; that his name is preserved, whether in Agnew's Hill, or in its older form Carnanagholy ; and that, having conquered and parcelled out the country, De Courcy and all his band fell under the displeasure of King John, and by him were declared rebels to the king. Had the accusation been one of actual rather than constructive treason, we can hardly suppose that Henry d'Agneaux would have been allowed to return, as he apparently did, to lands in Normandy,[2] and been allowed to compound for real rebellion by a fine.

However this may have been as respects this branch, we

The French account is : "Cinq bâtimens de la flotte dispersée sur la mer furent submergis avec quatre cent personages ; dans le nombre de passagers étaient Henri d'Aignel, Baron d'Angleterre "—Depping, *Hist de Normandie*, ii 80.

And the English version : "A great tempest arose ; a fleet of fifty ships which attended the king were dispersed and terribly shattered One of them sank, on board which was Radulph de Bellamont, the king's physician, and Henry de Agnis, who is called by a contemporary writer the most noble of the barons of England "—Lord Lyttleton, *Henry II*, iv. 292.

[1] In 1196, Henry de Agneux, being a rebel to King Richard, that king seized his lands and granted them to Ralph de Lenham for 200 marks, saving to Mabel de Agneux her dower —Bloomfield, *Norfolk*, iii. 248.

[2] "Le Manoir et Motte de la Roque ou demeuraient Henri d'Agneux et Jehan son fils, chevaliers "—Hozier, *Armorial Général de France*

Bloomfield tells us John Agneaux was heir to Redenhall, but failed to recover it.

substantiate from Bloomfield authoritatively these facts, that a Henry d'Agneaux, direct descendant of "Agneli" of the Domesday, owned Redenhall Manor in the reign of Henry II.; that a Henry d'Agneaux, for some cause untold, incurred the king's displeasure in the ensuing reign, and that his heir of line was John[1]

But whilst we find Henry and John of a now well-established English branch recrossing, from circumstances, the channel, it is interesting to note interchange of visits between the Norman stock and their connections in England.

In our last chapter we find intermarriages between the Agneaux, Bohun, Hommet, and De Saies. In particular we named a gift to an abbey for prayers to her husband's soul by Adeliza d'Agneaux, witnessed by her brother-in-law Engler de Bohun. A year or two previous we trace in English chartularies this same Hélie d'Agneaux, on a visit to the same Bohun, witnessing a gift of Engler's to the abbey of Quarr.[2]

In the first year of King John (1199) we find William de Humet, Constable of Normandy, making a grant at Stamford to the nuns of St. Michael there, in presence of Jordan de Humet, William de Saie, Rodolphus de Agnis, Gileberte du Val;[3] and within a year we find the same Rodolphus de Agnis signing in French form "Raoult d'Agneaux" as a witness to his kinsman Richard de Hommet of a grant in Normandy   Rodolph de Agneaux is styled of Kettering.

Thomas d'Agneaux is entered as an owner in county Buck-

---

[1] A clerical error seems to have crept into Bloomfield's text, writing Walter instead of Henry   His words are. "King Richard seized all his lands, and granted them to Ralph de Lenham, saving to Mabel de Agneau her dower, and to Peter de Leonibus (Lenham) his goods and corn sown on the land; and in 1199 Walter himself confirmed the grant. In 1200 Roger de Lenham owned one moiety, and Henry de Agnells settled it on him by fine —Bloomfield, *Norfolk*, iii 248.

From this it appears Lenham advanced the money for the fine. Henry being Mabel de Agneau's husband, and a Henry in possession in 1200, the "Walter himself in 1199" should obviously read Henry.

[2] Carta Engelgeris de Bohun de Hasilera in Insula de Victa (following several bishops), +Helie de Aignell, +Gaufrede Rufi, +Robert de Brehal, etc. —Dugdale, *Monasticon*, 1 761.

[3] Dugdale, *Monasticon*, i. 489; Peck, *History of Stamford*.

ingham of Chalfunte Sancti Petri, Chalfunte Sancti Egida, which last we take to be the pretty village of Chalfont, St. Giles, near Uxbridge,[1] of classic memory as Milton's favourite retreat. And early in the thirteenth century Robertus de Agnis gets seizure by royal mandate of lands in Suffolk and Essex.

To revert to Hertfordshire, besides the manors of Aignell in Redbourne and Hemel Hempstead, the Agneaux possessed Pentlai or Penley in the former parish, which was their usual residence.[2] The names of their neighbours in the reign of King John, as given by Chauncy, have a curious significance.

Near to Penley was the manor of Gadesden, the residence of Roger de la Zouche, who had inherited through the heiress of a daughter of a Bohun.[3]

Beyond Gadesden was Ware, lately inherited by Saier de Quenci from William de Saie[4] (lately named). It may be noted that the Priory of Ware half a century later was the house of his lady when her son Roger was Lord of Galloway.

Adjoining both manors were the lands of Hitchin, originally assigned to Peter de Valognes, a knight of the Cotentin, carried by his two daughters, co-heiresses, to David Comyn and Bernard Baliol.

The sons of the lords named of Ware and Hitchin married Helen and Dervorgille, daughters and co-heiresses of Alan, Lord of Galloway, and became Lords of Galloway in their turn. Roger de Quenci's daughters carried his honours to Alexander Comyn (son of David), and Alan, a son of Roger de la Zouche.

The son of Baliol's wife Dervorgille became King of Scotland, and a daughter married another Comyn, Justiciary of Galloway.

We have therefore the coincidence that the descendants of a knot of Anglo-Normans, first connected by ties of blood in

[1] Hardy, *Rotuli Literarum Clausarum in Turri Londonensi*, vol. 1 p 332

[2] Penley in Domesday Book, Pentlai between Tring and Berkhampstead, by the Bulburne river. King William granted this manor to Earl Morton. The next lord that I find is John de Aygnell.—Chauncy, *Hertfordshire*, fol. 590.

[3] Gadesden was previously owned by Edward de Saresburg, married to a Bohun; their daughter and heiress married De la Zouche.

[4] At the Conquest Ware was assigned to Hugh de Grantesmailer, of whom two daughters and heiresses married respectively Robert de Courcy and William de Saie.

France, and afterwards by those of property in Hertfordshire, gave to Galloway (to which some of them had probably at that period never turned a thought)—six overlords, a justiciary, and a line of hereditary sheriffs, as well as two crowned Scottish kings.[1]

The first move in the sequence of events by which these results were brought about seems to have been the appearance of Alan upon the scene to support the English barons in their rising against King John, of which Saier de Quenci was the moving spirit   The friendships formed round their camp fires led to renewed intercourse between the nobles who obtained the Magna Charta.   Alan's eldest daughter was married to De Quenci's eldest son; Baliol, who was also concerned at Runnymede, secured the hand of another, and through these heiresses all the lords named became directly interested in Galloway.

Although the Agneaux were not in the rank of the greater barons, such as De Quenci and Baliol, we have direct evidence that they supported these magnates with sufficient effect to incur the resentment of the king; and that, contrary to the engagements he had made with the leaders, he forfeited the estates of those who had assisted them, those of the Agneaux being named, and their lands in the eastern counties being especially ravaged by his mercenaries when on his march to Lincoln in 1217, which he reached to die on the 19th October, after having been half drowned previously in the Wash.

Within a week of his death we find Robert d'Agneaux (whom we believe to have been the owner of the Hertfordshire manor as well) restored to his privileges by a mandate from the council;[2] and three years later he is named a Lord of Assize.[3]

---

[1] Roger de Quenci, John Baliol, Alexander Comyn, Alan de la Zouche, John Baliol (2d), Edward Baliol, successively lords , Alexander and John Comyn, justiciaries ; John and Edward, crowned kings of Scotland , Agnews, hereditary sheriffs

[2] 26 Oct. ann 1 Henry III.   The Sheriff of Suffolk and Essex is desired to give sasine to Robertus de Agnis of all his lands and other pertinents, "qualiter inde habuit dre qua recessit a fide et servicio Domini Regis Johannis, prioris nostri "—Hardy, *Rotuli in Turri Londonensi*, i 332.

[3] The Sheriff of Norfolk and Suffolk is instructed to bring certain persons named before Robertum de Agneus, Robertum de Coleville, "justiciarios constitutos per preceptum nostrum "—16th October 1224, *ib.* p 633.

In the criminal records of the period we find several Agneaux figuring not as judges, but defendants, on charges very similar to those to which young Galloway lords were often called upon to reply at "Justici Aires" in their own province

Thus "Radulphus de Agneaux of Kettering" in 1277 comes in for the kings will at an assize at Lincoln for slaughter, paying therefore twelve solidi to Alexander Cacherel.[1]

"Robert, son of Aygnell of Multon," compounds with Adam Lepeter for goods spoiled (Scotice spulzeit) by the said Robert, and compounds for seven solidi (ut cancelerunt ejus latrocinum).

John Aignel is adjudged to pay Peter de Bures three solidi for assault. This points him out as of Penley, De Bures being a neighbour. This John was himself a pursuer in court for the manor of Redenhall, but the decision was against him.[2] Nevertheless he otherwise prospered, and we can trace his family continuously for several generations, until, whether from pecuniary or other difficulties, they migrated northwards.[3]

His son was a man of some note, as a knight serving his sovereign and his shire,—a soldier and a senator,—and, what would now seem incompatible with either, a judge of assize, as well as acting as sheriff.

From Parliamentary writs, and from the Pipe Rolls, we can trace minutely his doings in all these capacities. A few specimens will suffice.

In 1296 we find Johannes d'Aygnel summoned to perform military service in person against the Scots. Muster at Newcastle-upon-Tyne, 1 March, 24 Edward I[4]

A third letter to the same sheriff styles Robertus de Agneus "Justiciarius Noster," *ib.* p. 63   Quoted by a French genealogy as "Justicier du Roi" That may mean rather judge than grand justiciary

[1] *Rotuli Hundredorum, Co Lincoln*

[2] "In 1264 Peter de Savoy surrendered Redenhall into King Henry II's hands for the use of Prince Edward (he apparently held it in mortgage from the Agneaux). The prince granted it to Nicolas de Yatingdon. John de Agneux sued Bartholomew de Yatingdon as heir, but failed to recover.—Bloomfield, *Norfolk*, iii 248.

[3] Pedigrees, from old chartularies of St. Albans, of the greatest family interest, not otherwise readily accessible to him, were kindly communicated by Mr Cussans to the author.

[4] *Parliamentary Writs.*

Thence, as a matter of history, we know that the king made a rapid march, stormed and took the castle of Berwick, then held a Parliament, and summoned the clergy and laity of Scotland to swear fealty to himself. Among those that trooped in, John Aygnell may have renewed acquaintance with such of the Barons of Wyggeton and Dunfres as were of Hertford origin, scions of the Zouches, De Quencis, and Comyns, little thinking that a little later his own family would have a firmer foothold in Galloway than any of them. In short, though probably he was little aware of the historic interest destined for the display, he was a witness of the signing of the Ragman Roll.

In 1295 Edward I. summoned the English Parliament to meet at York, and on this John Aygnel sat as Knight of the Shire for Hertford.[1]

In 1300 Sir John Agynell was named one of the justices of Oyer and Terminer,[2] and the following year was elected to be one of the assessors and collectors of the fifteenth granted to the king by the Parliament at Lincoln.

Upon Edward I.'s death in 1306 a Parliament was summoned to meet at Northampton, when Sir John Aygnel was re-elected for Hertfordshire, and sat on this the first, also on the second Parliament of Edward II.[3]

In 1373 we find him by the Pipe Rolls serving the office of High Sheriff for Hertford,[4] and as such he appears in an entry in the chartulary of St. Albans. "Oliver de Burdigans granted all his lands called Le Troy to the Abbey of St. Albans, witnessed by Sir John Aignel, Sir Richard Chamberlain, and Sir Stephen de Cheyndut, the 18 July, 8 Edward II."[5]

By a pedigree compiled from entries of various requisitions in the chartulary of this Abbey, it appears that Sir John

[1] All these attendances are to be found in the Parliamentary Returns of Members for English Parliaments, moved for by Right Hon. Gerard Noel, M P , but in the text are usually quoted from Chauncy's *Hertfordshire*

[2] Commission tested at Bury St. Edmunds, 10 May, 28 Ed. I

[3] Commission tested at Linlithgow, 1 Nov , 29 Ed I.

[4] Then written John de Aygnel of Pentlai.

[5] Chauncy, fol 477.

Aygnell[1] had three sons—Peter, William, and Adam   The two eldest predeceased him ; but William left a son, John,[2] between whom and Adam he divided his estates.   Adam was succeeded by a son, also John.[3]   One of these Johns was the progenitor of the Agnews of Lochnaw, the only daughter and heiress of the other John being ancestress of the Earls Verney, now represented by Sir Harry Verney of Claydon.

The third John Aygnel married Katherine, daughter of John de Chilterne, of Rickmeresworth,[4] and stands thus on the family tree

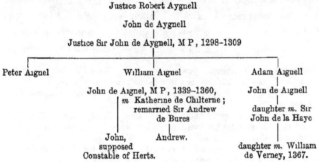

```
                    Justice Robert Aygnell
                            |
                      John de Aygnell
                            |
           Justice Sir John de Aygnell, M P, 1298-1309

Peter Aignel        William Aignel              Adam Aignell
                          |                          |
               John de Aignel, M P, 1339-1360,  John de Aignell
                m  Katherine de Chilterne ;           |
                  remarried Sir Andrew        daughter m.  Sir
                       de Bures               John de la Haye
                          |                          |
            John,        Andrew.
          supposed                           daughter m. William
        Constable of Herts.                   de Verney, 1367.
```

Katherine de Chilterne seems to have brought her husband considerable property,[5] and he appears to have lived in style

[1] Chauncy quotes this curious charter from the records of St. Albans: " Oliver de Burdigans, 8 Edward II (1315), granted all his land called Le Troy, and also his lands and tenements which Geoffrey Turkeyld and Alexander the Fool, his bond-tenants, held of him, to the abbot and convent of St. Albans, which deed was attested 16th July by Sir John Aignel, Sir Richard Chamberlain, Sir Stephen de Cheyndut, John de Lattene, Roger de Meredene, and many others "

[2] John de Aignell, who held this manor (Penley) an. 10 Edward II., without question was lord hereof, and grandson and heir of John de Aygnell, who served in Parliament held an. 26 of Edward I., and in the Parliaments of an. 1 of Edward II , and an. 2 of the same king —Chauncy, fol. 1364

[3] Roger de Messeworth held of the king land in Tring, which he alienated to Adam Aignel, which alienation Roger's son William confirmed to John Aignel, son and heir of Adam , and this John Aignel held of the king   John, son of William Aignel, was kinsman and next heir of the said John, the son of Adam —Extracts from minutes of evidence of an inquisition held at Aldebury, Co Hertford, 2d Oct 1364   *Gesta Abbati Sanc. Albani.*

[4] Now Rickmansworth.

[5] In her widowhood, 20th April 1376, Katherine, widow of Andrew de Bures,

at his manor house at Pentley, holding his courts,[1] and representing his county in Parliament from 1339 until his death [2]

Some years before this, however, he seems to have got into difficulties, and parted with one of his manors of Aignels to the Abbey of St. Albans,[3] and eventually with the manor place of Pentlai to Sir Andrew de Bures [4] He died in 1361, leaving a son under age to the guardianship of his brother-in-law, John de Chilterne, and was buried beside his father and grandfather, Sir John Aygnell, in the Church of Albury, the family burying-place, in the chancel of which their arms are (or were till lately) to be seen as given by Chauncy: azure two chevrons or, on a canton argent, a holy lamb gules, with staff and banner.

previously of John de Aygnell, grants to her brother Henry de Chilterne all her right in lands in Herts and Bucks which he had received from the said Henry, which had belonged formerly to her father John de Chilterne.—Cussans, *Hertfordshire*, iii. 138.

[1] John de Aygnel held a court in this manor in the nineteenth year of Edward II , and several other courts from an. 2 until the twenty-fourth year of Edward III.—Chauncy, f 594

[2] A catalogue of those eminent persons that are to be found upon record who served this county in Parliament .

Edward I

26	John de Aygnel.	Robert de Hoo.
30	John de Aygnel.	Ralph de Munchancey.

Edward II

1.	John de Aygnel	Gerard de Braybrock
2.	John de Aygnel -	Ralph de Monte Caviso.

Edward III

12.	John de Aygnel.	Philip de Aylesby
33.	John de Aygnel.	Ralph de Monte Caviso.

Chauncy, *Hertfordshire*, fol. 23.

[3] This is now known as St. Agnells, as to which Mr. Cussans, historian of the shire, wrote to the author . "There are at the present time two manors in Hertfordshire known as Agnells or Aynells in Redbourne and Hemel Hempstead, both called after the family of Agnell It is probable, after the two came into different hands, that the Abbey Manor was called St. Albans Agnells to distinguish it from the other, and that in course of time the 'Albans' was dropped —10th April 1879 "

[4] Of this manor in the history Mr Cussans says "This manor was possessed at a very early period by the family of Aignell—the name of a family in France, spelt in a variety of ways · Agnels, Agnes, Aygnell, Agneaux, Aynell. It is from this family Sir Andrew Agnew of Lochnaw, Wigtonshire, deduces his descent "—Cussans, *Hertfordshire*, iii 232.

There is reason to believe that the first English branches carried three lambs gules, differenced from those of Normandy, which were argent; these further differenced by the Hertfordshire branch with the chevrons which had been carried by the branches in Burgundy and Provence.

Notwithstanding dilapidations, we find from inquests that the younger John Aygnell was infefted into what may be called very pretty pickings from the family estates; those in Hertfordshire alone we give below.[1]   But his over-zealous guardian launched himself and ward into lawsuits with the powerful Abbot of St. Albans, urged with a bitterness that led to feud, from which the young heir suffered much in pocket and himself in person.

It is somewhat curious that whilst these entanglements were undoubtedly the cause of the last of the Hertfordshire Agneaux changing his domicile and setting out to push his fortunes farther north, the records of the actions at law in which he was worsted (lately brought to light) enable us satisfactorily to unravel matters connected with his pedigree which seemed difficult to reconcile and hopelessly forgotten.[2]

[1] The said John, son of William Aygnel, held at his death of the king:

One acre of meadow land in Rickmeresworth, called Le Estmade ; one acre and a rood in Rickmeresworth in the hamlet of Crookslee, his principal messuage in Rickmeresworth, called Le More, with forty acres of land and eighteen acres of meadow and three acres of pasture held by petty sergeantry of the king , in the town of Rickmeresworth half a hyde of land containing thirty acres held of the Abbot of St. Albans for military service ; in the hamlet of Danielside certain tenements ; and in hamlet of Crooklee a tenement called Elysonde held by military service of the Abbot.   One messuage, one carucate of land, fourteen acres of meadow, ten acres of pasture, five acres of wood with appurtenances called Asseles, and one virgate of land called Hanekwellesland, held in free socage of the heirs of Stephen-ath-grove ; fifteen acres called Le Stratefield held of John of Muridene in free socage

In the town of Caeshoo (Cashiobury) one water-mill called Tolfade, one meadow called Le Mullemade, a small croft called Le Mulm Croft, and one several bank of the river Colne held of John Chilterne.

In Redbourne one messuage, one carucate of land, three acres of wood, and twenty-one shillings rent held of the Abbot —Quoted by Cussans, *Hertfordshire*, iii 137

[2] John de Chilterne appears to have caused Thomas de la Mare, Abbot of St. Albans, much trouble.   De Chilterne was accused of farming certain tenements of the Abbey, which belonged to a minor John, son of John son of William Aygnel, and refusing to pay the accustomed dues to the Abbot.   The latter

Katherine de Aygnell shortly after this remarried with Sir Andrew de Bures, the purchaser of Penley manor house, to whom she bore a son, Andrew, and John de Aygnell returned to pass the years before entering upon manhood to the home of his infancy, over which his mother was thus again called to preside.

On reaching man's estate, although, as we have seen, he inherited various lands, it is probable there was upon them no manorial residency, and that these were heavily encumbered; and on his stepfather's death in 1365 the baronial hall of Penley passed, as a matter of course, to his brother Andrew, and he was only an inmate upon sufferance.

Realising, therefore, what he could from such lands as he had, whether arrangements for his final settlement in Galloway had been preconcerted with his many neighbours who had connections there or not, he bid a long adieu to his Hertfordshire haunts, and rode forth in search of adventure.[1]

Much about the same time John de Aignel, son of Adam, co-heir with his grandfather, died, leaving an only daughter, who carried his lands to Sir John de la Haye, whose great-grand-daughter married John, son and heir of Sir Ralph Verney, Member and Lord Mayor of London 1466. Ancestors of the Earls Verney, represented as before said by Sir Harry Verney, in whose hall of Middle Claydon, on an old shield above the mantelpiece, among the quarterings, are the arms of John de

enforced his claim by driving off fifty of De Chilterne's cattle, at the same time requiring him to send their fodder This the obstinate John de Chilterne refused to do, and they died of starvation   "Whereupon," the pious chronicler records, "De Chilterne became more obstinate than ever" At length it was adjudged that John should pay the Abbot a thousand marks as compensation, but instead of doing so he went off to join the king's army in France On his return the Abbot caused his arrest, and he was committed to the Fleet Prison While there he procured an inquisition to be taken to prove how little he owed the Abbey This was taken at Albury, 2d October 1365. The result, as showing the lands in Hertfordshire owned by John Aygnel, are given in the note above — *Gesta Abbatum Sancti Albani*, iii pp. 3-35   Quoted in Cussans's *Hertford-shire*, iii. 137.

[1] Mr. Cussans, the greatest authority of the day on Hertfordshire genealogies, writes . "The name (Aygnell) does not appear after 1359 on the Rolls of Parliament, it is probable, therefore, that shortly after this time the family either removed or became reduced"

Aignel, bearing the chevrons and holy lamb gules, with staff and banner, as in the burying-place at Albury.

Considering the many ramifications of the family in England, and how frequently the name occurs in rolls and inquests during the three centuries preceding, it seems somewhat strange that it should have suddenly disappeared by the failure of heirs-male in one branch of Sir John Aygnell's heirs, and the migration of the other.

Having been at pains to trace cadets of county families of older generations, we have only succeeded in recovering two names—Radulphus or Ralph Aignell, an ecclesiastic in County Hertford[1] in 1381 ; Andrew, son of George Aignell, in baptismal register of St Mary, Aldermary, 1575 The first of the Anglo-Normans of whom we have authentic record, as well as the last, south of the Tweed, being thus appropriately Andrew.

As before said, the Agneaux line thus ran in two manors of Aignell, as also further on Daynell and Danielside. Anglo-Norman surnames, when, as was not uncommon at the period, they were adopted by their retainers of humble rank, take curious forms ; thus De Aygnell became Daniels ; Pied-de-fer, Puddephatt ; De la Marc, the name of the haughty Abbot of St. Albans, is remembered in Dollimore ; and d'Ayeville, still more uneuphoneously as Devil.[2]

[1] Mr Cussans, specially referred to, adds "In 1587 Ralph Aignell, clericus, one of the executors of Thomas le Gros, conveys the manor of Furneaux Pelham to Thomas Bydeford "

[2] "Agneau, Agnell, Aynel, are identical I should be by no means unwilling to believe that Daniels is not D'Aynells. I took some pains to trace the common Hertfordshire names of Devoil (Devil sometimes) and Puddephatt. The former I traced through old deeds and registers through Devil, Deflle, Deovil, Devoile, to d'Ayeville , the latter from Puddephatt to Pedifat, to Pedifer, to Pied-de-fer ; the Dollimores are De la Mares.

" T. E. CUSSANS,
"179 Junction Road, 10th April 1875.

"To Sir Andrew Agnew, Bart "

In Galloway the population generally keep more correctly to original forms The "Bou o' Niel," Gordon, and Cumming (Comyn), are phonetically true , Fraser changes to Frissel, De Veir to Weir , Taillefer is little changed in Telfer. Among the baronage the changes are not for the better In Galloway, Vaux or De Vallibus (intermediately Woauss) is now Vans , d'Agneaux, and d'Aygnell, Agnew , Mondavilla (in England Mandeville), Mundwell , De Vesci, Vertel , De Monte Alto, Mowatt

CHAPTER X

A.D. 1365

His plate-jack was braced, and his helmet was laced,
And his vaunt-brace of proof he wore,
At his saddle-girth was a good steel sputhe
Full ten pound weight and more,

The Eve of St John.

A FEW stout English spearmen in his train, and a little gold in his pocket, John Aignell, bidding a long adieu to the Hertfordshire home, and his half-brother Andrew, made his way to the Scottish capital.

Scotland was still a field open to Anglo-Norman adventurers. Kings courted their society, encouraged their desire to hold under them, and, having still land in abundance to bestow, were only too glad to place on it these vassals, on whose performance of feudal duties they could rely, and who were moreover able to take possessions and hold them unaided.

Hence his settlement at Lochnaw. But before accompanying him thither, we must turn for a moment to the Irish traditions of the family. The salient points of these are that an Agneau, having accompanied Sir John de Courcy at the conquest of Ulster, received as his share of the spoil the "Tuagh of Latharna," and left his name there in Agnew's Hill which overlooks it; that these lands remained continuously in the possession of his descendants, not only up to the reign of Edward III., but after he had transferred his allegiance to a Scottish king.

All this rests entirely upon tradition, and is incapable of proof, no Irish charters or state papers of the date having been preserved. At the same time there are some old written notices of the matter, and the traditions connecting the family with Larne are so strong and definite on both sides of the water that we give them for what they are worth.

Scotch, English, and Irish, it is assumed as notorious that the Agnews had held Irish lands beyond all memory of man, and also that the first Agnew of Lochnaw passed by way of Ireland to the Scottish Court.

Sir George Mackenzie, one of the earliest Scottish genealogists, writes :

"Agnew.—The chief is Agnew of Lochnaw, whose predecessors came from Ireland, Rego Davidus 2do, being a son of ye Lord Agnews, alias Lord of Larne. There he gott the keeping of the king's castell of Lochnaw, and was made Heritable Constable yrof." [1]

Nisbet the herald [2] (whose inquiries were so far official that he was assisted by a grant from Parliament in their prosecution) repeats "The Agnews of Lochnaw were Lords Agnew alias Lords of Larne.   One of their sons came from Ireland to Scotland in the reign of David II., where he got the keeping of the king's castle of Lochnaw, and was made Heritable Constable thereof, and of the shire of Wigtown."

Chambers states as a matter well known : "We find an Agnew accompanying Sir John de Courcy in the invasion of Ireland." [3]

Repeated in the *Scottish Nation* . [4] "In the twelfth century Sir John de Courcy was accompanied, we are told, by an Agnew, , an Anglo-Norman like himself," both referring to their occupation of Larne.

Playfair, an English authority, whose notice of the French domicile of the family we have proved to be accurate, writes :

[1] Mackenzie's Genealogical MSS., Advocates' Library, Edinburgh.

[2] Nisbet's *Heraldry*, 160.

[3] Chambers, *Eminent Scotsmen*, vol. v.

[4] *Scottish Nation*, ii 679

"This ancient family were seated in Normandy about the end
of the tenth century, where they bore the name of Agneaux;
there is a tradition in the family, confirmed by some ancient MSS.,
that the first progenitor in England came from Normandy
with William the Conqueror.   How long they resided in
England is uncertain, but it is understood that they went to
Ireland soon after its subjection to the English Crown by
Strongbow, and it is very well known that they had extensive
possessions in the county of Antrim, where they were Lords of
Larne.   We are unable to prove this by any specific records, on
account of the unsettled state of that part of the kingdom in
those early times.   But in the time of David II. a son of the
family of Agnew arrived at the Scottish Court, where, being a
man of bravery and spirit, he got the keeping of the castle of
Lochnaw, of which he was made Hereditary Constable, and also
was appointed Sheriff of the County of Wigtown." [1]

The matter is more authoritatively put by the Rev. Classen
Porter, whose words carry weight from his known accuracy in
Irish antiquarian and genealogical research. [2]   "It would be
wrong to suppose that the first immigration of the Agnews into
Antrim took place on the settlement there of King James's
Scottish colonists.   They had been in Antrim centuries before,
and during all that time had retained their connection by
property with the neighbourhood of Larne, although, on the re-
distribution by King James among the Chichesters, MacDonnells,
and other families, the Agnews of Larne were obliged for the
first time to hold as tenants under the Earl of Antrim the lands
which their Norman forefathers had won by the sword." [3]

A letter addressed to the late Sir Andrew Agnew, seventh
baronet, [4] by an Irish resident gentleman, Mr. Farrell of Maghera-

---

[1] Playfair's *British Family Antiquity*.   The MSS which he alludes to are to
be found in abundance in the archives of La Manche.

[2] On tracing the subjoined article to the pen of Mr Porter, the author wrote
to Dr. Reeves, Dean of Armagh, now Bishop of Dromore, to know his opinion as
to its weight   The Dean's reply was.   "Mr Classen Porter is a good and reliable
antiquary "

[3] Published in the *Northern Whig*, 27th September 1864.

[4] The author's father

morne, dated 1818, has this passage : " There are few estates in Ireland that are not spoken of as having been the property of some Irish family not now in possession. But I have never heard the most distant idea being suggested that Kilwaughter was supposed to have been the property of any other family previous to the reign of Elizabeth. I do not know of any mountain in the north of Ireland that bears the name of a family, and no other name has been ascribed to it so far back as I have been able to obtain records." In reference to this Mr. Classen Porter (to whom the letter was shown by the author) stated that the townland of Mulloch-Sandal, within a few miles of Larne, took its name from one of De Courcy's followers, rendering it *prima facie* not at all improbable that Agnew's Hill may have got its designation from another. " We know, however," he subsequently wrote, " from retours of a very ancient date (one I believe reaching back to 1198), that it has been also called Carnanagholy."[1] Now Carnanagholy means the " Horse knight's Cairn " Horse knight on Celtic lips would well convey the idea of an accoutred Anglo-Norman. But a second local tradition respecting the name is even more suggestive —that the hill stood for a French officer who settled at Larne[2]

The only historical facts in the slightest degree corrobo- rative of these traditions being . (1*st*) The intimate connection between the families of De Courcy and Agneau; (2*d*) the association of the fathers of the Sir John de Courcys and Agnews of the day as fellow members of the royal household; and (3*d*) the further fact of Henry de Agnew being " declared rebel," and his manor in Norfolk forfeited to the Crown at the very time that De Courcy was imprisoned, and also declared rebel, for high-handed proceedings in Ulster.

[1] This was referred to Dr. Reeves, *facile princeps* in interpreting names, who unhesitatingly rendered Agholy, Each mhilidh, horse knight, Agholy being the recognised form of the vernacular.
[2] Mr. Classen Porter, writing to the author in 1864, says : "This form of the tradition I have got from Mr Burke at Larne, now eighty years of age, he having been told by a Miss Craig of Glenarm, she having seen it in an old book, viz that the first Agnew who settled at Larne was a French officer, whence the name of Agnew's Hill "

If a story can be constructed on so slender a foundation.
Henry de Agneau may be presumed to have been one of the
Norman knights who joined Henry II. at Milford Haven, the
rendezvous he had appointed for the Irish expedition in 1171,
Hence the king "took shipping, and arrived unto Waterford
in the kalends of November, being St. Luke's Day. The Irish
chieftains were greatly astonished at the magnificence of the
Anglo-Norman knights. Wonderful it was to the rude people
to behold the majesty of so gallant a prince . the pastime, the
sport, and the mirth, the continual music, the masking, mum-
ming, and strange shows; the gold, the silver, and plate, the dainty
dishes, furnished with all sorts of fish and flesh, the wines, the
spices, the delicate and sumptuous banquets, the orderly service,
the comely march and seemly array of all officers, the
gentlemen, the esquires, the knights and lords in their rich
attire, the running at tilt in complete harness."[1] "There were
three sundry sorts of servitors which served in the realm of
Ireland—Normans, Englishmen, and Cambrians. The first
were in most credit and estimation. The Normans were very fine
in their apparel; they could not feed but upon dainties, neither
could their meat digest without wine at each meal. They left
no means unsought how they might rule the roast, they would
not remain in remote places—a warm chamber, a ladie's lapp, a
soft bed, a furred gown, pleased them well"[2]

Prominent among these dainty gentlemen was Sir John de
Courcy, and he, quarrelling with Fitz Aldelme the viceroy,
started a few years later upon an expedition of his own ·
"By his wise confidence and witty persuasions, he allureth
and enticeth to him such as were the valiantest, honestest, and
chosen men of them all, and having so gotten into his company
two and twenty gentlemen and about three hundred others, he
boldly entereth and invadeth the Province of Ulster."[3]

Again Henry Agneau, we are to suppose, was one of this
little band of twenty-two, who followed his chief into this
unknown country. A prophecy of Merlin Colodine had fore-

---

[1] Hanmer's *Chronicle*   [2] Giraldus Cambrensis.   [3] Holinshed's *Chronicles.*

· told that a white knight sitting on a white horse, bearing birds on his shield, shall subdue Ulster. De Courcy rode forth on a white charger,[1] three eagles were emblazoned on his shield, and as place after place yielded to the Norman arms superstition helped to make the victory easier, and the whole province of Ulster submitted to this handful of adventurers. The king, fain to secure allegiance as best he might, instead of treating De Courcy as a mutineer, created him Earl of Ulster, and gave him a grant by patent to himself and his companions of all the lands they could conquer by their own swords, to be held and enjoyed by themselves and their heirs for ever.[2]

Acting as Lord Paramount, he granted the lordship of Howth to a Moricus de Sancto Lorentio, his brother-in-law, held by the Earl of Howth and Viscount St. Lawrence, his descendant, and to D'Agneau he allotted the lordship of Larne, a part of which was enjoyed by his descendants until the beginning of the eighteenth century.

The Norman conquerers introduced a species of civilisation to which the natives would no doubt gladly have remained strangers. "They builded many castles, made bridges, mended highways, repaired churches, and governed the country in great peace until the days of King John."[3]

It may be mentioned in connection with the name of Agnew in Ireland that the surname was assumed by a considerable sept of Celtic origin, the Ognieves or O'Gnives. These have no connection with descendants of the Norman Agneaus, who all became Protestant, whereas the O'Gnives are Catholics.

The O'Gnives were the bards of the minor branch of the Clanneboy O'Neills, and had their residence on a rock near Ballygelly on the Antrim seaboard The O'Gnive of his day is mentioned as appearing in his state dress and attracting much attention at the court of Queen Elizabeth. His descendants call themselves Agnews.

[1] He rode upon a white horse, as also did Bean, in his shield painted birds blazoned thus. argent, three griples or geires, gules, crowned gold —Giraldus Cambrensis, 16.

[2] Hanmer's *Chronicle.*   [3] *Ibid*

CHAPTER XI.

A.D. 1365 to 1366

You, my good yeomen,
Whose limbs were made in England—show us here
The mettle of your pasture.—SHAKESPEARE.

BY whatever route Aignell reached the Scottish Court, whether,
like his great-grandfather, by way of Newcastle-upon-Tyne, or, as
tradition has, by Dublin, Larne, and the estuary of the Clyde,
his mission was a success, as "their he gott the keeping of the
Castell of Lochnaw," furnishing him at once with employment
and a home.

As the writs in connection with his first infeftment were
lost in the rifling of the castle some years later, we can only fix
the date approximately.

King David II. had, on his return from captivity in 1347,
been prevented from taking steps for quieting Galloway by
disturbances elsewhere.   And it was not until 1363 that,—
having concluded a final and secret treaty with King Edward
III.,—he felt himself strong enough to attempt a settlement of
the turbulent districts of the west.   There his Castle of Lochnaw
was without a keeper, and young Agnew arriving opportunely
seemed exactly suited for the place.   Forthwith his commission
as Constable was made out, and with his charter of Crown lands
in his pocket, his Hertfordshire yeomen at his back, he set out
to take possession, his escort proving sufficient not only to guard
him by the way, but to keep the king's peace when settled on

the holdings which he and the family henceforth were to call their home.

The founding of the fortunes and scene of the settlement of the Scottish branch of the Agnews has been well and humorously described by a lively writer :

" The Isthmus of the Rhynns is guarded by the royal Castle of Lochnaw, the seat of the Agnews, Hereditary Sheriffs and Baillies of the county. Pleasantly placed among wooded hills by the side of a romantic loch, the ancient seat of the Agnews still boasts the square solid tower about whose battlements is spread a wondrous scene of land and water. The Agnews, as their name and arms imply, are of Norman origin, and bear upon their coat three lambs. They established themselves on both sides of the Irish Sea, having one foot, so to speak, on either island, and probably, after the Norman method, without much regard to the rights of the folk who were there before them. As a powerful, if alien family, they attracted the regards of the Scottish monarchs, who sought to strengthen their hold on the principality of Galloway ' And thus from an early date they were *par excellence* the king's men, and seem to have gone hammer and tongs, with anything but lamblike behaviour, against all other potentates in their neighbourhood.[1] . . . As a rule it must be said that the sheriffs were every bit as wild and lawless as the rest of the king's lieges in these parts Forays, feuds, sieges, and plunderings, curiously mixed up with pleadings and law-suits, went on from century to century. When the Douglasses were out of the way, there were the Kennedys to quarrel with. The Kennedys, Earls of Cassilis, were far more powerful than the sheriffs, but the Agnews held their own in

---

[1] The writer continues, though he anticipates our story · " When the Douglasses ruled at Threave, the Agnews had a hard time of it. Douglasses grim and black were altogether too strong for both king and sheriff, and Lochnaw was captured by the Douglas power and the Agnews driven into exile. They probably had some concern in that terrible scene at Stirling Castle, when the Douglas was done to death by the king and his attendants. Anyhow, soon after that event, the king granted by charter the hereditary sheriffdom to the Agnews." —" Chronicles of Scottish Counties," reproduced in *All the Year Round*, vol. xxxviii. p. 538.

many skirmishes and downright battles, both in the field and in the law-courts."

A tradition, though somewhat grotesque, of the first constable taking seizine of Lochnaw, seems not altogether inconsistent with the humours of the period.

When it was rumoured that a king's man had commission to take it, a native chief, it is said, named M'Clellan, was in occupation of the stronghold.

Denuding the country round about of all provision, and stocking well his own larder, he laughed in his sleeve as the stranger, with his armoured following, surrounded the lake, drawing up his boats upon his island. Vainly the titular constable tried to threaten or treat, the king's writs did not then run very freely in the province, and spearmen could not well conduct a siege with empty stomachs. Attack was impossible. Agnew's favourite henchman at last suggested a stratagem. A mutiny was enacted in their camp, and after a pretended scuffle, appeared to be quelled, and the henchman exposed to view as the ringleader dangling from a tree (the rope having been so arranged about his neck that he could for a while save himself from strangulation). The hanging scene arranged, the whole party mounted and made off; an ambush having been set. The plot succeeded to their heart's content. M'Clellan, who had been curiously watching the proceedings, as soon as the last lance pennon had disappeared behind Drumloccart, manned a boat and went to examine the victim. But hardly had he sprung ashore, before the lyers-in-wait cut off his retreat, and were after him sword in hand. The old Pict, however, was so supple and sly, that he led them a long chase through broken ground, and hours elapsed before they ran him in. His foe despatched, young Agnew bethought him of his lieutenant, who had been left far longer than he had bargained for. The farce, alas, was turned into a tragedy: the brave fellow whose wit had gained him the castle, hung stiff and cold.

The phonetic derivation of Lochnaw is Loch-an-atha, "lake

of the ford"; and that there was a submerged causeway from the island to the shore there can be no doubt. But in this there was nothing distinctive. Almost every lake in the province had its castle. Where there was not a natural island, a crannog was constructed, and whether built on an artificial or natural island, every such strength had a causeway to the shore.

In the oldest description of the shire extant, Lochnaw is described as a lake "belonging to the Sheriff of Wigtown, wherein ye kings of old had an house"; and as we find two Eochys among its Pictish kinglets, we are inclined to think that—as Lough Neagh in Ireland—it is from one of these that it takes its name.

Many place-names in its neighbourhood are suggestive of royal residence.

The eastern shore of the lake is Drumloccart,[1] the "ridge of the palace"; a large tract of land connected with the constabulary was Garthrie, "the king's enclosure"; Craigauch, "Eochy's rock," was the name of the old "tawar," or fortified lookout-post, already mentioned as one of Eochy's strongholds. The importance attached to the defence of Lochnaw is shown by many traces of Norse and Celtic spades in lands adjoining. Below the Tawar of Craigauch[2] is a Danish fort (curiously called Kemp's Graves) in Aldouran Glen, whence the parish name, Leswalt (Lios-uillt), "the fort of the glen"; and between this and Drumloccart, in the dry summer of 1880, a submerged causeway was discovered through the Black Loch, consisting of oak staves 6 feet 7 inches in length and 8 inches in diameter, evenly laid on a bed of hazel branches closely packed and in perfect preservation. Eastward of Lochnaw is also Dinduff, "the ox fort,"[3] and a castle site called also Craigoch   Above

[1] Lucairt is the conventional term in the Highlands for the residence of a kinglet

[2] Of the great conic mounds of defence, as we learn from the intrenchments that surround them, and the encampments on their summits, was the Tawar of Craigoch in Leswalt —*Cal.* iii. 356.

[3] So Clondoff, County Down. Damh, an ox, often changes to Duff.—Joyce, 1 473. In this case the soil is light sand and gravel Duff, from dubh, is applied to black or peaty soils.

Lochnaw, southward, the highest hill is Sleutennoch (Teinne-
ach), " the (watch)fire hill " ; and farther westward three contiguous circular raths almost within bowshot of one another, on
a hill-slope called Lashandarroch, which may mean either " the
old forts of the oak wood," or " the fort of the old oaks."   At

Tower
of Craigoch

Larbrax, due west, is the well-known Sea King's Camp, mapped
by Ainslie Kemp's Walks (obviously wark).   A little to the
north is the fort on Salt Pans Bay, under Millvaird (the bard's
hill), and farther north, Castle Bann,[1] evidently synonymous
with Carbantium or Carbantorigum.

[1] The site is remarkable, flattened from the rock, 216 feet in circumference ; this detached from the cliffs by a dry ditch 20 feet deep.   There is hardly

Of the sites of historic or legendary tales we have, on the shore near Lochnaw, Cave Ochtree, whence Uchtred was dragged by his ruthless brother Gilbert.   Tapmalloch (rather Taphmalloch) is the hillside where St Malachy o' Morgair reared his chapel and rath whilst waiting for a ship from Bangor.   Below it is St. Ringan's Well; Tringan, as it is called in the countryside, famous for its never-failing supply of the purest water.   On the eastern shore was the ancient Kilmorie, beside which was a wonder-working well of great repute on the lands still called St Mary's Croft, and Glen Mary, now Glenside.   Beyond Glen Mary, Loch Connell intervening, is Killiemaccuddican, where, as already mentioned, the saintly power of the infant Cuthbert first asserted itself; whilst nearer Lochnaw, the names are rather suggestive of early Anglo-Norman occupation.   Galdenoch,[1] "the place of the new comers"; Drummullin, "the mill ridge", and Slewnagel, "the chapel hill."

Of the neighbours, the Constable found on his arrival the nearest were the Lairds of Corswall, Dunskey, Garthland, and Killeser.

Corswall was owned by Alexander Campbell, a son of Sir Duncan Campbell of Loudoun, whose elder brother Andrew was Sheriff of Ayr.   The lands are named from a hill (Cor-siale, "the round hill of the brine"),[2] at the northern extremity of the Rhynns, against which the billows break in a north-western gale in one sweep from Labrador.

Corswall Castle lay in a hollow behind it, the lower story vaulted and serving as a cow fort.   A preposterous story passes current that in the well underneath this was a spring of such power that by raising the lid the owners could at pleasure flood the moat and approaches to the castle; the origin of which seems

a stone lying upon another, but many chisel-shaped stones lay on the beach below it.

[1] Gallda, as a living word in Ireland, now means "belonging to an Englishman"   In Galloway it is usually to be referred to Anglo-Normans.

[2] Previous to 1333 Corsiall belonged to Sir Alan Stewart of Dreghorn. Corsehill is more correct than Corsewell, the modern form   It is written Crosswell in Robertson's *Index*, Krosswell,—Pont

due to the corruption of the Celtic name to Corsehill, and afterwards to Crosswell, whence it became confounded with St.
Columba's Well, once a place of considerable resort at a short
distance from it.   It seems never to have occurred to the
inventors of the story to inquire what had occasioned the total
disappearance of this impetuous spring

Dunskey, here the equivalent of Portree, belonged to Adair,
as also the strongholds of Kinhilt and Dromore.

Dunskey [1] (dun-sciath), "the winged fort," stood on a beetling
crag on the lands of Portree (Port-righ, "the king's port," now
Portpatrick).

Kinhilt [2] (ceann-eiltte), the site of the castle of the hind's
hill, was on the lands of Kildonan, just beyond the point where
the line of the Colfin Glen cuts the road to Dumfries.[3]

Canting origins are proposed for the name of Adair and
Kinhilt, or, as it is corrupted, Kilhilt, in connection with his
acquisition of these lands.

Dunskey, it is said, had been long in possession of a robber
and pirate named Currie, who was outlawed for his excesses,
and his castle, deemed almost impregnable, was promised by the
king to whoever should bring him his head.

A Geraldine from Ireland, who had fled from justice there,
endeavoured to retrieve his fortunes by gaining the prize.   He
waylaid the robber chief, and surprising him one night, forced
him backwards, and after carrying on a running fight, struck
him down with the hilt of his sword at the end of Colfin Glen.
Securing his head, he hurried to the court, presenting his bleed-

---

[1] Scœodunum vulgo arx alata.—Blaeu.   So Liskeagh, Sligo, Donaskeagh,
Tipperary —Joyce, ii. 178
  The winged fort, or fort of shields; "the wing" or "shield" rather in the
sense of extended side-buildings than of a store of arms.
  [2] So Annahilt, County Down.   Near Lochnaw is the same place-name,
translated "hind's hill."   Adjoining Kinhilt is Barnchalloch (Bearn-na-scalg),
"the gap of the hunting"; and near this again Slewnark, "the hill or moor of
the hunting-horn," Sleibh-na-hadairce.   So Killeenark and Drumuahark, Ireland,
"the wood and ridge of the hunting-horn."—Joyce, ii. 218.
  Kynhylt, Chamberlain Rolls, 1455; Kynhelt, 1575; Kinhilt, War Com-
mittees, 1643, et seq., now corruptly Kinhilt.
  [3] New Stat. Acc., Wigtown, 142.

ing trophy at the point of his sword. He was infeft in Currie's lands forthwith, and building a castle where the fatal blow had been struck, called it suggestively Kilhilt.

"Who dare encounter Currie?" asked a courtier as the young Geraldine entered the royal presence. "I dare," he answered. "Good," said the king, "let that be your name." Heraldry favours the tradition, which at least is an old one; the Adans carrying for their crest a man's head couped and bloody, drops of blood falling from it [1] As a matter of fact, the origin of the name is neither the canting one, nor Athdara (ford of the oaks) from Irish lands, but it is simply a form of Edgar,[2] his progenitor being probably Edgar, son of Duvenald, a leader at the Battle of the Standard, grandson of Donegal of Morton Castle, a descendant of whom, Robert Edzear, had a charter from Robert Bruce of the lands of Kildonan, adjacent to which are those of Kinhilt. In confirmation of this we also find the name Edgar attaching to a hill on his property at Dromore.

Near Kinhilt was Garthland, the seat of the chief of the MacDoualls Though Norse in form, the name is Celtic Garbh- cluain, "the rough meadow," its older orthography being Gairach- cloyne, contracted at this time to Gaiaflan.[3] The name M'Dowall is usually derived from Dubhgall, "the son of the dark-haired stranger," presumably of the Norsemen. But Mr. Skene, with truer instinct, points for its derivation to a class of names in which gal stands for valour, the force in this case being "the dark-haired warrior."[4]

Next came M'Cullochs, occupying the strong houses of Killeser and Auchnaught. Killeser is from a dedication to St

---

[1] Adair of Kinhilt parted per bend dexter, or and argent, three dexter hands, gules. Crest, a man's head couped and bloody. It is said they carry the bloody head for killing one Carey of Dunskey, a proscribed rebel.—Nisbet's *Heraldry*.

[2] In the Lochnaw charter chest various deeds prove the name Edzear and Adair to have been interchangeable with the Galloway Adairs In a charter dated 1625 the name is spelled in both forms on the same page

[3] Garflan, Lochnaw charter chest, 1426 , Garflen, 1485 , Garthclone, 1488, ditto.

[4] The names Dubhgall and Finngall, Danes and Norsemen, must not be confounded with Dubhgal and Fingal, belonging to a large class of names ending with gal, signifying "valour."—*Celtic Scotland*, 1 28

Lassair, mother of St. Finian of Moville ; Auchnaught (nocht) meaning the bare field. The two principal families of M'Culloch were styled of Myrton and Torhouse (both in the Machers). On the lands of the latter were the well-known standing-stones beneath which their princely progenitor Gwalauc ap Lleenawg slumbered.

The earliest form of the name M'Culloch as a proprietor is M'Ulach, whence we trace it back in church calendars to Makwolok[1] (in the breviaries Volocus), thence to the Gwallawc of the Cymric bards, and the older Golgacus of the Romans, its Cymric root being gwalc, "the hawk of battle"

It is amusing to find how tradition travesties facts   It has been generally accepted that the root of M'Culloch is the Gaelic cullach, "a boar," and gravely stated that a Galloway chief who attracted notice by his valour at the Crusades had carried a boar as his device, whence Cullach became his *nom de guerre*. When returning home he was specially commended to William the Lion by Godfrey de Bouillon, who forthwith gave him the lands of Myrton, Glasserton, and Auchnaught ; and he, adopting M'Culloch as his surname, christened his son Godfrey after the King of Jerusalem, a name henceforward frequent among the M'Cullochs.

Unfortunately, besides various anachronisms, the earliest and the only arms registered of the M'Cullochs were Ermine, a fret ingrained gules

A more interesting tradition is that a ruin on Auchnaught is called by the peasantry "the hunting seat of the M'Cullochs." This is really a Celtic reminiscence, as, although the neighbourhood is by no means favourable to the chase, the ruins are mapped Castle Shell, which evidently the natives understood not long ago to be derived from seilg (hunting), just as the tribal name Selgova

---

[1] There is a Bishop Makwolok in the Kalendars, his day being 29th January Camararius places his death in 733, and names his mission as at Candida Casa. He was known also at Balveny, Mar, etc., where he is commemorated in the popular rhyme—

Wallafair in Logie Mar,
The 30th day of Januar

Forbes, *Scottish Saints.*

indicated hunters. The M'Cullochs had lately come into possession of Cardoness by the Water of the Fleet, as thus related.
A Border ruffian, having built up his house by violence and
rapine, took to himself a wife to perpetuate his name. His
spouse presented him with nine daughters in succession, each
new comer more unwelcome than the last. After a long pause
his wife was again as ladies like to be who love their lords.
Just before her lying-in he burst into her bower and brutally
declared that, unless she produced a son, he would drown her
and her whole progeny in the Black Loch. So capable was he
thought of acting on his threat, that great was the joy of the
whole countryside, as of the old rascal himself, when a boy was
actually born. It was midwinter, and the laird, in jovial mood,
ordered a feast to be prepared on the frozen surface of the loch.
The neighbours were bidden, and on a bright Sunday they and
his household assembled on the ice, the lady and her precious
babe being carried thither. The glass went merrily round, fun
was at its highest, when suddenly the ice collapsed, wife, son,
and the whole bevy of daughters save one, who was ill and had
been left at home, sank fathom deep in the dark waters, the
devil claiming the wicked laird as his own.

The little heiress, on growing to womanhood, gave her hand
to a M'Culloch, carrying to that family the lands and tower,
which thenceforth had the name of Cardoness, " the castle of
ill-luck." [1]

Besides the M'Cullochs and M'Dowalls, five families of
the Pictish blood still held lands in Galloway—the M'Clellans,
the MacKies, the MacGhies, the Accarsons, and the Ahannays.

The M'Clellans (Mhic Gille Phaolan), "sons of the servant
of St. Fillan," from whom was named the parish of Balmaclellan,
owned the two strongholds of Bomby and Raeberry, and their
chief was afterwards created Lord Kirkcudbright.[2]

---

[1] Caer-donais Donais, "mischief, misfortune, ill-luck" O'Ryley "the
devil, evil, mischief" MacAlpine: "Miltoness is Meall-donais, 'the devil's
hill'"

[2] Arms argent, two chevrons sable. Crest, a naked man supporting on the
point of a sword a Moor's head.

The MacKies (Mhic Aedh), "sons of Hugh," owned many lands, their chief being styled "of Larg"; and they carried two crows, with an arrow feathered thrust through their heads for a bearing, in commemoration of the feat of forestry performed by their ancestor before King Robert Bruce

The MacGhies were their cousins, the root of both names being similar. This branch of the family became fully the most powerful, and named the parish of Balmaghie[1]

In the names of Accarson and Ahannay the *a* stands for the equivalent to the Irish *o*, and has been dropped by their descendants. Of the Accarsons or Akersanes, the chief was of Rusco,[2] or Glenskairesburn. These lands were carried a century later by an heiress to the Gordons of Lochinvar.

The Ahannays or Hannays had superseded the Vipounts in Sorby, where they long occupied a strong house; as also at Kirkdale, in the Stewartry.[3]

Of Anglo-Normans Sir Walter Stewart, son of Sir John Stewart of Dalswinton, certainly *possessed* Garlies at this date, but it is doubtful if the family, as yet, were often or ever resident in Galloway.[4]

The Gordons (of whom more presently) ranged the Forest of Glenkens The Vaux were established in Wigtownshire, the Herries at Terregles, and the Maxwells on the Nith.

As a strong supporter of kingsmen in the shire, Sir John Kennedy warred sturdily on the northern marches, and in

---

[1] The bearings of the MacGhies differed entirely from that of the MacKies, being three leopards' heads, or.

[2] Rusco (Riascach), marshy Carsan is a living Celtic word for hoarse or asthmatic.

[3] Hannay is apparently an aspirated form of Sennach, a name common in the Kalendars, probably derived from sean, "old, venerable " Seannach is "lucky, fortunate, crafty "—O'Reilly.

The Ahannays carried argent, three roebucks' heads, azure, collared, or with a bell pendant, gules.

[4] The Stewarts had a charter of Garlies for the battle of the Largs. Sir John, as above, had a charter of renewal from Randolph, Earl of Moray. In October 1396 a contract was entered into between Sir Walter Stewart of Dalswinton and Garlies, and Sir William Stewart, Sheriff of Teviotdale, that Marian, daughter and heiress of Sir Walter, should marry John, son and heir of Sir William.—Wood, i. 116.

1365 his son, Sir Gilbert, acquired Cruggleton, Polton, and the two Broughtons.[1]

An important element in the Constable's society were the fraternities of Soulseat and Glenluce, whose lordly abbots took their places with the baronage in the field, the banqueting hall, and the council board.

There were also at this date many lands in occupation of the Knights Hospitallers of St. John of Jerusalem, some of which had previously been held by the Knights Templars, to whom they had fallen heirs. "Hospital" then had a wider sense than a place for the treatment of the sick, the hospice being a house of entertainment for the stranger and the traveller. Near Lochnaw was the Spittal Croft of Craichmore (now Burgess Croft),[2] Portes-spittal under Nashantee, "old houses," of the Novantæ, near Agricola's Doon of Kildonan ; Spittal, between Kirkcowan and Wigtown ; Temple-Croft, Kirkmaiden ; Temple-lands, Sorby ; with St. John's Croft adjacent ; St. John's town, now Dalry, on the river Ken ; and St. John's Croft, the site of the burgh of Stranraer.

At the coming of the Agnews Malcolm Fleming, Earl of Wigtown, a man of mark and character, had died, or was dying, and was succeeded by a grandson, Thomas, who has the character of being weak, and who had long been a hostage in England for the King of Scotland's ransom   He succeeded his grandfather before 1365, when he had a renewal of the grant of his earldom, in which the king expressly reserved the regality jurisdictions held by the first earl, which he now granted by commission to the Agnews.[3]

---

[1] Concerning this name it is out of all doubt the same proceeded from the name Kennethe.—Pitcairne.

[2] In the Lochnaw charter chest is a charter by Sir William Knowlys, dated from the Preceptory of the Order of St. John of Jerusalem, of "a certain croft, the Temple Land, vulgerly called the Spittal Croft of Craighmore," dated from Torfichen, *circum* 1487.

[3] Charter to Thomas Fleming, heir au Counte de Wigton.—Fr. David II Perth, 25 Jan. 1365-6

Sciatis nos dedisse et restituisse Thome Flemyng totum comitatum de Wygtoun cum pertinencus . .   sicut quondam Malcolmus avus prædicti Thome tenuit, salvo quod jus regalitatis in ipso comitatu non habeat, aut ipsa regalitate utatur, *quam ex certa causa in suspenso* remanere volumus.—*Great Seal Register.*

CHAPTER XII

THE DOUGLAS AT LOCHNAW

A.D. 1366 to 1424

> Grim Douglasse answered him agayne
> With great words up on hee,
> I have twenty men against they one,
> Behold, and thou mayest see.
>
> *Border Ballads.*

FROM the appointment of the Agnews to the keeping of Lochnaw by David II. to their restoration (after having been ousted by Earl Douglas) by James I., a hiatus occurs in family records as to the dates of the successions and marriages of three generations.

Charter evidence, however, suggests their connections during that period to have been with the Vauss, the Campbells, M'Dowalls, and Adairs.

The Vauss (Vaux, de Val, de Valibus) had been Norman neighbours of the Agnews; Vaux, whence their name, lying near Bayeux, almost adjoining Les deux Jumeaux; and we have already noted the association of the families on English soil, an acquaintance to be renewed in Galloway.

The first Vaus of Barnbarroch was a son or nephew of William de Vaus of Dirleton ; another son of whom, Alexander, was inducted into a living in Galloway in 1381, and was afterwards consecrated bishop; his brother or cousin marrying the heiress of Barnbarroch *circum* 1384.[1]

---

[1] Alexander Vaus was possessed of Church livings in Galloway as early as the year 1381, and was consecrated bishop of that diocese in 1420.—*Cor of Sir Patrick Waus.*

Previous to this, however, we find mention of an Andrew Vaus—as a Galloway baron—who fell at Poictiers 1356, fighting against the English.[1] And this date is perfectly consistent with the possibility of his having left a daughter of an age eligible for the wife of the first constable of Lochnaw.

In 1368 Archibald Douglas received hereditary gift of all the Crown lands in Galloway eastward of the Cree, and the rights of the Earldom of Wigtown were soon about to drop into his hands through the unfitness of its holder. This result was hurried on by a series of insults which we cannot but suspect the grim Archibald of encouraging. The last of these insults, whence Fleming's disappearance from Galloway, reads like a comedy. But it is quite obvious such pranks could not have been played with impunity had the Earl of Wigtown not lost the sympathy of his neighbours.

A cadet of the house of Dunure, Alexander Kennedy, closely connected with the baronage of the Rhynns, who, from his readiness to unsheathe his blade, was nicknamed Alschunder Dealgour (Sandy of the Dagger), having quarrelled with Fleming, committed such serious depredations on his land that the earl, in a rage, determined to take him dead or alive, or, as quaintly expressed by the chronicler, "This Alschunder fell in mislyking with the Erll of Wigtoune, quha wes ane werry gritt manne, and had ane gritt force in all the country, and wes so far offenditt at him that he offeritt to any that wald bring this Allexanderis heid, that suld have the fourty markland of Stewarttoune in Cuninghame!" This coming to Alexander's ears, he had the titles of the estate drawn up in legal form, "heffand all his rycht of the said xl mark land put in forme," "and convening to the number of ane hundred horse," he rode all night, timing his arrival at Wigtown for Yule-day morn,

[1] A French historian, writing of the period, says. "Dans ce temps-là le Comte de Douglas et son frère Archinbald Seigneur de Gallovay venait avec trois mille Ecossais au secours du Roi. Ils firent bon service à la Bataille de Poictiers. Des hommes de marque furent tués,—Andre Stevart très jeune mais très brave—Robert Gordon d'une grande famille—André Vaus de Gallovay le frère d'armes du Seigneur Archinbald. Le comte échappa mais Archinbald fut pris."—*Hist des Malheurs de la France sous le Roi Jean* Paris, chez Bard, 1611, vol. ii. 103

at the hour he knew the earl likely to be at morning mass
Bursting into the church, his charter in his hand, "My lord,"
he exclaimed, "you have promised this 40 mark land to whoever will bring you my head, and who so meet to offer it to
your lordship as your humble servant? And therefore I will
desire your lordship to keep your word to me, as you would to
any other." His dagger dangled at his side, the spurs and
scabbards of his followers clanked on the pavement as they
crowded in behind him. "The earl perceived that gif he refused it would cost him his lyffe, and therefore took pen and
subscribed the same." "Alexander thanked his lordship, and
taking his horse, lap on, and came his ways." [1]

That the earl should have been cowed and despoiled by such
a daring roysterer, we can readily conceive. But what were
the Sheriffs of Ayr and Wigtown about that he was not tracked,
and obliged to surrender his person and his charter to superior
force?

No hue or cry was raised; no blast of the horn denounced
him rebel, no kingsman stirred to avenge the majesty of the
law. Alschunder profited at least as much by Fleming's
unpopularity as by his own audacity The officials of Wigtown
and the shire of Ayr shrugged their shoulders, whilst Douglas,
who could easily have righted his fellow peer, laughing in his
sleeve, offered to relieve him of his responsibilities

As a result, Fleming, disgusted with the Galloway baronage,
who on their part openly despised him, fell in with the grim
Archibald's proposal [2] A bargain was speedily concluded. For
£500 he surrendered his lands, his castle, his powers and privileges, his very title (though this last was not eventually confirmed
by the king), to Archibald, who thenceforth became Lord Para-

---

[1] *History of the Kennedys*, p. 5. How far the story is founded on fact, it
would now be difficult to trace, but it is certain that the Earl of Wigtown made
a grant of the town of Kyikyntullach to Sir Gilbert Kennedy, which was confirmed 13th May 1372.—*Reg. Mag Sig* 104 · Pitcairn, *Hist of Kennedys*, 79.

[2] In the charter conveying his lands and offices to Douglas, dated 6th February
1371, Fleming expressly gives as the cause of his leaving, "propter magnam
atque gravem immicitiam inter me et majores indigenos dicti Comitatus "—Crawford's *Peerage*, 409.

mount both east and west of Cree, and gave special pro-
minence to his style of Lord of Galloway

His epithet "grim" notwithstanding,[1] there can be no
manner of doubt that the change from Fleming to Douglas
was for the advantage of the province, the sinister memories
attaching to his castle of Threave[2] belonging not to himself,
but to his great-grandchildren.

The death of David II. in 1371 further increased the
prestige of the Douglasses, as it was not until they had been
conciliated that the king's nephew could ascend the throne as
Robert II.[3]   It altered also considerably the status of all
Galloway officials who had held appointments directly from
the king.   For although Archibald governed in the king's
name, he considered himself solely responsible for order, with
the right of appointment to all offices vacant, requiring all
Crown vassals to acknowledge himself as their superior.

It was, however, an object with Archibald to make his
service popular, and attach the baronage to his person.   Himself a veritable Paladin, formidable in the field, and as sagacious
as he was strong, he easily won the admiration of the chivalry
of the province, who freely enrolled themselves under his
banners, their tastes being constantly gratified by adventurous
raids, in which they not only lived well at the enemy's expense,
but returned to their homes laden with spoils.

Meanwhile a son had succeeded the first Constable of Lochnaw, in the keeping of which he was in no way interfered with by
the Lord of Threave ; and there is reason to believe, although
all charters have disappeared, that the family had extended their

---

[1] "Archibaldus dictus Grym sive terribilis."—Bowmaker, *Continuation of
Fordun*, bk xv ch. xi.

Archibald the Grim was a natural son of the Good Sir James. He married
the daughter and heiress of Thomas Murray, Earl of Bothwell, on succeeding
to whose estates he assumed the three stars, the cognisance of the Murrays, in
addition to those of Douglas, argent a chief azure

[2] Tref. (Cym), Treabth (Celtic), an equivalent of Aros, "a house, a homestead " The Pictish evidently here approached the Cymric. Various deeds in
the Lochnaw charter chest are dated "Apud Treyf."

[3] King Robert II was the only child of Walter Stewart by the Princess
Marjorie, King Robert I.'s daughter.

possessions eastward of Lochryan, and had become possessed of the lands of Croach and Laight Alpyn.[1] Concurrently with the succession of this generation, William Douglas, a natural son of Archibald, was entrusted with the management of Galloway affairs.

The first swordsman of his day, handsome, hearty, and accessible, he was singularly fitted to take the lead in the raids and revels of the period. Faithfully followed by the youth of the province, he soon made himself such a name that, what with his prowess and good looks, he proved a successful rival to the King of France, whose hand the Princess Egidia, the fairest lady of her day, is said to have refused, for love of this Galloway knight.

A chronic war, due to the private rivalry of border chiefs, raged for years, which, owing to the prowess of Archibald and William, turned usually to the advantage of the Galwegians.

In 1378, an English army were carrying all before them in the eastern counties, under Sir Thomas Musgrave, when the Douglasses fell unexpectedly upon them. The Galwegians, couching their lances, charged with the cry of "Douglas and St. Giles!"[2] with a fury which bore down all opposition, almost all the English gentlemen of fortune being taken prisoners and held to ransom.

A meeting being agreed upon between the Lord of Galloway and John of Gaunt, Duke of Lancaster, to arrange a truce, this was kept for the appointed time, but the moment it expired Douglas pounced upon and took the castle of Lochmaben, which

[1] The Agnews of Croach on Lochryan were cadets of Lochnaw, in whose favour these lands were detached from the family estates as early as *circum* 1460 But though they notoriously so received them and held possession for three hundred years, all charters connected with these transactions have been lost.

[2] Then they shouted their war-cry, which I think was "Douglas and St Giles!"—Froissart, 1 224 St. Giles was patron saint of Edinburgh, Egidia was its feminine form . . The conduct of the Douglasses in these wars is thus described by Froissart: "Sir Archibald Douglas was a good knight, and much feared by his enemies. When near to the English, he dismounted and wielded before him an immense sword, and gave such terrible strokes, none were so hardy among the English as to be able to withstand his blows The battle was sharp,.the Scots took seven score good prisoners, and the pursuit lasted to the Tweed"—Froissart, 1. 225.

had long been in their hands. Further, following after them with clouds of light horsemen, the terrible Archibald recovered also the part of Teviotdale which the English had held since the battle of Durham.

In these years the ranks of the baronage of Western Galloway were recruited by the arrival of the Dunbars. As early as 1368 George Dunbar, second son of the ninth Earl of March, had a charter of lands in the Glenkens and Mochrum, but usually resided at Cumnoch or Blantyre in the shire of Ayr. By Alicia, daughter of Mure of Rowallan, he had two sons, to the second of whom, Patrick, *circum* 1375, he gave the lands of Mochrum, upon which his family continuously resided

The Earl of Fife, and James, Earl of Douglas, attacking the English in the east, Douglas, as a diversion, burst with his Galwegians unexpectedly on the lake districts of Cumberland, which, lying beyond the usual limits of border raids, afforded a rich booty to his army, who plundered the quiet homesteads with a will, ransacking wardrobes, cellars, butteries, and chapels. Wyntoun's minute description (who gives the date 1386) is worth attention:

> And Schyre Archebald that than was
> Off Gallway Lord : assemblyd then
> Thai war welle thretty thowsand men.
> Thai swne passyd Sullway ;
> Syne till Kokyrmowth held thai.
> Between the Fellis and the sé
> Thare thai fand a hale cuntré
> And in all gudis abowndand,
> For na ware was in till that land,
> Syne Robert the Brwys deyd away.
> Than all that cuntré can thai pray
> And duelt thre dayis in till that land,
> Quhill thai had fillyd welle thare hand
> Syne held than thai hame thair wayis
> Wyth thare eupresoneys and thare prays,
> And passyd Sullway but tynsell,
> For thai war wysly led and welle.[1]

The mention of Cockermouth, and between the " Fellis and sé," suggests that this expedition was partly a naval one, and shipping would greatly facilitate the removal of their prey.

[1] Wyntoun, bk. ix. ch. vii.

Other successes attended this campaign, the leading spirit being Sir William Douglas, then, as styled by Wyntoun, "a joly bachelare," but an ardent wooer too, and that of the beautiful Princess Egidia. He had now so greatly distinguished himself that the king no longer withheld his consent to his marriage with his daughter, who returned his love. Their nuptials were duly celebrated, and returning to Carlisle the knight proudly presented his bride to his comrades of a hundred tuilzies, thanking them for assisting him to win her,[1] and forthwith Egidia reigned supreme, the queen of all their hearts.

Her honeymoon was to have been spent in camp, but was fated to be of the shortest duration. News reached Carlisle from the west that a band of Ulstermen were harrying the Rhynns in the absence of its defenders, and leisurely freighting their ships with whatever they chose to carry off. Great was the indignation of the Galwegian mosstroopers on learning that a set of Irish gallowglasses had so presumed to ape their doings on the Derwent, and still greater their exasperation when, having made all possible speed, the royal bride heading the column as their forest queen, they only reached their destination in time to see the sails of the laden ships disappearing in the offing.

So great was the energy of William Douglas that in an incredibly short time shipping was collected sufficient to carry five hundred spearmen across the channel Availing himself of the castle of Lochnaw as a place of safety for Egidia, and leaving her with the keeper's lady (whose husband we may be sure accompanied him), he tracked the retiring raiders along the Ulster shores, and followed them into Carlingford[2] Here he

---

[1] William, basse son to Archibald Douglas, Lord of Galloway, for his singular valour and reiterate victories against the Englishe both by sea and land, Kyng Robert did give him his daughter Geilles, a werry beautiful ladye, in marriage —Balfour, 131.

The king settled £300 annually out of the customs of the great towns, dilecto et fideli nostro Wilhelmo de Douglas militi filio Domini Archibaldi de Douglas, Domini Galwidii et Egidiæ carissimæ filiæ nostri   26th December 1386

[2]   Five hundyrd fechtares as I heard say
            At Karlyngford arrived thai.
                                        Wyntoun, bk. ix. ch. vii

took the town by assault, and recovering his spoil, laid it under
contribution, and by his personal prowess and strength
repelled an attack made on him unawares by troops from
Dundalk.

Considering this attack treacherous, he seized all the shipping in the port, and loading it with the spoil, set fire to the place,
and stood out to sea with his prizes.

Having thus revenged himself on the Irish he remembered
he had some old scores to settle at the Isle of Man.

Landing there, he seized more ships, filling them also with
goods and animals, and then, although in sight of Burrowhead, on the Isle of Whithorn, making a long detour by the Mull
of Galloway, and rounding Corswall Point, his large flotilla
rode in triumph in the calm waters of Loch Ryan.

That he took this course, which quadrupled the distance and
added indefinitely to the dangers of the voyage, is easily but
only to be accounted for by reading between the lines and
remembering that the Lady Egidia was waiting for him near
these distant waters, and doubtless, daily from the Tawar, watching for the arrival of the avenging squadron.

Rhyming and graver historians are equally minute in describing the circuitous route taken, and that they returned to,
as they had started from Loch Ryan:[1]

> Syne bi se thair trade took thai
> Till Man and Harryde it in thair way
> And syne arrywyd in Loch Ryane.
> > Wyntoun, bk. ix. ch. viii.

Shortly after this William Douglas led his Galwegians
across the western marches to assist his father Archibald. And
whilst there, James, Earl Douglas, heading a column farther
eastward, was killed at Otterburn

By ordinary rules his title should have passed to the Earl
of Angus ; but these were not ordinary times, and Archibald
Douglas was no ordinary man. He demanded legitimisation,

---

[1] Buchanan is equally explicit "Atque obiter Manniæ insula spoliatus ad
Lacum Rianum qui partem Gallovideæ et Caractæ diremit, appellunt "

basing his demand on the right of the sword. The Galloway barons declared for him to a man , they were actually in the field ready and able to uphold him against all comers. The king consequently formally ratified the claim he was powerless to refuse.[1]

If Archibald had been almost equal in power to King Robert II. before he was served heir to his kinsman, after it he was practically master of the situation And two years later Robert III. had to give the hand of the Princess Royal to the eldest son of his great feudatory as the price of his acquiescence in his own coronation.

But whilst Archibald asserted himself as Lord Paramount in Galloway, barring all interference or appeal, his rule, though despotic, was just, and his ideas of government far in advance of his age. He habitually assembled his baronage in local parliament, when laws were discussed, framed, and promulgated, regulating intercourse across the Borders, military service, the keeping and burning of bales, and general order. And so well and so long was peace preserved under this system that young William Douglas, despairing of finding fighting nearer home, foolishly accepted an invitation from certain fire-eating Teutonic knights to assist in a war against infidel Prussians, and sailed for Dantzic, never to return. He fell in a few days after landing, not in battle, but by the hand of an assassin Though Quixotic in his contempt for a quiet life, his untimely death was a real loss to Galloway, where high and low long mourned him as a friend.[2]

He had long acted as his father's right hand man, and by the tact and kindliness of his disposition so administered affairs as to occasion the least possible friction between the ruler and ruled, between the autocratic overlord and those who claimed to be Crown vassals.

---

[1] The fact being that Archibald, Lord of Galloway, was a bastard, how came he to be Earl Douglas? The answer must be by the grant of Robert II.— *Caledonia*, iii 267

[2] The customs of the wool of Galloway is remitted to Egidia, daughter of the king, in her widowhood.—*Exchequer Rolls*, 1401.

After his death the demands of the Douglas, if not more peremptory, were more harshly pressed, their tenour being that all officials, whether appointed by the Crown or not, must acknowledge him as their sole superior. In Kirkcudbright he altered the style of Sheriff to Steward, as marking the holder as his personal officer. The baronage also were desired to renew their titles to their lands from himself under pain of confiscation.[1]

Most of the lairds complied. M'Douall of Garthland being among the first, was treated with distinction, and not only confirmed in his estates but named Steward of Kirkcudbright.

Agnew of Lochnaw, whether from real affection to the king, or emboldened by his close relations with the Kennedys, who were near at hand, and the distance and strength of his keep, neglected to bring in his commissions to be checked at Threave, and Douglas sent to fetch him. According to tradition, Archibald found his fortalice a harder nut to crack than he had expected. It was a far cry from Threave to Lochnaw, and the ways none of the easiest.

An inland road by Knockwhassan, under the beaten hill of Dindinnic,[2] leads to Lochnaw by the valley of the Piltanton Here the Agnews lay in ambush for a party of the Douglasses who were coming to attack them. A fight ensued, both being

[1] A tissue of nonsense has been written on this subject, as if Douglas went from house to house demanding charters, and burning them maliciously. In the first place, the native proprietors held allodially, and therefore had none, in the second, the actual charter was as valueless to himself as he declared it to be to the proprietor He asserted himself superior. If any one declined to accept his lands from him, because held from the Crown, he simply confiscated them, and put a vassal of his own in possession. Crawford, the antiquary, writes such stuff as this: "It is impossible that old charters could be preserved in that country; what might have escaped the mighty Edward were more fully rifled by Archibald, Lord of Galloway. This is the reason that, although there be many ancient families in Galloway, yet not one gentleman has any writings preceding the time that the lordship of Galloway came to the house of Galloway "—MSS Hist. of the M'Dowalls of Garthland.

[2] The tradition as told is that the M'Ewans had then lately come from Argyle. We should naturally have supposed that a victorious party of Highlanders would have been more likely to have kept the arms and thrown the men into the moss hole. Knockwhassan, Cnoc-chasan, "the hill of the pathway"; Dindinnie, Dun-teinie, "fort of the fires"; Lochnafolie, Loch-na-fola, "lake of the blood."

well matched, when a stalwart band of M'Ewans, holding under the former, took the Douglasses in the rear, who were made prisoners to a man. Having stripped them of their arms, they let them go, and afraid of retaining what might afterwards prove evidence against them, threw the weapons into a flow moss, called Loch-na-folie.

Whether this little episode is to be believed or not, there could but be one result to the unequal strength. The earl had but to beleaguer the island a few days more or less to starve the garrison into an unconditional surrender.

His day of triumph came. And considering the standard by which the actions of offended potentates were then weighed, it cannot be said that the earl treated the constable with any wanton cruelty He allowed him to leave with his family unmolested, and go where he pleased; though he dealt more roughly with the castle, firing whatever was combustible in its massive structure, and toppling over the battlements whence the flag had flown in defiance of his summons.[1]

Traditionally it is said that the Agnews when driven from Lochnaw retired to their lordship of Larne[2] Possibly they did, if they still possessed it. Though we believe that their journey was much shorter, whether by land or water, and merely across Loch Ryan to their lands of Croach. But however this may have been, the constable lost little time in repairing to Court to lay his grievances before the king. Robert III doubtless expressed much sympathy, but could give him no assistance, whether with money or men. He, however, allowed him to remain at Court, whether with or without an appointment, where he was fortunate enough to attract the favourable notice

---

[1] As stated curtly by the chronicler · "Reg. Davidis 2di, a son of ye Lord Agnews, gott the keeping of the king's Castell of Lochnaw. His great grandchild wes opprest by the Erle of Douglas, by whom the Castell of Lochnaw wes blown up."—Mackenzie MSS., Advocates' Library, Edinburgh.

[2] "The Agnews of Lochnaw being dispossessed by Archibald the Grim, and their lands given to William Douglas, emigrated beyond his influence to Ireland But not liking their new place of abode, the father and son removed to the Court of Robert III at Perth, the former becoming a member of the royal household, and the latter having the good fortune to attract the notice of the king's daughter Margaret "—Chron. of Lincluden, 63.

of the Princesses Margaret and Mary. He assisted probably at
the marriages of both—the elder to Archibald Douglas, son and
heir of his terrible lord; the latter to George, first Earl of
Angus (the date of which is 24th May 1397), and afterwards to
a Kennedy of Dunure.

Meanwhile the jurisdictions of the Agnews and their lands
of Lochnaw were bestowed on William Douglas (probably an
illegitimate grandson of the earl), who took possession of the
shattered keep, styling himself "Constable, and also Sheriff, of
Wigtown."

Shortly after these summary proceedings, the great Archibald
himself passed to his last account (1401).[1]

Heavy as his hand had fallen on our ancestor, candour
obliges us to repudiate the charges local authors have somewhat
loosely heaped upon him. In truth, he was neither brutal nor
rapacious. He was religious according to his light, and in his
administration as between man and man was scrupulously just.

Two indictments against him have been repeated *ad nauseam*
in exaggerated terms of reprobation. One, that, as an ogre
greedy of old charters, he went from house to house, where, if
his unnatural appetite was unsatisfied, he battered down the
walls to get at them This we have already shown to be ridiculous. The other, that he laid a tax on every parish of a fat
heifer yearly, to be salted for winter provisions for his garrison.
The record of this "vile oppression" being usually accompanied
by such a sensational sentence as, "Woe be to those who refuse
to pay." It is too absurd to talk of one bullock from a whole
parish yearly as oppressive.

His character as given by Froissart, an observant and impartial contemporary, may be accepted as a fair one . "Most

---

[1] Earl Archibald married Johanna, daughter and heiress of Thomas Moray,
Lord of Bothwell In her right he introduced into his shield the three stars so
well known afterwards as the Douglas achievement His arms previously were
argent, a chief azure

The Bothwells held the office of "Panetarius Scotiæ." In a charter to his
father, who married King Robert I 's sister, the office is written in the vernacular
"pantryman " "Charter by Andrew Murray, pantryman, and Christian Bruce,
his spouse "—Robertson's *Index*

upright was he in judgment, yet severe; faithful to his word; recommended to fame as much by his wisdom as his valour."

His successor, also Archibald, is distinguished from the grim Earl as the Tyneman, a soubriquet, we suspect, in facetious allusion to his loss of an eye, and another member, even more important, at the battle of Homildon [1]

At this battle, fought in Northumberland 14th September 1401, he received five severe wounds, and was taken prisoner, as well as his brother-in-law Angus ; and of the Galloway baronage, Fergus M'Dowall of Garthland, Roger Gordon of Lochinvar, and Robert Stewart of Durisdeer.[2]

Earl Douglas was released by his captor, Percy, on condition of his assisting him in an attack on his own king. The Lord of Galloway asked nothing better, but was again taken prisoner whilst performing this engagement.

Henry IV. of England quickly released him on his sending thirteen knights as hostages for his ransom, among whom were Sir Herbert Maxwell of Caerlaverock and Sir John Herries of Terregles.

Douglas's brother-in-law Angus, less fortunate, died whilst still a prisoner, and the hand of the Princess Mary being free, she gave it to James, son of Sir John Kennedy of Dunure.

A most scandalous story of how the princess was wooed was put into circulation by a member of another branch of the Kennedys, which has developed into a spurious tradition, the absurdities and anachronisms of which are patent: " King James I. send ane of his dochters to the Laird of Donour to foster, quha remaynit with him quhill sche was ane woman. At the quhilk time the ladyis owen son heffing mair creditt in his moderis house nor her stepsone, being in luff with the young ladye, gettis her with bairne. The king her father being far offendit thairatt, could find no better way nor to cause him

---

[1] Hume of Godscroft gives the reason for the nickname, "in that he tint all his men, and all the battles that he fought." But this is opposed to fact He was an able and redoubtable commander, and his services notoriously competed for by the kings of France and England, as well as by his own.

[2] Dorus-darie, "door of the oakwood," i.e. entrance to the forest

marie her. And sa the Laird Donour deshereist his eldest sone, and made his second son land." [1]

We have here a tissue of untruths. The princess was not fostered at Dunure; her first visit there was as a widow. James, her husband, was the eldest son and natural heir to his father. The only slight plank on which the scandal originally floated was that James Kennedy was actually killed some years later by an illegitimate brother, who may or may not have been older than himself [2]

James and the princess had three sons,—John, Gilbert, James, —and probably one daughter only, as their married life extended little over four years. [3]

We are enabled to fill in a few details as to the Galloway baronage from the record of courts held at Threave. In 1403 the Earl issued a precept of sasine to Thomas Herts, Steward of Kirkcudbright, desiring him to infeft Sir Archibald Gordon in the lands of Kenmure, as heir to his father Roger, killed at Homildon.

Previous to 1411 we find a charter of confirmation to Sir John Stewart and Elizabeth his daughter of the lands of Cally, [4] witnessed by William Douglas of Leswalt, Thomas M'Culloch of Myrtoun, Fergus M'Dowall of Garthland, Alexander Gordon of Lochinvar, John Keith, and Alexander Cairns, Provost of Lincluden. A tombstone of this provost, a valued and trusted servant of the earl, who styles him "Cancellarius noster," was lately recovered under a heap of rubbish in the Lady Margaret's Chapel at Lincluden—a massive slab of red

---

[1] *Historie of the Kenedys*, Pitcairn, 6.

[2] "Only one wife of Sir Gilbert Kennedy is mentioned in any of his charters, Agnes Maxwell; and she is described as mother of all his children except Gilbert, John, and Roland, these being called to the succession failing heirs-male of Sir Gilbert's body lawfully begotten "—*Historical Account of Kennedies from Charters*, 13-17.

[3] In all peerages and genealogies extant—Douglas, Wood, Pitcairn, and the *History from Charters*—all daughters are omitted for four generations, though there notoriously were many.

[4] Cally, anciently Kalacht, Girthon "Caladh," a port or landing-place A dispensation to the Elizabeth named, to marry her cousin Alexander Stewart, was granted by the Pope in 1411, which fixes the date.

freestone, 8 feet by 4, bearing this touching appeal to the passer by : " You that have (unwittingly) trodden upon my body, pray for my soul "—" Qui me calcatis pedibus prece subveniatis."

In 1414 Fergus M'Dowall resigned his lands of Gairachloyne, Lochans, and Longan, into his superior's hands, who thereupon reconveyed them by charter to his son Thomas, in presence of Sir William Douglas of Eskford, Sir John Herries of Terregles, Sir Alexander Gordon of Kenmure, Master Alexander Cairns, and John a-Kersone of Glen.

In the Lochnaw charter chest a writ of the earl's, dated 20th October 1421, confirms a deed of John de Crawford de Trarinzean to his cousin John de Cairns, scutifer to the earl, and son of William Cairns, of the lands of Cults, in the parish of Cruggleton, he paying yearly therefor a silver penny in name of blench farm. Though the pedigree cannot be traced, it is very possible that this De Cairns was an ancester of Lord Chancellor Earl Cairns. Before this, between 1415 and 1420, Alexander Vaus was consecrated Bishop of Galloway, in right of which he became superior of a large tract of Church lands, as well as of the stronghold in the island which gives its name to the parish of Inch.

CHAPTER XIII

THE DUCHESS OF TOURAINE

A.D. 1424 to 1440

After drought commeyth rayne,
After plesor commethe payne,
  But yet ıt contynyth nyt soo ;
For after rayne commyth drocht agayne,
  And joye after payne and woe.

THE second Archibald neither developed his father's administrative talents nor his liking for Galloway. His forte lay in the
direction of armies in the field ; and wearying of Threave, after
first coquetting with the warlike Henry V. of England, who
would fain have persuaded him to change his allegiance, he
came to terms with Charles VII. of France, the career thus
opening before him being more in consonance with Scottish
tradition.

This settled, committing the management of his affairs,
public and private, to his countess, he sailed for France. There
his reception was of the warmest, the king at once appointing him lieutenant-general of the kingdom, creating him Duke
of Touraine, and investing him heritably in the lands of the
duchy.

He enjoyed these dignities but a short time, as he fell in
the battle of Verneuil—against the English under the Duke of
Bedford—the 17th of August 1424.

By his will the superiority of Galloway devolved not upon
his son, now fifth earl, but upon his widow; and as, almost
simultaneously with her husband's death, James I., her brother,

was released from his long captivity, all rights and privileges connected with this lordship were confirmed by the king in their fullest sense to his " beloved sister"; (carissima nostra Margharita soror); and she, being henceforth known as Duchess of Touraine, ruled for nearly twenty years at Threave, a veritable queen.

Prominent among the members of her household, each of whom she addresses as her beloved squire (scutifer, the modern equivalent of which would probably be equerry), by a rather strange coincidence were Andrew Agnew, son of the constable driven from Lochnaw, and William Douglas, who was in the enjoyment of his rights.

Both gentlemen seem to have been on the best of terms, though William styled himself " sheriff" and retained possession of Lochnaw. There is reason to believe that the Agnews had been left undisturbed by the Douglasses in any of their lands which were unconnected with the constabulary, and at this moment the duchess's squire, when not in attendance on that lady, seems to have resided in the manor-place on the island which gives its name to the parish of Inch.[1] In this old strength we find him, A.D. 1426, completing the purchase of certain tofts and crofts, as well as a mill, described as all lying "between the torrents in the Barony of Innermessan," which we take to mean between the stream that discharges from the lochs of Inch and the Galloway Burn.

His new purchases adjoined the lands of Croach and Laight Alpyn, which he probably already possessed, and it is an undoubted fact that beyond all memory of man the Agnews owned the castle and old moat of Innermessan. Though no charter of its acquisition is extant,[2] there is frequent record of its occupation by them, as well as of its alienation to the Earl of Stair.

[1] The superiority of this strength, as well as of wide lands in the parish, lay with Alexander Vaus as Bishop of Galloway, several of which he granted to the Agnews in perpetual feu. It is curious that some of these have returned to scions of the bishop's family, notably Sheuchan and Tongue, by the marriage of a Vaus with an heiress of a branch of the Agnews.

[2] Andrew Agnew of Lochnaw, son of the duchess's squire, disponed the lands of Croych to his son William as early as 1460.—*Exchequer Rolls.*

A decree of the Lord Auditors towards the close of the century proves them to have had early occupation of the Aird, Culhorn, Glenhappel, and the Boreland of Soulseat, all lying in the Inch.[1]

The charter of this most recent purchase bears that " Gilbert M'Cambil and Nevin M'Gilbar, burgesses of the burgh of Innermessan, dispone the mill of Innermessan and certain tofts and crofts to Andrew Aignew[2] and his heirs for ever." And because the former has no seal of his own he borrows that " of an honourable man, Thomas M'Dowell of Garslew." And the latter also having no seal, "appends that of Sir Alexander Cambil, Lord of Corsevel, provost of the said burgh. Witnessed at the Inch the 14th day of October 1426 by Sir Patrick M'Men, late abbot of Dundrennan, David Ross, Gilbert M'Dowel, Duncan M'Maycan, Andrew M'Kelli, Duncan M'Nely, and many more '

This we believe to be the only record extant of the ancient Rerigonium having been once a regularly constituted burgh, having its provost, baillies, and burgesses, though it has long fallen into decay. It is also interesting to note that it is not without authority that Camden in his *Britannia* styles the early Sheriffs of Galloway Agnew of the Inch.[3]

At this conjuncture the Duchess of Touraine actively interfered in favour of her younger equerry's[4] restoration to his father's home. She offered William Douglas Cruggleton Castle, with its lands, as a fair exchange for Lochnaw. And owing to rumours in the wind of the young king's dealings with defaulters

---

[1] *Acta Auditorium*, 1490.

[2] This charter being printed in the official publication of national records, need not be quoted at length   The double *g* in Agnew evidently represents the *y* which the Aygnells in England inserted before the *g*.   In this, as in other early charters, it is impossible to distinguish between a double *l* and a *w* at the end of the word, the two being interchangeable in Scotland

[3] Galloway reckoned among the sheriffdoms over which Agnew of the Isle presides —*Britannia*, ii. 1199.

[4] Andrew Agnew obtained in the capacity of scutifer the good will of Lady Margaret Stewart, Duchess of Turenne, while she enjoyed Galloway as her dower.

in his absence, he was glad to divest himself of a dangerous possession, getting full value in exchange.[1]

James I. was a man of a very different mould from Robert III , especially jealous of any assumptions of his nobility (the duchess's son, his own nephew, Earl Douglas, had already been committed to prison on a suspicion of misbehaviour), and a whisper how William Douglas came to style himself Sheriff of Wigtown [2] or Keeper of Lochnaw in defiance of royal authority might have led to his being summarily justified on the dool tree before that castle gate. It is significant that in the papers which passed on this occasion William Douglas dropped the "Vice Comes" which he had invariably subscribed himself before the king's return, and the duchess simply styles him her scutifer.

As the result of the duchess's gracious intervention [3] we find Andrew Agnew on a happy day in the autumn of 1426 riding with a party of his kinsmen to the castle of Wigtown, where William Douglas set his seal to charters transferring to him the constabulary and lands of Lochnaw, and the privileges of the barony in the fullest manner : "By all ancient meiths and boundaries, in ways, paths, waters, pools, with fishings, huntings, hawkings, with power of holding courts, with herezelds, bludwiths, and merchets of women," etc. Approved and confirmed "delecto scutifero nostro, Andrew-Agnew by Margareti, Ducisse Turonne, Comitessi de Douglas et Domini Galvidii. Apud Treyf," and finally ratified by James I. by a charter under the great seal.

---

[1] William Douglas was Sheriff of Wigtown and Constable of the Castle of Lochnaw in March 1424 —*Cal* iii. 393   As late as March 1424 William Douglas witnesses a charter to the Bishop of Galloway as "Vice Comes de Wigtoun."— *Great Seal Register.*

[2] William Douglas held the lands of Lochnaw and constableship of the castle thereof, both which he transferred in 1426 to Andrew Agnew ; he obtaining from the said lady a charter to the lands of Balquhirry, Cults, and Craglyntown. —*Caledonia,* iii. 361.

[3] Margaret, daughter of Robert III., after the death of her lord held the whole lordship of Galloway   Under such rights she disposed of lands, granted charters, confirmed possessions, and settled transfers of property as Lady Superior —*Caledonia,* iii. 383.

William Douglas signs at his castle of Wigtown 10th November 1426, styling himself .Dominus de Leswalt. "Witnessed by Alexandro Cambill Domino de Corsewel, Thoma MakDonel de Garflen, Nigello Adare de Portre, Adam de Dalzel de Elliotston, et Magistro Gilberti de Park, Secretario."[1]

The first three, kinsmen of Agnew, have before been mentioned. Adam de Dalzel was second son of Sir John de Dalzel, ancestor of the earls of Carnworth.[2]

Some time before this James Kennedy, husband of the duchess's sister, the Princess Mary, had been killed in a family quarrel, and she had remarried Sir William Edmonstone of Kincardine,[3] leaving her children to be brought up by their grandfather at Dunure, and it may be well supposed that they, and especially the only daughter, were frequent visitors of their aunt at Threave. Here her young equerry availed himself of his opportunities of pressing a successful suit   Her interest in this may partly account for the haste of the kindly duchess in effecting the restoration of Lochnaw to the intended bridegroom

The proposed connection with the Kennedys accounts for her selection of the lands of Cruggleton as the exchange which

[1] All these charters are printed at length in the official publication of the *Great Seal Register.*

The duchess's confirming charter bears as follows

"Quam quidem cartam officia donationem et concessionem in eadem contentas in omnibus suis punctis, articulis, conditionibus, modis ac circumstanciis, approbamus, ratificamus et pro nobis et successoribus nostris Galvideæ domino in perpetuam confirmamus, dilecti scutiferi nostri Andrea Agnew, in feode et hereditate in perpetuam." Recapitulating "Per omnes rectas metas antiquas et divisas, in viis, semitis, aquis, stagnis, moris, mariscis, boscis, planis, pratis, pascuis, et pasturis; piscationibus, venationibus, et aucupationibus, cum curiis et eorum exitibus, herezeldis, bludwetis, et cum merchetis mulierum   Cum molendinibus multuris et eorum sequelis; cum libero introitu etiam et exitu ac cum omnibus aliis et singulis libertatibus, commoditatibus, asiamentis et justis pertinenciis suis quibuscunque," etc

[2] This charter of 1426 is the oldest producible in Galloway, and in the peerage pedigrees of the Earls of Carnworth, as well as those of the M'Dowalls and Adares, it is referred to as identifying the signatories.

[3] It is somewhat of a coincidence that by her third marriage the Princess Mary became the ancestress both of the Dukes of Montrose and of Grahame of Claverhouse, whilst by her second she was that of the Earls of Cassilis and Sheriffs of Galloway.

she offered to William Douglas for Lochnaw, Sir Gilbert
Kennedy [1] having ancient rights over part of these lands, which
he concurred in relinquishing to assist in his granddaughter's
settlement.

The signing of the charter above mentioned was almost
immediately followed by the marriage, and the happy couple
repaired to the Rhynns to re-establish themselves in the old
home. On their inspection, however, of the old king's castle,
it proved to have had so severe a shaking when in the grip of
the Black Douglas, that it was easier to build another than to
repair it

Civilisation had so far advanced that it was no longer
necessary to cling to the island as the only defensible position.
Not that raids were less frequent, but that the art of fortification was better understood.

A new site was therefore chosen on a slight elevation above
the lake, by which two sides were defended, the two others
being surrounded by a moat. Here the central keep was raised
five stories high, with thick rubble walls; a continuous stair-
case of rough whinstone leading to a watch tower, adjoining
which a portion of the parapet was corbelled out so as to form
"machicoulis," or apertures in the floor closable at pleasure,
overhanging the entrance door, through which missiles could be
hurled upon assailants.   Corbels also supported projections
round the chimneys, allowing free circulation to those on the
parapets, these being pierced by spy-holes. Built at the same
time as the tower, but with slighter walls, and capable of being
shut off from it in case of attack, was a dining hall, with a
ladies' bower above it—the former 28 feet 8 inches by 17 feet
6 inches. These proportions, although modest compared with
those of English barons, such as Haworth just across the
Borders, were probably larger than any in Galloway of the
period. Outside the court, overlooked by the keep, was the

---

[1] He had a charter of the lands of Cruggleton, Powton, and the two
Broughtons, 22d January 1365 —*Reg. Mag Sig.*

A part of these had been granted by Earl Douglas to the monks of Whithorn,
but had been apparently resumed.

barmkyn (Anglo-Norman barbican), serving the double purpose
of a defence of the drawbridge and place of security for cattle.
And within the outer lines were granaries, workshops, stable,
and the green.[1]   And again, within the courtyard were the
chapel, brewhouse, knocking-stone, hawk-perch, and the jouggs.
Happily no gallows knob disfigured the entourage, that ghastly
emblem of baronial state being relegated to the dool tree on the
island.

Altogether, the young couple at Lochnaw might truly say
the lines had fallen to them in pleasant places · overshadowed
by no more powerful neighbour, in the most cordial relations
with the lady superior, hence in favour with the king, whose
marked policy it was to support the lesser baronage against the
more powerful, beyond the reach of Border raids, secure at
nights from the prowling thief when their drawbridge was
raised, and ample calls of duty to occupy their days.   Housekeeping, when everything—woollen work, linen work, plaidings,
embroideries, were made at home—required the lady's constant
superintendence ; who, besides the supply of the grosser wants
of the mouths and bodies of her household, was expected to
be skilled in the mysteries of the still-room, and dazzle her
neighbours with proof of her maidens' taste in coverings and
tapestry.

Whilst for the laird, a constant practice of military exer-
cises, supervising his flocks and herds over a wide range, a
holding of courts, and even the chase itself, were matters as
much of necessity as of duty.   The law required every official
to have weapon-shawings four times in the year.[2]   Every baron
was enjoined to erect bowmarks near his castle, at which his

---

[1] A green before chiefs' residences, for drills, games, and receptions, was an
institution derived from Celtic times.   It was termed "faitche," pronounced
"faha"   Jamieson suggests it "as the root of 'fey,' that piece of inland on
which the dung was regularly laid and laboured"   It is possible that in its
secondary sense of a green field, it may have applied to this, but the "fey"
was the especial spot of perpetual cultivation, often called the "berefey,"
whereas the green in question was never cultivated at all, and might be more
idiomatically rendered "terrace "

[2] Acts, 3 Parlt James I. ch 27.

tenants were expected regularly to attend ; and there the lady's presence might tend much to popularise such gatherings, and by her smile enhance the value of the silver pennies given as rewards.[1]

A statute, promulgated as late as 1427, a year later than the period to which we refer, required the baron, "in gang and time of year," to chase and seek the whelps of the wolf[2] Whilst such names within an easy walk of Lochnaw as Hind Hill and Knocknamoak,[3] are suggestive of larger game than sportsmen would now find in these coverts. Another duty of the Constable of Lochnaw, which we may feel assured his lady was pleased to share, was attendance at Threave. And we may be allowed to try to realise the ordering of these journeys.

The roads of the period were the old pack-horse tracks, trodden perhaps by the beasts of burden which had supplied Agricola's commissariat ; any improvement during the intervening centuries being problematical. One idea governing the selection of a line for a highway was its directness , and so far from taking level into consideration, steep pitches were positively preferred, as affording some natural drainage where much of the level country was boggy. The sole engineering work in Galloway worthy of the name was the bridge thrown by Dervorgille across the Nith, one end of which rested on Galloway soil.

---

[1] That the bowmarks be made be lords and barronnes ; that each man schute sex schotts at the least , and that all men within fiftie, and past twelve years, use schuting · twa pennies to be given to them that comes to drink.—14 Parlt James II ch 64

[2] Ilk barronn to chase and seek quhelps of the woolfe, and gar slaie them , and the barronnes sall give to the man that slaies the woolfe and brings to the barronn the head, twa shillings ; and quhen the barronn ordaines to hunt and chase the woolfe, the tenants sall rise with the barronn, under the pain of a wedder each man.—7 Parlt. James II. ch. 105   Date 1427.

Though madadh requires the addition of alluidh to form the dictionary term for a wolf, maddy alone is generally held in nomenclature to mean wolf, not dog Thus Stockamaddie, Kirkmaiden, seems exactly translated in Wolf's Slock, Carsphairn , Claymoddie, Glasserton, by Wolf's Stone, Eskdale. Polmaddy, Forest of Buchan ; Glenmaddie, New Abbey ; Cormaddie, Holywood, are the pool or pit, glen, and hill of the wolf

[3] Cnoc-na-muick, "knoll of the wild boar or swine." Hind Hill = Kinhilt.

Other bridges, so-called, were simply logs thrown across smaller streams for foot-passengers, and causeways of mixed stone and wattle were occasionally laid across marshes and flow mosses

There were numerous fords where the passage had been artificially assisted, the larger streams being crossed at established ferries. The old establishment of these highways and their adjuncts is proved by the hold they have on our Celtic nomenclature.

The Pictish term for a highway is represented in Gaelic by "bealach"; a path, by "cassan," literally a footway; (cos) a causeway, by "çeis" and "ceisseath," primarily a basket or wicker-work; also by "cliath,"[1] a hurdle; a ford, by "ath" (t mute), a bridge, by "droichead."

As examples, Garvalloch and Ballochrae are the "rough" and "smooth" pass; Ballochbeathes and Ballochrush, the road through the birches and the brushwood; Ballochakip, through the tree-stumps; Ballochalee, the pass of the calves, and Ballochjargon, the red, or bloody pass.

Cassan, from cos, a foot, appears in Knockwhassan and Culquhassan, the knoll and back of the pathway; Cassandeoch (da each), the path of the two horses; Cassanvey, of the birches; Cassannaw, of the ford

Ceiseach, as a causeway, appears in Balkissoch, and Dernakissoch, and Knockeiche, the townland, oakwood, and knoll of the causeway.

Cliath appears in Barcly, Barchly, and the Cly—the former translated in the Ordnance map Causeway End.

We find fords innumerable : Darnaw, Craignaw, Knocknaw, Inshaw, popularly Lochnaw—wood, rock, knoll, island, lake of the ford. Annacarry and Annaboglish are Ath-na-Coradh, Boglach, ford of the weir and of the flow moss. Ashendram, near Portpatrick, is the ford of the old ridge (whence the term old?); it crossed the Pinminnoch Burn at Enoch, meaning an ancient place of assembly, or a fair.

---

[1] Dublin was anciently Acly (Athcliath), ford of the hurdles.—Joyce i. 362. This was over the Dubhlinn, the black pool, hence the city's name.

Droichart, or droichead, a bridge, is often applied sarcastically ; a dangerous ford in the Piltanton is Drochdhuil, the
devil's bridge.[1] A spot near Corswall Point, where a man at the
risk of his life might jump a chasm in the cliffs, is mapped
Drochhead. A similar gap in the beetling crags between
Castle Feather and Burrowhead is called in the vernacular,
probably a translation, the Devil's Bridge.

Drumdrochet and Kildrochat are the ridge and wood of the
bridge. Near the latter is Barsolas, indicating an eminence
where a light was placed to guide the belated traveller to this
passage of the Piltanton[2]

Bardrochwood, in Minnigaff, is simply a corruption for
Bardrochat.

Let us try to picture to the mind's eye a cavalcade bent on
traversing such ways defiling across the drawbridge from
Lochnaw. The advance guard fully accoutred (for travelling
was hazardous to those not well attended), pricking forward,
their lance pennons fluttering to the breeze. A troop of little
Galloways carrying the wardrobes and other luggage, hawks and
hounds with their keepers accompanying the party ; for where
the pace had to be regulated by baggage-drivers on foot, it was
usual for knights and their ladies on such journeyings to enjoy
sport by the way. The first halt of the worshipful constable
and his wife, we may place with confidence at Soulseat,—a ten-
mile trudge,—where all, gentle and simple, were made welcome
by the monks to their midday meal. Thence a nine-mile ride
would bring them to Drumacardy,[3] whence, after fording the
Luce, they were welcomed to the larger accommodations of the
Cistercian fraternity ; and there, in the garden or the bowling-
alley, pleasantly whiled away their time till called to the re-
fectory for the evening meal.

[1] Lough an doul, cavern, Loch an diabhil —Joyce, i 199.

[2] So Assolas, Cork, and Ballynasolus, Tyrone. "When roads were few and
bridges fewer, to be able to strike the fordable point, at night especially, was
a matter of life and death   To keep a light of some sort burning on the spot
would suggest itself as the most natural and effectual plan for directing
travellers."—Joyce, i. 217

[3] The ridge of the workshop or forge

The next morning, skirting a succession of mosses, whose
names keep green the memories of forests long entombed below
them,[1] fording the Tarf by the way, an eight-mile ride would
bring them to Craighlaw, the seat of the Mures.[2] Whence,
following the Bladenoch and crossing it by a boat or raft, "as
it was rarely fordable," near Spital, a pleasant ride past the
Stones of Torhouse would bring them to Wigtown, where, if at
home, William Douglas would doubtless claim the privilege
of entertaining them in his castle, or if absent on duty good
quarters would be cordially placed at their disposal by the
Black Friars.

The third morning's journey would commence with the long
ferry of the Cree, from Knockdown to Cassencarry,[3] their
route thence leading them past the old strengths of Carsluith
and Barholm to those of Cardoness and Cally, on either side of
the Fleet; and entertainment would doubtless be offered them
by a M'Culloch or a Stewart. Whence through the wood of
Cumston, across a second Tarf, they would reach the Priory of
Tongueland, from the doachs[4] of which the brethren would
draw salmon for their refreshment. Then leaving the priory,
and still following the banks of the Dee, the party would
presently catch a glimpse of the towers of Threave, where, as
has been happily said, "the widowed duchess demesned herself
so graciously as to rob the rugged pile of half its gloom."[5] But
turning from such pleasing imaginings, the domestic annals
of the period furnish records of sterner realities   The Lady of
Threave and her squire were alike plunged into the deepest

[1] As Darvaird, oaks of the bard , Dargoles, of the coals, i e charcoal ;
Darnain, Dernagee, of the wild geese, or of the winds , Darsnag (snaig), of the
woodpecker , and many more.

Although quite treeless, it is curious that a farm on the first spot is known
by the pleonastic name of Wood of Darvaird.

[2] Craighlaw, creaghlath, gray rock. Tarf, a bull, from a superstition of a
bull's spirit infesting the water   Tarbhuisge, the water bull of the Irish and
Scotch Highlanders , Tarrooushley, of the Manxmen.

[3] Cnocdonn, brown knoll. Cosancoradh, the foot of the weir

[4] The doachs of Tongueland are its fish-weirs. Coldoch, near it, is the back
of the weir

[5] *Chronicles of Lincluden*, p 62

anxiety by the double arrest of Earl Douglas and Sir John Kennedy, eldest brother of the Lady of Lochnaw. Both were seized on no averred charge, but, as supposed, for having let fall, unguardedly, words as to the Draconian code to which the nobility were being subjected. The Earl was released after several months' close confinement, and retired into voluntary exile, but Sir John Kennedy was seen no more.[1] A deep mystery hangs over his fate, as to which an entry in the Exchequer Rolls is little reassuring. "For £14 : 15 4, Sir John Kennedy's expenses in the Castle of Stirling," dated 1434, three years later. After that he apparently ceased to be an expense.

The unfortunate young man's crime seems to have been simply his deprecation of such severities as those to which he was himself subjected; and their frequent repetition afterwards drew down on James I. a terrible retribution. He was murdered at Perth A.D. 1437 by Sir Robert Graham and his accomplices, as the chronicler pithily puts it "The cause of the king's slaughter was that he was owre cruel to his lords."

Some communication, "though no record of it exists," was doubtless made to Sir Gilbert Kennedy of his grandson's death, as Gilbert the second was recognised as oldest surviving son before 1438, when he married Catherine, daughter of Lord Maxwell. In 1438 James Kennedy, his next brother, was consecrated Bishop of Dunkeld About the end of the fourth decade of the century Sir Gilbert Kennedy died at a great age, leaving three sons,—Alexander, John, and Thomas,— who founded the powerful houses of Ardstincher, Blairquhan, and Bargany, and was succeeded by his grandson Gilbert just mentioned. About the same time George Douglas, son of Agnew's fellow - scutifer William, married Christian, daughter of Sir William de Ruthven, who was infeft for

---

[1] For certain causes the king caused Archibald, Earl of Douglas, and Sir John Kennedy, his nephews, to be arrested. The earl he sent to the Castle of Lochleven ; Kennedy he kept in the Castle of Stirling.—Goodall, *Contin. of Fordun*, ii 490.

her dower in the lands of Berbeth, Dinduff, and Balquhirry, adjoining those of Lochnaw.[1]

Immediately after James I.'s assassination, Earl Douglas hasted back from France, and was named one of the Council of Regency; Sir Alexander Livingstone being appointed the boy king's governor, and Sir William Crichton chancellor. He did not, however, survive his mother, and therefore was only in name Lord of Galloway, though he affected the style[2] He died of fever in 1439, leaving David his son and heir, a boy of fifteen, William, and Margaret, "the fair Maid of Galloway." Soon after, the Duchess of Touraine died, "the exact date has been lost," and was buried with much pomp and pageantry[3] and real grief in the Abbey of Lincluden, where a magnificent monument was erected to her memory. All chroniclers concur in stating that she was truly and rightly beloved by all classes in her little dominion,[4] where she was deeply and generally mourned, and by none more sincerely than by her faithful squire Andrew Agnew of Lochnaw

[1] Bar beith, birch hill; Dundamh, ox fort: Baile coue, townland of the hollow.

[2] On his tomb was the inscription "Hic jacit Archibaldus Douglas, Dux Turoniæ, Comes de Douglas, et de Longoville, Dominus Gallovidiæ, Wigtoniæ et Annandiæ"

[3] The remains of the deceased lady were conveyed from Threave to Lincluden, a distance of fifteen miles; never before had such a grand pageantry, at once so solemn and imposing, entered the college grounds All accounts that have come down to us concur in stating that she combined in a remarkable degree sweetness of disposition with strength of purpose — *Chronicles of Lincluden*

[4] The Princess Margaret lived in the Castle of Threave and mitigated the rigours of her husband and his father. When she died does not appear. She was certainly buried in the chancel of the Church of Lincluden, where an elegant tomb was erected to her memory, without ascertaining the time of the Galloway people losing so great a blessing "—*Caledonia*, iii 270, 383

There can be little doubt that the chronicler of Lincluden is right. The duchess survived her husband about sixteen years, her death occurring some time in 1440.—*Chronicles of Lincluden*, 63.

CHAPTER XIV

THE FIRST HEREDITARY SHERIFF

A.D. 1440 to 1455

Oh curse confound the Deil o' Threave,
His neebors he doth harry,
But Gallowa ne'er will be his slave,
Nor the braw Laird o' Raeberry.

Galloway Song.

ALMOST concurrently with the duchess's death, her nephew, James Kennedy, was promoted from the see of Dunkeld to that of St. Andrews, becoming at once Primate of Scotland and a prominent member of the Council. And, probably by his good offices, both Andrew Agnew of Lochnaw and his son received appointments in the royal household.[1]

About this time also we find the Murrays taking a place in the Galloway baronage as of Broughton, they being scions of the family of Cockpule.

David, who had succeeded on his father's death as sixth Earl of Douglas, on the duchess's decease was now the recognised Lord of Galloway, and seems to have served himself heir to some of his grandmother's popularity; as, although during his short life he lived principally at Douglas's castle of Dalkeith, he was favourably regarded in the province as a gay and generous youth.

Unfortunately he incurred the envy and illwill of Crichton

---

[1] Andrew Agnew of Lochnaw, son of the scutifer of the duchess, was scutifer to James II.—*Caledonia*, iii. 361. This, though true, carries a wrong impression, as the father as well as the son was long in the royal household, receiving the gift of the hereditary sheriffship as a reward of his services

and Livingstone, who, agreeing in nothing else, concurred in arranging a fiendish plan for his destruction. This, they would have had it believed, was necessary for the safety of the state; but that he was either a crafty or dangerous conspirator (be it remarked he was just fifteen years old) is pretty clearly negatived by the ease with which he allowed himself to fall into the snare. He was decoyed to Edinburgh (24th November 1440)along with his brother William, and both were murdered at a banquet. The earnest pleadings and bitter tears of the boy king—"the king grat very sore"—showed a truer instinct of the arts of governing than the calculating barbarity of the regent and chancellor.

The sympathy evoked for the victims increased the popularity of the Douglasses in Galloway, and rendered them more really formidable than they had ever been before.

The victim of the "black dinner,"[1] was succeeded by a granduncle, Lord Balvany, known as James the Gross. His years and corpulence inclining him to placidity, he made no effective protest against the crime, but was succeeded in 1443 by a son William, who, when eighth earl, played a stirring part upon the scene.

Earl William succeeded in entirely supplanting both Crichton and Livingstone in influence with the king, boldly accused both of malversation, on which they fled the country, and he himself was named Lieutenant-General of the kingdom.

For this appointment he was well fitted, having a clear head and a strong will. Up to this point public sympathy was entirely with him, but he now forfeited the good opinion of many in Galloway by his conduct towards the only sister of his murdered kinsman.

She had inherited vast estates and the titular lordship of Galloway,[2] which Earl William coveting, although the "Fair

---

[1] Edinburgh Castle, Town and Tower,
God grant thou sink for sin,
And that e'en for the black dinner
Earl Douglasse got therein.

Galloway Ballad.

[2] Margaret, daughter of fifth Earl Douglas, celebrated as the Fair Maid of Galloway, enjoyed all Galloway and other domains. The marratagium of this

Maid" was a mere child, repudiated his wife (a lady of irre-
proachable character), and induced the king to concur in an
application to the Pope to sanction an unholy alliance with
the infant, which was granted, Margaret herself being the only
party not consulted.[1]

Thenceforth William made Threave his usual residence.
And there, heartless as he had shown himself in domestic relations, his bearing toward the baronage was uniformly gracious,
and his rule popular and firm. In his earliest essays at administration he seemed following in the footsteps of his sagacious
ancestor, the first Archibald. Convening the baronage of
Galloway and Annandale in Border Parliament, he presided in
person, whilst statutes and usages of march were considered and
codified. At such a meeting in 1448 statutes were set down for
regulating bales and beacons, the assembling and arranging of
the host, of prisoners, and ransoms. These were approved and
promulgated by the earl on the 18th of December, he having
made all present to swear solemnly that they would maintain
the laws they had concurred in framing[2]

These statutes are so illustrative of the habits and ideas of
the period, forming also the military code in force in Galloway
for many a year after, that we insert them in the Appendix.

One only we quote, as amusingly characteristic of a Galloway
weakness, which is historical: "If there happens any chase,

lady was granted by James II. in presence of Parliament, 2d February 1449-50
On the death of her brother she had inherited the lordship of Galloway, which
was not entailed, but the earldom went by entail to her granduncle James.—
Caledonia, iii. 271.

[1] In February 26, 1452-53, Pope Nicholas granted a dispensation for the
marriage of James, Earl of Douglas, with Margaret, widow of Earl William.
This is stated to prove that she was actually married to William, which is
disputed, although a dispensation for it was granted in 1444

As the Fair Maid was only twelve years old when the dispensation was granted
for her marriage with Earl William, she must have been born in 1432.—*Caledonia*,
iii. 271

[2] 18th December 1488 Earl William Douglas assembled the lords, freeholders, and eldest Borderers, and caused those lords and Borderers to be sworn,
the Holy Gospel touched, that they justly and truly, after their cunning, should
decreet, decern, deliver, and put in order and writing, the statutes, ordinances,
and usages of march that were ordained in Black Archibald of Douglas's days.—
The Harleian MSS.

either fleeing or following, whatever he be that takes his fellow's horse, if he wins any goods on him, either prisoner or other goods, he that owned the horse shall have the half of it; and he shall bring the horse again to the stake, and failing that he shall be noted as a traytor and punished. And if it happens him to fly on that horse as soon as he comes home, he shall pass to the market of the shire, and proclaim him, and immediately deliver him to the sheriff; and if he does not this he shall be punished as a traytor."

A hundred and thirty years later the Galloway contingent at the battle of Langside improved their position by exchanging their small and weary nags for the larger and fresher horses of their Lothian comrades in the front, and "as it happened to them to have to fly upon them" in the rout that followed, they were all the richer for the defeat, as we much doubt whether conscience induced any to deliver their stolen horses to the sheriff. Well had it been for Earl Douglas if the wisdom of which he gave promise at these Lincluden assemblies had been as conspicuous in his after career The efficacy of the ordinances that had just been enacted was soon put to the test. Flames shooting up from the "white· wynd of Drifesdale," Trailtrow, and Kindleknock, were responded to from Criffel, and taken up in detail on Bengairn, Cairnsmore of Cree, and the Knock of Luce; and by the next evening's sun the baronage from the marches of Carrick, Rhynns, Machars, and Glenkens, had kept tryst at Lochmaben Stane.[1]

Earl Douglas greeted their arrival; Percy, the hereditary foeman of his house, had already crossed the Sark with an English host, and as quickly as the earl could set battle in array he joined issue with him.

He himself led in person the men of the Stewartry, Lord Maxwell those of Nithsdale and the Borders on his left, whilst the spearmen of "Wyggeton and Carrick" formed the right

---

[1] This was the usual trysting-place for warden raids. It is a standing stone 8 feet high, 21 feet in circumference, near the seashore, between the Kirtle and the Sark. It has no connection whatever with the lake, castle, or parish of Lochmaben.

wing under Craigie Wallace, a "knycht of sovereign man-hood."

The main body under Douglas in their advance were sorely galled by the arrows of the English bowmen, and wavered, when Wallace rushing past them, closed with the archers, who were now at disadvantage, the combat being between English swords and Scottish spears   At this crisis of the battle the Bore of the Solway rushed up the Sark [1] with a loud roar, threatening the retreat of the English, and causing a momentary panic. The spearmen of Wigtown pressed them home, utterly routing them with considerable loss, and taking all the remainder prisoners.   So many persons of wealth were among the latter that, what between the plunder of the camp and the ransoms of those who had surrendered, "thair was such abundance of gold and silver broght to Galloway that the lyke thereof was never seen in no man's time before." [2]

The Battle of the Sark was one of the few Scottish successes against the English in a fair field, one happy result of which was a year's truce unusually well kept.

Shortly after this the leading barons of the realm were summoned to Edinburgh to assist at the nuptials of the king with Mary of Gueldres.   Among those connected with Galloway were Earl Douglas himself, his laurels green from the late battle, his brother Lord Ormond, Sir Gilbert Kennedy, James Kennedy the Primate, Stewart of Garlies, Vaus, Bishop of Galloway, Andrew Agnew of Lochnaw, and his sons Andrew and Gilbert   The feast was spread in the great hall of Holy-rood, course after course was disposed of (without forks) during five long hours, "strong drinks were as plentiful as sea water," and it is gravely recorded, as an incident creditable to the clerical head, that "a legate, a mitred abbot, and three bishops sat at a table by themselves, all drinking out of the same cup, and with-out spilling any." [3]

[1] "The water boldening with the filling of the sea."
[2] The account of the battle and sentences between inverted commas are from Lindsay of Pitscottie
[3] Pinkerton, i. 432.

Hitherto Douglas had exercised regal powers in support nominally of the royal authority, though unquestioned. But now, as the king grew into manhood, and wished to take the reins into his own hands, the earl declined to submit to any control. In short, he deliberately organised a party pledged to support himself under all contingencies, he engaging to defend his partisans from attack, whether from persons they had outraged, or from officers of the law. Such a partaker Douglas had in John of Auchinleck, who, having frequently raided on Colville of Ochiltree's lands, and as often been saved by Douglas from pursuit, was at last encountered personally by Colville, and killed in a skirmish Douglas upon this grossly maltreated many of Colville's tenants, carried his castle by storm, hung him at its gate,[1] and not satisfied even with blood for blood, massacred every male within the defences.

This was certainly carrying matters too far, even for the rough ideas of the times, and aroused popular indignation to so high a pitch that Douglas found it prudent to ask leave to travel, a permission which the king, powerless to punish, was too happy to give. And he retired to France, leaving his brother Lord Balvany in charge of his affairs, who, however, eventually proved the most contumacious of the two. Insolent and oppressive to his neighbours, and flatly refusing, though summoned repeatedly, to come to Court and answer charges laid against him, "the king caused ane companie of men of warre to bring him in against his will,"[2] which they having done, Balvany ate humble pie, promising to restore to every one his own, and to amend his conduct. But being released on these conditions, "he keipt never a word that he had spoken for the repairing of his offences,"[3] but further maltreated his accusers.

"The king hearing of this proudness," caused Orkney, the Chancellor, "to pass into Galloway, and gather up all the rents

[1] The unusual joy for victory, peace, and the royal nuptials was interrupted by the death of Richard Colville, an eminent knight, not so much because it was unmerited, as that the manner in which it was perpetrated afforded a most pernicious example to the people —Buchanan, bk xi. chap 32
[2] Pitscottie, 87 et seq   [3] Ibid

in these parts to the king's use." But Orkney arriving with
only a small bodyguard, Balvany found means to prevent any
payments to be made to him, and openly insulted him.[1]

The king, stung to the quick, passed to Galloway in person,
and threw himself upon the loyalty of the baronage.

There can be no doubt that the majority of those east of
Cree remained "servants" of the house of Douglas, but the king
found sufficient support in the west to enable him to drive
Balvany beyond the marches, obliging his partisans to shut
themselves up in the castles of Lochmaben and Douglas, both
of which at last he took, razing the latter to the ground.[2]

As few family names are mentioned in the record of these
struggles, no lists of those on either side can be fully made ; but
we know as a fact that among the king's men to whom rewards
for services were afterwards dealt out were the Kennedys and
the Agnews. Meanwhile Earl Douglas, hearing of the entanglements in which his brother had involved him, hurried home,
and confessing his faults on his knees before both king and
queen, so worked upon their feelings that a free pardon was
accorded him ; and, still more weakly, all his castles were restored. The injudiciousness of this indulgence was quickly
shown by its being ascertained that hardly had he left the king's
presence than he entered into treasonable correspondence with
the English.

Fortunately for James II., at this conjuncture he allowed
himself to be guided by the advice of the Primate, James
Kennedy, who, having satisfied himself as to the earl's treachery,
strongly counselled his master no longer to allow his too
powerful feudatory to set him at defiance, nor longer try to
avert the inevitable struggle, in which any delay was to be to

---

[1] But when the Earl of Orkney passed to Galloway and Douglasdaill,
accompanied by ane small number of folkis, not only was he disobeyed, but also
mocked and injured be the Erle of Douglas's friendes.—Pitscottie, i. 88.

[2] The king with ane armie passed into Galloway, at whose cuming the thieves
took sic fear that they fled to strongholds and strengthis for safety. But the
king sent an armie to pursue them, who were repulsed, on the quhilk the king
took so great anger that he seized all the fortalices and castles in the countrie,
and won the castles of Lochmaben and Douglas.—Pitscottie, i. 89.

Douglas's advantage. The king lost no time in acting on this advice. Whether summoned specially to consult as to the state of feeling in the west, or in the ordinary performance of their turn of duty at court, we find the Agnews, father and son, along with Gilbert (afterwards Lord) Kennedy in Edinburgh in May 1451, and in the company of Crichton the Chancellor. And within a few days of their signing a family deed, which both indicates their presence there and fixes the date,[1] the king, in presence of his principal officers of state, asserted the royal authority in Galloway by naming his trusty squire Sheriff of Wigtown, in direct contempt of Douglas's pretensions, his commission empowering him " to embody troops, and if need be to lead them in person to oppose those in rebellion and defend our lieges." [2]

At the same time, if we are to believe tradition, although no record of the transaction remains, Patrick M'Clellan, tutor of Bomby, accepted a similar commission as Sheriff of Kirkcudbright.[3] The sheriffship of Western Galloway seems to have been in abeyance for some years previously. It is stated to have been held by the Agnews of Lochnaw till transferred by Archibald the Grim to William Douglas. He dropped the title

---

[1] At Edinburgh, 18th May 1451, a charter is signed by Gilbert Kennedy of Dunure of the lands of Largentin and Brocklach to the collegiate church of Minybole for the health of the soul of Catherine Maxwell his wife, in presence of William Lord Crichton, Sir Walter Scot, Andrew Agnew, Alexander Wardlaw, Patrick Agnew, George de Schoreswod our clerk, Thomas Brown clarc. not. pub —*Great Seal Register.*

[2] The commission is addressed · "Dilecto familiari nostro scutifero Andrei Agnew. Cum potestate ad summonendum et excitandum omnes et singulos inhabitantes, ac si necesse fuerit ipsos pro resistantum nostrorum rebellium conducendum . . . testibus "

William, Lord Crichton, our Chancellor , George, Earl of Angus , Alexander, Earl of Huntly , Alexander, Earl of Crawford , Patrick, Lord le Glammis ; Alexander, Lord Montgomerie ; William, Lord Somerville , with the bishops of Glasgow, Moray, and Whithorn. Sealed 25th May 1451. At length in *Great Seal Register,* vol. 1 [1]

[3] That the M'Lellans in ancient times were Sheriffs of Galloway is beyond a doubt —Crawford's *Peerage,* 237. He is always styled sheriff in local histories, but all charters of the old M'Lellans have disappeared.

---

[1] In acknowledgment of the services of various members of the family, " Pro suis suorumque filiorum gratuitis servitiis multipliciter impensis "

on James I.'s return from captivity, and there is no mention of a sheriff in the interval. The commission of 1451 reinstated the Agnews permanently in the position, constituting the holder a royal officer, responsible to the king alone, and entirely independent of the house of Douglas. As respected the new sheriff and the Kennedys, with whatever part-takers, it was now war to the knife with the potentate of Treave.

In the words of the chronicler :

"All this tyme the Earle of Douglas cast himselfe to be stark against the king, and therefor sought and persuaded all men under his opinion and servitude, and in speciall the gentlemen of Galloway, with Coile, Carrick, and Cuninghame, and all other pairtes that were neir adjacent unto him, desyreing them daylie to ride and goe with him as his own household men and servantis, and to assist him in all things whatsomevir he had to doe, whither it was ryght or wrong, with the king or against him. Bot some wyse men, seeing the danger of the Earle of Douglas's proceedings, would not take part with him, nor ride, nor gang with him, nor be his man." [1]

Woe to those who did not obey his call, unless they could make their defences sure. The king sent his quota towards the strengthening of Lochnaw, by the hands of Sir Gilbert Kennedy, the keeper's brother-in-law, in the shape of £5 out of the crown dues in Carrick. The sum seems ridiculously small, but we may suppose was not then thought inadequate; at all events a crown charter signed and sealed was required for its transference.[2]

As for M'Clellan, his castle of Raeberry, on a cliff overhanging the Solway, was supposed to be impregnable.

Disloyal as Douglas was, and vindictive against those who opposed him, it cannot be disguised that large numbers of all ranks were attached to his interest; as it must have been by his personal popularity chiefly that he was able to cope on equal

---

[1] Pitscottie, 96.

[2] Gilberti Kennedy per solucionem factam Andree Agnew, de firmis terre de Turneberdy £v per cartam Regis suo magno sigillo sigillatam.—*Exchequer Rolls,* 1452.

terms with the national forces; indeed the "wyse men" who refused to ride with him were notoriously in the minority.

For long the issue of the struggle was doubtful. No sooner was the king's flag raised at Lochnaw than the earl's bands beleaguered it; and though unable to force the drawbridge, the sheriff's cattle-pens were plundered and his barns destroyed.[1]

And not only were the lands of Gilbert Kennedy overrun, but the earl incited his partisans in the north to ravage those of the primate. He even contemplated the consignment of the good bishop to his dungeon.[2]

What the fate of either of the brothers might have been may be gathered from his treatment of Herries[3] of Terregles, one of the few who had dared to call himself "a king's man" in the east, as had the Kennedys in the west. Sir John Herries[4] having sustained many injuries from Douglas's partisans, and vainly sought redress, took the law into his own hands, and having followed some "limmers," recovered from them (a part only) of his own goods which they had stolen. Upon this they complained to their lord, who forthwith summoned Herries to his court, at which, as a mockery of justice, he was condemned as a thief for stealing what was really his own. And the sentence was carried out in defiance of express orders from the king. M'Clellan, as in duty bound, publicly protested against this judicial murder. Herries's crime had really been his support of the king's sheriff; and Douglas, enraged at the said sheriff intervening, ordered his arrest. M'Clellan naturally defending himself from those sent to seize him, one of Douglas's men was

[1] Four years later compensation was paid to Andrew Agnew, Sheriff of Wigtown, out of the Exchequer, in consideration of the burning of his grain — *Exchequer Rolls.*

[2] Bishop Kennedy's lands were plundered at the instigation of the Earl of Douglas, who had further instructed Lords Crawford and Ogilvy to seize if possible the person of the bishop and to put him in irons.—Chambers, *Eminent Scotsmen,* iii 308

[3] He is so called in various histories and by Sir Walter Scott, but is not to be traced in the direct line of the Herries of Terregles in Douglas's peerage

[4] John Herreise was castin in the yrrones and thairafter schamefullie hangit, as he had been ane thief, notwithstanding the king's commandment to the contrair —Pitscottie, i 96

killed in the scuffle, and the tutor fled to Raeberry. The
infuriated Douglas instantly besieged him, when a wicket of his
castle was found to be not proof against the golden key. Brib-
ing a warder, he got access to his victim, and personally seizing
him, carried him to Threave. Adam, Lord Grey, and his brother
Patrick, fellow members with the sheriff of the royal household,
uncles of M'Clellan, were on duty at court when the news of
their nephew's capture arrived from Galloway. Realising the
imminent danger of their kinsman they passed straight to the
king, imploring his assistance; and James II., waiving his
dignity in anxiety to save his officer, "caused right ane sweit
letter to the Earl of Douglas," not commanding, but imploring
him to deliver the Tutor of Bomby to Sir Patrick Grey, who
forthwith started on the errand.

He arrived at Threave just as the earl was rising from table,
who, divining his message, went to meet him with mock
cordiality in his hall. And under the plea that it was ill talk-
ing between a full man and a fasting, gained time to have
M'Clellan's execution carried out before the messenger had had
his say. He expressed himself honoured by a visit from the
king's familiar servant, "made him good cheere," and dinner
over, reverently received and carefully read the king's letter.
Then saying that as to any desire or supplication it should be
thankfully granted to the king, and all the rather for his (Sir
Patrick's) sake; and taking his hand led him forth to the
green, on which lay a white cloth, and on this being raised the
Tutor's corpse was exhibited. With affected surprise the earl
exclaimed, "Sir Patrick, you are a little too late, your sister's
son wants his head, but his body is entirely at your service."
Grey called for his horse, and having leapt on, he then fiercely
retorted, "My lord, if I live, you shall pay dearly for this
day's work."

"To horse and pursue him," shouted the Douglas, and had
not Grey's horse been an unusually good one the next morning's
sun would have surely seen his own body dangling from the
gallows knob of Threave. "The king was heavilie disap-

pointed," yet we cannot approve his having fought the earl with his own weapons. Douglas was enticed to Stirling with solemn promises of safety, received with pleasant words, and on the 20th of February 1452 sat down merrily to supper with the king and his household. Supper ended, those in attendance withdrew, and James, with blandishments reminding the earl of the loyalty of his forbears, urged him to break his treasonable leagues. Douglas scornfully replied that nothing should make him break his engagements to his friends. "If nothing else can," said the king, "this shall," and plunged his dagger into his heart. The gentlemen in waiting, hearing the scuffle, rushed in, foremost among them Patrick Grey, who seeing his nephew's murderer in grips with his sovereign, finished the killing with his battle-axe. Thus fell William, eighth Earl of Douglas, a man of brilliant parts, but through ambition first faithless to his wife, and then to his king. Overweening pride led him on to deeds of violence, for which he had well deserved to die, though the king was utterly unjustified in acting as executioner. The deed done, the mangled body was thrown from the window, and the castle garrison had to gird for the fight. Four stalwart brothers of the deceased soon knocked at the door. The besiegers were far more numerous than the besieged, but a messenger crept out in the darkness to tell Bishop Kennedy of their plight, and happily their bolts held good. The bishop rallied the Gordons of the north to the king, sent Huntly to intercept Crawford on his march to support the Douglases, and with his usual tact,[1] when Crawford was then defeated, induced him to make his submission. He then detached Angus from the cause of his kinsman ; and raising men in all quarters, as thousands rallied to the royal standard, Douglas's partisans commenced to melt away. Angus's important and somewhat unexpected adhesion to the king's men gave rise to the jocular saying, since proverbial, that the Red Douglas has put down the Black.

[1] Kennedy, Bishop of St. Andrews, guide and councillor of the king, a man whom it is not unreasonable to believe that God had mercifully provided for the occasion —*Lives of the Lindsays*, 126.

An assembly of his states—not very fully attended—at Edinburgh in June declared that the assassination of Earl William was a legal act,—in short, that the killing was no murder; and further declared his four brothers to be enemies to the Commonwealth, and their estates forfeited. Whereupon James II., feeling himself firmly established on the throne, proceeded to reward his friends with a lavish hand.

Of those connected with Galloway, Sir Gilbert Kennedy got the keeping of the castle of Lochdoon, Herbert Maxwell was temporarily appointed Steward of Kirkcudbright, and Andrew Agnew of Lochnaw had a renewal of his charter [1] to himself and heirs for ever.

Why this second charter was necessary it is difficult to understand, the substance being almost identical with that he received the previous year. However, the charter exists, with a great seal attached to it, witnessed by the Lords of the Council, much as was the other, though the Primate, Lord Lindsay of the Byres, Lord Grey, and Patrick, Lord Graham of Kincardine, are witnesses to the second, not present at the previous one.

The charter is as follows, the translation being an old one among the family papers :—

"PENES DOMINUM DE LOCHNAW.

"James, by the grace of God, king of the Scots, to all good men (etc.), greeting—Know that for the singular favor, love, and affection we bear to our lovit friend and esquire (scutifer) Andrew Agnew ; and for his and his son's gratuitous services, manifoldly rendered, and to be rendered, to us . . . by these

---

[1] It has been stated " the Agnews had probably some concern in that terrible scene at Stirling Castle, when the Douglas was done to death by the king and his attenders. Anyhow, soon after that event, the king granted by charter the hereditary sheriffdom to the Agnews."—*Chronicle of Scottish Counties.*

The loyal barons received lands and honours ; at the same time Andrew Agnew of Lochnaw was appointed Sheriff of Wigtownshire.—Mackenzie, i. 376.

Although they were probably present as stated, it is satisfactory to note that the services of himself and sons, gratuitously rendered, had been acknowledged in a royal charter at least a year previous to the terrible scene.

presents we make, constitute, and ordain the said Andrew Agnew
to be our Sheriff of Wigtoun.

" The said office of Sheriff of Wigtoun, with all the pertinents,
to be held and possessed by the said Andrew Agnew for the
whole term of his life, and after his decease by Andrew Agnew,
son and apparent heir of the said Andrew, and by the heirs-male
of his body, lawfully begotte ; whom failing, by Patrick Agnew,
natural son[1] of the said Andrew, and the heirs of his body, lawfully begotten; whom failing, by Gilbert Agnew, natural son of
the said Andrew Agnew senior, and the heirs of his body, law-
. fully begotten, in fee and heritage for ever (the which foresaid
persons failing, then freely to revert to us or our successors),
with the fees, profits, emoluments, liberties, commodities, easements and just pertinents whatsoever, as well unnamed as
named, in any way justly held to be belonging to that office,
or that may hereafter belong to it, freely, quietly, fully, entirely,
honourably, well and in peace, with no let or hindrance whatsoever

" With full and free power to them of ordering, beginning,
holding, ending, and (when needful) of continuing Sheriff's
Courts, of summoning parties, and causing them to be summoned, with power of levying fines, issues of court and escheats,
and of destraining, if need be, for the same, and of punishing
delinquents

" With power of receiving and calling on pleas, and receiving and opening the breves from our chapel (presented to Andrew
himself or his heirs), and duly doing desert thereto, of hearing,
deciding, and duly determining suits and questions moved in
and belonging to the said courts, with power of removing
mayors and serjeants from their offices and appointing others
as oft as to them may seem expedient; of deputing one or more

---

[1] Scottish legal authorities, we believe, are of opinion that " filius naturalis "
does not necessarily imply illegitimacy   It is possible that this was the case
as to Patrick, but he was undoubtedly a member of the royal household, and his
services specially acknowledged by the king   As to Gilbert, it is almost certain
that the words applied to himself are a clerical error, as his name was that of all
others most likely to be given to a legitimate son of the family whose mother
was a Kennedy.

deputy or deputies under them as often as it shall please them, for whom they shall be responsible, who shall have the like powers in the matters premised.

"And also with power of ordering parades, and summoning gatherings of armed men, and raising the bondmen (vincinarios), all and singular, within the sheriffdom, for the defence of the country; and, if need be, of leading the inhabitants in person to us or our lieutenant to oppose our rebels and to defend our lieges. With power of correcting and punishing the absent, remiss, and disobedient, as their defections deserve. And generally with power of doing, exercising, consummating, and executing all other things known to pertain to the office of Sheriff, whether by law or by usage.

"Wherefore we straightly command, and hereby apprize, all whom it may concern, that they promptly respond to, obey, and apply to the said Andrew, and after his decease to his heirs foresaid, in all matters pertaining to the said office; under all the penalties to which they shall otherwise be subject.

"In testimony whereof we have caused our great seal to be appended to this charter before the Reverend Fathers in Christ, James,[1] William, John, and Thomas,[2] Bishops of the churches of St. Andrews, Glasgow, Moray, and Quhithorne; our dearest cousin George, Earl of Angus; William, Lord Creichtoune,[3] our chancellor and well-beloved cousin; our dear cousins Patrick, Lord Graham;[4] Thomas, Lord Erskine; William, Lord Somyrvile; John, Lord Lindesay de Biris[5]; Andrew, Lord Gray, the master of our household; Master John Arons, Archdeacon of Glasgow, and George de Schoriswod, rector of Cultre, our clerk.

"At Edinburgh, the twenty-ninth day of the month of July, in the year of our Lord the One thousandth, four hundredth, fiftieth secondth, and in the sixteenth of our reign."

---

[1] James Kennedy the Primate.

[2] Thomas Spence, Bishop of Galloway on Vaux's resignation.

[3] Lord Crichton, reappointed Chancellor 1447.

[4] Lord Graham, ancestor of the Duke of Montrose.

[5] Lord Lindsay of the Byres, High Justiciary of the north of Scotland. A scion of his was Sir David Lindsay of the Mount.

In the fifteenth and sixteenth centuries the powers and privileges of a sheriff in his own province were nearly as unlimited as those of the great justiciars. The emoluments also were considerable. When a sheriff-principal held his court by proclamation, all barons, knights, and freeholders within the shire owed him suit and presence. Neither bishops, mitred abbots, nor barons might hold their own courts unless the sheriff had been duly notified. So that if he chose either he himself or one of his deputes might be present.

One of the rights named in the Agnew commission is suggestive, viz "the power of raising the bondmen, all and singular, for the defence of the country." The chartered term is "vincinarios," otherwise termed "nativi adscripti glebæ," a class, apparently descendants of the native Picts, hereditarily transferred by sale or gift along with the soil which they cultivated [1] It is curious thus to find the existence of these bondmen recognised in Galloway at this date, and it is equally curious to learn that by the end of the following century slavery (for it was nothing else) had entirely disappeared. a change effected so quietly and gradually that it is unnoticed in contemporary history, and no exact date can be assigned for the final manumission of the serfs.

James, Earl Douglas, having continued quiet for several months, James II suddenly endeavoured by indulgence and blandishments to attach him to his person

The first instalment of the royal favour was in the very objectionable form of the gift of marriage of his sister-in-law, this in spite of the indignant protest of the widowed "Fair Maid." The second was the impolitic act of accrediting him as envoy to the English Court, this being then Lancastrian, and the earl having been notoriously long in correspondence with the Yorkists. Douglas gladly accepted the mission, as a pleasant chance for whiling away the time till the Papal dispensation arrived to sanction his unholy marriage. And such good use did he make of his time, that he was able suddenly to

---

[1] Cosmo Innes, *Early Scottish History*, 98.

surprise the confiding James by besieging him in Stirling with
a much larger force than the king could muster to oppose him.

Happily the King had the Primate with him in this emer-
gency, whose strong head proved more than a match for
Douglas's irresolute hand.

Had the earl struck home at once, it is generally believed
he might have made himself master of the kingdom; but,
calling a halt when he should have sounded the charge, Bishop
Kennedy found time to work upon the fears or feelings of his
partisans, and detached many of them from his ranks. Some
joined the king, others slunk silently away, till Douglas, almost
deserted, had no option but to betake himself to flight.

He and his brothers lurked in Annandale a while, but there
the demands made for their supply became so oppressive that one
after another of the numerous vassals of their house renounced
fealty and craved protection of the king.

The host of the west was ordered to be put in array. The
Sheriff of Wigtown summoned the baronage of Western Galloway. Herries of Terregles headed those of the Stewartry,
who, joining the assembled Maxwells, Johnstons, and Carlyles
from the Borders, took up a strong position at Arkenholme,
near the confluence of the Ewes and the Wauchope with the
Esk.

Upon the morning of the 1st of May the Douglas brothers
swooped down fiercely upon the gathering. A hotly contested
battle ensued, the Galloway spearmen at last succeeding in
forcing their opponents to give back, when, as in all such hand-
to-hand fights, the vanquished were utterly dispersed with great
slaughter.

Douglas's next brother, the Earl of Moray, fell upon the
field; the Earl of Ormonde surrendered to Sir John Carlyle;
Lord Balvany disappeared unattended in the forest; and the
earl himself, so lately all but master of the kingdom, made his
way as a fugitive to the Earl of Ross, who, eager to rid himself
of so compromising a guest, passed him on to England, whence
he never returned.

The losses of the victors seem to have been comparatively few, but we learn from the Exchequer Rolls that the Sheriff of Galloway fell in the performance of this last and not least important service to the king. Great was the rejoicing at Court at this crowning victory. Moray's head, sent in token of the complete success, was exhibited to the populace with savage glee, whilst Ormonde was hurried to the scaffold, lest his wounds should cheat the gallows.

The Galwegian commanders came in for large shares of the spoil. Herries of Terregles got the keeping of the Castle of Lochmaben; Johnston and Carlyle, joint captors of Ormonde, received grants of land, the latter in the Stewartry; and Andrew Agnew of Lochnaw, now second hereditary sheriff, received gifts in money and kind in consideration of his father's services.[1]

---

[1] To Andrew Agnew, Sheriff of Wigtown, six chalders of meal in consideration of the burning of his grain and the death of his father in the king's service. To Andrew Agnew the escheat of the grain of William Dunbar, etc. Per concessionem factam per dominum Regem Andree Agnew per literas suas sub signeto camerario de Bute directas. . . . et pro feodo suo xx Li.—*Exchequer Rolls*, 1456-68.

CHAPTER XV

A.D. 1455 to 1484

Trowit and lovit wel with the king,
This ilke guid and gentle knycht
That wes baith manful, lele, and wycht.

A FEW days after the battle of Arkenholme, Andrew Agnew, now second Sheriff, was served heir to some of his father's lands, his uncle Gilbert, now Lord Kennedy, acting *in loco parentis*. The record of the service is interesting, as being worded in the vernacular, then very unusual; also as being among the last occasions in which any of the Douglas's nominal rights were held legally admissible in the province. Earl Douglas was a fugitive, though Threave Castle still held out in his name, and his kinsman George Douglas here gives infeftment of the lands of Lochnaw in virtue of a superiority recognised by the Duchess of Touraine, though acquired by George's father, William, in an act of defiance of the Crown.

The precept is worded thus:

"George of Douglas of Leswalt till his luffit Cusing Fergus M'Gachin, Gretyng, & for als mekyll as it is funing be an Inquest of ye best & ye worthiest of ye Rands[1] before me in my Curt of Witsunday of my lands of Leswalte haldyn at Cors M'Gachin in Glenluse, y^t Androw Agnew, was nerrest & lachful ayr to quylum Androw Agnew, his fayr, Schyrraff of Wigtoun, & of lachful eld, w^t al ye laiffe of ye pnts. of ye bryff,

---

[1] The Rhynns.

beand ful & haile of ye lands of Salcare, Lochnaw, & Garkerue, w^t ye offices of Balzare of my Barony of Leswalt : My
wil is, & I charge zhou to gyff heritable state & sesing to ye
said Androw or his att^{r}na berer of y^r lris of ye said lands of
Salcare, Lochnaw, & Garkerue, w^t y^r pertinants yir lett'is se^y
for owty delay —In witnes herof, becauss I had na seile to put
of my awyn, I haff procurit a^t instance ye seile of ane Honorable
& a wyrschipful man Gylbert Kennedy—Dinowyr in my said
Curt of Whitsunday ye xvi. day of ye moneth of May, ye zer of
our Lord M four hund fychte and v. zers—to be huning to y^r
letteris—befor yr witness, Thomas M'Dowell, Gebon M'Dowell,
Gebon Kennedy, Alexr. son, Gebon, Rollandson, Andrew Neilson,
Fynlaw M'Culach, Ferg^s M'Gachin, Alexand^r Gordon, Pat^k
M'Dowell of Logan, and Willm of Wyna notar, & oyr more " [1]

Of the cadets of the Kennedys, Gilbert Kennedy was of
Kirkmichael.[2] " Gebon, Alexander's son," was son of the
Laird of Ardstincher.[3] " Gebon, Roland's son," was son of
Roland Kennedy of Leffnoll.

Thomas M'Douell was Laird of Garthland, whose daughter
there is reason to think afterwards was married to the young
sheriff. Patrick M'Douell, founder of the Logan branch, was
probably his son, this being the first time that style appears.
Finlay M'Culloch was of Torhouse, the most powerful of his name
after the Laird of Myrton. Alexander Gordon was of Airds, a
brother of Lochinvar. M'Gachan's ancestors were landowners
in Wigtown at the signing of the Ragman Roll. Neilson was of
Craigcaffie.

---

[1] In notes on the Lochnaw charters by Mr. John Vans of Barnbarroch, c.
1810, as to this precept, he writes : " I cannot believe this man (George of
Douglas) to be George, fourth Earl of Angus , he is possibly the son of a natural
son of that house " [A very good guess.] Of the worshipful man Gilbert :
" This was Gilbert, first Lord Kennedy, son of the Princess Mary, and half-
brother to Angus."

[2] The pedigrees of the cadets we take from the historical account of the
Kennedys, compiled from charters at Culzean   The first Gilbert was son of
David Kennedy, son of Sir Gilbert, Lord Kennedy's grandfather. In charters
of 1455 he is styled Gilbert Kennedy of Kirkmichael.

[3] Gilbert, son of Alexander Kennedy of Ardstincher, had a charter, 31st
December 1456, of the 25 shilling land of Beoch, in the parish of Inch

George Douglas had apparently had no complicity in the treasonable doings of his kinsman, and had probably supported the king's sheriff against the earl. It seems therefore to have been found convenient to admit this superiority, his father having done so, his signature thus facilitating the service.

Moreover the rights of the Douglasses were not formally annulled till three months later, when Galloway was annexed to the Crown by Act of Parliament.[1] And even when this was done, George Douglas was allowed a life interest in the lands of Leswalt, a dower also being reserved for his wife. This lady, Katherine Ruthven, long survived him, and on her death the lands were assigned to the queen for her life.

The Act which deprived the Douglasses for ever of their semi-independent power, was passed the 4th of August 1455. And the king passed forthwith in person to accept the homage of the lieges, which was everywhere joyfully accorded except at Threave, whose gates were closed against the royal train This was done in the name of the countess, though her position in the castle was rather that of a prisoner than its mistress. Threave was accordingly besieged; but the walls proving too thick for the mild artillery of the period, the lieges of Kirkcudbright subscribed to furnish the king with heavier metal. A local blacksmith named M'Min succeeded in welding together that triumph of Scottish ordnance, yclept "Mons Meg," which, charged with a peck of powder and a stone ball the weight of a Carsphairn cow, swept the castle from end to end, and, were we to believe tradition, carried along with it the hand of the "Fair Maid," as she was in the very act of raising the wine-cup to her lips. Whereupon the castle instantly surrendered.[2]

---

[1] These are the lordshippes and castells annexed to the Crown: the hail lordshippe of Galloway, with sic freedomes, commodities, as it wes thir daies, togedder with the Castell of Triefe."—11th Parliament James II chap iv

[2] The loss as described of the guilty hand may have suited the ideas of a credulous age, though it might even have occurred to a monk of the fifteenth century that a lady delicately nurtured could hardly have survived the shock of a ball from Mons Meg, much less have borne children after the mutilation But it is really too ridiculous that the finding of a ring among some rubbish under

Little as the latter part of the story requires refutation as repeated in monkish gossip, it involved a most unfair reflection on the countess; the insinuation being that Providence had thus punished that very guilty hand which had wickedly been given to two brothers.

Poor lady, she had indeed been more sinned against than sinning   Happily, history utterly belies the tale, as it is categorically stated that the castle being taken, she forthwith threw herself at the king's feet, implored and obtained his mercy. Certainly had her arm been carried away, she would not have been in a condition to make her obeisance.   It is pleasant, moreover, to be able to add that brighter days dawned on the "Fair Maid." The king gave her in marriage to his half-brother, the Duke of Athole, with whom she lived happily, and by whom she had two daughters—Janet, married to Alexander, third Earl of Huntly, and Katherine to John, sixth Lord Forbes.

The loyalty of the lieges of Kircudbright was rewarded by the erection of their town into a royal burgh, M'Clellan of Bomby being its first provost   The keeping of the castle of Threave was given to Maxwell of Terregles, and a new office created, that of Chamberlain (collector of the royal revenue), bestowed on William, Abbot of Dundrennan; whilst all landowners holding formerly under Douglas, who made unconditional submission, were confirmed in their estates as vassals of the Crown.

Henceforward sheriff and steward followed their avocations undisturbed.   In 1456 we find the sheriff giving sasine to Sir William Stewart of Dalswinton and Garlies of the lands of Glasserton : interesting as the first mention of the family with this place, for three centuries after their principal residence [1]

the castle a few years ago should be gravely mentioned as authenticating the story.   "Threave Castle was partially repaired under the superintendence of Sir Alexander Gordon   On clearing out some rubbish the workmen discovered a massive gold ring inscribed 'Margaret de Douglas, the Fair Maid of Galloway.' This singular relic is supposed to have been on her hand when blown away at the siege of the castle "—Mackenzie, vol 1 App 35

[1] Andrew de Agnew, Vicomes de Wigtoun, onerat se de xxv libris de relevio

The administrative duties of a sheriff were sufficiently complex. With woeful ignorance of the rudiments of political economy, the king and his council endeavoured to benefit the exchequer by instructing sheriffs to interfere in every conceivable turn of commercial transactions.

So many difficulties were placed on exporting in any shape, as greatly to prejudice the producer; whilst merchants, if they had the slightest success in speculation, had hanging over their heads indefinite penalties for usury or forestalling.[1]

Crude Acts on such lines drawn up by the Lords of the Articles, ratified as a matter of course by Parliament, were referred to the sheriffs for execution.

Among those especially affecting Galloway were such as follows :—

1. The sheriff was to forbid the exportation of wool, if in his judgment it might be required at home.

2. No bullion might cross the borders, even to purchase the necessaries of life ; no cattle might be sold out of the realm, however high a price might be offered for them ; no cloth might be bought from Englishmen, however desirable the bargain.

3. Even salmon[2] might not be sold out of the country, but with the singular proviso that half the value must be paid in English coin, the other half in Gascoigne wine.

And every court he held the sheriff was expected to ascertain what persons within his shire bought victuals , and on the slightest suspicion that any dealer "held back with dearth," his goods were to be escheated to the king, and he to be subject to the pains of usurers (ockerrares).

Sheriffs also were required to hold the barons answerable to

terrarum de Glasserton regi debito per sasinum datum dno Willelmo Stewart de Dalswyntone militi.   Apud. Edin 4 Nov. 1426

[1] That schiriffis enquire quhat persons within their bounds byes victuals and halds it till dearth ; and gif it bees founden, that they be punished and demained as ockerrares suld be, and the victual escheated to the king —6th Parlt James II c. 22.

[2] That na salmond be sauld nor bartoured with ony man, that hes it out of the realme, bot for English money allanarlie gold and silver for th' ane halfe, and Gascoigne wine or sic gud pennie worth for the other half.—10th Parlt. James I c 132.

themselves for the proper cultivation of the land, it being enacted that every baron should insist that every tenant on his lands owning a yoke of eight oxen should sow at the least a firlot of wheat, half a firlot of peas, and forty beans, under a penalty to himself of ten shillings. " And if the barronne be found negligent in the receiving of that pain from his husbandmen, then this shall be raised on him to forty shillings, and that as oft as he defaults without remission to the king." [1]

This statute soon became a dead letter, if indeed it was ever endeavoured to be enforced at all, as also another, more unreasonable, though frequently re-enacted, "that the football, golf, and all sic unprofitable sports be utterly cried down."

Statutes against sorners, that is persons extorting entertainment by threats of violence, though startling in their severity, seem to have been really called for and frequently enforced.

Beggars on horseback, now talked of as a joke, seem to have been by no means uncommon : jolly beggars in every sense, with hounds following them as well.   The very wording of many Acts is suggestive of the masterful manner in which this sorning was carried on   Such as " that sornares be punished to the death " ; " that sornares taken in time coming shall be delivered to the king's sheriffs, who shall forthwith do law upon them " ; "that sheriffs are to take an inquisition at ilk court as to sornares and masterful beggars with horse and hounds. And gif any sik be founden, that thair horse, hounds, and other gudes, be escheat to the king, and thair persons put in the king's ward, quhile the king has said his will upon them."

" Fenzied fools, bards, and other sic like runners " were to be kept in prison in irons, " any money being found upon them to be used for their support ; but their funds exhausted, their ears were to be cut off, and they banished from the country; and if they reappeared they were to be hanged.[2]

Early in 1460 the sheriff was sent on a mission to an Irish court, that of Shane O'Neill, representative of the famous Aedh Buidhe (Yellow-haired Hugh), whilome King of Ulster.   It

---

[1] 14th Parlt James II. c. 81.   [2] 6th Parlt. James II c. 2.

might be supposed that his being chosen to go there favours the
notion of the Agnews's continuous possession of lands at Larne
But it is far more probable that he was selected simply in
consequence of the king's long and entire confidence in him as a
member of his household.   The object in view seems to have
been to obtain O'Neill's co-operation in a war projected against
England.   James II. thought that the dissensions between
Yorkists and Lancastrians there rendered the moment propitious
for his recovery of the Border fortresses which the English had
wrested from the Scots, and an Irish raid on Lancashire or
Cumberland would occasion a useful diversion in his favour,
should he make a descent on Berwick

The sheriff visited the Irish potentate at Edenduff,[1] Shane's
Castle, overlooking Lough Neah.   Whether he succeeded in his
object or not, we are not told, the only record of the visit being
an entry for a considerable sum allowed for his expenses.[2]
Soon after his return, the king entered in full confidence on his
campaign, took the town of Roxburgh, and was besieging the
castle when the sight of reinforcements arriving in numbers
made them " so blyth " that he ordered a general volley to be
fired as a *feu de joie.*   But standing too near his clumsy artillery
(in the quaint words of Lindsay), " his thigh bone was dung in
two be ane piece of a misframed gune, that brak in the schutting,
be the which he was strucken to the ground, and died hastily
thairafter."

The arrangements incident to a government for the long
minority entailed by this sad event were soon completed, and
the sheriff was fortunate in having many friends among its
members.

Bishop Kennedy was the young king's tutor.   Lords Kennedy,
Boyd, and Graham (sworn friends and part-takers) were three

---

[1] Endendubh = black hill brow—Aidhe-buidh—whence Clann (or Tribe) of
Aidhe Buidhe, in the vernacular Clanaboy or Clandeboye, a name preserved in the
seat and title of Lord Dufferin

[2] To Andrew Agnew, Sheriff of Wigtoun, for expenses · Eundo in Yberniam
versus Regulus O'Nele, by mandate of the king of good memory, xx li   The Lord
Chancellor attesting the mandate.—*Exchequer Rolls,* 6th March 1460.

out of the six regents ; [1] the Bishop of Glasgow was a fourth, and him the sheriff was able to oblige by appointing his nephew, John de Muirhead a sheriff-depute of Galloway. Angus, half-brother of Kennedy and the sheriff's mother, was Warden of the Western Marches.

Very shortly after this the sheriff was summoned to assist at the meeting of the two queens—Margaret of Scotland, just widowed, and Marguerite of Anjou, the high-spirited wife of Henry VI.—one of the most romantic episodes in Galloway story.

After the capture of her husband and rout of the Lancastrian army at Northampton, the English Margaret, with her boy,— titular Prince of Wales,—sought and received an asylum at Lincluden. Lyndsay its provost, the bailies of Dumfries, and neighbouring Galloway baronage, vied with one another in providing good cheer and comfort for their guest ; [2] the Scottish queen, sending before her a quota of provision, [3] appeared to welcome and condole, and on her arrival at once summoned her Sheriff of Wigtown and the Steward of Kirkcudbright [4] to assist her in entertaining.

Among civic dignitaries present at the board we find the name of Herbert Gledstanes, a forbear possibly of the Right Honourable William Ewart Gladstone.

Private griefs do not appear to have diverted the royal ladies' minds from practical politics ; a match for the Scottish Princess Royal with the English heir-apparent being proposed by the one, the restoration of Berwick suggested by the other.

And further, the Sheriffs of Galloway, Dumfries, and

[1] The lords of the regency were the Earl of Orkney, Lords Graham, Boyd, and Kennedy, Andrew Muirhead, Bishop of Glasgow, Thomas Lauder, Bishop of Dunkeld. The Bishop of Glasgow was one of the commissioners sent to Denmark for procuring King Christian's daughter in marriage for King James III.

[2] (*Inter alia*) A bedcover and pan of sheets lost at Lincluden when the queen was there with the Queen of England —The accounting of Herbert Gladstanes, bailie of Dumfries, 1461 —*Exchequer Rolls*

[3] For 3 pints of white wine of Poitou, £13 : 10s. For carriage of the same to College of Lincluden, 32 shillings. Also for 3 boles of salt for use at the time the Queen received the Queen and Prince of England —*Exchequer Rolls*

[4] The expense of two servants, the one to the Rhynns, the other to Kirkcudbright from the College of Lincluden, 12 shillings.—*Exchequer Rolls*, 1460-61

Roxburgh, with the Sheriff of Kirkcudbright and the Warden of
the Marches, were convened to discuss in conclave in the hall of
the college various burning questions of the Borders with the
English queen   Everything seemed settled to mutual satisfaction; tender adieux were exchanged, and the royal heroine of
the red rose, sanguine of success, rode forth from the peaceful
cloisters to court the din of the battlefield.

The fortune of war proved against her cause, and the crushing defeat of Towton rendered all these negotiations useless,
and sent her back to Scotland powerless to give effect to the
carefully drawn protocols of Lincluden.   Her husband too,
separated from her in their flight, sought refuge in Galloway,
having, with a young child and a meagre retinue, crossed the
Solway in an open boat and landed at Kirkcudbright [1]

Thither, as an old courtier, the sheriff repaired to give the
forlorn monarch what comfort he could and assistance in tracing
his belongings   The party were hospitably entertained by the
Grey Friars in their convent (afterwards the castle), till news
was obtained of his queen's whereabouts, and orders arrived to
escort the royal fugitive to Linlithgow.

In 1462 the Abbot of Dundrennan was succeeded as Chamberlain of Galloway by Alan Muir, of the house of Rowalan.[2]
In his first accounting there is an entry of a large sum paid to
the Sheriff of Galloway (no less than £180) from the Crown
rents, apparently in consideration of the various services above
mentioned, and others rendered to the queen regent.[3]

In 1463 George Douglas died, the last of that inferior branch
of the Douglasses. His lands of Leswalt reverted to the Crown,
the dower being reserved for Christian Ruthven, his wife.

[1] "The King Herry is at Kirkhowbre with four men and a childe. Queen
Margaret is at Edinburgh, and hir son   30th August 1461."—A letter of Sir
Robert Whytinghame —*Original Letters of the Paston Family*. Doubts are expressed as to this visit in preface to vol. vii. of the *Exchequer Rolls*, apparently
on authorities quoted by Miss Strickland. But any loose notices can hardly
weigh against a contemporary letter of unquestioned authenticity

[2] The chamberlain had three sons : Alexander, Archibald, and Rankine
Members of his family once owned Craighlaw, and afterwards Torhouse Mure

[3] Paid by Master David Guthrie, treasurer to the king, to Andrew Agnew,
from fermis of the Crown in Galloway, super Cree, £180 : 3 8.—*Exchequer Rolls*.

Lord Kennedy was appointed receiver of the rents of the barony, afterwards acquired by the family in fee; the Agnews continuing—as they had been beyond all memory of man—to be bailies of the barony under the Crown. This is to be specially noted, as Lord Kennedy's grandson, on acquiring full possession of the barony,[1] claimed the sole right of holding courts at Leswalt, which, though successfully resisted by the Agnews, led to bitter quarrelling, and a complete estrangement between the families

Successive Earls of Cassilis were powerful enough to set decisions of the High Courts at defiance, and it was not until the reign of Charles I. that the arm of the law was strong enough to restrain the Kennedies from violating the Agnews's chartered rights. At this date no one in the west country could compare in influence with Lord Kennedy. Besides his own many vassals and wide domains, he held letters of revenue or "man-rent" from the powerful cadets of his house, the Kennedys of Blairquhan, Bargany, Ardstincher, Leffnoll, the Coiff, Knockdaw, and Drummellar, and had bonds of mutual assistance and defence from Lords Boyd, Hamilton, Maxwell, and Montgomery; himself a regent of the kingdom, and deriving additional prestige from the position of his "wyse and religious" brother, the bishop. Unfortunately, however, that

---

[1] The barony of Leswalt is thus described in Lord Kennedy's first accounting. "Compotum Gilberti Domini Kennedy, receptoris firmarum de Leswalt de terminis Penthecostes, 1464".—

£8 de firmis terrarum trium Largbrecks;[1] £3 : 6 : 8 de Masmore[2] et Knocnargade de dictis baronie. Et de 18s. de le Glakis[3] de dictis baronie. Et de 18s de firmis de Achnocharth.[4] Et de £3 de duabus Glenstokdalis Et de £3 · 6 : 8 de le Tallaich.[5] Et de £3 . 6 . 8 de Barbeth Et de £3 : 6 · 8 de Dunduffis et duarum Balcurvis.[6] Et de £3 . 6 : 8 de le Mule. Et de 16s. 8d. terrarum de Garthrowan Et de £3 : 6 : 8 de firmis de le Flote Et de £5 de Kerowmacgill[7] and Kildonane. Et de 40s. de Drumfad. Et de 30s de Callonnis[8] and Dalyewanach.[9] Et de £6 · 13 : 4 de firmis baronie de Bartonny[10] de dictis terminis.

Summa hujis expense, £52 : 2 . 8.

---

1 Larbrax	2 Now Knock and Maize	The original "silver hill," a large meadow.
3 Glac, a hollow		4 Auchnotteroch, upper or Uchtred's field
5 Challoch, the knoll, or perhaps the forge		6 Balquhirry, townland in the corrie.
7 Clerical error for Kirk or Caer MacGill.		8 Caldons, the hazel wood
9 Dalmannoch, monk's field		10 Barwhanny

good man died in 1466, mourned by all parties, an irreparable loss to the State, and to the king especially, who was not so happy in his future councillors.

As to local doings, a fierce encounter took place in 1467 between many Galloway gentlemen near Synniness. A M'Dowall was killed in the fight, for which John Agnew, Thomas and Nigel Adair, and Niven Mackenzie, were amerciated[1] in £10 each.

In 1469 the sheriff's heir, Quentin, married Marian, daughter of Robert Vaus of Barnbarroch.[2] The lady's three sisters married the Lairds of Garthland, Corswall, and Kinhilt. About the same time John de Muirhead, sheriff-depute, married a daughter of Lord Hepburn of Hailes, and Andrew M'Dowall of Eldrig was named another sheriff-depute.

The lordship of Galloway, with the customs of the burgh of Wigtown and Kirkcudbright, were settled upon Queen Margaret of Denmark by Parliament in 1471. Two years later her majesty made a progress through the province to receive the homage of her new vassals and propitiate St Ninian

The burgesses of Wigtown, anxious to have fresh confirmation of their privileges, among which was the lucrative one of levying toll on all horses, cattle, sheep, and bales of wool crossing the Cree, elected the sheriff provost of the borough, hoping that, as a *persona grata* to the royal pair, he might assist in forwarding their views. He accepted the office, and we afterwards find him for several years consecutively attending for the borough's interest at the capital.[3]

---

[1] Pro morte quondam Thome M'Dovele et aliorum interfectorum apud Synons, commissa ad septem annos.—*Lord Treasurer's Account*, 1474

[2] On the occasion of his son's marriage, the sheriff resigned his lands of Craighmore to the Crown , which were regranted ("Quentino Agnew et Mariote Waus, sponse sua ") by charter under the Great Seal, 28th January 1469.
In 1473 the Lord Treasurer compounds with Andrew Agnew for the renunciation of the third part of the lands of Drumjergane , as also for the renunciation of Ardnamord (properly Airynamord), airadh na mairt, sheiling of the oxen — *Exchequer Rolls.*

[3] In the *Exchequer Rolls*, 1474-76 respectively, are the entries . "Compotum ballivorum per Andream Aggnew, burgi de Wigtoune redditum ex parte Andree Agnew, prepositi dicti burgi."
1481   For the baillies of Wigtoun, £xx.
1483.   Per Andream Aggnew for the baillies of Wigtoun, two years, £xl.

Their majesties travelled in considerable state;[1] ferrying the Ken at St. John's Kirk of Dalry early in November;[2] a crane being purchased to grace the royal table by the way! leaving Wigtown for Whithorn on the 12th November, where, it is to be remarked, the king bought two Galloway horses for £2 and £7 . 10s. respectively.

On the 15th of November they slept at the Abbey of Glenluce, and on the 18th crossed the Bridge of Ayr, which seems to have then only just been built, as 10s. were given to the masons.[3]

Ninian Spot, who had succeeded Thomas Spence as Bishop of Galloway in 1459, lodged a complaint in 1466 against Finlay M'Culloch of Torhouse, and his sons, "for having wrongously spulzeit his corn, cattle, and goods." The Lords Auditors allowed the case to drag on for several years ; and at length, on his repeated application, referred the whole matter "to Andrew Agnew of Lochnaw, sheriff," with an order that "the said M'Culloch should restore as much as the reverend father could prove had been taken from him before the said sheriff."[4]

A serious difference arose between Bishop Spot and the sheriff as to the latter's tenure of various church lands, which

[1] 1473, xx August   To Andro Balfoure for lyveray goonis to sex ladys of the quenis chalmire et hire passing to Quhytehirne: xxj elne of gray, fra Dauid Gill, price elne £x, summa £x : 10s —Lord Treasurer's Accounts

[2] At Sanct Johnis Kirk, for the ferrying of horses and men owre at the water, 5s.

Till a man for a cran be the way passand to Quhitherne, 5s.

xii. November, in Quhithern   To Johne of Kynloycht, to buy him a horse, ijli.

xv. November   For a horss boycht to the king, be the way cummand fra Glenluss, £vii . 13s.

[3] 18th November 1473.   To the massonis of the Bryg off Ayre, 10s —Lord Treasurer's Accounts.

[4] We may here mention that, in the Exchequer Rolls we find Andrew Agnew, Sheriff of Wigtown, accounting at Edinburgh 1471 for sasines he had given of Auchlawn [1] (now Auchleand) to William M'Gye of Skeoch , and chapel croft of Altoune [2] to Roland Kennedie of Barjerroch , and of Barowar to Patrick M'Kie ; of Clugstone to John Clugstone ; of Glenturk [3] to Alexander Mure , of Cotlands to David Faullerton ; of Logan to Uchtred M'Douall —Act. Aud

---

[1] Acha leathen, broad field
[2] Altoune, often Auld Toun, is not broad Scotch, as it seems, but Alltan, little glen
[3] Gleantorc, wild boar's glen

had been acquired by his father from Bishop Vaux. Lands held nominally under lease from the Church were considered almost equivalent to freehold; and this holding was especially popular with the baronage, as involving fewer military services than those held under the Crown.

Bishop Spot seems to have demanded larger sums for the renewal of his leases than the sheriff was inclined to pay; but in declining to come to terms, he refused to give up occupation. The bishop consequently raised an action against him before the Lords of the Council, "for his wrongous occupation, labouring, and manuring of the lands of Sheuchan and others" The case was called on the 25th of October, but the sheriff took the easy course usual with Galloway barons, and failed to appear or give any answer to the charge. But he had friends at court, and instead of the decision going against him by default, we find the entry, "The Lords of Council assign to Andrew Agnew, the 17th of January following, with continuation of days, to produce and shew such evidents and rights as he will use, and shew anent his rights which he claims to the said lands." [1]

That these "evidents" were sufficient seems proved by the fact that the bishop gave him no further trouble, and, five years later, we find by records in the charter chest that his son was infefted in these very lands,[2] by right of inheritance, as heir to his grandfather, 10th June 1478. Elizabeth Hamilton, spouse of umquhile Helise M'Culloch, brought an action before the Lord Auditors against "Andrew M'Culloch, Quentin Agnew, Duncan Mackmakyn, James Hert, Andro M'Culloch's man, and Henry Mundwel, chaplain, for their wrongous withholding of 66 bolls of clene braddit oats"; both parties being present by their procurators, and the allegations heard at length, the Lord Auditors decree that the said parties shall restore and deliver again the said 66 bolls of oats.[3]

---

[1] *Act Dom Concil*

[2] The precept granted by the succeeding bishop of these lands is worded "Dilecto Quentino Agnew, vicecomiti, juxta formam et tenorem cartæ quondam Andrea Agnew, avo dicti Quentini "—*Retour*, 25th February 1485.

[3] *Act Aud*

This year also Lord Kennedy died, and was succeeded by his son John, who had been married first to a daughter of Lord Montgomery, and secondly to a daughter of the Earl of Huntly.

An entry in the Wigtown Borough Records introduces us to the sheriff's second son, William, acting there as a bailie.[1]

The Head Court books chronicle an exploit of his eldest son Quentin,—who, probably then occupying Innermessan, led a party through Glen App to the lands of Ronald M'Neil, whence he drove back a rich booty before him.

Ronald carried his case before the Lord Auditors, who on hearing both parties ordered, "that Quentene Agnew should restore and deliver again to Ronald M'Neile, thirty-three great kye, price of the piece 24s.; eight oxen, each 30s.; one bull, 30s.; seven two-year-old kye, and three fed veals, each 13s. 4d, which the said Quentene spoiled from the said Ronald out of the lands of Areshene."[2]

As simple restitution was merely ordered with no fine, we presume Quentin's visit to Ronald to have been a return one

About 1481 the Maxwells first appear as Wigtownshire landowners. Edward, grandson of Herbert, first Lord Maxwell, married Margaret, one of the four coheiresses of William Mundwel (De Magnavilla), who brought to her husband, with other lands, part of the barony of Monreith. A precept to Andrew Agnew, Sheriff of Wigtown, from Robert Boyd, prays him to give sezine to Edward Maxwell of a fourth part of the barony of Monreith,[3] as formally possessed by Hawysai Mundwel.

Among the witnesses are Herbert Maxwell and Rankine

[1] 14th December 1478   Maurice Anderson, burgess of Wigtown, by the delivery of a silver penny into the hands of William Agnew, one of the bailies of the said borough, resigned 12s rent out of his tenement, lying between that of Mr Gilbert Maghellan, chaplain, and Mr John Machon.

[2] Arnsheen, airidh sidhein, "the sheiling or place of the fairy hill."—*Act. Aud.*

[3] Monreith, moine riabhac, but anciently written Murrith and Murrief, which, if the true name, would be "gray walls" (mur), house or stronghold.

Mure, termed "baillies," and Fergus M'Lymphquhaia (a quaint form of M'Clumpha).[1]

In 1483 the Lord Auditors addressed letters to Andrew Agnew, Sheriff of Wigtown, "to take prufe before him, and warn all parties to be present," in a case in which George Vaus, now Bishop of Galloway, sued Sir William Stewart of Garlies and Lady Euphemia Graham or Vaus his wife, for "withholding the males, farmez, profits, gressums, and other duties, from Patrick Vaus his nephew, and Lady Euphemia's son." She and her second husband had occupied Barnbarroch during her son's minority, and were disinclined to make it over to him when he came of age. The Lord Auditors, on the sheriff's report, adjudged that "they did wrong in the occupation of the said lands, and shall restore the back rents and duties so far as Patrick Vaus can prove before the sheriff that they have retained them."

The sheriff received also letters under the Privy Seal to warn all the lieges to be equipped for war, and ready to join the royal standard at eight days' notice; the king undertaking to find them in victual for twenty days. And should they not be required to take the field, the sheriff nevertheless to muster all men capable of bearing arms, and give the king notice of the day he fixed for that parade, that the king might send a confidential servant to report if "the lieges be well bodin."

John Montgomery, nephew of Lady Kennedy, had married an Adair, and a dispute arose between him and his wife's family as to his rights under marriage settlements. The sheriff seems to have sided with the Adairs, as "Johne of Muntgumre"[2] raised an action against Andrew Agnew, sheriff, and "Newyn, his son," Finlay M'Allon, Gilbert Neilson, Mitchell M'Ilvayne, Gelcallon,[3] Patrick and Thomas Adair, and Sir Thomas M'Ilvayne, "for the wrangous occupation and manuring of the lands of Dromore and Kildonan, pertaining to him be reason of his spouse."

---

[1] Ramage.—*Drumlanrig and the Douglasses*, 186.
[2] A younger son of the second Lord Montgomery
[3] Gilla Colm, servant of St. Columba.

The Lords decreed that the said persons were in the wrong, and "ordained that they devoid and red the same. Sir Thomas (the reverend) to pay a fine of 25s., Gelcallon and Patrick Adair of 12s. 6d. each."

Very shortly after this deliverance, the second sheriff died. During his lifetime he had infefted his second son William in the lands of Croach and Laicht Alpyne, by whose direct descendants in the male line they were enjoyed for nearly 300 years.[1]

[1] Sasine given to William Agnew, "de firmis terrarum de Creach," 1460.— *Exchequer Rolls.*

CHAPTER XVI

THIRD HEREDITARY SHERIFF

A.D. 1484 to 1498

He was lord of the huntin horn
And king o' the covin tree,
He was lo'ed in a' the westlan waters,
And oh ! he was dear to his ain menye.

A MANDATE under the Great Seal, dated 30th January 1484,
directed Andrew M'Dowall of Elrig[1] as sheriff-depute, to give
Quentin Agnew of Lochnaw heritable state and seizine of the
lands and offices which his father held under the Crown.

And a precept issued by Bishop Vaus on the 25th of February following, empowered Uchtred M'Dowall of Garthland, as
bailie of the bishop lands in Galloway, to infeft him in the
properties which his family held under the Church, by virtue
of a "charter granted by Alexander, Bishop of Galloway, to
Andrew Agnew, grandfather of the said Quentin. Sealed
in the presence of Adam Hepburn,[2] and William Colvel of
Cumston."

[1] Honorabilis vir Andreas Macdowall de Elrig, Vicecomes, habeas mandatum
supremi domini nostri regis sub testimonio sui magni sigilli cum alba cera
sigillatum et virtute ejusdem mandati ad conferendam sasinam hereditatum
Quentini Agnew . . est legitimus et propinquior heres ejusdem quondam
Andreæ patris . . . una cum officio Vice-comitatis de Wigtown, et officio
balliatus de Leswalt, et quod de nobis tenantur in capite.

[2] Son of Sir Patrick, first Lord Hailes. His sister was married to Andrew
M'Dowall of Elrig ; his elder brother was created Earl of Bothwell.

Elrig, Eldrig = Alderich (curates), according to situation has exactly opposite
meanings , often Auldridge, implying old cultivation, otherwise Elrick—haunted,
eerie, wild.—Jamieson. In glossary to Ramsay's *Gentle Shepherd* : wild, unin-
habitable.

On the 5th of February the formal infeftment of the Crown lands was carried out in presence of William Agnew younger of Croach, Robert Ahannay of Sorby, Patrick M'Culloch of Larg, John M'Christin, William Wallace, Jacob Hert, and Henry Mundwel, chaplain at Lochnaw; "whilst about 11 o'clock in the forenoon of the 12th of March" the Laird of Garthland, "by delivery of staff and stone," gave him possession of the lands of Dalzarran, Sheuchan, and Tongue, before John M'Kie of Myrtoun, Andrew M'Dowall of Myroch,[1] Uchtred M'Dowall of Dalreagle, Uchtred M'Dowall in Knockincross, and Thomas M'Dowall in Stronrawer.[2]

In these sasines it is to be observed that the royal mandate recognises the baillierie of Leswalt as held heritably by the Agnews under the Crown, which was afterwards disputed by the Kennedys

The orthography of some of the place-names deserves notice: Garthclone reflects the Celtic root "garbhcluain," rough meadow, equivalent to Garryclone in Ireland.

Kockincross, now Craigencross, "the knoll or hill of the cross," a conspicuous knoll in the Spital Croft of Craichmore (now Burgess Croft), once belonging to the Knight Templars. Cross in topography oftener indicates a gallows than a religious symbol; but in this case a real cross may have crowned the hillock, as we identify the lands with "a certain croft, the Temple land, vulgarly called the Spital Croft of Craighmore," sold at this time to M'Dowall by Sir William Knolys, Preceptor of the Order of St. John: "There being paid to us at our house of Torphichen the dues accustomed to be paid at the time appointed to the Templars" A son or kinsman of this M'Dowall remained as tenant, whence his designation "in" not "of," Knockincross; and the croft was soon after sold to the Agnews.

---

[1] Murbhach, pronounced Murrach, flat land by the sea-shore, a salt marsh (Joyce, 166); variously written Murrough, Murreach, further softened in "The Murrowe" of Wicklow

[2] Dare sasinam hereditatum de dilecto nostri Quentino Agnew . . . juxta formam et tenorem cartæ quondam recolendi memorii Alexandri nuper Candidæ Casæ episcopi . . . quondam Andreæ Agnew avo.

We here find an interesting identification of the name of Stranraer   Robert I gave the lands of Stranrever in the Rhynns of Galloway to Fergus de Mondewilla (whence Mundwell); but these have not hitherto been recognised as a site of the royal borough, owing to the hamlet which first sprung up there having been known as Chapell and St. John's Croft

Stranrawer next appears in the charter for its erection as a borough under Adair of Kinhilt, *circum* 1595 ; and this it has been supposed was a new name then given, meaning "the row on the strand."

Such a derivation is most unlikely, as, if from the vernacular, the form would not probably have changed. The discovery of the word on the very spot a full century before seems to fix it as Celtic "Sron Reamher," the broad snout (Promontonium Crassum), sufficiently applicable to a gravelly bank raised by the confluence of a stream, the bank having now been levelled and built upon, and the stream course covered over.

The Adairs at this time were numerous   there were Adairs of Altoun, of Curghie, of Maryport, of Dromore, of Creechan, of Genoch, and Kinhilt,[1] their family traditions being strangely tangled with legends of the early Church. Of the latter, none is more definite than that of Medana , and despite its absurdities, there can be little doubt that she was a real personage, and that her name survives in-three Kirkmaidens, which local tradition ascribes to three maiden sisters of a fictitious Bishop Adair. This bishop, whose name will be vainly searched for in Keith, is said to have presided over a monastery near Kinhilt; and wishing to add a library to his suite of rooms, he had a large boulder brought from Portesspital to form the lintel of his doorway. Next morning the stone had disappeared. He sent for another, when, to the surprise of the messengers, they found

---

[1] Altoun, little glen ; Curghie, Cor-gedh or gaeth, hill of the wild geese, or windy hill ; Creechan, Cruachan, the stack-shaped hill   Of this last, Simpson preserves an odd piece of folklore . "At a piece of ground called Crichen, the sheep have all their teeth very yellow, yea, and their very skin and wool are yellower than other sheep in the country, and will be easily known, though they were mingled with any other flock of sheep "   Genoch, Gaineach, a sandy place ; Kinhilt, hind hill

the first stone lying on the shore, brought it back, and replaced
it. Next day it was gone again; but knowing where to look for
it, it was soon traced, and the bishop, equal to the occasion,
ordered a Bible and a sword to be engraved upon it before building it in again. Its erratic tendencies thus effectually stopped,
the stone remained firm until involved in the ruin of all Popish
houses

The sceptical are recommended to visit the adjoining farm
of Colfin,[1] where, doing duty as a coign to his steading, the
intelligent tenant will show them this very stone

Symson offers a third derivation for one of the parishes:
"Kirkmaiden, so called because the kirk is dedicated to the
Virgin Mary, the point of whose knee is fabulously reported to
be seen on a stone somewhere about a place called Maryport."
This is altogether a confusion. At Maryport there may have
been a dedication to the Virgin, but the parish "maiden" is
Medana. The Breviary of Aberdeen gives a true legend which
connects her with the three parishes so called. The daughter
of an Irish king, the beautiful Medana (or Modwene) was sought
in marriage by many, and especially by a knight more per-
sistent than the rest; but Medana, unknown to her friends,
had taken vows of celibacy, and to avoid the soldier's importunity
fled, attended by two handmaids. Embarking in a helmless skiff,
she was wafted by providential guidance to a creek in the Rhynns
of Galloway, still called Portankill, from the chapel that she
reared there. Here, a cave serving for her bower and oratory,
she led a life of poverty and labour. Time flew by, till one day
she was startled by voices on the shore, and her knight rushed
in, entangling her in his embraces. With one wild scream she
freed herself from his grasp, and, followed by her handmaids,
plunged through the surf, and took refuge on a boulder. The
lover sprang after her; but ere he could reach it the stone floated
miraculously, and bore her across the billows to Monreith Bay.
Here she found shelter and repose, and lay fast asleep, when at

---

[1] Cul-fionn, white (that is, arable land, or grassy) corner, so Coolfin, Ireland.
—Joyce, ii. 265.

cockcrow her persecutor reappeared, and she with difficulty gained time for a moment's parley by climbing a tree. "Why persecute me thus?" she tearfully exclaimed "Those eyes oblige me," began her knight sentimentally; but ere he could finish his sentence Medana had torn her eyeballs from their sockets, and sobbing out, "Take then what you want!" dashed them at his feet. Maddened, broken-hearted, penitent, when too late, he slunk away. Medana now came down, asking for water to bathe her aching face. She was told there was no well near, when lo! where her eyes had fallen, up bubbled a fountain of limpid water, its origin attested by its healing power. She washed and saw The remainder of her days were happy; she living a life of devotion and good works in the enjoyment of the society of the saintly Ninian and the congenial brotherhood at Whithorn.[1] And when she died she was in due course canonised, and the chapels she had reared on either side of the Bay of Luce became the mother churches of the parishes which bear her name.

The ruined church of Kirkmaiden in Ferns has rather an eerie[2] reputation. When its parish was absorbed by Glasserton the fabric was allowed to fall into decay, but the burying-ground, which was that especially of the houses of Myrtoun and Monreith, remains.

It is alleged that a guest at the mansion-house of Moors[3] made a bet that he would ride at midnight to Medana's Chapel

[1] In Kirkmaiden in the Rhynns "there is a small cave, though one of no little note, between the bays of Portankill and East Tarbet, called by Chalmers St Medan's Cave, together with a pool in the adjacent rock, called the Well of the 'Co' From the superstitious observances connected with the spot it seems likely it was the abode of some Druid or recluse To bathe in the well as the sun rose on the first Sunday of May was considered an infallible cure for almost every disease, and till no very remote period it was customary for almost the whole population of the parish to collect on this spot on the first Sabbath of May (which was called Co-Sunday) to bathe in the well."—*New Statistical Account, Kirkmaiden*

For a minute description, and views of St. Medana's Cave and Chapel, see *Ayrshire and Galloway Archæological Collections*, vol vi art 2

[2] "Terror" (Jamieson), "fear of beings of a supernatural stamp" (M'Taggart)

[3] Moor, Moore, Mur, "the tower", whence Murrith, corrupted to Monreith, "the gray tower" "The Mower, together with the whole parish of Kirkmaiden, belonging to Sir William Maxwell of Muirreith"—Symson.

and bring away the Bible. He started, but was never again
seen alive.   Next day his body lay cold beside that of his
horse.   The corpse had been neither stripped nor plundered, but
the entrails of both man and beast were garlanded over the old
thorn bushes near the kirk.

Again, when the parish was suppressed, the pulpit and bell
were taken down with the view of being utilised in a new kirk
in a sister parish across the bay. They were put on board a boat,
which sailed on a fine day with a fair wind, everything promising
a good passage.   But the bell had been consecrated for use in
" Halie Kirk," and was thus being unceremoniously transferred
to an unconsecrated building ,—the Papists say the Patron Saint,
the Presbyterian guidwives say the Devil—raised a storm which
sent boat, bell, and cargo to the bottom of the sea.   Yet even
there this lusty bell clings to the memories of Medana's Chapel,
and, not unmindful of the duties for which it had been set apart,
sends forth a knell from the watery depths whenever the last
breath is passing from the bodies of any of the old family of
Myrtoun.   So say the lieges of Portwilliam.

Lawlessness becoming very rife among the upper classes, an
Act was passed instructing the coroners when they received
their " Porteous Rolls," [1] and found persons named therein " that
they dared not, and had not power to arrest," to pass to the
sheriff and inquire whether he will become surety for their
appearance at the next Justice Aire. If the sheriff agree, well ;
but if the sheriff refuse, he shall require the said sheriff in the
king's name to send his officers and familiars in sufficient
numbers to enable him to arrest them   And when arrested, if
the coroner had no safe place to keep them in, he should bring
them to the sheriff, who should charge himself with their custody,
and who on delivering them at the Justice Aire should be
allowed his expenses.[2]

A sheriff-depute of Galloway furnishes an apt instance of a

---

[1] A list of persons indicted to appear before the Justiciary Aire.—Jamieson.
Chaucer uses " portos " for a missile.
[2] 14 Parlt James II chaps. 99-101.

mighty and disobedient person with whom minor officials might find it difficult to deal.

John Muirhead, one of Quentin Agnew's deputes, and William his brother, and Rankine Mure, son of the chamberlain, are charged with the masterful spoliation of Sir Alexander Scott, parson of Wigtown, "of the whole lamb teinds, cheese, and dues of kirk since the feast of Pasch, last by-past; and the wrangous occupation and manuring of his kirkland and glebe."

The Lords and Council decree that Rankine, John, and William, should "red and devoid the same," and pay the parson the proper rent.[1]

The same year we find the account of the bailies and borough of Wigtown up to 1st July 1488 "rendered at Edinburgh by Quentin Agnew, Sheriff of Wigtown, and provost of the said borough"[2]

In 1488 civil war had broken out. Angus getting possession of the person of the Prince Royal, headed an insurrection against the father in the prince's name. Angus having been always popular in Galloway, the baronage there generally sided with him. Indeed, Earl Bothwell, his right-hand man, was then Steward of Kirkcudbright.

The final struggle took place on the 8th of June. Angus's advance guard, formed of the spearmen of the Merse and the Lothians, under Bothwell, met that of the king, formed of High-landers, in greatly superior force, who staggered Bothwell's advance by a well-directed volley of arrows, then closed, and used their claymores with such deadly effect that his line broke, and victory for the king seemed certain, when suddenly the Galloway men came into action, mounted on small but hardy steeds, wielding their long spears, with which the broadswords could not cope, and charging into the Highland host with terrific cries, drove back all before them.[3]

---

[1] *Act. Dom Concilii.*   [2] *Exchequer Rolls*

[3] The Homes and Hepburns having the vanguard, with thame in company, Mers, Tividaill, and East Lothian ; and next thame the Liddisdale and Annandaill, with manie of Galloway.—Pitscottie, i. 219

The king fled, his whole army dissolved in panic; and before that day's sun was down James III. had been cruelly murdered and his son proclaimed king. The Galloway men, having exchanged the title of rebels with those they had opposed, cheering for James IV., marched back as tried and trusted loyalists, rich in glory and the spoils of war. ·

Just previous to this insurrection, the sheriff had resigned his lands and offices into King James III.'s hands, with a view of their being bestowed upon his eldest son (a fashion of the times, which answered the purpose of entails). It is of some historic interest to note that there were duplicate warrants for this transaction in the Lochnaw charter-chest. The first, in the name of James III, dated April 26 (which apparently the rebellion prevented from taking effect); the second, in that of James IV., dated 6th August 1488. This second precept is addressed to Uchtred M'Dowall, sheriff-depute, desiring him "to give heritable state and seizine to Patrick Agnew, son and apparent heir of Quentin Agnew, Sheriff of Galloway, of the lands of Lochnaw, Salquhirry, and Creachmore, as also of the offices of Sheriff of Wigtown, Baillie of Leswalt, and Constable of the Castle, Lake, and manor-place of Lochnaw, reserving to the said Quentin the life-interest in the lands and offices, and to Marian Vaus her rights as a Tercer, should she survive him." The delivery to the minor was made by Nevin Agnew, his uncle, at "five o'clock on the afternoon of the 16th August, before William Agnew junior, of Croach, James M'Dowall, Elias Gordon, Sir Finlay M'Bryd, chaplain at Lochnaw, James Hert, Thomas Cruikshank, John Makgarue, notary public."

On some cause of quarrel unknown, the sheriff, one fine autumn day, mustered his retainers on the green at Lochnaw, and passing by Dindinnie, Knockwhassen, Crailoch,[1] Knock-glass, and the slopes of Craignaquarroch,[2] to Kinhilt, seized a considerable prey of cattle, and passing on by the Caldons[3] and

---

[1] Crailoch, Crithlach, "a bounding in shaky places, a shaking bog "
[2] Craignaquarroch, na-chaoroch, "rock of the sheep "
[3] Caldons, "the hazelwood "

Kirkmadrine [1] to Ardwell, stormed the house, stripped it, appropriated four horses in the stable, sundry oxen, such cows as he
fancied from the byres, and returned with his spoil. It seems
probable that this raid was in retaliation, and that the provocation must have been considerable, as Adair, one of the parties
attacked, was the sheriff's brother-in-law; and the Lord Auditors,
to whom the case was referred, simply ordered the restoration
of the property taken, and imposed no fine.   "The Lord
Auditors decreets and delivers that Quentin Agnew, Sheriff of
Wigtown, shall restore, content, and deliver to William Adare
of Kynhilt, and Archibald M'Culloch of Ardwall, 28 oxen, price
of the piece, 24s., 22 ky, the piece, 18s. 4d.; 88 sheep, price
of the piece, 3s 4d.; 4 horses, £3:6 8, and for gudes and
insicht of household, 16 merks spulziet and taken by the said
Quentin" [2]

Moderate as this valuation seems, the sheriff demurred,
alleging its excess as an excuse for withholding the whole sum
awarded; and, strange to say, the Lords of Council, on appeal,
seem to have reduced it by the price set on the furniture, provided this was given back.   "5th May 1489, the Lords of
Council ordain that letters be directed to distress Quentin
Agnew, Sheriff of Wigtown, his lands and guds, and make
payment to William Adare and Archibald M'Culloch of the
sum of £48:2:8, rastand the award of the guds taken by the
said sheriff. But gif the guds of household be delivered again
as gude as taken, that they defalk 16 merks."

By one of the earliest Acts of the new reign ships were forbidden to "come and make merchandize" at any ports in
Galloway, excepting Wigtown and Kirkcudbright; thus arbi-
trarily preventing the lieges enjoying the advantages of their
situation whether on Loch Ryan, the Bay of Luce, and the
many creeks between the Cree and Nith upon the Solway

In 1489 an Act was passed enjoining sheriffs to take strin-

---

[1] Kirkmadrine, "St. Medran's Church." This was the parish church of Toskerton, Tuaiscairt, "a northerly place" (as compared with Kirkmaiden).

[2] *Act. Aud.*, 17th October 1488.

gent measures to prevent salmon-poaching, and regulate cruives, "that they stand not in forbidden time, and let the midstream be always free for the space of 5 feet, and that the Setterdaies slop[1] be observed and kept."[2]

Another Act of local significance is "for undooing of caupes in Galloway." Caupes were exactions in addition to those legally imposed, such as herezelds and grassums, and are interpreted as "pretended benevolences of horses, cattle, or the like, accustomed to be wrested from the poor by the landlords in Carrick and Galloway." For which the Estates declare "they see no reasonable cause," and the sheriffs are desired to protect those so oppressed: "all such abusions, evil use, and extortions, to be punished henceforward as theft." An admirable statute, but for long a dead letter.

About this time Lord Kennedy made his usual residence at the Manor-place of Inch.[3]

In 1488 he had given Quentin M'Dowall a tack of the lands of Culmore, and of the Larg, the latter probably as a "kyndlie rowme" (a holding given on easy terms as to rent, but for which the tenant was expected to support his superior in the field). Having either repented of his gift or been dissatisfied with the occupier, Lord Kennedy annulled the tack, but M'Dowall declining to remove, his lordship seized some hundreds of his sheep by way of fine. The tenant appealed to the Lord Auditors, who decided that Lord Kennedy must abide by the tack, and leave Quentin undisturbed in the said lands. The Lords further "adjudge that Lord Kennedy does wrong in withholding five score sheep from Quentin M'Dowall."[4]

Lord Kennedy appears to have treated their decree with contempt. Two years later, the matter came before the Council,

---

[1] The Setterdaies slop is the time in which it is not lawful to take salmon between evensong on Saturday, until the rising of the sun on Monday.

[2] Parlt. 2, James IV. c 15 and 18.

[3] In the charter history of the Kennedys, the first notice of the Kennedys being appointed captain and keeper of the Manor-place of Inch is dated 1516 But the family notoriously resided there before, as evidenced in many cases before the Courts. [4] *Act. Aud.*

who issued a summons to "John, Lord Kennedy, to show why
he had not fulfilled the articles ordered by the Lord Auditors,"
allowing him till the following March to prove that he had
contented the said Quentin; [1] which it is to be presumed he
did.

About this time many influential persons, ladies among
their number, stongly advocated reform in the Church. Presbyterianism, as subsequently developed, was not then so much as
thought of, "Halie Kirk," with the Pope as its avowed head,
being had in reverence ; the sovereign Pontiff being respect-
fully requested to suppress disorders in his household, and to
allow the very few persons capable of doing so to read the
Holy Scriptures as authorised by the Church. As the more
conspicuous members of those preferring these claims belonged
to Ayrshire rather than Galloway, they were nicknamed "The
Lollards of Kyle." Among those most prominent was Marian,
Lady Stair, wife of William Dalrymple, and daughter of John
Chalmers of Gadgirth

In the year 1494 a meeting of these so-called Lollards was
invaded by Blackadder, Bishop of Glasgow, and cited to appear
before the king It might have been a serious affair had the
fourth James been as pitiless an enforcer of the law as was the
first, who had acquiesced in Paul Craw being burnt alive, gagged
with a ball of brass, for simply expressing sympathy with
the Lollards of England. With a kindlier disposition, and more
real chivalry, the king gave the accused a fair hearing, allowed
their defence to be undertaken by Read of Barskimming, "a man
of firm mind and facetious repartee," which he so conducted
"that the greatest part of the accusation was turned into
laughter." [2]

Though somewhat of a bigot personally, James IV. jealously
resisted any encroachment of the Church on the royal authority
Of this Bishop Vaus had early experience, when complained of
for opposing the king's authority in Galloway in the person of
his sheriff, under circumstances as follows :—

[1] *Act Dom Concil*   [2] Calderwood, 154.

Sir Alexander M'Culloch had been appointed by Quentin Agnew a sheriff-depute, and he, in the ordinary exercise of his functions, had ordered a distraint on Mitchell M'Brair. M'Brair appealed to the bishop, who took upon himself to intervene, and threatened to excommunicate the sheriff's sergeants if they obeyed their orders.   They at once told their chief, who returning with them, personally superintended the distraint

Vaus, furious at being held of so little account, sought to terrify Sir Alexander by the thunders at his command. Mounting the high altar, he cursed sheriff, clerk, and sergeants, by candle, book, and bell, and after charging the air with his curses, had the curses committed to writing, and served "letters of cursing" to each of them.

> Never was heard such a terrible curse
> But what gave rise
> To no little surprise,
> No one seemed one penny the worse

M'Culloch duly reported these doings to the sheriff principal; and although against Quentin Agnew spiritual thunders fell very flat, he resented the affront put upon his office, and complained to the king.

Vaus was instantly summoned to meet the charge in court; and the humbled prelate had the mortification of hearing it declared before his accusers and the public, that the king's Highness was greatly angered at his presumption, and that the Lords of the Council, having heard both parties, refer the punishment of the bishop to the king himself, as an example to others[1]

Notwithstanding the high words that passed at this pretty little quarrel, cordiality was soon restored between the disputants.   The bishop did not long refuse to 'take a cup of kindness for auld lang syne" in his sister's hall; and the king

---

[1] The Lords of the Council refers the corrections thereof to the king's Highness, and counsels his good grace to provide for remedy thereintil, that it may be an example in time coming to others not to make stop or impediment to the king's officers in the execution of their office —*Act. Dom. Concil.*

was so entirely satisfied with his subsequent bearing, that when he founded a chapel royal at Stirling a few months after, he named George Vaus its first chaplain, who thereafter had much influence over him.

This chaplaincy became a permanent appendage to the see of Galloway ; its salary, a welcome additon to the income of its bishop.

1st of June 1494, the Snowdon herald "passed with haste"[1] to the Sheriff of Wigtown, bearing letters from the king "anent the schip at Brak at Quhitherne." These were not written with any view of protecting the property of the owners, but to assert the king's privilege as wrecker-in-chief against any local pilfer.

A more unpleasant letter soon followed from the tax-gatherer, the Lord of St. John, reminding the sheriff of an unsettled score "of the rest of the first tax granted for our Sovereign Lord's marriage," and for arrears of payment by some of the neighbours, "for whom the said Quentin Agnew became pledged to the said Lord."[2]

The sheriff was long in replying to this, probably because he had no money to send. Consequently he was cited to appear before the Lord Auditors, but treated their summons with similar neglect : "The said sheriff being ofttimes called, and not compeering."

A warrant was therefore issued to distrain upon his lands and goods for the sum required; and, in legal phrase, he was declared rebel. His lady, intuitively grasping the gravity of the situation, rode at once post haste to Edinburgh, and succeeded in obtaining a counter order, staying action. "In presence of the Lord Auditors, Marian Wauss, spouse of Quentene Agnew, and Master James Henderson, procurator for the same Quentene, permission was given to delay all execution of any decreet, gif any happit to be given"

[1] For which he received 40s.—*Exchequer Rolls.*
[2] Owed to the Lord Thesaurer by the Sheriff of Galloway, £19 : 6 . 8. Also by the three M'Cullochs, £10 each , by Patrick Black, £10 ; by Andrew Lauchlaneson, £10 , for the quhilk the schirriffe became pledged.

Letters, however, though not issued, had been made out, and had somehow come into the possession of Symon M'Culloch, who, owing a grudge to the sheriff, collected a band of wild spirits, and these, to their great solace and divertissement, organised a day's sport in sweeping the sheriff's outlying pastures, and seizing and pounding such booty as they could find. They scoured a wide range of country ; but from the smallness of the bag at the end of their long day's sport it is obvious that their amusements were not altogether undisturbed. The records of the Supreme Court, to which they were after cited to answer for their conduct, minutely recount the lands gone over and the amount of prey secured.

When placed at the bar, they endeavoured to plead the king's letters as a warrant for the outrage. But this was not for a moment entertained by their judges, who fined them smartly for their frolic, adjudging them to make good the full value of all that they had taken, paying besides the travelling expenses of the sheriff and his lady, as well as the expenses of the trial.

The judgment is as follows :

"The Lord Auditors deliver that Symon M'Culloch, Neil Neilson of Carcalffy, Alexander Campbell of Auchiness, Uchtred M'Dowall of Dalregill, Uchtred M'Dowall of Mindork, sall restore and deliver again to Quentine Agnew, and Marian Vauss, his spouse, xxiiij^{ts} ky with calffs, price of the piece, 3 merks ; 3 horses, price of the piece, 3 merks, 8 oxen, price of the piece, 30s.; 9 score sheep, price of the piece, 4s.; quhilk goods were spulziet and taken be the said persones fra the said Quentine and his spouse out of the lands of Lochinall, Marschlach, Clannerry, the Ard, Culurborne, Glencapill, Suthquhen, Drumregget, and the Bordland of Salset. As was sufficiently pressit before the Lords, the quhilk gudes were allegit to haf been taken be the said Symon Mackculloch and his complices, be virtue of our Sovereign Lord's letters. The quhilk letters and endorsation thereof beand seen and understood be the Lords, were declared to be unorderly execut, as was pressit be

the execution thereof; and ordains that letters be written to
distress the said persones, the wuds and goods therefor, and for
£40 for the said Quentynes costs, dampnages, and scaith, sus-
tenit be him and his spouse through the wanting of the said
gudes; and for 40s to the expences of the four witnesses that
deponet in his matter." [1]

As far back as 1487 a resignation by Quentin Agnew, in
favour of his son Patrick, and Catherine Gordon, is witnessed
by the lady's father Robert Gordon, and his elder brother Sir
Alexander Gordon of Lochinvar.[2]

This we must suppose to have been on the occasion of the
betrothal rather than the marriage of the young couple ; Patrick
then being only sixteen years of age.   The wedding followed in
due course; the bride's father, afterwards Sir Robert Gordon,
being styled of Glen (and on his brother's decease became
of Lochinvar), and her mother was the heiress of John Accarson
of Glenskyreburn, now Rusco [3]

The Skyre or Skirsburn, which named this barony, is classic,
as pointing to two Galloway proverbs of great antiquity ; "Skirs
Burn warning" being suggestive of calamities sudden and
overwhelming· "By reason," says old Andrew Symson, "that the
Skirs Burn having its rise from Cairnsmuir, will swell by sudden
inundation, even in the summer time, almost in a moment."
In the other case, the folklore takes the form of rhyme.

> When auld Cairnsmoor wears his hat,
> Palnure and Skirs Burn laugh at that.

---

[1] *Act Aud.* 9th December 1494.

Carcalfly, Craigcaffie , Auchiness (Auchness), Eachines, horse isles ; Mindork,
Moinedorch, dark moor, or tore, of the wild boar , Claunerry (Clendry), Claon-
iach, sloping land , Culurhorne, Culhorn, Culk'corna, angle of the barley ;
Glencapill, Glenhapple, of the horses ; Suthquhen (Sheuchan), Suidpeachan,
the little seat, Carzarane (Cairnzarran), Guerran, the horses' cairn ; Drumregget,
Dunragit, Ragat's fort , Bordland (Boreland), "Bordlands signifie the demesnes
lords keep in their hands for the maintenance of their tables "—Cowell's *Law
Dictionary*

[2] The original, with a very perfect impression of Quentin Agnew's seal attached,
was recovered by the author when examining the family charter chest at Kenmure
Castle in 1874 ; and was kindly presented to him by the Hon Mrs Bellamy
Gordon

[3] Riaseach, an adjective form of riasg, "a marsh or fen."

This is matched by a couplet used a little farther eastward :

> When Tintock tap puts on a cap,
> Criffel wots fu' weel o' that.

A rather melancholy story connects itself with a cousin of the bride. The Gordons of Huntly were still near of kin to those of Lochinvar, and still retained their Border properties.[1] There was another Katherine Gordon at this date, whose rare beauty, as well as her name, accounts for the alacrity with which the chivalry of Galloway were ready to ride in her favour, and which nearly led to an English war. At the moment when the golden youth of Scotland were at the feet of the lovely Katherine,—known as the "White Rose," the King of France, to suit his own purposes,[2] palmed Perkin Warbeck on James IV. as the real Duke of York, and the Scottish king falling into the snare, married Katherine Gordon to the pretender, rightly judging that the young nobility would gladly don the badge of his Gordon bride, now similar to his own, but which proved of ill omen to the lady.

There was mustering in hot haste from the Merse to the Rhynns of Galloway : none more ready to maintain his fair cousin's cause against all comers than the young sheriff.

The din of preparation reached the English court, whence an army was soon in full march upon the Borders. Their approach was announced by bale-fires flashing east and west from a hundred hills ; the king's sheriffs urging every available lance from their respective districts to the front.

Happily, for once sense prevailed over sentiment, and the

---

[1] It is not generally remembered that the Huntly, as well as the ducal title of the Gordons, was derived from the Borders Huntly was a village in the parish of Gordon in Berwickshire, the only vestige of which is a farm named Huntly, and Huntly Wood in Gordon parish. The Gordons, on getting possession of their earldom in Aberdeenshire, carried it with them : whence the name of the parish there so called

[2] 1496 the French king, Louis XII , discovers to King James a notable piece of apocrypha called Edward, Duck of Yorke : this masked comedian proved a notable counterfeit .   This year the counterfeit Duck of Yorke is married to the Earl of Huntlie's daughter, and gets a good armey of Scots for his aide. They invade the English borders, King Henry prepares a grate armey to invade Scotland, but no blood was shed one ather syde.—Balgoni, i. 220

English succeeded in convincing the Scots of the futility of
Warbeck's pretensions; that the beauty of his wife could in no
way assist in his legitimation ; and that the people of England
repudiated him *en masse.* A formal truce was signed, and the
army simultaneously withdrew: recorded rather boastfully in
official accounts, the intimation made to the Sheriff of Galloway
being worded "Repulse of an English Raid."[1]

The White Rose was not a name to conjure with in England ,
for poor Katherine the coincidence was unfortunate. Perkin
Warbeck was taken and executed soon after; but Henry VII.,
struck with the beauty of Katherine, recommended her to his
queen, who retained her about her person, and eventually
married her to Sir Matthew Cradock, ancestor of the Earls of
Pembroke

The king had now commenced a series of pilgrimages, almost
annual, to Whithorn, generally attended by a large retinue,
including minstrels, to beguile the way. In Wigtownshire he
usually lodged in the religious houses , though he occasionally
slept in the house of Myrtoun, as a charter exists erecting the
place into a burgh of barony in favour of Sir Alexander
M'Culloch "in consideration of the hospitality the king had
received there on the occasions of his passing to and from
Whithorn."

In the ruined tower of Myrtoun an unglazed and unplastered
closet, now used as a pigeon-house, is pointed out as the "King's
chalmer."[2]

Almost immediately after "the scaling of the Englishmen "
(September 1497), we trace the king taking his midday meal on
the Loch Ryan shores, on the return from such a pilgrimage,

[1] 20 August 1497. David Green receives 32s to pass with the king's letters
to the schirifs of Wigtown and Galloway, to warn them of the scaling of the
Englishmen Docketed "Notice of the Repulse of an English Raid."—*Lord High
Treasurer's Accounts.*

[2] The other Myrtoun in Penninghame, now Myrtoun M'Kie, had been
previously constituted a burgh of barony by James III., A D. 1477, subject to the
Kennedies of Blairquhan : both burghs have entirely decayed.

In the Chamberlain Rolls is an entry, "Alexander M'Callauch, Miles de Myrtoun
et Marian Sinclair ejus sponsa." Marian was daughter to Sir John Sinclair, the
Queen's knight

from an entry for compensation paid to some of the sheriff's
tenants near Innermessan, for bites taken by his horses from
their growing oats, when turned loose during the king's repast.[1]

The same year Patrick M'Culloch attacked the house of
Ardwell, and slew his kinsman Archibald, the owner, in the
fray ; the only particulars as to which are to be gathered from
a respite to the said Patrick for the slaughter " committed under
the silence of night." A still more serious crime is to be
gathered from the same sources,[1] namely, a remission to Sir
Alexander M'Culloch of Myrtoun, the Laird of Garthland, and
twenty-nine others, for the burning and reefing of the houses
of Dunskey and Ardwell   The attack must have been made in
great force and with much persistence, which resulted in the
capture of a fortalice of such strength as Dunskey.

Owing to the increasing infirmities of his father, the duties
of sheriff were now generally performed by Patrick Agnew,
already infefted conjunctly with Quentin in the office.   Reared
as he had been among scenes of feud and violence, such audacious
proceedings as not only plundering, but firing and razing old
strengths, were too much even for the lax code of conduct then in
vogue ; and he bestirred himself with laudable activity.   Three
blasts of a sergeant's horn constituted the culprits " fugitive "
The officers of the law were on their tracks , and so hot was the
pursuit, that the offenders, powerful as they were, found it
necessary to tender their submission and make reparation to the
aggrieved parties, upon which they received a " remission." This
word, mild in form, implied no small amount of pain and
penalty endured , as, in the case of " fugitives" of baronial
position declared rebel, their lands and holdings were left open
to be ravaged and distrained upon with rough justice ; moreover,
they had to find good security for the fines and compositions
imposed.   A good round sum must have passed from the
pockets of the lairds of Garthland and Myrtoun, into those of
Ninian Adair, who restored his castle of Dunskey in a style
highly creditable to his taste.

<hr>

[1] Pitcairn, *Criminal Trials.*

Other lairds of smaller means, implicated in the outrages—notedly several of the M'Kies,—wandered as outlaws for many years before they found securities to be answerable for their share in the damage.[1]

Whilst west of the Cree such strongholds were levelled in private warfare, eastward, Loch Fergus, the palace of the old Lords of Galloway, belonging to the powerful Laird of Bomby, was nevertheless destroyed by fire by Cairns and others[2]

After such daring crimes, a simple theft from a high ecclesiastic almost raises a smile. On the 18th of November 1497, John Dunbar, son and apparent heir of the Laird of Mochrum,[3] is charged with resett of feft with his servitors William Fleming, James M'Culloch, and John Core, 'quhilk was with Elizabeth Kennedy that time she took away £43 gold and silver, a silver sele, and other small gere, had in her keeping for the Reverend Father in God, George Vaus, Bishop of Galloway."[4] We read also of a minor crime, but which was always punished with disproportionate severity . "the refe of certain haliks out of Dundrennan by John Herries of Barclay, aggravated by the binding of the men keeping them."[5]

About this time the sheriff was struck down by disease (probably paralysis), and in the interests of his family his affairs were put in trust, a precept under the Privy Seal constituting Robert Ahannay of Sorby and Niven Agnew younger of Croach

---

[1] Duncan M'Kie and several others received a remission in 1503 ; and three more of the M'Kies were not finally "relaxed" till 1510, the Laird of Lochinvar becoming surety for the parties —Pitcairn, *Criminal Trials*

[2] Remission to John Carnys in the Copwood, and Thon Hutchenson, for art and part of the burning of Loch Fergus, belonging to the Laird of Bomby.—25th February 1498.

[3] The young Laird of Mochrum was son of John, the second son of Sir James Dunbar of Westfield, who had married Margaret, heiress of Sir Patrick Dunbar of Mochrum, she thus carrying her lands to her kinsman, and dying in 1483, her husband remarried a Stewart of Garlies.

[4] Bishop Vaus's nephew, Patrick of Barnbarroch, had a charter to himself and his spouse, Marian Kennedy, of the lands of Longcaster, with the lake and isle of the same, by John Dunbar of Mochrum, 20th November 1498 — Pitcairn, *Criminal Trials*

[5] Pitcairn, *Criminal Trials*

curators for the management of his affairs until his recovery or death.[1]

His death followed soon after. Of younger children we only trace Michael, a canon of Whithorn, and Mariotta, married to John de Murehead of Lawchop and Ballies.

[1] A precept of ye office of curatory of Quintyn Agnew, Sheref of Wigtown, be a retour ob made to Robert Ahannay of Sorby, and to Nevin Agnew, sone and ar apperande to Wilze Agnew of Croich, upon his lands, rents, possessions, and guds. Ay and quhill God provide of his hele or ded. 19 Januari, anno regis xi. (1498).—*Privy Seal Register*, lib. i. fol. 58.

We find an Andrew of the period, probably a younger brother, and copy the extract, especially with a view to the form of "Kirkmedyn" (Medana).

1493. King confirms charter of John Kennedy of Ladycroft, Kirkmedyn, to Nevin Agnew, son and heir of William Agnew of Croach, to be held of the king. Witnessed by Uchtred Edyare of Crachine, John Gordon, Andrew Agnew, Patk. Edyare, And. Maecallane, Richard Edyare.—*Great Seal Register*, vol. i. p. 455, No. 2057.

SEAL OF QUENTIN AGNEW, 1487.

CHAPTER XVII

BARONIAL BANQUETINGS

A.D. 1498 to 1506

The lieges all did till their lady lout,
Wha was conveyed with ane royal rout
Of barroness and lusty ladies sheen.
Welcome our Queen! the commons gave ane shout.
                                        DUNBAR.

THE year of the fourth sheriff's accession, Cuthbert Baillie succeeded Lindsay of Fairgirth as Chamberlain of Galloway.[1] Soon after we find him styled of Dunragit, which he must have purchased from the sheriff or his father, as the only earlier notice of the property extant is in a decree of the Lord Auditors (1494), in which it is catalogued among lands belonging to Quentin Agnew and Marian Vaus his spouse.

The dwelling-house was not on the site of the present mansion of the estate, but about a mile eastward, where the names and holdings of "Old Hall" and "Orchard" indicate the family residence. The new Laird of Dunragit, who in his first accounting is styled Canonicus Glasguensis, was of a family having a common origin with those of Lamington, Dochfour, and Polkemmet. Among the first items in these accounts is one to Sir Alexander M'Culloch and Marian Sinclair his wife,[2]

---

[1] Mure had been chamberlain from 1462 to 1496, when he was succeeded by James Lindsay of Fairgirth, a cadet of the house of Balcarres, who held the office two years.

Fairgirth is Norse from "faar," a sheep, as in Fair Isle and Faroe.

[2] Alexander M'Callauch, Miles de Myrtoun, et Marian Sinclair ejus sponsa.— *Chamberlain Rolls.*

the lady apparently a daughter of Sir John Sinclair, "the Queen's Knight."

In 1501 we find James IV. varying his route, entering Galloway by Dumfries, entertained on the 23d of April by the friars of Kirkcudbright, to whom he gave eight French crowns, passing the next day to Whithorn, to do which he must have ridden betimes, having to commence his journey by ferrying the Dee, next to ride to and cross the Fleet, thence pass to Cassencarry, and ford or ferry the Cree to Wigtown, whence a good twelve miles remained to his journey's end[1]

Sir John Dunbar, who had married as his second wife Janet, daughter of Sir Alexander Stewart of Garlies, had by her two sons: Archibald, founder of the house of Baldoon, and Gavin, afterwards tutor to James V., and Archbishop of Glasgow. He obtained in 1502 a nine years' grant of the keeping of the castle of Threave, certain fishings in the Dee, and the office of Stewart of Kirkcudbright; but was unfortunately killed in a quarrel (probably as to these very fishings) by the young Laird of Lochinvar, and was succeeded by his son John This John, from the very circumstances of his succession, fell heir to a blood feud with the Gordons. He inherited also the remainder of his father's term of the Stewardship of Kirkcudbright, and in due course "letters of slains" having been granted to Alexander Gordon for the assassination of his father, according to the curious ideas of administration then current, the whole clan of Gordons were exempted from his jurisdiction, on the ground that "neither of the two parties could be competent judges in actions affecting one another, owing to the discord and unkindness existing between them."[2]

[1] 22 April 1501   To the Freiars of Kyrkcudbricht, eight Franesche crowns. Item the same day in Whitherne, to Sir Andrew MacBeek, to dispone among priests, £5 —*Lord Treasurer's Accounts.*

[2] An exemption to Alexander Gordon of Lochinvar, himself, friends, tenants, and partakers, from the jurisdiction of the Steward of Kirkcudbright and his deputes —*Privy Seal Register.*

In Sir John Dunbar's accountings as chamberlain we find, A.D 1504, £30 as dues for Leffinnolls (so spelt, Lefnoll), Laucht Alpine, and Mekell Laucht.

John Dunbar married Catherine, daughter of Thomas M'Clellan of Bomby.

About this time a feud between the Agnews and M'Kies attained such considerable proportions that the Crown ordered an inquiry, and the High Justiciary of Scotland summoned both parties to meet him at Dumfries where, after much ado, he induced both (on the 13th August 1504) to enter into recognisances to keep the peace; John Murray of Cockpule standing surety for the sheriff, and Thomas Kirkpatrick of Closeburn for the M'Kies. The former is now represented by the Earl of Mansfield; the latter is believed to be a progenitor of the Empress Eugenie of France.

In April 1505 the king made one of his many pilgrimages to Whithorn; starting from Ayr early on the 29th, and fording the Doon, the Girvan, and the Stincher, he entered Galloway by Glenapp, and arrived early in Glenluce. The same afternoon we read of his enjoying a game of bowls at the abbey with such of the baronage as the abbot had invited to assist at his entertainment.

The entry as to this in the Lord Treasurer's accounts seems to give a touch of reality to the scene. The king was unlucky, and lost 17s. at the game, which was honourably discharged.[1] A Galloway horse was also presented to his majesty on the occasion, which he was graciously please to accept.[2]

Early the following year, "the queen in her thraws of birth being near the last agonies of death," the king started on foot for St Ninian's shrine. His progress was now necessarily slower, and no conviviality was indulged in by the way.

On the 15th March he reached Dalry and paid 18s. for his supper and bed. Next day he dined at a halfway-house between the Ken and Cree in his long walk to Minigaff, paying 9s. for his "belcheir" On the 17th he walked to the Clachan of Penninghame, where was the bishop's palace, where he

[1] 29 Aprile. To the king to play at the kyles at Glenlus, 17s. Kyles=bowls, more strictly skittles, from the French *quilles.—Lord Treasurer's Accounts.*

[2] To the Abbot of Glenluce his man of bridal silver of ane gray horse giffen here to the king, 13s —*Ibid*

probably slept, giving 9s. to the man that bore St. Ninian's bell

On the 18th he got to Wigtown, paid 28s. at the inn, and leaving in the middle of the night, walked fasting and barefoot to Whithorn, giving 13s. to his guide.[1]

The faith of the royal pilgrim had its reward in the queen's recovery; and in token of gratitude the queen and king together made a progress to Whithorn the following year in royal state. Queen Margaret's wardrobe required seventeen horses to carry it, the king's three, and a twenty-first for the chapel gear.

The queen, not strong enough to ride, was borne in a litter, entered in the accounts as the queen's chariot.[2]

Gentle and simple from Rhynns and Machars donned their best to give the royal pair a befitting welcome. The clerical element, represented by the bishop, the priors of Whithorn and Wigtown, the abbots of Soulseat and Glenluce, friars black, white, grey, red, and parti-coloured ; the lay, by the sheriff, the chamberlain, coroner, and baronage, "all dighted in their braws."

> Their pleasant ladyes prancing ower the bents,
> In costly clothing to their hiche contentes.

Great were the acclamations when the king and queen passed to St. Ninian's shrine, and placed their gifts over the relics of the saint. The king, leading her by the hand, presented the Tudor Margaret to her lieges, radiant in gems and health, which she acknowledged as due to the intercessions of their favourite saint.

> "Welcome our Queen ! the commons gave ane shout"

The return journey of the royal pair, accompanied by the

---

[1] 16th day of March. To the king's belchior in Dalry, 18s. For the king's belchior quhen the king dinit be the gait, 9s. Item, that night the king sowpit at Menegouf for the belchior there, 9s.—*Lord Treasurer's Accounts.*

The-phonetic spelling Meneguif tallies with the Celtic Moine-Gamp, or Cymric Myned-Gauaf, "the wintry moor."

[2] 17 July. Three dozen points to the quene's chariot, 13s , a quartar carsay quhilk mendit the quene's letter graith, 13s ; Galloway carsais, kersey or woollen stuff, a frequent item in ancient book-keeping.

sheriff and a bodyguard from the Rhynns, was by the Mochrum shore to Glenluce, where they passed the night; the abbot doing the honours of the monastery grounds; the king, well pleased that the English ladies of the suite (notably my Lady Musgrave) should see the acres of esculents, many of them not yet common in the north, the orchards and trimmed borders, gave a douceur of 4s. to the gardener.

These were days of fun and feasting, any incidental notices of which are doubly agreeable; because, whilst the wrong-doings and bickerings of society are minutely chronicled, we are told little of the merry-makings and lighter occupations of our ancestors. Yet, if our forbears were somewhat violent and prone to enter into "bands" in gendering feud, they were fully alive to the claims of hospitality. If the baron was too often to be seen issuing from his gate, "boden in fere of wear," the baronial halls were frequent scenes of the friendly rivalry of their ladies, whose red-letter days were those which marked their triumph of culinary skill; and we shall for a moment try to penetrate the mysteries of the kitchen and housewifery, with the aid of the slight clues we have to guide us. A proverb in use among the Anglo-Norman baronage gives us a guide to their hours:

> Lever à cinq, diner à neuf,
> Souper à cinq, coucher à neuf,
> Fait vivre d'ans nonante et neuf

Freely translated by a later generation:

> Early to bed and early to rise,
> Makes a man healthy, wealthy, and wise.

In the fourteenth century, in England as well as Scotland, nine, poetically the hour of prime, was the usual dinner hour; whence Chaucer—

> And let us dyne as sone as ye may,
> For by my chilindre it is prime of day.[1]

In the fifteenth century it is believed the higher classes usually

---

[1] "The Schipmanne's Tale"

dined at ten; and for long five o'clock was the recognised hour
for the evening meal: arrangements which made artificial light
unnecessary for dinner at any season, and not often wanted for
supper—an important consideration when ordinary candles and
oil were bad, and wax both scarce and dear.

The dining-halls of Galloway gentry were less imposing than
those of the English. Rarely, if ever, were to be seen there the
raised dais and the deeply recessed fireplaces, examples of which
are to be seen at Naworth Castle, the nearest to the Borders.

The hall of Lochnaw, built about 1426, was 29 feet by
17½, that of Dunskey, rebuilt nearly a century later, 36 feet
by 17.

English and Scottish living-rooms were alike without lath
and plaster; the halls of ordinarily good houses having hangings
of worsted, and those of the wealthiest, tapestry.

A polished dining-table (now almost mediæval) was then
unknown, as was mahogany itself. The festive board was
formed of deal planks loosely placed together on trestles, and
covered with a cloth. This, if somewhat inelegant, had the
advantage of elasticity; as when, as it not unusually happened,
the dining-hall was overcrowded, free circulation was afforded
by moving a part of the table when eating was done; and when
the party broke up, the part remaining was lifted from its
trestles and laid against the wall, whence the mediæval phrase
"closing the tables."

Plain deal cupboards, ranged round the room, held the
various requisites for repasts. · These, with increasing wealth
and refinement, developed into the buffet: an ornamental open
stand with shelves, on which china, pottery, and plate, were
arranged for show. From the centre of the ceiling depended
the chandelier, consisting in primitive times of two transverse
boards, but usually in the fourteenth and fifteenth centuries
made of latten or copper,[1] carrying four candles stuck on

---

[1] Latten, an alloy of brass In 1495 Henry Mundwell and Janet Buyt sued
Rankin Mure for the detention of a brazen chandelier at Wigtown The Lords of
the Council referred the matter to Quentin Agnew, desiring him or his deputes to
value it, which they did at 3s.—*Act. Dom. Concil.*

spikes, a third bar being sometimes added so as to carry six lights.

Candlesticks of brass were often placed simply against the walls, having a motto beneath the bracket;[1] and when much lighting was required, especially for the passages or court, this was usually provided by torches carried by the retainers.

The lady of the house usually furnished napkins plentifully for her guests; and when a feast was being prepared, the style of the entertainment was primarily gauged by the amount of

"Domik work (damask) on buird desplayed."[2]

Of silver plate the most essential was the saltcellar; and second in importance was a round dish similar in size, divided into compartments for sugar and various spices. Silver punch-bowls were usual; or if made of other material, with silver edges. A silver basin was always if possible procured to hand round to guests for ablutions; but only a very few of the wealthiest land-owners had silver trenchers for their joints. Silver drinking-cups were also in use; indeed, the baron frequently carried his own cup with him; but few could supply these to many guests · ordinary drinking-vessels being wooden, sometimes with a metal rim, sometimes of porcelain, all such described as macers.[3] Glass bottles, of an enormous size, were early used as decanters. Many a laird could boast his

"Pair of bossis gude and fyne
They hold ane gallon full of Gascon wyne."[4]

But a wineglass was a curiosity. It is said, whether jokingly or not, that one wineglass sometimes went round the table.

In an inventory of 1492 is "my candel beme with six bellys of laton," i.e. six brazen holders.

[1] In an inventory of 1463 we find "a candylstick of laton with a pyke", Also "a candylstick of laton whereupon is wretyn, 'Grace me governe.'"

[2] Lyndsay, vol. ii. p. 279.

[3] In inventories "maser" seems equivalent to drinking-cup They are sup-posed to have been sometimes of earthenware, sometimes porcelain A plausible derivation is the Dutch "maiser," maple wood, of which fancy cups were often made A "mazer gilt" in inventories seems often to mean silver gilt.

[4] Dunbar

We find Adair of Kinhilt borrowing from Sir Patrick Vaus —both being Galloway lairds—"ane silver basin, gilt abune the edges, weighing seven score and ten ounces; and one laver of silver." [1]

Lord Cassilis, in the middle of this century, was able to spare from his plate-chest, over and above what he required for his own use, as a loan to his mother, "a silver basin and a laver, a double gilt cup, a gilt macer, two silver trenchers, two little salt fatts in their nooks, a silver salt fatt and cover thereof ungilt." [2]

Where plates were scarce, thick slices of bread did duty instead, and soaked up the gravy. In frugal houses, these formed part of the repast; in greater families and at feasts these trenchers were collected in the alms baskets by servants, when the tables were closed, and distributed to the poor.

In the matter of cutlery the host only felt himself bound to provide table-knives for his own household. Every guest brought his own knife in a leathern sheath attached to his girdle; whence the caution to a diner-out in an old book of etiquette, "Bring no knyves unscoured to the table." [3] Forks, to a much later period than we now write of, were totally unknown as a medium of conveying food to the mouth : those mentioned in inventories were solely used for carving and serving. When gentlemen of refinement endeavoured to introduce the custom from abroad as cleanly and convenient, it was abominated as a foreign innovation, ridiculed as an affectation, and—what seems almost incredible—denounced from the pulpit as wrong. In Ben Jonson's comedy of *The Devil is an Ass*, first acted as late as 1616, the use of forks in the highest English society was so little known that we find the following dialogue between Sledge and Meerecraft, a speculative adventurer :

Sledge. "What ?"
Meerecraft. "My project o' the forks"

---

[1] *Correspondence of Lord Barnbarroch,* p. 261
[2] *Charter History of the Kennedys.*   [3] Lydgate

Sledge. " Forks ? what be they ? "

Meerecraft " The laudable use of forks brought into custom here, as
    they are in Italy,

To the sparing of napkins . . .

                                    . 'twill be

A mighty saver of linen through the kingdom."

When the cook had put the finishing touches to their
" subtilties," [1] dinner was announced by sound of trumpets
(this in itself being a baronial privilege); and a servant handing
round a basin, another following with napkins, the guests
washed their hands before, as they subsequently did after meat.
They then filed off to their places, hand in hand, each couple
eating off the same trencher.

The bill of fare on which a Galloway baron might draw was
as enviable for its excellence as for its variety. Plums in his
savoury broth, red fish, oysters, beef and mutton of the best,
venison and wild boar, grouse, partreck, duck, plover, and game
of every sort, varied by such *hors d'œuvres* as haggis and Har-
rest brose, there being this difference, however, between his
tastes and ours, that what we consider coarser articles of food,
porpoises and sturgeon, were held to be more lordly food than
smelt and salmon, whilst, not to mention cormorants, coots, and
hedgehogs, all included in his menu, cranes and swans, purchased at exorbitant prices, were preferred to moorfowl and
mallard to be had for the taking near his own gates, and an
old peacock, first skinned, then roasted and farced, and redecked
in his gorgeous plumage, was more esteemed than the fattest
capon or turkey.

" Bread of mane," fancy loaves, spiced and sweetened jelly
(the art of extracting which from the feet of calves, sheep, oxen,
and pigs, was well understood), pastry, and comfits, were placed
plentifully on the table. But the triumph to the lady of the
house depended upon the skill of her cooks in the production of
the " subtilty," a mighty compound of the elements of cakes and

[1] An ornamental device in pastry These were often very bold, such as a
ship filled with birds, surrounded by a sea full of fishes, having a tall mast with
sails of silk and ermine

sweatmeats, formed into edible models of sculptured groups, castles, ships, or heraldic devices, set down as an epergne, to be eaten with the dessert.[1]

We have been fortunate in recovering the details of a feast given by George Neville on his installation as Archbishop of York in 1491, to which many of the officials and baronage of Galloway were invited, and notably the bishop, his claim over him as his suffragan being foregone on the occasion, under protest. A great company of the gentry from both sides of the Border were present, for whose entertainment was purveyed 104 oxen, 1000 sheep, 2000 pigs, and other animals in proportion, 104 peacocks, 204 cranes, 12 porpoises and seals, besides game and poultry of all sorts, 1000 partid dishes of jelly, 3000 plain dishes of jelly, 4000 cold baked tarts, 2000 hot custards

Music was a usual accompaniment of feastings. In King James's numerous journeys to Galloway, he presses into his service the musicians of the burghs and the baronage. Thus we read of the Prior of Whithorn's clarsha, Redman the lutar, William the tambroner, Ainslie the tambroner, Quhynbore the tambroner, and his marrow, a piper that playet with the schawmes (cornet), Pate Harper the clarsha at Whithorn, two trumpeters of Whithorn, the pipers of Wigtown, Lord Fleming's tambroner, and numerous fithlers; all these, in the years 1497-98, the usual minstrels playing at merrymakings in the countryside When dinner was over the attendants handed round the ewer, and all washed · a very necessary process where all had eaten with their fingers. Abundance of napkins were

---

[1] In a manual of such Scottish matrons of the fifteenth century as could afford such entertainments, called the Menagier de Paris, minute directions are given for cooking hedgehogs, rooks, magpies, jackdaws, sheldrake, coots, cormorants, and others innumerable

We subjoin a bill of fare from the Sloane MSS. of the fifteenth century, which has a Scottish ring.

1st Course —Umbles of a heart Side of a heart roast Swan Fesaunt. Bytore (Bittern) Pike Great gurnard. Haggisse. Blanche custard. A subtilty

2d Course.—Gelee Cream of almonds. Kid Chickens larded Pertrick Larks. Perch. Porpoise roast. Frytours lombard Payne puff. A subtilty (a castle of silver with veins of gold).

provided, but only one basin for the whole. As a contemporary
poet puts it .

Then they toke eche other be the hand and weshed.

If this small provision at Galloway entertainments sounds un-
refined, we find that even a century later there was but one
basin, and that only once filled with water, supplied at baronial
banquets in more wealthy England.

When Cosmo III, Duke of Tuscany, travelled through the
southern counties of England in 1663, one of his suite, whilst
acknowledging the abundance and good quality of the provisions set before them by the west country proprietors, remarks in parenthesis that they thought the cooking not so
good as that of France, adds, "There is a great want of that
gentility at English tables which is practised in Italy .   .
There are no forks, nor vessels to supply water for the hands,
which are washed in one basinfull of water, which serves for
all the company "[1]

Lastly, as to wines. Dunbar the poet adjures the king to
leave dull Stirling and come to more luxurious Edinburgh

To eat swan, cran, patrik, and plever,
And every fish that swims in river,
And drink with us the new fresh wine
That grew upon the river Rhine,
Fresh fragrant clarets out of France,
Of Angiers and Orleanse.

The importations of wines direct to Galloway was limited
by law to the ports of Wigtown and Kirkcudbright, the lieges
having the advantage of buying it cheaper than in the eastern
shires, Gascon wines being retailed at 6 and 8 pennies the pint
against 8 and 10 elsewhere[2] Rhine wines were not unknown,
nor those of Spain and Portugal, called sack (i.e. sec = dry), as

[1] *Travels of Cosmo III , Duke of Tuscany, in 1663*, by Count Lorenzo Mega-
litto, p. 464   Quarto   1821
[2] That na wines that is cum in at the west seas be bocht of onie dearer price
nor £16 the tun of Burdeaux wine, and the Rochel wine for £12 or thretteen
pounds the tun, and that nane of them sell the samin of onie dearer price nor
aucht pennies the pynt of Burdeaux wine, and 6 pennies the pynt Rochele wine
—5 Parlt Queen Mary, c. 1.

also Malmsey Madeira, called Malvoisie, and Muskadill, which
were sweet; and a strong liqueur called Hippocras, mixed with
spices and sugar, was much drunk. Distillation was not then
general in Scotland, but aqua vitæ, *i.e.* brandy, appeared occasionally on the tables of the wealthy.

Lyndsay, describing the reception of a traveller at a Scottish
country gentleman's house, writes:

> He found his chalmar well arrayed
> With dornik work on buird desplayed.
> Of venison he had his weill,
> Gude aqua vitæ wyne and aill,
> With nobile comfeittes, bran and geill,
> And sua the Squyer fuir richt weill.[1]

Whilst on another occasion a host is described as entertaining
his guests

> With mirth, music, and minstrallie,
> With wyld fowle, venison, and wyne,
> With tail and flam and fruitage fyne,
> Of bran and geill there was na stent,
> And Ipocras he could not want.[1]

Another Lyndsay (the historian), in giving details of a feast
given in 1528 by the Earl of Athol, where we should hardly
look for greater luxuries than at the command of Galloway
barons, enumerates " all kinds of drink, as aill, beer, wyne, both
white and claret, malvasie, muskadaill, eligant hippocras, and
aqua vitæ; farder, thair was of meattis, weat bread, maine bread,
and gingebread, with fleshis beiff and mutton, lamb, veill and
venison, goose, gruse, capon, cunning, cran, swan, pairtrick, plever,
duik, drake, brissel, cock and pannies, blackcock and muirfoull,
capercailles; all delicat fishes, as salmond, trouts, pershes, pikes,
eels. Syne were there proper stuarts, cunning baxters, excellent cooks and potingaris; with confections and drugs for the
desserts "

---

[1] Squyer Meldrum; bran, brawn; geill, jellies; skent, scant, scarcity; flam,
custard, a pudding baked in a dish.

CHAPTER XVIII

THE FOREST OF BUCHAN

A.D. 1506 to 1510

> The Kennedys wi' a' their power,
> Fra Cassilis to Ardstencher towers,
> May rise and flock like screeching craws,
> Fra heighs an' hous, fra homes and ha's,
> An' hither come wi' blawing crack;
> They'll bear anither story back.

THE Isle of Man had, till the fifteenth century, belonged to Scotland.

In earlier days Olave the Swarthy, an independent kinglet, had wedded Affrica,[1] daughter of Fergus, Lord of Galloway, who was recognised as Queen of Man; but later Alan, Lord of Galloway, and his brother the Earl of Athol, held the island in subjection. Much intercourse consequently took place between the Galwegians and the Manxmen, till the latter, throwing off the yoke of Olave's successors, confiscated the property of such Galwegians as had settled there, and banished them for ever from their isle.[2] As a consequence the "wild Scots" made occasional piratical descents upon the Manxmen, who rarely retaliated.

About 1506, however, the English Earl of Derby obtained rule there, and carried the war into the enemy's country.

---

[1] Knockeffrich, Kirkinner, near Fergus's strength of Loncaster, is supposed to take its name from her.

[2] The legislature in 1422 enacted "that all Scottish men do avoid the land of Manx by the next vessel that goeth to Scotland, upon paine of forfeiture of their goods and bodyes to prison."

Then came Thomas Derby, born king, 'twas he wore the golden crupper,
There was not one lord in England itself with so many knee-guinea men [1]
On Scotland he revenged himself, and went to Keelchoobragh,
And there made such havoc on houses, that some are yet unroofed. [2]

An owre true tale: he laid Kirkcudbright in ashes; but, encouraged by a visit of sympathy from King James IV., on which occasion he made the corporation a gift of the Castle,[3] it rose phœnix-like from its ashes, and it was found that happily the freebooters had spared the marcat cross, which still stands, purporting to have been erected in 1504.

Lord Derby's fillibustering energy was overmatched by Cutlar M'Culloch, a cadet of Myrtoun, and a born sea-king. He induced the Celts to build and man many more boats, and envelop the Isle of Man with his flotilla.

Again and again he ravaged it, carrying off all that was not too hot or too heavy for removal, till his very name became a bugbear with young and old, his ubiquity being such that a Manxman presiding at the board would warn his guests to begin with the meat and finish with the broth, so as to make sure at least of a substantial bite before M'Culloch could disturb them.

And so closely did they believe him to match Satan himself in his powers of mischief, that it was proverbially said that the family prayers of a Manx patriarch might be epitomised in the couplet—

> God keep this house and all within
> From Cut M'Culloch and from sin

An evidence of his audacity and success is preserved in the deposition of a governor of Peel Castle, the strongest in the island, but which he had taken and stripped :

[1] The soubriquet "knee-guinea men" is matched by as funny a one in Galloway a century later, when a moss-trooping laird on the Galloway marches was known as "Gibby with the gowden garters," he being Gilbert Elliot of Stobs, who married Margaret, daughter of Sir Walter Scott of Harden, she being known as "Maggie Fendy (i e handy) —Life of First Earl of Minto, vol. 1 p. 4.

[2] Translation of a Manx poem in Train's History of Man.

[3] It was granted by David II, to Archibald Douglas in 1369. On forfeiture of the Douglases it reverted to the Crown In 1582 Sir Thomas M'Clellan acquired it and built the Castle, the ruins of which now remain upon its site.

"Taken by Collard M'Culloch and his men, by wrangous spoliation, two box beddes and ayken burdes, a feder bouster, a cote mailzie, a mete burde, twa kystes, five barrels, a gyle-fat, xx pipes, twa gunys, three bolls of malt, a quern of rosate, certin petes, viii boll of thraset corn, xii of unthraschen, xl knowtes.
(Signed) "JOHN MACHARIOTIC, Governor, 1507." [1]

M'Culloch's [2] achievements having freed the landowners of the Galloway sea-board from anxiety of invasion, they expended their energies in quarrels with one another. Those which obtained the greatest notoriety were passages of arms between Sir David Kennedy and the sheriff, resulting in a feud which, if temporarily laid, burst forth again and again and dragged its course for more than a hundred years. The Kennedys and Agnews for two generations were very near of kin; and for three, the most cordial relations had existed between them The power of the Kennedys would have been irresistible in the west country, could the stem of the branches have lived in harmony. But it was not so. The powerful houses of Bargany and Blairquhan were in chronic feud with that of Dunure, which they almost rivalled in influence; and the numerous Kennedy cadets were perpetually entering into bands with one faction or the other, changing sides whenever it suited their whims or convenience. It may have been well for their neighbours that it was so; as, if the clan had acted as one body, there would no doubt have been truth in the ancient rhyme—

Fra Wigtoune to the toun of Aire
And laigh down by the cruives o' Cree,
Ye shall not get a lodging there
Except ye court a Kennedie. [3]

---

[1] The barrels were probably ale, a gyle-fat, a still; the pipes of wine, knowtes, nolt or black cattle.—Challerson, 47
[2] In a note to *Peveril of the Peak*, Sir Walter Scott writes "The redoubtable Cutlar is now represented by James M'Culloch of Ardwell, the author's friend and near connection."
[3] Besides the three great families named, there were Kennedys of Girvan Mains, of Drummennan, of Leffnoll, of Coiff, of Glentig, of Lenzie, of Gillespie, of Knockdolian, of Carslo, of Balmaclanahan, of Bennane, of Knockreoch, of Knockdaw, of Kirkmichael, of Pinwhirry, of Drummerchie, of Garriehorn, of

Lord Kennedy's eldest son, Sir David,[1] had in his father's lifetime been infefted in the lands of Leswalt, which his family had purchased from the Crown, and had taken up his residence at the Inch, which he held under the Church. Oblivious of, or rather ignoring the rights of the Agnews as Crown Bailies of Leswalt,[2] he claimed exclusive right of holding court there.

A Galloway sheriff had to find his own troopers, whether to protect the lieges or assert his own private rights, and Patrick Agnew could only resist Sir David's pretensions by summoning his friends and part-takers to come to his assistance. Both parties were resolute, Sir David's apparently much the strongest; and we find from official records that he attempted over and over again to hold these courts, but was foiled by the sheriff and his friends. Five faction fights, waged with great severity, occurred, and were adjudicated upon by the Supreme Courts between the years 1506 and 1513.

Sir David called up numerous kinsmen from Carrick. The sheriff was supported by his kinsmen the lairds of Lochinvar, Garthland, Corswall, Barnbarroch, Kinhilt, Sorbie, and Broughton. Patrick Mure and Nevin Agnew, youths who delighted in a tuilzie, seem to have acted the part of aides-de-camp.

The campaign was opened by Sir David Kennedy riding, after formal announcement, in force from the house of Inch to Leswalt. The court-house of Leswalt lay about two miles from Lochnaw, at the foot of Aldouran Glen; and no sooner had Sir David come in sight of it, by way of St. John's Chapel, than the sheriff's party appeared descending from the so-called "Danish Camp" in superior force, and warned him off. The

Daljarroch, of Auchtralure, of Barquhanny, of Cloncaird, of Guiltree, of Skeldon, of Synniness

The Coiff, or the cove, is now Culzean ; Leuzie, the wet meadow , Carslo, the calves' carse , Knockdaw, knoll of the ox , Garriehorn, barley croft , Daljarroch, reddish field , Cloncaird, tinkers' meadow.

[1] He was knighted by James III on the creation of his second son Alexander, Duke of Ross, 29th January 1497.

[2] Patrick Agnew had been personally infefted in this office by Crown precept, as mentioned before "Officio Ballivatus de Leswalt *de nobis* tenendo in capite"

conduct of the sheriff on this occasion seems to have been unimpeachable. Backed by numbers able to enforce his rights, he made a dignified protest, and retired.

Such a peaceful ending to the day's work seemed too tame to wilder spirits, such as Mure, who after seeing the sheriff safely housed, doubled back at full speed, overtook the Kennedys, and had a glorious tussle, in which he had the best of it, and returned in triumph with the spoils of war.[1]

Sir David, however, was not to be thus diverted from his purpose. He proclaimed another court, and proceeded to hold it with a larger retinue. The sheriff accepted the challenge, donned his armour, met him by the way, and effectively prevented his holding his court, but this time with considerable violence.

Kennedy thereupon appealed to the Supreme Courts, which as usual played fast and loose, and whilst not admitting his right to hold the court at all, fined the sheriff's followers slightly for appropriating their opponents' accoutrements. In short, tacitly admitting the sheriff's chartered rights, but giving Sir David some solatium for the bruises of his jackmen.

The sheriff, having paid the penalty incurred by the over zeal of his followers, considered old scores against him cancelled, and proceeded to open a new account.

Kennedy soon gave him the opportunity. He again rode along

---

[1] At a Justice Aire, held July 1510, Patrick Waus of Irsick, Nevin Agnew, Ninian Adair, with the Lairds of Killeser, Corswall, Mindork, and twenty-three others, Alexander Hannay, brother-in-law of the Laird of Capenach, and ten others, are indicted for "riding with the Sheriff of Wigtown, and oppression done to Sir David Kennedy."

The indictment in the first case only charges the sheriff with "riding forth in rowting." But Patrick Mure, Nicholas Fresle (Fraser), and others, are charged "with forethought felony done to Sir David Kennedy, coming upon him in warlike manner with invasive weapons, and for hereschip of cloaks and other goods from his servants."

Patrick Agnew, Sheriff of Wigtown; Alexander M'Meiken, Nevin Agnew, John Adau, George Cruikshank, Thomas Porter, Patrick Agnew, servants of the said sheriff, are charged with convocation of the lieges with warlike arms, jakkes, and splents, and the oppression done to Sir David Kennedy, coming to Leswalt and hindering him from holding his court. In both cases the sheriff is permitted to compound.—Pitcairn, *Criminal Trials.*

the same highway, again was interrupted by the sheriff's friends, more "cloaks" taken from his servant, his court-book seized, and its blank leaves scattered ignominiously to the winds, the sheriff prudently keeping himself out of sight.   Again Kennedy appealed to the council, and again the sheriff was permitted to compound with his followers by a fine.[1]

It would be tedious to detail all those collisions, which are entered in the criminal records, and which may be well supposed to represent only a small part of such as actually occurred.   It is remarkable that in every case adjudicated upon, the sheriff's party had the advantage of the Kennedys: a clear proof of his popularity and the readiness of his neighbours to support him.

We shall pass to what seems to have been the last encounter, and which settled the question in the sheriff's favour for the lifetime of all parties concerned.

Sir David Kennedy, finding that convictions for undue violence in no way assisted his pretensions, determined in a final effort to prove that might was right.   All that owed him suit and service were summoned from Kyle and Carrick; and such a squadron was soon assembled as he believed would make the audacious sheriff understand who was master.   The sheriff proved equal to the occasion · keeping his larder full as well as his powder dry, he invited his part-takers to banquet with him the evening previous to the day fixed by Sir David for the trial of strength.

The records of the High Court of Justiciary supply us with the names of his guests, which included the lairds of Garthland, Corswall, Killeser, Broughton, Mindork, Sorby, Ninian Adair, the young Laird of Creaken, the Prior of Soulseat, Thomas Waus his brother, and twenty-six others.[2]   Cheerily the cup went round in the crowded dining-hall of Lochnaw that night; and bravely the band mustered on the green the following morning   The fair Katherine handed them the stirrup-cup; the

[1] Patrick Vaus for oppression, coming upon Sir David Kennedy, stouthrief of cloaks and other goods from the servants of the said lord , court-books, etc.— Pitcairn.

[2] Pitcairn, *Criminal Trials.*

Abbot of Soulseat gave his blessing; the young Laird of Kinhilt, a suitor for the hand of the sheriff's daughter, led the way—all happy in anticipation of a fray .

> The battle is their pastime, they go forth ·
> Gay in the morning as to summer's sport

The road from the manor-place of Inch to the court-house of Leswalt led past the hamlet of Chapell (now Stranraer) and across a little stream entering Loch Ryan beyond St. John's Well.

> Here the Kennedys in a' their power

were met by the sheriff's men, who barred their passage; and a *mélée* ensued, in which spear and sword-thrust were so freely exchanged that the brook is figuratively asserted to have run red, and that day got the name of the "Bloody Burn," which has clung to it ever since. Again the Agnews were victorious; and again Sir David entered an indictment, charging many of those present, who had no call to interfere, with "coming upon him in a warlike manner" and "forethought oppression." The Court admitted the breach of the peace to have been a "heinous one"; but they simply fined certain of the defendants ten marks each, to be paid at their leisure, accepting the sheriff himself and the lairds of Garthland and Craighlaw as "sureties for the parties."

Sir David found himself no nearer obtaining any admission of his claims on the Baillierie of Leswalt, the action he had entered furnishing a lasting and authentic record of his defeat.

So great was the exultation of some of the younger of the victors, that we find Nevin Agnew playing most audacious pranks, carting hay out of the great man's barns, and even making an attack upon his person; as in the Court Records "Nevin Agnew comes in for the king's will for breaking His Majesty's protection granted to Sir David Kennedy," and on several occasions is charged with "oppression to Sir David Kennedy," such terms as "protection" and "oppression," reading rather strangely as applied to the conduct of this pugnacious little laird towards so great a magnate as the heir of Cassilis. Meanwhile Sir David had succeeded his father as third Lord Kennedy, and *circum* 1511 was created Earl of Cassilis   Being now beyond all dispute paramount in Carrick and in Kyle, he seems to have ceased to concern himself about holding courts in Leswalt.

Sir John Kennedy of Blairquhan had now become a power in Galloway. He acquired wide lands in Penninghame, and about 1508 built and endowed a chapel on the Cree, which he dedicated to St. Ninian.[1]

The Kennedys of Blairquhan, however, rarely supported their cousin, Lord Kennedy, in his feuds.

Bishop Vaus died in 1508, and was succeeded by David Arnot,[2] and from him Lord Cassilis formally obtained the keeping of the manor-place of Inch,[3] as well as a regality jurisdiction over wide Church lands, of which many Galloway barons were " kyndly " rentallers.[4] The earl was also titular ranger of the Forest of Buchan, a style he much affected, of which he was undisputed owner, and might well exult in this lordly possession. A grander range for the field-sports of a feudal chief could hardly be imagined, comprising within its limits peaks almost within the snow range, the haunts of ptarmigan,[5] deep dens for deer,

---

[1] Near the ruins of St. Ninian's Chapel is Clachaneasy, which Sir Herbert Maxwell suggests is from the root Iosa (Jesus) ; if so, equivalent to Kirkchrist.

[2] On Vaux's death, James, son to John Beton of Balfour, became Bishop elect of Galloway ; but before consecration was advanced to the Archbishopric of Glasgow ; and David Arnot, son to John Arnot of that ilk, was preferred to the see.—Keith, 164.

[3] Gilbert, second Earl of Cassilis, was appointed by the Bishop of Galloway baillie of all the lands belonging to the bishopric, and captain and keeper of the manor-place and loch of Inch in 1516 —*Historical Account of Kennedys*, 32.

But it is evident that the father had the appointment previously, and notoriously resided at the manor-house.

[4] The Agnews had possession of the Dougaries (black enclosure), Craigbernach (the gapped craig), and Kylfeather (St. Peter's Chapel), all in the parish of New Luce

[5] " In the remote parts of the famous mountain of the Mearroch, a very large red deer, and about the top thereof, that fine bird the mountain partridge, called by the commonalty the tarmachan ; that bird feeds on the seeds of the bulrush, and makes its protection in the chinks and hollows of thick stones from the insults of the eagles, which are plenty about that mountain "—M'Farlane's MSS , Advocates' Library.

and lochs and streams innumerable. It included the whole
of the large parish of Carsphairn, and portions of those of
Straiton, Dalmellington, Kells, and Minnigaff.

The following modern farms formed but a small portion of
the Forest: Buchan, of which the steading is on Loch Trool,
known by the shepherds as the Four Nines, its extent being
held to be 9999 acres, Portmark, Arrow,[1] Lamloch, Palgown,
Stroan, Dungeon o' Buchan, Glenhead, Castle Maddie, Powmaddie, the Bush, the Cooran Lane.

Much of the so-called Forest was heath and hill-pasture, a
few arable spots intervening among thickets of primeval oak,
birch, and the rarer pine, with breaks of coppice; romantic glens,
where the rowan, and thorns black and white, picturesquely
contrasted with the juniper and holly; the only vegetation not
indigenous being an occasional ash tree planted for "policie"
near the lodges.

Wild lochs at various levels reflected the hills which backed
the panorama, of which the highest peaks, frequently snow-clad,
were Benyellarry, the Dungeon of Buchan, Curleywee, Millfore,
and the Merrick (Giant's Fingers).[2]

Numerous hunting-lodges were scattered through the Forest,
of which a favourite one of Earl David's is known as Hunt Hall,
its ruin crowning a green knoll, surrounded by three lakelets.
Garrary was another of his haunts; and Powmaddie is still
pointed to by the herds as the place where food was prepared
for Cassilis's hounds.

The old names have much significance. The range as seen
from a distance resembles the fingers of an extended hand.
Powmaddie and Castle Maddie recall the days when the barons
raised their tenantry to hunt the wolf. Pulnnee (pol phiadh) is

---

[1] Arrow, a place of corn; Lamloch Lom, a bare place; Palgown, the smith's
pool; Castle Maddie, Powmaddie, the wolf's castle and pool; Buchan, if Pictish,
seems to approach nearest the Cymric form Buwch-an, a place of cows

[2] Benyellarry, Iolaire, the eagle's peak, Cooran might be a diminutive of
currach, the little marsh, but more probably caorainn, the mountain ash; Millfore, meall-four, the cold hill, Mearich, Meurag, the finger, Loch Goosie (within
the Forest's bounds), Guisach, of the pine wood, is the only old local place-name
taken from the Scotch fir, which certainly existed in the native forest.

the pool of the red deer (and "deer's den" is mapped four times within the limits of the Forest). Benyellarry is still haunted by eagles.

The bounds of the Forest gradually contracted. In the seventeenth century a large portion had been acquired by the Lords of Garlies and Lochinvar. In 1678 "a procuratory of resignation was granted by John, sixth Earl of Cassilis, to Sir John Gordon of Lochinvar, of his free forest of Buchan." All that now retains the name belongs to the Earl of Galloway. In the eighteenth century there was much litigation between the Earls of Cassilis and Galloway as to its marches: of this, funny traditions have been preserved. "You will not allow yourself to be talked out of a rood of my rights," says my Lord John to his chamberlain. "My Lord," quoth that functionary, "there's nae living man could fix the bouns within twa or three thousan' acres"

Lord Cassilis's agent took more energetic steps to vindicate his master's interests, producing a "wabster body," a great oracle in the countryside, who swore upon his soul that on a particular spot he stood upon Cassilis's soil. His testimony was accepted by the arbiters in the case, and the bounds marked off. But long afterwards, when in his cups, it is said the old rascal would recount the story with a twinkle in his eye, adding, "It was truth that I swore to on my soul, for that very morn I had put a pickle of Cassilis's soil on the sole of my boot."

In the days of which we write, the marches of the Forest were for miles ill-defined between Cassilis and Lochinvar. But disputes arising were settled in a much more high-handed way than references to any "wabster body," though those with official power frequently tried to influence law-courts in their own favour.

About 1509 Lord Cassilis had a seat at the council board, whence from a coigne of vantage he fought over again the battle of Leswalt Knowing the carelessness of officials in conforming to Acts of Parliament, he raked up a series of charges of oppressions and malversation against the Sheriff of Galloway, founded on breaches of these, upon which he was called to plead

He was accused of oppression done to James Kennedy, Mariotta M'Ewen, Thomas M'Dowall, and Roger M'Crochat, for causing them to plough and harrow his lands in the years 1504-8, to build his dykes with their peats, and with plundering them yearly of a swine ; also with oppression done to Thomas Mak-william in taking and harrying ten bolls of barley ; of the hereschip of a young riding mare from Thomas Kennedy. The sheriff's retainers, George Cruikshank and Thomas Mure, striking the said Thomas ; and with the heirship of a jument from John M'Roy in the Forest of Buchan.[1]

Though no doubt the sheriff was not immaculate, a know-ledge of the circumstances and habits of the times go far to show that his exactions, if illegal, at least were customary; and certainly the High Courts did not regard the charges as serious. In the first place they were retrospective, the aggrieved parties being Cassilis's tenants in Leswalt · the so-called oppressions were the exactions of accustomed dues to the bailies of Leswalt, of which in reality the earl illegally disputed the right. A baron-bailie by law and custom was entitled to so many days ploughing and harrowing, leading, carriages, peat-cutting, and hens. The swine were probably taken as " caupes," although doubtless an Act had passed " for undooinge of caupes in Galloway ", [2] and of a breach of this he had to plead guilty, but with the mildest results ; " being permitted to compound," and the Laird of Loch-invar accepted as his surety;[2] which is the more amusing, as the taking of the horse in the Forest of Buchan was probably in support of his kinsman's claim on those marches disputed by the earl, a mere outcome of the feud between the Gordons and Kennedys.

And as to this especial case, the entry in the court-books is that the Laird of Orchardton, the sheriff's son-in-law, should become surety that he would satisfy the parties.

At a Justice Aire held at Wigtown in 1510, there are several

---

[1] Pitcairn, *Criminal Trials.*   [2] *Ibid.*

convictions for killing "red fish in close time." Also John
Maklumphaire[1] in Kirkmeren (Kirkmadrine) was convicted of
stouthrief of the wood of Garthlone,[2] and of the barking thereof.
Fined £3, afterwards remitted, he being a pauper.   There were
three other convictions for cutting and carrying away timber
from the woods of Barnrawer, Glensiche, and Croschrie, proving
that there were still some remains of the native forest; as we
may assume that there had been little replanting, the many
statutes to that effect notwithstanding.

[1] Same name written M'Lymphquay in 1401.   M'Clumpha, often abbreviated
M'Clue

[2] Garthlone, Garthland; Barnrawer, Baraer, Penninghame, the bluff top;
Croschrie, Crossarie, Kirkcowan, cross-roads, or place of crossings.

CHAPTER XIX.

FLODDEN

A.D. 1510 to 1527

In suith he was a barronne bauld,
For tuilzies tough in days of auld.
                                        BOSWELL.

LEFT to maintain his position among a turbulent baronage as
best he might, a Galloway sheriff had no choice but to enter
into bonds offensive and defensive. The highest legal functionary in the province was thus compelled not merely to do that
which was in itself illegal, but in so doing he became bound to
involve himself in the quarrels of his part-takers, rendering him
liable to attack from parties who were at feud with these ; the
impartiality of a judge in such circumstances being impossible.

The complications thus induced were endless. We find it on
record that the sheriff suffered from depredations on his estates
from M'Clellan of Gelston, from no personal quarrel of his own,
but because the M'Clellans were in bands with the Dunbars,
who had a blood feud with the Gordons, who were in alliance
with the Agnews.

Sir John Dunbar, who had been unhappily killed by Alexander Gordon, had left two daughters ; the elder married to
M'Clellan of Bomby, the younger to the Laird of Gelston, whose
son entered *con amore* into the feud. The sheriff, unable to
adjudge in his own case, remanded him to the higher courts,
where the charges proved were so serious, that judgment was
(with a severity very unusual against a man of baronial rank)

entered that "Patrick M'Clellan for art and part of stouthrief of twenty oxen from the Sheriff of Wigtown, under silence of night," should have "his hede stricken fra his body." The sheriff proved not revengeful, for, satisfied with the wholesome lesson thus read him, he exerted himself to procure a reprieve, and this so effectually, that not only was his life spared but the other penalties remitted [1] Gratitude may have kept M'Clellan from further attempts on the cattle pens at Lochnaw, but society had little reason to thank the sheriff for his clemency.

Shortly after, Patrick M'Clellan, with two kinsmen, was declared rebel for the killing of Robert Mure; and again he was denounced from the Market Cross of Edinburgh for the "cruel slaughter of George Frere"

The only notices we have of social life at this period are to be gathered from the defaulter's book. These certainly are ample, but, it must always be remembered, show only one side of the picture.

About 1510, Sir William M'Clellan of Bomby and M'Ghie of Plumptoune were fined £4, conjointly and severally, "for convocation of the lieges at the court held at the Standarde Stone of Dundrennan," i.e. assembling there armed to overawe the judges.

John M'Clellan was convicted of the theft of two hogsheads of Gascony wine from John Foster, in Kirkcudbright, the Laird of Bomby becoming his surety, he himself being further charged with "art and part of oppression done to Sir William Shanks, monk of Dundrennan, casting him down from his horse during the time of the above said court; and further, for detaining and taking Andrew Drury, officer of the Abbot of Dundrennan" For the latter offences Sir William and M'Ghie were fined six marks each, and Alan and John M'Clellan ten.

[1] 1510 The kingis grace rehabilis Patrick M'Clellan of Gilestoune to his warldly honours, dignities, and uther privileges, and lauchfully to succeed his fader and utheres his predecessors, notwithstanding the dome given that the said Patrick's head suld be strucken fra his body, for the rief and stouth of twenty oxen and ky frae Patrick Agnew, Sheriff of Wigtoune, and his servantis, under silence of night.

Patrick Mure, previously mentioned as a free lance, open to engagements with every faction, was summoned within a limited period on a variety of charges, which we quote as a curiosity. First, for forcibly occupying the lands of Andrew Dunbar in Mochrum; second, spulzying the annual rent of lands belonging to the Laird of Bomby; third, contempt done to the king in taking one called Lang M'Kie out of the stocks wherein he had been placed by the sheriff-depute for hurting a Spaniard; fourth, for heirschip of five oxen from John M'Clean; fifth, breaking up the doors of Mr. Richard Aikenhead, Vicar of Wigtown, and keeping him furth thereof, and with Thomas Mure and Nicholas Mure, his servants, casting the vicar's servant over his own stair; sixth, for forethought felony done to Symon M'Chrystine, sheriff-depute in Wigtown, by chasing him with a drawn quhinzear; seventh, stealing a young gray horse from Andrew Boyd; eighth, for carrying off ten bolls of victual and twenty-four threaves of fodder; ninth, stouthrief of five score sheep from Andrew Dunbar in Derry of Mochrum; tenth, theft from James Porter of ten score bolls of wheat, eleventh, robbery of goods from Andrew Mure; twelfth, forcible occupation of the Laird of Bomby's farm, near Wigtown, for two years.[1]

The M'Kies of Myrtoun seem to have lived in chronic feud with the sheriff, whence we find the "sheriff's servants" (which may simply mean friends in bands with him) charged with robbing John M'Kie of seven cows with their calves, wounding John and his men, "with loss of thumb to the said John." At the same Justice Aire they produced a "remission" for the slaughter of Patrick and Thomas M'Kie, who seem to have been killed in the fray.

Symon M'Chrystine, a sheriff-depute, is charged with going forth of burgh in convocation to the place of Myrtoun, of the stouthrief of oxen, horses, and sheep there, from John M'Kie,

---

[1] Spulzying, carrying off a spoil; heirschip, the act of plundering, stouthrief, carrying off by force (Pitcairn) Robbery, accompanied by violence, in all cases punished capitally.—(Erskine, *Institutes*)

breaking the said John's barn door and taking all his beir and
oats forcibly from him.   This active sheriff-depute is charged
on other occasions with "oppression done to the community of
Wigtown," with "taking the best merchandize out of ships coming to the said burgh, and keeping the same in his own cellars."[1]
In 4th November 1510 "Patrick Agnew, Sheriff of Wigtown,
came in for the king's will for usurping his authority by putting
James Porter to the knowledge of an assize for the slaughter of
John M'Myane, and from taking pledges to purge the said
Thomas of the said slaughter."   James Porter was a brother to
the Laird of Lagg, and a "servant" of the sheriff.   The Crown
was very jealous of reserving jurisdiction over the "four pleas,"
of which murder was one; and the suggestion is further of
partiality that the sheriff indicted his friend for the minor
offence of slaughter instead of murder.   At the same court,
Patrick Waus of Irsack[2] was allowed to compound for "the
stouthrief of six silver tasses from the Lord Bishop of Galloway.
Item, for oppression done to the bishop for houghing his oxen
Item, for oppression to John M'Ilvaine, in Whithern for the
detention of his crops.   Item, for the southrief of certain oxen
and cows from the executors of unquhile Mr. Alexander Waus."
The bishop was David Arnot.

Nevin Agnew of Croach continued his predatory attacks on
his neighbours.   He admitted before the Lord Justices his complicity in coming upon the Lairds of Ardwell and Kinhilt
severally, in a warlike manner, and sundry acts of "oppression,"
the cool impudence of one of which excites a smile   "the
stouthrief of tymmer of twa houses, with the windows and
doors thereof."   Yet for all his misdemeanours he was permitted
to compound.

These ridings in routing were suddenly brought to a close
by the summons to arms sounding forth from the capital.   Instantly local bickerings ceased, feuds were forgotten, and the

[1] Pitcairn
[2] Ersoch (arseach), a ploughed place or arable land; literally, abounding in
tillage.

baronage assembling, rode forward shoulder to shoulder to wield their arms for king and country.

Many a manly hand grasped that of a neighbour in unaffected friendliness after years of strife; and well that it was so, as many of these restless spirits were destined to meet no more on the scenes of their old forgatherings. Within a few days they all fought, and many of them fell, on the fatal field of Flodden. The Galloway baronage bore their full share of the national loss, "in this sorrowful battell strichen and cudit the nynth day of September, the year of God 1513[1]

Of the sheriff's neighbours and kin there fell: his uncle, Sir Alexander Gordon of Lochinvar, Sir Alexander Stewart of Garlies; the M'Dowalls Lairds of Garthland, Freuch, and Logan; Adair of Kinhilt, M'Culloch of Myrtoun, Sir William M'Clellan of Bomby; the Earl of Cassilis; Lords Maxwell and Hernes; Sir William Douglas of Drumlanrig; the Master of Angus; and his brother, William Douglas. Poor old "Bell the Cat" was so overwhelmed with grief at the loss of these, his only sons, that, riding back with the surviving remnant of Galloway lairds as far as their routes lay together, he entered the Priory of Whithorn, and passed there the remainder of his days in contemplation and prayer.[2] The body of M'Culloch was mistaken for that of the king, and hurried off to London in hope of a reward, where, however, the mistake was discovered.[3]

There were no lists in these days taken of the wounded; but there is reason to believe that the sheriff did not escape scatheless, as he died within a few weeks of the battle; his eldest son, Andrew, being under age

---

[1] Pitscottie, i. 281.

[2] The Earl of Angus had implored the king not to attack the English in the rash way which he proposed. The king's answer to the venerable peer was: "Angus, if you are afraid, you may go home." Thus publicly insulted, he left the camp, but returned on hearing that his sons were killed.

[3] Alexander M'Callo (of his awin guard) was very lyke in make to the king, and so they tuik and kest him in ane chariott, and had him with them into England. But trew it is they gote not the king, because they had never the token of his yron belt to schow.—Pitscottie, i. 281.

Of three daughters, the eldest married William Cairns of Orchardtown; another, Katherine, married Ninian Adair of Kinhilt (whose mother, Euphemia, was a Stewart of Garlies). This Ninian built the square tower once styled a manor-place, afterwards the gaol of Stranraer. Tradition avers that—no stones being procurable at hand, and wheeled carts unknown,— Adair placed retainers in rows some three miles to the quarries, whence the stones were passed singly from hand to hand to the builders.[1] A third daughter, Christian, married Blaise M'Ghie (presumably of Balmaghie) We find a charter in the lady's favour of the lands of Egerness.[2]

The fourth sheriff is a fair type, reflecting at once the vigour and the weaknesses of an hereditary official in the fifteenth century.   If an injury had to be redressed, especially that towards a friend, he was ready to spring into his saddle and deal out justice with his own right arm at a moment's notice. Little he troubled himself with studying the statute book, much less with the technicalities of law.

Help thy friend and do nae wrang

was his motto, and against great odds he maintained the king's authority in the person of his sheriff, handing down all the rights delegated to his forbears by the Crown unimpaired to his successor

The case has been humorously and happily put in an article already quoted : " As a rule, it must be said that the sheriffs were every bit as wild and lawless as the rest of the king's lieges in these parts.   Forays, feuds, sieges, and plunderings and lawsuits, went on from century to century.   When the Douglases were out of the way there were the Kennedys to quarrel with.   The Kennedys, Earls of Cassilis, were far more powerful than the sheriffs ; but the Agnews held their own in

---

[1] In a deed it is styled the tower, fortalice, manor-place, yards, and orchards of Chappell.—*Adair MSS*

[2] 1527 There is a charter, " Blaisii M'Ghie et Cristina Agnew, sponsa sua," of the lands of Egerness and Brochtonwall —*Great Seal Register*.

Michael M'Ghie submitted to Edward III. in 1389.—*Rot. Scot.*

many skirmishes and downright battles, as well in the field as in the law courts."

Andrew Agnew, the fifth sheriff, as a minor was given sasine of the lands and offices he held heritably by a mandate from the Crown, dated 20th May 1514,[1] Nevin, Thomas, and William Agnew being witnesses to the service; and a precept from David (Arnot), Bishop of Galloway, directed his infeftment in the various lands his father had held under the Church, carried out before Michael Agnew, Martin M'Meiken, Thomas Agnew in Clone, and Thomas M'Geych, presbyter of Whithorn.

Gilbert, who succeeded a second Earl of Cassilis on his father's death at Flodden, maintained the kindliest relations with his kinsman at Lochnaw; and the quarrel as to the Courts of Leswalt was allowed to slumber.

Sir Alexander Stewart, who had also fallen at Flodden, was succeeded by another Alexander, who had married Elizabeth Kennedy of Blairquhan, by whom he had nineteen daughters, five of whom married in Wigtownshire, to the lairds of Mochrum, Garthland, Sorby, and Corswall: the fifth shortly after this date to the young sheriff. The aunt of this lady of Lochnaw was Agnes Lady Maxwell, whose husband in 1520 was appointed Steward of Kirkcudbright.

Within a year of fatal Flodden, and a few weeks after the death of poor old Bell the Cat at Whithorn, the queen dowager had married his grandson Archibald, now Earl of Angus; by which act her regency terminated, and fell by her first husband's will to the Duke of Albany. Both queen mother and regent now concurred in appointing Gavin Dunbar, Prior of Whithorn, tutor to the young king. a duty which he performed to the satisfaction of his pupil, the Council, and society at large. Entries in the Lord Treasurer's accounts show that he was entrusted with all arrangements for his royal pupil; as examples: 16th February 1517—"Given to Maister Gavin Dunbar, the

---

[1] In the case of the Baillierie of Leswalt, "quod de nobis tenetur in capite" is applied equally as to the sheriffship

king's maister, to buy necessar thingis for the king's chalmer, 9 h."

"Item—28th August. To Maister Gavan Dunbar, for expences maid by him in reparating the chalmer in the quhilk the king now lives, £3."

In 1522 Dunbar was promoted to the Archbishopric of Glasgow, and in 1528 was Lord Chancellor. Albany, disgusted with the strife of factions, had retired to France, but now unexpectedly turned up in Galloway. Here the barons received him with distinction, sided with him in his wranglings with the queen dowager, and escorted him in force to Edinburgh.

In 1522, having returned to France to ask for King Francis's assistance, he suddenly reappeared at Kirkcudbright with fifty ships, and disembarked great store of arms and ammunition. The Gallovidians flocked to his standard in such numbers that he marched eastward in sufficient force to raise the siege of Jedburgh.[1]

The same year a judgment of the Lords of the Council stands on record against the sheriff for injury done to Waus, Parson of Wigtown; but his name seems only to be introduced as a formality, his son's being mentioned along with him, who was an infant in arms. The real culprit seems to have been a kinsman of the parson, Nevin Vaus, son of Robert Waus, supported by Nevin Agnew of Croach, the sheriff's kinsman.

In the Court books the action stands against Andrew Agnew, Sheriff of Wigtown; Patrick Agnew, his son; Nevin Vaus, Gilbert Hughan, John Reed, and Nevin Agnew, for the houghing, slaughter, and destruction of three of his oxen, price of the piece £3, stopping the labouring and tilling of his mailing, and damage and scaith further sustained to the amount of £20.

The Lords of Council deliver that the said parties have

[1] The Duck of Albany this yeare returns from France; he ships at Brest and lands at Kirkcudbright the 7th of October.—Balfour, i. 250.

The French king could not spare him many men, but gave him 3000 pikes and 1000 launces. The Duke, to the number of fifty sail, embarks at Brest the 21st September, and lands at Kirkcudbright.—David Scott, 325.

Having escaped the English fleet which lay in wait for him, he landed at Kirkcudbright 7th October 1523.—Mackenzie, i. 443.

done wrong, and shall content and pay the damages claimed,
and exempt the said Master John from the jurisdiction of the
sheriff and his officers. (Nevin Agnew was a sheriff-depute.)

In 1525 much brawling occurred between the queen's
faction, of whom were the Earls of Argyle and Arran, and
Angus, the queen dowager's husband, who conjointly with
Lennox, getting possession of the young king's person, temporarily got the upper hand.

One of their acts was a wise one. They sent Lord Cassilis,
accompanied by two churchmen, to negotiate for peace with the
queen's brother Henry VIII., who cordially received Cassilis
and entertained him at Greenwich; and on his return a Parliament was summoned to meet at Edinburgh to discuss the
proposals he brought back

Hither the barons of Galloway repaired ; among those recorded as present, beside Cassilis, being the Laird of Lochinvar,
the Laird of Bomby, Lord Maxwell, the Sheriff of Galloway,
besides many powerful cadets of the Kennedys, the M'Dowalls
of Garthland and Freuch, M'Culloch of Torhouse, Cairns of
Orchardton, Gordon of Craighlaw, all accompanied by armed
retainers.

The swashbuckler style in which these gentlemen habitually
paraded the streets, their respective followers armed to the
teeth, led to encounters of the most serious nature. In two of
the frays which attained most notoriety, the west country barons
were prominent.

In the first, certain partisans of Cassilis killed a Dutch
nobleman Of the cause of the quarrel no record remains ; but
the extraordinary number of remissions for his slaughter,
amounting to over two hundred and fifty, gives a startling idea
of the fierceness of these street battles, as the opposing forces
may be presumed to have been considerable. As usual, some of
the Kennedys are found fighting on both sides. The official
record is drawn in form of a respite to Gilbert Earl of Cassilis,
William Lord Semple, and thirteen others, Fergus M'Dowall of
Freuch, Alexander M'Dowall, tutor of Garthland, M'Kie of

Myrtoun, Ahannay of Sorby, thirty-four others named, and 233 others, origin unknown, for the treasonable slaughter of Cornelius de Machitima, Martin Kennedy, and Gilbert M'Ilwraith.[1]

A day or two later, old Lochinvar, with his nephew, the Sheriff of Galloway, and Sir James Douglas of Drumlanrig, the young laird of Orchardton, M'Culloch of Torhouse, and other kinsmen, when sauntering well attended down the High Street, met face to face Sir Thomas M'Clellan of Bomby, also with a band of friends and followers   Between Bomby and Lochinvar a blood-feud raged.   Both parties must needs keep the crown of the causeway.   Neither would yield an inch.   A desperate struggle ensued, Lochinvar eventually keeping the place of honour, but ending in the Laird of Bomby lying dead at the door of St. Giles's Church,   Much litigation ensued in these days of weak government.   The resource of the Courts was to incline aggressors to make compensation to the aggrieved, achieved by refusing to grant remissions for slaughters till "letters of slains" were procured from the families bereaved. And although persons of position were not easily arrested, they were formally put to the horn and declared rebel, implying that any one strong enough to do so might seize their persons. It was consequently a convenience to aggressors, however powerful, to obtain such a remission.

A good instance of the procedure in question is furnished by the present case.   The Laird of Lochinvar and the Sheriff of Galloway were indicted, summoned, failed to appear, declared rebel, but remained at large for some eleven years with little inconvenience to themselves, till the matter was settled and the outlawry recalled in the shape of "a remission to James Gordon of Lochinvar, Andrew Agnew, Sheriff of Wigtown, James Douglas of Drumlanrig, William Gordon of Crichlaw, George M'Culloch of Torhouse, William Cairns, young laird of Orchardton, David Gordon, John Gordon, called John of Whitherne, and twelve others, for art and part of the slaughter

[1] For the treasonable slaughter of umquhile Cornelius de Machitima at the Tolbooth of Edinburgh at the time of seat of our Parliament.—Pitcairn

of Thomas M'Clellan of Bomby, committed eleven years by-
past, in the burgh of Edinburgh. Dated 13 January
1538."

This settlement was hastened by a romantic incident. The
Laird of Bomby, heir to the slaughtered man, met and fell
desperately in love with the daughter of his father's slayer.
Old Lochinvar wisely smiled upon his suit, and soon parties
who had long been vainly summoned to underlie the law, sat
with the pursuers at the wedding-feast, the bridegroom presenting his new relatives with "letters of slains" formally
endorsed by "Thomas M'Clellan, son of Thomas M'Clellan
deceased, to Sir James Gordon of Lochinvar, and all his
assisters in the slaughter aforesaid."

And so the tomahawk was buried.

To revert to 1526, Lennox broke with Angus; the young
king escaped from the latter's keeping; civil war broke out,
Angus being supported by Arran, whilst Lord Cassilis declared
for Lennox and the queen. The Galloway lairds being friendly
with Cassilis, he was able to bring nearly two thousand men
into the field

The parties met at Linlithgow; Lennox was worsted, and, as
asserted by Cassilis, killed in cold blood after the fighting was
over by Sir James Hamilton.

Angus, having now recovered the king's person, summoned
all who had sided against him in the king's name to appear for
judgment for helping the king to escape. Cassilis among others
came in, made his submission, and was permitted to compound.
But whilst he paid his fine, he unguardedly used some very
hard words against Sir James Hamilton. He mounted to ride
home, but was waylaid in his journey, and killed near Prest-
wick by the hand of the Sheriff of Ayr,[1] but, as was generally
thought, at the instigation of Hamilton. Earl Gilbert was truly
mourned in Galloway, his two daughters being married to the

---

[1] Earl Gilbert wes killed at the Pow of Preisetick in Kyll, by Hugh Campbell
of Loudoun, Sheriff of Ayr, 2d Dec 1527.—Balfour, *Genealogical Collections*,
Pitcairn, *History of the Kennedys*, 84.

Lairds of Freuch and Kinhilt, besides whom, by his wife Isabella, daughter of the second Earl of Argyle, he left Gilbert his heir, David of Culzean, and Quentin, who was Abbot of Crossraguel, and became famous for his public disputation with John Knox as to the sacrifice of the mass.

The following year James V.'s power was fully established. Angus, having stood at bay awhile in his strong castle of Tantallon, fled to England; and by an Act of Parliament 1528, himself, his kin, and friends, were forfaulted, and their lands annexed to the Crown.

In connection with this, we find by the criminal records that many persons of rank were pursued " for abiding from the king's host and army at Tantallon." Almost all of these were Galloway lairds, there being especially mentioned Andrew Agnew, Sheriff of Galloway, the lairds of Garlies, Balmaghie, Torhouse, Creachan, Barclay, Larg. The matter probably went no further; but it is difficult to account for their conduct. There is no hint in history of any disaffection in the province : it was certainly from no want of stomach for a fight; and we can only suppose that there was still a lingering affection in Galloway for the name of Douglas, and especially for the branch of Angus.

CHAPTER XX

THE DAWN OF THE REFORMATION

A.D. 1528 to 1545

> For, Esayas into his wark
> Callis thame lyke doggis, that can nocht bark,
> That callit ae preistis, and can nocht preche
> Nor Christis law to the pepill teche.
>
> LYNDSAY, *The Complaint.*

GILBERT, third Earl of Cassilis, when staying at St. Andrews, a boy of twelve years old, was forced by Beaton[1] to countersign the death-warrant of Patrick Hamilton, the proto-martyr of the Scottish Reformation. The archbishop had much miscalculated the effect which his act of faith would produce either on his young pupil or the general public. Cassilis, from the part thus forced upon him, was led to enquire into, and afterwards to approve of, Hamilton's creed; and so loudly was the popular disgust expressed against such barbarities perpetrated in the name of religion, that one of Beaton's most trusted familiars warned his master in the form of a grim jest against ordering a repetition of such scenes: "If you needs must burn many more heretics, my lord, pray burn them in deep cellars below ground; for you must know that the smoke from Mr. Hamilton's body has infected all upon whom the wind has blown it." The words of the merry gentleman were sober truth; the easterly

---

[1] James Bethune or Beaton, was named Bishop of Galloway on the death of George Vaux; but before he was consecrated to that see he was advanced to the Archbishopric of Glasgow. In 1505 he had become Lord High Treasurer, and was one of the principal ministers of state.

haar of St. Andrews had carried the infection far into the
western shires, and deep mutterings from Ayr and Galloway
presaged the coming storm.   The days had gone by when the
great monasteries were centres of charity and learning.   The
shepherds of the period were prone to shear, but seldom fed
their flocks.   Their uselessness and rapacity were scathingly
exposed, not by heretics, but by decorous churchmen, such as
Sir David Lyndsay of the Mount ; and so notorious were their
delinquencies, and so true to the life, that they were read with
acceptance before the king and queen, and specially applauded
by cardinals and spiritual lords—veritable Gallios—in Court
circles.

The universal complaint in the west was that the clergy—
regular and secular alike—impoverished the people by bare-
faced exactions, for which they gave no religious consolation in
return ; hovering round a death-bed, not to solace the sufferer,
but to secure the corpse present [1] from the survivors ; such dues
being heartlessly extorted, even if the sorrowing relatives were
half-starved by the exactions.

All good Catholics deplored such scandals.   Lyndsay lays
the scene of a pitiable case, in which a yeoman, once well to do,
traces his ruin to church dues, heartlessly levied in the hour of
his affliction, on the Earl of Cassilis's lands, near Ayr :

> We had three kye that was baith fat and fair,
> Nane tidier came into the town of Ayr.

He tells at length how, having first buried his father and his
mother, and then sickness suddenly bereaving him of his wife—

> The vicar tuik the best cow by the heid
> Incontinent when my father was deid.
> And when the vicar heard tell that my mother
> Was deid, for haud he tuik to him another.
> Then made my wife did mourn baith e'en and morrow,
> Till at the last she died for very sorrow.
> And when the vicar heard tell my wife was deid,
> The third cow he cleikit by the heid

---

[1] The corpse present was the best cow and "upmost cloth," *i.e.* coverlet, of
the bed of the deceased.

> Their upmost clais that was of raplock gray,
> The vicar gart his clerk them bear away.
> When all was gone, I micht make nae bebate,
> But with my bairns passed till by my meat.[1]

To their unapostolic rapacity was added the inability to
preach, whence the satirist makes a countryman explain—

> Schir God nor I be sticket with a knife
> Gif ever our parsoun prechet in all his life.

When such sentiments were freely expressed in the highest
society, the spirit of enquiry was stimulated rather than checked,
by the persecution of humble Reformers   It soon was whispered
that their doctrines were none other than those of the Bible ; and
it seemed an enigma that to read the Bible, even privately, much
more to communicate its contents to others, should be deemed
a capital crime by dignitaries of that Church.   Consequently a
curiosity to see a Bible pervaded all ranks, especially in the west
country.

Gordon of Airds, a near kinsman of the sheriff, having gone
on some errand across the borders, met with some of Wycliffe's
followers, from whom he obtained a copy of that divine's translation of the Testament.   On returning, he invited such of his
neighbours as he could trust to come to secret readings in the
woods, where the subject was discussed, and the reformed
doctrines quietly made their way.   It must be understood that
the sweeping changes afterwards demanded were not even
wished for at this period.   It was no question of Presbyterianism or Episcopacy ; neither Calvin nor Knox had as yet made
their voices heard ;[2] to strengthen and improve the Catholic
Church by a reform of abuses was all they asked for, with this
one step only in advance, that the Bible, on which the Church
was avowedly founded, should no longer be withheld from its
adherents.

"Airds" was a remarkable man: brought up at Clanyard,[3]

---

[1] Lyndsay's *Complaint*
[2] Calvin was born in 1509 ; Knox, in 1505.
[3] Claon ard, "the inchning steep"

the third son of Alexander Gordon of Auchenreoch,[1] and when a youth, from his great size and strength, he was known as "Sanie Rough." In time he became the father of a numerous family, all like himself zealous for the Reformation; and as a third generation grew up about him, his designation was changed to the "Patriarch."

An amusing story is current as to the use to which he turned his progeny. There being a law that any beast labouring on Church holidays should be forfeited to the king, and Gordon habitually neglecting to stop his work on the numerous saint-days, fasts, and feasts, an order was obtained to enforce the statute. In response he assembled a large party at Airds upon Christmas Day, yoked ten of his sons to the plough, an eleventh acting as coller, ploughed a ridge of land before the astonished spectators, and dared either priest or layman to distrain his team. Years rolled on, the Patriarch grew gray, and great-grandchildren had sprung up around the grand old man.

A benighted traveller of gentle mien craved one evening hospitality at his gate. He was courteously received by a stalwart man, who referred him to his father,—the father indicated referred him to *his* father, and he forthwith accosted a white-locked grandsire, who again referred him to *his* father. Completely mystified, he was passed on to the venerable laird, seated in the old armchair, who vouchsafed him a hearty welcome.

Presently the board was spread; but whilst partaking of the good things set before him, our traveller could not divest himself of an undefined dread that there was something unearthly about his hosts; and it was not until supper ended, the household assembled, and family worship was conducted with a simple earnestness by the Patriarch, that the uneasy guest was fully convinced that there could be nothing uncanny about the family.

---

[1] "Auchenreoch, the gray field " Alexander Gordon, second son of William de Gordon of Stichel, had a charter to Alexander Gordon, brother of John Gordon of Lochinvar, of the lands of Auchenreoch, 1490. From him descend the Gordons of Aird, now of Earlston.

The Patriarch is said to have attained the age of 101; having been born in 1479, and surviving until 1580. His grandson married Margaret Sinclair, who brought him the lairdship of Earlston; the honour of which house is in safe keeping in the person of his descendant of the twelfth generation—Sir William Gordon, one of the heroes of the death-ride of Balaclava.[1]

King James V. about this time set himself, with more energy than judgment, to stanch the theft and reiving prevalent on the Borders. No doubt the mosstroopers required chastisement; but hanging wholesale batches of men—born dragoons, forming a ready-made buffer to English aggression; patriotic, if thievish—was both unstatesmanlike and cruel[2]

Messengers rode post haste to the sheriffs of Galloway, Ayr, Roxburgh, and Dumfries, to desire them to warn all lords, barons, and freeholders, to arm and equip themselves, and pass with the king on his bloody assize. And all gentlemen that had "dogges that were good" were charged to bring them with them, that the king might hunt by the way.

The tale of the royal sport in the intervals of hunting men was "18 score of harts, pulled down by the dogs, besides all manner of small game killed by hawks"

The blending of sterner business with field-sports was exemplified in its acutest form in the hanging of Johnny Armstrong and his men;[3] and in a less tragic phase in the case of Lord Maxwell, who, riding in unsuspiciously, bringing his dogs to share in the fun, was instantly seized, and placed in durance

[1] Earlston, said to have been a hunting-seat of James, Earl of Bothwell. Sir William Gordon served in the 17th Lancers in the Crimea; for which he has a medal, the Ribbon of the Legion of Honour, and the Order of the Medjidie. He afterwards served with distinction with his regiment in the suppression of the Indian Mutiny.

[2] The king marches and surveys the Borders, apprehends 48 of the principallest rogues, and hangs them all.—Balfour, ii. 260.

This is only one of many executions following, which we are told "manie Scottismen heavily lamented."—Pitscottie, ii 342

[3] Efter this hunting, the king hangit John Armstrang, als guid ane chieftain as ever was upon the Borders, and albeit he was a lous leivend man, yett he never molested no Scottisman.—Pitscottie, also Pinkerton.

vile, very narrowly escaping with his life.[1] The charge against
Maxwell was that he had "winked at the villainies of the
limmers on the marches."

But whilst dealing so severely with sins of omission in the
eastward, James took no adequate steps to punish crimes of commission in the west   The Macdowalls of Freuch and of Mindork
audaciously invaded Arran with fire and sword, and burned
Brodick Castle to the ground.   The success of this flagrant
attack, conducted by two Galloway lairds against one of the
most powerful nobles of his day, is evidenced by the very terms
of the warrant issued against them, and commanding them to
underlie the law.   And yet, as far as we can learn, they neither
surrendered nor were arrested, nor even suffered any serious
inconvenience for their contumacy, as Freuch's name appears in
various records of the period as pursuing his ordinary occupations undisturbed on his estates.

This outrage was the outcome of the feud engendered by the
murder of Cassilis (who was father-in-law of Freuch) at Prest-
wick, which Arran was believed to have abetted.   And as
plunder was not the object, the deed was generally applauded in
Galloway.

A few years later we find the sheriff called upon to make
good damage done by his kinsman, the young laird of Croach.
On the 8th of July 1532, the Lords of the Council decree "yat
Andrew Agnew, Sheriff of Wigtown, pledge and souritie for
Nevin Agnew, sall restore, content, pay, and deliver, to Dene
Andro Stevenson, sub-prior of Quhithorn, and Vicar of Clauch-
shant, ye guids underwritten, spuilziet and reft fra him by ye
said Nevin and his complices, and fra his tenants furth of his
kirkland of ye said vicarage—that is to say, 12 kye and oxen,
price of the piece, 40s ; as also that Andro Agnew, sheriff of
Wigtown, is pledge and suretie for John M'Kewin in ye
parish of Leswalt, shall content and deliver to Dene Andro
Stevenson the guids spulziet and reft fra him be the said John

---

[1] The king causes behead Cockburn of Hindarland and Adam Scot, and
imprisons the Earl of Bothwell, Lords Maxwell and Home, and the lairds of
Buccleugh, Ferniehurst, Pollard, Johnston, and Marker.—Balfour, 1. 260.

furth of his mansion-house of the said vicarage, twa hors, price of the piece, £20 "   The price the dean put upon his horses seems exorbitant, as the king not long before had purchased at Whithorn a "lady's pad" for one of the queen's suite for £5.[1]

About this time, M'Dowall of Logan being a minor, his wardship was granted to Vaux, Abbot of Soulseat,[2] who assigned it to John Vaus of Barnbarroch.   To this the chapter of the abbey demurred, appealing to the king, in whose name a letter was addressed to the sheriff.

"James, be the grace of God, King of Scots, to our Sheriff of Wigtown, greeting.

"As it is shewn to us by our lovet, John Vaus of Barnbarroch, that Dean David Vaus, Abbot of Soulseat, having by our gift the wardship of Logan, and he having made the said John his assignee thereto, yet nevertheless the incumbrance of the abbey troubled the said John in the brooking of the said ward-lands. Our will is, and we charge you that incontinent these our letters seen, ye call both parties before you, and take cognisance in the said matter, and do them justice.

"Given under our signet at Edinburgh, the 19th day of August, and of our reign the 28th year" (1533)

In 1535 an Act of Parliament recapitulating the statutes as to re-aforesting the land, ordained that "the breakers thereof be taken cognisance of by the sheriff at his first head court after Pasche," attaching terrific penalties against all destroyers of growing wood : £10 fine for the first offence ; £20 for the second ; for the third, death.[3]   We doubt whether the lieges took much more note of it than to turn it into rhyme :

---

[1] We find a charter of resignation of the lands of Croach and Brockloch by Gilbert Agnew and Margaret Muir, his spouse, to their son Nevin, dated 16th December 1528.

Brockloch is not the badger's lake, but the badger warren   Clayshant, Clachseanta, the holy stone—holy, used in the superstitious sense of a charm, auspicious.—O'Reilly.

[2] In 1525 a venerable father in God, David Vaux, is named as coadjutor and successor to Quentin Vaux, Abbot of Soulseat   In 1531 there is an obligation by Henry M'Culloch of Killaster to infeft David, Abbot of Soulseat, in the lands of Drumbreddan, to be held of his own lord, the laird of Myrtoun.

[3] Fourth Parlt James V. chaps 10 and 11.

> The oak, the ash, the elm tree,
> Hang a man for all the three ,
> For a branch ye may win free,
> But for a root ye'll hangit be

The most important Act of the period was the institution of
the College of Justice (1537), popularly known as the Court of
Session; a leading feature of which Act was "that all processes
be taken in order, the unpriveleged to be tabulat with the
priveleged." The realm being divided into four circuits, the
western comprising "Striveling, Aire, Renfrew, Lanark, Wigtoune, Dumfreis, Kirkcudbright, and Annandale."

About this time Sir Alexander Stewart of Garlies was sent
as ambassador to the English Court. Previous to setting out
he obtained renewals of his charters of Garlies and Glasserton,
with remainder to his eldest son Alexander, failing whom to his
second son John, parson of Kirkmahome.[1] Sir Alexander had
married first Katherine, daughter of Sir James Crichton, without
issue ; secondly, Margaret Dunbar, heiress of Clugston. Their
second son is the progenitor of the Stewarts of Physgill.

In 1536 the king sailed for France incognito, in search of a
wife, taking among his companions Gordon of Lochinvar, and
Stewart, Bishop of Aberdeen, granting extraordinary indul-
gences to certain of their relations, among whom are named
Andrew Agnew, Sheriff of Galloway, the lairds of Garlies and
Sorby, and John Vaus of Barnbarroch — in the shape of
"exemption from answering to the courts of law for any
misdemeanour whatever committed by them during the king's
absence." An indulgence with a vengeance!

The royal knight errant did not speed smoothly on his
course, being blown north instead of south, and having rounded
Cape Wrath instead of the North Foreland, be suddenly cast
up at the Isle of Whithorn, his ship being damaged, and,
escorted by the baronage, rode back to Leith   Here he em-

---

[1] The ancient form of the name was Kirkmacho and Kirkmagho   The saint
seems to be the Mahasans, whose church in Edinburgh was despoiled by Edward
I , otherwise St Machut, to whom the parish church of Wigtown was dedicated
as well as Lesmahagow.

barked in another ship, leaving Archbishop Dunbar and Lord
Maxwell among others to act as regents, and arrived safely at
Dieppe, where he was met by the Earls of Cassilis, Moray, and
Lennox, sent forward as ambassadors to ask the hand of the
Princess Magdalene of France.

Four years before this, Lord Cassilis having gone to Paris to
finish his education, had fallen in with Buchanan, who had fled
from Scotland owing to his faith, and who was offered and
accepted the position of Cassilis's tutor, and remained attached
to his person till 1537.[1]

In 1542 is chronicled the " Solway Rout," where the Scottish
leaders suffered themselves to be taken prisoners, and their
10,000 followers were dispersed by 300 English horse; this
inglorious result being attributed to pique and pride of ancestry,
outraged by Oliver Sinclair—a roturier—being placed in command.

But though this was the cause alleged, the truth seems to
have been that many of these lairds being Protestant at heart,
were disgusted with the cold-blooded cruelty with which the
king's clerical advisers were urging him to stamp out the new
doctrines.   It was the clergy who had hurried the king into
this war with England, having been so imprudent as openly to
suggest that the expenses of the war might be met by exacting
the fines to which the law subjected heretics.   The Scottish
baronage well knew that a serious war could not be maintained
with England without help from France, and success, with
French assistance, meant the riveting of the Papal yoke upon
themselves, which the English had just thrown off.

Many Scotch lords with Protestant leanings had already
entered into correspondence with the English, and it is more
than probable that Cassilis and Garlies inwardly felt what Lord

---

[1] Lord Cassilis was occasionally at home in the interim; as in 1536 his name
appears in company with the laird of Freuch, as attacking John Dunbar.

Fergus M'Dowall also had to underlie the law for coming on John Dunbar of
Blantyre with the Earl of Cassilis, assaulting and wounding him.   In 1538 there
is a respite to Fergus M'Dowall of Freuch for the cruel slaughter of John M'Culloch, in both cases the Earl of Cassilis becoming surety.

Maxwell openly expressed, when urged by a bystander to put spurs to his horse and escape capture: "It is better to be a prisoner abroad than hang at the market cross at home."[1]   At all events all three surrendered, and were sent to London, where they were exceedingly well entertained; Cassilis being assigned to Archbishop Cranmer, Maxwell to Sir Antony Brown, and Garlies to his kinsman the Duke of Lennox, himself a fugitive established in England, who had been already employed by Henry VIII. to intrigue with the Scottish lords; and he now assisted in arranging the terms of ransom for the captives.   A letter of his to Lord Shrewsbury on the subject is exceedingly interesting, dated from His Majesty's castle of Wressel, 13th June 1543   "My Lord—I have received the King's Majesty's letter from your Lordship this Mondaye, being the 13th of the month, commanding me to certify your lordship in writing of the names of all such pledges and prisoners as I have in my custody.

"My Lord, truth it is that my first journey to Dumfries there came into the King's Majesty's service by my procurement the most part of the Lairds of Gallowaye · such as the Laird of Garles, the Laird of Lochynwar and Tutor of Bomby, who I brought with me to Carlele, where they did enter their pledges to the Lord Wheirton; and forasmuch as the Laird of Garles is my near kinsman, I did take into my custody, by my Lord of Somerset's licens, the said Laird's son being of the age of 16 years, but by my judgement his father may spend 1500 marks Scots, which is all I can certify your Lordships in this matter."

Lord Wharton, as Warden of the Western Marches, thus names the several Galloway lairds taken prisoner in his official report to the king:—

"The names of suche Scotishe pledges and prisoners as wes taken on these Western Marches [24th November 1542], with

---

[1] Balfour, i. 274   His version is "The Scots, in disdain of their general, Oliver, render themselves captives to the English at Solwa Moss, and were led captive to London, such as the Earls of Cassalis," etc.

an estimate of their values and estimation [we extract Gallo-vidians only]:

"Robert Maxwell, nowe Lord Maxwell, an ancient baron of greate lands, his self remayneth as yet in Carliell.

"The Lord Carlishe[1] [Carlyle], a man of 300 merks and more, and little thereof in his hands, but holden from it by rebells in his country. His selfe remayneth at Pontefrett Castle in the custodie of Sir Henry Savell, besides that he is a prisoner, as aforesaid, his pledge his son and heyre with my Lord Latimer for 101 men.

"The Larde of Dabatie [Dalbeattie], of 20 markes land, his pledge his brother with Sir John Tempest for 41 men.

"The Larde of Orcherton, of ten pounds lands or more, his pledge with Sir William for 112 men.

"The Larde of Carlies [Garlies], of an hundred pound land and more, and of good estimation, his pledge his son and heyre with the Earl of Lennox for 206.

"The Larde of Loughinware [Lochinvar], a man of two hundred markes lands, and in goods better than a thousand pounds, his pledges his cousins, two of them with my Lord Scrope, and one with my Lord Conyers, for four score and fifteen.

"James Macklenyne [M'Clellan], Tutor of Bombye, a man of good estimation and small living, his pledge his sonne and heyre with Doctor Bransbye for 151.

"John Maxwell, the Lord's brother, who answers for all uppon his brother's lands, his pledge Hewghe Maxwell, his nephew, for 1000 men and more.

"The Abbot of Newe Abbey, of two hundred merks ster-

[1] Michael, fourth Lord Carlyle of Torthorwald, owned Kelhead, Cummertrees, Dornock, Torduff, Middleby, Lees, Kirkconnel, etc, and his forbears, if not himself, Colyn and Rowcham in Galloway. His ancestor held these by charters "to the king's sister's son," Sir William de Carlyle having married a sister of Robert Bruce. In 1487 Robert Carlisle had the keeping of the Castle of Threave and the stowardship of Kirkcudbright Of this fourth lord it is on record that at the signing of the bond of association for the support of James VI. in 1567, he was the only peer who could not write his name, and was obliged to have recourse to the assistance of a notary.

ling in right of his house, his pledge Richard Browne and
Robert Browne, his cosyns, for 241 men.

" The town of Kyrcumbre, a prety haven, pledge for it
Baryby Douglas son, worth nothing, for 36.

" Town of Dumfresse, a fair market town, pledge for it
Cuthbert Murray, worth litill or nothing, for 221 men.

" The Abbot of Salsyde, his house of an £100 yearly, his
pledge James Johnston his son and heyre, for 20 men."

The Scottish prisoners were thrown into company which
confirmed their Protestant leanings; Cassilis living chiefly with
Cranmer and Latimer, Garlies associating openly with the followers of Wycliffe, and (so contagious was the spirit of enquiry)
Lord Maxwell, though still professing himself a Catholic,
signalised himself by moving from his place in Parliament, immediately on his return from Scotland, "that it sall be lawful
to all the lieges to have the Holy Writ in the vulgar tongue"

But we are anticipating, this occurring in 1543, James V.
having died the 16th of the previous December, and the Scottish
prisoners having been allowed to return.   Maxwell's bold
course occasioned a fierce debate.   Archbishop Dunbar started
to his feet, and in the name of his brother prelates protested
against such a proposition, the more especially coming from a
Catholic.

The queen, much dismayed, threw in her influence with the
churchmen, but all in vain.   For the first time in Parliamentary
strife the prelates found themselves in a minority in the Estates.

Arran, the Regent, for a time encouraged the Reformers,
and all the lords who had been taken prisoners had returned
pledged to support a match between their infant princess and
the heir to the English crown; the significance of which proposal lay in the fact that it indicated sympathy with church
reform   At this moment, when for a short interlude religious
opinions might be discussed openly without danger to the disputants, George Wishart made his appearance in Galloway, his
coming there being due to the folly of the churchmen in the
east, he having been banished from St. Andrews for teaching

the Greek Testament.   This, to thinking men, showed that the ground on which Beaton and his party stood was so utterly without foundation that it obliged them to prevaricate and to contradict themselves : hitherto the demand for the Scriptures in the vulgar tongue had been constantly met by the reply that the Church allowed the reading of the Bible in Hebrew, Greek, and Latin, whereas the moment that Greek was brought within the reach of ordinary students, they violently suppressed it, and no doubt would have done the same with Hebrew had its study become popular.

Wishart was supported in the west by Lord Cassilis, Lord Glencairn, and his son Lord Kilmaurs, and notably by the young Laird of Garlies, who, when threatened with proceedings for encouraging heretical preachers, boldly answered, " I *do* avow them, and will maintain and defend such against any or all kirkmen that may be put at them."

Knox tells an amusing story at Dunbar's expense.   Beaton having written to the archbishop to keep an eye on and oppose the dangerous heretic in the west, he repaired to Ayr.   There finding that Wishart was announced to preach, he mounted the pulpit before he arrived.   The people were inclined to use him roughly.   " Let him alone," said Wishart, " he will do us more good than harm."   Silence was obtained ; but the archbishop found it easier to occupy the Reformer's seat than to match his eloquence.   He became confused, words refused to come, till at last he stammered out, " They say we should preiche [1]   Quhy not ?   Better lait thrive than never thrive.   Haud us still for your bishop, and we shall provyde better next tyme."

Though the narrator cannot be called impartial, it probably embodies the popular report of his discourse.   The habitual neglect of preaching was one of the causes which hurried the Roman Catholic Church to its fall.

Two hundred years before, a Galloway bishop had acquitted himself better, immortalised by Wyntoun in his *Rhyming Chronicles* :

[1] Knox's *History of the Reformation*, I. 48

The Bishop of Galloway thare Thomas,
A Theolog solempne he was,
Made a sermond richt plesant,
And to the mattere accordant.

Soon after his affair at Ayr Wishart was confronted at Dunbar, in a court where the bishop was more of a match for him than in the pulpit   Having wandered from Galloway, where neither bishop nor cardinal had been allowed to touch him, Wishart was arrested by Beaton's orders, carried to St. Andrews, arraigned before the Primate, Dunbar, and Durie, Bishop of Galloway—unpitying judges where heresy was a crime.   He was of course condemned to die, and the reverend trio assisted at his burning.   Vainly had the Bible been appealed to before men whose earnest caution to those whom they really loved was, " If ye will read ye must burn."   As useless was eloquence in a case where its possession rendered the speaker the more dangerous ; any mental recognition by the prelates of his shining ability taking possibly the form of the thought once audibly expressed by a famous judge to a less worthy prisoner . " Ye're a vera clever chiel, man, but ye wad be nane the waur o' a hangin'."

Dunbar was doubtless conscientiously a persecutor, attached to the old religion, and believing it to be the duty of the State to punish treason to the Church with death.   The Reformers themselves held blasphemy to be a capital crime : a dangerous admission when partisans had to define the precise legal meaning of the term.

Archbishop Dunbar was an able and estimable man, though neither liking nor liked by the Reformers.   It must not be supposed that his failure in the pulpit arose from any want of culture   George Buchanan, one of the most resolute opponents of his theology, has the candour to state than an evening spent in converse with the archbishop was to be compared to supping ambrosial nectar with the gods.   Dunbar died about 1546. Peace to his memory.

CHAPTER XXI

A.D. 1544 to 1547

" Fight on, my men," Sir Andrew said,
   " A little I'm hurt, but not yett slaine,
I'll bot lye down and bleed awhile,
   And then I'll rise and fight agane "

THE rulers of Galloway—Pictish, Saxon, Norse alike—had from
the earliest times realised the advantage of free trade with
England, whilst the policy of the Scottish kings, finding expression in Acts of Parliament, was to restrict all communications across the Solway as much as possible. The Church party,
more concerned for orthodoxy than protection, alarmed at the
very whisper of a blood union between their princess royal and
a heretical prince, threw their whole influence into the scale of
breaking with the English and establishing the closest relations
with France.

In Galloway, however, so paramount was the importance
felt to be of a good understanding and free commerce with their
neighbours, that the staunchest Catholics joined hands with the
most advanced Reformers to promote the marriage between their
royal Mary and the heir-apparent to the English crown. For
this Lord Maxwell was not less keen than the young Laird of
Garlies. Divergence of opinion here had not yet been accentu-
ated by blows ; and religious matters seem really to have been
treated more calmly in this province than elsewhere.

Arran, the Regent, though a Catholic, had sided with those

who called for reform, till, suddenly alarmed at the free expression of opinions he had himself encouraged, he threw himself into the arms of the reactionaries, and the union of interests on either side of the Borders was postponed for many a long day.

The English negotiations were rudely broken off, and Panther, Abbot of St. Mary's Isle, sent to France to give effect to the policy diametrically opposed to the interests of the province in which he lived. The unwisdom of their rulers was soon brought home to the nation at large when two avenging columns, sent by King Henry, crossed the Borders, one of which ravaged Galloway up to the gates of Panther's priory, and laid Dumfries in ashes, while the second placed Edinburgh under contribution, and applied the torch to the Palace of Holyrood. This was indeed a national calamity, a mass of public and private records being thus irretrievably lost—the mischief all being due to the vacillations of Arran.

Many Galloway barons were now made to feel individually the effects of Henry's wrath. All the prisoners of the Solway Rout had received their liberty on the condition of promoting the royal marriages, and had given hostages for its performance These were summoned to surrender themselves forthwith under penalty of execution of the said hostages : no empty threat; Cassilis, who had lingered by the way, received a pitiable appeal from his uncle and two brothers not further to neglect them.[1] He returned at last ; and so favourably was the king impressed with the young lord's sincerity that he immediately released the

[1] His hostages were his uncle, Thomas Kennedy of the Coiff, and his brothers David and Thomas. Their letter is as follows —

"My Lorde—We commende all oure services to yor Lo^P. quhon plesit to wit yat we all comfortles doo complaine of oure miserable case, for wee arre chargit for zor intrys—in all haste possible. For gif ze doo not, we sall sufere dethe and yat ryt certly . My Lorde, remember quhat pane and sorrow we doo sufar—tarying on yor coming in all possible hast, to have sowm comfort of zou, that ye will relieve us and bring us out of yis great dyspayr

(Signed) Thomas Kenydie, sometime Land of Coiff
David Kenedie of Carrick, ye ane
Archibald Kynnidy.

Copie of L^{rs} sent to the Erle of Cassils from his pledges, 1543.—Lodge's *Illustrations*, 1 46

hostages, entertained them himself right royally, and allowed the earl to return with his suite to the house of the Inch. Lord Maxwell found himself in a more serious dilemma : literally between the devil and the deep sea. He could not obey his order of recall, because Arran had imprisoned him for his importunity in advocating this same English marriage ; whilst Henry, unaware of this, or discrediting it, issued orders to his warden to take him dead or alive

The warden[1] went to work with a will ; and when at last Maxwell was released by Arran, Wharton bribed his hereditary enemies, the Johnstons, to entrap him ;[2] and having him in his power, in order to make him sign the surrender of Caerlaverock, he treated him with scandalous severity.

Lord Hertford thus deprecatingly reports the matter to secretary Paget :

" My Lord is in such a state of perplexity, he can neither eat, drink, nor sleep."

In short, the unfortunate Lord Maxwell was tortured till, "to effect his deliverance, he gave up his castle of Caerlaverock to the English on the 28th October 1545."

Lord Wharton, however, had two to reckon with · old Lochinvar, though wishing for good relations with the English, had no idea of allowing them to become joint owners within the marches. Summoning his numerous kin, among whom were his nephew the sheriff and Drumlanrig, he so closely beleaguered Caerlaverock that Wharton with all his forces by sea and land vainly endeavoured to relieve it ; and, strange to say, the Johnstons, who had not been unwilling to pocket English money for making their hereditary opponent a prisoner, entirely dis-

[1] In 1542 Lord Wharton was Governor of Carlisle, and in 1543, as Warden of the Western Marches, defeated the Scottish invaders at Solway Moss, to the number of 15,000, himself only leading 300 men —Lodge's *Illustrations*, i. 202

He was ancestor of Philip, Duke of Wharton, at whose death in 1731 the direct line became extinct

[2] " I have ordered Lard Johnson 300 crowns ; the Abbot of Selsid, his brother, 100 , and to my special 100 crowns, if by his draught I may have in my hand Robert Maxwell. I would be glad to trap him "—Lord Wharton to Lord Shrewsbury, 10th February 1544 —Lodge's *Illustrations*, i 85.

approved of his fortalice becoming an English garrison, and came promptly to the rescue.

So strong was the fortalice that Lochinvar failed to storm it ; but his Galloway troopers persistently investing it, the defenders were starved out the following May.

It was then handed over to the Regent ; but he being now satisfied of the loyalty of Maxwell, restored it to him, renewing his commission of Warden of the Marches. Lord Maxwell only survived the turn of his fortunes a few weeks, dying the 9th of July 1546, leaving by his wife Janet Douglas of Drumlanrig a son, Robert, fifth Lord Maxwell. The Johnstons were quite a power west of the Nith, giving their name to the parish in which stood the residence of their chief, the strong house of the Lock-wood, whose decendants were Earls of Hartfell and Annandale.

The brother of the laird was abbot as well as commendator ; and we find record of his dealings with the sheriff, in which he grants him church lands in " kyndlie tenancy," which after the Reformation were confirmed to the Agnews by the Crown in fee

The original grant, shorn of tautology, runs as follows . " Us James, by the permission of God, parson of Johnston, Com-mendator of the Abbey of Soulseat, grants us to haif setten to our lovit Andrew Agnew, Sheriff of Wigtown, Agnes Stewart his spouse, and Patrick Agnew, sone and apparent heir to the said Andrew, their heirs, executors, and assignees, a half of the lands of old extent of Olbrick, lying in our barony of Drum-mastoun, as it lyes in length and breid, in houses, biggings, feylds, lesurs, pastures, moss, medow, and with common pasture, and with all and sundry other commodities and purtenance quhatsoever, far and neir, with power to the said sheriff, Agnes Stewart his ladye, his son, and their heirs and executors, to input and output cottrals and undersetters, who are to remove and change as oft as shall be thocht expedient by the said Andrew Agnew and Agnes Stewart, etc., for the sum of fyve marks, good and usual money, at the usual terms of the year, in equal portions In witness thereof, we have appended the common seal of our said abbey, together with our subscription manuals of us and our said convent, at the Abbey Saulset ye xiii day of ye month of Februar, ye year of God 1543, before Master Gilbert Johnston, Roger Johnston, Andrew Agnew in Kylstay, Sir Andrew Quhyıt, Michael Murray."

The abbot and commendator as has been already mentioned was taken prisoner at the Solway Rout, and released on giving his son and heir, James Johnston, as his pledge, and ıt is probable that he was now disposing of Auldbreck to the sheriff[1] to raise the sum required to set him free.

In the Barnbarroch charter-chest is a discharge, dated 1st December 1456, "from Andrew Agnew, Sheriff of Wigtown, to Johnne Waus, parson of Wigtown, of the sum of fyf pound usual money, for the Martınmas maill of Culquhoıc."

Master Johnne Waus had resigned his benefice the previous year ın favour of his kinsman Patrıck, who beıng only fifteen years of age, was allowed to perform his duty by deputy, and to travel to Paris to finish his education.

The young cleric, second son of John Vaus of Barnbarroch by a daughter of Sır Simon M'Culloch of Myrtoun, rose to consider-able note as a Lord of Session, best known as Lord Barnbarroch When appoınted parson of Wigtown he was a schoolboy at Mussel-burgh, whence he wrote a letter to his mother, interesting as a specımen of famıly correspondence of the period, and also in proof of our assertıon that a greater freedom in relıgıous dıscussıon seemed to have been then allowed ın Galloway than elsewhere.

Here we find a boy allowed by parents of undoubted orthodoxy to purchase a New Testament and to read it unre-

[1] Olbrıck, or Auldbreck as now wrıtten, falls readıly ınto the Celtıc Allt Breac, "the trout stream," but the absence of a stream of any sıze, or of any trout, rather tells agaınst such an etymon, as also agaınst the Saxon Old Brıdge In a secondary sense, however, thıs may be the derıvatıon, the name beıng a translation of Vetereponte, an old proprıetor, *circum* 1190. Ivo de Veterepontı granted the church of Great Sorby, whıch ıs adjacent, in pure alms, to the abbot and monks of Dryburgh ; hıs charter beıng confırmed by Roland, Lord of Galloway Aygıston, corrupted from Inglestoun on these lands, was probably one of hıs seats

As an example of such derıvatıons, whıch are unusual, we have Mold on the Welsh borders, from de Monte Alto, a famıly name, corrupted ın Galloway to Mouat And Buttevant ın Ireland ıs derıved from Boutez-en-avant, "push forward," the war-cry of the Lord Barrımores, ıts former owners.

proved, moreover acknowledging the possession of a book, for writing which its distinguished author, Buchanan, was in exile.[1]

Letter from Patrick Waus from School to his Mother, 3d January.

Most louing mother, eftir my hairthe commendaciounnis, ye sall vit that I am in good helth, praissit be God, vissing this sam to yow and all youris. Ye sall vit that I am verie skant of linine cloth of sarkis and aurlairis.[2] I haine vrytin verie oft to yow about them, and ye haine never send me ane anser. I pray yow vat[3] ye vaild send me sum mo schankis, for them that I haine vill be schone doine. I mervell that ye send vs not out the ssingill sollit schone, quhilk ye promissit to them out till vs. Nocht ellis, bot commitis you to God; and my most hairthe commendaciounis to yourself, and to my sisteris, the third day of Januar—Your loving sonne.   PATRICK VAUS.

   To my loving mother this
        Be derecit.

Letter by Patrick Waus written from School.

The count of the silver quhilk I haine receauit from Jhamis Challmiris.

Item mair reseuit from Jhamis Challmiris xxiij[s] for till bay ane ovid. Item mair iiij pundis for till giue for iiij pair of schoune, quhilk I gait or ever Vattie Scot furnishit me at your avine command. Item mair receiuet xxx[s] for till bay ane boue[4] the quhilk boue the tuteris sune brack hir befoir yor mother or ever I cam out of the toune, and Jhamis Challmiris gaiue for ane other xxx[s], and for vi arouis everi arroui iiij[s]. Item mair receiuit xxxx[s] for till bay ane hait and ane string   Item mair iij pundis for till bay thrie pair of bleue hois, quhilk I haid nene quhill I gait them   Item mar receauid xxxii[s] for ane neu

---

[1] Among his necessary expenses he accounts for 28s. "for ane silva" This was a treatise written by Buchanan *circum* 1536, satirising the Franciscans, on reading which Archbishop Beaton was so enraged that he compelled the author to flee the country and remain in exile for twenty-four years

[2] Neckcloths.   [3] That.   [4] Bow.

testament and ane sam buck. Item mair receuit xxiij[s] for ane
silva. Item mair receuid xviij[s] for the commenteris of ceser.
Item mair for ane salust xij[s]. Item mair for ane half dusane of
arouis ta me and sandiris xx[s].

The soum xxix pundis.

The youth, it will be observed, expresses himself anxious to
have a pair of dress shoes. These, unlike riding-boots, were
supplied very sparingly to young ladies and gentlemen as
expensive luxuries : a story of which,—although the scene is
often shifted,—is usually associated with the house of Murray of
Broughton, Vaus's nearest neighbour, and amusingly illustrates
the difficulty.

As the laird was standing about his doors one day, a
well-to-do neighbour, not in his *première jeunesse*, rode up,
unusually sprucely dressed, and answered the invitation, "Will
ye licht?" by saying, "First ye shall hear my errand," which
was no less than to ask leave "to coort Miss Jean." The host,
looking rather sheepish, muttered something about Jean being
still owre young. "Just as ye please," retorted the fat buck,
and turned away in a huff. No sooner was he gone than
Murray rushed into his wife's room to tell the story. "Are ye
daft?" roared the lady, ere he had half done, "three lasses to
marry, and sma' tocher for one! rin for your life, and ca' back
the laird." "But, my dear," interposed the husband, "hoo can
he see her the day? Jeanie's shoon are at the mending The
thought came across me as the laird was speaking, and I was
just dumfoundered." "Stuff," said the dame, "I'll gie her mine."
"And whatever will ye do yersel?" "Do? I'll just pull on your
boots, and let doon my lang petticoats, now rin! I'se warrant
ye he's no far off." The dame was right. Like his prototype
Cockpen, the big laird had "ridden cannily," and was easily
called back. Miss Jean received him smilingly, in her mother's
shoes ; little the old beau thought what the old lady had on ,
the young one did not say him nay, and Miss Jean's shoes came
back from the mending to be danced in at her bridal.

In the course of 1546, in answer to a petition from the Abbot of Glenluce, the Lords of the Council instructed the sheriff to take possession of the abbey, and prevent Lord Cassilis from occupying the precincts.

Of the circumstances of the abbot's quarrel with Lord Cassilis we know nothing; but the sheriff could only carry out his instructions, in opposing his powerful neighbour, by calling in his part-takers, amongst whom were the lairds of Lochinvar and Garlies; and the former, being already at feud with the Kennedys, serious complications might have ensued. Lord Cassilis in his turn complained; and, with their usual vacillation, the Lords desired the sheriff to retire forthwith, and the retreat was effected without any breach of the peace.

The official record of the transaction is somewhat involved: "My Lord Governor, and Lords of Council, understand that Gilbert, Erle of Cassilis, Baillie of the Abbey of Glenluce, intending to hold a court upon the lands and lordship of Glenluce, and to that effect has made convocation of the lieges: and that, on the uther part, Andrew Agnew, Sheriffe of Wigtown, be assistance of the Laird of Lochinvar and others, his friends, *at command of my Lord Governor and Lords of Council*, has taken the place and Abbey of Glenluce, and holds the same, tending to make convocation of their kin and friends, for staunching of inconvenientis in the countrie, and for the wele and quietness of the realm, it is ordained by the Lord Governor and Lords of Council that the Sheriff of Wigtown shall remove furth of the said abbey and place of Glenluce, and leave the same void and red.

"And anent the supplication of the Reverend Father in God Gilter, Abbot of Glenluce, against Gilbert, Erle of Cassalis, John M'Dowall of Garthland, William Adair of Kinhilt, Fergus M'Dowall of Freuch, making mention wherein that to resist the invasion of their place and abbey, Andrew Agnew, Sheriff of Wigtown, at command of the Queen's letters, entered with certain friendis and servants in the said place, and remaynit thair quhill laythe, it is ordained that the keeping of the said

place shall cease simpliciter, and the invasion thereof be superseded quhill the 8th day of July next to come." [1]

Lochinvar, having readily come at his nephew's call to assist
him in his little difficulties at Glenluce, we next find him calling
on the sheriff, and his other cadets and king, to strengthen his
hands in better defined operations in the marches.   Lord Maxwell had provisioned and garrisoned his strong fortalice at
Lochmaben, and here the board was daily spread, to which all
old comrades were welcome, where schemes were discussed for
keeping the English in check, the tempting proposal being
added that they should try to recoup themselves for the ransoms
of the Solway Rout.

Old Lochinvar entered heartily into the plans; and where
such pastimes as tuilzying and moss-trooping, business and
pleasure blending, were in the wind, there was no difficulty in
attracting the daring spirits of the district.

Long details of these Border skirmishes are to be gathered
from the English archives, but as they are very wordy and
somewhat dry one specimen may suffice, in the form of a
letter from Lord Wharton to Lord Eure : [2]

"On Saturday last aforeday, John Maxwell, Lord Maxwell's
brother, the Laird Drumlangairt (Drumlanrig), the young Lochinvar, and others of their garrison lying at Lochmaben, to the
number of a thousand men, assembled themselves at a place
called Tordofe, near to the water bank which divideth the realms,
and sent a hundred light horsemen in the daybreaking to
Glasson in England, and laid the rest in ambush at Tordofe
But the watch descried and encountered them; there was a
sharp skirmish, and they have slain Watty Bell, and two or
three of their geldings, and taken one notable Borderer. Thanks
be to God, no damage done to any Englishman, except a gelding slain under a servant of mine"—Carlisle, 14th June 1547.

More serious work, however, was in store for the Border

---

[1] *Register of Privy Council,* i. 3
[2] Sir William Eure, commander-in-chief 1542, created a baron 1544, was of
an ancient Northumbrian family He had a son, Sir Ralph, killed in one of
these skirmishes with the party at Lochmaben.

chivalry who were thus enjoying themselves in Lord Maxwell's
hall.   "The Protector Somerset threatening the capital with
both an army and a fleet, the Scottish regent puts out the fyerie
crosse."[1]

Bale-fires gleamed from Criffel to the Knock of Luce,
sheriff and steward had peremptory orders to push forward the
Galloway levy forthwith, to join the great gathering encamped
on the banks of the Esk, where an impromptu Parliament
held at Monkton Hall, the 8th day of December, enacted as
follows :—

"The Lord Governor, noblemen, barons, freeholders, and
gentlemen, convened to pass forward for the defence of the
realm, in Parliament assembled, statute, devise, and ordain, that
gif it shall happen (as God forbid) that any lord, baron, or
freeholder be slain, that their heirs shall freely have their own
wards, reliefs, and marriages in their own hands, to be disponed
upon as they shall think convenient."

This Act passed, and a most important one it proved to be
to the families of many of those there present.   The host was
marshalled and manœuvred in the presence of the enemy, with
the view to immediate battle.

The advantage seemed entirely with the Scots, they repulsed
an onset of English horse with such heavy loss that Somerset
determined on sending a flag of truce to treat for peace.   But
as he was on the point of sending his messenger, a bold flank
movement initiated by Angus, which would have completed his
discomfiture, was mistaken by the main part of the Scottish
army for a retreat ; and a want of central authority being the
vice of the Scottish military system, instead of maintaining
their ground and waiting for orders, small parties, each led by
local chiefs, rushed helter skelter to a furious but ill-directed
encounter, which occasioned the wildest confusion, and lost
them irreparably the advantages of their position.

Somerset instantly saw and took advantage of their mistake.
Recalling his flag of truce, he launched his serried ranks against

[1] Balfour, i 283

the broken groups of eager Scotchmen, 'each fighting for his own hand. Discipline prevailed over ill-directed valour; the Scots gave way before well-conducted charges *en masse*, the English following on, striking till their arms were tired of slaying, quarter being seldom asked for or given.

Sad was the news which the few survivors of the Galloway force carried back to their desolated homes. " In the fallow fields of Inveresk," writes an eye-witness, "the dead bodies lay as thick as a man may notte cattell grazing in a full plenished pasture" [1] There the Sheriff of Galloway met a soldier's death, and near him lay his uncle, the Knight of Lochinvar, the Lairds of Garthland and Freuch, the Laird of Bennane and his son, Vaux of Barnbarroch, and George, Master of Angus

Of the fifth sheriff's family we trace three sons : Patrick, his heir; Gilbert, afterwards of Galdenoch, and Alexander of Ardoch, and a daughter, Helen, Lady of Torhouse.

By virtue of the last Parliamentary Act, at which he had assisted on the eve of the battle, his eldest son was immediately infefted in his lands and offices ; otherwise, being a minor, the revenues of his estates would have been the perquisite for five years of some needy courtier to whom would have been assigned the nominal wardship.

On the 5th January 1548, George M'Culloch of Torhouse, the late sheriff's son-in-law, acting as sheriff, in conjunction with Gilbert Agnew of Croach, gave effect to a Crown mandate ordering him to give heritable state and seisine to the youth, dated 26th December preceding [2]

George M'Culloch was grandson to Finlay M'Culloch, a

[1] Patten's *Expedition*.
[2] Maria D G R S dilectis nostris Georgio M'Culloch de Torhouse, David Crauford de Park, Gilberto Agnew de Croach, salutem   Quia per inquisitionem de mandato nostro per vos factam ad capellum nostrum retornatam compertum est quod Patricii Agnew latoris presentiam, obiit ultimo vestitus et sasitus, ut feode ad pacem et fidem nostrum sub nostro vexillo in campo juxta Pynkecleuch decimo die mensis Septembris ultimo elapsis de totis et integris, terram de Lochnall, etc.   Et de officiis vicecomitatis nostri de Wigtoun, Constabularie de Lochnall et Balliæ hereditarie de Leswalt.

Apud Edinburgh vicesimo die mensis Decembri anno regni nostri sexto.

witness at the second sheriff's service. Torhouse at this time
comprised all the lands which a little later furnished out three
baronies : Torhouse M'Culloch, Torhouse M'Kie, and Torhouse
Mure.   Upon his lands stood the famous standing-stones of
Torhouse, below which there is little doubt rest the ashes of
Gwallwc-ap-Lleenaug, the eponymous of his race. Gwallwc, "the
hawk of battle," was, as mentioned before, not the King Galdus
of Boece, or the Galgacus (though the name is the same) who
confronted the Romans, but the nephew of Caradoc (whence
Carrick in Ayrshire), who flourished in the sixth century—the
progenitor of the Galloway M'Cullochs.   The mansion-house
was standing at the end of the seventeenth century.[1]

[1] In Wigtown parish there are no considerable edifices, except Torhouse, situated on the north side of the Blendenoch, belonging to George M'Culloch ; not
far from whose house is a plain on which there is a monument of three large whin-
stones, called King Galdus's tomb, surmounted at about twenty paces distance
with nineteen considerable great stones, erected in a circumference.—Symson's
Large Description.

CHAPTER XXII

A.D. 1548 to 1559

The Pape, that Pagan full of pryd,
He has us blinded lang ;
For where the blind the blind do guide,
No wonder both go wrang.

Spiritual Songs

THE first judicial act of Patrick Agnew, now sixth hereditary sheriff, was to preside at the service of Uchtred M'Dowall to the baron of Garthland, who lay beside his father on the field of Pinkey.[1]

The late laird had left two sons, and two daughters—Florence and Helen—married to the Lairds of Freuch and Logan, so that the heads of the three principal branches of this ancient house were all for the moment brothers.

The young sheriff was soon called upon to perform the more serious duty of "summoning gatherings of armed men." The bale-fires announced the advance of the English, under Lord Wharton, who, having driven Lord Maxwell out of the way with great slaughter, had taken possession of Dumfries, whence he summoned the towns westward to surrender. He sent forward Sir Thomas Carleton, who, according to his own report, "rode one night [in February] for the town of Kircobree, and coming there a little after sun-rising, they who saw us coming

---

[1] Uchtred, John M'Dowall's son and heir, is retoured at Wigtown before Patrick Agnew, the High Sheriff of the county, upon the last day of February 1543, as lawful heir to John M'Dowall of Garthland, slane at Pynkey Cleuch.—Crawford's MSS.

barred their gates, and kept their dykes, for the town is dyked on both sides with a gate to the westward," so that he was only able to invest it   The Laird of Bomby presently issued from his neighbouring stronghold, and took the English in the rear, but was beat off, when suddenly, "west of Dee," they observed, to use Carleton's words, "a well-appointed force of Galloway folks" who had marched at speed from Wigtown with the sheriff, whereupon Carleton thought it best for the present to secure the booty he had taken : "about 2000 sheep, 200 kye, 40 or 50 horses, mares, and colts." So after showing a bold front at the "difficult ford of the Dee" till after dark, he drew off, and marched all night to Dumfries.[1]

The good folks of Kirkcudbright now opened their gates to their succourers from the Shire, and joyfully filled the wassail bowl for their reception.   Though checked at Kirkcudbright, Carleton surprised and took the Lockwood with great address. He writes that, "learning that the Laird of Johnston, and his brother the Abbot of Soulseat, were still detained in England, he thought good to practise some way by which to get hold of the castle.   It was a fair large tower, able to lodge all our company, with a barnekin,[2] hall, kitchen, and stables, all within the barnekin, and was kept but by two or three fellows and as many wenches."

Timing his arrival for an hour before sunrise, he left the bulk of his squadron outside.   "Twelve men stole into the barnekin and took the wenches, the only persons in it, and kept them close till daylight.   Two men and a wench slept in the tower. At dawn, one of the men, rising in his shirt, went to the tower head, carefully scanned the horizon, and there being no one to

---

[1] MSS. account of a foray into Scotland in February 1548. Reprinted in Nicholson's and Burns's *History of Scotland.* Of this retreat, Carleton says · "We left our sheep and put our worst horsemen before the nowte and nags, and sent thirty of the best horsemen to prick at the Scots if they should come over the water at the forehead ford , which the Scots perceiving, stayed.   So we passed quietly that night to Dumfries, leaving the goods in safety with a good watch Thus, with wiles, we beguiled the Scots "

[2] Barbican, an advanced work before a castle gate, especially intended to defend the drawbridge.

be seen, called to the woman who laid in the tower to rise
and open the tower door; she so doing, and opening the iron
door and a wooden door without it, the men who lay concealed
rushed forward, but brak a little too soon; for the wench, perceiving them, leaped back into the tower, and almost got the
door closed to, when they got a hold of it, so that she should
not close it, and so we won the Lockwood"

Here he tells us they found good store of beef, meal, malt,
butter, and cheese, with luxurious quarters, and fortifications
which, when well manned, were almost impregnable; and
Wharton, well pleased, named him Keeper of the Lockwood

The laird of Bomby mentioned by Carleton was Sir Thomas
M'Clellan, son of the laird killed in the streets of Edinburgh by
old Lochinvar; and he who was killed at Pinkey had left besides
his heir a second son William, who succeeded by remainder to
the lands of Penninghame in Wigtownshire, and four daughters
—Helen, Lady M'Clellan; Katherine, married to M'Culloch of
Cardoness; Margaret, Lady Douglas of Drumlanrig (whose
grandson was created Earl of Queensberry); and Janet, who
shortly after this English foray married the young sheriff, and
became lady of Lochnaw.[1]   The laird of Bomby, Helen Gordon's
husband, in 1569 acquired the house and grounds of the Grey
Friars Monastery in Kirkcudbright, on the site of which he built
the castle, still picturesque in its ivy-clad ruins

When we consider how clumsy and inefficient were the firearms of the day, it provokes a smile to read that the baronage
of 1550 seriously complain that they "can get no pastime,
hunting or hawking, by reason that the wylde beasts and wylde
fowls are exiled and banished by them that schuttes with guns"

Whereupon Parliament enacts that "whosoever of our
sovereign's lieges of whatever degree take upon hand to shoot a
deer, roe, or other wild beasts, or any wild fowls with half-hap,

---

[1] 3d September 1550   Patrick Agnew, Sheriff of Wigtown, with consent of
John Dunbar of Mochrum, one of his curators, settles on Joneta Gordon, sister
of John Gordon of Lochinvar, the lands of Salquharry on her viduity

Witnesses. Gilbert Agnew of Croach, Patrick M'Cracken of Shuchane, Malcolm
M'Culloch.

culverine, or pistol, in ony times to come, shall incur the pains of death, and confiscation of their goods. And whoever brings such culprit to the sheriff of the shire shall have escheat of his goods, and be otherwise rewarded as the sheriff may think fit." [1]

As a rider to this the sheriff was to satisfy himself that the poulterer did not sell game too dear; a sumptuary law fixing the prices as follows: "The crane, 5s.; the swan, 5s.; the wild goose of the great breed, 2s ; the claik (barnacle), quink (golden-eye), and rute (rude goose), 1s. 6d each; the plover and small moorfowl, 4d.; the blackcock and gray hen, 6d.; the dozen of powtes, 12d ; the quhaip (curlew), 6d.; the cunning (rabbit), 2s. till Shrove Tuesday, thenceforth, 1s.; the lapron, 2d., the woodcock, 4d.; the dozen laverocks and other small birds, 4d., the snipe and quailzie, 2d ; the tame goose, 16 pennies; the capon, 12d.; the hen and poultry, 8d.; the gryce (young pig, wild or tame), 1s. 6d."

A feud broke out in 1554 between the Lairds of Garlies and Lochinvar; as an episode in which Alexander Stewart, young Laird of Garlies, accompanied by Michael M'Cracken, a burgess of Wigtown, forgathered with Simon Gordon, a kinsman of Lochinvar's, and killed him, wounding his servant also, in revenge for which Lochinvar, with the laird of Barskeoch, Roger Gordon, David Gordon of Marbreck, Roger Gordon of Hardland, Gilbert M'Dowall of Machermore, Patrick M'Kie of Larg, and Eliseus Gordon, attacked and forced open M'Cracken's house in Wigtown, gutting it, the owner flying for his life.

Both parties presented themselves for trial at a Justice Aire in Kirkcudbright; the Laird of Garthland becoming surety for his son; the Laird of Lochinvar's own recognisances being accepted for the appearance of his part-takers to answer to the charges "of hame sucken and searching for Michael M'Cracken for his slaughter." [2]

---

[1] 4 Parliament, Queen Mary, chap. 9. By an Act, 15th June 1555, 6 Parliament, Queen Mary, chap. 51, there was this addition. "That na man ryde or gang in their neighbour's corn in halking or hunting fra the Feast of Pasche, and that na pairtrich be taken unto the Feast of Michaelmas "

[2] Pitcairn, *Criminal Trials*, 1554-55.

At the same court Sir James M'Culloch is replegiated by the Bishop of Whithorn for resetting, supplying, and intercommuning with Godfrey M'Culloch, rebels at the horn for the cruel slaughter of Patrick Mure, and Thomas M'Clellan of Bomby, his brother, Godfrey M'Culloch of Ardwell, John M'Culloch of Barholm, Ninian Glendonwin in Parton, Richard M'Kie of Myrtoun, and John Akinzean (M'Kinnon) had already been summoned to underlie the law as principals in the said slaughter, the Laird of Lochinvar becoming surety.

Such was the feebleness of the Government, that at this very date Sir John Gordon of Lochinvar, a party or principal in so many disorders, was invested with a special commission as Justiciary for Eastern Galloway, apparently in illustration of the adage, " Set a thief to catch a thief"

This year we find the sheriff in Edinburgh arranging a settlement of two years' accounts, not an agreeable process, as, although a sheriff shared in the fines and dues which he had to collect, he was often obliged perforce to give long credit to neighbours, coin being very scarce ; and in this matter he seems to have been helped by Master David Carnegie, a fact interesting to note from the close connection afterwards formed between the two families. A formal deed was executed by the sheriff to this effect ·

" Be it kend till all men, me, Patrick Agnew, Sheriff of Wigtown, to be bound and straitly obliged to Master David Carnegy, Parson of Kynnoull," who " has relieved me at the hands of John, Archbishop of St. Andrews, treasurer for the time, of the sums following viz £389 : 6 8, resting-owing by me in my counts made in the Chekker-rolls, the year of God 1553, and of the whole sums contained in the Book of Respondie owing by me since making my said count unto the tenth day of April 1554 years. Therefore I bind me, my heirs and assignees, and with me John Dunbar of Mochrum and Alexander Stewart of Garuleis, cautioners and sureties for me, conjointly and severally, to pay to the said Master David £210 usual money of Scotland, betwixt the day of the date hereof and the first day of September *nextocum*, but longer delay.

" And if we fail in making thankful payment thereof at the said term, I and my sureties oblige us to pay to the said Master David the whole sum of £389 : 6 : 8, of which he has relieved me at ye said Reverend Father's hand.

"Provided always, that gif the said John, Archbishop of St. Andrews, give any discharge subscribed with his hand after the date hereof to any person of any part of the said sum of £389 6 . 8, the same to be allowed to me, the said Patrick, as for payment.

" I and my sureties subscribed this with our hands at Edinburgh, 6 February 1555 years."

David Carnegie was the second son of Sir Robert Carnegie of Kinnaird His acquaintance with the sheriff commenced from his having been appointed a few months before, along with Maxwell of Terregles, a commissioner to settle disputes upon the Borders Though titularly parson, he practised as a lawyer, rose high in his profession, and served in various commissions in matters affecting the Laws, the Church, and the Exchequer. Freed by the Reformation from vows of celibacy, he married in 1560 Elizabeth Ramsay, heiress of Colluthie. Surviving his elder brother Sir John, he succeeded to Kinnaird in 1595 His first wife dying, he married Euphame, daughter of Sir John Wemyss, and had by her four sons David, created Earl of Southesk; John, created Earl of Northesk; Sir Robert Carnegie of Dunnichen, Lour, and Auchterlony , and Alexander, Laird of Balnamoon—a most prosperous family truly.

A direct descendant of his, daughter of Sir James Carnegie, and but for the attainder eighth Earl of Southesk, became the wife of Sir Andrew Agnew, seventh Baronet of Lochnaw.

We read that in 1557 "the Queen Regent raisses a great armey to invade England, and the nobility flatly refuses to invade it."[1]

This refusal, which arose from reluctance to augment the queen mother's powers, had its echo in Galloway, where several lairds, prominently Stuart of Garlies and Dunbar of Mochrum, were summoned to underlie the law "for abiding from a warden

---

[1] Balfour, i. 308.

raid summoned to convene at the Lochmaben Stane."   In reply
they alleged " that at the day of Trew, they raid to the water of
Annan, to have passed forward with the warden, but the water
was so great they might not ride it without danger of life."
Their plea was accepted.

Meanwhile the Protestant doctrines had been making great
progress in the west; the Queen Dowager, ill advised by the
clergy, allowed the time to go by when reforms might have
strengthened the old Establishment.

As early as 1548 John M'Brair, a canon of Glenluce, having
embraced the reformed doctrines, attracted great attention as a
preacher.   The see of Glasgow having remained vacant for
some years after the death of Dunbar, and Dury, Bishop of
Galloway (being also Abbot of Melrose) preferring residence at
Court to his house at Claire, evangelical doctrines were sown
broadcast in the province without check.   Presently, however,
Hamilton, Bishop of St. Andrews, making a progress in the
west, astounded at what he heard, instituted a vigorous search
for " the Apostate Heresiarch," M'Brair, and at last tracked him
to Lord Ochiltree's,[1] where, in spite of the owner's resistance, he
was arrested and carried to Hamilton Castle.   The archbishop,
however, was unable to retain his prisoner, his bolts being
forced and his victim rescued by " John Lockhart of Barr, a
stout gentleman," who saw the preacher safely across the
Borders.   The preachers had long been openly encouraged and
entertained in Galloway; and no generous-minded baron, be he
Protestant or Catholic, cared to assist in the arrest of men who
had broken bread at their tables, well knowing that they would
be dragged before tribunals where they would get short shrift.
The Lords Cassilis, Glencairn, and Ochiltree; the Stewarts,
Gordons, Agnews, Kennedys, Dalrymples of Stair, and Chalmers
of Gadgirth, all interested themselves actively in the safety of
the Reformers, as was quickly shown.   The Queen Dowager
allowed herself to be over-persuaded, against her better judgment,

---

[1] Andrew, Lord Ochiltree, was a determined reformer.   One of his daughters
married John Knox , another Kennedy of Bargany.

by the bishops to summon all known preachers to Edinburgh,
they fondly supposing that they would thus place them on the
horns of a dilemma, either of running their heads into the noose,
or else by disobedience subjecting themselves to the pains of
outlawry. However, to the confusion of the Council, the
preachers obeyed, but attended by serried files of spearmen
under the leading of the western lairds, eloquent in jakkis.
The Council were dumfoundered. A doggerel rhyme of the
Bishop of Galloway,[1] who seems to have been a funny fellow,
amused the bystanders so much as to have been thought worthy
of preservation; when the arrival of their retinue was reported
in the Council Chamber, turning to the queen:

> Madame! because they are come without order,
> I redeye send them to the Border

Excellent advice, had the said lairds been amenable to discipline. Her majesty proved more equal to the situation than
her ministers, and tried soft words, saying according to an eye-
witness: "'My joys, my hearts, what aileth you?' Whereupon
a bold man, James Chalmers of Gaidgyrth, upspake, 'We know
that this is but the malice of thae jevells and (pointing to the
clerics) those idle bellies; they trouble our preachers, and
would murder both them and us!' 'My lords,' said the queen
to the bishops, 'I forbid you to trouble these good men or their
preachers.' So she dismissed them with a good grace."[2]

Archbishop Hamilton had to content himself for the loss of
M'Brair by burning Walter Mill, a heretic of much inferior note,
at St. Andrews, where he was still supreme; though the good
people of the East Neuk showed much exasperation, and as a
mark of opinion closed every cellar door in the city so that the
executioners had much ado to find materials for the fire.

In Galloway, Bishop Dury bore himself more discreetly, and
no collision between churchmen and reformers is recorded
during this phase of the religious struggle in the province.

---

[1] "The Bishop of Galloway, after his accustomed manner, said in rhyme to
the Queen" (as above) —Calderwood, 1. 344.

[2] Calderwood, i. 345   "Jevell," a contemptuous term.—Jamieson.

The spirit of the period, however, showed itself in the compilation and singing of grotesque and even ribald ballads, but which were actually published under the title of "godly and spiritual songs." Though not without humour, and himself a wit, Dury must have been scandalised at hearing such verses as these before an admiring crowd in contempt of the Pope :

> His cardinals has cause to mourn,
> His bishops are borne abacke,
> His abbots gat an uncouth turn
> When shavelings went to sacke
> With burgess wifes
> They led their lifes,
> And fare far better than we.
> Hey tricks trim goe tricks under the greenwood tree.

Whilst, however, indignation was rightly directed against the extortions, idleness, and immoralities of churchmen, the Reformers were as yet far from grasping those ideas of tolerance and Christian liberty which underlie the very name of Protestant If the Romish clergy had been too lax on the score of amusements, the Reformers fell into the opposite extreme. Not satisfied with insisting on the sanctity of the Sabbath, they decried innocent diversions on every day of the week, and dancing was held by them in such abhorrence, that had their maxims been pushed to their logical conclusions, any one taking the father for an example in the parable of the Prodigal Son must have incurred Church censures.

Up to this time the fame of Robin Hood had been celebrated regularly in May, always upon a Sunday or saint's day. The whole burgh populations in Galloway, as elsewhere, turned out to some neighbouring field, two worshipful bailies being usually selected as Robin Hood and Little John, the most respectable citizens joining as performers, when various scenes in the famous outlaw's life were acted.

Jack in the Green also arrived at the proper season ; and at Christmas an Abbot of Unreason (the Scotch representative of the English Lord of Misrule) appeared upon the scene and played his part.

The reforming party might with great propriety have introduced an act forbidding these diversions upon Sundays; but in
place of this a law was drawn by which such amusements were
forbidden altogether, and sheriffs were strictly enjoined to see
that "sic unprofitable sports be utterly cried down." Further,
that for the future "no manner of person be chosen Robin Hude
nor Little John, nor Queens of May, the choosen of such to tine
their freedom for the space of five years, and be otherwise
punished at the queen's grace's will, and the acceptor of sic like
offices to be banished furth of the realm." Monstrous as this
appears, a clause appended was almost worse: "If any women
or others make perturbation for skaipie of money or otherwise,
they shall be taken, handled, and put upon the cuckstules."

Though these Acts were extorted from the Lords of the
Articles, the Reformers could not always command a majority.
Legislation took the form of a see-saw; and another Act of the
same year, apparently in retaliation, forbids the eating flesh in
Lent and other days forbidden by the Church, under pain of confiscation of the eater's goods, "and gif the eaters has na guids,
their personis to be put in prison, there to remain for a year
and a day."

Lord Cassilis had been sent to France to attend Queen
Mary's marriage with the Dauphin, and was named a Lord of
the Bedchamber to Henry II. of France in honour of the event.
But afterwards he and his colleagues greatly offended the French
king by opposing the giving of the crown matrimonial to the
royal bridegroom.

Cassilis and two other of these Scotch lords died at Dieppe
on the 18th of November 1558, as was generally suspected by
poison, suggested in all contemporary chronicles. But for the
credit of French hospitality it is pleasant to be able to state that
an affecting letter from the earl, written on his deathbed to
Lord Barnbarroch, clearly contradicts the scandal. It ends
thus:

"Fair ye weil, off Dieppe this vii. of November. Item, ye
sall wit my fevir is callit the cotedicene, and hes bene thir ix.

dayis paist, quharbe I am groving sa waik that I dow do na thing—Youris,   "CAISSAILLIS."[1]

The Earl left by Margaret, daughter of Alexander Kennedy of Bargany, Gilbert, fourth earl; Sir Thomas Kennedy of Culzean; Jean, married to Robert, Earl of Orkney, and Katherine, married in 1574 to Lord Barnbarroch as his second wife.

Among the last acts of this amiable Earl of Cassilis before starting on his mission for France was, at the request of Sir Patrick Agnew, acting along with Sir John Gordon in an arbitration between members of the Adair family, to one of which Sir Patrick was curator. The matter is of but trifling importance, but philologically interesting, as proving with certainty the derivation of the name Adair to be from the christian name Edgar rather than the Celtic ath darach "ford of the oaks." The Adairs of Crichane and Kinhilt were of the same stock, and of the cousins at this date we find the one branch adhering to the older spelling, whilst the other uses the new.

"At Edinburgh, the 19 day of May, ye year of God 1557 years, we, Gilbert, Earl of Cassilis, Lord Kennedy, and John Gordon of Lochinvar, judges, arbitrators, and amicabell compositors.

" Chosen betwixt an honourable man Patrick Agnew, Sheriff of Wigtoun, for himself, and taking the burden upon him for Margaret Edzear and Janet Edzear, dochteris lawful to Niniane Edzear, son of Niniane Edzear of ye Creechane, on the one part, and William Adair of Kinhilt for himself, and taking upon him the burden for Quinten Edzear, son of the said Ninian elder, on the uyr parte, anent the tocher to be given by the said William and Quenteni to the said Margaret and Janet.

" Dearce, deliver, and for final sentence arbitrall, decern, and ordain ye 2d William and Quenteni to pay and thankfully deliver to the 2d Margaret the sum of 200 merks in manner following: 100 merks at Whitsunday next the time after she

---

[1] *Correspondence of Sir Patrick Waus,* p. 12.

have completed the bond of matrimony with any man of possession, and 100 merks at the feast of Martinmas therafter.

"In witness whereof we have subscribed this our decreet arbitrall with our hands, day, year, and place foresaid, before these witnesses : Alexr. Stewart of Garleis, Hew Kennedy of Drummellan, Hew Kennedy of Barquhinny."

In 1558 Bishop Dury died, and was succeeded by Alexander Gordon, son of the Master, and brother of the fourth Earl of Huntly.   He was titular Archbishop of Athens, and subsequently embraced Protestantism, but, rightly or wrongly, was never thought very earnest in the matter.

The queen regent died the following year, and Mary and Francis summoned a Convention of Estates, which met in August 1560, in which the Reformers being in a majority adopted a Protestant confession of faith.   In this Parliament there sat the Earls of Cassilis and Glencairn, the Master of Maxwell, the Lairds of Lochinvar and Garlies, and the Bishop of Galloway.

Unsettled as was the state of society, we find the good folk of Wigtown embarking in commercial enterprise with a spirit they hardly maintain at the present day.

Certain burgesses having entered into copartnery to supply their fellow-townsmen with wines, spices, laces, furs, and other luxuries, every possible restriction was in these days placed on trade, and these good folk could not get the required authorisation until the Laird of Lochinvar became bound, under a penalty of £1000, that they would allow no rebels to the sovereign authority to purchase any of their good things.   How they were to discriminate loyal from disloyal persons under the circumstances of the period would have sorely puzzled the wisest heads; as the Laird of Lochinvar himself, who was their security, and the sheriff who had to certify to the bond, were alike members of the "Congregation," in direct antagonism to the religion of the regent.[1]

[1] The bond bears as follows :—

"Forasmuch as the Regent has granted to Patrick M'Blane, John M'Cracken,

Alexander Hannay, John Hannay, William Gordon, John M'Allenay, and John Waus, a passport and testimonial that they are true and obedient subjects to our sovereign lord and lady, and sua may saiflie pass to ye ports of France, and use leifful trafect and business, but truble or impediment: Therefore we, John Gordon of Lochinvar, becomes caution and security for the said persons, that they shall bring their goods and merchandize, which they shall happen to bring furth of the realm of France, to the port and haven of Wigtown, so that our sovereign lord and lady's true and obedient subjects shall be furnished y^{r}w^t, and that the said persons shall not change nor trafect any of their goods with any persons that have rebelled against our sovereign's authority.   Obliging me and my heirs, yat gif the said persons doiss in ye contrar of ye premiss, to pay to the said princes the sum of £1000 money of this realm

" Before Patrick Agnew, Sheriff of Wigtown :

" Master Robert Stewart and John Stewart, witnesses.

" At Edinburgh, 13th Jan 1559. Sic. Subr.   LOCHINVAR."

CHAPTER XXIII

THE KING OF CARRICK

A.D. 1559 to 1570

The Gordon, Hay, and brave Agnew,
Three knights of high degree,
Unto the ladye courting came,
All for her fair beautie.

ALTHOUGH Lord Cassilis was considered a Protestant in the Parliament of 1560, he had not decidedly declared himself for the Congregation. It was a great object with the Court party to gain him ; and among the last acts of the queen regent was the absurd though not uncommon one of granting an exemption from the jurisdiction of the Sheriff Principal of Galloway, which was as follows :

AN EXEMPT FOR THE EARL OF CASSILIS AND HIS DEPENDENTS FROM THE SHERIFF OF WIGTOWN.

" We, understanding that thair standis sum variance, discord, and unkyndness, betwix oure cousing, Gilbert, Earl of Cassilis, his kin, friendis, and servandis on that ane part ; and our Schiref of Wigtoun, his kin, friendis, and servandis on that uther part, quhairthrow he and his Deputtes may be na jugeis competent to thame in ony action concerning thame : Therefore, We, for eschewing of grettare inconvenienttis, be thir presentis exemes our said cousin, his kin, friends, allies, tenants, servants, and par-takers fra our said Schiref and his Deputes, thair jurisdiction, office, and power, anent any action concerning them als weill

crimmal as civil in time coming indurng our will; charging
therefore our said Schiref and his Deputes that they desist and
cease fra all calling, persewing, or proceding upon any action
concerning our said cousin, his kin, friends, allies, tenants, servants or part-takers either crimmal or civile in time coming ay
and quhill they have command of us in the contrair; discharging
them utherwayes of all proceedings thairintill, and of their
offices in that part during the said space, notwithstanding any
commission of justiciar given or to be given by us in the contrair
to our Schiref; anent the quhilk we dispense in so far as con-
cerns the premises by thir presents, given under our signet, and
subscrivit by our dearest mother Marie, quene dowriare and
regent of our realm.   At Edinburgh, to the yeir of God one
thousand fyve hundred and fifty-nyne years, and of our reign
the 2d and 18th years   Marie R."

A copy of this found its way into the Barnbarroch charter-
chest, on which the accomplished editor of his ancestor's correspondence pertinently remarks. "Sir Patrick Agnew of Lochnaw
was the representative of the royal authority, but being seemingly
at feud with the earl, the regent says that he and his deputies
would not be competent judges in actions between them"[1] The
absurdity is even greater than appears on the surface: the
"discord" was prospective; the earl had as yet not even been
served heir to his father of happy memory, who moreover had
not left him a single feud to inherit.

As there is little on record creditable to the fourth earl, it
is pleasant at least to find that he was a better son than a
neighbour; and we quote the details of the ample provision he
made for his mother, which is interesting as bearing on the
social habits of the period.[2]

On the 29th August 1559 he assigned her "the place of
Cassalis, with garden and orchard, and yearly for her life 110
bolls meal, 52 bolls bear, 115 marks money, 89 capons, 36

[1] *Correspondence of Lord Barnbarroch*, p. 16
[2] He was under age when he made the provision quoted in the text. He
was served heir 16th October 1562.—*Charter History of Kennedys*, p. 38

salmon (and the yearly rent of various holdings), 111 milk ewes, 77 yeld ewes, 108 wedders, 40 gimmers, 40 dinmonts,[1] 11 old goats, 2 kids, 114 head nolt in the Forest of Buchan, 16 nicol cows and as many calves, 77 farrow and 9 yeld cows, 5 three-year-old cows, 22 old oxen, 2 bulls, 6 three-year-old oxen, 2 bulls, 5 two-year-old oxen, 11 queys, 9 stirks (during her life), a silver basin and a laver, a double gilt cup of silver, 2 cases of silver, the one gilt the other ungilt, a gilt macer, 2 silver trenchers with two little salt fatts, 12 silver spoons, a silver salt fatt, a black velvet bed with curtains black damask, 4 pieces of tapestry, 4 feather beds and their bolsters, etc. Ratified on 5th Nov. 1559 by Quentin Kennedy, Abbot of Crossraguel, Sir Hugh Kennedy of Girvan Mains, David Kennedy of Culzean, and Mr. Thomas Hay, pastor of Spynie, the earl's curators."

Quentin Kennedy, the earl's uncle, was one of the few Church dignitaries of the day who could preach : a man of parts and learning, even by the Protestant chroniclers admitted to be "ane guid man and ane that feared God after the manner of his religion."

In 1562, when the opposing parties were nearly evenly balanced, Quentin Kennedy challenged John Knox to an open discussion as to the doctrine of the Mass, "Which," says Calderwood, "was granted, and held at Mynibole[2] three days; the abbot undertook to prove that Melchizedek offered bread and wine," and adds, "he could adduce no proffe." Most un-biassed persons would now admit that Kennedy was right, though he naturally failed to convince a west country audience that the Mass as then celebrated was the necessary outcome of that act of patriarchal worship. Both parties were satisfied with their champions : the Roman Catholics permanently so , and Quentin Kennedy has since been canonised

Notwithstanding the blandishments of the queen dowager,

---

[1] Gimmer, a ewe two years old.   Dinmont, a wether in the second year.

[2] Calderwood, ii. 203.   The old form Mynibole points to the derivation moine-buaile, "moor of the dairy place "

Earl Gilbert, persuaded, it was said, by his young wife, Margaret, daughter of Lord Glammis, declared himself a Protestant. Unfortunately he did not adorn the doctrine he professed.

By a letter dated at Amboise, 25th March 1559, the young Queen Mary and her husband Francis had asked Cardinal Sermoneta to confirm Thomas Hay (second son of Hay of Dalgety, a cadet of the Errols) as Abbot of Glenluce, as also an annuity of £100 out of the revenues of the abbey to Mr. Patrick Vaus. Both were conceded. This Abbot was the progenitor of the Hays of Park.

In 1562, for a matter unexplained, we find Patrick Agnew, Sheriff of Galloway ; John Gordon of Lochinvar, Finlay Campbell of Corswall, William Adair of Kynhilt, Master Patrick Vaus, Parson of Wigtown , John Gordon of Barskeoch, Matthew Campbell, Sheriff of Ayr ; and Hugh Kennedy, "fader-brother" to the Earl of Cassilis, denounced for not appearing as witnesses before the Council when summoned. In 1563 Queen Mary married secondly her cousin Lord Darnley, who, with his father, the Earl of Lennox, had a common ancestor with the Stewarts of Garlies ; Sir Alexander (of Garlies) and his son being both present at the marriage, the latter being one of the fourteen knighted on the occasion. Sir Alexander was presented with a snuff-box, still preserved at Galloway House, inscribed · "The gift of Henry, Lord Darnley, to his cousin Sir Alexander Stewart of Garlies."

The close connection of the Garlies Stewarts with the king consort accounts for their having, alone among their Galloway neighbours, remained unsoftened to Mary during her subsequent troubles.

During twenty years preceding these times, many men of blameless life had been cruelly sacrificed for endeavouring to bring the Church practice to the touchstone of the Bible. When, therefore, the reforming party became masters of the situation, · they would have been more than human had they accorded their opponents that full toleration which Catholics themselves denounced as wrong. Consequently we find, in 1563, the Bishop of St. Andrews arraigned for "saying and hearing Mass," and forty-seven others charged with attempts to restore Popery.

The Kennedys of Culzean and Barquhanny were charged with coming with two hundred persons "bodin in fear of weir" to the parish church of Kirkoswald. And Malcolm Fleming, Commendator of Whithorn, Sirs the Reverend Thomas Montgomery and William Tailzefeir, had to underlie the law "for indecently and irreverently abusing the Sacrament of our Lord's body and blood, in contravention of our Sovereign Lady's proclamation."

The Lords of Assize were Andrew Stewart, Lord Ochiltree, Maxwell of Terregles, the Laird of Lochinvar, the Sheriff of Galloway, Dunbar of Mochrum, Dunbar of Baldoon, and four other lairds of Ayrshire; the doom pronounced being that the two Kennedys be put in ward in Edinburgh Castle, and the Whithorn churchmen in the Castle of Stirling, there to remain during the pleasure of the queen.[1]

When the government was taken out of Mary's hands the regent courted the co-operation of the Galloway baronage. They were frequently summoned for assistance and consultation; thus we find in 1567, letters ordered to be directed severally "to Patrick Agnew, Sheriff of Wigtown; John Gordon of Lochinvar, Thomas M'Clellan of Bomby, John Gordon of Ardes, Alexander Gordon of Troqueer, William Gordon of Craighlaw, and Michael, Lord Carlisle, desiring them to appear before my Lord Regent, be the 6th day of October next to come, to give their advice and judgement anent the establishment of universall justice and goodness within the bounds of the said marches, and for remeid of divers disorders and disobediences committed by the inhabiters of the west country."[2]

We mentioned the enterprise of certain merchant burgesses of Wigtown in trading to France: it seems greater dangers attended much shorter voyages. The sheriff was obliged to address a remonstrance to the English government, praying "that compensation and redress be made to William Wauss,

[1] Pitcairn.   [2] Privy Council Register.

John Martin, and William Gordon, merchants of Wigtown, whose ships had been seized and spoiled by Shane O'Neil and others in Ireland" Also "for a cargo plundered in the harbour of Carlingford by the said Shane and Ferdonagh Macgenis" The good Queen Bess graciously acknowledged receipt of the petition, which she desired her Lord Justice to reply to and remedy. It is calendared in the State Paper Office, "The complaint of certain merchant burgesses of Wigtown, commanding Sir Thomas Cusacke to deal in the matter," dated 9th January 1595.

When Mary was deposed on her marriage with Bothwell, the Galloway baronage generally signed the bond, recognising the prince as king. But when the beautiful queen effected her escape from Lochleven Castle, most of these same lairds donned her colours, the Stewarts of Garlies, Dunbars, and M'Kies only excepted. In the east, Lords Herries and Maxwell, the Abbot of Dundrennan, Lochinvar, M'Clellan of Bomby, the Laird of Drumlanrig, in the west, the Sheriff, the Bishop, the Abbots of Soulseat and Glenluce, Baillie of Dunragit, Patrick Vaux, M'Culloch, Gordon of Craighlaw, and many Kennedys, flocked to the queen's standard Cassilis was there, and shook hands with Lochinvar ; and Lord Fleming as cordially fraternised with the Sheriff, who had so lately thinned his breeding stock in the church lands of Cruggleton.

The queen's partisans outnumbered the king's, but so hotheaded were the Galloway knights, that in their haste to break a lance for their fair mistress, they joined battle without order or concert on the 13th May 1568, and were totally defeated.

An amusing incident of the retreat shows that the instinct to appropriate their neighbour's horse was as strong in the true Gallovidian as in the days of the Black Douglas. When the Galloway spearmen saw that the battle was lost, with great presence of mind passing quickly to the rear, they remounted themselves on the pick of the spare horses of the other divisions, and thus easily distanced their pursuers, among whom were many of their former allies, who joined their opponents in the useless chase.[1] With these they furnished a bodyguard, which, headed by Lord Herries, accompanied Mary in a rapid flight to Dundrennan;[2] whence she crossed the Solway, to return no more to Scotland.

Their adherence to the losing side proved a serious matter to the Galwegians. The following year the Regent Murray entered the province from the eastward, and easily took Dumfries; but Lochinvar refusing to yield, he burned Kenmore Castle to the ground. Fortunately for the Wigtownshire barons the regent's army fell short of supplies, and instead of advancing turned backwards and lived at free quarters on the lands of the Maxwells and Drumlanrig.

A fiery summons, however, was issued, ordering them all to come in and make their submission, which appears to have been unattended to in the first instance, and reissued by Lennox two years later. The summons is dated 1569, but endorsed "The charge of Lennox upon certain barons and gentlemen in Galloway, 1571."[3] It was as follows.

"James, by the grace of God, with advice and consent of our dearest cousin, our regent,—We charge straitly Patrick Agnew, Sheriff of Galloway; Hugh Kennedy of Chappell, Master Patrick Vaux of Barnbarroch, Thomas Baillie of Little Dunraggit, Andrew Bailzie of Dunraggit, Alexander Gordon of Craighlaw, Thomas Hay, Abbot of Glenluce, Archibald Kennedy of Sinnyness, William Kennedy, M'Culloch of Ardwell, M'Culloch of Kelleser, to compeer personally before our dearest goodsir and Regent, upon the 20th of March inst., at Ayr, to answer such things as shall be laid to their charge, under the pain of tresson; with certification to any of them gif they failzie, ye said day being by-past, they shall be repute, halden, esteemit, demesnit, and pursuit with fire and sword, as

---

[1] If there happens to be any chase, either fleeing or following, whoever he be that takes his fellow's horse, and does not as soon as he comes back deliver it to the sheriff, he shall be treated as a traitor.—Douglas's Border Ordinances, No. 5

[2] She, seeing herself deprived of the day, fleies with the Master of Maxwell and his company of Galloway men quho escaped on their fellows' horsses that had endured the brunt of the battell.—Balfour, i. 344.

[3] State Paper Office.

traitors and enemies to God, us their sovereign, and their native countrie."

The day after the arrival of Mary and her attendants at Carlisle she wrote to Cassilis, pleased with her reception, and blissfully ignorant of her future fate. The letter is in the Culzean charter-chest, and we believe has never before been published.

"Traist Cusing,—Forsamekle as I for the salftie of my bodie findand na suir acces nor place within my realme to retire me at this tyme, as ye may knaw, I was constraignit to leve the samin and to pas in this cuntrey of Ingland, quhair I assuir yow I have bene Rycht weill Ressauit and honorablie accompaigned and traicted. I have deliberit to pas fortherward in France to pray the King my gude broder to support and help me to delyuer and Releue my Realme of sic Rebelliouis troublis and oppressionis that now regnis within the samin, and to depart furth of this toun the xxiij day of this Instant moneth, Thairfore I pray you effectuouslie traist cusing that ye in the menetyme hald yourself constant in my seruice and aduerteiss your freinds and neighbouris to do the samin, and to be in readienes to serue me quhan the occatioun sall offer as ye have done trewlie afoir this tyme, Speciallie at the last battall quhair (as I am adwerteist) ye have done Rycht weill your deuoir, ye beand on your featis quhilk sall nocht be forgit be me in tyme coming. With the help of God I houp to retuine agane about the xv day of August nixt with gud company for the effect foresaid God willing. This I beleve ye will do as my traist is and wes ay in you, And for to mak ane end of my bill I will commit you to the protectioun of the eternall God   AT Carlell the xx day of Maij 1568.   MARIE R.

"I pray you my lord excuss this stamp because the quene hes na uthir at this tyme.

"To my lord Erle of Cassilis"

The queen from her English prison sent Lord Barnbarroch "a grant of the escheat of Alexander M'Kie, because of his assisting James, Earl of Moray, in the downcasting of Lochinvar's place of Kenmure." This, of course, from the circumstances, was inoperative.

The "unlaw" of this period was much aggravated by the fact that whilst the government was carried on in the name of James VI., Mary's partisans were the most influential in .Galloway, where, the Sheriff himself being a "queen's man," the "king's men" ran riot. Gradually the former opened their eyes to the hoplessness of Mary's cause, and made their submissions to the regent, but great had been the complications when the royal authority was thus in abeyance. Official documents suggest situations which would seem extravagant in pages of fiction

Sir Alexander M'Kie of Myrtoun was a "king's man," and having insufficient provision for a second son, saw his way of setting him up at the expense of a partisan of the queen's.

Alexander Vaux, when killed at Pinkey, had left as his heiress an infant daughter, Helen, who was brought up by her uncle Patrick (the future Lord of Session), who was out for the queen, leaving his wife and ward in his house of Carscreugh

M'Kie formed the bold plan of seizing this infant heiress and marrying her to his son. It is evident that he secured some assistance through political partisanship, from the fact that the Stewarts of Garlies, the Dunbars, and the Johnstons, the only "king's men" of note in the west, were proved to have been alone cognisant of his intentions.[1]

Under silence of night, on 31st July 1568, a band of M'Kies forced an entrance into Carscreugh, and, despite the elder lady's tears, not only robbed her of her charge, but deliberately plundered the place and premises, carrying away jewellery, ornaments, the family plate, a large sum of money, and the title-deeds.

For this they were formally put to the horn on the 11th of August; but the whole machinery of law was out of gear, and no arrest was made

[1]-Mr. Vans Agnew tells us that the plotting was suspected, and a letter written to put Patrick Vaus on his guard, also that Alexander Stewart younger of Garlies, a week after the outrage was committed, wrote that he had been told that his own father and the Laird of Mochrum were both privy to M'Kie's enterprise —Barnbarroch's *Correspondence*, 47.

It should be premised that immediately after her father's death the gift of Helen's wardship and marriage had been granted to Sir John Bellenden, the Lord-Justice Clerk, so that the aggrieved parties seemed to have unusual facilities for bringing the outrage to the knowledge of the government Nevertheless much delay followed the horning, and it was not for several weeks that the regent despatched special messengers to the sheriffs of Ayr, Galloway, and Dumfries, with warrants for the arrest of the abductors. That to Sir Patrick Agnew is as follows :

"Forsamekle as it is shewn to us that Sir Archibald M'Kie of Myrtoun M'Kie, Patrick M'Kie his brother, Duncan M'Kie, burgess of Quhithorn; John M'Kie, son to Isabel Mure, in Torhouse , Sandy M'Kie (and other household servants named), in maist awful and cruel manner assieged Mr. Patrick Waus's dwelling-place of Carscreugh in his absence, his wyf and his pupill Helene, with convocation of Lieges bodin in fear of weir, and thereafter perforce broke up the doors thereof, and maisterful reft and ravished, the said Helene being under the age of eleven years; had her away with them, and yet uses her in thraldom and captivity at their pleasure , and also theftuously by way of stouthrief, under silence of night, away took furth of his coffers in gold and silver marks the sum of 8000 marks, together with gold and silver work, jewels, and others, to the value of £3000 , and since they, denounced as rebels and put to the horn, yet haunts, frequents, and repairs within the said town of Wigtown, and resorts to kirks and markets, we charge you straitly thir our letters sene, to search, seek, and take them whenever they may be apprehended, and gif any of them pass to strengths and houses to lay siege thereto, and gif they refuse to be taken, or on taking happen slaine, our sheriffs shall not incur danger nor skaith in their persons or goods : And we charge all barronns, gentlemen, and freeholders to assist our said Sheriff of Wigtown and his deputes, under pain to be called assisters in rebellion, as will answer to us thereupon. At Edinburgh from under our signet 7th Sept. 1568 "

A proclamation was consequently made from the market cross at Wigtown, warning all the lieges neither to buy, advance money or goods on, or assist in concealing or disposing of, any of the spoils of Carscreugh; but long before this was read the prize for which the M'Kies had risked their heads was far beyond the sheriff's jurisdiction. Helen was where sheriff-sergeants would find it difficult to follow—in the Johnston's stronghold of the Lockwood. Here the ceremony of marriage between the frightened child and the needy cadet had been gone through before an assembly of persons in good position, not one of whom seems to have protested.

Now what action did my Lord Justice-Clerk take when he heard of this abduction of his ward, whom, if legally entitled to fatten on, he might at least have been expected to protect?

Outrunning the regent's messengers, penetrating with soft words or a silver key the defences of the stronghold which sets all sheriffs' officers at defiance, a limb of the law in his lordship's interest found his way into the inmost recesses of the ladies' bower, and there, before a family circle of Johnstons and M'Kies (who were laughing in their sleeves), as if the Lockwood was her usual home, and ignoring the fact of the marriage, with perfect gravity he stated that the Lord Justice-Clerk, solicitous for the comfort of his ward, had sent him to offer her the choice of four elder sons of good family in marriage, namely those of the Sheriff of Galloway, the Laird of Garthland, M'Culloch of Myrtoun, and M'Culloch of Killeser. The sheriff's son was not of marriageable age; whether the others were so or not we cannot tell. Helen was no longer free to choose; but for this he little cared, having thus publicly, and evidently by preconcerted arrangement, made the above proposal, following it forthwith with a protest as follows:

"Ane honourable man, James M'Clellan of the Nuntown, procurator to ane noble man Sir John Bellendon of Auchinoule, having offered the said Helene to choose whether she would marry one of the four persons stated, equal to her in living and blood, and of the quhilks personis the said Helene refusit to tak ony of them in marriage, wherefore the said M'Clellan claims for the said nobleman the double and treble of the avail of marriage. This done at the Lockwood, about 12 hours of noon, 6th day of Sept. 1658, before thir honourable men: John Johnston of that ilk, James Johnston of Corry, John Johnston of Gretno, David Johnston in the Clairquhite, Herbert Johnston, servant to Mr. Patrick Waux of Cascrew." [1]

The whole affair is scandalous. Sir John Bellenden must have been aware of the impossibility of Helen's compliance; moreover, though he was Lord President of the Council, the M'Kies were never brought to justice.

Shortly after Alexander M'Kie, in whose interest the crime had been committed, wrote to the uncle apologising and offering to make terms. This Patrick Vaux seems to have thought it best to do. The marriage was acknowledged, and 8350 marks given by the guardian as his niece's tocher.

The one redeeming feature in the case is that the M'Kies seem to have used the young lady well, and that her married life was happier than her rough wooing might have led her to expect.

The charter-chest discloses another act of turbulence in the province resulting from the issue of Langside.

Lord Fleming, the great Chamberlain of Scotland, had by a grant, dated 1567, received a-gift of the rents of the Priory of Whithorn, including the lands of Cruggleton, either in co-partnery with, or on the forfeiture of, Malcolm Fleming, the former commendator. But after the queen's defeat the regent's half brother, Robert Stewart (afterwards Earl of Orkney), super-

---

[1] Some recollection of this strange incident seems reflected in a genuine old Galloway ballad Carscreugh is altered to Craignarget, and there are other changes in the names One of these couplets heads the present chapter, the next was as follows —

" Which of these men," they asked her then,
  " That should her husband be ",
But scornfully she did reply,
  " I'll wed nane of the three "
With scorn and pride she answer made,
  " You'll ne'er choose one for me,
Nor will I wed against my mind
For all their high degree "
(At full in Sharpe's rare *Ballad Book.*)

seded both as Commendator of Whithorn. The Flemings refused to give up the abbey lands; and Lord Fleming, mustering his forces, marched off to maintain his pretensions. The sheriff on being appealed to sided with Lord Robert Stewart, and exercising his functions in a style worthy of his great-grandfather, swooped down on the pastures of Cruggleton, and swept off the whole of Fleming's stock upon the disputed lands.[1]

The regent had already written to Barnbarroch : " Traist friend . . . We understand that certane futemen and horsemen ar presentlie cum in Galloway, direct be the Lord Flemyngis, quhilkis intendis or ar alreddy assegeing the hous of Crugiltoun, pertening to our brother the Commendator of Quhithorne. . . . We pray you therefore maist effectuusly, as ye will euir schaw us plesser and guidwill, that with all possible diligence ye convene your kin, freindis, seruandis, . . . and releve our said brother of the said assege, and persew the authouris thairof with all hostilitie.——At Edinburgh, the xxiij of Aprile 1569.—— In traist your assurit freind,   JAMES, REGENT.[2]

Lord Fleming raised the siege, leaving his kinsman Malcolm in the sheriff's hands.

Lord Robert Stewart (a natural son of James V.) was connected with Galloway by his marriage with Lady Janet Kennedy, daughter of the third (good) Earl of Cassilis. He greatly profited by the temporalities of the Church, being Commendator of Holyrood as well as of Whithorn, exchanging some of these with great advantage for those of the Bishopric of Orkney. He was created Earl of Orkney 1581, still drawing an income from Galloway, as in the Great Seal Register there is a letter of provision to Patrick Stewart, fifth son of Robert Earl of Orkney, from the Priory of Whithorn. His half-brother the Regent Murray was murdered 21st January 1570, and succeeded

---

[1] In a testament-dative of Malcolm, Commendator of Whithorn, given up by John Lord Fleming, executor (catalogued among debts doubtful of recovery), are item : By Patrick Agnew, Sheriff of Wigtown, for 17 score yowes and 17 tupes spulziet be him in ye tyme of my being in Cruggleton. Ye said yowes and tupes with the proferts estimat to £1000.——*Cumbernauld Papers.*

[2] Barnbarroch's *Correspondence*, 61. A copy of this letter is in the Lochnaw charter-chest.

by the Earl of Lennox, father of Darnley. He in his turn was
attacked and killed at Stirling, where the gallant Alexander
Stewart of Garlies fell fighting bravely in defence of his kinsman [1]

Meanwhile the fourth Earl of Cassilis, who in the sense of
an unchecked tyrant had come to be called the King of Carrick,
had misdoings of every sort attributed to him.   In the words of
an old history of the Kennedys, "this last Gilbert was a very
greedy man, he cared not how he got land so that he could
come by the same."   He entered into "bloking" (that is
bargaining) with the Abbot of Glenluce for perpetual feu of
some of the abbey lands, but before the deeds were signed the
abbot died.   The earl, fearing his successor might prove less
pliable, "dealt" with a monk who undertook to draw out a
pretended agreement and forged the necessary signatures, armed
with which Cassilis took possession.   Not choosing, however,
to be any way in the power of a libertine monk, "he caused a
carle called Carnochan to stick him," and then fearing the carle
might peach, he moved a relative to accuse Carnochan of theft,
on which he gave him an assize in his own courts and hanged
him.   "And sa," concludes the relator, "wes the lands of Glenluse conqueist." [2]

If the above charges are to be received with a grain of
salt, a tale of daring wickedness issued from the "Black Voute"
of Dunure, which the earl himself never affected to deny.

Shortly after the death of Quentin Kennedy a Master Alan
Stewart obtained the abbacy of Crossraguel, of the temporalities
of which the earl determined to possess himself by fair means or
by foul.   Stewart having taken possession, was, on the morning
of the 27th of August 1570, walking unsuspicously in the wood
of Crossraguel, when he was surprised by Lord Cassilis with
sixteen armed men in his suite, who after some "flattery and
deceitful words" persuaded him to go with him to Dunure; he

---

[1] Alexander Steward, young Laird of Garlies, carried away prisoner, was
slaine, but it is uncertain whether by the enemie or negligentlie by the pursuers.
—Calderwood, iii. 140

[2] Pitcairn, *History of the Kennedys*, p 9.

well knowing that if he refused they would have taken him by
force.   Arrived there, he was for a season honourably entreated,
"gif," as he ingenuously remarked, "a prisoner can think any
entertainment pleasing."   Six persons were specially appointed
to wait upon him; but he felt they were simply his keepers.
From time to time he was civilly asked to sign a feu-charter
the abbey lands (a nineteen and five year tak of the whole
fruits, duties, and teinds, of all the kirks and parsonages pertaining to it); he replying that this was impossible, as he had already
disponed them to "kyndlie tenants"; the earl, finding blandishments fell flat, said, as a ghastly joke, that "he would now prove
whether a collation could work that which his previous good
cheer had not," and had him taken to a secret chamber, with such
as were bidden to the banquet.   In the victim's own words, "On
the first of September, after long boasting, he caused me to be
carried by John Kennedy his baxter, John M'Clue his cook,
Alexander Richardson his pantryman, Alexander Eccles, and Sir
William Todd (chaplain), to the Black Voute, where the
tormentors denuded me of my clothes perforce, except only my
sark and doublet, and then bound my hands at the shackle
banes with a cord, as he did both my feet, and bound my soles
betwixt an iron chimney and a fire.

"The first course was: 'My Lord Abbot, will you please
confess here that with your own consent you remain in my
company,'—'Would you, my lord, that I should lie for pleasure?
It was against my will I came, and against it that I stay.' 'But,'
said the earl, 'you shall remain.'—'I am not able to resist your
will and pleasure.' 'You maun then obey me,' said the earl,
and certain parchments were offered me to subscribe. I declined.
Efter the erle espyed repugnance and that he could not come to
his purpose by fair means, he commanded his cooks to prepare
the banquet.   And first they fleeced the sheep even to his skin;
and next they bound him to the chimney, his legs to the one
end, his arms to the other: and as they began to bait the fire
that the roast should not burn, but might roast in soppe, thye
spared not flambing with oil."

In that torment they held the poor man, " who ofttimes cried, 'Fye upon you ! will ye ding whingares into me, and put me out of the world, or put a barrel of powder under me. There is as meikle gold in my purse as will buy enough to put me out of pain.'

"On this the said earl bade his servant Richard put a serviette in his throat that the voice might be stopped   At length the King of Carrick, perceiving the roast to be enough, commanded it to be taken from the fire ; and the Earl said grace thus : 'Benedicite, Jesu Maria : You are the most obstinate man ever I saw.   Had I known ye wad have been so stubborn I would not for £1000 have handled you so.' "

The half-roasted abbot was however still kept a prisoner. The earl " resorting to the same practices on the 7th of September, which being performed at the 11 hours at night," as the abbot continues, " seeing that my flesh was consumed and burnt to the bone, where through I shall never be well in this life time, I condescended to their purpose, and the Earl got all his pieces subscribet as weel as a half roasted hand could do it " [1]

Kennedy of Bargany, whose sister-in-law was Stewart's wife, hearing of the outrage, had procured "letters of deliverance " from the Court, which the King of Carrick despised, and " for his contempt was put to the horn," he caring as little for the one as for the other

Bargany, who had only been partially informed, getting wind of what had really happened to the abbot, and "perceiving that the ordinary justice could neither help him nor yet the afflicted man," attacked the house of Dunure in such force that he broke in and released the abbot—the earl disappearing by a back way. " The brute," as he is deservedly called in the record, " flew fra Carrick to Galloway, and there so suddenly assembled herd and hyreman that pertained to the band of the Kennedys," that in an inconceivably short time he in turn besieged Bargany

---

[1] Act of Privy Council anent the complaint made by Mr. Alane Stewart   Also *Memorials of Transactions in Scotland from* 1569 *to* 1573, by Richard Bannatyne.

with the abbot in the house of Dunure, beside himself with
rage, and vowing vengeance.

The Laird of Bargany meanwhile had had letters granted him
calling on all the king's good subjects to assist, which found so
ready a response in Kyle and Cunninghame that the servants
of the earl were outnumbered ; " perceiving which, the earl's
brother and the Master of Cassilis in their heat would lay fyre
to the dungeon, with no small boasting that enemies within the
house should die." [1]   Those within remonstrated ; but they per-
sisted in their attempts till " the wind of an hagbut " blasted the
Master's shoulder, when they desisted, and the earl's company
drew back from the house.

Bargany carried the Abbot to Ayr, where, at the market cross
he declared how cruelly he had been entreated, and publicly
revoked the acts done in his extremity.   On the 27th April
1571 the earl was arraigned before the Regent and Lords of
Privy Council at Stirling, who ordered him to be detained until
he found surety in £2000 that neither he nor none that he may
lett shall molest Mr. Alane Stewart."

Beyond this detention, no further punishment was inflicted
for his barbarous act ; but even for this he unblushingly complains
to his kinsman Vaus of Barnbarroch, as if he had been harshly
treated, for the " little matter," as he styles it, between himself
and the abbot.

He even asks for his advice as to whether he may not be
demeaning himself by making any submission to the regent :

" Traist cusin.—I have received no word of you since coming
here. The Abbot has written to me that he is willing the business
take end which is between us, but he has not written in what
manner. The Regent is very urgent in the retaining of me until
I give obedience, quhair I must do after the advice of men of
honour.

" I am somewhat disappointed that you may not have resort

[1] The earl's brother was Thomas, afterwards Sir Thomas Kennedy of Culzean,
tutor to his nephew the fifth earl.   On the failure of the elder branch, 1759, the
title went to his direct descendant, who became ninth earl.

to where I am, that I might confer with you and have your advice on such great affairs as I have to do. I would you should come and speak with me if you could guide me any way.— You assured cusin and good friend,   CASSALIS.

" Off Dumbarton Castle, 26th June " [1]

The end of the whole matter was, that the abbot, despairing of any redress from the government, negotiated through Lord Boyd, who arranged that Cassilis should pay £500 to Stewart of Cairndonald, to whom the abbot had previously feued the land, 3000 marks to the abbot himself, giving a bond of 300 marks to Hugh Kennedy, which Lord Boyd himself had borrowed, for which consideration Lord Boyd undertook to procure the abbot's signature to a charter embodying all the conditions against which he had held out in the Black Voute. The author of the *Historie*, who evidently had not heard all these particulars, states, " My Lord gave the abbot some money to live upon, quhilk contented him." Concluded, "and thus were the lands of Crossraguel conqueist."

We next find the earl himself invoking the law, and that in a manner peculiar to the period, in the case of a supporter of his own, M'Dowall of Garthland, killed in one of the many feuds then carried on. He thus writes to Lord Barnbarroch—

" Cusin.—This is to advertize you that there is a law day appointed against the 27th of April at Edinburgh, on those who are suspected and known to be guilty of the unhonest slaughter of my special friend and servant Uchtred M'Dowall.[2] Whereat I intend, God willing, to be accompanied with such friends and servants as I think needful to that effect, seeing that I can do no less than to suitt and get such remedy as the law will provide ; desiring you, effectuously as you would serve me, to be ready to

---

[1] Bannatyne's *Memorials ; Privy Council Records ;* Barnbarroch's *Correspondence*, p 76   Some of the last deeds mentioned are in Lord Ailsa's charter-chest.

[2] The M'Dowall's of Lochinvar are the parties pointed at   The slaughter of M'Dowall was committed in the struggle of the Gordons with Cassilis for the abbey lands of Glenluce.   There is no record of their appearing to defend the case. At that period all justice was in abeyance.

pass with me, and meet me at Ayr the 6th of April next. I believe nether you nor any other that pertains to me will grudge that journey, any more than if you or any of yours had fallen on such evil handling, which God forbid, I should grudge any labour to see some order done for it.

"I think it meetest *that every man should have his jak.* I commit you to God.   CASSALIS.

"From the Inch, 22d March 1570."

From the above it would appear that the king of Carrick thought, and probably rightly, that the military maxim "Victory usually falls to the largest battalions," was as applicable in his days to battles in the law-courts as in the field.

SEAL OF PATRICK AGNEW, 1575.

CHAPTER XXIV

SUPPRESSION OF PILGRIMAGES

A.D. 1570 to 1584

Ane gat a twist o' the craig;
Ane gat a bunch o' the wame,
Jamie Young got lamed o' a leg,
And syne ran walloping hame.

Border Minstrelsy.

HAVING alienated the affections of the powerful branches of his house, Earl Cassilis seems to have issued from his short detention in Stirling "a sadder and a wiser man." We have seen that from his prison he had entreated the Laird of Barnbarroch to come and see "gif ye may guide me in any wise."

A better counsellor he could not have chosen; Barnbarroch, afterwards his father-in-law,[1] being remarkable during a long life for keeping on good terms with his neighbours; and we may feel assured that it was by his advice that the Earl's first act when released from Dumbarton Castle was to ride straight to his house of the Inch and endeavour to place the relations between the Sheriff and his friends on the footing that they had been with his family of old. His approaches were made in a spirit which ensured success; he offering to grant to the Sheriff and the Lairds of Garthland, Kinhilt, and Myrtoun kyndlie tenancies of a large portion of the Church lands he had acquired in the very questionable way already mentioned.

---

[1] Lord Barnbarroch's mother was Marian, daughter of the second Lord Kennedy. He married first Elizabeth, daughter of Hugh Kennedy of Girvan Mains, who died 1572; and secondly, 1574, Katherine, daughter of the third Earl of Cassilis, sister of the present earl.

Those which came into the sheriff's occupation were Kylfeather, Craigburnoch, and the Dougaries.[1]

Shortly after, the sheriff sublet a portion of these to his second son. We make an extract from the tack, as useful in verifying the family pedigree : "Mr. Patrik Agnew, Sheriff of Wigtown, having in tack and assedation all and haill the lands underwritten of ane nobbell and potent Lord, Gilbert, Earl of Cassalis ;—with express consent and assent of Andro Agnew, my son, lets to my weel beloved second lawful son Patrik, all and haill the lands of Craigberanoche, together with their purtenance and teind charges for the years and terms of 19 years," etc. "Signed at Wigtown the 23d January 1575, before Alexander Agnew of Croach, Gilbert Agnew of Galdenoche, Quentin Agnew my son, and Sir Herbert Anderson, notary-public."

On the 6th of September of the same year the sheriff acquired from John Johnston, Commendator of Soulseat, the lands of Auldbreck, which he, as his father had hitherto, held as tenant to the Church,—in fee-simple.[2]

Transcriptions were made of seisines of Dalzerran, Meikle and Little Toung, Sheuchane,[3] Marsloch, Garchlerie,[3] by which the sheriff had been infefted by precept from the Bishop of Galloway in 1550, and which were now confirmed to him by charters from the state.

---

[1] Kylfeather, Cilpheadair, "Peter's church," or "the piper's grave" ; Craigburnoch, "Creagbearnoch, "cloven craig"; Dougaries, dubh garadh, "black enclosure," *i.e.* peaty soil. The number of clerical names on the lands is remarkable, there being Altaggart and Altibrair, "the priest's and the friar's glen"; Knockiebrair, "the friar's knoll"; Kilmacfadzen, "M'Fadyen's cell or church "; Kilmalloch, "St. Malachy's chapel"; Lagnabanie, beannacht, "the hollow of the benediction."

There is also the Eyes of Kylfeather, from the Norse oe, "a green oasis in the moor"; as well as Larachane, " the side of the red deer"; Altigonskie, "the cuckoo's glen"; with the numerical combinations, Bardeoch (da each), and Altryoch (tri each), "the ridge of the two horses," and "the glen of the three horses."

[2] Charter by Commendator, dated 6th September 1675. Confirmation by the Crown 1586.

[3] Sheuchane, Suidheacan, the little seat ; Garchlerie, Garthclearach, the cleric's enclosure. It is now corrupted to Garthleary.

The principal witnesses to these "transumpts" are · Master Patrick Vaus of Barnbarroch ; Robert Johnnestown, his servant , Alexander Vaus, burgess of Whithorn ; Nevin Agnew, of Craloch ; Gilbert Agnew, of Galdanoch, with many more.

Acts of Parliament were fulminated again and again against the leagues entered into, and the overgrown military establishments resulting from them, kept up by private parties.

" Na person of whatsoever quality, estate, or degree should raise bands of men of war on horse or foot, with pistolets, picks, spears, jaks, splents, steel bonnets, white harness, or other munition, or make sound of trumpet or talbrone, or use culvennes with banners desplayed, under pain of death to the raisers, as also to those who rode with them."[1]   Also that none of the lieges should enter into leagues or bands ; that all bonds of manrent, and that all who gave or took them, should be put in ward.[2]

Acts serving only as historic curiosities, and proving the inveteracy of the offences condemned ; whilst in a somewhat contradictory spirit the government constantly urged the sheriffs to ascertain that every man, gentle or simple, "should be weaponed effeirand to his honour," these weapons to be shown twice in the year, "at sic day and place as shall please the sheriff"[3]

Non-possession of arms was a rare delinquency indeed, but as any attention to law "was long out of use," few of the barons we should imagine troubled themselves to parade at place or time "as it pleased the sheriff," for the Earl of Morton, apparently well aware of this, on becoming regent, immediately issued a proclamation commanding the sheriffs rigidly to enforce such a weaponschawing the incoming year. Further, desiring that such inspection might be held simultaneously over the country, on the 20th July and 10th October 1675. " And further, that none should be obliged to travel

[1] 9 Parl. Queen Mary, chap. 83.
[2] 6 Parl Queen Mary, chap. 43
[3] 6 Parl James V , chaps. 85 and 87.

an unreasonable distance, the sheriffs should furnish names of persons of note to assist them, so that there might be several meeting-places in every shire." For that of Galloway, the sheriff named Sir Alexander Stewart and the Laird of Garthland, who are entered in the record accordingly.

In the autumn of 1575 Katherine, the sheriff's eldest daughter, was married to the heir of Larg, head of the M'Kies, whom Symson writes of " as a very ancient name and family in this country." The marriage-settlements, signed 8th October, are as follows :

"It is agreed, appointed, and finally ended, betwixt the the honourable parties following, to wit : Patrick Agnew, Sheriff of Wigtown, taking burden on him for Katheren Agnew his daughter, on the one part, and Patrick M'Kie of Larg, taking the burden upon him for Alexander M'Kie his son and apparent heir, on the other part, in manner following; to wit, the said Patrick M'Kie of Larg shall infeft the said Alexander his son and Katheren Agnew his future spouse in her viduity in all and haill the lands of Larg (and others) lyand within the Stewartry of Kirkcudbright, and parish of Monygaff, to be holden of our Sovereign Lord the King's Majesty and his successors according to the said Patrick's auld infeftment.

"And the said Patrick Agnew obliges him, his heirs and assignees, to pay to Patrick M'Kie the sum of thirteen hundred merks in name of tocher.

" And attoure gif it happens that the auld lady the foresaid Patrick's guid wife leiff after the yeirs of the said fynding, in that case the said Patrick M'Kie shall find Alexander M'Kie and his future spouse the ane yeir in his house, and the said Sheriff another yeir enduring her lifetime.

" Before these witnesses—Thomas M'Culloch of Torhouse, Patrick Vaus of Barnbarroch, Patrick M'Kie, James M'Kie in Corsbie.   (Signed)   PATRICK AGNEW.
                                    PATRYK M'KIE of Larg."

The Laird of Torhouse was the sheriff's nephew ; Patrick

M‘Kie was the elder brother of Alexander, famous for the abduction of Helen Vaus. The tocher, though only 1300 marks, was large for the times. When the sheriff's eldest son shortly after married the only daughter of Stewart of Garlies he only received 1000 marks with his bride. "The auld lady" mentioned, was Margaret, daughter of Sir Alexander Stewart of Garlies by Margaret Dunbar, heiress of Clugston

On the 14th December 1576 the King of Carrick passed from the scene, leaving a son, a minor, to whom his brother-in-law Lord Glammis became tutor, Hugh Kennedy of Auchterlour managing the estates. But Glammis the chancellor dying in 1578, Sir Patrick Vaus, who the previous January had been nominated one of the senators of the courts of justice, thenceforward called Lord Barnbarroch, assumed entire charge of the young earl's affairs

Hugh Kennedy having taken up house at the Inch, and calculating on the sheriff's reconciliation with the late Earl, endeavoured unadvisedly to renew claims to holding courts at Leswalt, and sent an officer in the chancellor's name to order the attendance at this court of all who owed feudal casualties to the young earl. The sheriff at once deforced the baron-officer, and refused to allow any proclamations to be made in Leswalt court-house but by himself. Hugh Kennedy wrote word of this "to his special lord and master, my Lord of Glammis, concerning the fear of the fermes within the parochins of Inche and Leswalt: I sent an officer in your lordship's name to the effect that payment should be in readiness, and to proclaim the same in writing; the quhilk was taken from the officer by the Sheriff of Wigtown, and he discharged (forbid) the said officer to proclaim any fear[1] there by word or writing, the which I thought good to advertize your lordship of, for I know not the lyk done by any friend or servant of the house of Cassalis. I understand the said sheriff to mislike onything that may work by him in that country of Galloway, to the

---

[1] The money dues.

effect that he may hif things in use to his own commodities, which use he would be leath to be alterit of."

This epistle was fortunately submitted by the chancellor to Lord Barnbarroch (among whose papers it was found), a councillor who above all things was discreet, and who advised his lordship to check the zeal of his subordinate, especially in the matter of the court-house.   It is to be observed that the point in Hugh Kennedy's letter against the sheriff lies in the words "friend and servant of the house of Cassalis"; his holding the lands lately mentioned from the earl in kyndlie tenancy being put forward as a reason for expecting to yield something of his rights.   One sentence of his letter to the chancellor is interesting as an agricultural reminiscence.   "As to the corn in this country, they say it will nocht gif us bot horse corn, quhilk will nocht be worth 20 shillings the boll." But adds afterwards, "Blessed be God we are this year als gude as any countrie is, and no appearance of ony great dearth." [1]

The following letters are partly in connection with the incidents above, and are given as specimens of the sheriff's epistolary style :

LETTER FROM SIR PATRICK AGNEW, SHERIFF OF WIGTOWN, TO THE LAIRD OF BARNBARROCH.

"My lord, eftir my hartlie commendatioun, I resawit your (l) writting fra ane boy of kinheltis,[2] tuichand my awin bissines, that your (l) is catioun for me.   Your (l) sall wit that on my treuth and honestie the tutour hes tane that silwer of the tenentis ; and as for the rest that the tresourar sould haif, I haif

---

[1] Nevertheless Hugh Kennedy seems to have been rather a mischief-maker. He writes to Lord Barnbarroch : "My Lord, I have received your L. writing, declaring that the Sheriff of Wigtown and the Laird of Garflen had offered to my Lord Chancellor 4 marks for every boll of finne maill, and twa marks for every boll of teind maill ; quhereof the Sheriff has made his vaunt in Galloway, and stays the tenant of payment.   I desire your L. that I may make proclamations in your L. name and mine to the effect we be na further scornit or mockit in the country, and nocht to prevail to us.   And gif it be otherwise, prays your L. to advertize me."   The answer is unknown.

[2] Adair of Kinhilt.

wryttin yit as befoir for the sam to master alexr. knowis to maik
sum raleif to me in that.   Me lord, sa laing as I haif land or
gear, your (lo) salbe raleifit as honestie wald godwilling, and
geif I can get na raleif, bot to mak payment, your (lo) man help
me at the tresourar hand, for I haif na other quantancie [1] bot
your (lo) to charg; albeit I haif nocht done my dewtie to your
(lo), your (lo) salbe na losar for me godwilling farther quhair
your (lo) wryt to me to be in edr. the aucht of agust to my
chakar compt, I sall asuire your lordschip I haif nocht gottin
my presept of chakar as tuirsday the penult of this instant; and
as to my compt this yeir, I haif na thing ado bot the supiroritie
of the lady corswall [2] of the tua mark land of knokiname,[3] and
the quarter of the mill of the galdenoche,[4] quhilk my lord
argyllis geift [5] will tak away, that he gat quhen the lard of
corswall died; for scho entret air to hir father [6] quhen he died;
Sua I will nocht be cummerit this yeir.   I pray your (lo) haif
me excusit, for I haif nocht done my dewtie to your (lo); your
lo salbe satisfeit at your cuming to this cuntrie in all thingis to
your (lo) awin contentment, for I haif no other to scharg bot
your (lo), quhen ye haif to do, lyk as I salbe redy to your (lo)
at power on the auld maner.   And sua committis your (lo) to
god.   At lochnaw, the penult of July, be your (l) at power on
the auld maner.   PATRIK AGNEW.[7]

"To my the honorabill and my maist speciall
    my lord of barnbarroche."

---

[1] ? Acquaintance.

[2] Finlay Campbell of Corswall, Chamberlain of Galloway, died in 1565, leaving two grand-daughters co-heiresses.   The elder, Jane, was served heir to her
giandfather, and must be the person here meant.

[3] A farm in Portpatrick parish.   [4] A farm in Stoneykirk parish.

[5] The gift was that of her ward and marriage   Sir Hew Kennedy "oblist"
him to present Jane Campbell, one of the heirs of Corswall, to the Council, the
Earl of Argyle, donatour to her ward and marriage, consenting thereto —Reg
Privy Council, January 1564-65

[6] John Campbell of Lundy —(Ibid   vol i. p. 326.)

[7] Sir Patrick Agnew of Lochnaw succeeded his father as Sheriff of Wigtown
in 1547, and died in 1590   Sir Thomas Kennedy was tutor of Cassilis from
about 1577 till about 1590.   This letter was therefore written between those
dates, but it contains nothing to show in what year.

LETTER FROM PATRICK AGNEW TO SIR PATRICK WAUS, ABOUT 1577 OR 1578.

" My Lord, efter my maist hartle commendatioun, efter my
writing to your L with hew, I reseuit ane writing of my Lord
Chanslaris the xxix day of october, desyring me to be at his L
in edinburch the first of november, quhilk your l may schaw
my Lord Chanslar it was over schort warning. And in respect
I haid appoyntit befoir the dayat betwix his L and the lard of
Lochinvar, as I writ to your L befoir with hew, I could not be
able to keipe his L writing for schortnes of tyme ; Thairfoir
your L man haif me excusit at my Lord chanslar. And farther,
gif my Lord chanslar rydis over the watter, ye may causs his L
speik the comtrollar and thesaurar with your aun diligence,
quhilk I lippen maist to continew my comptis quhill his (L)
bak cuming, and to adverteiss me of his (L) dayat to Edr. agane,
that I may causs the lard of Lochinvar keipe the same ; and
your l anser in writ with the berar, with my hartle commenda-
tiounis to your ladie my ant. Off Lochnaw be your gud frend at
power on the auld manner.   PATRICK AGNEW.

" Your L will delyver this other writing of myne to my Lord
Chanslar, and excuiss the same as your L wysdom thinkis gud.
To my ryt speciall frend my lord of barnbarroch."

There is something hearty in the sheriff's subscription " Your
good friend after the auld manner."   Within a few months of
this, Lord Barnbarroch, as a friend of both parties, assisted in
drawing up the pre-nuptial contract between the sheriff's eldest
son, and Agnes daughter of Sir Alexander Stewart younger of
Garlies (killed, as already stated, at Stirling 1571,) and Lady
Katherine Herries ; the Laird of Garthland with others being
among the witnesses, by which the sheriff bound himself to
infeft " Andrew Agnew my son and apparent heir, and Agnes
Stewart his future spouse, in the lands of Dindinnie and Auchneel." The lady's tocher being 1000 marks, for which her
grandfather, Sir Alexander Stewart, made himself responsible.

Lady Katherine Herries had remarried secondly Wallace of Dundonald, and thirdly M'Dowall of Mindork, which she seems to have regretted ; for we find a letter from her to Lord Barnbarroch, dated " Mundork, 2d day of July " (year unnamed), in which she tells him her husband intends " wodsetting sum land " of her late husband, and " quhat he means to do," she adds, " is contrair to my will and plesor."

In the following generation Mindork passed to the Stewarts, as to which an absurd story is told, that the last laird of the old tower, which has long disappeared, failing to pay certain crown-dues was put to the horn, and that the Laird of Garlies taking advantage of this endeavoured to arrest him, with a view to keeping his land   That the outlawed M'Dowall [1] confided his distress to a publican, who found him a hiding-place near the Spittal of Bladenoch, saying that there the devil himsel would be hard set to find him.   Boniface, however, proved false, and betrayed him to the more powerful laird, who sent a party to seize him, and he showing fight, was roughly treated, and among other indignities his captors singed his beard, and lodged him in Wigtown gaol, where he died, utterly neglected, his body even not receiving Christian burial.   The moral pointed by the story is that Providence did not let the outrage pass altogether unavenged, as henceforth for many generations the beards of the Stewarts were singularly scanty.

It is hardly necessary to point out the absurdity of the whole story.

Alexander Gordon, Bishop of Galloway, died 1576, having founded a family on the spoils of his diocese, styled Gordons of Glenluce   He may have been sincere in his religious convictions, but he had the misfortune to be looked upon, alike by the church he had left and that which he joined, with scant respect. The former styled him " a time-serving heretic ", the latter subjected him to various suspensions, and mortifications innumerable. On the 6th August 1573, he was sentenced to make public re-

---

[1] There is a signature of Uchtred M'Dowall of Mundork to a paper in Barnbarroch charter-chest, date 28th March 1596.

pentance in sackcloth three several Lord's days, and it was only on his making humble entreaty that the sackcloth might not be worn in his own diocese, backed by the regent's personal request, that it was conceded that he should confess his offences in presence of a congregation specially convened in the Abbey Kirk, on a Lord's day, but without sackcloth.

By his wife, Barbara Logie, he had a son John,[1] to whom he resigned his lands, which were confirmed by charter. By the act of annexation of 1587, the lands became vested in the Crown, but were regranted to Laurence Gordon, brother of the above John, by James VI. 1602.

Some odd traditions are preserved of the baronial courts of this family. A certain M'Clumpha and his daughter were there convicted as sheep-stealers, the father's doom being to be hung upon a gibbet till he was dead, and the girl to be branded with S.S.[2]—a legend of very different import across the Border. Whilst awaiting execution of their sentences a "supple rascal" named Douglas, arrested for brawling, was thrust into their cell, and with his assistance they all managed to break out, but were soon re-arrested, and Douglas was condemned to be dragged with them on the hurdle to the gallows, and afterwards to be banished to Barlure. As the three started on their dreary journey, the old man with great *sang froid* made it his dying request that the executioner should brand the lassie as far back as possible, "sae that her mutch may cover the scar." The interest in the tradition lies mainly in following Douglas to his destination—Barlure, the hill of the leper. The spot is mapped by Pont, Libberton, the name giving some colour to the tradition as a spot to which outcasts might be consigned; neighbouring place-names, such as Eldrig of Libberland, and Libberland Burn, all pointing to the fact that wretched lepers

[1] John seems to have resigned in his brother's favour, he being Dean of Salisbury, to whom the property reverted in 1610, and was carried by his only daughter to Sir Robert Gordon of Gordonstown, who disposed of it to the Crown, and the revenues were annexed to the see of Galloway.

[2] The collar of S.S. is that worn by the Chief Justices of England. Dugdale says it is from St. Simplicius. The wearers of the collar of S.S. is a classical style for Chief Justices.

were consigned to this place rather for separation than for
treatment. Ochtreloure was possibly a leper hospital ; Pullour, a
pool, probably supposed to possess some virtue in curing leprosy.[1]
Douglas on his way to his penal residence by the old pack-horse
track leading to Killgalhoch (the church of the standing stones),
before crossing the Tarf would pass the two remarkable standing
stones at Laggangarn.   These were once part of a complete
circle, but having been frequently plundered for building purposes, crosses were cut on the last remaining three, which
were consequently spared.   A strong-minded mason, however,
regardless of the charm, carried off one of them as a lintel
for his house.   Despite all advice he built it in ; but soon
his children sickened and died one by one, his sheep-dog went
mad, and he boldly seized him by the tail and dashed out
his brains against the lintel.   His doom was now sealed ; the
dog bit him in its dying struggles, the fell disease attacked him,
and at his own request his wife and wife's sister " smoored him
atween twa cauf beds."

In 1579, at a Justice Aire in Wigtown, Uchtred M'Dowall
younger of Garthland, is charged with " riding furth and con-
voking the lieges bodin in fear of weir, and with the cruel
slaughter of James Gordon of Barskeoch."   Andrew M'Dowall
of Dalreagle, and George his eldest son, were heavily fined as
abettors in the matter.   These were results of the " dishonest
slaughter " of another Uchtred M'Dowall, mentioned in the last
chapter, for which, even though backed by Cassilis, his relatives
had probably been unable to obtain any redress.

A lively incident of the feud is thus alluded to in a letter
from Lochinvar to Lord Barnbarroch ·   " Efter maist hertlie
commendationis, ye sall wit that the Laird of Barguny and Garthland has come to my friend's house Sanderis Campbell, and has
schot furth of the same his wyff and bairns." [2]

---

[1] I suppose everywhere we find a name containing this word Lobhair (Lour),
we may infer lepers were connected with it —Joyce, ii 80

[2] Barnbarroch's *Correspondence*, p 229.   The parties to this were Uchtred
M'Dowall of Garthland and Thomas Kennedy of Barguny, on the one part ; Sir
John Gordon of Lochinvar, John Gordon of Barskeoch, and Alexander Gordon

The greatest change of the century in the usages of the people at large was now brought about by a series of legislative measures in the name, though hardly in the spirit, of religion

Hitherto kings had vied with one another who could go the oftenest and offer the most at St. Ninian's shrine; special legislation provided for the safety of travellers, even aliens, to the province. Now, a change had come over the spirit of the dream, and in 1581 Acts were promulgated which must have filled the beadles of Whithorn with dismay.

Pilgrimages to St. Ninian's Church, and wells, or crosses, were no more to be resorted to, even those of Medana or St. Columba were prohibited, under severest penalties

The preamble set forth that the dregs of idolatry yet re-remained by usage of pilgrimages to chapels, wells, and crosses, by observing festival days of saints, by singing of carols within and about kirks at certain seasons, and observing certain other superstitious and Papistical rites. For remede thereof the sheriff was to search and seek the persons passing on any such pilgrimages, and apprehend them in the actual deed of transgressing of the Act, and condemn them, Ilk gentleman or gentlewoman landed in a £100, the unlanded in 100 marks, for the first offence; and for the second the offenders to suffer the pain of death as idolaters. Superstitious observers of saint days, and singers of carols, when caught in the act were to be put in prison, and speedy judgment passed on them by the sheriff, and if not able to redeem their persons by fine then to be kept in prison, irons, or stocks, upon bread and water, for a month at the least, and then to find caution for better behaviour.[1]

The sheriffs were to receive one-half of the fines, the other half to go to the poor of the parish   The framers of this statute, who had laudably struggled to have the Bible brought within the reach of all in the vulgar tongue, had been strangely oblivious of the toleration which its pages inculcate, and of the charity "not easily provoked."

of Portencorkerie, on the other. All were bound over to keep the peace. October 1579.   [1] Seventh Parliament James VI., chap. 104.

Many of the superstitions they laboured to remove were truly ridiculous; but it was simply wicked that their exercise by quiet inoffensive persons should bring them within reach of the hangman. Happily their bark was worse than their bite, and though not a few Popish priests suffered death for administering the mass, we have read of none executed for bringing their children to holy wells.

So deeply, however, were these usages ingrained in the habits and traditions of the people, that though these laws frightened people from parading such practices in public, for long the wells especially were privately visited at particular days and hours; and no doubt in certain nervous diseases cures were effected in those who implicitly believed in their efficacy. Of such wells we can mention but a small proportion · Near Lochnaw was Kilmorie, St Mary's well, "to which," as Symson writes a century later, "people superstitiously resorted" St. Columba's well, known also as the Crosswell (though this has no connection with the name of Corswall), was in the parish which he names Kirkcolm; in which also was St Bride's well, besides a dedication to her as Kilbride   There is St. Malloch's well at the foot of Tapmalloch (tiebh-malloch), "the hillside of St. Malachy o' Morgair," whence he watched for a vessel coming for him from Bangor; below it Tringan, St Ninian's, or Ringan's well; and a little farther on the Culdees' well, at Knockaldy (cnoc-ceilede).   A few miles farther on, in Dunskey Glen, is St. Kain's well, whence the name Ochtriemakain (ma and mo indicating a saint), his name interesting as connecting Galloway with Cornish tradition, where St. Keyn is identical with Cainnech or Canigus of the Scoto-Irish Church.   In Cornwall the tradition attaching to St. Kain's well is, that if a bridegroom on his wedding-day drinks from it before his bride he will be master; but that, if the lady gets the first draught, the gray mare will be the better horse.   By Chappell Patrick there was St. Patrick's well; and at Stranraer St. John's well, below high-water mark, was in much repute   In Stoneykirk and Glenluce there were two St. Katherine's wells, and a third in Kirkmaiden, its name strangely disguised in the corruption Kibbertie Kite, though really the chief alteration is in the change of the initial K for T (Tiobar-tighe-Ceat), "Katherine's well house." What makes the identification certain is that "St. Kathcrine's croft" (so mapped) adjoins. Near Kibbertie Kite is Chipper dingan. Here again we have St. Ninian's name in an unusual disguise, the conventional R being changed to D. But this substitute is not without ecclesiastical authority, as Geoffrey Gaimer writes .

> A Witernam (Whithorn) gist Saint Dinan
> Longtens vint devant Columban.[1]

Near the last two there is Muntloch well;[2] and another, St. Bride's; and a still more famous one, really Medana's, but known as "Well of the Co," largely resorted to within the memory of the present generation on the first Sunday in May. Across the Bay of Luce, in the other Kirkmaiden, now a part of Glasserton parish, is the Chincough well (whooping-cough) well, whose original source flowed from the eyeballs of St. Medana, "superstitiously resorted to" long after the passing of the Acts In Kirkinner was Malie's well, sacred to St. Patrick's nephew Malidh, who names the Water of Malzie Besides others too numerous to mention, there was the Gout well in Minigaff, Mount Horeb well in Kirkmabreck, the "Brownie's well," Dalry , St. Mungo's well, Carsphain; St Lawrence's, Colvend.

The cool indifference of a Galloway baron to summonses from law courts is amusingly illustrated in a case in which the sheriff himself was defendant.

Bishop Gordon had claimed certain sums from him as teinds of Church property in Glenluce; but as the bishop himself had secularised and appropriated many of these, the sheriff, thinking

---

[1] *Estoire des Engles*, Geoffroi Gaimar, eleventh century

I am indebted for this identification of St. Ninian as Dinan, i e. Dingan, to Sir Herbert Maxwell.

[2] About a mile and a half from the parish kirk is a well called Muntluck well, in the midst of a little bog, to which persons have recourse to fetch water for such as are sick, asserting that if the sick person shall recover the water will so buller and mount up when the messenger dips in his vessel that he will hardly get out dry shod

he should have *his* share in the spoil, declined to pay. The bishop dying in 1576, his widow remarried Alexander Gordon of Grange, who, discovering this debt to the late bishop's estate, conjointly with his wife raised an action against the sheriff, and obtained a decree for the amount. To this the sheriff opposed a passive resistance, and did nothing, whereupon "letters of horning" were raised against him, but with no further effect.

A year and a day elapsed, and under the renewed application from Gordon, the court declared the liferent of his estate forfeited to the king. Nevertheless, the sheriff kept possession : the sum probably was small. From his papers we find he had no difficulties as to money, but he was simply contumacious ! Presently, however, his eldest son, being about to receive a commission as justiciar, thought it unseemly that his father should remain under the category of those with whom that commission enjoined him specially to deal, and either paid it out of his own pocket or induced his father to compromise, resulting in his getting as a grant from the Crown the escheat of Lochnaw in his own favour. The whole proceeding reads like a legal farce, Sir Patrick being apparently neither the better nor the worse for the settlement.

"Under our privy seal, at Haliruid Hous, the 3d of March 1584: Wot ye us to have given to our lovit Andro Agnew younger of Lochnaw his heirs and assignees the escheat of all guids moveable and unmoveable, debts, tacks, steadings, rowmes, possessions, corns, cattle, insicht plenishing, acts, contracts, actions, obligations, reversions, decreets, sentences, sums of money, jewels, gold, silver, coined and uncoined, and other goods and geir whatsoever, which appertained of before to Patrick Agnew of Lochnaw, and now pertaining to us, falling and deciding in our hands and at our disposition be the laws and practice of our realm; and the liferent, mails, farms, profits and duties of all lands, tenements, and annualrents, which appertained before to the said Patrick Agnew of Lochnaw, *holden by him immediately of us*, induring the said Patrick's lifetime which now appertains to our disposition by our Acts of Parliament, through the said Patrick wilful and obstinate lying and remaining under the process of horning without lawful relaxation, attour the space of a year and a day next after that he was denounced our rebel and put to our horn, To be halden and to be had the escheat goods and the liferents by the said Andrew Agnew."

Far from the sheriff being in any disgrace at Court through these irregularities, we find him named as taking a prominent part as an assizer in the trials consequent on the defeat of the conspiracy known as the Raid of Ruthven, in which his friend M'Dowall of Garthland was gravely implicated

The so-called raid was the seizure of the young king's person by Ruthven, Earl of Gowrie, and his accomplices (in 1582), to compel him to dismiss his favourites the Earls of Arran and Lennox   It was momentarily successful, but ended in the discomfiture of all concerned.

The state trials consequent commenced in 1584, and lasted many months.

On the panels of assize were the Master of Cassilis, Patrick Agnew, Sheriff of Galloway, John Gordon of Lochinvar, William M'Culloch of Myrtoun.[1]   It is noteworthy that Sir John Gordon was at first placed on another panel, but was challenged by Lord Gowrie himself, the reason alleged being the enmity known to exist between Garthland and Lochinvar.

The Laird of Garthland, who had first married a Kennedy of Girvan Mains, on her death had remarried a daughter of Lord Methven, sister of the Countess of Gowrie   Most of those implicated lost their lives, but Garthland managed to escape and never returned, his enforced exile bringing the feud with the Gordons to a close   This trial was followed by a non-political one, in which Patrick M'Kie of Whitehills was charged with "forging, feuzening, and stryking false moneys. half-marks, 30s., 20s, 10s, and 40-penny pieces." The assize, by mouth of William M'Culloch of Myrtoun, found him guilty "of counter-feiting the half-marks and 40d pieces in great quantity," but

[1] Pitcairn's *Criminal Trials.*

acquitted him of the other charges : a qualification by which he took little, being sentenced "to tynt life, lands, and goods, and to be hanged at the market cross of Edinburgh.[1]

Great cordiality existed between the sheriff and Sir Thomas Kennedy of Culzean, a letter from whom we insert thanking the sheriff for his having become security for some of his kin and dependants for money due to them, assuring him he will take care that he shall not be the loser

LETTER FROM SIR THOMAS KENNEDY OF COLZEAN TO THE SHERIFF OF GALLOWAY.

"Traist freind, efter my hartlie commendationes, I ressauit your lettre, and consideris be the same that the laird of barnbarocht is ernest with you for that hundreth pundis that he wes cautioner for.   It is trew my seraundis hes ressauit ane part of it , alwyiss I sall relief yow at the laird of barnbarochtis handis howsone he cumis to edr., and thairof ye salbe certane without langar delay.   And as to the males, quhilkis he craveis out of the barony, as I persaue be thair lettre, he willbe awand me twyss alsmekle malc out of glenluce, quhilk salbe allowit to him, ane part of the ane for the other.   Alwyiss nather ye nor the tennentis sall ressaue truble for ony of thir causis.   Swa that howsone he cumis to edr. ye salke fred.   Haveing na forder occasionn for the present, I committ yow en godis protectionn. Off blaknes this satirday Be youris assurit freind,

"THOMAS TUTOR OF CASSILLIS.

"To my richt traist friend the Sereff off Galloway."

[1] Pitcairn's *Criminal Trials.*

CHAPTER XXV

THE ARMADA

A.D. 1584 to 1598

> Go tell it in Wigtoun, in Carrick, in Kyle,
> Although the proud Dons are now passing the Moil,
> Wi' this magic clue
> Of the indigo blue
> That Eleine de Aggart has at her command
> A foreign foe never shall win to our strand

To check the lawlessness generally rampant, Government, feeling itself somewhat stronger, issued a commission of Justiciary of Wigtown to the sheriff's eldest son, who had previously been associated with him in his office.[1]

Entrusting him thus with privileges overshadowing those of Sheriff Principal, there being no reservation in his jurisdiction of the former pleas of the Crown, the said commission prefaced with the words: "As we are certainly informed that there are very many persons in our shire of Wigtown who cannot behave orderly, we therefore appoint our lovit Andrew Agnew our justiciar in these parts, giving him full power from us of holding courts, and of continuing them, as often as need is, and of causing all to be summoned who owe suit, amerciating the absent, and indicting persons accused."[2]

His selection for such an appointment requiring a cool head

[1] Among the Barnbarroch papers we find that Sir Patrick Vaus requiring a decreet of removal against certain of his tenants, carried his case before "ane honourable man, Andrew Agnew, Sheriff of Galloway, 23d May 1586."

[2] The commission, which is under the quarter seal, constitutes him our justiciar in that part known as the Sheriffdom of Wigtown, for a term of nineteen years. It is dated "From Halyrude House, 30 April 1586."

and unflinching courage proves him to have acquired a name for energy and capacity. It was doubtless to his advantage that he had a Stewart of Garlies for his wife and a Gordon of Lochinvar for his mother, so that he might calculate on the support of these two powerful rival factions; and, what was pleasing in the result, he seems consequently to have had a hand in their reconciliation[1] Moreover, some time before his brother-in-law Lochinvar had been appointed Justiciar of the Stewartry, the disorders of the time were aggravated by the disaffection of many men of position, engendered by the severity of the laws against Roman Catholics.

Lord Maxwell was imprisoned for allowing a single mass to be said at Lincluden Abbey on Christmas Day, and was only liberated on the impolitic condition that he should instantly leave the country. He did so, and going to Spain, in his wrath urged the king to utilise the Galloway ports for the purpose of invasion, undertaking to make a diversion in his favour.

In the meantime King James VI. appeared in person on the Galloway marches, summoning justiciars, sheriffs, and steward to meet him at Lochinvar. The sheriff and his son received him. Lord Maxwell was necessarily absent. The king pushed on to Kirkcudbright, where the party were doubtless entertained by the Laird of Bomby, brother-in-law to both the Sheriff of Galloway and Lochinvar. It was on this occasion that the king presented to the burgh the famous "siller gun" as an heirloom, which bears on its barrel the initials T. M. C. for Sir Thomas M'Clellan, and the date 1587.[2]

The next year Maxwell suddenly appeared in Galloway, and believing the Armada to be close behind him, hoisted his flag at his castles of Threave, Caerlaverock, and Lochmaben

---

[1] Grizzel Gordon, daughter of Sir John and niece to the elder Lady Agnew, married Alexander, first Earl of Galloway, nephew of the younger Lady Agnew, the justiciar's wife

[2] In some accounts the year of the king's visit is stated to be 1588, but the date on the gun itself, 1587, seems conclusive The Galloway historian speaks depreciatingly of the trophy: "This trinket, like a penny whistle seven inches in length, has been only shot for three times in the memory of the oldest inhabitant"—Mackenzie, i 529.

He was mistaken indeed. As he vainly scanned the horizon to the westward for the coming Spaniards, the dust of the king's squadrons announced their advancing from the east. Maxwell fled, and hurriedly embarking in a ship at St. Mary's Isle, stood out for the Irish Channel in his hopeless quest. Sir William Stewart, brother of the Laird of Garlies, was at his heels, and unmooring another vessel, gave chase, and ran him to ground on the seaboard of Carrick.

The king's troops bringing artillery with them, Threave and Caerlaverock instantly struck their colours. Lochmaben held out for another day, but before the evening of the second, cannon having forced its defences, David Maxwell, its keeper, dangled from the castle gate.

As it proved, the Armada went by the way of the English Channel, only appearing on the Galloway shores in a condition of hopeless discomfiture, as to which there are some dim traditions, particles of truth underlying the spurious element.

That best authenticated is that a first-class man-of-war was driven ashore in the Bay of Luce, near Portwilliam, at a spot mapped "Philip and Mary Point"

A second was said to have been wrecked under Cruggleton Castle, and that a stallion getting ashore was the progenitor of the Galloway breed.

A third is believed to have been driven on the Ardwell shore, and Float Bay is said to take its name from the wreckage , and this local. quidnuncs hold to be further proved by the adjoining place-name, "Money Head," derived, as they say, from the doubloons which were to be gathered there by the handful when the ship broke up.

Nothing can be more absurd than all these latter statements. Not only did Shakespeare write "Know we not Galloway nags?" but they were praised by Froissart two centuries before the building of the Armada.[1]

[1] Taylor, who should have known better, adopts this absurdity, and under head of words derived from place-names, names Galloways, writing, "One of the galleons of the Armada, which had succeeded in weathering Cape Wrath, was lost on the coast of Galloway, and tradition avers that a Spanish stallion rescued

"Money Head" is an attempted translation of Barnammon, and Cairnmon (Cairn nam ban) the woman's, *i e.* the "witch's cairn"; Jeanie's Cairn, close by, being another attempted rendering; the "women" in such names implying either fairies or witches.

Tradition credits local witches (though of a far later date than those which named these places) with assisting in the defeat of the Armada. Elsie M'Taggart, immortalised by Train as Eleine de Aggart,[1] was believed to have watched for ship after ship as they rounded the Mull of Cantyre, perched on a rock, holding a blue ball of worsted in her hand, which as she unwound the storm became more and more serious, until at last they sank into the seething waves under her spell.

A few sentences from a letter of Lady Katherine Vaus to her son-in-law Kennedy of Barquhanny, taking charge in her absence, gives us some inkling of the cares of a housewife of the period

"Ye write me that ye have gotten aucht mais of herrings for Barnbarroch; we must hold us content of the same for this year. I pray you fail not, but gar make us 12 bolls of meal and half a, brewing of double ale against our hame-ganging, and God preserve you. Further, I pray you not to fail to send me out silver with the first that comes, for we are very skant thairoff. Also ye shall receive rattoun poison and gae give the same to the rats—Yours at power.

"DAME KATHERINE KANNADY,
Lady Bairnbarroch.

"Off Edinburch, 23 Februar 1506."[2]

The last sentence absolutely contradicts Symson's assertion

from the wreck became the ancestor of the strong and serviceable breed of Galloways "—Taylor's *Words and Places*, 5th Edition, 285.

We might answer him with Pistol, "Thrust him downstairs! Know we not Galloway nags?"—Shakespeare, *Henry IV*, act iv sc 2.

[1] Train's *Mountain Bard*. It need hardly be repeated that Float has no connection with wreckage, being old Saxon fledt, "where a vessel can float," marking a naval station of the Northumbrian Saxons.

[2] Barnbarroch's *Correspondence*, 345.

that rats were unknown in Kirkinner before his coming there a century later.[1]

The Lady Katherine's husband had in 1587 been one of the ambassadors who negotiated the marriage of Princess Anne of Denmark, which having been solemnised by proxy, the young king, in daily expectation of her arrival, writes thus to the Laird of Barnbarroch :

" At Edinburgh, the penult day of August 1589. The Queen our bedfellow being hourly looked for to arryve, we earnestly desire that ye will send hither to the help of the honourable charges to be made in this action, sic quantity of fate beef and muttoun on fute, wild fowlis, and vennysonn or other stuff meet for this purpose, as possibly ye may provide and furneiss of your awen, or be your moyane, and expeid the same here with all diligence after the receipt of this one letter."

But before the hampers could be packed, all this was countermanded. News had arrived that the royal bride was storm-stayed in Norway, and Sir Patrick was ordered at once to attend the king thither They went to Norway accordingly, and reaching Upsala the 19th November, we are told that the king immediately at his coming "past quyetlie with buites, to hir hienes. His majestie myndit to give the Queine a kisse efter the Scottis faschioun at meiting, quhilk scho refusit as not being the forme of hir countrie.   Marie ! efter a few wordis prively spoken betwix his majestie and hir, thair past familiaretie and kisses." [2]

They were married on the 24th November, but did not return to Scotland till May-Day of the following year ; immediately after which, in recognition of his services, Lord Barnbarroch was given " the advocation, donation, and right of patronage of the kirks of Kirkinner, Kirkcowan, Cammanell, and Wigtown."

About this time Thomas Hay, late Abbot of Glenluce, settled on secularised church lands, and took the style of Park.   His

---

[1] In the Presbytery of Wigtown, although we have mice good store, we have no rats —Symson's *Large Description.*

[2] Moysie's *Memoirs,* p 80 ; Barnbarroch's *Correspondence,* 377.

son, who hád married a daughter of the Laird of Garthland, built the house so called, which still stands, though used only as a farmhouse, placing over the doorway the inscription : " Blessit be the name of the Lord, this verk vas begun the first day of March 1590, be Thomas Hay of Park, and Janet Makdoval his spouse." [1]

Consequent upon the assumption of church property by the Crown, royal charters were granted to the Agnews of Lochnaw of the lands of Kerronrae and Marsloch, which had been held from the bishops, as well as of the office of the bailliene of Soulseat.[2]

This office carried jurisdiction over Portpatrick, the landward part of which parish was then known as the " Black Water of the Inch," although it was not constituted a separate parish until 1620, when Chapel Patrick became its kirk. On its extinction the revenues of the Abbacy of Soulseat amounted to £343 : 13 : 4 silver rent, 13 chalders and 4 bolls of meal, 7 of bear, 6 of oats, 1 lb of wax, and 13½ dozen capons.

In connection with the secularisation of these abbey lands, we find an inquisition held by the justiciar on the 30th November 1589, " in Pretorio," as his court-house of Wigtown is termed, to ascertain the values of the church lands of the Inch. The principal interest in the document lies in the names of the assizers in the roll, as follows ·_

" Before the most honourable Andrew Agnew, Sheriff, in the court-house of Wigtown, with Gavin Dunbar of Baldoon, and Alexander Agnew of Croach his deputes, there sat the following : Alexander Ahannay of Sorby, Alexander Gordon, Tutor of Craighlaw ; Simon M'Christine of Clonche, John Ahannay younger of Sorby, William Kennedy of Gillespie, Patrick M'Kie of Larg, Pattrick M'Kie of Drumbuie, Gilbert M'Clanachan in

[1] M'Dowall MSS., to which Cranford adds "She was the youngest that was married to Parke, and not verie sprightly."
[2] Kerronrae (Ceath-ramhaidh Riabhach), the gray quarter. The charter of confirmation under the Great Seal dated 12th May 1587, in favour of Patrick Agnew, Sheriff of Wigtown, recapitulates the lands of Marsloch, Kerronrae, Clendrie, Sheuchan, Garchlerie, and Holymark, as granted by Alexander, Bishop of Galloway, to the said sheriff, 14th July 1566

Culerain, Gilbert Boyd of Leswalt, Fergus M'Clanachan in Machquhar, John M'Culloch 'of Torhouse, John Gordon of Crequhan, Robert Maxwell, brother of John Maxwell of Mureith ; John Dunbar of Midwig."

About this time the sheriff's third son, Patrick, became Laird of Barmeill (a name which may be translated "the top of the hill"), the lands all in Glasserton parish ; and he afterwards acquired those of Wigg, founding the branch of the family so called.

In days when the number of kinsmen able to "ride and gang" with him added greatly to the prestige of the family chief, it was of no small interest to the sheriff that the various cadets of his family should prosper.[1] And besides the acquisition of these lands by his son, Agnew of Croach now found the wherewithal to purchase the lands of Culmalzie from the Commendator of Whithorn, whilst Agnew of Galdenoch had a purse sufficiently well filled to be able to accommodate the powerful Laird of Barnbarroch.[2]

In the Barnbarroch charter-chest we find an odd contract between "the Laird of Barnbarroch and Sir Andrew Agnew, Sheriff of Wigtown, dated at Glenluce 29th March 1588," by which the Laird of Barnbarroch, taking burden on him for John his son and apparent heir . . . touching the thieves apprehended with red hand in the barony of Mochrum Loch, the profit of their escheat shall be equally divided betwixt both parties, their respective officers to have free power in searching and ryping in the said lands, but stop or impediment.—John Hannay of Kirkdill, James M'Culloch of Drummorrell, witnesses."[3]

[1] From the chief family of Agnew of Lochnaw there sprang various families who constituted much of the baronies of Wigtownshire —*Caledonia*, iii 395.

[2] In the Barnbarroch charter-chest is a discharge by Gilbert Agnew of Galdenoch to Thomas Kennedy of Barjarg for £100 on behalf of Mr. Patrick Waus of Barnbarroch, "quha was adebted to me for the same. Gilbert Agnew, 22nd April 1583."

[3] Under the date 11th July 1588 there is a letter from the Clark Register to the Right Honourable the Sheriff of Galloway, asking him to exempt the Laird of Barnbarroch from taxation as being a Lord of Session.

Ninian Adair of Kinhilt had a large family, and a prosperous one, by Elizabeth of Lochinvar, sister of the Lady of Lochnaw. His second son became Laird of Maryport, his third of Curghie; his fourth was successively Dean of Raphoe and Bishop of Killaloe, of Waterford, and of Lismore. His fifth son is styled of Cardrine, a small estate near the Mull of Galloway.

In a letter dated from Lochnaw 29th November 1582, the sheriff addresses him as "brother", tells him he has been saying a good word "concerning your plea" to the young Laird of Mochrum and the Laird of Barnbarroch, and signs himself "your brother at power, Patrick Agnew."

During Sir Patrick's sheriffship, the Hathornes—written also Halthorne and Hawthorn—established themselves in Airies. The name occurs as far back as in the Chamberlain Rolls 1455, in which the Chamberlain accounts for "15 bolls farinæ avenaticæ (oatmeal) of the escheat of David Halthorn. "Quentin Halthorne and Alexander Halthorne" were summoned "to compeer before the Lords of Council, 22 Jan. 1484,—and compeered not." The family became kyndlie tenants of the lands of Airies under the Church, and on the 6th November 1562, we find a bond of maurent between Harry Hawthorne of Airies and Alexander Waus of Barnbarroch. "Harry Hawthorn becoming servant to the said Alexander Vaus, to ride and gang with him in all his leisum causes and actions; for which cause the said Alexander gives to the said Hary his parsonage of his 6-merk land of Mickle Aries, for the yearly payment to him of 14 marks.

"Simon M'Culloch of Myrtoun; Patrick Mure of Cairnfield; Alexander M'Culloch of Kyllasser; Alexander Vaus and Sir Herbert Anderson, notary public, witnesses"

A Michael Hawthorne was a "reader in Toskerton" in the first list of reformed clergy, probably the brother of Harry, mentioned with the clerical "sir," by Lord Barnbarroch in a letter to his agent: "Always ye will remember to provide Sir Michael Hawthorne's silver against Paice (Easter) at the latest. 9 Feb 1586."

The Hawthornes acquired Airie Hemming in the parish of Glenluce, retaining Airies till the present century. Eventually John Hawthorn of Airies married in 1738 Agnes Stewart of Physgill, and took her name. His descendants are the Stewarts of Glasserton

Beyond the mere mention of the second hereditary sheriff having been employed in negotiations with the Regulus O'Neill, A.D. 1460, there is no record of any communication kept up by the Agnews with the north of Ireland. In an historical notice, however, it is assumed as notorious that some of the Scottish baronage in the west held lands in Ireland. It is as follows . "A D. 1540, King Henry VIII. takes the title of King of Ireland, whereat King James somewhat grumbles, but keeps himself quiet in respect King Henry makes no use of this title for expelling the Scots there from their inheritance." [1]

The question of the Agnews' possession of Larne still remaining entirely dependent on tradition, and that especially Irish.

Forty years later, however, such Scots as had land there had a more active foe in a Celt from their own side of the water, "Sorley Boye," [2] by whom Anglo-Norman and Lowland Scots were alike termed the Sassenach. To him Queen Elizabeth made a more vigorous resistance than James V., sending Essex with a large force to confront him; but the picturesque barbarian made good his hold of the seaboard from Strangford Loch to the Giant's Causeway.

The queen afterwards accepted his submission; and James VI. treated his son with great distinction, eventually creating him Earl of Antrim (in 1603), with the over-lordship of the entire regions known as "The Route" and "The Glynns," extending

---

[1] Balfour, i. 272

[2] This was Somhirle M'Donnell. Somhirle or Somerled, a name composed of two Norse words, Sumar lidi, "summer soldiers or wanderers," equivalent to sea-kings or vikings The name has been incorrectly rendered Charles, and still more so Samuel. Sorley Boye is the golden-haired Somerled

That part of Antrim extending from Ravel Water northward, at the present day "The Route"—Latin ruta—is considered to be a corruption of the latter part of Dalradia

landwards from Larne to Coleraine. Connected with this there seems indirect evidence of the Agnews having been ancient owners of a part of these domains, in that one of the first acts of Sir Randall M'Donnell, the son in question, before he was created an earl, was to offer Sir Patrick Agnew leases of various townlands in the baronies of Glenarm and Larne.

The last notice we find of the sixth sheriff is an entry in the Privy Council Records of special commissions granted to Patrick Agnew of Lochnaw, Sheriff of Wigtown; John Kennedy of Blairquhan, Sheriff of Ayr, and John Gordon of Lochinvar, Sheriff (sic) of Kirkcudbright, to convene the freeholders for choosing commissioners to meet at Edinburgh the 6th October following, and to report the result of the elections.

The sheriff died in 1590. The first of his line buried in the churchyard of Leswalt with Protestant rites. He left, besides his heir, Patrick of Sheuchan (reproduced by his grandson), William of Barmeill; Thomas, whose son was heir of his uncle William, Quentin, who had various properties near Stranraer; Alexander of Ardoch in the Stewartry, then sheriff-depute; and two daughters—Katherine, the Lady of Larg, and Helen, wife of John M'Dowall, presumably of Garthland [1] Gilbert Agnew of Galdenoch, in virtue of two Crown precepts, invested his eldest son in his lands and rights, the ceremonies extending over two days—the 22d and 23d April 1590. The witnesses the first day being David Kennedy, Alexander Agnew of Croach, James M'Ewen in Leswalt, Robert Boyd in Largbrak, George M'Callum, and Niven Adair younger of Kinhilt. On the second, Nevin Agnew in Mais, William Dunbar in Culmalzon, Finlay M'Cracken, Patrick M'Kie, William Gordon in Bernernie, William Agnew, brother-german of the sheriff; Thomas M'Dowall, Alexander M'Dowall, Michael M'Cracken, notary to sheriff-clerk. [2]

[1] There is a charter in the Great Seal Register of the lands of Portensak (Portnessoch) to John M'Dowall and Helen Agnew his spouse, 20th January 1581.

[2] Both charters in the Great Seal Register. Largbrak, Lairbrax; Mais, Maize, Cymric maas, "meadow", Barnnernie (n-airne), "hill-top of the sloe bush."

The seventh sheriff as justiciar had already gained himself a good name by his activity, and at the date of his succession the local historian relates "that the condition of the inhabitants had considerably improved   Law had assumed some vigour, and both the persons and property of individuals were held more sacred.   The execution of justice had become more certain, and the chances of escape diminished.   The courts of justiciary had principally contributed to produce this salutary change in Galloway." [1]

In recognition of his services he was moreover appointed Chamberlain of Galloway, an office of considerable emolument, and which, except in his case, had never been conjoined with that of sheriff.   His accountings, as preserved in the Chamberlain Rolls, extend continuously from 1595 to 1609.   He was knighted previous to the earlier date.   We doubt if he considered this a privilege, but rather as an attempt of the heralds for extracting a fee.   It is observable that all the principal Galloway lairds registered as knights, such as Garlies, Lochinvar, Myrton, and the sheriffs, never use the "sir" in their signatures, considering the baronial position the more honourable, except in the case of being conferred personally by the sovereign for service in the field   The knightly prefix is invariably given to the clerics, and often to the notaries public.   In 1591 we find the sheriff serving Sir Patrick Vaus heir to George, Bishop of Galloway (his good-sire's brother), who had died at the age of ninety at least, in 1570.   The record is as follows .

"The Sheriff's head court at Wigtown, holden in the Tolbooth of the same be ye honourable Andrew Agnew, Sheriff of Wigtown, the 12th day of October 1591.

'. *Suits called.* — The court affirmed absence amerciate · Dempster, Patrick Wardlaw.

---

[1] Mackenzie, vol. ii p 2

The Privy Council Records supply many facts useful in filling in the links in pedigrees   Thus 1592 : " Bond by Andrew Agnew, Sheriff of Wigtown, that James M'Kie of Drumbuy shall not harry Alexander Gordon, Tutor of Craighlaw. Subscrivit at Lochnaw, 3 July, before Archibald Gordon and Alexander Agnew "

Jurors.

George M'Culloch of Torhouse.
Patrick Hannay of Kirdaill.
William Dunbar in Culmalzow.
Alexr. Gordonn, apparent of Balcray
Simon M'Christine of Clonsche
Gilbert Gordon of Polmallairt
Malcolm M'Kie in Dyrrie.

William Campbell of Kerrintray.
Harrie Halthoirne of Aries.
Mr. William M'Gowyne, Commissar
of Wigtown.
Johnne Baillie in Dunragat.
John Ramsay of Boghouse.
William Muir, tutor of Cairnfield

" The quhilk day compeerit the right honourable Sir Patrick Waus, Barnbarroch, desiring the honourable inquest above written, to serve him as nearest and lawful heir-male to umquhile and Reverend Father in God, George Wawss, sometime Bishop of Quhithorne, quha decesit the year of God 1570. Our Sovereign Lord's brief verified be William M'Culloch, king's officer upon the 28th day of September last.

" The said inquest passed furth of Court as the use is being rypelie advicit, with the said brief and claim ; and on entering again all on ane voice, but variance, servit the said Sir Patrick as heir-male nearest and lawful to the said umquhile George conforme to the said claim."

On this, Mr. Vans Agnew remarks : "This good-sire succeeded in 1482 ; therefore at that date his Father and the Bishop's was dead, and this Bishop George must have lived for nearly 90 years." [1]

But, as seen in our pages, Bishop George Vaus was brother-in-law to the present (the sixth) sheriff's great-great-grand-mother, which Mariotta became Lady of Lochnaw in 1469; at which date she must have been somewhere about nineteen years of age, and it is highly improbable that George could have been more than twenty years younger than his sister, or that he was consecrated bishop before he was himself thirty-three. On either of which calculations he seems certainly to have been a centenarian. [2]

In 1591 the Laird of Larg died, leaving to his widow, the

---

[1] *Correspondence of Sir Patrick Waus*, Introduction, p 34

[2] The startling fact being that Bishop George Vaux died 101 years after his sister was married and established as Lady of Lochnaw

sheriff's sister, the whole of the revenues of Larg and other
lands. On the 13th of July 1593 Catherine M'Kie, late Agnew,
was married at Lochnaw to Alexander Gordon of Clanyard,
the settlements then signed conveying to the sheriff, in trust
for his sister, a life interest in the lands of Clanyard, Garroch-
tree, and Portencorkrae [1]

Whilst Catherine Agnew was its lady Clanyard Castle was
famed as the "best halding house" in all the country side, and
she herself as a "notable spendar" [2]

Kitchen and hall are now alike silent, but her old dinner-
bell is still as sonorous as ever, it having been removed to the
parish church of Kirkmaiden, where it now weekly summons
the lieges for more serious purposes.

The bell had been cast in 1534 for Lord Dalhousie, from
whom it had been acquired by the Laird of Lochinvar, who
made it a wedding-gift to the bride and bridegroom on their
taking up house at Clanyard. The following letter from the
sheriff is in the Barnbarroch charter-chest:

LETTER FROM SIR ANDREW AGNEW TO THE LAIRD OF BARNBARROCH, 24th June 1592.

My Lord, eftir my hertlie commendatioun, the berar heirof
Mr. Williame Turner, as I am Informit, hes agreit with the
commisser, and hes satisfeit him in all things, according as he

---

[1] Clanyaid, claonard, "the high slope."

In a charter under the Great Seal, from Stirling, 1594, both settlements are
recapitulated. By the first Katherine Agnew receives the lands of Larg, Mark,
Tarff, Polbrecks. Dated 9th December 1591. Witnesses. Patrick M'Kie, apparent
of Larg, Sheriff of Galloway, Patrick Heron, Robert Gordon of Bernerney. The
second is to Andrew Agnew, Vice Comes, and Katharina Agnew, soror ejus,
giving Clanyard, Portencorkrae, Garrachtrie, etc Signed by Alexander Gordon
and the sheriff as principals ; Quentin Agnow the sheriff's son, and others,
witnesses.

Port au corcuir, "the port of the crimson " ; above it red granite crops out in
the cliff   Bamcorkrae, "the height of the crimson or red."

[2] Cloneyard, of old a very great house

Rather more than a couple of centuries ago Alexander Gordon had brought
home to Clanyard as his wife the richly dowered sister of Sheriff Agnew. They
kept house with baronial splendour and profusion ; for every day in the year a
Galloway nowt was killed, and not "a peck " but a boll of malt brewed. Clan-

will testifie and mak knawin unto your (L.) Quhairfoir I will
desyre your (L.) that as your (L.) has bene ane guid freind and
favourer of him hitherto so in lyke wayis your (L.) will forder
him to get his besines exped. This nocht dowting bot your (L.)
will do for my requiest, as I salbe habill to do for your (L.)
requeist agane. Nocht trubling your (L) with farder at this
present quhill the nixt occasioun, committis your (L) to the
protectioun of the lord ffroume the wigtoun the xxiiij day of
Junij 1592.   ANDRO AGNEW.

"To the rycht honorabill and my speciall my lord of barne-
barroch."

In a charter of renewal in the Great Seal Register in favour
of Ninian Adair, dated 12th November 1595, "Portray," the
"Clachane of Stranrawer," is named as part of his barony.

In 1596 "Stranrawer" was erected by Act of Parliament
into a burgh of barony under the Adairs of Kilhilt, the
charter just quoted having been overlooked. It has been generally assumed that the name was a new one given at this erection,
and, as Symson suggests, descriptive of the situation , as by the
town "there runs a bourn or strand, so that perhaps the town
should be spelled Strandrawer." But good Andrew Symson
notwithstanding, neither "row" nor "strand" lie at the root of
the name, but "sron," the "nose or snout," and "reamhar," the
"bluff point." The Celtic form Stronrawer is to be found in the
Lochnaw charter-chest a century before this, and is obviously
identical with the "*Stranreier* in the Rhynns" in charters of the
days of Robert Bruce. The bounds assigned by charter to the
burgh are "St. John's Croft, extending to 6 acres, from the
burn which comes from the Loch of Chappell to the Loch of Loch
Ryan, and to the lands of Airds to the east. The tower, fortalice,
manor-place, and yards of Chappell on the west. The water-
gang which was to the mill of Chappell on the south; and

yard must have been a pleasant residence : it is sheltered from westerly gales by
Barncorkrae Fell, and from bitter east winds by the heights of Garrachtrie
Around it are fair arable lands, and half a mile to the west is Clanyard Bay, with
its broad sandy beach —MacIlwraith's *Guide to Wigtownshire*, 148.

the Loch of Loch Ryan on the north; reserving to Elizabeth Kennedy, heretrix of the said croft, the tower, fortalice, manor-place, yards, and orchards of Chappell." In 1595 we find the rising town styled "Clachane de Stranrawer", in 1596 it becomes "Librum Burgum Regalium."

Within a few years of its foundation, Stranraer became quite a social centre, a knot of county lairds habitually frequenting it; the Laird of Garthland building a large town house, as also Quentin Agnew the sheriff's brother, as well as Lynn of Larg and the Kennedys of Chappell; John Kennedy of Creach being among its first provosts, and cadets of the Agnews, M'Dowalls, and others among its bailies. In later years it is traditionally said that the George Hotel was once the town house of the Earls of Stair.

The cordial relations established between Sir Thomas Kennedy of Culzean and his "traist friend," Sir Patrick Agnew, were drawn even closer with his son.

Sir Thomas, known as the "Tutor of Cassilis," is written of even by a bitter opponent as "indeed a very potentious man, and a very wise man." The heir whom he had educated seems to have inherited a large share of his father's (the fourth earl's) greed, and hardly was he free from his uncle's leading-strings than he showed himself as unscrupulous in making money, and more careful to keep it, than his father. He gave early evidence of this ruling passion, when, in 1597, being barely twenty years of age, against all remonstrances, he married the widow of Lord Maitland of Thurlston, a lady old enough to be his mother, but largely dowered. As pithily put, "Ye 3d of November 1597 Earl Cassilis married ye Chancellour Maitland's widow, of gude yearis, not like to bear children, daughter and heir to Lord Fleming."[1] And at his wife's instigation he further accepted the office of Treasurer of Scotland, from which the tutor vainly tried to dissuade him[2]

[1] Cottonian Manuscript.
[2] The 22d March 1598 the Earl of Cassilis is made great Treasurer, persuaded thereto by his wyfe, quha had been the chancellor's wyfe before, and thought she would have her last gudeman Treasurer. But his majesty thinking him right

Before this the tutor's eldest daughter Margaret had married Patrick, the sheriff's eldest son; and shortly after her sister married the younger Mure of Auchendrane under extraordinary circumstances.

Sir Thomas Kennedy had obtained a decree in court against this young man for 12000 marks, "not intending to put the same in execution, but as an awband above his head," which greatly incensed his family They meeting to consider the matter, Auchendrane, his father, suggested a simple mode of dealing with the debt. Sir Thomas had a house at Maybole, and the laird's advice was to waylay him on his return from a supper-party to which it was known he was engaged for New Year's night 1597 The accomplices watched accordingly, and tracking their victim to a narrow close, discharged a volley point blank at the party, the tutor escaping their bullets by a miracle. "He flees, they chase him; but by the mirkness of the night he escapes." The noise aroused the neighbours, and friends rallying to Sir Thomas, Mure and his party had in turn to fly The misdemeanants were summoned to appear before the council, and not attending, were declared rebel and put to the horn. Whereupon the tutor seized the "House of Auchendrane, destroyed the plenishing, and wrecked all the yarding" [1] Ruin stared the Auchendranes in the face, when the bold idea occurred to the laird to propose a marriage between his son and heir and the tutor's daughter; at the same time expressing himself in language of the most abject penitence for his misdoings Young Mure was of good repute, his expectations large, and there may have been previous love passages between the young folks. At all events the damsel proved not unwilling. The tutor took the matter *ad avizandum*, and as the result kith

rich, and that she might furnish sums of money, and using words to this effect, put them to such a fright that she moved him forthwith to give the place up He had to pay 8000 marks to be allowed to do so.—Pitcairn's *Historie of the Kennedyis*, p 112

Lady Cassilis died 1609, aged fifty-five, having had issue by her first husband John, created Earl of Lauderdale, of whom one was ancestor of the Maitlands of Freuch

[1] Pitcairn's *Historie of the Kennedyis*, p 27.

and kin from far and near were summoned to the bridal ; and
so thorough did the reconciliation appear that the historian of
the opposing faction writes that " the Laird of Culzean did now
so affect the good of the Laird of Auchendrane and his house,
that it was no less dear to him than his own." [1]

An unfortunate quarrel occurred about this time between
the Master of Cassilis and the tenant of Auchnotteroch.   These
lands, now a part of the Lochnaw estate, then the Earl of
Cassilis's, had been let by Sir Thomas Kennedy to one M'Ewen,
the Master of Cassilis having previously engaged that they
should be given to his foster brother, Patrick Rickard.   Hearing
this, the Master sent a message to M'Ewen warning him not to
accept the farm, " else he would make all his harness clatter."
But this M'Ewen, " being a proud carle, and having the Sheriff
of Galloway as well as Culzean to back him," defiantly answered
" that he would take any land my lord chose to give him.
Thereupon the Master, forgathering with M'Ewen, slays him,[2]
whereat my lord was far offendit."   Afraid of returning to his
brother, the youth claimed and received hospitality at Garthland,
where, falling in love with his host's sister, he married her,
" whereat," we are told, " my lord was even more offended than
he had been before."   It is a curious coincidence that after the
lapse of nearly three centuries, a M'Ewen is still tenant of
Auchnotteroch.

[1] The marriage complete, Auchendrane relaxed from the horn, and all their
folk made free that was with him and made friends —Pitcairn's *Historie of the
Kennedyis*, p. 36 , from which are taken all the notices in inverted commas
above.

[2] Three years later, 14th September 1601, we find a remission to the Master of
Cassilis, John Boyd his servant, and Hugh Kennedy of Chappell, for the
slaughter of Andrew M'Ewen in Auchnotteroch

CHAPTER XXVI

THE FEUDS OF THE KENNEDYS

A.D. 1598 to 1616

Few were the words, and stern and high,
  That marked the foemen's feudal hate ;
For question fierce and proud reply,
  Gave signal soon of dire debate.

Lay of the Last Minstrel.

SIR JOHN KENNEDY of Blairquhan, whose family had long owned
lands on the Cree, towards the close of the century acquired
from Sir John Vaus various lands in Sorbie. He had married
Lady Margaret Keith, daughter of the Earl Marshal, by whom
he had two sons, John and James, and a daughter, married to
Andrew, third Lord Ochiltree. About 1605, this second son
married the sheriff's daughter Jane, and his father settled the
lands of Cults and Baltier upon the young couple, with Cruggleton Castle for their residence.[1] Of the branches of the Kennedys
none were more respected than the Laird of Blairquhan. He,
alone of all the clan, keeping himself clear from the frequent
bickerings and meetings between relatives, ending in blood,
which kept the province in a state of continual turmoil. Of
the family holding baronial position in Galloway we trace a
Kennedy of Leffnoll, of Knockybay, of Arioland, of Auchtra-

---

[1] In the Lochaw charter-chest are various charters to James Kennedy and
Jaine Agnew his spouse. No. 1 of Baltier, No. 2 of Cults, of 23d September 1606,
confirmed "and to be holden of his majesty by royal charter, 5 Nov. 1606."
Also Nos. 3 and 4 of Cruggleton Castle and contiguous lands, one from M'Dowall
of Machermore, another from Sir John Wauss of Longcastle, confirming the
former as superior. John Kennedy of Blairquhan had built and dedicated a
chapel to St. Ninian at the Cruives of Cree in 1508.

lour, of Chappell, of Airiehemming, of Grennan, of Synnieness, of Gillespie, of Airds, of Creach, and of Cairngaarn.

The feud between the earl and Bargany had led to such disorders that, on the complaint of the local officials, the king summoned both to Edinburgh, and there "gart them shake hands." But hardly were their differences composed, than the earl plunged into a serious quarrel with the whole baronage of the shire. His father, it will be remembered, had in one of his softer moods propitiated the good-will of these gentlemen by granting them kyndlie tenancies which, if they did not bring as much rent to his coffers as what was marketably obtainable, yet secured him their good-will, often of more than money's worth to a superior. Greed being the new earl's weak point, he did not see the matter in this light, and determined to break the leases Accordingly he "obtenit ane decreitt aganis all the gentill menne of Galloway, of all thair kyndlie rowmis, sik as the Lairdis of Gairfland, Kenhilt, and Meirtonne, with the Schereff of Galloway, and thair freindis, rydis to his house of Inche in Galloway, with forty horse in geir, on intentione to put the same decreite of his to executiounne. . . . The quhilk, the gentill menne of Galloway perseiffing, send and desyritt me Lord to wse thame kyndlie; bot he refuissit the samin, and wald wse na thing bot the rigour of the law", and singling out Garthland for his first attack, proclaimed a court at Glenluce for next day, thinking there to enforce the decree against him.

From his intimate relations with Culzean, the sheriff might probably have made terms for himself; but this he scorned to do, and deciding to make common cause with his neighbours, the friends met, and engaging to support one another to the death, made arrangements for putting a superior force in the field on the following morning

Cassilis's summons was therefore responded to in a manner as prompt as unexpected. As he was preparing to leave his house with his troop of forty horse, he was informed that the gentlemen had already ridden past his gates on the way to Glenluce with one hundred horse in geir

M'Dowall's family under the Church had been baron bailies of the district; and the gentlemen entering the court, and my lord not appearing, Garthland facetiously remarked "If my lord would come there, he should be welcome, and he should be his depute." The earl meanwhile occupied his morning in recruiting his forces ; and as the party jubilantly returned, endeavoured to disperse them by a flank attack. A mêlée ensued, ending in the earl's men being driven back within their defences.[1] Where a garrison being ill provisioned, their increased numbers rather told against them, for the gentlemen knowing this, invested the island so closely that no one could get out, and food was running scarce. In this dilemma the earl determined to throw himself upon the generosity of his cousin Bargany, who was actually at the moment in hostile bands against him; and having with him as his chaplain the minister of Colmonell, he despatched him on an embassage to Bargany.

The reverend gentleman sped so quickly on his errand that he reached Ardstincher before Bargany had retired to bed, who, hearing his story, at once "lapp on with forty horse," desiring a further detachment to follow, and, riding all night, arrived at Craigcaffie by break of day Hence he sent desiring the sheriff and gentlemen to confer with him. They soon appeared, explaining that they were not assembled "to pursue my lord to his injury," but simply to defend themselves from wrong. Bargany expressed sympathy with them, and especially with Garthland (who indeed was in bands with him), promising to deal with my lord, adding, " Gif me lord be to do you wrong, and not use you kyndlie by the sight of friends, I will not only leave his lordship, but defend you to the last drop of my blood "

---

[1] "Now, the vay that thay war to cum bak was be the Loch-end of the Insche, quhair me Lord wes , and me Lord had gaderitt sum ma of his menne to him or thay com bak , and sa, isschit out of the loch, and thocht to put thame about the way thay com Bot thay com that way and wald nocht be stayitt. The Galloway menne com that nycht, and inclossitt the Loche , and wald not latt nane out or in , for thay knew he wes not weill prowydit. .   . My Lord of Caissallis wes hiche offenditt .   . bot heffing ane minister in the Yll with him, callit James Zoung, minister of Camnell (who) com out, and said he was going to his kirk For the quhilk effect thay sufferitt him to pass."—Pitcairn's *Historie of the Kennedyis*, p. 31

All agreed "that they would abyde by his judgement"; and
Bargany passed to the Inch.   Here my lord thanked him for
having proved a friend in need, and promised to be entirely
guided by him in his dealings with the baron's kyndlie rowmis.
Upon this Bargany returned to the gentlemen, and suggested
that they should send their followers home and come with him
to discuss their matters with my lord; he undertaking to be
answerable for their safety, and to make doubly sure, passed on
forty of his own men armed into the island.

The earl received them affably, promising to stand by whatever "his eame" should settle.   Their grievances being thus
discussed in an amicable spirit, and the laird entering into
particulars with my lord, "agreed them all to their contente-
ments," it being understood that the decreit against Garthland
should be forthwith withdrawn.

The mansion-house being now provisioned, my lord insisted
that they all should stay and dine, which they did, nothing loth,
and dinner over, all mounted and rode off, the Galloway gentlemen, as a mark of goodwill, escorting his lordship to Glenapp.
All seemed now happily settled, when, a few days later, having
waited on the earl with the conditions reduced to writing,
Cassilis, to his astonishment, coolly told him that he did not feel
himself bound by promises extorted by superior force, and
should fulfil them only so far as he chose.

High words ensued; the indignant Bargany challenged the
earl,[1] who agreed to give him satisfaction, but played him
as false in this matter as the former, never appearing "at the
time or place," and again setting the law in force against his
kyndlie tenants.   He took out king's letters against Garthland,
which the sheriff was bound, in virtue of his office, to enforce;
but he being himself in "bands" with Garthland, he took no
step in accordance with these to compel his removal or distrain his
effects, for which, consequently, he became personally liable

---

[1] "And efter his way-cuming, writ to me Lord, 'that his lordschip wald,
according to his word, apoynt him tyme, place, and maner.'   Bot me Lord geff
na ansuer, bot lat the samin pass ouer withe sylense."—Pitcairn's *Historie of the
Kennedyis*, p. 34

A summons was consequently served upon him by orders of the Lord Treasurer, requiring him to account for the money he had been desired to collect, and failing to reply, he had a visit from the Carrick pursuivant, with a demand for the surrender of the keys of his castle to the king, as if he had been an ordinary debtor.[1] The sheriff obeyed, and for the said keys he asked and received a receipt. It is to be presumed they were handed back to him, as we can find no suggestion of his having been in any way further inconvenienced by the visit. This receipt, bearing date 19th September 1601, is in the charter-chest at Lochnaw ·

"Compearit Robert Campbell, Carrick Pursewant, quha, be virtue of our Sovereign Lord's letters directed at the instance of his Highness's Treasurer and Comptroller, had charged an honourable man, Andrew Agnew of Lochnaw, Sheriff of Wigtown, to render and delyver to him in our said Sovereign Lord's name his Castle, Tower, Fortalice, and Dwelling Place of Lochnaw, and to deliver him ye keys thereof, conforme to the said letters quhilk are of ye date at Striveling ye 21st day of August last bypast, under the pain of treesone, ye said Robert granted that the said Andrew Agnew, Sheriff foresaid, for obedience of the said letters has rendered and delivered to him the said Castle, Tower, and Fortalice, with the keys thereof, conform to the said charge, and granted the same fulfilled concerning the delivery of the said place. Done at my dwelling-house at 10 hours before noon, in presence of Thomas Agnew, Baillie of Stranrawer; James M'Morland, smith; John Smyrlie, servitor to the said Robert, and Thomas Agnew, merchant burgess of Stranrawer.

"ROBERT CAMPBELL, Carrick Pursewant."

Though the whole proceeding reads much like a farce, entanglement in the meshes of the law might have proved a serious matter for the uncaring sheriff, had not Sir Thomas

---

[1] The law of Scotland did not permit imprisonment for debt, but by a legal fiction transmuted a refusal to make payment into a question of disloyalty, equivalent to treason.

Kennedy intervened, and brought these unseemly wrangles to a close. Inviting the earl, his nephew, to meet at his mansion of the Coiff, or Culzean, he got both to consent to submit their matters to mutual arbiters, and abide by their decision, and in the result the earl seems to have kept better faith than in the former question of arbitration at Lochinch.

Both parties signed the following paper :—

"At Maybole, the 12th day of November 1601.—A noble and potent Lord, John, Earl of Cassilis, on the one part, and Andrew Agnew of Lochnaw, Sheriff of Wigtown, on the other part, have faithfully submitted and compromised themselves by signing the blank on the other side of the paper, to be filled by the final sentence arbitral of Gilbert Ross on the part of the noble Earl, and John Kennedy of Baltersone on the part of the Sheriff, as judges, arbiters, and amicable composers, equally chosen by both the said parties to decern and ordain · what satisfaction in sums of money or other ways the said Andrew shall give to the noble Earl for the heritable fews of the lands of Kylfeather, Craigberrinoch, and the Dougarie, within the barony of Glenluce, appertaining to the said Sheriff in kindlie stedding, and which he alledges should be set to him in few, according to a decreet-arbitral pronounced by the late Earl of Murray betwixt the Earl's late father and the Laird of Lochinvar.

"The said Judges have presently accepted these presents, and shall fill in the blank betwixt this and the twenty-fifth day of December next to come . and by what the Judges decern and ordain by that the said parties are bound and obliged to abide

"In witness whereof both parties have subscribed the blank within, and they, with the Judges, have subscribed these presents, time, place, and day foresaid, before Sir Thomas Kennedy of Culzeane, Knyt., John Kennedy of Balneil, Thomas Kennedy of Sinniness (and their servants).

"JOHN EARL OF CASSILIS.
"ANDRO AGNEW."

The details of the arbitration are not forthcoming, but we have ample proof that the sheriff was satisfied, and that the earl kept faith, by a charter under the Great Seal confirming the assignment of the lands of Kylfeather, Craiburnoch, and the Dougaries, by the Earl of Cassilis in feu-farm to Andrew Agnew of Lochnaw, Sheriff of Galloway, and his heirs for ever   Cordial relations were thus re-established between the house of the Inch and Lochnaw.[1]

We find a note as to the Justiciar of Galloway, when in Edinburgh in 1600, intervening to clear a brother from a scrape in a manner hardly consistent with judicial propriety.   It is as follows . "Robert Maxwell, merchant in Edinburgh, having been disappointed of a sum of £100 due to him by Alexander Agnew, brother of the Sheriff of Wigtown, apprehended the said Alexander in Edinburgh, and consigned him to ward till he found caution to answer the law.   But while the town officers were conveying the debtor to the Tolbooth, the Sheriff of Wigtown, accompanied by Sir Robert Gordon, apparent of Lochinvar, and all his friends and servants who were in town, violently rushing upon the said officers with drawn swords and quhinzears, released the said Alexander Agnew, and carried him off to John Gordon's house.   The King and Council decern Sir John Gordon by the 20th of the month, till he find security for the sum adjudged." [2]   The matter was compromised

The ties between Sir Thomas Kennedy and the sheriff's family, which had subsisted for two generations, were drawn even closer in a third, by the marriage of the sheriff's eldest son Patrick with Margaret, the Laird of Culzean's daughter, by Elizabeth, daughter of David M'Gill of Cranstoun Riddell. As a result, which was no doubt considered natural, we observe in the Privy Council Register, a relation that Patrick Agnew, younger of Lochnaw, becomes responsible by a bond of £1000, that James Kennedy of Culzean (now his brother-in-law), should

---

[1] *Privy Seal Register*, vol. 74, folio 300   "Apud Halyrude Hous," 26th December 1602

[2] *Reg. of Privy Council*, vol. i p. 102.   The assault seems to have been made in 1598, but not adjudged upon till two years later.

not harm John Dalrymple of Stair, or James Dalrymple, his brother.

The relationship of the families of Garlies and Lochnaw had been for some generations very close. The sheriff was married to Sir Alexander Stewart's aunt, whose mother was a Douglas of Drumlanrig by Margaret Gordon of Lochinvar, sister of the sheriff's mother.

In 1600, being then under age, young Sir Alexander Stewart obtained the consent of his curators—Walter, Commendator of Blantyre, and Robert Douglas, Provost of Lincluden—to marry Grizel, daughter of Sir John Gordon of Lochinvar. The marriage-contract was signed at Wigtown the 15th October, no one being present besides the principals but the sheriff and Alexander Stewart of Clary; and was solemnised the December following at Kenmure Castle "in face of Haly Kirk," the witnesses signing thus. "Blantyre," "Lyncloudon," Sir John Gordon of Lochinvar, Sir Andrew Agnew, Sheriff of Wigtown, Alexander Stewart.[1]

The young Sir Alexander was in 1607 raised to the peerage as Lord Garlies, and further advanced in 1623 to the Earldom of Galloway. A second marriage seems to have been the result of the wedding-party at Kenmure; Rosina Agnew, second daughter of the sheriff, espousing William M'Clellan of Glenshannoch, brother and next heir to the Laird of Bomby, who was shortly after created Lord Kirkcudbright. Rosina's husband did not live to inherit, but her eldest son Thomas succeeded his uncle as second Lord Kirkcudbright, well known as a dashing cavalry officer in the civil wars.

The law, so inert in graver matters, was set in motion in one which now sounds ridiculous ; Uchtred M'Dowall of Garthland, Alexander Hannay of Sorbie, Sir John Vaus of Barnbarroch, and Alexander Gordon, being all summoned, in March 1600, " to compear before the Lords of Session to hear themselves decerned as having incurred the pains for boarding themselves

---

[1] This contract is in the charter-chest of Kenmure Castle, and a copy was kindly given to the author by the Hon. Mrs. Bellamy Gordon in 1874.

in oistlar houses"; the penalties for which were serious indeed —"500 marks the Lord and Prelate, and 300 the Barons, to be uplifted for the King."[1]

The chronic feuds of the Kennedys were meanwhile troubling the marches. The intensity of the disorders is to be gathered from such notices, among dozens of others, "of the young Laird of Bargany gathering to the number of 600 men and horse with twa hundert hagbutteris, and many basses" (*i.e.* cannon); my Lord Uchiltree joining him with an hundred horse, "so that in all he wes the number of nine hundred men on foot and horse," to oppose my Lord Cassilis, who was coming with nearly an equal number to distrain the crops at Dangart, for which he had obtained a decreet   The necessarily sanguine result of such a meeting was only prevented by the intervention of Lord Cathcart (married to a near kinswoman of Lord Cassilis), who "travelled among them" and composed their differences.[2]

It was but a truce. Very shortly afterwards Bargany, with the Kennedys of his faction, and the Laird of Auchendrane, hearing of my Lord Cassilis being about to ride to Galloway, lay in wait for him at a ford of the Stincher, and would have taken his life had they not been overawed by the unexpected presence of his uncle, Sir Thomas Kennedy, who they strangely seem to have thought would have kept out of sight and connived at their attempt.

The earl's party passed unchallenged, little aware of how narrow had been their escape, and arrived safely at the Inch, where, next morning, who, of all men, should present himself at the tutor's bedside, but Auchendrane, the chief conspirator himself, who coolly reproached the tutor for not having played into their hands.

The earl, hearing of his coming, had sent orders that he should not be allowed to leave; and presently joining him and the tutor in the courtyard, accused him of plotting to take his

---

[1] 2 James VI.'s seventh Parliament, chap. 115.
[2] *Historie of the Kennedys*, pp. 37-38.

life, which Auchendrane audaciously denied. The earl, however, determined to detain him as a prisoner; and as he was telling him this, dinner was announced, to which he invited him. As, however, the earl entered the house, Auchendrane's servant beckoned to him to make for the boat, which he had unfastened, and both he and Ardmillan's brother, who was also in the yard, jumped in and pushed off, the earl supposing they were following him; and before he was aware of their escape they were already on horseback and away.

Shortly after Cassilis rode from Galloway to his Castle of Craigneil, "where he remained ane space"; which castle lying close to that of Ardstincher, Bargany's residence, both swarming with armed men, encounters were of daily occurrence. In one of these, Bargany being surrounded by superior numbers, of whom he struck down many, Hugh Kennedy of Garriehorn "brak a lance on him, Quentin Crauford strak at him with swords, and ane fellow called John Dick hackitt a lance at him, and strak him through the craig and the thropill."

Carried home in this uncomfortable state, the poor young man died of his wounds, being barely twenty-five years old; much lamented by his partisans; the chronicler of his house adding that "he was of his age the most wise he mycht be, and gif he had time to add experience to his wytt he had been by his marrows."[1] That he was a brave young man there can be little doubt, but we can hardly with the chronicler admit him to be an example to all posterity, except in the sense of quoting his untimely fate as a warning against playing with edged tools.

Bargany was far too important a personage to die unavenged, and my Lord Cassilis was summoned to answer a charge of being accessory to his death; whereupon my lady rode into Edinburgh, and dealt with her friends at court. Nevertheless things might have gone hard with him had not the Laird of Culzean followed, and "*by his moyane*" obtained for my lord an Act of

---

[1] *Historie of the Kennedyis*, p. 51. "Had been by his marrows," would have surpassed all his contemporaries.

Council, declaring "all my Lord had done good service to the King," because Bargany's brother was at the horn for other slaughters at the moment of the fatal encounter.

Having thus righted his nephew's affairs, the Laird of Culzean rode into Galloway, and "there remaynit a great space" with his daughter, destined to be his last visit to Lochnaw, for, according to the monstrous usages of the day, the friends of Bargany had solemnly sworn that a man of note of the Cassilis faction must die, and the occasion to them came very shortly after.

Sir Thomas Kennedy, having to go to Edinburgh, unsuspectingly wrote a note to Auchendrane, telling him so, and asking him to meet him by the way. On getting the letter he at once communicated its contents to Drummurchie, Bargany's brother, and Mure of Cloncaird. All along Mure, under a disguise of gratitude, had nursed a deadly hatred to Culzean, and it was soon settled that this was an opportunity not to be lost, and that they should waylay the tutor the following morning.

Sir Thomas started merrily from Culzean on his journey, attended by one servant only; and when among the sandhills, beside St. Leonard's Chapel, the four assassins fell upon him, "and slays him maist cruelly wi' shots and strakes, and took from him efter he was slain his purse and ring, and sundrie diamonds, with his golden buttons of goldsmith work." These "honourable" men plundered him also of "eleven score rose nobles, his swordbelt and hangar, and left him", when his man Lancelot "brings him with him to the Grennan, and there gets ane horse litter, and takes him to Maybole."

Public feeling, lax as it was in matters of feud, was outraged by the circumstances of this murder. Mure, the instigator, should have been bound by ties of gratitude as well as of kindred to his victim, and indignation rose to a boiling-point when he was further suspected of a second murder on a poor scholar, who had been an unwilling, and the only witness to Mure's conference with Drummurchie.

The Mures, father and son, were arrested, and as no direct

evidence was forthcoming, they were put to the torture, under which, however, they held out bravely; and as most persons "much misliked that form of trial," they were on the point of being liberated, when one of the accomplices in the scholar's murder, wishing to secure his own safety, turned king's evidence, and all three were convicted, mercy being denied to the informer, and the Mures made a full confession of both their offences, much to the satisfaction of the public.[1]

The tutor left four sons, the second, Alexander, eventually carried on the line, and his great-grandson, on the failure of the senior branch, was served heir as ninth Earl of Cassilis, the present Marquis of Ailsa being his direct descendant.

The chronicler tells us "his dochteris warre thrie · Margaret married the young Sheriff of Galloway, Helen married the young laird of Auchendrayne, and Susanna was efter Lady Larg"

This Laird of Larg being Sir Patrick M'Kie, son of Katherine Agnew; and his son represented the Stewartry in Parliament during the civil wars. Margaret, with her husband Patrick Agnew, resided during the sheriff's lifetime at Innermessan, a position commanding the road from Ayrshire, by which Cassilis was constantly passing to the Inch, rendering it difficult for young Agnew to avoid taking part in the tuilzies in which the earl was engaged with the slayers of his wife's father; the more so as the Bargany faction loudly proclaimed their intention of offering a second victim to the manes of their chief.

Their next attack was a most ungallant one upon a lady. Cassilis having occasion to go to London, his lady took the opportunity of paying some visits in Galloway, arriving by Innermessan on the 16th April 1604, and returning probably from Lochnaw about the 21st of May. Kennedy of Drum-

---

[1] Lord Cassilis gave this extraordinary bond to his brother to induce him personally to revenge his uncle's death, should law fail to do so: "We, John, Earl of Cassilis, binds and obliges us how soon our brother Hugh Kennedy with his complices takes the laird of Auchendrane's life, that we shall make good and thankful payment to him of the sum of 1200 marks yearly, together with the corn for six horses, and herein we oblige us upon our honour. Subscribed at Maybole, 3d September 1602."

murchie, his hands red with the tutor's blood, getting notice of
her plans, arranged with Sir James Stewart (who was married
to a daughter of Garthland) and Mure of Cloncaird to waylay
her when beyond call of her Galloway friends.   Lady Cassilis
meanwhile had asked her brother-in-law "the Master" to escort
her, which he readily agreed to do, bringing with him fifteen of
his brother's horse.   Deeming their number sufficient, they
parted from their Wigtownshire friends, fording the Stincher, and
getting safely beyond Maybole, when, on the moor of Auchendrane, Bargany attacked them with a party of nine horse,
twenty-four hagbutt men being drawn up on either side of the
way   Outnumbered as to firearms, the Master effected a retreat
upon the mansion-house of Auchensoul, belonging to a friend
Duncan Crawford, who fortunately had "three stalwart friends
with him : the young laird of Grimatt, a brother of the Laird of
Polquharne, and Quentin Crawford of Sill."

Drummurchie quickly invested the place, but so garrisoned
they refused to surrender; whereupon a torch was procured,
and "it being but a thak house," they were soon smoked out,
but still made a stand in the walled yard.   My lady came
forward to parley, when Drummurchie coolly informed her
that among her retinue was one John Dick, who, as before
mentioned, was concerned in his brother's slaughter; and
that he would discuss no terms unless he was delivered up
to him.

John Dick, overhearing this, speedily made a "slop in the
dyke" behind them, dashed through, and, assisted by the smoke
which partly concealed him and his horse, was off in an
instant.   Thereupon Drummurchie's party made off after him,
chasing him "four or five myle", but he distanced them all,
never drawing bridle till far on the road to Loudon, where he
arrived in an incredibly short time, telling his master of the
plight in which he had left the countess.

The earl told his story to the king, which put his majesty
in "sic a rage" that letters were sent forthwith to the Sheriffs
of Galloway and Ayr, ordering them instantly to pursue and

arrest the misdemeanants, and further desiring the matter to
be brought before the Parliament.

The sheriffs acted with a will; yet in Galloway so much
more efficient were private bands than legal procedure, that the
release of Lady Cassilis had already been brought about, not
by the action of the sheriff's officers, but by pressure brought to
bear by the Laird of Garthland and Lord Ochiltree, who had a
private understanding with Drummurchie. Summons of treason
nevertheless went forth in due time against Thomas Kennedy
and Walter Muir for the double crime of burning Auchensoul
and the abduction of Lady Cassilis; and on the 11th of July
Parliament adjudged Drummurchie "to have tint his fame,
honours, and dignities, and that he be punished as a traitor, and
all his lands, gudes, and geir forfeited to the king."[1]

The Earls of Cassilis had hitherto inhabited the old strength
of the Inch, which had sheltered the Agnews when driven from
their home. The present earl now set about building a new
house on a tongue of land between the two lakes, well known
as Castle Kennedy.

Whilst the building was in progress, the earl, riding up
thither near Girvan Bridge, stumbled suddenly on Thomas
Dalrymple (brother of the Laird of Stair), who was then at the
horn for having lain in wait to kill Cassilis himself a few
months previously. The youth was "hard at my lord's men
in the twilight" ere ever he knew them. The earl carried
him to Craigneel, where he halted for the night, and
before starting next morning "gave him an assize and
hanged him on a tree" Though the act was severe, the
earl was perfectly within the law;[2] but in revenge for the pro-

[1] Their indictment was "pro malevolo, crudeli, nefario, abominabili et
scelesto incendio manerii Auchensoul—ubi Domina Joanna Comitessa de
Cassilis, Hugo Kennedie, etc , captivi facti sunt. Et vi abducti et in privatis
carceribus detenti "

[2] Lord Cassilis's act may seem harsh, but the chronicler had somewhat
hazy ideas as to the spirit of kindness and what might be cause of offence,
having himself related, without a word of disapprobation, as a fact, that on the
6th December 1606 the youth had lain in wait to murder Cassilis as he passed,
for which he was a fugitive when caught, and for which the Baron Court condemned him

ceeding, Muir of Cloncaird, himself also at the horn at the moment for other slaughters, rode off to Galloway, and there killed David Girvan, the master of the works at the castle, in cold blood, though he had no concern whatever in Dalrymple's seizure.

Lady Cassilis, the victim of Drummurchie's escapade, died in 1609, and her husband the fifth earl in 1615. He was succeeded by his nephew John, son of the Master of Cassilis, who had married Margaret, daughter of M'Dowall of Garthland. This sixth earl resided more constantly at Castle Kennedy than his father. He is known in family tradition as the "solemn earl;" but, as we shall see, he too could don his armour and "ride forth in routing" on occasions.

Sir Thomas Kennedy, father of the Lady of Lochnaw, had been predeceased by his eldest son. After his murder, his second son, James, was served his heir, who, for some reason unknown, sold Culzean to his next brother, Alexander. This brother acquired other estates by marrying Agnes, heiress of Kennedy of Ardmillan, and his descendants eventually succeeded to the Cassilis title.

Requiring some immediate advantage in respect to his purchase, he was assisted by his brother-in-law, as shown in a bond : " I, Alexander Kennedy of Culeane, grants me by the tenour hereof from the hands of Sir Patrick Agnew, knight, Sheriff of Wigtown, the sum of seven hundred and fourscore marks money usual of this Realm, whereof I grant my receipt, and bind me my heirs and executors thankfully to refund and deliver the same to the said Sir Patrick, and the Dame Margaret Kennedy his spouse. With ten marks money yearly for the annual rent of ilk hundred marks of the principal

"At Innermessane the 20th day of April before thir witnesses . Robert Weir, servitor to the said Sir Patrick, and James Glover, notar, writer hereof."

In 1606 James Kennedy acquired the lands of Cults, as shown by a charter executed at Glenluce, granted by Vaus of Barnbarroch, the 25th of November, in favour of James

Kennedy of Cruggleton, and Jane Agnew his spouse. Witnessed by Andrew Agnew, Sheriff of Wigtown, John M'Dowall of Garthland, Thomas Hay of Park, and James Glover, notary public.

We also find a disposition of Mellan, now Molland Hill, in the parish of Penninghame,[1] to Alexander Agnew, the sheriff's third son, by James Gordon of Hazelfield, dated 21st November 1609 ; and on the 26th January 1611 his father purchased for him the lands of Barvennan from Sir John Vaus. Of these the Bishop of Galloway was superior; and we find a second charter of confirmation by William, Bishop of Galloway, confirming Alexander Agnew's right to Barvennan, dated 27th January 1614

This " Reverend Father in God " was William Couper, son of John Couper, merchant in Edinburgh. Very different characters are given him by Calderwood and Keith; the former sneeringly remarking, " None fracker against the Estate of Bishops in the purer times, than he, none now fracker for the present course and corruptions of the times " ; the latter intimating " that he rested from his labours, Feb. 1619," adds, " he certainly was a man of worth."

In 1608 Ninian Adair had died, and was succeeded by his son William, married first to a M'Clellan of Gelston, and thirdly to a daughter of Cathcart of Carleton By the first he had Robert, his heir; by the third, William, well known as minister of Ayr from 1640 to 1684.

William Adair succeeded Sir John (the Reverend) Johnston as Commendator of Soulseat : an office which must have been purely honorary, the lands having been secularised when the abbey was suppressed. William entered into close relations with Sir Hugh Montgomery of Broadstone, who had received a part of one-third of the O'Neil lands in the north of Ireland, to which he led a colony of western Scots. Quite an exodus of Galloway cadets ensued to this paradise of confiscations.

The following Galloway lairds made application to be

---

[1] Drummolyn, "mill ridge "—Pont.

enrolled as undertakers in the intended plantation and distribution of forfeited lands in the province of Ulster :—

George Murray of Broughton for 2000 acres, with Alexander Dunbar of Egerness as cautioner.

Alexander Dunbar for 2000 acres, with Murray as his cautioner.

James M'Culloch of Drummorell for 2000, with Broughton cautioner.

Andrew Lord Stewart of Ochiltree for 2000, his uncle Robert Stewart cautioner.

James Dalrymple, brother to the Laird of Stair, 2000 acres, and though not a Gallovidian, one who had traversed it in its length and breadth. Mr. Timothy Pont for 2000 acres.

The sheriff had dealings with the new Lord Antrim as to his Irish claims, of which we shall say more presently.

Some years after this the sheriff purchased the reversion of Cults and Baltier from James Kennedy, who had no family, and which ever since have been known as a part of the estate called the Sheriff's lands. The charter was signed and sealed at Lochnaw, the 10th day of January 1615, bearing . " Wit ye all and sundrie whom it effeirs : me, Sir Andrew Agnew of Lochnaw, Sheriff of Wigtown, forsamekle as my belovit sone in law, James Kennedy of Crugiltoun, has sauld, disponit, and dimitted to me, my airs and successors, bot any manner of regres, reversion, or right of redemption quhatsoever. The five pound land of Cults, and three and a half mark land of Baltier lyand in the parochin of Cruggleton. The said James has heritably infeft me in ye said lands. The charter containing the precept of seizing of the daitt at the place of Lochnaw, the 9th January 1615, for the sum of 5000 marks usual of Scotland.

" Subscrivit with my hand, written by William Gardner, my seal is hung and affixed at Lochnaw, before Quentene Agnew, my sone ; Gilbert Agnew, my servitor domestic ; Thomas Baillie, servitor to the said James ; and the said William Gardner, notary."

There was a residence on the land of Cults, as we find the

sheriff's daughter-in-law dating a discharge from the Cults, subscribing herself "Dame Margaret Kennedy, Lady Lochnaw."

The sheriff seems also to have been able—very unusual in
those days—to pay down to his sons their respective portions
before his death, as proved by the following registered discharge: "Be it kenned to all men, be thir present letters, we,
Andrew, Alexander, and Quentene Agnew, lawful sons to the
rycht honourabill Sir Andrew Agnew of Lochnaw, knycht,
Sheriff of Wigtown; forsamekle as ye said Sir Andrew Agnew,
our father, has contented and payit to us, and ilk ane of us, the
full and haill soums of money quhereupon we were infeft in
wadsett in our said father's lands, in satisfaction of all portions
natural and bairns' part of geir, which befell and appertenit to
us be right of umquhill Agnes Stewart, our mother, Be the
tenour hereof, we discharge the said Sir Andrew Agnew, his
heirs and successors, all and haill of the said lands.

"At Lochnaw, the 13th day of November, the year of God
1616, before yir witnesses: Sir Patrick M'Kie of Larg, knycht;
William Agnew of Croach; Mr. Thomas Garvey, minister of
Leswalt; and Gilbert Agnew, merchant in Stranraer."

The Sheriff died before the close of 1616.

CHAPTER XXVII

THE KING'S BAILIE OF LESWALT

A.D. 1616 to 1630

Oh! we have the noble Stewarts that have lived here
For more than the space of four hundred year;
Agnews, and M'Dowalls, and Gordons so gay,
And Maxwells, and Murrays, and likewise Park Hay.
Galloway Shepherds.

THE entry of the eighth sheriff's service is as follows :—

"The Sheriff-Court of Wigtown, holden in the Tolbooth there-of by John Ahannay of Sorbie, and William Agnew of Barmeil, sheriff-deputes.

"Ye quhilk day, anent ye public edict raised at the ainstance of the right honourable Sir Patrick Agnew of Lochnaw, Sheriff of Wigtown, son and heir of unquhill Sir Andrew Agnew of Lochnaw, Sheriff of Wigtown, his father, summoning and charg-ing all and sundry be open proclamation at the Market Cross of Wigtown and other places needful, to have compeirit this day. To have heard and seen the instrument of seizine insert and registrat" (which instrument is then recapitulated with lists of lands and offices, the seizing of the former being by delivery of earth and stone; of the latter, by rod and staff). "On the 17th March 1617, about 2 in the afternoon, in presence of John Kennedy of Crichane;[1] Archibald Gordon in lands of Luce; Alexander Agnew in Kerronrae; William Agnew of Croach; Ninian Agnew in Craigauch; Antony Stewart, servant

---

[1] He seems to be the husband of the sheriff's cousin Jane, daughter of Sir Alexander Stewart of Garlies, father of the first Earl of Galloway.

to the said Sir Patrick, and Alexander Templeton, servant to the said John Kennedy."

Among the sheriff's papers is a precept from the Court of Exchequer for the infefting of Sir Patrick Agnew of Lochnaw, Sheriff of Galloway, in a house and yard in the town of Stranrawer, which belonged formerly to John Adair, burgess thereof, *who being a bastard, died without issue or making a settlement.*

A query here suggests itself : Was this a usual perquisite of sheriffs ?

In 1619 Bishop Cowper was succeeded by Andrew Lamb, Bishop of Brechin.   On King James's accession to the English crown he had appointed Gavin Hamilton to the see of Galloway, which had been without a titular bishop for twenty years ; gifting him also with what revenues remained to the priory of Whithorn, and the abbacies of Tongland and Dundrennan.

Hamilton died in 1614, and was succeeded by Cowper, who, as his predecessors, had been constituted also Dean of the Chapel Royal.   When King James, moved by his " salmon-like desire," revisited the land of his birth in 1617, Cowper officiated, and it is said to have given peculiar offence that the bishop administered the Sacrament there to the Court and courtiers kneeling, though we can hardly see how he could have done otherwise if he used Episcopal services at all.

A General Assembly was called at Perth in 1618, which adopted by a majority certain reversions to ancient usages : namely, kneeling at the Sacrament, and observance of Easter and Christmas Day.   Bishop Cowper supported these changes, and, according to Calderwood, " upbraided Mr. Thomas Provane, minister of Leswalt ; Mr. James Symson, minister of Tongland ; and exceeded all bounds in abusing Mr. David Pollock, minister of Glenluce, for voting against them." [1]

More impartial observers, however, declared that Cowper always exhibited a laudable moderation ; with Calderwood, "purity of worship" meant Presbyterianism.

Cowper's successor was Andrew Lamb, two of whose daugh-

[1] Calderwood, 7, 334-349.

ters married respectively Murray of Broughton and Lennox of Cally . a son of the former, in a succeeding generation, married his cousin, the heiress of the latter, and thus combined the properties.

The acrimony engendered by sectarian differences colours all the annals of the period, panegyric or abuse being bestowed entirely according to the writer's religious bias. Thus Row and Calderwood, good men, but certainly violent partisans, retail with glee ribald sayings against all the bishops. We shall only quote one :

> Vinum amat Andreas, cum vino Glasgua amres ;
> Ros cœtus, ludos Gallua, Brichæus opes.

Thus translated for us by the first-named divine :

> St. Androes loves a cup of wine,
> Wine Glasgow with an whoore ,
> Rosse companie, play, Galloway,
> Brechin not to be poore [1]

It is but fair to add that the "play" with which Cowper is taunted was neither with cards nor dice , he was not a gambler, but fond of a game of golf on the links of Leith. Almost all the Galloway proprietors had accepted the leading doctrines of the Reformation ; but when James, alarmed at the power the General Assembly wielded, employed his kingcraft to assimilate the churches of the two kingdoms, he found many, both of the clergy and the laity, in sympathy with himself. The Presbyterian divines, from an exaggerated craving for so-called purity, had reduced the church services to a baldness distasteful to those who had been accustomed to more ornate ritual; and even a considerable section of the clergy preferred a moderate Episcopacy to extreme Calvinistic Presbyterianism.

The leaders of the ultra-Presbyterians were good and earnest men, but prone to denounce all who differed with them in

---

[1] Row, 259 and 292.   George Gledstanes, Archbishop of St. Andrews ; John Spottiswode, Archbishop of Glasgow , David Lyndsay, Bishop of Ross , William Cowper, Bishop of Galloway ; Andrew Lamb, Bishop of Brechin, and afterwards of Galloway.

matters of ritual as wicked, classing together Prelacy and Popery as deadly sins.

The Bishops, thus abused, not satisfied with retorting from the pulpit, somewhat ill-advised, profited by their position to get laws framed for their assistance. Hence law, strained to reusurp unfair powers over conscience, fell into disrepute, and under the imposing protests of assertion of the law on the prelatical side, and conscientious resistance to it from the presbyterian, life in Galloway was embittered, and the province impoverished for three generations. No actual outbreak occurred until 1638.

Meanwhile the sheriff's attention was called officially to more trivial matters. Commissioners appointed to examine the weights and measures used in the realm had reported that the greatest diversity from the standards existed in the sheriffdoms of Wigtown, Dumfries, and the border counties. The Sheriff of Wigtown was therefore desired to convene a court in his shire within twenty days, and there "embraced the met," and decreed that none shall presume in time to come within any sheriffdom, to sell, block, bargain, contract, or deliver, with any other met or measure but that by the Act then approved.

It is amusing to have to state that, notwithstanding his exertions, the teinds of Leswalt, of which the hereditary sheriffs were principal heritors, have continued to this day to be paid in Galloway met, which is exactly double of that ordained by statute.

Gallovidians indeed have been always proverbial for "good weight." Within the present century a stranger presented himself at a "farm toun" among the hills, and asked for a pound of butter. The moorman was out, and his gudewife, though ready to serve him, could nowhere find the "pun-stane." The meal-stone quarter, her only weight available, obviously would not do. They searched long and vainly for the "ouncel weights," when the woman's eyes brightened. "I ken hoo we'll manage it the noo," she exclaimed, seizing one of the fireirons. "The gudeman brought hame a pair o' tangs yestreen fra the

smiddy, which then just weighed twa pund.   Wi' them I'll
weigh your pund o' butter."   Raising the tongs in triumph, she
intelligently put one leg in the scale and let the other hang.
The beam got its swing, the butter was plastered in till it
righted, and the new-comer carried off his purchase with a light
heart, well pleased with his experience of Galloway weight.

In the criminal records of 1618 we find a county proprietor
convicted of a cruel murder.   Maxwell of Garrarie having got
possession of another man's estate (probably by way of wadsett),
and being bound to make some provision for the penniless ex-
owner, became irritated at the annuitant's tenacity of life, and
took effectual steps to make it a terminable annuity   The man
was murdered and thrown into a moss-hole.   Lord Garlies and
M'Kie of Larg assisted his relatives in tracing the murderer.
Circumstantial evidence was obtained sufficient to authorise the
Sheriff to arrest him, who sent him before the High Court of
Justiciary, where " the dittay" as follows tells its own story :

" Johne Maxwell of Garrarie having, in his politic and crafty
manner, upon conditions best known to himself, conqueist and
acquired from Johne M'Kie of Glassock his haill worldly
moyane and estate, and thereby drawn him to his daily company and attendance : He, furth of his avaricious and churlish
disposition, loathing and wearying of the said John M'Kie's
company, in the month of July 1618, to rid and exoner himself
of his company devised and concluded in his develish heart the
pitiful and treasonable murder of the said John M'Kie as follows :—finding the said John for the most part making his
daily residence with him at bed and board within his place at
Garrarie, upon the 18 July, knowing the time of John M'Kie's
dyet in coming to his house, under silence and cloud of night,
accompanied by George Maxwell his son, and others, with
swords and invasive weapons, on John his coming to the said
place, put violent hands on his person, bound both his hands
and feet, and thereafter in most cruel and merciless manner
playing the part of hangman, with a hair tether strangled and
wirreit him to death; and having by that violent and cruel

meane bereft him of his life, thereafter carried him to a peat
moss or burn called the Burn of Ravenstoun, wherein they
flang him."

On this charge, upon full consideration, Maxwell of Garrarie
was found guilty, and was beheaded, as he justly deserved, on the
2d of April 1619.

As an incident in connection with this trial, it is stated that
seventeen gentlemen of the district, among whom were Sir John
Dunbar of Mochrum, James Kennedy of Cruggleton, Alexander
Dunbar younger of Mochrum, George Gordon of Barskeog, and
Alexander M'Culloch younger of Myrtoun, were all fined one
hundred merks each for declining to serve upon the assize.

The Lynns of Larg, owning a small lairdship on the Water
of Luce, were in the habit of fishing with small regard to their
neighbours' marches The Rosses of Balneil and Hays of Park
remonstrated, but in vain ; the Lynns daring them to try to turn
them back. At last they accepted the challenge, and came
upon the poachers in the act of trespass in a bend beyond the
Muir Kirk of Luce. A tuilzie ensued, in which it is said three
of the combatants fell dead upon the river banks, and few
retired unwounded The name of "the Bloody Wheel," impressed upon the battlefield, is held to authenticate the story.

A less tragic tradition connects itself with the Hays and the
valley of the Luce.

There was a wedding-party near the abbey of Luce, and a
young Hay of Park was amongst the company. In the course
of the feast one of the few articles of plate was suddenly missed ;
and a blacksmith present, expressing more loudly than any one
his indignation at the fact, ended by a solemn prayer that
"cauld iron might be his hinner en' quhaever took it." He
became much excited, and later in the evening rudely called upon
Hay to pay for the shoeing of a horse he owed him, and irritated
the young man so much by his insulting manner that at last he
drew his sword and ran him through the body. As those present
raised the corpse, the missing article fell from the dead man's
pocket ; and their indignation at his murder was momentarily

married respectively the Lairds of Freuch and Logan. Uchtred M'Dowall, the former, was son of a daughter of Lord Barnbarroch. His branch of the family was especially prosperous, possessing, in addition to Freuch, the lands and strength on Dowalton Loch, besides the extensive barony of Loch Ronald with its two picturesque lakes. Agnes Agnew's grandson married Lady Betty Crichton, in her own right Countess of Dumfries, her great-grandson inheriting that earldom, and his only daughter carried the title to the Earl of Bute.

Alexander M'Dowall, Laird of Logan, settled upon his bride as her dower the lands of Grennan, Balgown, Chappell Rossan, and Auchness. The same year we find Gilbert Agnew disposing on the 26th September to Quentin Agnew, designed brother of the sheriff, lands lying within the burgh of Stranraer, with consent of Agnes M'Dowall his spouse; "to his name" this amusing declaration being used instead of the modern, "his mark," "with my hand at the pen, as held by the notary underwritten, because I cannot wryte myself."

In the Barnbarroch charter-chest there is a discharge by Lady Agnew, mother of the M'Dowall brides, to Sir John Vaus, worded thus ·

"I, Dame Margrett Kennedy, Lady Lochnaw, grants me to have resawitt fra my eam the Lord of Barnbarroch ten bolls beir at £8 the boll, and ten bolls corn at 5 marks the boll, and shall cause my husband allow the same to him in part payment of the annuals that he is caution for. Subscrivit with my hand at the Cultis, 25 April 1625, before this witness, Alexander Agnew in Marslache."

The memorandum proves beyond dispute that in the west country at least eme or eam had a wider sense than uncle. Sir John Vaus was undoubtedly her cousin, and Kelly in his *Old Scotch Proverbs* rightly glosses eam "relation," though this has been disputed by Jamieson.

Dame Margaret Agnew must be held to be an authority as to the idioms of her day.

Her eldest son was married in the summer of 1625

to the only daughter of Lord Galloway, by Grizel Gordon of Lochinvar. The substance of the marriage-contract is as follows:

"It is agreed between ane potent Erle, Alexander, Erle of Galloway, for himself and taking burden upon him for Lady Agnes Stewart, his lawful daughter, on the one part; and Sir Patrick Agnew of Lochnaw, Knycht, Sheriff of Wigtoun, and Andrew Agnew his son and apparent heir, on the other part; forsameiklc as the said Andrew shall, God willing, marry and to his lawfull wyfe take the said Lady Agnes, and solemnize the bond of matrimony in presence of Christ's congregation between the date hereof and the last days of July next to come. . . . The said Sir Patrick binds himself to infeft duly and sufficiently the said Andrew and Lady Agnes in the lands of Craichmore, Auchneel, etc., in the parish of Leswalt,—the lands of Calquhirk, lying among the borough acres of Wigtoun,—the lands of Craigbirnach in the parish of Glenluce, etc. etc., for the quhilk solemnization and other causes specified the said noble and potent Erle binds himself, his heirs, etc., to content and thankfully pay to the said Sir Patrick Agnew, the sum of eight thousand merks in name of tocher with his said daughter—to witt, 2000 merks at the feast and term of Whitsunday 1626; 3000 merks at Whitsunday 1627; and the sum of other 3000 merks at the term of Whitsunday 1628. And in like manner, after the accomplishing of the said marriage, to entertain the said Andrew, his future spouse, their servants and retinue, according to their rank, for the space of two years next thereafter, which being expired, the said Sir Patrick binds himself to entertain them and their servants in the same manner for the space of one year thereafter.

"Written by Wm. Stewart notary and servitor to the said noble Earl, at the place of Glastoune, the 22d day of March 1625 years, before these witnesses—John Ahannay of Sorbie; Mr. James Adamson, minister of Penninghame; Mr Abraham Henryson, minister of Quhithorne; Alexander Stewart in Larg; and William Agnew of Barmeill."

By these provisions the young couple were saved all the cares and expenses of housekeeping for three years.

It is a proof of the scarcity of money that a potent Earl could promise no more than 8000 merks (less than £450 sterling) to an only daughter for her portion; and that even this sum was only to be paid by instalments. And, more surprising still, we find that, eleven years after, not one farthing of the money had been paid; and that, after vainly trying to obtain a settlement, the sheriff sued the noble earl for the amount, and obtained a decree from the head courts commanding immediate payment.[1]

John Ahannay, a witness to the young sheriff's marriage-contract, unfortunately renewed an old blood feud with the Murrays of Broughton, through which his family had already suffered much; and from excesses committed he, incurring further fines and escheats, was obliged to part with the remainder of his lands. The barony of Sorbie, with "the old place," was sold to Lord Galloway, and his lands of Crailloch.[2] John Ahannay himself was killed in a quarrel. His younger brother Patrick was a man of literary as well as military note. He served with distinction under the King of Bohemia, and rose to the rank of general. He published a volume of poems, so highly esteemed that, seventy years ago, a copy fetched at the sale of Sir Mark Sykes's effects £42 : 10s.; and in 1864 a copy

---

[1] "Charles, by the Grace of God, etc.—Forasmuch as by a contract made and perfected betwixt our rt trustie Cousin and Councillor, Alexander Earl of Galloway, and Sir Patrick Agnew, of Lochnaw, Knight, Sheriff of Wigtown, of the date 22d March 1623, anent the marriage then contracted and thereafter solemnized between Andrew Agnew and Lady Agnes Stewart, the said Earl bound himself to have paid Sir Patrick the sum of 8000 merks in name of tocher,—we will therefore and command the said Alexander Earl of Galloway to pay to the said Sheriff the foresaid sum of 8000 merks within six days next after he be charged by me thereto, *under the pain of rebellion and putting of him to our horn.* —15 day of April and of our reign the twelff year 1636."

[2] Creloch, now Crailloch, written in the curates' lists Crelaugh. Crith-lach, "a shaking bog" so Creelaugh, Galway; Crylaugh, Wexford.—Joyce, ii. 367.

We find in the Lochnaw charter-chest, first: Contract entered into betwixt Sir Patrick Agnew of Lochnaw and John Ahannay of Sorbie, whereby the said John, with consent specified, sold, and, under reversion by way of wadsett, disposed the lands of Creloch to the said Sir Patrick, 29 June 1625.

Second · Sassine following on the above contract in favour of Sir Patrick Agnew, dated the 7th and registered the 14th July 1626.

bound in vellum, "printed for Nathaniel Butler 1622," was
knocked down for the startling price of £96. A third brother
was created a baronet in 1629 by the style of Sir Robert of
Mochrum, and was killed in the Civil War in 1642. To him
Sir Samuel Hannay of Kirkdale was served heir of line in 1762.
On the 24th of May 1627 we find sasine in favour of Sir Patrick
Agnew and his lady of the lands of Knocktinnie in Kirkcowan
(the hill of the bale fires), proceeding on a contract between the
said parties and the Earl of Galloway. And the same year the
sheriff acquired the mill of Auchrochar, and the year following
the lands so called from William Boyd.[1]

We find several notices of purchases made by the sheriff's
eldest son. As: "Disposition by Robert Weir to Andrew Agnew
apparent of Lochnaw of ane heritable right upon the lands of
Crooch, Minigaff, and houses and yards in the said Kirktown."
And under date 6th April 1627: "Sassine of the houses in
Wigtown called Turnpeick and Blackhall, and the yeards thereof,
to Andrew Agnew apparent of Lochnaw."

In 1627 the king ordered the surrender of all the tithes
throughout the country to himself: doubly rash, because, whilst
it offended many, it pleased few   The bulk of them were held
by the more powerful barons, who were little disposed to give
them up, whilst the lower orders saw in it only a scheme for
endowing Episcopacy, which they detested. Charles, however,
never did things by halves. Royal commissioners were appointed
forthwith to value these teinds, and every shire was desired to
send two of the barons to confer with them.

Sir Patrick Agnew and Sir John M'Dowall of Garthland
represented the shire of Wigtown; their commissions dated at

[1] In a charter of confirmation of these lands to the sheriff, the Bishop of
Galloway makes it clear that Crochaire, "the hangman," is the true root of the
name: "Be it kent till all men, we Andrew, Bishop of Galloway, for certain
soums of money, other gratitudes, pleasures, and gyd deeds made payment and
done to us be Sir Patrick Agnew of Lochnaw, Knight Baronet, be the tenor
hereof, we give, grant, and dispone to the said Sir Patrick his heirs and assignees
the escheit of William Boyd of Ardcroquhart, and all and haill the 40s. land of
Ardcroquhart with the purtenance, corne mill thereof, milne lands, and multures.
At Edinburgh the 2d day of August 1630."

warrants to apprehend; and brought the Petitioner's officer that
morning out of his own house and bed to proclaim at the said
Church a Court to be holden in his Lordship's name within the
foresaid Bailliary, and immediately after caused a number of
armed men to go unto that place where the Petitioner used to
keepe his Courts, and there entrenched and fortified the same,
placing musketeers and pikemen garrison-wise there. And
upon the 2nd of July then following, the earl being charged at
the Petitioner's instance by letters of Lawsuitry granted by the
Lords of your Majesty's Council, and on the 3rd day of the said
month being likewise charged by the Privy Council to desist from
holding or keeping Court or approaching unto the said place
under his Highnesses will, yet nevertheless the said earl did
most contemptuously disobey both the said strict charge from
the Lords aforesaid and without having any respect unto the
letters signed by your Majesty's royal hand in the Petitioner's
behalf, did on the 3rd day of the said month, having convocate
three hundred horse and foot with musketts, hagbotts, pistolls,
lances, and such other warlike and invasive weapons prohibited,
come and in most hostile manner upon the Petitioner's own
domains upon a part of the Petitioner's own land which was
opposite to where the Court was to be kept, and there, to the
great terror and disquieting of the country and in contempt of
the Petitioner and the foresaid letters they did shoote off their
pieces; and there (the earl) kept his men upon your suppliant's
lands for the space of two days, destroying the Petitioner's corn
and grasse to his exceeding great losse and hinderance.

  "Whose most humble suite is—

  "That your Majesty will take the said earl's high contempts,
ryotts, and oppressions unto your royall consideration, or give
order to your Majesty's most Honourable Privy Council to take
a course for the condigne punishing thereof, to the end others
by his example may be warned not to commit the like insolence
and outrage; and that speedy order may be taken for the Petitioner's restitution unto the foresaid lands tithes and office;
and such satisfaction made him for his wrongful sufferings, great

losses, charge and damage as shall be agreeable to conscience
and equity.   Without which your suppliant cannot return home;
many of the said earl's men being very dangerous people, lately
brought out of Ireland and placed in the lands the Petitioner is
now dispossessed off.   The said earl and his men having done
what in them lies to vex the Petitioner, purposely to have him
forfeit his bond of ten thousand merks, which the Lords of your
Majesty's Privy Council then enforced them both to enter into
for the preservation of the peace.

"And as in duty bound he will daylie pray for your Majesty's
longe and happy wraigne.   PATRICK AGNEW."

Upon receipt of which the king referred the matter to the
chancellor.—

"To our trusty and well beloved Cousin and Councillor,
the Lord Viscount Duplin, Chancellor of the Kingdom of
Scotland—

"Charles R.—Rt. trusted and well loved Cousin and Councillor, we greet you well.   Whereas, Sir Patrick Agnew Knight
hath complained unto us of divers oppressions done unto him by
the Earl of Cassilis, as by the enclosed petition doth appear,
our pleasure is that you consider thereof, and after exact trial of
what is therein mentioned, if you find that our law and authority have been contemned and broken by the said earl, or that
he hath oppressed the Petitioner in his Office, Estate, or Person,
that you censure, fine, or cause punish him as you shall find the
nature of his offence to have justly merited : And that you make
him give sufficient satisfaction to the Petitioner for what losses
he hath sustained by him, that others may be restrained from
attempting the like hereafter and that our peace in those parts
may be duly preserved for the general good of all our loving and
well disposed subjects there.

"Which recommending to your care we bid you farewell, from
our Court at Bagshotte the 15th of August 1629."[1]

---

[1] This letter was forwarded by the Chancellor to the Sheriff of Galloway, and
is preserved among the Lochnaw Papers

The sheriff, in his petition, graphically sets before us the scene of the quiet of the Sunday morning disturbed by the appearance of Lord Cassilis with his host, largely recruited amongst the wild Irish from the opposite shore; and pithily describes their reckless proceedings as they bivouacked on his own lands, to the special detriment of his standing corn!

There had been much previous correspondence about similar quarrels; but into this it is not necessary to enter, as the sheriff indicated in this petition the result of former bickerings; in consequence of which both the earl and himself, at the very moment of his writing, were bound over under heavy penalties mutually to keep the peace.

Another cause of these disputes arose from the claim of bishop's teinds. Cassilis had become tacksman to the Bishop of Galloway; and the sheriff, apparently with reason, argued that the earl was bound to stand by any such commutations in money as were customary and *sanctioned by previous agreement*. To this Cassilis demurred, claiming the tithes in kind in full, and raising an action "for spoliation of tythes" against the sheriff; who retorted that the "Earl was but a tacksman interposed betwixt the Bishop and himself, contrary to the spirit of the Royal Proclamation for the surrender of all tythes to the King, in which it is set forth, that 'what favor is granted in Bishops' teythes, is onlie to the Bishop himself,'" and not to the interposed tacksman.

The sheriff ably states his own case in a petition to the king, also extant; setting forcibly before his Majesty the fact that subjects living in remote districts may be much oppressed if liable to be vindictively summoned to the head courts, even supposing the decision to be given in their favour:

"Your Petitioner, and his predecessors, are heritable proprietors of certain lands immediately halden of your Majesty, and hath, in all tyme bipast, had the teythes of the said lands for sixteen pounds Scottis money payit to the Earl of Cassilis as tacksman to the Bishop of Galloway. Until now of late most rigorously the said earl hath called and pressed the Petitioner for spoliation of the said teythes—notwithstanding of your Majesty's royal reformation and good course of your revocation, registrate and published to your subjects,—upon which your Majesty was graciously pleased to direct your royal letters in favor of your suppliant advysing his Lordship to forbear such rigorous dealing . . . nevertheless, without any regard to your Majesty's letter he hes *kept the Petitioner in plead of law*, both exacting inordinate dues and intruding himself in the Petitioner's heritable office halden of your Majesty.

" And now after valuation and approbation of the Petitioner his teinds before the Commissioners appointed by your Majesty the Petitioner will have real security in the Petitioner's lands for the valued bolls—otherways the Petitioner would become one perpetual fermorer to the said earl of unliquidat bolls,—and by *this means byd intollerable process of law ilk year, and be in worse case than he was before; the Petitioner's residence being near ane hundred myles distant from the seate of Justice, to his great damnage and overthrow.*

" Whose humble suite is that your Majesty would be pleased to give warrant what right the Petitioner shall give to the earl, and what right the Petitioner shall receive from the bishop or interposed tacksman. Lykeas your suppliant most humbly craves your Majesty to convert the valued bolls to a constant money rent; your suppliant freed of continual plead of Law. Humbly craving your Majesty to this effect to stay all action at the said earl's instance against the Petitioner."

As a result, Sir Patrick not only had restitution made of the lands of which he had been dispossessed, but, by a precept from the Court of Chancery, was retoured as heir to his father in the bailiary of the barony of Leswalt,[1] to the earl's entire discomfiture.

Some of the by-play which occurred during the great bailie-court quarrel is extremely amusing. A series of petitions appeared against the sheriff, of some of which it is to be suspected that the earl was instigator.

---

[1] Dominus Patricius Agnew de Lochnaw, hæres Domini Andreæ Agnew patris in officio balliæ hæreditariæ de Leswalt.—*Inquis Spec*

which for mettall and riding may rather be tearmed bastard
barbs than Gallowedian nagges   Likewise their nobility and
gentry are as courteous, and every way generously disposed, as
eyther discretion could wish, and honour command. . . . Certainly Galloway is become more civill of late than any maritime
country bordering with the westerne sea." [1]

Montgomery, the Galloway bard, also gives contemporary
experience as to the fauna with which he was familiar among
the woodlands of the Dee.

> The con, the coney, and the cat,
> Whose dainty downs with dew were wat,
> With stiff mustaches strange
> The hart, the hind, the doe, the rae,
> The fulmart, and false fox
> The bearded buck clamb up the brae,
> With birsie bours and brocks. [2]

In 1629 the sheriff was created a Baronet of Scotland and
Nova Scotia   The charter by which a certain tract was erected
into the barony of Agnew is still preserved, and its seal as
entire as the day of its issue.   Moreover, he got actual infeftment of his lands and honours on the Castle Hill at Edinburgh.

The enumeration of various rights "in nubibus" thus conferred upon him is amusing ; for with his lands he was endowed
with "castles, towers, fortalices, manor-places, houses, mills,
teinds great and small, with right of Patronage of the Churches,
and mines and minerals of gold and silver, lead, iron, and other
metals, with all precious stones, gems, pearls, christals, alums,
corals, and others whatsoever."

With power "to build cities, burghs, ports, naval stations,
batteries, watch-towers, and fortifications . . . with free Justiciary,
office of sheriff and power of making laws . . . punishing all
crimes . . . and with customs of all goods and merchandize."

"To be called the Barony and Regality of Agnew to be holden

---

[1] Lithgow, *Nineteen Years' Travel*, quarto, 1632, p 495.   He was received
with great distinction at the courts of both James VI and Charles I.   His
visit to Galloway was probably in 1628

[2] *The Cherrie and the Slae*   First edition, printed in 1607   The con is a
squirrel, the cat the formidable wild one long extinct.

by the said Sir Patrick in free barony and regality for ever, by all just marches, as the same lie in length and breadth, in houses, buildings, bushes, plains, moors, marshes, ways, paths, waters, stanks, rivers, meadows, grazings, pastures, mills, multures, hawkings, huntings, fishings, peats, turfs, coals, coal-heuchs, rabbits, warrens, doves, dovecots, smithies, maltings, breweries, brooms, woods, trees, quarries, stone and lime, with courts and their issues, amercements, herezelds, bloodwits, and merchets of women; with furk, foss, sock, sack, thole, thame, vert, wrack, waith, wair, venison; infangthief, outfangthief, pit and gallows, with common pasture and free ish and entry, with all and sundry liberties, commodities, profits, easements, and their just pertinents, as well not named as named, as well below the earth as above."

On the 4th of May 1624 we find a sasine given to Sir Patrick Agnew of Lochnaw, and Dame Margaret Kennedy his spouse, of the lands of Knocktym,[1] in the parish of Kirkcolm, acquired from the Earl of Galloway.

---

[1] Tom, genitive tuim, "a bush, tuft, or thicket." Knocktuim, "the bushy knoll."

END OF VOL. I.